WILEY PLUS

www.wileyplus.com

ALL THE HELP, **RESOURCES**, AND PERSONAL **SUPPORT** YOU AND YOUR STUDENTS NEED!

www.wileyplus.com/resources

1st DAY OF **CLASS** ... *AND BEYOND!*

2-Minute Tutorials and all of the resources you and your students need to get started

WILEY PLUS Student Partner Program

Student support from an experienced student user

WILEY FACULTY NETWORK

Collaborate with your colleagues, find a mentor, attend virtual and live events, and view resources www.WhereFacultyConnect.com

WILEY PLUS *QuickStart*

Pre-loaded, ready-to-use assignments and presentations created by subject matter experts

Technical Support 24/7 FAQs, online chat, and phone support www.wileyplus.com/support

Your *WileyPLUS* Account Manager, providing personal training and support

ERNST & YOUNG
Quality In Everything We Do

AUDITING
A PRACTICAL APPROACH
CANADIAN EDITION

Robyn MORONEY
Monash University, Caulfield East, Australia

Fiona CAMPBELL
Ernst & Young, Melbourne, Australia

Jane HAMILTON
La Trobe University, Bendigo, Australia

Valerie WARREN
Kwantlen Polytechnic University, Surrey, British Columbia

With contributions from

Luke BAXTER
Darrell JENSEN
Stephanie LAMONT
Anilisa SAINANI
Ernst & Young LLP, Toronto, Ontario

John Wiley & Sons Canada, Ltd.

Library and Archives Canada Cataloguing in Publication

Auditing : a practical approach / Robyn Moroney . . . [et al.]. — Canadian ed.

Includes index.
ISBN 978-0-470-67890-9

1. Auditing.   I. Moroney, Robyn

HF5667.M697 2012   657'.45   C2011-904630-X

Production Credits
Acquisitions Editor: Zoë Craig
Vice President and Publisher: Veronica Visentin
Senior Marketing Manager: Aida Krneta
Editorial Manager: Karen Staudinger
Production Manager: Tegan Wallace
Developmental Editor: Daleara Hirjikaka
Media Editor: Channade Fenandoe
Editorial Assistant: Luisa Begani
Interior Design: Mike Chan
Typesetting: Thomson Digital
Cover Design: Interrobang Graphic Design, Inc.
Cover Photograph: © Getty Images/Photographer's Choice
Printing and Binding: Edwards Brothers

Printed and bound in the United States of America

1 2 3 4 5 EB 16 15 14 13 12

John Wiley & Sons Canada, Ltd.
6045 Freemont Blvd.
Mississauga, Ontario L5R 4J3
WILEY Visit our website at: www.wiley.ca

ABOUT THE AUTHORS

Robyn Moroney, B.Ec. (Hons), M.Com., Ph.D., CA, CPA, is an Associate Professor in the Department of Accounting and Finance at Monash University, Australia. Before commencing her academic career, Robyn worked as an auditor at Arthur Young, now Ernst & Young. With over 25 years' academic experience, Robyn has previously held positions at the University of Melbourne, the University of Auckland, the University of New South Wales, and La Trobe University. As a member of the board of the Accounting and Finance Association of Australia and New Zealand, which represents the interests of accounting and finance academics in both countries, Robyn has taken on a number of roles including co-chairing the conference technical committee and the doctoral symposium. Her areas of research are the behavioural aspects (auditor decision-making processes) and economics of auditing.

Fiona Campbell, B.Com., FCA, is an Assurance Partner with Ernst & Young in Melbourne Australia. Fiona has been serving clients in the assurance practice since 1991 and has worked on audit clients primarily in the manufacturing, consumer, and industrial products industries, as well as not-for-profit sector organizations. She has considerable experience providing professional services to Australian and foreign-controlled companies, including large publicly listed and private companies. Fiona is also responsible for assurance methodology and technology at Ernst & Young in Australia, and has been involved in designing the firm's global audit methodology for the past 14 years, including ensuring compliance with both international and local auditing standards.

Jane Hamilton, B.Bus., M.Acc., Ph.D., is Professor of Accounting at the Bendigo campus of the Regional School of Business, La Trobe University, Australia, and previously held academic positions at the University of Technology, Sydney. Jane has 20 years' experience in teaching and has published the results of her auditing research in several Australian and international journals.

Valerie Warren, B.Comm., MBA, CA, is an Accounting Instructor at Kwantlen Polytechnic University in British Columbia. Before commencing her academic career, Valerie worked as an auditor with KPMG. As well as teaching a variety of accounting courses including auditing, advanced accounting, and accounting theory, Valerie also serves as a Practice Review Officer for the Institute of Chartered Accountants of British Columbia, where she conducts practice reviews of national, regional, and small CA firms to ensure compliance with current accounting and assurance standards.

PREFACE

Welcome to the first Canadian edition of *Auditing: A Practical Approach*. This is not just another auditing text. As the title suggests, the textbook focuses on how audits are conducted in practice. As authors, we bring our diverse experiences to this book to provide a very different approach to teaching and studying auditing. In addition to covering the essential topics of auditing, the text provides greater insight into how an audit is conducted and the issues that are of greatest concern to practising auditors.

As each chapter unfolds, students are introduced to the various stages of an audit. Key auditing concepts are addressed in a succinct manner, making them easily understandable. To underpin this approach, each chapter begins with a diagrammatic representation of the stages of an audit, with the current stage highlighted as we progress through the text. The diagram provides a useful reference point to ground the discussion in each chapter to the relevant stage in the audit process. To underpin our discussion of how an audit is conducted, we use a case study of a hypothetical client, Cloud 9. The discussion in each chapter is kept general, with our case study providing an example of how the general principles behind each audit may be applied in practice. By using this approach, students are provided with a continuing example of how the concepts discussed may apply in practice.

The Cloud 9 case study provides a flexible learning tool to be used within an auditing and assurance course. Details about Cloud 9 and its audit are provided in each chapter to give an insight into how an audit is conducted, the issues that auditors face at each stage of an audit, and the processes used to gather evidence and arrive at conclusions. The Cloud 9 case materials can form the basis of class discussions, student role plays, or online exchanges between students. At the end of each chapter, a case-study problem is set using Cloud 9 as a basis. These problems can be used as part of the weekly tutorial program, or as an assignment for students to work on individually or in groups (or some combination of the two). This textbook contains 12 chapters. An overview of each chapter is now provided, followed by a description of the structure used in each chapter.

Overview of the text

Chapter 1: Introduction and overview of audit and assurance. This chapter begins with a definition of assurance engagements, an explanation of how they can differ, and the different levels of assurance and opinions that can be provided by auditors. The role of the financial statement preparer is contrasted with that of the auditor, which leads into a discussion of the source of the historical and ongoing demand for audit services. The regulations surrounding the provision of assurance services are outlined and the expectation gap is explained. This chapter provides the background that underpins the remainder of the text.

Chapter 2: Ethics, legal liability, and client acceptance. This chapter provides an overview of the fundamental principles of professional ethics that apply to all accountants. Particular attention is given to auditor independence, including threats and safeguards. The auditor's legal liability to their client and third parties is explained, together with the concept of contributory negligence. This chapter ends with a discussion of the factors to consider in the client acceptance or continuance decision, which marks the commencement of our discussion of how an audit is conducted.

Chapter 3: Audit planning I. The first stage of every audit involves planning. This important topic is covered in two chapters. Chapter 3 begins with a discussion of the different stages of an audit. The key components of the planning stage are gaining an understanding of a client, identifying the risk of fraud, assessing the extent of related party transactions, evaluating the client's going concern assumption, gaining an understanding of the client's corporate governance structure, and evaluating how a client's information technology can impact on risk. These components of audit planning are described in detail in this chapter, along with a discussion of how client closing procedures can impact on reported results.

Chapter 4: Audit planning II. This chapter continues our discussion of audit planning. Specifically, this chapter includes a definition of audit risk and describes its components. The concept of materiality, the development of planning materiality, and how it is used when conducting an audit is then described. The process used by auditors in arriving at their audit strategy, which provides a blueprint for the remainder of the audit, is explained. The chapter concludes with an overview of the use of analytical procedures during the planning phase of an audit.

Chapter 5: Audit evidence. This chapter contains an overview of the different types of audit evidence and the processes used by auditors to gather that evidence throughout the audit. The audit assertions, which aid in risk identification and the design of audit procedures, are defined. The concept of sufficient appropriate audit evidence is explained. The procedures when using the work of an expert or another auditor are described. This chapter concludes with a discussion of how auditors document the details of evidence gathered in their working papers.

Chapter 6: Overview of tests of controls, substantive procedures, and sampling. This chapter provides the backdrop for chapters 7 to 11, where tests of controls and substantive procedures are described in detail. This chapter commences with a description of the difference between tests of controls and substantive procedures and the factors that impact the nature, timing, and extent of audit testing. Audit sampling is then described.

Chapter 7: Gaining an understanding of the client's system of internal controls. This chapter provides an introduction to and an overview of internal controls and the background to understanding how they are tested. In this chapter, internal control is defined and the seven generally accepted objectives of internal control activities are outlined. Internal control at the entity level and the transaction level are explained and contrasted. A description is provided of how an auditor documents their understanding of their client's system of internal controls. Based upon that understanding an auditor will then identify strengths and weaknesses in their client's system of internal controls and communicate their findings to those charged with governance in the organization.

Chapter 8: Execution of the audit—testing of controls. This chapter provides a description of how an auditor conducts their tests of their client's internal controls. The description includes a discussion of how an auditor determines when to conduct their tests, how they identify different types of controls, how they select the techniques to use when testing controls, how they select controls to test, and how they design their tests of controls. Once controls testing is completed an auditor must interpret the results of their testing and the implications of the findings for the remainder of the audit. A description is provided of how an auditor does this along with how they document the details of their controls testing.

Chapter 9: Execution of the audit—performing substantive procedures. This chapter provides an overview of the substantive procedures used by auditors when testing the details of their client's transactions and account balances. This chapter provides a backdrop to the detailed discussion in chapters 10 and 11. This chapter includes a discussion of the link between audit risk and the nature, timing, and extent of substantive procedures conducted by the auditor. An overview is provided of common substantive audit procedures used in practice and the level of audit evidence obtained when conducting different tests. This chapter concludes with a description of the documentation of the conclusions reached by auditors as a result of their substantive procedures.

Chapter 10: Substantive testing and balance sheet accounts. This chapter provides an overview of the types of substantive procedures commonly used in practice when testing the contents of a client's balance sheet. The relationship between risk for a significant account and the extent and timing of substantive procedures for that account is described. The procedures commonly used by auditors when testing balance sheet accounts are then explained. Specifically, the procedures used by auditors when testing cash; trade (accounts) receivables; inventory; property, plant, and equipment; and payables are described in detail in this chapter. An overview is then provided of how substantive testing is used for other balance sheet accounts before an explanation is provided of the processes used by auditors when assessing the results of their substantive procedures to determine whether additional substantive tests are necessary.

Chapter 11: Substantive testing and income statement accounts. This chapter provides an overview of the types of substantive procedures commonly used in practice when testing the contents of a client's income statement. The relationship between an auditor's overall risk assessment for a client and the consequent extent and timing of substantive procedures when testing income statement accounts is explained. These procedures are compared and contrasted to the procedures outlined in chapter 10 when testing balance sheet accounts. The procedures commonly used by auditors when testing income statement accounts are then explained. Specifically, the procedures used by auditors when testing revenue, cost of sales, and significant expense accounts are described in detail in this chapter. Finally, an overview is provided of how the results of these substantive procedures are used by auditors to determine whether additional substantive tests are necessary.

Chapter 12: Completing and reporting on the audit. This final chapter of the text marks the conclusion of the audit. An explanation of the procedures performed by an auditor as part of their wrap-up, including gathering and evaluating audit evidence, is provided. The going concern concept is revisited in the context of finalizing the audit. Subsequent event testing is explained. The procedures used by auditors when evaluating material misstatements uncovered during their audit are outlined. A description is provided of how auditors evaluate the conclusions drawn throughout the audit in relation to evidence gathered and its impact on the overall opinion formed on the financial statements. The form and content of the audit report is outlined. Finally, a description is provided of the types of reports an auditor will provide to the client's management and those charged with governance at the conclusion of the audit.

Structure of each chapter

Each chapter commences with an overview of the *learning objectives* addressed in the chapter. These learning objectives are highlighted throughout the chapter as the discussion unfolds. After each learning objective is covered in the text, three *before you go on* questions are set for students to confirm they recall the main issues covered. As these questions come directly from the text, it is straightforward for students to check their understanding of the key concepts covered before progressing to the next learning objective (section) in the chapter. Specific learning objectives are also linked to end-of-chapter professional application questions. This approach means that tutorial questions can be set to ensure coverage of the learning objectives considered most important.

Following the list of learning objectives is a summary of the Canadian and international *auditing and assurance standards* discussed in each chapter. The listed standards are incorporated in the discussion within the textbook. Other pronouncements and guidance statements are also listed and discussed where applicable.

The summary of standards is followed by a diagram of the *overview of the audit process*. This figure aids in understanding the structure of the textbook, which mirrors the process generally used when conducting an audit. The diagram highlights the stage to be covered in the current chapter, which aids in understanding what has come before and what is still to come.

Following the overview diagram is an *audit process in focus* section, which includes a brief overview and outline of the chapter. As *key terms* appear in the text for the first time, their definitions appear in the margin, which aids studying and revision.

The *Cloud 9* case study appears throughout each chapter. Students can choose to incorporate Cloud 9 in their reading of each chapter or to go back and read through the case study after reading the main text. As Cloud 9 is easily distinguishable from the main text, either approach can be adopted when studying a chapter.

Descriptions of the *professional environment* in which auditors operate appear in each chapter. These vignettes provide some details of the auditing profession and various challenges faced by auditors.

Each chapter concludes with a summary, list of key terms used, and end-of-chapter questions. The *summary* provides a brief recap of each learning objective covered in a chapter. The end-of-chapter questions include *multiple-choice questions*, review questions, professional application questions, a Cloud 9 case study question and a research question.

Solutions to multiple-choice questions appear at the end of each chapter, so students can use these as part of their independent study. The *review questions* test student understanding of the key concepts covered in the chapter. The *professional application questions* are problems designed around the learning objectives set for the chapter. Each question is graded as basic, moderate, or challenging and indicates the learning objective(s) covered. A selection of the professional application questions are based upon problems set by the Certified General Accountants of Canada (CGA) professional studies, the Canadian Institute of Chartered Accountants (CICA) for the Uniform Final Exam, and the Australian Institute of Chartered Accountants as part of their chartered accountants program. The Cloud 9 *case study* builds from one chapter to the next and is based on the information provided in each chapter, in the case study at the end of each chapter, and in the appendix to the textbook. The use of a case study in this text aids in the appreciation of how each topic covered fits in to the context of an audit as a whole. Together with the practical approach used in the body of the text, this allows a deeper understanding of how audits are conducted in practice. *Research questions* provide an opportunity for students to gain a deeper appreciation of the role of academic research in providing greater insights into audit practice. Sample documents and forms are included in *Appendix A* at the end of the text and provide students with useful examples of the forms and templates that they would encounter during an audit.

Technology for Teaching and Learning

Auditing: A Practical Approach Canadian Edition offers instructors and students a unique and comprehensive set of technology tools to aid in instruction and learning. These have been carefully developed and integrated with the text and serve to expand the educational experience.

WileyPLUS is an innovative, research-based online environment for effective teaching and learning.

WileyPLUS builds students' confidence because it takes the guesswork out of studying by providing students with a clear roadmap: what to do, how to do it, if they did it right. Students will take more initiative so you'll have greater impact on their achievement in the classroom and beyond.

WileyPLUS and the *Auditing: A Practical Approach* Canadian Edition website at http://www.wiley.com/go/moroney provide a wealth of online resources including quizzes, chapter PowerPoint slides, and videos for classroom use accessible to both instructors and students. Instructors also have access to the Solutions Manual and the Testbank in Word and computerized formats.

Acknowledgements

We thank the following reviewers for their valuable feedback:

Sally Anderson, *University of Calgary; Mount Royal University*

Greg Caers, *Ryerson University; McMaster University*

Shiraz Charania, *British Columbia Institute of Technology*

Peggy Coady, *Memorial University of Newfoundland*

Heidi Dieckmann, *Kwantlen Polytechnic University*

Robert Ducharme, *University of Waterloo*

Susan Fisher, *Algonquin College*

Teresa Gallant, *British Columbia Institute of Technology*

Don Jones, *University of Windsor*

Michael Kudolo, *Humber Institute of Technology and Advanced Learning*

Erin Marshall, *University of Alberta*

Julie McDonald, *University of Toronto; Ryerson University*

Ted Nowak, *Concordia University*

Patrick Ounlert, *Brock University*

Wendy Popowich, *Northern Alberta Institute of Technology*

Fred Pries, *University of Guelph*

Garth Sheriff, *Carleton University*

D. Rand Rowlands, *George Brown College*

Rik Smistad, *Mount Royal University*

Joe Toste, *Centennial College*

Joan Wallwork, *Kwantlen Polytechnic University*

Brad Witt, *Humber Institute of Technology and Advanced Learning*

We would also like to thank the following contributors for preparing the ancillaries to the book and for their useful suggestions and comments:

Shiraz Charania, *British Columbia Institute of Technology*

Angela Davis, *Booth University College*

Robert Ducharme, *University of Waterloo*

Ian Farmer

Richard Michalski, *McMaster University*

Ted Nowak, *Concordia University*

We would like to thank Ernst & Young LLP, Toronto, specifically Luke Baxter, Darrell Jensen, Stephanie Lamont, and Anilisa Sainani for reviewing the text and for offering valuable suggestions for improvement as well as for providing us with real-world exhibits to include in the text.

We also thank the staff at John Wiley & Sons Canada, Ltd., for their support and expertise. We would especially like to thank Zoë Craig, Acquisitions Editor; Deanna Durnford, Supplements Coordinator; Channade Fenandoe, Media Editor; Daleara Hirjikaka, Developmental Editor; Aida Krneta, Marketing Manager; and Tegan Wallace, Production Manager. We also wish to thank all the sales representatives for their tireless efforts in promoting this book. We would also like to extend special thanks to Darren Taylor, Executive Publisher, Higher Education, Australia for all his help and support. We would like to specially thank Laurel Hyatt, Julie van Tol, and Merrie-Ellen Wilcox for their editorial contributions.

We also thank our families for their support and patience. A special thanks to the "guys," Oliver, Matthew, and Nicholas.

We have tried to produce a text that is error-free and that meets your requirements. Suggestions and comments from users are always welcome.

Valerie Warren
October 2011
valerie.warren@kwantlen.ca

HOW TO USE THIS BOOK

Auditing: A Practical Approach has been designed with you—the student—in mind. This textbook has been designed to enhance your learning experience and is our attempt to provide you with a book that both engages you with the subject matter and encourages a greater understanding of the auditing process. We have tried to accomplish these goals through the following elements.

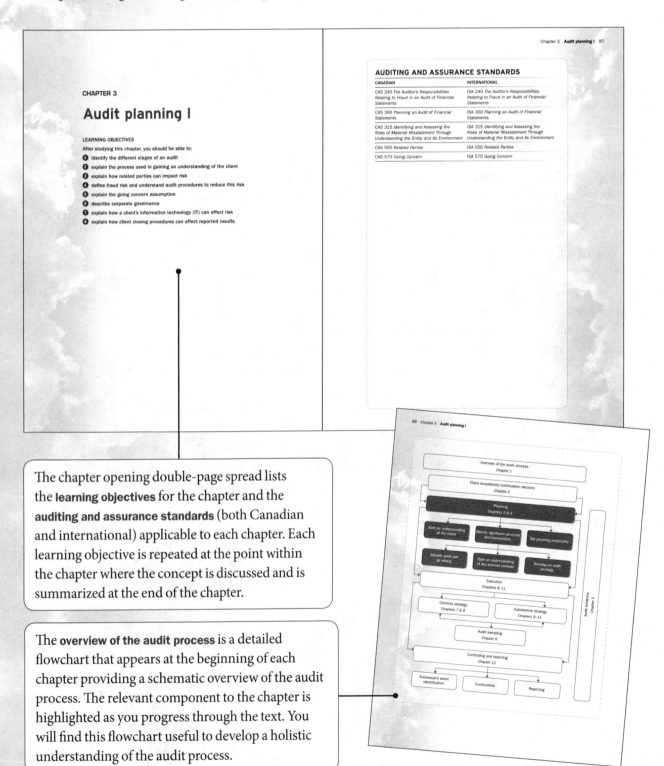

The chapter opening double-page spread lists the **learning objectives** for the chapter and the **auditing and assurance standards** (both Canadian and international) applicable to each chapter. Each learning objective is repeated at the point within the chapter where the concept is discussed and is summarized at the end of the chapter.

The **overview of the audit process** is a detailed flowchart that appears at the beginning of each chapter providing a schematic overview of the audit process. The relevant component to the chapter is highlighted as you progress through the text. You will find this flowchart useful to develop a holistic understanding of the audit process.

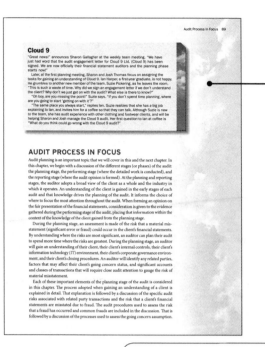

Cloud 9 is an integrated case study that aligns with the audit methodology detailed in each chapter. The case appears several times in each chapter, providing a continuing practical insight into how the topics discussed can be applied in an audit. The **audit process in focus** provides an introduction to the topics covered in the chapter.

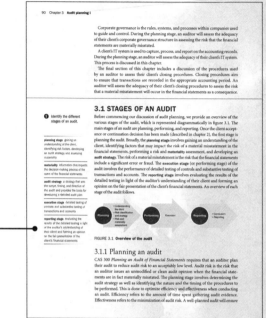

Key terms are bolded in the text at first mention and defined in the margin, listed again at the end of the chapter, and defined in the end-of-book glossary.

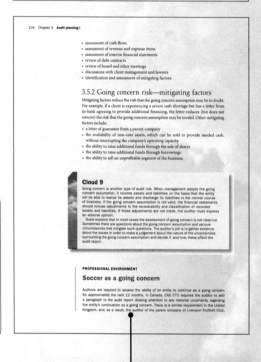

Before you go on questions are presented after each section and contain questions for review of the key points covered.

Professional environment boxes apply the key topics and processes discussed in the chapter to current events locally and internationally.

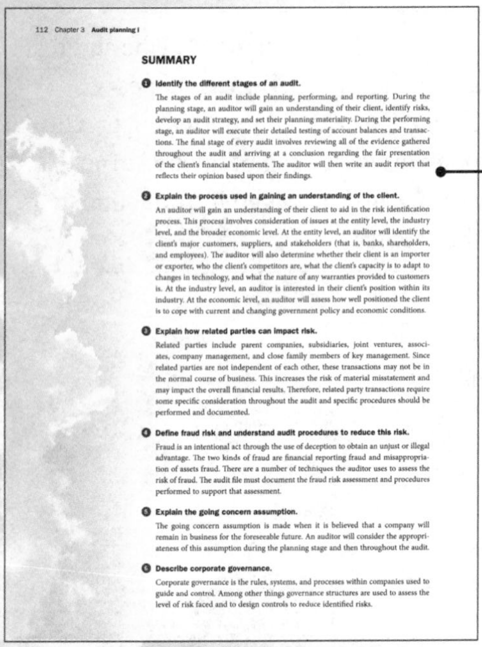
112 Chapter 3 Audit planning I

SUMMARY

1 Identify the different stages of an audit.
The stages of an audit include planning, performing, and reporting. During the planning stage, an auditor will gain an understanding of their client, identify risks, develop an audit strategy, and set their planning materiality. During the performing stage, an auditor will execute their detailed testing of account balances and transactions. The final stage of every audit involves reviewing all of the evidence gathered throughout the audit and arriving at a conclusion regarding the fair presentation of the client's financial statements. The auditor will then write an audit report that reflects their opinion based upon their findings.

2 Explain the process used in gaining an understanding of the client.
An auditor will gain an understanding of their client to aid in the risk identification process. This process involves consideration of issues at the entity level, the industry level, and the broader economic level. At the entity level, an auditor will identify the client's major customers, suppliers, and stakeholders (that is, banks, shareholders, and employees). The auditor will also determine whether their client is an importer or exporter, who the client's competitors are, what the client's capacity is to adapt to changes in technology, and what the nature of any warranties provided to customers is. At the industry level, an auditor is interested in their client's position within its industry. At the economic level, an auditor will assess how well positioned the client is to cope with current and changing government policy and economic conditions.

3 Explain how related parties can impact risk.
Related parties include parent companies, subsidiaries, joint ventures, associates, company management, and close family members of key management. Since related parties are not independent of each other, these transactions may not be in the normal course of business. This increases the risk of material misstatement and may impact the overall financial results. Therefore, related party transactions require some specific consideration throughout the audit and specific procedures should be performed and documented.

4 Define fraud risk and understand audit procedures to reduce this risk.
Fraud is an intentional act through the use of deception to obtain an unjust or illegal advantage. The two kinds of fraud are financial reporting fraud and misappropriation of assets fraud. There are a number of techniques the auditor uses to assess the risk of fraud. The audit file must document the fraud risk assessment and procedures performed to support that assessment.

5 Explain the going concern assumption.
The going concern assumption is made when it is believed that a company will remain in business for the foreseeable future. An auditor will consider the appropriateness of this assumption during the planning stage and then throughout the audit.

6 Describe corporate governance.
Corporate governance is the rules, systems, and processes within companies used to guide and control. Among other things governance structures are used to assess the level of risk faced and to design controls to reduce identified risks.

The **summary** restates and summarizes the learning objectives set for the chapter.

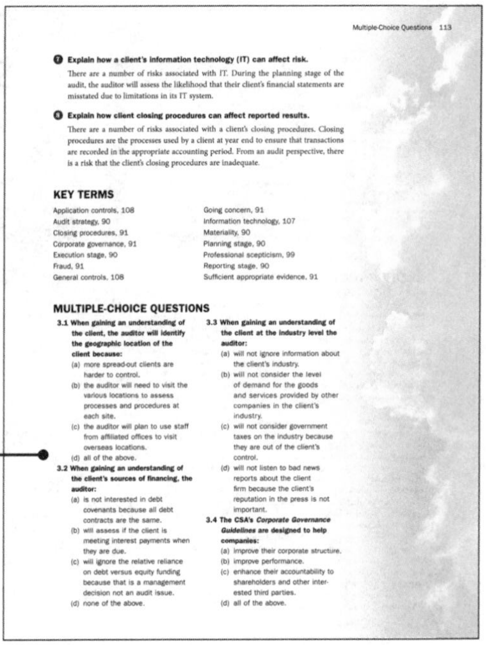
Multiple-Choice Questions 113

7 Explain how a client's information technology (IT) can affect risk.
There are a number of risks associated with IT. During the planning stage of the audit, the auditor will assess the likelihood that their client's financial statements are misstated due to limitations in its IT system.

8 Explain how client closing procedures can affect reported results.
There are a number of risks associated with a client's closing procedures. Closing procedures are the processes used by a client at year end to ensure that transactions are recorded in the appropriate accounting period. From an audit perspective, there is a risk that the client's closing procedures are inadequate.

KEY TERMS

Application controls, 108	Going concern, 91
Audit strategy, 90	Information technology, 107
Closing procedures, 91	Materiality, 90
Corporate governance, 91	Planning stage, 90
Execution stage, 90	Professional scepticism, 99
Fraud, 91	Reporting stage, 90
General controls, 108	Sufficient appropriate evidence, 91

MULTIPLE-CHOICE QUESTIONS

3.1 When gaining an understanding of the client, the auditor will identify the geographic location of the client because:
(a) more spread-out clients are harder to control.
(b) the auditor will need to visit the various locations to assess processes and procedures at each site.
(c) the auditor will plan to use staff from affiliated offices to visit overseas locations.
(d) all of the above.

3.2 When gaining an understanding of the client's sources of financing, the auditor:
(a) is not interested in debt covenants because all debt contracts are the same.
(b) will assess if the client is meeting interest payments when they are due.
(c) will ignore the relative reliance on debt versus equity funding because that is a management decision not an audit issue.
(d) none of the above.

3.3 When gaining an understanding of the client at the industry level the auditor:
(a) will not ignore information about the client's industry.
(b) will not consider the level of demand for the goods and services provided by other companies in the client's industry.
(c) will not consider government taxes on the industry because they are out of the client's control.
(d) will not listen to bad news reports about the client firm because the client's reputation in the press is not important.

3.4 The CSA's *Corporate Governance Guidelines* are designed to help companies:
(a) improve their corporate structure.
(b) improve performance.
(c) enhance their accountability to shareholders and other interested third parties.
(d) all of the above.

Multiple-choice questions provide a self-test opportunity to confirm understanding of the concepts presented in the chapter. Solutions are provided at the end of the chapter.

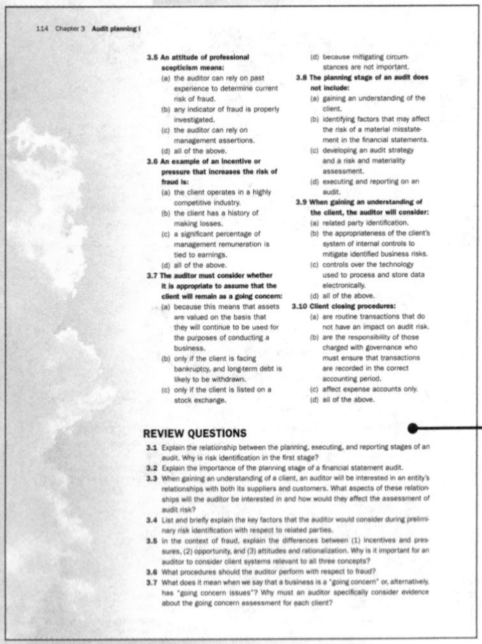
114 Chapter 3 Audit planning I

3.5 An attitude of professional scepticism means:
(a) the auditor can rely on past experience to determine current risk of fraud.
(b) any indicator of fraud is properly investigated.
(c) the auditor can rely on management assertions.
(d) all of the above.

3.6 An example of an incentive or pressure that increases the risk of fraud is:
(a) the client operates in a highly competitive industry.
(b) the client has a history of making losses.
(c) a significant percentage of management remuneration is tied to earnings.
(d) all of the above.

3.7 The auditor must consider whether it is appropriate to assume that the client will remain as a going concern:
(a) because this means that assets are valued on the basis that they will continue to be used for the purposes of conducting a business.
(b) only if the client is facing bankruptcy, and long-term debt is likely to be withdrawn.
(c) only if the client is listed on a stock exchange.
(d) because mitigating circumstances are not important.

3.8 The planning stage of an audit does not include:
(a) gaining an understanding of the client.
(b) identifying factors that may affect the risk of a material misstatement in the financial statements.
(c) developing an audit strategy and a risk and materiality assessment.
(d) executing and reporting on an audit.

3.9 When gaining an understanding of the client, the auditor will consider:
(a) related party identification.
(b) the appropriateness of the client's system of internal controls to mitigate identified business risks.
(c) controls over the technology used to process and store data electronically.
(d) all of the above.

3.10 Client closing procedures:
(a) are routine transactions that do not have an impact on audit risk.
(b) are the responsibility of those charged with governance who must ensure that transactions are recorded in the correct accounting period.
(c) affect expense accounts only.
(d) all of the above.

REVIEW QUESTIONS

3.1 Explain the relationship between the planning, executing, and reporting stages of an audit. Why is risk identification in the first stage?
3.2 Explain the importance of the planning stage of a financial statement audit.
3.3 When gaining an understanding of a client, an auditor will be interested in an entity's relationships with both its suppliers and customers. What aspects of these relationships will the auditor be interested in and how would they affect the assessment of audit risk?
3.4 List and briefly explain the key factors that the auditor would consider during preliminary risk identification with respect to related parties.
3.5 In the context of fraud, explain the differences between (1) incentives and pressures, (2) opportunity, and (3) attitudes and rationalization. Why is it important for an auditor to consider client systems relevant to all three concepts?
3.6 What procedures should the auditor perform with respect to fraud?
3.7 What does it mean when we say that a business is a "going concern" or, alternatively, has "going concern issues"? Why must an auditor specifically consider evidence about the going concern assessment for each client?

Review questions test your understanding of the material presented in the chapter and encourage considered comment.

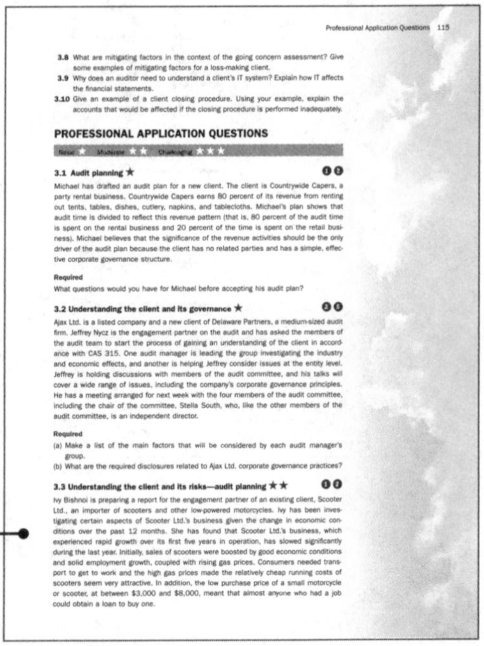
Professional Application Questions 115

3.8 What are mitigating factors in the context of the going concern assessment? Give some examples of mitigating factors for a loss-making client.
3.9 Why does an auditor need to understand a client's IT system? Explain how IT affects the financial statements.
3.10 Give an example of a client closing procedure. Using your example, explain the accounts that would be affected if the closing procedure is performed inadequately.

PROFESSIONAL APPLICATION QUESTIONS

Basic ★ Moderate ★★ Challenging ★★★

3.1 Audit planning ★ 1 2
Michael has drafted an audit plan for a new client. The client is Countrywide Capers, a party rental business. Countrywide Capers earns 80 percent of its revenue from renting out tents, tables, dishes, cutlery, napkins, and tablecloths. Michael's plan shows that audit time is divided to reflect this revenue pattern (that is, 80 percent of the audit time is spent on the rental business and 20 percent of the time is spent on the retail business). Michael believes that the significance of the revenue activities should be the only driver of the audit plan because the client has no related parties and has a simple, effective corporate governance structure.

Required
What questions would you have for Michael before accepting his audit plan?

3.2 Understanding the client and its governance ★ 2 6
Ajax Ltd. is a listed company and a new client of Delaware Partners, a medium-sized audit firm. Jeffrey Nycz is the engagement partner on the audit and has asked the members of the audit team to start the process of gaining an understanding of the client in accordance with CAS 315. One audit manager is leading the group investigating the industry and economic effects, and another is helping Jeffrey consider issues at the entity level. Jeffrey is holding discussions with members of the audit committee, and his talks will cover a wide range of issues, including the company's corporate governance principles. He has a meeting arranged for next week with the four members of the audit committee, including the chair of the committee, Stella South, who, like the other members of the audit committee, is an independent director.

Required
(a) Make a list of the main factors that will be considered by each audit manager's group.
(b) What are the required disclosures related to Ajax Ltd. corporate governance practices?

3.3 Understanding the client and its risks—audit planning ★★ 2 3
Ivy Bishnoi is preparing a report for the engagement partner of an existing client, Scooter Ltd., an importer of scooters and other low-powered motorcycles. Ivy has been investigating certain aspects of Scooter Ltd.'s business given the change in economic conditions over the past 12 months. She has found that Scooter Ltd.'s business, which experienced rapid growth over its first five years in operation, has slowed significantly during the last year. Initially, sales of scooters were boosted by good economic conditions and solid employment growth, coupled with rising gas prices. Consumers needed transport to get to work and the high gas prices made the relatively cheap running costs of scooters seem very attractive. In addition, the low purchase price of a small motorcycle or scooter, at between $3,000 and $8,000, meant that almost anyone who had a job could obtain a loan to buy one.

Professional application questions are graded as basic, moderate, or challenging and specifically test your understanding of the material presented in the chapter on the learning objectives indicated.

Financial facts

- The November 30, 2012, unadjusted financial statements show CLL's current ratio is 1.64:1.
- If the long-term debt is re-classified as a current liability, the current ratio would be 0.42:1.
- The $500,000 shareholder loan to Martin Roy is also classified as long term; however, if it is classified as current, the ratio would decline further.
- The debt-to-equity ratio is 85.8%.
- The company has traditionally had a history of positive earnings; however, in the last two years, it has reported a net loss.
- Cash on hand is $1,094,000.
- Accounts payable has increased by more than 100%.
- Share capital is reported on the 2012 balance sheet at $10,386, 000.
- CLL's long-term debt includes the $6,000,000 secured operating line of credit. The line of credit is a revolving loan, which the bank can call on three months' notice if certain financial covenants are not met. It had been classified as long-term debt in 2011 because the bank waived its right to call the loan before December 1, 2012.

Required

(a) What facts indicate that CL may not be a going concern? What facts indicate that CL may be a going concern? Make a conclusion on whether you believe it is appropriate to assume the company will remain a going concern.
(b) What are the risks related to the shareholder loan? What are three recommended procedures the auditor should perform related to the shareholder loan?
(c) What type of report should be issued if management refuses to disclose the share-holder loan as required by IFRS and ASPE? Why?
(d) Discuss the decisions made by the board. Are they ethical? Do they comply with the requirements of CSA's *Corporate Governance Guidelines*?

Source: Adapted from the Uniform Final Exam (UFE), The Institutes of Chartered Accountants in Canada and Bermuda, Paper 3, 2005.

CASE STUDY—CLOUD 9

You are a graduate working for W&S Partners, a Canadian accounting firm with offices located in each of Canada's major cities. W&S Partners has just been awarded the December 31, 2012, statutory audit for Cloud 9 Ltd. (Cloud 9). The audit team assigned to this client is:
- Jo Wadley, partner
- Sharon Gallagher, audit manager
- Josh Thomas and Suzie Pickering, audit seniors
- Mark Batten, IT audit manager
- Ian Harper and you, graduates.

As a part of the planning process for the new audit, the audit team needs to gain an understanding of Cloud 9's structure and its business environment. By understanding the client's business, the audit team can identify potential risks that may have a significant effect on the financial statements. This will assist the team in planning and performing the audit.

Required

Answer the following questions based on the additional information about Cloud 9 presented in the appendix to this book and in this and earlier chapters. You should also consider your answer to the case study questions in earlier chapters where relevant.

Your task is to research the retail and wholesale footwear industries and report back to the audit team. Your report will form part of the overall understanding of Cloud 9's structure and its environment.

Case study—Cloud 9 questions continue the Cloud 9 case presented in the textbook and encourage detailed evaluation of the scenario presented. These challenging exercises are ideal for group discussion and build professional communication skills. In addition, longer case-type questions allow students to analyze information and pull together concepts from the chapter and apply them to real-world situations.

RESEARCH QUESTION 3.1

The auditor and the Ponzi scheme

Bernard Madoff was convicted in 2009 of running a Ponzi scheme, the biggest in U.S. history. A Ponzi scheme is essentially the process of taking money from new investors on a regular basis and using the cash to pay promised returns to existing investors. The high and steady returns received by existing investors are the attraction for new investors, but they are not real returns from investments.

As long as new investors keep contributing and existing investors do not seek redemptions, or the return of their money, the scheme continues. However, eventually, as in the Madoff situation, circumstances change, the scheme is discovered, and the remaining investors find that their capital has disappeared.

At age 71, Madoff was sentenced to prison for 150 years and will die in jail. Now that Madoff is behind bars, attention has turned to Madoff's auditor, David G. Friehling. Friehling is accused of creating false and fraudulent audited financial statements for Madoff's firm, Bernard L. Madoff Investment Securities LLC. Prosecutors allege that these fraudulent reports covered the period from the early 1990s to the end of 2008.

Required

(a) Research the progress of the case against David Friehling. Write a report explaining his alleged role in the Madoff Ponzi scheme and the current (at the time you write your report) state of the legal action against him.
(b) Friehling was subject to U.S. auditing standards and legislation. Explain if, and how, Friehling's alleged actions would violate Canadian auditing standards and professional ethics.

Sources: D. Searcey and A. Efrati, "Sins and admission: getting into top prisons," *The Wall Street Journal: Europe* 17–19, July 2009, p. 29; C. Bray and A. Efrati, "Madoff ex-auditor set to waive indictment," *The Wall Street Journal: Europe* 17–19, July 2009, p. 29.

RESEARCH QUESTION 3.2

Public company financial statements

The financial statements for public companies are available through the website SEDAR (www.sedar.com). This is the official site that provides access to information filed by public companies and investment funds with the CSA. The objective in making public this financial information is to enhance investor awareness of the business and affairs of public companies, and to promote confidence in the operation of capital markets in Canada. Achieving this objective relies heavily on the provision of accurate information on market participants.

Required

Go to www.sedar.com and select the most recent set of *audited annual* financial statements for a Canadian public company. Using this set of financial statements, answer the following:

(a) When planning the audit, the auditor needs to gain an understanding of the entity's structure and its business environment. To do this, the auditor focuses on identifying potential risks that may have a significant effect on the financial statements. Prepare a memo for the audit planning file and discuss the entity, industry, and economy-level factors that the auditor should consider to plan the audit for this entity.

Research questions take you beyond the text and encourage you to complete various research-based activities.

BRIEF CONTENTS

CONTENTS

4 Audit Planning II 126

5 Audit Evidence 168

6 Overview of Tests of Controls, Substantive Procedures, and Sampling 214

7 Gaining An Understanding of The Client's System of Internal Controls

8 Execution of The Audit—Testing of Controls

9 Execution of the Audit—Performing Substantive Procedures

12 Completing and Reporting on the Audit 460

CHAPTER 1

Introduction and overview of audit and assurance

LEARNING OBJECTIVES

After studying this chapter you should be able to:

1 define an assurance engagement

2 differentiate between types of assurance services

3 explain the different levels of assurance

4 outline different audit opinions

5 differentiate between the roles of the preparer and the auditor, and discuss the different firms that provide assurance services

6 explain why there is a demand for audit and assurance services

7 identify the different regulators, legislation, and regulations surrounding the assurance process

8 describe the audit expectation gap.

AUDITING AND ASSURANCE STANDARDS

CANADIAN	INTERNATIONAL
Canadian Standards for Assurance Engagements, s. 5000–5790	*International Framework for Assurance Engagements*
CAS 200 *Overall Objectives of the Independent Auditor, and the Conduct of an Audit in Accordance with Canadian Auditing Standards*	ISA 200 *Overall Objectives of the Independent Auditor and the Conduct of an Audit in Accordance with International Standards on Auditing*
CAS 210 *Agreeing the Terms of Audit Engagements*	ISA 210 *Agreeing the Terms of Audit Engagements*
CAS 220 *Quality Control for an Audit of Financial Statements*	ISA 220 *Quality Control for an Audit of Financial Statements*
CAS 240 *The Auditor's Responsibilities Relating to Fraud in an Audit of Financial Statements*	ISA 240 *The Auditor's Responsibilities Relating to Fraud in an Audit of Financial Statements*
CAS 610 *Using the Work of Internal Auditors*	ISA 610 *Using the Work of Internal Auditors*
CAS 700 *Forming an Opinion and Reporting on Financial Statements*	ISA 700 *Forming an Opinion and Reporting on Financial Statements*
CAS 705 *Modifications to the Opinion in the Independent Auditor's Report*	ISA 705 *Modifications to the Opinion in the Independent Auditor's Report*
CAS 706 *Emphasis of Matter Paragraphs and Other Matter Paragraphs in the Independent Auditor's Report*	ISA 706 *Emphasis of Matter Paragraphs and Other Matter Paragraphs in the Independent Auditor's Report*
Canadian Standards for Assurance Engagements s.7050	ISRE 2410 *Review of Interim Financial Information Performed by the Independent Auditor of the Entity*
	IAPS 1010 *The Consideration of Environmental Matters in the Audit of Financial Statements*
CSQC 1 *Quality Control for Firms that Perform Audits and Reviews of Financial Statements, Other Financial Information, and Other Assurance Engagements*	ISQC 1 *Quality Control for Firms that Perform Audits and Reviews of Financial Statements, and Other Assurance and Related Services Engagements*
Canadian Standards for Assurance Engagements, Review Engagements, s. 8100–8600	
Canadian Standards for Assurance Engagements, Compilation Engagements, s. 9200	

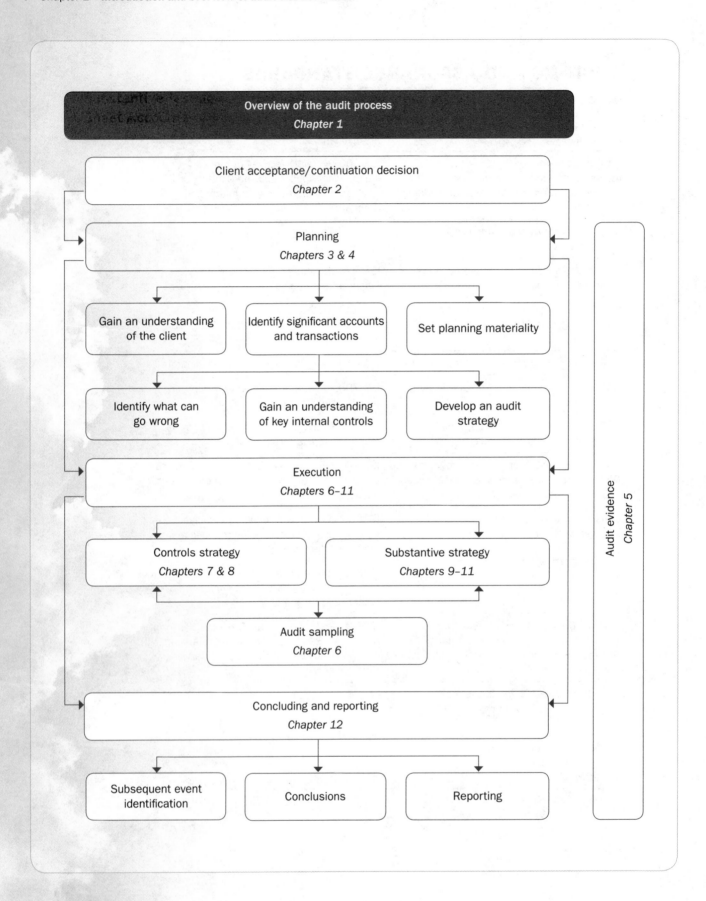

Cloud 9

This book is designed to provide students with the opportunity to learn about auditing by using a practical, problem-based approach. Each chapter begins with some information about an audit client—Cloud 9 Ltd. (Cloud 9). The chapter then provides the underlying concepts and background information needed to deal with this client's situation and the problems facing its auditor. As students work through the chapters, they gradually build up their knowledge of auditing by studying how the contents of each chapter are applied to Cloud 9. The end-of-chapter exercises and problems also provide students with the opportunity to study other aspects of Cloud 9's audit, in addition to applying the knowledge gained in the chapter to other practical examples.

Cloud 9 Ltd., a subsidiary of Cloud 9 Inc., a listed company in Canada, is looking to expand. McLellan's Shoes is seen as a potential target.

In 1980, Ron McLellan starts a business in manufacturing and retailing customized basketball shoes. Ron calls his business McLellan's Shoes. Ron borrows from the bank to start the business, using his house as security, and over the years he works very hard to establish a profitable niche in the highly competitive sport shoe market. Ron is able to repay the bank in 1990, just before the recession. As he watches interest rates soar above 20 percent, he vows never to borrow again.

As the business grows, Ron's wife and three adult children start to work for him, with responsibility for administration, marketing and sales, production, and distribution. By the early 1990s, Ron's business employs 20 people full-time, most of whom work in production. There are also several casual employees and part-time staff in the retail outlet, particularly during busy periods.

In February 1992, Ron receives a call from Chip Masters, the senior vice-president of Cloud 9 Inc. Chip expresses an interest in buying McLellan's Shoes. Ron is getting tired, and his children are starting to fight among themselves about who is going to take over from their father. Ron has had enough, but he does not want Chip to know that. He asks if Chip is ready to talk about the price. Chip says he is, but first he needs to see the audited financial statements for McLellan's Shoes.

Ron asks for some time. He tells Chip that he needs to talk to his family and will get back to him. When Ron puts the phone down he immediately rings his friend from the golf club, Ernie Black, who is a chartered accountant. For years, Ernie has been quietly suggesting to Ron that his business affairs need attention. Ron is skilled at making deals and working hard, but he has never bothered with sophisticated financial arrangements. He has never had a formal set of financial statements prepared for McLellan's Shoes. Ron is in a panic—he wants to sell McLellan's Shoes, but what is he going to do about Chip's request for audited financial statements?

AUDIT PROCESS IN FOCUS

The purpose of this chapter is to provide an overview of audit and assurance services. As the focus of this book is the audit of financial statements, we begin with an overview of what an audit is, and why and how it is done. We also introduce some of the assurance and audit terms that will be used throughout the text. We then go on to define assurance engagements and differentiate between the various types of assurance engagements. The assurance engagements explained in this chapter include financial statement audits, compliance audits, operational audits, comprehensive audits, and internal audits. We also discuss the emerging area of assurance of corporate social responsibility disclosures. We then provide an overview of the different levels of assurance that can be provided when conducting assurance procedures. The levels of assurance discussed in the chapter include reasonable, moderate, and no assurance engagements.

Next, we provide a brief overview of the different audit opinions that an auditor can arrive at after completing an audit. An auditor can provide either an unmodified or a modified audit opinion. Unmodified or modified opinions can include an emphasis of matter paragraph, which is intended to draw the reader of the opinion to a specific matter. If a modified opinion is used, the auditor has the choice of three types of modifications: qualified, adverse, or a disclaimer of opinion. These concepts are explained further in this chapter.

The roles of the financial statement preparer and auditor are explained and contrasted. An overview of the different firms that provide assurance services is then given. That section contains details about both accounting and consulting firms and the different services they provide. The reasons why there is a demand for audit and assurance services are then described, and an overview of assurance regulators and their regulations is provided. The audit expectation gap is explained in the last section of the chapter.

1.1 AUDITING AND ASSURANCE DEFINED

Cloud 9

Chip Masters has asked Ron McLellan for audited financial statements of McLellan's Shoes. He has heard about tax audits, efficiency audits, and financial statement audits. Are they all the same thing? Ernie explains to Ron that there are several services that people call "audits" that are different from financial statement audits. However, all these services, including financial statement audits, can be defined as assurance engagements.

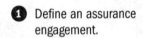 **1** Define an assurance engagement.

assurance engagement an engagement performed by an auditor or consultant to enhance the reliability of the subject matter

accountability relationship situation in which one party is answerable to another for the subject matter

According to the CICA Handbook, an **assurance engagement** is an engagement where a practitioner is engaged to issue a written report and concludes on a subject matter for which the accountable party is responsible. Therefore, a prerequisite for an assurance engagement is the existence of an **accountability relationship**, where one party is answerable to another for the subject matter (s. 5025.04).

An assurance practitioner may be an auditor working in public practice providing assurance on financial statements or a consultant providing assurance about environmental disclosures. As illustrated in the triangle in figure 1.1, there must be an accountability relationship where a person or organization is responsible to the users for the subject matter. For a financial statement audit, the company is the accountable

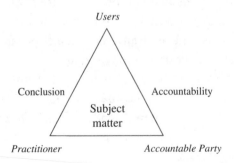

FIGURE 1.1 **Parties involved in an assurance engagement**

party, its shareholders are the users, and the subject matter is the financial statements. Engagements where the practitioner is hired to provide advice to clients, such as management and tax consulting, are not assurance engagements, as there is no accountability relationship between management and users.

While the audit of a company's financial statements is one of the most common types of assurance engagements and the focus of much of this book, it is not the only type of assurance engagement.

The next section of this chapter provides a description of some of the different types of assurance services.

1.1.1 Auditing and assurance terms defined

When you are acquiring a new skill, it is often necessary to become familiar with new terminology. This section presents a number of key assurance and audit terms to introduce you to the language of auditing.

Term	Definition
applicable financial reporting framework	The financial framework chosen by management to prepare a company's financial statements. For example, an applicable framework for a reporting issuer would be International Financial Reporting Standards (IFRS). An applicable framework for a private enterprise could be Accounting Standards for Private Enterprises (ASPE), or it could be IFRS.
assertions	Statements made by management regarding the recognition, measurement, and presentation and disclosure of items in the financial statements.
audit evidence	Information used by the auditor to support the audit opinion.
audit file	The file where the evidence and documentation of the work performed is kept as a permanent record to support the opinion issued.
audit plan	The list or description of audit procedures to be performed.
audit risk	The risk that the auditor may express an inappropriate opinion. This means the auditor may indicate that the financial statements are not materially misstated when in fact they are.
financial statements	A structured representation of historical financial information, including the related notes.
independent auditor's report	The auditor's formal expression of opinion on whether the financial statements are in accordance with the applicable financial reporting framework.
internal control	The processes implemented and maintained by management to help the entity achieve its objectives.
material	An amount or disclosure that is significant enough to make a difference to a user. For example, if a company reports a profit of $100,000 and the auditor finds an error resulting in an overstatement of net income by $10, this probably wouldn't affect an investor's decision. However, if the auditor finds an error overstating revenue by $50,000 or 50 percent of the profit, this likely would affect the user's decision and would therefore be considered material. The concept of materiality is one of the reasons why an audit never provides 100 percent assurance.

(continued)

Term	Definition
materiality	The maximum amount of misstatement or omission the auditor can tolerate and still issue an unmodified or "clean" audit opinion.
sufficient and appropriate evidence	The quantity (sufficiency) and quality (appropriateness) of the evidence collected by the auditor.
unmodified opinion	The auditor concludes that the financial statements are fairly presented.
working papers	Paper or electronic documentation of the audit created by the audit team as evidence of the work completed.

BEFORE YOU GO ON

1.1 What are two examples of assurance providers?

1.2 What might an assurance provider express a conclusion about?

1.3 What is an accountability relationship?

1.2 DIFFERENT ASSURANCE SERVICES

2 Differentiate between types of assurance services.

In this section, we provide an overview of the different types of assurance services that an assurance practitioner can provide. Common types of assurance engagements are financial statement audits, compliance audits, operational audits, comprehensive audits, and internal audits. We will also briefly consider assurance on corporate social responsibility (CSR) disclosures. Each will now be explained in turn.

1.2.1 Financial statement audits

financial statement audit an audit that provides reasonable assurance about whether the financial statements are prepared in all material respects in accordance with the financial reporting framework

According to CAS 200 *Overall Objectives of the Independent Auditor and the Conduct of an Audit in Accordance with Canadian Auditing Standards,* the objective of a **financial statement audit** is for the auditor to express an opinion about whether the financial statements are prepared in all material respects in accordance with a financial reporting framework (CAS 200, para. 11). Within a Canadian context, this means that the financial statements have been prepared in accordance with Canadian generally accepted accounting principles (GAAP) and any relevant legislation, such as the Canada Business Corporations Act.

This means that when a set of financial statements has been audited, the information presented has been verified by an independent auditor. To do this, the auditor methodically gathers evidence to corroborate the financial information presented by management. At the end of an audit engagement, the auditor issues a report indicating whether the financial information is fairly presented in accordance with the financial reporting framework. This lends credibility to the information.

listed entity an entity whose shares, stock, or debt are listed on a stock exchange

fair presentation the consistent and faithful application of accounting standards when preparing the financial statements

The Canadian Securities Administrators (CSA) requires **listed entities** to publish audited financial statements annually. It is the auditor's responsibility to form an opinion on the fair presentation of the financial statements. **Fair presentation** refers to the consistent and faithful application of the accounting standards. In fulfilling their role, the auditor must be independent of the company audited and exercise due professional care.

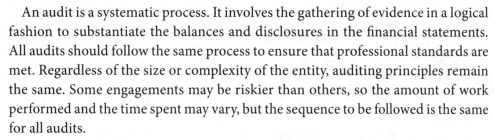

Cloud 9

Ron believes that his business has good, reliable financial records. Ron's wife helps him keep tight control of the cash and other assets, and together they prepare some simple reports on a regular basis. Ron believes he knows exactly what is happening in the business and monitors the business's cash flow and profit very closely. However, he has not prepared financial statements that comply with Canadian generally accepted accounting principles (GAAP). Is this a problem? Ernie explains to Ron that some businesses must apply the accounting standards. For example, if a company requires audited financial statements to meet regulatory requirements or as part of a loan agreement, then the financial statements must comply with Canadian GAAP.

An audit is a systematic process. It involves the gathering of evidence in a logical fashion to substantiate the balances and disclosures in the financial statements. All audits should follow the same process to ensure that professional standards are met. Regardless of the size or complexity of the entity, auditing principles remain the same. Some engagements may be riskier than others, so the amount of work performed and the time spent may vary, but the sequence to be followed is the same for all audits.

The first step in this sequence is the planning stage. This involves performing an overall risk assessment. The auditor documents an understanding of the business, its environment, and its processes to determine where the greatest risks may be. The auditor then devises an overall audit strategy, taking these risks into consideration. This allows the auditor to plan when to perform the "field work" (the work to be done at the client's premises), who will do it, and what exactly needs to be done. Tasks are usually divided by business cycle or financial statement groupings (for example, purchasing cycle, cash, property, plant, and equipment). The financial statement accounts related to each cycle are divided into sections. For each section there should be an "audit working paper program" that lists the procedures to be performed for that area.

During the execution stage, the auditor typically works at the client's premises. When the auditor is not a sole practitioner, and carries out the engagement as part of a team, staff members are assigned sections to complete, which generally involves obtaining information, assessing it, and having discussions with the client's staff regarding systems, procedures, and clarification as required. As the work is done, it is documented in the audit working paper file (which may be electronic or paper). The documentation is done through the use of narrative, memos, or schedules with audit "ticks" (common conventions used by auditors to indicate the work performed). The audit programs are "signed off" or initialled by audit members once completed. Each completed section is then reviewed by a more senior auditor, as work must be properly supervised.

Once the field work has been completed, the auditor leaves the client's premises; however, there remain a number of completion procedures to be done. Once all of the required procedures have been performed, the completed file and financial statements go to the partner responsible for the audit for review. If the partner believes there is sufficient and appropriate evidence in the audit file, and the financial statements appear fairly stated, he or she will approve and issue an unmodified audit opinion on the financial statements.

Limitations of a financial statement audit

An audit is conducted to enhance the reliability and credibility of the information included in the financial statements. It is not a guarantee that the financial statements are free from fraud and error.

The limitations of an audit result from the nature of financial reporting, the nature of audit procedures, and the need for the audit to be conducted within a reasonable period of time and at a reasonable cost (CAS 200).

"The nature of financial reporting" refers to the use of judgement when preparing financial statements, because of the subjectivity required when arriving at accounting estimates. Judgement is also required when selecting and applying accounting methods.

"The nature of audit procedures" refers to the reliance on evidence provided by the client and its management. If an auditor does not have access to all the information relevant to the audit, there is a limitation in the scope of the audit. If the auditor is unaware of this situation, he or she may arrive at an inappropriate conclusion based on incomplete facts. Evidence may be withheld or modified by perpetrators of fraud. It can be difficult for an auditor to determine whether fraud has occurred and documents altered, as those committing fraud generally hide evidence. Sampling is used when testing transactions and account balances. If a sample is not representative of all items available for testing, an auditor may arrive at an invalid conclusion.

"The timeliness and cost of a financial statement audit" refers to the pressure an auditor faces to complete the audit within a certain time frame at a reasonable cost. While it is important that auditors do not omit procedures in an effort to meet time and cost constraints, they may be under some pressure to do so. This pressure will come from clients wanting to issue their financial statements by a certain date, from clients refusing to pay additional fees for additional audit effort, and from within the audit firm, where there are pressures to complete all audits on a timely basis to avoid incurring costs that may not be recovered. By taking the time to plan the audit properly, an auditor can ensure that adequate time is spent where the risks of a significant error or fraud are greatest.

1.2.2 Compliance audits

compliance audit an audit to determine whether the entity has conformed with regulations, rules, or processes

A **compliance audit** involves gathering evidence to ascertain whether the person or entity under review has followed the applicable rules, policies, procedures, laws, and regulations. There are a number of examples of compliance audits. A tax audit is used to determine whether an individual or company has completed a tax return in accordance with the Income Tax Act. Within an organization, management may specify that certain processes be followed when completing a function. For example, a company may have policies and procedures for the hiring of new staff. In that case, the organization's internal auditors may be called upon to determine whether employees are following the specified processes appropriately.

1.2.3 Operational audits

operational audit an assessment of the economy, efficiency, and effectiveness of an organization's operations

Operational audits are concerned with the economy, efficiency, and effectiveness of an organization's activities. Economy refers to the cost of inputs, including wages and materials. Efficiency refers to the relationship between inputs and outputs; specifically, efficiency refers to the use of the minimum amount of inputs to achieve a given output. Finally, effectiveness refers to the achievement of certain goals or the production of a certain level of outputs. From an organization's perspective it is important to perform well across all three dimensions and not allow one to dominate. For example, if buying cheap inputs results in an inefficient production process, efficiency may be seen to be sacrificed to achieve economic goals.

Operational audits are generally conducted by an organization's internal auditors, or they may be outsourced to an external audit firm. Operational audits are sometimes referred to as value for money audits, performance audits, or efficiency audits.

1.2.4 Comprehensive audits

A **comprehensive audit** may encompass elements of a financial statement audit, a compliance audit, and an operational audit. For example, an auditor may report on whether an entity has met its efficiency targets. Comprehensive audits most commonly occur in the public sector, where compliance with various regulations is examined as part of the financial statement audit.

> **comprehensive audit** an audit that encompasses a range of audit and audit-related activities, such as a financial statement audit, operational audit, and compliance audit

1.2.5 Internal audits

Internal audits are conducted to provide assurance about various aspects of an organization's activities. The internal audit function is typically conducted by employees of the organization being audited, but can be outsourced to an external audit firm. As such, the function of internal audit is determined by **those charged with governance** and management within the organization. While the functions of internal audits vary widely from one organization to another, they are often concerned with evaluating and improving risk management, internal control procedures, and elements of the governance process. The internal audit function often conducts operational audits, compliance audits, internal control assessments, and reviews. Many internal auditors are members of the Institute of Internal Auditors (IIA), an international organization with more than 120,000 members that provides guidance and standards to aid internal auditors in their work. When conducting a financial statement audit, the external auditor may consider the work done by the internal auditors (CAS 610 *Using the Work of Internal Auditors*).

> **internal audit** an independent service within an entity that generally evaluates and improves risk management, internal control procedures, and elements of the governance process

> **those charged with governance** generally the board of directors, and may include management of an entity

1.2.6 Corporate social responsibility (CSR) assurance—An emerging area

Corporate social responsibility (CSR) reporting is voluntary. However, it is becoming more widespread (see section 1.6.4 of this chapter for a discussion of the demand for assurance in a voluntary setting). CSR disclosures include environmental, employee, and social reporting. Some organizations choose to have their CSR disclosures assured by an independent assurance provider. For example, Vancity Savings and Credit Union, part of the Vancity Group, voluntarily issues a CSR report, and it is formally assured by an independent third party. The assurance of CSR disclosures can be carried out by both auditors and specialist **consulting firms**. As these disclosures include non-financial as well as financial information, the skill set required to conduct these assurance services is quite broad.

Whether a company chooses to provide additional voluntary environmental disclosures or not, an auditor must still consider the impact of environmental issues on a

> **corporate social responsibility (CSR)** a range of activities undertaken voluntarily by a corporation; CSR disclosures include environmental, employee, and social reporting

> **consulting firms** non-audit firms that provide assurance services on non-financial information, such as corporate social responsibility and environmental disclosures

client's financial statements when conducting the financial statement audit. However, as investors demand more relevant information in this area, further guidance is expected.

PROFESSIONAL ENVIRONMENT

Assurance engagements on carbon emissions information

Many companies now present CSR information in their annual reports or in separate corporate sustainability reports. In some cases, the reports include information about carbon emissions. However, the reporting and assurance of these reports is voluntary and largely unregulated, raising concerns about the quality of the information. One of these concerns is that the information being provided in CSR reports is not sufficiently quantitative, particularly with respect to carbon emissions data.

There is little guidance for assurance providers with respect to carbon emissions. Canadian Standards for Assurance Engagements s. 5025 (*Standards for Assurance Engagements other than Audits of Financial Statements and Other Historical Financial Information*) provides general guidance for assurance engagements, but it is not specific to engagements that assure either carbon emissions information or corporate sustainability reports.

Due to the increasing demand for assurance on greenhouse gas information, the International Auditing and Assurance Standards Board (IAASB) is in the process of developing a standard for this topic. The rationale for the project is related to the growth in carbon or emissions trading schemes around the world, and the need for reliable information and a global approach for their efficient and effective operation. The IAASB claims that the "robustness of such schemes is subject to the rigor with which emissions are measured, which in turn is affected by the measurement criteria and the assurance systems used." The IAASB released a consultation paper in late 2009 seeking views on key issues in developing the standard, specifically on the form of assurance report that users would find most useful, as well as technical aspects of applying the assurance process to carbon emissions. While the timing of this project has not been finalized, an exposure draft has been released and comments received. The IAASB is in the process of reviewing the exposure draft responses.

As Canada has adopted the international standards, the Auditing and Assurance Standards Board (AASB) has issued an exposure draft based on the international standard, with minor modifications considered necessary for the Canadian environment. The final standard is expected to be released in 2012.

Sources: International Federation of Accountants. "IAASB Issues Consultation Paper to Enhance Reporting on Greenhouse Gases." (October 22, 2009) www.ifac.org/MediaCenter.

Cloud 9

Ron is not concerned about internal audits—his business is too small for a separate internal audit function. He is also not worried about CSR reporting or compliance and operational audits. His priority at the moment is to close the deal with Chip Masters, and he still does not know what he has to do about the audit.

BEFORE YOU GO ON

2.1 What are the three elements of an operational audit?

2.2 What is the objective of a financial statement audit?

2.3 What are the most common functions of the internal audit function?

1.3 DIFFERENT LEVELS OF ASSURANCE

In this section we describe the different levels of assurance that a practitioner can provide when conducting assurance procedures. An assurance practitioner can provide reasonable assurance, moderate assurance, or no assurance. When providing reasonable and moderate assurance, the practitioner's report is addressed to the party requesting assurance (for example, a company's shareholders). When an assurance practitioner performs a non-assurance engagement, a report on the findings is sent to the responsible party (that is, the organization that prepared the information under consideration). The differences between reasonable, moderate, and no assurance are now explained.

3 Explain the different levels of assurance.

1.3.1 Reasonable assurance

The objective of a **reasonable assurance** engagement is to gather sufficient evidence upon which to form a positive expression of an opinion regarding whether the information being assured is presented fairly. This means that the auditor has done adequate work to report with reasonable certainty that the information being assured is, or is not, reliable. This does not reflect absolute assurance, as an auditor can never be 100 percent certain that there are no errors or omissions. For example, an auditor is in the position to say whether in their opinion the financial statements are in accordance with relevant laws and accounting standards and they present fairly the financial position of the reporting entity. Auditors can only make such a positive statement if they are reasonably sure that the evidence gathered is sufficient and appropriate. The audit of a company's financial statements is one example of a reasonable assurance engagement. CAS 700 *Forming an Opinion and Reporting on Financial Statements* provides guidance on the form and elements of the audit report.

The audit opinion will depend upon the auditor's findings while conducting the audit. A brief overview of the different opinions that an auditor may form when conducting a financial statement audit is provided in the next section of this chapter. Reasonable assurance is the highest level of assurance provided; again, note that it is high but not absolute assurance. An example of an audit report is provided in figure 1.2.

reasonable assurance assurance that provides high but not absolute assurance on the reliability of the subject matter

1.3.2 Moderate assurance

The objective of a **moderate assurance** engagement is to perform sufficient procedures and gather sufficient evidence upon which to express a negative assurance form of communication regarding the reliability of the information being assured. This means that the auditor has done adequate work to report whether or not anything came to their attention that would lead them to believe that the information being assured is not worthy of belief. The auditor is not in a position to say that in their opinion the financial statements are in accordance with the relevant law and accounting standards, and does present fairly the financial position and performance of the reporting entity. The auditor is only able to say that the information is plausible, in that nothing makes them believe otherwise. To make a negative statement, auditors do not need to obtain as much evidence or perform as many procedures as when they make a positive statement.

The review of a company's financial statements is called a **review engagement**. A review engagement may be requested when the client requires some assurance over the financial statements but does not require an audit level of assurance. For example, a lender of a small business may not want to approve a loan based on financial statements with no assurance, but it may not require the same level of assurance that an

moderate assurance assurance that provides negative assurance on the reliability of the subject matter

review engagement engagement in which the auditor does adequate work to report whether or not anything came to their attention that would lead them to believe that the information being assured is not fairly presented

FIGURE 1.2 **Example of an audit report**

Source: Ernst & Young LLP, 2011

Ernst & Young LLP
Chartered Accountants
Ernst & Young Tower
222 Bay Street, P.O. Box 251
Toronto, Ontario M5K 1J7

Tel: 416 864 1234
Fax: 416 864 1174
ey.com/ca

INDEPENDENT AUDITORS' REPORT

To the Board of Directors of Skyward Ltd.

We have audited the accompanying consolidated financial statements of Skyward Ltd., which comprise the consolidated statements of financial position as at December 31, 2012 and 2011, and the consolidated statements of comprehensive income, changes in equity and cash flows for the years then ended, and a summary of significant accounting policies and other explanatory information.

Management's responsibility for the consolidated financial statements

Management is responsible for the preparation and fair presentation of these consolidated financial statements in accordance with International Financial Reporting Standards, and for such internal control as management determines is necessary to enable the preparation of consolidated financial statements that are free from material misstatement, whether due to fraud or error.

Auditors' responsibility

Our responsibility is to express an opinion on these consolidated financial statements based on our audits. We conducted our audits in accordance with Canadian generally accepted auditing standards. Those standards require that we comply with ethical requirements and plan and perform the audit to obtain reasonable assurance about whether the consolidated financial statements are free from material misstatement.

An audit involves performing procedures to obtain audit evidence about the amounts and disclosures in the consolidated financial statements. The procedures selected depend on the auditors' judgment, including the assessment of the risks of material misstatement of the consolidated financial statements, whether due to fraud or error. In making those risk assessments, the auditors consider internal control relevant to the entity's preparation and fair presentation of the consolidated financial statements in order to design audit procedures that are appropriate in the circumstances, but not for the purpose of expressing an opinion on the effectiveness of the entity's internal control. An audit also includes evaluating the appropriateness of accounting policies used and the reasonableness of accounting estimates made by management, as well as evaluating the overall presentation of the consolidated financial statements.

We believe that the audit evidence we have obtained in our audits is sufficient and appropriate to provide a basis for our audit opinion.

Opinion

In our opinion, the consolidated financial statements present fairly, in all material respects, the financial position of Skyward Ltd. as at December 31, 2012 and 2011, and its financial performance and its cash flows for the years then ended in accordance with International Financial Reporting Standards.

Toronto, Canada

February X, 2013.

"Ernst & Young LLP"

Chartered Accountants
Licensed Public Accountants

ERNST & YOUNG

Ernst & Young LLP
Chartered Accountants
Ernst & Young Tower
222 Bay Street, P.O. Box 251
Toronto, Ontario M5K 1J7

Tel: 416 864 1234
Fax: 416 864 1174
ey.com/ca

REVIEW ENGAGEMENT REPORT

To the Board of Directors of Skyward Ltd.

We have reviewed the consolidated balance sheets of Cloud 9 Ltd. as at December 31, 2012 and the consolidated statements of income, retained earnings and cash flows for the year then ended. Our review was made in accordance with Canadian generally accepted standards for review engagements and, accordingly, consisted primarily of inquiry, analytical procedures and discussion related to information supplied to us by the company.

A review does not constitute an audit and, consequently, we do not express an audit opinion on these consolidated financial statements.

Based on our review, nothing has come to our attention that causes us to believe that these consolidated financial statements are not, in all material respects, in accordance with Canadian accounting standards for private enterprises.

Toronto, Canada

February X, 2013.

"Ernst & Young LLP"

Chartered Accountants
Licensed Public Accountants

FIGURE 1.3 **Example of a review engagement report**
Source: Ernst & Young LLP, 2011

audit would provide. CICA Handbook sections 8100–8600 provide guidance on review engagements and the form and elements of the review report. An example of a review report is provided in figure 1.3. The review report highlights the responsibilities of the auditor to comply with Canadian generally accepted standards for review engagements and that the financial statements comply with Canadian GAAP or another appropriate financial reporting framework. An explanation of the procedures used in conducting the review is provided. The report states explicitly that an audit was not performed and therefore an audit opinion is not being expressed. Finally, the review report includes the conclusion of the auditor that they were not aware of any matter that made them believe that the financial statements were not in all material respects in accordance with GAAP or other appropriate framework (negative assurance).

In conducting a review, an auditor will obtain an understanding of the entity under review; identify potential material misstatements where effort should be concentrated; and conduct analytical procedures, enquiries of entity personnel, and other tasks to aid in the formulation of their report. The work done when conducting a review is less extensive than the work done when conducting an audit. Specifically, an auditor will make enquiries of key personnel, apply analytical procedures, and hold discussions with client staff. That is why an auditor can provide only moderate (limited) assurance after completing a review. It is also why this engagement is less time-consuming and therefore less costly.

1.3.3 No assurance

An assurance provider may perform other services for clients for which **no assurance** is provided. In such circumstances an assurance provider must ensure

no assurance what results when an auditor completes a set of tasks requested by the client and reports factually on the results of that work to the client

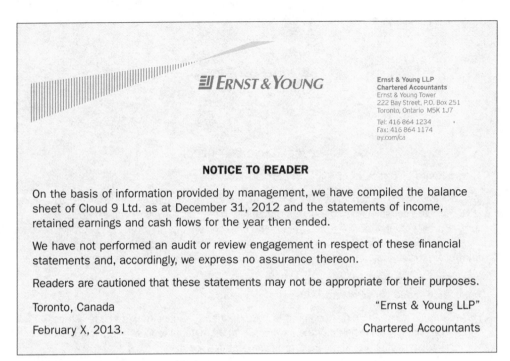

FIGURE 1.4 **Example of a Notice to Reader**
Source: Ernst & Young LLP, 2011

compilation engagement
engagement in which an auditor
compiles a set of financial
statements based on the
information provided by the client,
ensuring mathematical accuracy

when reporting to users that they make clear that they are merely reporting the activities that they have performed (and in some engagements, their findings) and are not providing assurance. An example of an engagement where no assurance is provided is a **compilation engagement**, where an auditor compiles the financial information as provided by the client and arranges it into a set of financial statements. The accountant ensures that the information is mathematically correct but does not perform any procedures to assure that the information is not materially misstated, and therefore no expression of assurance is provided. However, the auditor must ensure that they are not associated with information that may be false or misleading.

To ensure that users are aware that no assurance is being provided, the auditor attaches what is called a **Notice to Reader** report to the financial statements. The Notice to Reader report explicitly states that no assurance is being provided. An example of a Notice to Reader is provided in figure 1.4.

Table 1.1 summarizes the differences among the three types of engagements.

Notice to Reader the
communication issued when the
auditor performs a compilation
engagement

TABLE 1.1 **Types of
engagements**

Characteristic	Audit	Review	Compilation
Objective	To reduce the assurance engagement risk to an acceptably low level so that a positive opinion can be provided. Reasonable assurance means a high, but not absolute, level of assurance.	To reduce the assurance engagement risk to an acceptable level to allow the practitioner to express a negative form of expression in that nothing has come to their attention.	To compile a set of financial statements based on information provided. No assurance provided.

(continued)

Characteristic	Audit	Review	Compilation
Procedures	Sufficient appropriate evidence is obtained as part of a systematic process that includes: • obtaining an understanding of the assurance engagement circumstances • assessing risks • responding to assessed risks • performing further evidence-gathering procedures using a combination of inspection, observation, confirmation, re-calculation, re-performance, analytical procedures, and inquiry.	Sufficient appropriate evidence is obtained as part of a systematic process that includes obtaining an understanding of the subject matter and other assurance engagement circumstances, but in which evidence-gathering procedures are limited to discussion, analytics, and inquiry.	Mathematical accuracy is checked. There is no requirement for sufficient appropriate evidence; however, the auditor must not be associated with anything false or misleading.
Financial reporting framework	Must be in accordance with Canadian GAAP or other appropriate financial reporting framework.	Must be in accordance with Canadian GAAP or other appropriate financial reporting framework.	GAAP not required.
Level of assurance	High	Moderate assurance	No assurance
Report	Independent Auditor's Report	Review Engagement Report	Notice to Reader
Cost and time	Most time-consuming, highest cost	May take less time, as less work required; lower cost	Least amount of work, lowest cost

Cloud 9

As Ernie explains the differences between reasonable and moderate assurance, Ron wonders if Chip will accept a review, rather than an audit, of the financial statements. If he will, it will be much easier and cheaper for Ron. However, Ron also realizes that Chip would not get as much assurance from a review as he would get from an audit. Ron thinks Chip would know the difference between an audit and a review; because he asked for an audit, Chip must need the additional assurance it provides.

BEFORE YOU GO ON

3.1 What are the main differences between reasonable and moderate assurance engagements?

3.2 What is the level of assurance required for an annual financial statement for a reporting issuer?

3.3 What does negative assurance mean?

1.4 DIFFERENT AUDIT OPINIONS

4 Outline different audit opinions.

Chapter 12 contains a detailed discussion of the different types of audit opinions an auditor can arrive at when completing an audit. The purpose of this section is to present a very brief overview of those opinions.

The most common audit report is unmodified and contains an unmodified opinion. An **unmodified opinion** is also known as a clean opinion. The audit report in figure 1.2 is an example of such a report. Auditors arrive at this type of opinion when they believe that the financial statements are not materially misstated and that they present fairly the financial position of the company, and that the information provided is in accordance with Canadian GAAP.

unmodified opinion a clean audit opinion; the auditor concludes that the financial statements are fairly presented

An audit report may have an unmodified opinion and include an **emphasis of matter** paragraph. An emphasis of matter paragraph draws the attention of the reader to an issue that the auditor believes has been adequately and accurately explained in a note to the financial statements. The purpose of the paragraph is to ensure that the reader pays appropriate attention to the issue when reading the financial statements. The audit report remains unmodified and users of the financial statements can still rely on the information contained in the financial statements (CAS 706 *Emphasis of Matter Paragraphs and Other Matter Paragraphs in the Independent Auditor's Report*).

emphasis of matter what results when an auditor will issue an unmodified audit opinion when there is a significant issue that is adequately disclosed and there is a need to draw the attention of the user to it

All other audit reports are modified. There are three types of modifications (CAS 705 *Modifications to the Opinion in the Independent Auditor's Report*).

qualified opinion opinion provided when the auditor concludes that the financial statements contain a material (significant) misstatement

The first is called a **qualified opinion** and is issued when the auditor believes that "except for" the effects of a matter that is explained in the audit report, the financial statements can be relied upon by the reader. A qualified opinion is used when the matter of concern can be identified, quantified, and explained in the audit report. In this case the matter of concern is material but not pervasive to the financial statements. In this context, "pervasive" refers to misstatements that are not confined to individual accounts or elements of the financial statements, or, if confined, the misstatements affect an extensive portion of the financial statements or there are missing disclosures that are vital to a user's understanding of the financial statements.

More serious matters require an adverse opinion or disclaimer of opinion. An adverse opinion is appropriate if the auditor has evidence that identified misstatements, individually or in aggregate, are material and pervasive to the financial statements. A disclaimer of opinion is used when the auditor is unable to obtain sufficient appropriate audit evidence on which to base the opinion, and concludes that the possible effects on the financial statements could be material and pervasive. Although these opinions are used in different circumstances, in both instances the matter or matters of concern are so material and pervasive to the financial statements that the auditor cannot issue a qualified, "except for" opinion.

The different possible audit opinions are illustrated in table 1.2.

TABLE 1.2 **Different audit opinions**

Source: CAS 705 *Modifications to the Opinion in the Independent Auditor's Report,* para. AI

Nature of the matter giving rise to the modification	Auditor's judgement about the pervasiveness of the effects or possible effects on the financial statements	
	Material but not pervasive	Material and pervasive
Financial statements are materially misstated	Qualified opinion	Adverse opinion
Inability to obtain sufficient appropriate audit evidence	Qualified opinion	Disclaimer of opinion

Cloud 9

Ron worries that an auditor might not be able to give a clean opinion on his business's financial statements. The whole point of getting an audit would be to give Chip sufficient assurance that the financial statements give a true and fair view of his business's financial position and performance, and thus agree to pay a good price for the business. If the auditor gives a disclaimer of opinion or an adverse opinion, Chip could either change his mind about the business or offer only a very low price because he can't be sure that the business is as profitable and as solvent as Ron claims. Even getting a qualified opinion would be serious. Ernie assures Ron that disclaimers are extremely rare; in fact, he has never seen one. Adverse opinions are also rare, and if Ron's belief about his good financial records and tight control over assets is well founded, then there should not be any major problems.

BEFORE YOU GO ON

4.1 What are the different types of unqualified audit opinions?

4.2 What are the different types of modified audit opinions?

4.3 What type of audit opinion is unqualified and modified?

1.5 PREPARERS AND AUDITORS

In this section we explain and contrast the different responsibilities of financial statement preparers and auditors. We provide details of the role that each group plays in ensuring that the financial statements are a fair representation of the company in question. Following this discussion, there is an overview of the different firms that provide assurance services.

A complete set of financial statements includes the balance sheet (statement of financial position), income statement (statement of comprehensive income), statement of cash flows, statement of changes in equity, and the accompanying notes. It is the responsibility of those charged with governance (generally the board of directors and management of an entity) to prepare the financial statements. They must ensure that the information included in the financial statements is fairly presented and complies with Canadian accounting standards and interpretations. According to CAS 200 *Overall Objectives of the Independent Auditor and the Conduct of an Audit in Accordance with Canadian Auditing Standards*, those charged with governance are responsible for:

- identifying the financial reporting framework to be used in the preparation and presentation of their financial statements
- reporting, establishing, and maintaining internal controls that are effective in preventing and detecting material misstatements finding their way into the financial statements
- selecting and applying appropriate accounting policies and making reasonable accounting estimates.

5 Differentiate between the roles of the preparer and the auditor, and discuss the different firms that provide assurance services.

1.5.1 Preparer responsibility

It is the responsibility of those charged with governance to ensure that the information contained in their financial statements is relevant, reliable, comparable, understandable, and fairly presented. Each of these concepts is now discussed.

Relevant

The information included in the financial statements should be relevant to the users of that report. Information is relevant if it has an impact on the decisions made by users regarding the performance of the entity. Users require information that helps them evaluate past, present, and future events relating to the entity. They are interested in evaluating past decisions made by management and predicting whether the entity will remain viable (that is, a going concern) into the future. Users can use current information to estimate future share price movements, like dividend payments, and the ability of the entity to meet its immediate obligations.

Reliable

The information included in the financial statements should be reliable to the users of those statements. Information is reliable when it is free from material misstatements (errors or fraud). If users perceive that the information presented is unreliable, for whatever reason, the financial statements cannot be used to make the types of decisions outlined above. The information must be unbiased; it must not be presented in such a way as to influence the decision-making process of the user. An independent audit of the financial statements is one method of improving the reliability of the financial statements.

Comparable

The information included in the financial statements should be comparable through time. Users need to be able to trace an entity's performance to identify any trends that may influence their perception of how well the entity is doing. Users also need to be able to benchmark the performance of the entity against other similar organizations to assess its relative performance. To enable such comparisons, information must be presented consistently across time and across entities. Any changes in accounting policies must be clearly disclosed so that appropriate adjustments can be made. Consistent application of Canadian generally accepted accounting principles by all entities over time aids these comparisons.

Understandable

The information included in the financial statements should be understandable. Users need to understand the information presented in order to make appropriate decisions. The notes to the financial statements are used to provide additional details to aid in the interpretation of the accounting information provided. The details included in the notes must be phrased in such a way as to impartially inform users to aid their decision-making.

Fair presentation (true and fair)

The information included in the financial statements should be fairly presented. "Presented fairly" or "truth and fairness" refers to the consistent and faithful application of the accounting standards or an applicable framework when preparing the financial statements.

It is the responsibility of the auditor to form an opinion on the fair presentation or the truth and fairness of the financial statements. In doing so, the auditor will assess the accounting policies selected by those charged with governance of the entity. Specifically, the auditor will evaluate whether those accounting policies are consistent with the financial reporting framework used by the entity. The auditor will also consider the accounting estimates made by those charged with governance and management to determine whether the estimates are reasonable. The auditor will assess the relevance, reliability, comparability, and understandability of the information presented in the financial statements.

1.5.2 Auditor responsibility

When undertaking an audit, the auditor should use professional scepticism, professional judgement, and due care. Each of these concepts is now defined and explained.

Professional scepticism

Professional scepticism is an attitude adopted by the auditor when conducting the audit. It means that the auditor remains independent of the entity, its management, and its staff when completing the audit work. In a practical sense, it means that the auditor maintains a questioning mind and thoroughly investigates all evidence presented by the client. The auditor must seek independent evidence to corroborate information provided by the client and must be suspicious when evidence contradicts documents held by the client or enquiries made of client personnel (including management and those charged with governance).

Professional judgement

Professional judgement relates to the level of expertise, knowledge, and training that an auditor uses while conducting an audit. An auditor must utilize their judgement throughout the audit. For example, an auditor must determine the reliability of an information source and decide on the sufficiency and appropriateness of evidence gathered, the procedures to be used in testing, and an appropriate sample size.

Due care

Due care refers to being diligent while conducting an audit, applying technical and statute-backed standards, and documenting each stage in the audit process.

1.5.3 Assurance providers

Assurance services are provided by accounting and other consulting firms. The largest accounting firms in Canada are known collectively as the "Big-4." The firms that make up the Big-4 are Deloitte, Ernst & Young, KPMG, and PricewaterhouseCoopers (PwC). These four firms operate internationally and dominate the assurance market throughout the world. There were once eight international firms, but after a series of mergers and the collapse of Arthur Andersen, the Big-8 became the Big-4. These four firms dominate the audits of Canada's largest companies.

The next tier of accounting firms is known as the national accounting firms. The firms in this tier have a significant presence nationally and most have international affiliations. National firms in Canada include, among others, Collins Barrow, BDO, PKF Canada, Grant Thornton, DMCL, Myers Norris Penny, RSM Richter, and Nexia Canada. These firms service medium-sized and smaller clients.

The next tier of accounting firms is made up of regional and local accounting firms. These firms service clients in their local areas and range in size from single-partner firms to several-partner firms with professionally qualified and trained staff.

All of these accounting firms provide non-assurance (or non-audit) services as well as assurance (or audit) services. Non-assurance services include management consulting, mergers and acquisitions, insolvency, tax, and accounting services. The Rules of Professional Conduct specify a number of requirements that restrict an accounting firm from providing non-audit services to its audit clients. These rules were established to increase the transparency of the extent of services being provided by an accounting firm to its audit clients after the collapse of several high-profile companies, including Enron and WorldCom (in the United States). The collapse of Arthur Andersen (previously an international accounting firm) raised concerns that the provision of non-audit services to an audit client could affect the independence and objectivity of the auditor.

Accounting firms are not the only providers of assurance services. A number of consulting firms provide assurance services primarily in areas of corporate social responsibility, including some combination of environmental issues, carbon emissions, community engagement, charitable activities, and employee welfare as well as disclosures in other areas. Consulting firms employ staff with a variety of expertise, including, for example, engineers, accountants, sociologists, scientists, and economists. An example of an assurance report on a corporate social responsibility disclosure is provided in figure 1.5.

FIGURE 1.5 **Example of an assurance report on a corporate social responsibility disclosure**
Source: Vancity's 2006–07 Accountability Report

Report of the Independent Social Auditor (Assurance Statement)

Introduction

The Vancity Group has commissioned InterPraxis to provide it with external assurance of its Accountability Report and the supporting web-based material (together hereafter referred to as the 'Report'). The Report presents the Vancity Group's sustainability performance over the period January 1, 2006, to December 31, 2007.

Responsibilities of the Vancity Group and InterPraxis

The Report is prepared solely by the Vancity Group, which is responsible for its entire content. This Assurance Statement and the Opinion is the sole responsibility of InterPraxis. The aim of the Accountability Report is to permit the Vancity Group to report on its social, economic and environmental performance. The objective of the assurance assignment is to perform sufficient work to provide assurance as to whether the Report, in all material respects, gives a balanced and fair view of the Group's social, economic and environmental performance measured against the assurance principles set out in the AA1000 Assurance Standard and the criteria established in the Group's Statement of Values and Commitments.

InterPraxis: Our Independence and Competence

InterPraxis (interpraxis.com) is an established social and economic consulting firm specializing in ethics, corporate social responsibility and social auditing. Our three-person multi-disciplinary audit team included subject-matter experts in law, environment, financial auditing and economics, and were led by a Certified Sustainability Assurance Practitioner with the International Register of Certificated Auditors (IRCA). All members of the assurance team are governed by our code of ethics and declare themselves to be independent, with no financial interest or consulting relationships with Vancity Credit Union, or its subsidiaries, that would influence their ability to act impartially.

(continued)

Approach

We have based our assessment against the principles of the AA1000 Assurance Standard.

In addition, we have relied on guidance contained in the Global Reporting Initiative (GRI) Sustainability Reporting Guidelines (2006). We planned and performed our work in order to obtain a reasonable level of assurance for information and explanations that we considered necessary for our Assurance Statement. As part of our work we developed a measure of significance in the context of the Report, and a risk assessment tool to help us assess what is material and where the risks of misstatement or error are greatest. When risk is assessed as low, and when processes are assessed as sound, less detailed audit work is performed and vice versa.

Scope

Our assurance work deals with the years ending December 31, 2006 and 2007. While our work covers all of Vancity Credit Union and Citizens Bank of Canada, our work on Vancity Enterprises Ltd., Vancity Community Foundation, Vancity Capital, Vancity Insurance Services Ltd., Vancity Investment Management Ltd., Inventure Solutions Inc., and Inhance Investment Management Inc., was carried out using a lower level of assurance procedures.

Our conclusions and commentary should not be used to form any judgments or make any decisions of a financial nature.

Limitations of Scope

The following represents limitations in the scope of our work that could affect our conclusions.
· As described in the previous paragraph, our work on Vancity Credit Union subsidiaries (with the exception of Citizens Bank) was carried out at a lower level of assurance
· Stakeholder consultations were focused primarily around employees and members/clients of Vancity Credit Union and Citizens Bank with lesser emphasis on the stakeholders of other subsidiaries
· Text box narratives in the Report have been reviewed for reasonableness but are otherwise not audited
· Our work did not include the verification of financial data, other than that relating to social, environmental or broader economic performance. However, financial data was cross-referenced to audited financial statements, when applicable.

Nature of Work Performed

InterPraxis obtained a general understanding of the Vancity Group's business practices and Statement of Values and Commitments, including key performance indicators and systems and processes in place to measure and report on performance. Based on this information, we considered its impact, and designed an evidence-gathering process for all significant assertions in the Report. This included the following procedures:
· Reviewing the entire content for reasonableness and completeness
· Obtaining an understanding of the processes used to develop data in the Report
· Reviewing press clippings, external media, blogs, web and legal databases
· Interviewing key managers and employees who either held managerial responsibility for specific areas and/or were responsible for developing the data, and other selected employees, reviewing the resulting information and comparing it with other knowledge obtained during our assurance work
· Reviewing the results of stakeholder focus groups and the results of surveys conducted by other independent bodies
· Where relevant, agreeing information to the minutes of the Board of Directors and other formal committees
· On a test basis, agreeing information to supporting documents such as invoices, internal reports, and correspondence
· Agreeing financial information to the annual audited financial statements when possible or, when not, to accounting records from which the financial statements are derived
· Observing premises and activities in the main head offices of Vancity Credit Union and Citizens Bank (located at 183 Terminal Avenue and 815 West Hastings Street, Vancouver)
· In some cases reviewing the work performed by the internal audit department on information contained in the report

(continued)

FIGURE 1.5 **Example of an assurance report on a corporate social responsibility disclosure** (continued)
Source: Vancity's 2006–07 Accountability Report

- Considering the completeness and relevance of the information in the Report from the point of view of key stakeholders
- During the course of our assurance work, when we questioned the accuracy or clarity of proposed Report content, we either received satisfactory answers to our questions or management made appropriate changes to the Report.

Key Findings: Alignment to the AA1000

We have assessed the quality and scope of information in the Report, the evidence that supports it, and the underlying management systems used to monitor performance against the following criteria of the AA1000 Assurance Standard.

Materiality

In developing materiality criteria we considered issues and concerns identified through internal regulations, stakeholder consultations, peer reviews and current and emerging societal norms. Based on our work, we believe that issues material to the Vancity Group's stakeholders have been considered and communicated in the Report.

Completeness

All companies in the Vancity Group have been included in this Report. While the Report focuses on social, environmental and economic impacts over which the Group has operational control, it has also made an effort to understand its upstream and downstream impacts and these are captured in this Report.

Responsiveness

Overall we found that the Vancity Group demonstrates a high degree of responsiveness to material stakeholder issues by integrating its responses into management goals and developing future commitments and through measurable and publicly stated targets.

Our Opinion

Based on our audit work and except for the effect, if any, of issues not identified due to the limitations of scope identified above, it is our opinion that the Vancity Group's 2006 – 07 Accountability Report presents a balanced and fair representation of its social, economic, and environmental performance.

Certified Lead Sustainability Assurance Practitioner
International Register of Certificated Auditors
(IRCA): No. 1188531
InterPraxis Consulting
June 6, 2008

Cloud 9

Ernie stresses to Ron that any financial statements prepared for McLellan's Shoes are Ron's responsibility, even if they are audited. The auditor has to be sceptical about the claims made by Ron in the financial statements. These claims include, for example, that the assets shown on the balance sheet exist and are valued correctly, and that the balance sheet contains a complete list of the business's liabilities. In other words, the auditor is not just going to believe whatever Ron tells him or her. Auditors must gather evidence about the financial statements before they can give an audit opinion. Ernie also explains to Ron that because his business is relatively small, he has a choice between large and small audit firms. Very large companies would be expected to select a larger audit firm because often smaller firms may be too small to effectively maintain their independence. If a small audit firm audits a large company it is open to the criticism that it will not be sufficiently sceptical because it does not want to lose the fees from that client. A large audit firm has many other clients, so the fees from any one client are a relatively small part of its revenue. Ron likes the idea that the smaller audit firms may be less costly.

5.1 A financial statement must be relevant and reliable. What do these terms mean in this context?

5.2 What three characteristics should an auditor have when conducting an audit?

5.3 What are non-audit services?

1.6 DEMAND FOR AUDIT AND ASSURANCE SERVICES

In this section we will provide an overview of the key financial statement users and their requirements. This is followed by a description of why these users may demand an audit of the financial statements. Next, three theoretical frameworks that have been used to encapsulate these sources of demand are described. Finally, the demand for assurance services in a voluntary setting is explored.

6 Explain why there is a demand for audit and assurance services.

1.6.1 Financial statement users

Financial statement users include current and potential investors (shareholders if the entity is a company), suppliers, customers, lenders, employees, governments, and the general public. Each of these groups will read the financial statements for a slightly different reason. Each group of users and their reasons for reading a company's financial statement is described below.

Investors

In the case of a company, investors generally read the financial statements to determine whether they should invest in or buy, hold, or sell shares in the entity being reported on. They are interested in the return on their investment and are concerned that the entity will remain a going concern into the foreseeable future. Investors may also be interested in the capacity of the entity to pay a dividend. Prospective investors read financial statements to determine whether they should buy shares in the entity.

Suppliers

Suppliers may read the financial statements to determine whether the entity can pay them for goods supplied. They are also interested in whether the entity is likely to remain a going concern (that is, it is likely to continue to be a customer of the supplier) and continue to be able to pay its debts as and when they fall due.

Customers

If customers rely on the entity for their business, they may read the financial statements to determine whether the entity is likely to remain a going concern.

Lenders

Lenders may read the financial statements to determine whether the entity can pay the interest and principal on their loans as and when they fall due.

Employees

Employees may read the financial statements to determine whether the entity can pay their wages or salaries and other entitlements (for example, holiday pay). They may also be interested in assessing the future stability and profitability of the entity, as this affects their job security.

Governments

Governments may read the financial statements to determine whether the entity is complying with regulations and paying a fair amount of taxation given its reported earnings, and to gain a better understanding of the entity's activities. An entity in receipt of government grants may provide a copy of its financial statements when applying for a grant and when reporting on how grant funds have been spent.

The general public

The general public may read the financial statements to determine whether they should associate with the entity (for example, as a future employee, customer, or supplier) and to gain a better understanding of the entity, what it does, and its plans for the future.

1.6.2 Sources of demand for audit and assurance services

information risk the risk that users will rely on incorrect information to make a decision

Financial statement users and their needs, as outlined in the previous section, are many and varied. There are a number of reasons why some or all of these users would demand audited financial statements. The primary reason is to reduce **information risk**, which is the risk that users will rely on incorrect information to make a decision. The causes of information risk include remoteness, complexity, competing incentives, and reliability. Each of these concepts is now explained.

Remoteness

Most financial statement users do not have access to the entity under review. This makes it difficult to determine whether the information contained in the financial statements is a fair presentation of the entity and its activities for the relevant period.

Complexity

Most financial statement users do not have the accounting and legal knowledge to enable them to assess the complex accounting and disclosure choices being made by the entity.

Competing incentives

Management has an incentive to disclose the information contained in the financial statements in a way that helps them achieve their own objectives—for example, to present their performance in the best possible light. Users may find it difficult to identify when management is presenting biased information.

Reliability

Financial statement users are concerned with the reliability of the information contained in the financial statements. As they use that information to make decisions that have real consequences (financial and otherwise, such as assessing the future viability of the company), it is very important that users are able to rely on the facts contained in the financial statements.

An independent third-party review of the information contained in the financial statements by a team of auditors, who have the knowledge and expertise to assess the fair presentation of the information being presented by the preparers, aids users across all of these issues. Auditors have access to entity records, so they are not remote. They are trained accountants and have detailed knowledge about the complex technical accounting and disclosure issues required to assess the choices made by the financial statement preparers. Independent auditors have no incentives to aid the entity in presenting its results in the best possible light. They are concerned with ensuring that the information contained in the financial statements is reliable and free from any significant (material) misstatements (error or fraud).

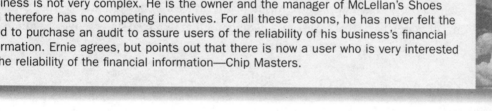

Cloud 9

Ron tells Ernie that he has no remote users, such as shareholders or lenders, and his business is not very complex. He is the owner and the manager of McLellan's Shoes and therefore has no competing incentives. For all these reasons, he has never felt the need to purchase an audit to assure users of the reliability of his business's financial information. Ernie agrees, but points out that there is now a user who is very interested in the reliability of the financial information—Chip Masters.

1.6.3 Theoretical frameworks

The reasons for demanding audit and assurance services outlined in the previous section have led to the development of three theoretical frameworks that have been used to explain why audits occurred prior to regulations requiring that they be done, why users may demand an audit from a certain type of firm (for example, an international or an industry specialist firm), and why users may demand assurance of voluntarily disclosed information (for example, environmental reports). The three theories are agency theory, the information hypothesis, and the insurance hypothesis. Each is described in turn.

Agency theory

When an individual is an owner-manager of his or her own business, there are no competing incentives. The owner (principal) and manager (agent) are one. When an owner hires a manager to run the business on his or her behalf, potential conflicts arise. The manager has an incentive to provide favourable results. If there is one owner, he or she can more easily monitor the activities of the manager. When there are several owners (such as shareholders of a large company), it is difficult for the owners to monitor the activities of the management. Agency theory tells us that due to the remoteness of the owners from the entity, the complexity of items included in the financial statements, and competing incentives between the owners and managers, the owners (principals) have an incentive to hire an auditor (incur a monitoring cost) to assess the fair presentation of the information contained in the financial statements prepared by their managers (agents).

Information hypothesis

Financial statement users require access to high-quality information to make a variety of decisions. That information is used to determine whether to hold or sell shares in the entity, whether to lend money to the entity, what rate of interest to charge the entity on money lent, and so on. The greater the perceived quality of the information contained in the financial statements, the more likely it will be relied upon by the users of that information. The information hypothesis tells us that due to the demand for reliable, high-quality information, various user groups, including shareholders, banks, and other lenders, will demand that financial statements be audited to aid their decision-making.

Insurance hypothesis

Investors take on a risk when buying shares. If the entity fails, investors could lose the money invested. According to the insurance hypothesis, an audit is one way for investors to insure against at least part of their loss should the company they invest in fail. As auditors are required to take out professional indemnity insurance policies, they are seen as having "deep pockets" (that is, access to money), should an investor be able to prove that audit failure was to blame, at least in part, for a loss. The insurance hypothesis tells us that investors will demand that financial statements be audited as a way of insuring against some of their loss should their investment fail.

Cloud 9

Cloud 9 is considering buying McLellan's Shoes from Ron. In effect, it is considering investing in the business. If the business fails, the shareholders of Cloud 9 will lose their money. The new investors have incentives that are in competition with Ron's. If Ron purchases an audit, he is providing assurance to the potential new investors about the fair presentation of the financial statements. The audit also increases the perceived reliability of the information in the financial statements. For example, the outsiders know that Ron will have to convince an auditor of the appropriateness of the reporting decisions he is making.

Purchasing an audit is also a way of taking insurance against any possible loss by creating the opportunity for investors to recover their investment from the auditor. In reality, the auditor is not guaranteeing the success of the business, only providing reasonable assurance that the financial statements comply with the relevant laws and standards and gives a fair presentation of the business's financial position and performance. There is little chance of a successful legal action against an auditor unless it can be established that the auditor failed to perform to a reasonable standard.

1.6.4 Demand in a voluntary setting

While the main focus of this book is the audit of company financial statements, assurance providers (including auditors and consultants) provide other assurance services (as outlined in section 1.2). The theories outlined above are now being used to understand more about the demand for assurance of corporate social responsibility (CSR) disclosures, including environmental, sustainability, and carbon emissions reports.

It is becoming more common for companies to voluntarily disclose CSR information in their annual reports, on their websites, and in separate stand-alone reports. This trend toward increased disclosures has been in response to stakeholder (shareholder, lender, employee, customer, supplier, and public) demand that companies be more accountable for their impact on the environment and on society. Stakeholders are concerned about more than just profits and returns on shareholder funds. They want to know what impact companies are having on our environment and what actions are being taken by those companies to reduce that impact.

Stakeholders are concerned about the reliability of environmental and other CSR disclosures. Just as the provision of these disclosures is voluntary, so is the assurance. Companies are not required to have their environmental and other CSR disclosures assured. Yet a number do (see, for example, the assurance report in figure 1.5). Assurance is provided to meet user demands for high-quality, reliable information and to demonstrate a high level of corporate responsibility.

BEFORE YOU GO ON

6.1 Who are the main users of company financial statements?

6.2 Why might financial statement users demand an audit?

6.3 What are the three most common theories used to explain the origins of the demand for audit and assurance services?

1.7 THE ROLE OF REGULATORS AND REGULATIONS

In this section we discuss the regulators and regulations that have an impact on the audit process.

7 Identify the different regulators, legislation, and regulations surrounding the assurance process.

1.7.1 Regulators, Standard Setters, and Other Bodies

The accounting profession in Canada is primarily self-regulated; however, it does rely on legislation to some extent. Currently, a number of organizations have an impact on the auditing profession, either directly or indirectly. They include the Auditing and Assurance Standards Oversight Council (AASOC), the Auditing and Assurance Standards Board (AASB), the Canadian Securities Administrators (CSA), and the various provincial securities commissions, the Canadian Public Accountability Board (CPAB), the provincial practice inspection programs, the Canadian Institute of Chartered Accountants (CICA), Certified General Accountants Association of Canada (CGA-Canada), and the Society of Management Accountants of Canada (CMA Canada). Each group will now be discussed in turn.

The Auditing and Assurance Standards Oversight Council (AASOC)

The AASOC is an independent body that oversees the Accounting and Assurance Standards Board (AASB). The board is made up of 9–12 members from various constituencies, including users, preparers, and auditors. The AASOC helps determine the strategic direction and the priorities of the AASB. Part of its mandate is to ensure that the standard-setting process is focused on the public's best interest.[1]

Auditing and Assurance Standards Board (AASB)

The purpose of the Canadian AASB is to serve the public interest by setting high-quality auditing and assurance standards.[2] To accomplish this, the AASB adopted the International Standards on Auditing (ISAs), which are issued by the International Auditing and Assurance Standards Board (IAASB). The ISAs have been redrafted by the IAASB and placed in a "clarity" format to improve the consistency of application worldwide. The Canadian version of the ISAs is now referred to as the Canadian Auditing Standards (CASs). In addition to issuing the CASs, the AASB is responsible for issuing the Canadian Standards for Assurance Engagements (CSAEs), as well as the Canadian review engagement and compilation engagement standards.

PROFESSIONAL ENVIRONMENT

International Auditing and Assurance Standards Board (IAASB)

The IAASB develops and issues International Standards on Auditing (ISAs). The IAASB claims that many countries either adopt ISAs as the national auditing standards or base their national auditing standards on the ISAs. ISAs have been recognized by securities and derivatives markets around the world, although the stock exchanges in the United States use the Public Company Accounting Oversight Board's (PCAOB) auditing standards.

The Clarity Project to redraft the ISAs began in 2003 with the objective of improving the clarity and consistent application of international auditing standards. This was seen as essential to the adoption of ISAs for statutory audits in Europe. The project has resulted in the redrafting of 36 international auditing standards. The final seven redrafted standards were released in early 2009, with application to audits for periods beginning on or after December 15, 2009.

The IAASB operates under the auspices of the International Federation of Accountants (IFAC), the global organization for the accounting profession, representing 157 associations in 123 countries (see www.ifac.org). Simnett argues that one of the hurdles that the IAASB faces in achieving greater acceptance of the ISAs is the perception that it is captured by the accounting profession. IFAC's members are accounting organizations and, in the past, most members of the IAASB have been practising auditors.

To increase the confidence of investors and others, IFAC has created a Public Interest Oversight Board (PIOB) to oversee the operations of the IAASB (and other standard-setting bodies associated with IFAC) (see www.piob.org). The PIOB was established in 2005 with the goal of increasing the transparency of the standard-setting arrangements in a manner that reflects the public interest. The PIOB reviews and approves the terms of reference for the standard-setting boards, evaluates the boards' due process procedures, oversees the work of the committees responsible for nominating members of the boards, and suggests projects for the boards. In an effort to increase international acceptance of the PIOB, and thus the ISAs, the members of the PIOB are drawn from a broad range of professions and regulatory agencies.

Source: International Federation of Accountants, "International Auditing and Assurance Standards Board–Fact Sheet, May 2011." www.ifac.org/IAASB; Simnett, R. "A Critique of the International Auditing and Assurance Standards Board." *Australian Accounting Review* 17 (July 2007), pp. 28–36.

Canadian Securities Administrators (CSA)

In Canada, securities regulation falls under provincial jurisdiction. However, securities regulators from across the provinces and territories have joined together to form the CSA. The CSA is a voluntary umbrella organization with the objective of improving, coordinating, and harmonizing regulation of the Canadian capital markets.[3] Part of its mandate is to regulate listed entity disclosure requirements. As such, it requires the annual filing of audited financial statements in accordance with Canadian GAAP, which in Canada is now IFRS for listed entities. It also requires that the CEOs and CFOs of reporting issuers certify that the annual financial statements are fairly presented. In addition, the CSA issues staff notices to provide reporting issuers with guidance on various issues, such as environmental disclosures.

Canadian Public Accountability Board (CPAB)

CPAB was incorporated in 2003 under the Canada Corporations Act. It was formed by the CSA, CICA, and Office of the Superintendent of Financial Institutions (OSFI) with the objective of promoting high-quality audits. The CSA requires that auditors of reporting issuers register and be a member in good standing with CPAB. To be a member in good standing, a firm must pass a CPAB inspection, which includes a review of the firm's compliance with its quality control policies and a sample of engagement files for compliance with professional standards.

Practice inspection programs

Accounting bodies have practice inspection programs to ensure compliance with professional standards. These are peer review programs, where members review each other's work and, in instances of non-compliance, take follow-up or remedial action. A review of a firm's quality control policies and procedures (for firms performing assurance engagements) and a selection of engagement files identify areas where a practising member may require assistance in maintaining prescribed professional standards.[4]

Toronto Stock Exchange (TSX)

The TSX is the largest stock exchange in Canada. It aims to help listed companies raise funds, provide opportunities for investors to build wealth, and enable buyers and sellers to transact with confidence. In order to remain listed on the TSX, a company must meet the requirements of the Securities Act of Ontario, the relevant provincial securities acts, and the CSA. Companies listed on the TSX must file all required documents through the SEDAR (System for Electronic Document Analysis and Retrieval) electronic filing system.

Canadian Institute of Chartered Accountants (CICA)

The CICA is a professional body with more than 77,000 members in Canada and Bermuda. Its members work in public practice (including global and national chartered accounting firms), industry, academia, and government. A not-for-profit entity that supports the setting of accounting, auditing, and assurance standards in Canada, CICA is a founding member of the International Federation of Accountants (IFAC).

Certified General Accountants Association of Canada (CGA-Canada)

CGA-Canada is a globally recognized, self-regulating professional association of over 75,000 students and certified accountants. Certified general accountants work throughout the world in industry, commerce, finance, government, public practice, and other areas where accounting and financial management is required.[5]

Society of Management Accountants of Canada (CMA Canada)

The Society of Management Accountants of Canada (CMA Canada) is a professional association that represents approximately 50,000 designated accountants and students. Certified management accountants integrate accounting expertise with advanced management skills in organizations of all sizes and types.[6]

Each of the three latter accounting bodies grant professional designations after the completion of an extensive training program. Students combine study and mentored work experience to develop technical competence and skills. The successful completion of a rigorous professional exam is required before a designation is conferred.

1.7.2 Legislation

In Canada, a company can be incorporated under either federal or provincial jurisdiction. If a company is incorporated federally, then it must follow the statutes of the Canada Business Corporations Act (CBCA) (excluding banks and insurance and trust companies). The CBCA calls for audited financial statements for federally incorporated companies that are listed on Canadian stock exchanges. The CBCA statutes also require that these financial statements be in accordance with Canadian generally accepted accounting principles, and audits must be conducted in accordance with Canadian generally accepted auditing standards as defined by the CICA Handbook. In addition, the CBCA provides regulation for auditor independence, auditor appointment, and auditor access to information and company records.

1.7.3 Regulation

Auditing standards are issued by the Auditing and Assurance Standards Board (AASB) in Canada. The standards provide minimum requirements and guidance for auditing engagements. The 36 Canadian Auditing Standards (CASs) constitute Canadian generally accepted auditing standards (GAAS), and apply to all audits of historical financial information where audit assurance is provided. They are based on the International Standards for Auditing (ISAs); however, they may be modified to comply with Canadian legal or regulatory environments.

The Canadian Standards for Assurance Engagements (CSAEs) are the engagement standards that apply to engagements other than audits of financial statements and other historical financial information. These standards provide general and specific guidance for assurance engagements other than historical financial information, such as the effectiveness of internal controls, where either reasonable or limited assurance is provided. Assurance engagements that comply with the CSAEs are also in compliance with Canadian GAAS. In addition, there are standards for review and related services, including compilation engagements.[7] Figure 1.6 provides an overview of the CICA Handbook—Assurance.

Cloud 9

Ernie explains that, in general, the regulators and regulations that apply to companies are not relevant to McLellan's Shoes. However, any auditor Ron engages would be also performing company audits and would be a member of at least one of the professional accounting bodies. The auditor would apply the auditing and accounting standards that are relevant to an audit engagement when auditing a small business. The auditor would apply strict professional standards to Ron's audit and should perform the audit to a reasonable standard.

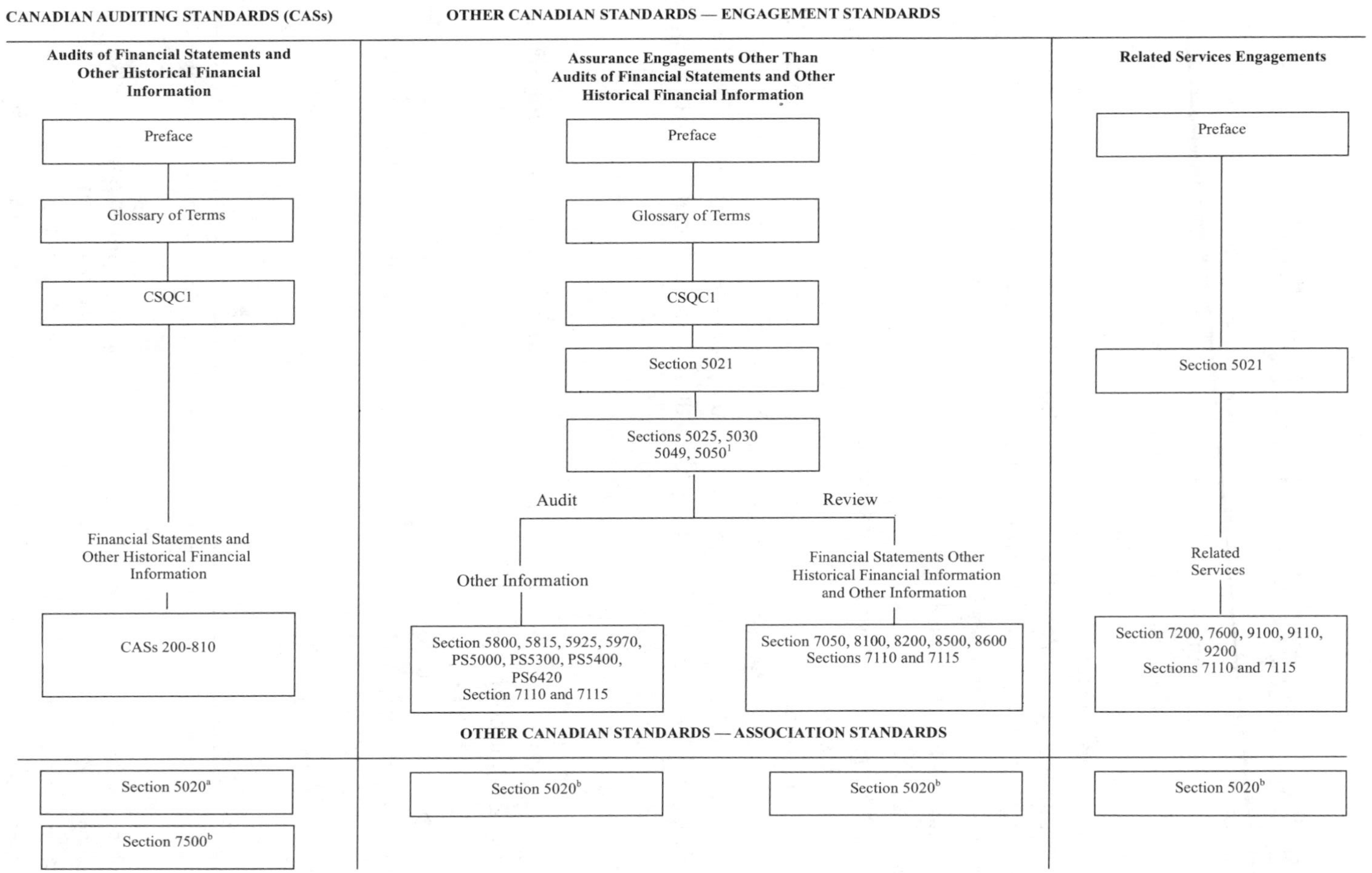

CANADIAN AUDITING STANDARDS (CASs)

OTHER CANADIAN STANDARDS — ENGAGEMENT STANDARDS

Audits of Financial Statements and Other Historical Financial Information

Preface

Glossary of Terms

CSQC1

Financial Statements and Other Historical Financial Information

CASs 200–810

Section 5020[a]

Section 7500[b]

Assurance Engagements Other Than Audits of Financial Statements and Other Historical Financial Information

Preface

Glossary of Terms

CSQC1

Section 5021

Sections 5025, 5030 5049, 5050[1]

Audit

Other Information

Section 5800, 5815, 5925, 5970, PS5000, PS5300, PS5400, PS6420 Section 7110 and 7115

Review

Financial Statements Other Historical Financial Information and Other Information

Section 7050, 8100, 8200, 8500, 8600 Sections 7110 and 7115

OTHER CANADIAN STANDARDS — ASSOCIATION STANDARDS

Section 5020[b]

Section 5020[b]

Related Services Engagements

Preface

Section 5021

Related Services

Section 7200, 7600, 9100, 9110, 9200 Sections 7110 and 7115

Section 5020[b]

[a] USING THE WORK OF INTERNAL AUDIT IN ASSURANCE ENGAGEMENTS OTHER THAN AUDITS OF FINANCIAL STATEMENTS AND OTHER HISTORICAL FINANCIAL INFORMATION, Section 5050, provides guidance on using the work of internal audit in carrying out an audit engagement other than an audit of financial statements and other historical financial information. The guidance may be useful for other types of engagements.

[b] ASSOCIATION, Section 5020, provides guidance on the public accountant's association with information, which may occur irrespective of the type of engagement.

[c] AUDITOR'S CONSENT TO THE USE OF THE AUDITOR'S REPORT IN CONNECTION WITH DESIGNATED DOCUMENTS. Section 7500, provides guidance on the auditor's responsibilities, after the completion of the audit of the entity's financial statements, when the auditor agrees to consent to the use of the auditor's report in connection with a designated document.

FIGURE 1.6 **Overview of the Assurance Handbook**

Source: Canadian Institute of Chartered Accountants, "Overview of the Assurance Handbook," *CICA Handbook—Assurance, Part I*, "Preface to the *CICA Handbook—Assurance*, Copyright © 2001, Canadian Institute of Chartered Accountants. References to the *CICA Handbook* are reprinted with permission from *The Canadian Institute of Chartered Accountants*, Toronto, Canada. Any changes to the original material are the sole responsibility of the author and/or publisher and have not been reviewed or endorsed by the CICA.

1.8 THE AUDIT EXPECTATION GAP

8 Describe the audit expectation gap.

The audit expectation gap occurs when there is a difference between the expectations of assurance providers and financial statement users. The gap occurs when user beliefs do not align with what an auditor has actually done. In particular, the gap is caused by unrealistic user expectations, such as:

- the auditor is providing complete assurance
- the auditor is guaranteeing the future viability of the entity
- an unqualified (clean) audit opinion is an indicator of complete accuracy
- the auditor will definitely find any fraud
- the auditor has checked all transactions.

  The reality is that:
- an auditor provides reasonable assurance
- the audit does not guarantee the future viability of the entity
- an unqualified opinion indicates that the auditor believes that there are no material (significant) misstatements (errors or fraud) in the financial statements
- the auditor will assess the risk of fraud and conduct tests to try to uncover any fraud, but there is no guarantee that they will find fraud, should it have occurred
- the auditor tests a sample of transactions.

  The audit expectation gap is represented graphically in figure 1.7.

  The audit expectation gap can be reduced by:
- auditors performing their duties appropriately, complying with auditing standards, and meeting the minimum standards of performance that should be expected of all auditors
- peer reviews of audits to ensure that auditing standards have been applied correctly
- auditing standards being reviewed and updated on a regular basis to enhance the work being done by auditors
- education of the public

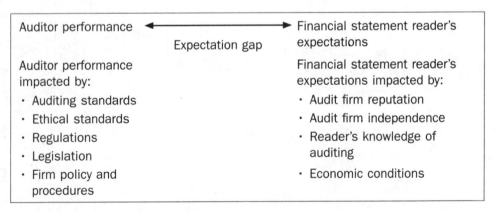

FIGURE 1.7 **Audit expectation gap**

- enhanced reporting to explain what processes have been followed in arriving at an audit (reasonable assurance) or a review (limited assurance) opinion (significant improvements have been introduced by standard-setters improving assurance reporting)
- assurance providers reporting accurately the level of assurance being provided (reasonable, limited, or none).

As described in this chapter, financial statement users rely on audited financial statements to make a variety of decisions. They use the statements to assess the performance of the company, the appropriateness of the remuneration paid to management, the adequacy of dividends declared, and the likely future viability of the company. Following the corporate collapses of the early 2000s (for example, Enron and Worldcom), user confidence in auditors and audited financial statements hit a low. In Canada and the United States, increased regulation was imposed on the auditing profession. The United States passed the Sarbanes Oxley Act (SOX) and created the Public Company Accounting Oversight Board (PCAOB). These organizations focus on corporate governance and accounting and audit regulations. In Canada, increased regulation resulted in the creation of the Canadian Public Accountability Board (CPAB). The standard-setters have also responded to public demands that auditors pay greater attention to the risk that a material fraud may occur. CAS 240 *The Auditor's Responsibilities Relating to Fraud in an Audit of Financial Statements* requires that auditors consider the risk of material fraud on every audit. The auditor must assess the risk that a material fraud could occur and gauge the adequacy of the client's system of internal control to prevent or detect such a fraud. If the auditor is not satisfied with the client's system of internal control, their audit procedures must be designed to aid in the detection of any material suspected frauds.

While highlighting the importance of considering fraud in every audit, standard-setters also highlight that the primary responsibility for fraud prevention and detection remains with those charged with governance (generally the client's management) (CAS 240, para. 4). They also emphasize the inherent limitation of any audit, making fraud detection less than certain (CAS 240, para. 5).

Cloud 9

Ron believes that Chip Masters would know what an audit can provide and what it cannot, because Chip is an experienced vice-president of a large international company. He would deal with auditors on a regular basis. Ron thanks Ernie for his time. Ernie has helped him to understand that preparing more detailed financial statements and engaging an auditor to perform a financial statement audit would not be as bad as he first thought. Ron now understands why Ernie thinks audits are valuable, and not just another business expense. If Chip Masters thinks that Ron's financial statements are more credible with an audit, then it is likely that he will be prepared to pay a higher price for Ron's business.

BEFORE YOU GO ON

8.1 Define the audit expectation gap.

8.2 What has caused the audit expectation gap?

8.3 What can be done to reduce the audit expectation gap?

SUMMARY

❶ Define an assurance engagement.

An assurance engagement involves an assurance provider arriving at an opinion about some information being provided by their client to a third party. A financial statement audit is one type of assurance engagement. This engagement involves an auditor arriving at an opinion about the fair presentation of the financial statements. The audit report is addressed to the shareholders of the company being audited, but other users may read the financial statements. Learning about auditing and assurance requires an understanding of auditing and assurance terminology, including terms such as audit risk, materiality, internal controls, listed entity, and assertions.

❷ Differentiate between types of assurance services.

Assurance services include financial statements audits, compliance audits, performance audits, comprehensive audits, internal audits, and assurance on corporate social responsibility (CSR) disclosures.

❸ Explain the different levels of assurance.

The different levels of assurance include reasonable assurance, which is the highest level of assurance, moderate assurance, and no assurance. Reasonable assurance is provided on an audit of a company's financial statements. Moderate assurance is provided on a review of a company's financial statements that provides negative assurance. No assurance is provided in a compilation engagement.

❹ Outline different audit opinions.

An auditor can issue an unmodified and unqualified opinion, also known as a clean report, an unqualified opinion with an emphasis of matter opinion, or a modified and qualified opinion, which is issued when the financial statements contain a material (significant) misstatement (error or fraud).

❺ Differentiate between the roles of the preparer and the auditor, and discuss the different firms that provide assurance services.

It is the responsibility of a company's governing body to ensure that their financial statements are relevant, reliable, comparable, understandable, and true and fair. It is the responsibility of the auditor to form an opinion on the fair presentation of the financial statements. In doing so the auditor must maintain professional scepticism and utilize professional judgement and due care.

The firms that provide assurance services include the Big-4 international firms, the national firms (with international links), local and regional firms, and consulting firms that tend to specialize in assurance of CSR and environmental disclosures.

❻ Explain why there is a demand for audit and assurance services.

Financial statement users include investors (shareholders), suppliers, customers, lenders, employees, governments, and the general public. These groups of users demand audited financial statements because of their remoteness from the entity, accounting complexity, their incentives competing with those of the entity's managers, and their need for reliable information on which to base decisions. The theories used to describe the demand for audit and assurance services are agency theory, the information hypothesis, and the insurance hypothesis.

7 **Identify the different regulators, legislation, and regulations surrounding the assurance process.**

Regulators of the assurance process include the Auditing and Assurance Standards Oversight Council (AASOC), the Auditing and Assurance Standards Board (AASB), the Canadian Business Corporations Act (CBCA), Canadian Securities Administrators (CSA) and the various provincial securities commissions, and the Canadian Public Accountability Board (CPAB). Relevant legislation includes the Canadian Business Corporations Act (CBCA). The three organizations responsible for accounting designations in Canada are the Canadian Institute of Chartered Accountants (CICA), the Certified General Accountants of Canada (CGA-Canada), and the Society of Management Accountants of Canada (CMA Canada).

8 **Describe the audit expectation gap.**

The audit expectation gap occurs when there is a difference between the expectations of assurance providers and financial statement or other users. The gap occurs when user beliefs do not align with what an auditor has actually done.

KEY TERMS

Accountability relationship, 6

Applicable financial reporting
   framework, 7

Assertions, 7

Assurance engagement, 6

Audit evidence, 7

Audit file, 7

Audit plan, 7

Audit risk, 7

Compilation engagement, 16

Compliance audit, 10

Comprehensive audit, 11

Consulting firms, 11

Corporate social responsibility (CSR), 11

Emphasis of matter, 18

Fair presentation, 8

Financial statement audit, 8

Financial statements, 7

Independent auditor's report, 7

Information risk, 26

Internal audit, 11

Internal control, 7

Listed entity, 8

Material, 7

Materiality, 8

Moderate assurance, 14

No assurance, 15

Notice to Reader, 16

Operational audits, 10

Qualified opinion, 18

Reasonable assurance, 13

Review engagement, 14

Sufficient and appropriate evidence, 8

Those charged with governance, 11

Unmodified opinion, 8, 18

Working papers, 8

MULTIPLE-CHOICE QUESTIONS

1.1 The parties relevant to an assurance engagement are:

(a) assurance practitioner, users, responsible party.

(b) assurance practitioner, responsible party, subject matter.

(c) assurance practitioner, users, criteria.

(d) assurance practitioner, subject matter, criteria.

1.2 Under the Canada Business Corporations Act the auditor has a responsibility to:

(a) form an opinion on the subject criteria.

(b) form an opinion on the independence of the company.

(c) form an opinion on the fair presentation of the financial statements.

(d) all of the above.

1.3 Performance audits are useful because:

(a) they include an internal audit.

(b) they are concerned with the economy, efficiency, and effectiveness of an organization's activities.

(c) they involve gathering evidence to ascertain whether the entity under review has followed the rules, policies, procedures, laws, or regulations with which it must conform.

(d) none of the above.

1.4 The function of internal audit is determined by:

(a) the external auditor.

(b) the Institute of Internal Auditors.

(c) those charged with governance and management.

(d) the government.

1.5 Negative assurance means:

(a) the auditor disclaims responsibility for the audit opinion.

(b) an adverse audit report.

(c) the auditor has conducted an audit and provides an opinion that the financial statements are not materially misstated.

(d) the auditor has done adequate work to report whether or not anything came to their attention that would lead them to believe that the information being assured is not fairly presented.

1.6 A "clean" audit report is issued when:

(a) the auditor has no independence issues.

(b) the audit opinion is unqualified and the auditor includes a paragraph in the audit report to emphasize something important.

(c) the audit opinion is unqualified and unmodified.

(d) the users cannot rely on the financial statements.

1.7 Those charged with governance have a responsibility to ensure that the information in financial statements is:

(a) relevant and reliable.

(b) comparable and understandable.

(c) fairly presented.

(d) all of the above.

1.8 Agency theory explains that audits are demanded because:

(a) conflicts can arise between managers and owners.

(b) conflicts can arise between managers and agents.

(c) conflicts can arise between owners and principals.

(d) conflicts can arise between auditors and owners.

1.9 The insurance hypothesis means:

(a) managers must take insurance.

(b) owners must take insurance.

(c) an audit acts as insurance.

(d) none of the above.

1.10 The audit expectation gap occurs when:

(a) auditors perform their duties appropriately and satisfy users' demands.

(b) user beliefs do not align with what an auditor has actually done.

(c) peer reviews of audits ensure that auditing standards have been applied correctly and the standards are at the level that satisfies users' demands.

(d) the public is well educated about auditing.

REVIEW QUESTIONS

1.1 What does "assurance" mean in the financial reporting context? What qualities must an "assurer" have in order for you to feel that their statement has high credibility?

1.2 Why do audit firms offer consulting services to their audit clients? Why don't they just do audits and let consulting firms provide the consulting services?

1.3 An assurance engagement involves evaluation or measurement of subject matter against criteria. What criteria are used in a financial statement audit?

1.4 Who would request a performance audit? Why?

1.5 Are internal auditors independent? Which internal auditor would be more independent: an internal auditor who reports to the chief financial officer (CFO) of the company, or an internal auditor who reports to the audit committee?

1.6 What is an "emphasis of matter" paragraph? When do you think an auditor would use it?

1.7 Compare the financial statement users and their needs for a large listed public company with those of a sporting team (for example, a football team).

1.8 What standards or guidelines are relevant to the assurance of corporate social responsibility disclosures?

1.9 Describe the expectation gap.

1.10 Explain the system of reviewing the quality of audits performed by listed company auditors.

PROFESSIONAL APPLICATION QUESTIONS

Basic ★   Moderate ★ ★   Challenging ★ ★ ★

1.1 Audit reports ★

A sample audit report is provided in figure 1.2 in this chapter. A sample review engagement report is provided in figure 1.3.

Required

(a) Explain the relevance of the paragraphs "Management's responsibility for the financial statements" and "Auditor's responsibility" in the audit report to the audit expectation gap.

(b) Find the lines in the audit report that express the auditor's opinion. Is it an unqualified or modified audit opinion?

(c) Find the lines in the review report that express the auditor's conclusion. Is it an audit opinion? Is it a positive or negative statement?

(d) Make a list of the other differences between the audit report and the review report.

1.2 Corporate sustainability reporting assurance ★ ★

The corporate sustainability assurance report for Vancity Credit Union is provided in figure 1.5 in this chapter. The provider of the report states that the work was performed in accordance with a methodology based on AA1000AS.

Required

(a) Who wrote the report?

(b) What level of assurance is provided?

(c) What is AA1000AS?

(d) Compare the AA1000 principles of completeness, materiality, and responsiveness with the financial statement qualitative criteria of relevance, reliability, comparability, understandability, and truth and fairness. Which set of characteristics would be more difficult for an entity to comply with?

1.3 Assurance providers ★ ★

Most audit firms maintain a website that explains the services offered by the firm and provides resources to their clients and other interested parties. The services offered by most firms include both audit and non-audit services.

Required

(a) Find the websites for (1) a Big-4 audit firm and (2) a national audit firm. Compare them on (i) the range of services provided, (ii) geographic coverage (that is, where their offices are located), (iii) staff numbers and special skills offered, (iv) industries in which they claim specialization, (v) publications and other materials provided to their clients or the general public, and (vi) marketing message.

(b) In times of economic recession would you expect the demand for audits to increase or decrease? Would you expect clients to shift from large (Big-4) auditors to national auditors or from national auditors to Big-4 auditors? Why or why not?

1.4 Canadian designations ★ ★

Each of the accounting bodies maintains a website that explains their designation process. Each designation requires both educational and work experience.

Required

Find the websites for (a) the Canadian Institute of Chartered Accountants, (b) the Certified General Accountants Association of Canada, and (c) the Society of Management Accountants of Canada. Compare them on (1) educational requirements and (2) work experience requirements.

1.5 Demand for assurance ★ ★ ★

In 2002 the audit firm Arthur Andersen collapsed following charges brought against it in the United States relating to the failure of its client, Enron. Some other clients announced that they would be dismissing Arthur Andersen as their auditor even before it was clear that Arthur Andersen would not survive.

Required

Using the theories outlined in this chapter on the demand for audits, give some reasons why these clients took this action.

1.6 Being an auditor ★ ★

You have recently graduated from university and have started work with an audit firm. You meet an old school friend, Kim, for dinner—you haven't seen each other for several years. Kim is surprised that you are now working as an auditor, because your childhood dream was to be a ballet dancer. Unfortunately, your knees were damaged in a fall and you can no longer dance. The conversation turns to your work and Kim wants to know how you do your job. Kim cannot understand why an audit is not a guarantee that the company will succeed. Kim also thinks that company managers will lie to you in order to protect themselves, and as an auditor you would have to assume that you cannot believe anything a company manager says to you.

Required

(a) Write a letter to Kim explaining the concept of reasonable assurance, and how reasonable assurance is determined. Explain why an auditor cannot offer absolute assurance.

(b) Explain in the letter to Kim the concept of "professional scepticism" and how it is not the same as assuming that managers are always trying to deceive auditors.

1.7 CPAB ★ ★ ★

You are a trainee auditor working for a small audit firm. You completed your accounting degree at the end of last year and although you have not yet had much experience, you are concerned about some of the practices and procedures adopted by your audit firm.

You overhear the two partners, Anouk and Riley, discussing some problems they are facing with a particular client. Anouk is advising Riley to "get the paperwork right" on the audit, otherwise they will be in trouble with CPAB's inspection program. After the conversation, Riley comes to you to ask if you, as a recent graduate, know anything about the CPAB inspection. Riley confesses that he hasn't been keeping up to date.

Required

Write a report to Riley explaining CPAB's audit inspection program.

Questions 1.8 and 1.9 are based on the following case.

Securimax Limited (Securimax) has been an audit client of KFP Partners (KFP) for the past 15 years. Securimax is based in Waterloo, Ontario, where it manufactures high-tech armor-plated personnel carriers. Securimax often has to go through a competitive market tender process to win large government contracts. Its main product, the small but powerful Terrain Master, is highly specialized, and Securimax does business only with nations that have a recognized, democratically elected government. Securimax maintains a highly secure environment, given the sensitive and confidential nature of its vehicle designs and its clients.

Clarke Field has been the engagement partner on the Securimax audit for the last five years.

The board of Securimax is considering changing from an audit engagement to a review engagement and has approached the audit partner, Clarke Field, to discuss the implications of this change. Clarke suggests that KFP could perform the review engagement.

Securimax's financial year end is December 31.

Source: Adapted from the Institute of Chartered Accountants Australia's CA Program's *Audit and Assurance Exam,* May 2008.

1.8 Types of assurance engagements ★ ★

Required

What is a review engagement? Why would a review be appropriate for a set of financial statements for Securimax?

1.9 Expectations gap ★ ★

Required

Discuss the expectations gap that could exist for the audit of Securimax. Consider the existence of any special interests of the users of Securimax's financial statements.

1.10 Performance and compliance audits ★ ★ ★

Fellowes and Associates Chartered Accountants is a successful national accounting firm with a large range of clients across Canada. In 2011, Fellowes and Associates gained a new client, Health Care Holdings Group (HCHG), which owns 100 percent of the following entities:

- Shady Oaks Centre, a private treatment centre
- Gardens Nursing Home Ltd., a private nursing home
- Total Laser Care Limited, a private clinic that specializes in the laser treatment of skin defects. Year end for all HCHG entities is June 30.

Total Laser Care Limited (TLCL) owns two relatively old laser machines used in therapy. Recently, staff using these machines have raised concerns that they have adverse impacts on patients.

TLCL also wishes to purchase a new, more technologically advanced machine. The Ministry of Health has agreed to fund half the purchase price on the basis that TLCL followed the ministry's "Guidelines for Procurement of Medical Equipment" when purchasing the accelerator. The Ministry of Health has engaged the Auditor-General to check that TLCL met the terms of the funding agreement.

Source: Adapted from the Institute of Chartered Accountants Australia's CA Program's *Audit and Assurance Exam,* December 2008.

Required

Discuss the relevant criteria against which the Auditor-General will check TCCL's compliance with the terms of the funding agreement.

1.11 Types of assurance engagements ★ ★

DDD Motor Sales Inc. is privately owned. It wants to expand its business and has approached its bank for a loan. DDD wants the funds to purchase additional inventory and will be able to provide excellent security to the bank. The bank has agreed that since DDD can provide good security for the loan, an external audit will not be required. The bank manager has insisted that DDD hire a firm of professional accountants to examine DDD's financial records and provide some level of assurance.

Required

(a) What type of engagement is required? Explain your answer.

(b) Assume that DDD contracts with Cicak & Jones, CGA's, to perform the required services. What is the title of the report or communication that Cicak & Jones will prepare?

(c) Identify the type of procedures Cicak & Jones will be required to conduct.

Source: Adapted from the Uniform Final Exam (UFE), The Institute of Chartered Accountants in Canada and Bermuda, Paper 2, 2000

1.12 Audit opinions ★ ★ ★

Required

What type of audit report would be appropriate in each of the following scenarios? Explain.

(a) There is uncertainty relating to a pending exceptional litigation matter that is adequately disclosed in the notes.

(b) The client's records are inadequate and the auditor is unable to obtain sufficient appropriate evidence.

(c) There is a material uncertainty that casts a significant doubt on the entity's ability to continue as a going concern and this uncertainty is adequately disclosed.

(d) There is a GAAP departure concerning a highly material item.

(e) The client will not allow the auditor to contact the client's legal counsel.

(f) The client's accounting records have been destroyed.

(g) There is a material misstatement in the client's inventory account. The misstatement is deemed to be material but not pervasive to the financial statements.

(h) Inventories are misstated. The misstatement is deemed to be material but not pervasive to the financial statements.

1.13 The expectation gap ★ ★ ★

Certek Technologies Inc. (Certek) is a biotechnology company whose stock traded on a major Canadian stock exchange. Over the 22 months following its initial public offering in May 2009, Certek's stock rose an astounding 1,350 percent. In mid-March 2000, Certek's stock began to decline. Then, in April 2000, the stock price plummeted when it was announced that Certek had stopped all research activities on its major projects due to unsatisfactory scientific results. You, CA, are sitting with some friends who make the following comments:

Ruby: I lost a bundle on the Certek stock. The stock went up with every press release. It seemed like the company was going to solve every medical problem in the world.

I thought the auditors had a responsibility to investors and the capital markets for information released to the public.

Omid: I don't understand how audited financial statements are the least bit useful. Certek was investing huge amounts of money in researching new pharmaceutical products, yet the financial statements provided no information on whether its research would develop into viable products. Couldn't the auditors take some responsibility for evaluating the research that companies are doing?

Required

(a) What is the auditor's responsibility for information released to the public?

(b) Discuss Omid's comment with reference to the expectation gap.

(c) What can auditors do to reduce the expectation gap?

1.14 Types of audit reports ★ ★

Situation 1

The accounting firm of Aschari and Di Tomaso was engaged to perform an audit of the financial statements of Pammenter Inc. During the audit, Pammenter Inc.'s senior managers refused to give the auditors the information they needed to confirm any of the accounts receivable. As a result, Aschari and Di Tomaso were not able to confirm the accounts receivable balance. However, they did not encounter any other problems during the audit.

Situation 2

The accounting firm of Jovanovic and St. Pierre has discovered, during its audit of Robson Chemicals Inc., that the client is being sued for $3 million. Allegedly, one of its products exploded and severely injured a customer. In the firm's discussion with Robson's lawyers, Jovanovic and St. Pierre ascertained that it is very likely that Robson will indeed have to pay this entire amount when the lawsuit is resolved. To provide for this, Robson's chief financial officer has included information relating to the lawsuit in the notes to its financial statements, but did not otherwise reflect it in its financial statements.

Required

For each of the independent situations presented above:

(a) state what type of audit report should be issued and

(b) explain your reasoning.

Source: Adapted from the Uniform Final Exam (UFE), The Institute of Chartered Accountants in Canada and Bermuda, Paper 2, 2000

1.15 Different audit opinions ★

C. D. Hodgson and Associates Chartered Accountants audited the financial statements of Tallender Company, a sporting goods retailer. As with all of his firm's audits, Carl Hodgson conducted the Tallender audit in accordance with generally accepted auditing standards, and, therefore, wrote a standard audit description in his audit report.

   On Saturday afternoon, just as he was about to write the audit opinion relating to this audit, Carl received an emergency telephone call from his wife regarding an accident involving their only child. He had to leave the office immediately and was not sure when he would be able to return. Since the only other person in the office at the time was a junior accountant, Khaled Nersesian, who had also worked on the audit, Carl handed him the completed financial statements and working papers and asked him to make sure it is appropriate to write an unqualified opinion.

Required

What should Khaled Nersesian take into consideration in deciding whether an unqualified opinion is appropriate for Tallender Company?

CASE STUDY—CLOUD 9

Ron McLellan established his business, McLellan's Shoes, in 1980. Ron keeps records and his wife helps him prepare basic accounting records. As McLellan's Shoes has no outside owners, Ron has never seen the need to have his books audited.

When Chip Masters from Cloud 9 Inc. expressed an interest in buying McLellan's Shoes in 1992, Ron was asked to provide audited financial statements. Ron discussed his concerns about having an audit with his friend Ernie Black. Ernie is concerned that Ron may forget their conversations and has asked you to prepare a summary of the issues listed below for Ron.

Required

(a) What are the main differences among a financial statement audit, a review engagement, and a compilation engagement?
(b) What is the difference between reasonable assurance and moderate assurance?
(c) Why would Chip ask Ron to have the financial statements for McLellan's Shoes audited rather than reviewed?
(d) What factors should Ron consider when selecting an accounting firm to complete the McLellan's Shoes audit?

RESEARCH QUESTION 1.1

Chong and Pflugrath conducted a study of different audit report formats and their effects on the audit expectation gap. They investigated whether report length (long or short), the location of the audit opinion (at the start or the end), and plain language (instead of technical language) affect shareholders' and auditors' perceptions of the audit. They surveyed a sample of shareholders and auditors and concluded that the responses indicate that different report formats have only minor effects on the audit expectation gap.[8]

Required

(a) In your view, what should be contained in an audit report that conveys realistic explanations of the auditor's role and the assurance provided by the audit report?
(b) Do you believe that auditors are correct in dismissing users' expectations as "unrealistic"? Should auditors be trying to meet these expectations by rethinking their role and changing their approach?

RESEARCH QUESTION 1.2

Required

Access the CICA Handbook and locate the following:

(a) What number is the CAS for audit documentation?
(b) How many sections are there to each CAS?
(c) What is the name of Section 5025?
(d) What numbers relate to review engagements?
(e) Where specifically can the required wording for the Notice to Reader be found?

SOLUTIONS TO MULTIPLE-CHOICE QUESTIONS

1. a, 2. c, 3. b, 4. c, 5. d, 6. c, 7. d, 8. a, 9. c, 10. b.

NOTES

1. Auditing and Assurance Standards Oversight Council. "Terms of Reference." October 2010, http://www.aasoc.ca, [accessed June 2011]
2. Auditing and Assurance Standards Board. "Terms of Reference." October 2010, http://www.aasbcanada.ca/, [accessed June 2011]
3. Canadian Securities Administrators. "Who we are." October 2010, http://www.securities-administrators.ca, [accessed June 2011]
4. Institute of Chartered Accountants of Ontario, 2011, *Members Handbook*, "Practice Inspection Program."
5. http://www.cga-canada.org [accessed June 2011]
6. http://www.cma-canada.org [accessed June 2011]
7. Ethical standards are also important regulations concerning auditors. These are discussed in detail in chapter 2 of this book.
8. Chong, K.M., & Pflugrath, G. "Do different audit report formats affect shareholders' and auditors' perceptions?" *International Journal of Auditing* 12 (2008), pp. 221–41.

CHAPTER 2

Ethics, legal liability, and client acceptance

LEARNING OBJECTIVES

After studying this chapter, you should be able to:

1 describe the fundamental principles of professional ethics and list some of the specific rules professional accountants are required to follow

2 define and explain auditor association and independence

3 explain the relationship between an auditor and key groups they have a professional link with during the audit engagement

4 explain the auditor's legal liability to their client, contributory negligence, and the extent to which an auditor is liable to third parties

5 identify the factors to consider in the client acceptance or continuance decision.

AUDITING AND ASSURANCE STANDARDS

CANADIAN	INTERNATIONAL
CAS 210 *Agreeing the Terms of Audit Engagements*	ISA 210 *Agreeing the Terms of Audit Engagements*
CAS 220 *Quality Control for an Audit of Financial Statements*	ISA 220 *Quality Control for an Audit of Financial Statements*
CAS 610 *Using the Work of Internal Auditors*	ISA 610 *Using the Work of Internal Auditors*
CSQC 1 *Quality Control for Firms that Perform Audits and Reviews of Financial Statements, Other Financial Information, and Other Assurance Engagements*	ISQC 1 *Quality Control for Firms that Perform Audits and Reviews of Historical Financial Information, and other Assurance and Related Services Engagements*

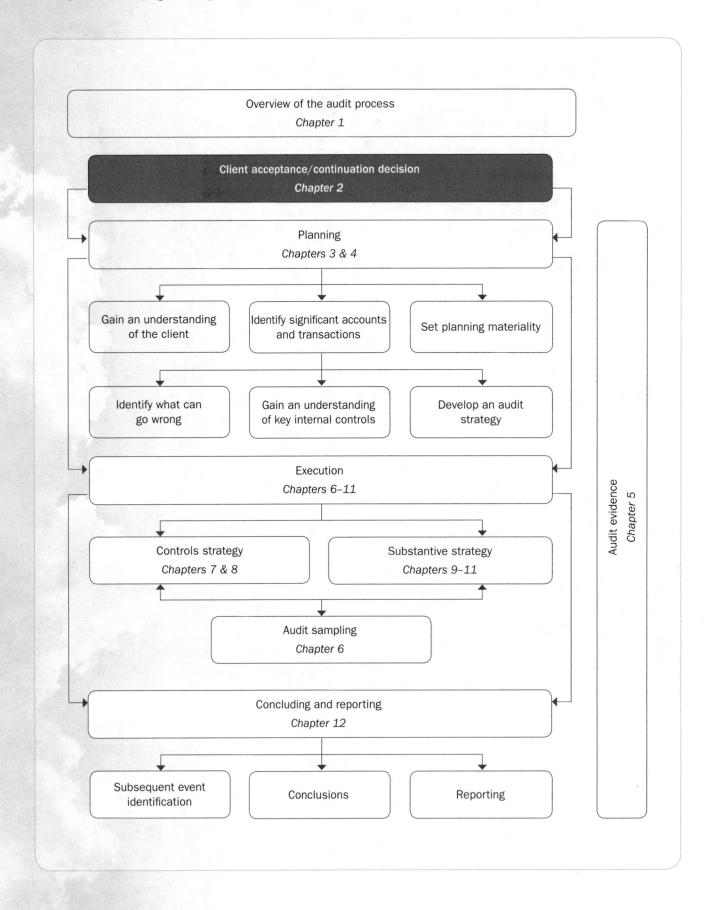

Cloud 9

Ron McLellan came to an arrangement with Chip Masters and sold McLellan's Shoes to Cloud 9 Inc. in 1993. The new business is named Cloud 9 Ltd. (Cloud 9). As part of the sale agreement, Ron McLellan was appointed to the Cloud 9 board of directors.

Cloud 9 has approached the accounting firm W&S Partners about performing the December 31, 2012 audit. If the client is accepted, the partner responsible for the audit will be Jo Wadley. She has asked Sharon Gallagher and Josh Thomas to assist with the client acceptance work. Sharon is an audit manager. Her task is to make sure that there are no nasty surprises for the audit team if they accept the audit. Sharon knows how crucial this is. She still has nightmares about an audit she worked on when she was a new graduate at another audit firm. The client in that case threatened to dismiss the auditor when the auditor wanted him to recognize an impairment loss on some assets. The client was the firm's largest account and the partner was under a lot of pressure to keep the client.

Josh is an audit senior. He has not been involved in the client acceptance process before, and needs the experience so he can be promoted to audit manager. Sharon and Josh do not know anything about Cloud 9 other than that it manufactures and retails customized basketball shoes; it is a subsidiary of Cloud 9 Inc., a publicly listed Canadian company; and it was purchased from Ron McLellan in 1993. Sharon stresses to Josh that they want to know that the client is not going to be difficult to deal with, and that W&S Partners can do a good job of the audit. Josh asks how they can know that now, before they start the audit.

AUDIT PROCESS IN FOCUS

The purpose of this chapter is to provide an overview of the current audit environment. We start by considering the fundamental principles of professional ethics. In particular, we discuss the principles of integrity, objectivity, professional competence and due care, confidentiality, and professional behaviour. We will also discuss some of the specific rules that incorporate these principles.

Auditor association is defined and how it may come about is discussed. Auditor independence is then described and its importance is explained. Independence of mind (actual independence) is compared and contrasted with independence in appearance (perceived independence). The factors that can threaten auditor independence are then explained. Safeguards that can reduce these threats are also discussed. These safeguards to auditor independence have been established in the law, in professional standards, or in accounting firm policies and procedures.

Financial statement auditors liaise with a number of groups when completing their audit. Apart from their client's management and staff, who aid the auditor directly throughout the audit, other groups are fundamental to the successful completion of an audit. These groups include the client's shareholders, board of directors, audit committee, and internal auditors. The nature of the relationship that the auditor has with each of these groups is explored in this chapter.

An overview of the legal liability of the auditor is provided next. In that summary, we explore the current status of an auditor's liability to their client and third parties. The concept of contributory negligence is also explained.

Finally, we consider the factors that impact the auditor's client acceptance/ continuation decision. This section of the chapter marks the beginning of our substantive overview of how an audit is conducted, since the first step for any audit is the decision to accept a company as a new audit client or continue as the auditor of an existing client.

2.1 THE FUNDAMENTAL PRINCIPLES OF PROFESSIONAL ETHICS

① Describe the fundamental principles of professional ethics and list some of the specific rules professional accountants are required to follow.

Generally speaking, ethics are the standards of behaviour that promote human welfare or the overall public "good."[1] When we speak of ethics with respect to professional accountants, we are therefore referring to the standards of behaviour that promote the welfare of society and the accounting profession.

In Canada, each of the three professional accounting bodies has a code of professional conduct. While the wording of each code of conduct may vary between designations, each is based on the same fundamental ethical principles. Accounting professionals are expected to use these principles to guide their behaviour, as they reflect the values deemed critical to the accounting profession. These principles are to act with integrity, objectivity, professional competence and due care, confidentiality, and professional behaviour. Compliance with these fundamental ethical principles is mandatory for all members of the accounting profession. Non-compliance can lead to disciplinary measures by a member's professional body.

> What Makes a Profession?
>
> Many people refer to themselves as professionals; however, a true profession should encompass the following characteristics:
>
> - There is mastery of an intellectual skill due to extensive education and training.
> - Services are offered to others for a fee.
> - There is an independent society or institute that sets and maintains the standards to ensure members are qualified and competent.
> - There is a code of conduct established and enforced by the society or institute.

integrity the obligation that all members of the accounting professional bodies be straightforward and honest

objectivity the obligation that all members of the professional bodies not allow their personal feelings or prejudices to influence their professional judgement

professional competence the obligation that all members of the accounting professional bodies maintain their knowledge and skill at a required level

due care the obligation to complete each task thoroughly, document all work, and finish on a timely basis

Integrity

Integrity refers to the obligation that all members of the professional bodies be straightforward and honest. Members should not be associated with information that is materially false or misleading.

Objectivity

Objectivity refers to the obligation that all members of the professional bodies not allow their personal feelings or prejudices to influence their professional judgement. Members should be unbiased and not allow a conflict of interest or the influence of others to impair their decision process.

Professional competence and due care

Professional competence and **due care** refer to the obligation that all members of the professional bodies maintain their knowledge and skill at a level required by the professional bodies. Members must attain a level of competence and keep up to date with changes in regulations and standards. The attainment of competence comes from education and work experience. Competence is maintained through continuing education and work experience. Members must also act diligently, taking care to complete each task thoroughly, document all work, and finish on a timely basis.

Confidentiality

Confidentiality refers to the obligation that all members of the professional bodies refrain from disclosing information that is learned as a result of their employment to people outside of their workplace. An exception is made where a client has allowed this disclosure to occur or where there is a legal requirement to disclose such information. Members are also not allowed to use information to their advantage or to the advantage of another person that has been gained as a result of their employment and is not publicly available. An example is using information learned from a client to trade shares.

confidentiality the obligation that all members of the professional bodies refrain from disclosing information that is learned as a result of their employment to people outside of their workplace

Professional behaviour

Professional behaviour refers to the obligation that all members of the professional bodies comply with rules and regulations and ensure that they maintain the reputation of the profession. Members should be honest in their representations to current and prospective clients. Members should not claim to be able to provide services that they are not able to provide. They should not claim to possess qualifications that they do not possess. They should not claim to have gained experience in areas where they have little or none. Finally, members should not undermine the quality of work produced by others or question their reputation.

professional behaviour the obligation that all members of the professional bodies comply with rules and regulations and ensure that they do not harm the reputation of the profession

Cloud 9

Josh is confident that he understands the fundamental principles of professional ethics. They apply to all of their audits and to their professional behaviour as accountants. Josh and Sharon can see no reason why they would not be able to abide by these fundamental principles in the audit of Cloud 9.

2.1.1 Specific rules incorporating the principles of professional ethics

In addition to the guiding ethical principles for professional accountants, there are also a number of specific rules that incorporate these principles. These are important because the principles are not specifically enforceable, but the rules of professional conduct are. Some of these rules are described below.

Fees and pricing

A fee can be provided only when requested by the potential client. Fee quotes cannot be provided to a client without adequate knowledge of the work to be performed. Fees quoted cannot be significantly lower than the fees charged by a predecessor firm. Contingency fees (based on outcome of service) are not permitted.

Advertising

Advertising must be in good taste. It cannot be false or misleading or make unsubstantiated claims.

Contact with predecessor

Before accepting a new engagement, the new auditor is required to contact the predecessor auditor and ask if there is any reason he or she should not accept the engagement. The rules of professional conduct require the predecessor auditor to reply on a timely basis. Due to the requirement of confidentiality, the response will be limited to a yes or no unless the client gives permission to the predecessor auditor to provide more information.

Firm names

Firm names are not to be misleading. They must be in good taste, and they cannot be self-laudatory.

Professional conduct

If a public accountant becomes aware that another designated accountant has breached the rules of professional conduct or has acted in a way that would discredit the profession, the public accountant has a duty to inform the relevant institute of the breach. However, before informing the appropriate institute, the public accountant should contact the other accountant and inform him or her of the criticism and request an explanation.

PROFESSIONAL ENVIRONMENT

Ethical decision-making

Ethical dilemmas are commonplace in both life and workplace. It is therefore likely that a professional accountant will face an ethical dilemma at some point during his or her career. While the above principles of the code of conduct guide behaviour, the resolution to an ethical dilemma usually involves making a choice between alternatives where there may not be an obvious right or wrong answer. To help make the best possible decision when facing an ethical dilemma, one should follow a structured decision-making process such as the one outlined below:

1. Obtain the relevant facts.
2. Distinguish the ethical issues from the facts.
3. Determine who is affected by the outcome of the dilemma and how each individual or group is affected.
4. Identify the likely alternatives available to the person who must resolve the dilemma.
5. Identify the likely consequence of each alternative.
6. Decide on the appropriate action.

This will ensure all of the issues, affected groups, alternatives, and consequences are considered before a final decision is made.

Apply the above six steps to the following scenario:

You are a recently designated accountant. As a result of having your designation, you have been hired as the controller at a national manufacturing company. Due to a recent economic slowdown, the company has been struggling to meet earnings targets. These targets are the basis for senior management bonuses. You report directly to the CFO.

This is your second month with the company; however, it is your first year end (December 31). The auditor will be coming to audit the books in three weeks. You have finalized the financial statements, and you have reviewed them with the CFO and the CEO.

The week before the auditor is expected to arrive the CFO comes to your office and explains that the financial results are very disappointing. He would like you to make the following journal entry:

On December 31, a sales contract was signed for $500,000 of goods with delivery to take place January 3. You are asked to record the revenue for this contract on December 31, the date the contract is signed and before the work is performed. This will result in early revenue recognition and doing so, will eliminate the overall net loss for the year.

You are married with a stay-at-home spouse and two small children. To celebrate your success, you recently purchased a new home. It cost a little more than you planned to spend and the mortgage payments are pretty hefty.

BEFORE YOU GO ON

1.1 What does it mean to act in the public interest?

1.2 List and explain the five fundamental ethical principles in the *Code of Professional Conduct* for professional accounting bodies.

1.3 What are the rules with respect to fees?

2.2 ASSOCIATION AND INDEPENDENCE

According to the Canadian Standards for Assurance Engagements (CSAEs), **association** is the term used to indicate a public accountant's involvement with financial information. There are three ways in which association can happen:

❷ Define and explain auditor association and independence.

association occurs when a public accountant is involved with financial information

1. When the public accountant performs a service or consents to the use of his or her name implying that a service was performed with the information.
2. When a third party indicates, without the consent of the public accountant, that he or she is associated with the information.
3. When a third party assumes that the public accountant is associated with the information.

When a public accountant is associated with information, he or she must comply with the rules of professional conduct and with the requirements of the CICA Handbook. The level of the public accountant's involvement with the information must be clearly communicated. This is very important because public accountants must take care to ensure that they are not associated with anything false and misleading.

The concept of **independence** is essential to a public accountant. It is a requirement to comply with the ethical principles to act with integrity and objectivity. Independence is defined as acting with integrity, objectivity, and professional scepticism. It is fundamental to every audit and must be adhered to by every auditor who provides assurance services. An external auditor is often referred to as an independent auditor, which highlights the importance of independence in every audit engagement. Financial statements must be relevant, reliable, comparable, understandable, and fairly presented (refer to chapter 1 for a detailed description of these terms). It is the responsibility of those charged with governance in a company (the **board of directors** and management) to ensure that the financial statements meet these requirements. It is the responsibility of the external auditor to form an opinion on the fair presentation of the financial statements. If an auditor is not independent of their client, it will affect the credibility and

independence the ability to act with integrity, objectivity, and professional scepticism

board of directors the group that represents the shareholders and oversees the activities of a company and its management

reliability of the financial statements. It is vital that financial statement users believe that the external auditor is independent of the company they audit. If that independence is compromised in any way, it will detract from the ability of users to rely on the financial statements to make decisions.

There are two forms of independence:

- *Independence of mind* is the ability to act with integrity, objectivity, and professional scepticism. It is the ability to make a decision that is free from bias, personal beliefs, and client pressures. Independence of mind is also referred to as actual independence.
- *Independence in appearance* is the belief that independence of mind has been achieved. It is not enough for an auditor to be independent of mind; they must also be seen as independent. Auditors must consider their actions carefully and ensure that nothing is done to compromise their independence both of mind and in appearance. Independence in appearance is also referred to as perceived independence.

Both independence of mind and independence in appearance are important for every auditor on every audit engagement. It is the responsibility of every auditor to consider potential threats to their independence and to seek out appropriate safeguards to reduce those threats to the extent possible. If a threat to an auditor's independence appears insurmountable for a particular client, an auditor should consider discontinuing as the auditor of that client.

The next section includes a discussion of the various threats to auditor independence for all assurance engagements as well as some of the additional threats to be considered for reporting issuers. That discussion is followed by a review of some of the safeguards that have been put in place by regulation, the profession, and accounting firms to minimize the threats to auditor independence.

Cloud 9

Sharon tells Josh about her experience at another audit firm where the client tried to pressure the audit partner into dropping a request to write down the asset values. It was an example of a threat to the auditor's independence. Although it is difficult to stop a client asking for a favour, the audit firm needs to have safeguards to prevent a simple request from turning into unreasonable pressure on the audit team to meet that request. Sharon and Josh agree that they need to consider the specific independence threats and safeguards for the audit of Cloud 9. The audit must be independent, as well as be seen to be independent.

2.2.1 Threats to independence

The rules of professional conduct identify five key threats to auditor independence. They are self-interest, self-review, advocacy, familiarity, and intimidation threats. Section 161 of the Canadian Business Corporations Act also deals with the requirement of the auditor to be independent. This section focuses on independence as it applies to *all* assurance engagements.

Self-interest threat

self-interest threat the threat that can occur when an accounting firm or its staff has a financial interest in an assurance client

Self-interest threat refers to the threat that can occur when an accounting firm or its staff has a financial interest in an assurance client. Some examples include:

- assurance team members involved in the assurance engagement (and their immediate families) own shares in the client's business
- firm members not involved in the assurance engagement (and their immediate families) own more shares in the client than the minimum number of shares permitted by the relevant governing body
- a loan to or from the client outside of normal lending terms
- fee dependence, where the fees (from assurance and other services) from one client form a significant proportion of the total fees earned from all assurance clients
- a close business relationship with the client, unless the relationship is limited to an immaterial financial interest for the client, the firm member, and the firm.

Cloud 9

Sharon's old firm had a fee dependence problem. The audit fees they earned from the client resisting the recommended accounting treatment for asset values were a significant proportion of the firm's total fees. W&S Partners is a much larger audit firm than Sharon's old firm, and Cloud 9's fees will not be a significant portion of total fee revenue.

Self-review threat

Self-review threat refers to the threat that can occur when the assurance team forms an opinion on their own work or work performed by others in their firm. Some examples include:

- an assurance team member having recently been an employee or a director of the client and therefore able to influence the subject matter of the assurance engagement
- information prepared for the client that is then assured, such as creating source documents, or preparing and recording journal entries without first obtaining management's approval
- services performed for the client that are then assured, such as internal audit services, information technology services, legal services, human resource services, and corporate finance services and valuations.

self-review threat the threat that can occur when the assurance team needs to form an opinion on their own work or work performed by others in their firm

Cloud 9

Josh and Sharon do not know of any current work being done for Cloud 9 by W&S Partners, or of any other relationships between members of the audit team and the client's staff. However, they will check with all other departments at W&S Partners, particularly the consulting department. They will also ask any new member of the audit team to disclose their interests and relationships with the client before they join the team.

Advocacy threat

Advocacy threat refers to the threat that can occur when an accounting firm or its assurance staff acts, or is believed to act, on behalf of its assurance client. In such a

advocacy threat the threat that can occur when a firm or its staff acts on behalf of its assurance client

case, the objectivity of the assurance provider may come under question. Some examples include:

- encouraging others to buy shares or bonds being sold by the client
- representing the client in negotiations with a third party
- representing the client in a legal dispute.

Cloud 9

The partner, Jo Wadley, advises Sharon and Josh that the audit firm is not acting for Cloud 9 in any other matter.

Familiarity threat

familiarity threat the threat that can occur when a close relationship exists or develops between the assurance firm (staff) and the client (staff)

Familiarity threat refers to the threat that can occur when a close relationship exists or develops between the assurance firm and the client, or between members of the assurance team and directors or employees of the client. The result can be that the assurance team becomes too sensitive to the needs of the client and loses its objectivity. Some examples include:

- a long association between the assurance firm and the client
- a long association between members of the assurance team and their client
- an assurance team member with a close relative who holds a senior position of influence at the client
- a former partner of the assurance firm holding a senior position with the client
- the acceptance of gifts by members of the assurance team from the client, other than very minor tokens
- the acceptance of hospitality (for example, a meal or tickets to a sporting competition) by members of the assurance team from the client, other than very minor gestures.

Cloud 9

Familiarity is usually a greater issue for existing clients than for new clients, such as Cloud 9 for W&S Partners. However, there could be personal familiarity issues in any audit engagement. Josh is worried about asking the senior staff to declare their relationships with the management of Cloud 9. He thinks they might regard that question as impertinent. Sharon tells Josh that she knows the senior staff at W&S Partners are very committed to ethical behaviour. If they were not to ask this question as part of the process of accepting the new client, Sharon and Josh would be disciplined for poor performance.

Intimidation threat

intimidation threat the threat that can occur when a member of the assurance team feels threatened by client staff or directors

Intimidation threat refers to the threat that can occur when a member of the assurance team feels threatened by the client's staff or directors. The result can be that the assurance team member is unable to act objectively, believing that if he or she does so there may be some negative consequences based upon the threat received. Some examples include:

- the threat that the client will use a different assurance firm next year
- undue pressure to reduce audit hours to reduce fees paid.

Cloud 9

The partner at Sharon's old firm was threatened with dismissal from the audit, and Sharon has heard of other clients pressuring auditors to reduce their fees. Sharon is confident that the firm of W&S Partners does not rely unreasonably on any one audit and is therefore less vulnerable to threats. She also knows that auditors at W&S Partners keep very detailed records of time spent on any audit tasks and can justify their fees if a client questions the amount.

While the above apply to *all* assurance engagements, there are additional prohibitions for auditors of reporting issuers. A **reporting issuer**, in accordance with the independence standard, is a public company with a market capitalization and a book value of total assets greater than $10 million. Some of the additional requirements to ensure auditor independence for reporting issuers include the following:

- Audit partners must be rotated every seven years, with a five-year break from the audit engagement.
- Audit committee must pre-approve all services provided to the client by the firm.
- Audit partners may not be directly compensated for selling non-assurance services to the audit client.
- Where an engagement team member accepts employment in a financial reporting role with a client, the firm must refrain from being the auditor of that client for at least one year from the date the financial statements were filed with securities regulators.[2]

When any of these threats are recognized, steps should be taken to remove or reduce the threat to an acceptably low level. This can be achieved by utilizing an appropriate safeguard.

> **reporting issuer** a public company with a market capitalization and a book value of total assets greater than $10 million

2.2.2 Safeguards to independence

Safeguards are mechanisms that have been developed by the accounting profession, legislators, regulators, clients, and accounting firms. They are used to minimize the risk that a threat will surface (for example, through education) and to deal with a threat when one becomes apparent (for example, through reporting processes within the assurance firm).

Safeguards created by the profession, legislation, or regulation

The accounting profession, legislation, and regulation have created a range of safeguards, including CSQC 1 *Quality Control for Firms that Perform Audits and Reviews of Financial Statements, Other Financial Information, and Other Assurance Engagements.* Safeguards include education of accountants about the threats to independence and the establishment of a code of ethics. For reporting issuers, legislation requires that an auditor be independent and that a communication of independence be issued to the client annually. Figure 2.1 is an illustration of the auditor independence letter.

March 1, 2012
        The Audit Committee
        Cloud 9 Ltd.
        Dear Audit Committee Members:
    I have been engaged to audit the financial statements of Cloud 9 Ltd.
Limited (the Company) for the year ending December 31, 2012.
    Canadian generally accepted auditing standards (GAAS) require that
I communicate at least annually with you regarding all relationships between
the Company and me that, in my professional judgement, may reasonably be
thought to bear on my independence.
    In determining which relationships to report, these standards require
me to consider relevant rules and related interpretations prescribed by the
appropriate provincial institute/order and applicable legislation, covering such
matters as:
(a) holding a financial interest, either directly or indirectly, in a client;
(b) holding a position, either directly or indirectly, that gives the right or
    responsibility to exert significant influence over the financial or accounting
    policies of a client;
(c) personal or business relationships of immediate family, close relatives,
    partners or retired partners, either directly or indirectly, with a client;
(d) economic dependence on a client; and
(e) provision of services in addition to the audit engagement.
    I am not aware of any relationships between the Company and me that,
in my professional judgement, may reasonably be thought to bear on my
independence, that have occurred from January 1 to December 31, 2011.
    GAAS requires that I confirm my independence to the audit committee in
the context of the *Rules of Professional Conduct of the Institute of Chartered
Accountants of Ontario*. Accordingly, I hereby confirm that I am independent with
respect to the Company within the meaning of the *Rules of Professional Conduct
of the Institute of Chartered Accountants of Ontario* as of March 31, 2012.
    This report is intended solely for the use of the audit committee, the board
of directors, management, and others within the Company and should not be
used for any other purposes.
    I look forward to discussing with you the matters addressed in this letter at
our upcoming meeting.

Yours truly,

CHARTERED ACCOUNTANT

FIGURE 2.1 **Sample independence letter**

Safeguards created by clients

Clients can put in place appropriate mechanisms that will reduce the threat to independence. They can introduce appropriate **corporate governance** mechanisms (discussed further in chapter 3), such as the establishment of an audit committee to liaise between the assurance partner and management to enhance independence. (See section 2.3.3 for a discussion of the role of audit committees.) Clients can ensure that the responsibility for the appointment and removal of an auditor rests with **independent directors** on the audit committee or the board. They can establish policies and procedures dedicated to ensuring that the financial statements are fairly presented. Finally, clients can put in place policies and procedures dedicated

corporate governance the rules, systems, and processes within companies used to guide and control

independent directors non-executive directors without any business or other ties to the company

to ensuring that the assurance team has access to all required documents and records when required. These safeguards can reduce but not eliminate the threat to independence. To ensure their effectiveness, clients must ensure that policies and mechanisms established are working effectively.

Cloud 9

Sharon explains to Josh that one of their key tasks will be to discover, document, and evaluate any independence safeguards created by Cloud 9. She explains that safeguards created by the profession and W&S Partners apply to all audits, so the relative success of an audit with respect to independence problems is significantly affected by the safeguards created by the client. The greater these safeguards, the less likely there will be any problems with the audit. The auditor needs to know that if a problem does arise, the client has committed to protect the integrity of the audit.

Sharon asks Josh to document the governance structure at Cloud 9, including background information on the directors and senior management. Sharon will investigate the structure governing the relationships between the directors and management of Cloud 9 and the parent company, Cloud 9 Inc.

Safeguards created by accounting firms

Accounting firms have in place a range of safeguards to ensure independence. They have policies and procedures to ensure the quality of their service, and they provide continuing education for their staff regarding these policies and procedures. Firms have client acceptance and continuance procedures to ensure that they identify any threats to independence on a timely basis. Firms have partner rotation policies to ensure that audit partners remain independent of their clients. They also have a policy of peer review, where audit partners review the work files of other partners and provide comment and feedback. Finally, firms establish procedures for staff to follow if they become aware of a threat to their independence. These safeguards can reduce but not eliminate the threat to independence. To ensure their effectiveness, accounting firms must ensure that policies and mechanisms established are working effectively.

Table 2.1 lists the five threats to independence, together with some of the safeguards that can help to remove or reduce each threat to an acceptably low level.

Threats to Independence	Safeguards to Independence
Self-interest threat	• Policies and procedures within an accounting firm identifying any staff with financial interest in an assurance client. • Regular review of assurance and other fees earned from each client in comparison to total fees from all assurance clients. • Minimizing the provision of non-audit services to assurance clients. • Policies and procedures prohibiting business relationships with clients.

TABLE 2.1 **Summary of independence threats and safeguards**

Source: Based on Accounting Professional and Ethical Standards Board 2010, APES 110, section 290. Reproduced with the permission of the Accounting Professional and Ethical Standards Board (APESB), Victoria, Australia.

(continued)

TABLE 2.1 **Summary of independence threats and safeguards** (continued)

Threats to Independence	Safeguards to Independence
Self-review threat	• Minimizing the provision of non-audit services to assurance clients. • When providing non-audit services, ensuring that the client is responsible for overseeing and guiding that work and making any final decisions regarding the outcomes of that work. • Having a cooling-off period before an audit partner can be employed in a senior role at an audit client.
Advocacy threat	• Policies and procedures prohibiting business relationships with clients. • Policies and procedures prohibiting the representation of clients in any disputes or legal matters. • Rotating staff assigned to clients so they do not spend too much time at any one client's premises.
Familiarity threat	• Partner and staff rotation policies. • Education regarding acceptance of gifts and hospitality from assurance clients providing examples of what is and what is not acceptable. • Procedures when assigning staff to assurance clients ensuring no close personal relationships exist between assurance team members and client personnel. • Education regarding socializing with client personnel.
Intimidation threat	• Avoidance of fee dependence. • Appropriate corporate governance structures within clients, such as an audit committee, to liaise with senior assurance team members and client management. • Adherence to stringent procedures regarding the removal of assurance providers.

PROFESSIONAL ENVIRONMENT

Quality control

CSQC 1 *Quality Control for Firms that Perform Audits and Reviews of Financial Statements, Other Financial Information, and Other Assurance Engagements*

Canada adopted the CSQC 1 on December 15, 2009, to complement its adoption of the CASs. The CSQC 1 deals with a firm's responsibilities to establish, document, and maintain a system of quality control if it performs audits and reviews of financial statements and other assurance engagements. The purpose of this standard is to ensure firms comply with legal and regulatory requirements and to ensure firms issue appropriate opinions.

As a result, firms that offer assurance services must have a quality assurance manual that outlines policies and procedures in the following areas:
• leadership responsibility to promote a culture of quality
• compliance with ethical requirements including a requirement to assess independence
• client acceptance and continuance to ensure firms perform engagements within their competencies and that they have adequate resources available
• human resource policies to ensure personnel are capable, competent, and ethical
• criteria for performing and documenting engagement quality reviews: while an engagement quality review (more commonly known as second partner review)

is required for all listed entities, firms need criteria to assess the need for an engagement quality review for non-listed entities. An engagement quality review involves a review of the financial statements and the work performed, and an evaluation of the opinion formed.

- monitoring: there are two requirements a firm must meet with respect to monitoring. First, a firm must perform an ongoing assessment of its compliance with the policies and procedures set out in its quality assurance manual. Second, every one to three years, a firm should have a "monitor" (someone not involved in the assurance engagements) review a selection of assurance files, as well as assess the quality control activities of the firm. A report should be issued identifying any weaknesses or deficiencies.

Source: The *CICA Handbook* – Assurance, Effective as of December 15, 2009

BEFORE YOU GO ON

2.1 What are the three ways an auditor can become associated with financial information?

2.2 Why is auditor independence so important?

2.3 What are some examples of circumstances that may cause a familiarity threat?

2.3 THE AUDITOR'S RELATIONSHIPS WITH OTHERS

The external auditor has the responsibility to form an opinion on the fair presentation of the financial statements prepared by their client. In conducting their audit, the external auditor comes into contact with client staff and management on a regular basis. The key groups that the external auditor will have a professional link with are the client's shareholders, the board of directors, the audit committee, and the internal audit team.

3 Explain the relationship between an auditor and key groups they have a professional link with during the audit engagement.

2.3.1 Auditors and shareholders

The audit report is addressed to the **shareholders** of the company being audited. This means that the shareholders are acknowledged as the main recipients of the financial statements and the attached audit report. Shareholders own the company. If the company fails, shareholders stand to lose most, if not all, of their investment. Shareholders rely on the audit report and the opinion contained within it to inform them about the reliability of the information provided by the management of their company in the financial statements. Auditors will not often meet the shareholders they report to except when they attend their client's annual general meeting. Exceptions include major shareholders, whom the auditor may meet with from time to time, and shareholding board members and client personnel, whom the auditor will meet with during the course of their audit. Shareholders are responsible for the appointment and removal of their company's auditors. The board of directors will facilitate this process on behalf of shareholders. Generally, the board will select an audit firm that they believe is appropriate or will propose when it is time to appoint a new audit firm. The board will then make a recommendation to shareholders. Shareholders generally follow recommendations made by the board of directors.

shareholders owners of the company

2.3.2 Auditors and the board of directors

executive directors employees of the company who also hold a position on the board of directors

non-executive directors board members who are not employees of the company. Their involvement on the board is limited to preparing for and attending board meetings and relevant board committee meetings

The board of directors represents the shareholders and oversees the activities of a company and its management. It is the role of the board to ensure that the company is being run to benefit the shareholders. The board will generally comprise a mixture of executive and non-executive directors. **Executive directors** are also part of the company's management team; they are full-time employees of the company. **Non-executive directors** are not part of the company's management team; their involvement is limited to preparing for and attending board meetings and relevant board committee meetings. It is the directors' responsibility to ensure that the financial statements are fairly presented and provide a true and fair view. It is the responsibility of the external auditor to audit the financial statements. The audit partner will meet with members of the board when necessary throughout the audit.

It is important that the board of directors have a mixture of executive and non-executive members; however, the majority of the board should be independent directors. The executive members have a deeper understanding of the company and its workings. Auditors meet with executive directors throughout the audit. The non-executive members are better representatives of shareholders as they are not employees of the company and can be more impartial in their dealings with management. The external auditor will read the minutes of board meetings to learn about the key decisions regarding the strategic direction the board plans to take the company in the future. Other information that may be found in the minutes includes the level of dividends declared, plans for significant asset purchases, purchases and sales of major investments, and major agreements with other companies that may be contemplated.

Boards of larger companies will also have a series of committees made up of various members of the board. It is the role of these committees to efficiently deal with specific important issues. The main board committee that the auditor deals with is the audit committee. The audit committee is described in more detail in the next section.

2.3.3 Auditors and the audit committee

audit committee a subcommittee of the board of directors. The audit committee enhances auditor independence and ensures that the financial statements are fairly presented and that the external auditor has access to all records and other evidence required to form their opinion.

An effective **audit committee** will enhance the independence of the external audit function: an audit committee acts on behalf of the full board of directors to ensure that the financial statements are fairly presented and that the external auditor has access to all records and other evidence required to form their opinion. While ultimate responsibility for the fair presentation of the financial statements rests with the full board, an audit committee can improve the efficiency of achieving this goal.

In Canada, the Canadian Securities Administrators (CSA) require that all listed companies have an audit committee. The role of this committee is to oversee the accounting, financial reporting, and audit of the financial statements. The audit committee should be established by the board and should consist of at least three independent directors who are financially literate.

From an audit perspective, it is important that the audit committee be independent of the remainder of the board and of the financial reporting function. The audit committee should consist of only non-executive independent directors. As noted earlier, a non-executive director is not part of the company's management team. An independent director is a non-executive director without any business or other ties to the company that could impede his or her ability to act impartially.

An audit committee should consist of members who can read and understand the contents of the financial statements. It is important that audit committee members have some understanding of the accounting policies used by the company and can communicate easily with the auditor about those choices. The audit partner will report to the audit committee when they have a significant disagreement with management regarding accounting choices made and/or with the content of the notes to the financial statements.

A formal charter sets out the structure, composition, and responsibilities of the audit committee. When a company does not have an audit committee, the audit partner will meet with members of the board of directors.

The responsibilities of the audit committee include the following:

- to recommend the auditor and their fees to the board
- to oversee the audit and resolve any differences between the auditor and management
- to pre-approve all non-audit services to be provided to the entity or its subsidiaries by the independent auditor.

2.3.4 Auditors and internal auditors

The role of internal audit (and **internal auditors**) is determined by those charged with governance, ideally the audit committee. The role of the internal audit function was explained in chapter 1. The external auditor views the internal audit function as part of the company being audited and, as such, the internal audit function can never be wholly independent of the company. However, if a company has an effective internal audit function, the external auditor can consider modifying the nature and timing of their procedures and reduce the extent of their audit testing. The final opinion on fair presentation of the financial statements remains with the external auditor, as does the responsibility for gathering and evaluating sufficient appropriate audit evidence to form that opinion. If the external auditor intends to use the work of the internal audit function, they should consider various internal audit characteristics (CAS 610 *Using the Work of Internal Auditors*), including the objectivity, technical competence, and due professional care of the internal audit function and the effectiveness of communication between internal and external audit. These characteristics are described below.

internal auditors employees of the company who evaluate and make recommendations to improve risk management, internal control procedures, and elements of the governance process

Objectivity

Objectivity refers to how the internal audit function fits within the client's organizational structure. This is important as it establishes the level of independence of the internal audit function from the rest of the organization. The more independent the internal audit function, the more reliance that can be placed upon it by the external auditor. Ideally, internal auditors should report directly to the audit committee or the board of directors.

Technical competence

Technical competence refers to the skills, training, and ability of the internal audit team. The external auditor may consider the background and qualifications, the level of training undertaken, and the extent of the experience of the internal audit staff. The external auditor will also be concerned as to whether internal audit staff are appropriately qualified for their roles.

technical competence the skills, training, and ability of the internal audit team

Due professional care

Due professional care refers to the documentation, planning, and supervision of the internal audit function. The external auditor is interested in the level of planning undertaken by internal audit. They will also want to see evidence of the procedures undertaken by internal auditors in formulating their conclusions.

Communication

Communication between internal and external auditors is achieved through the scheduling of regular meetings, the external auditor having access to internal audit documentation as needed, and the external auditor informing internal auditors of any issues affecting their work that arise during the external audit. It is important that internal and external auditors are free to communicate without interference from client management or staff.

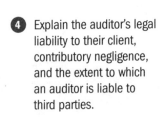

Cloud 9

Understanding the board of directors and its subcommittees will be a part of Josh and Sharon's work in documenting Cloud 9's governance structure. In particular, they have to find out whether Cloud 9 has an audit committee and the background of the directors who sit on the board. They also have to check for the existence of an internal audit department at Cloud 9, and find out what they can about the role and function of the internal audit department at Cloud 9 Inc. (the parent company) as it relates to Cloud 9.

BEFORE YOU GO ON

3.1 What is the difference between a non-executive and an independent director?

3.2 Why is it important that an audit committee be independent?

3.3 Why might an external auditor want to use the work of the internal audit function?

2.4 LEGAL LIABILITY

④ Explain the auditor's legal liability to their client, contributory negligence, and the extent to which an auditor is liable to third parties.

negligence failure to exercise due care

As noted in chapter 1, the external auditor must exercise due care when conducting an audit. This means that the auditor must be diligent in applying technical and professional standards, and must document each stage in the audit process. If the auditor is found to be **negligent** (to have not exercised due care), they may be sued for damages by their client or a third party.

Under tort law, to prove that an auditor has been negligent, it must be established that:

- A duty of care was owed by the auditor.
- There was a breach of the duty of care.
- A loss was suffered as a consequence of that breach.

Tort law is a body of rights, obligations, and remedies that is applied by courts in civil proceedings to provide relief for persons who have suffered harm from the wrongful acts of others. The person who sustains injury or suffers pecuniary damage is known as the plaintiff, and the person who is responsible for inflicting the injury and incurs liability for the damage is known as the defendant.[3]

2.4.1 Legal liability to clients

An auditor can be sued by their client. To sue the auditor, the client must prove that the auditor owed them a duty of care. A client can establish that the auditor owed them a duty of care in one of two ways: (1) under contract law for breach of contract or (2) under tort law for negligence.

1. Under contract law, a client can sue the auditor for breach of contract. This action may be taken when the auditor fails to live up to their responsibility implicit in agreeing to act as the auditor and explicit in the engagement letter. For example, if the auditor withdraws from an audit without cause, before completing the audit and issuing the report, the client can sue the auditor for breach of contract.

2. Under the tort of negligence, a client can claim that the auditor failed to take reasonable care in the performance of the audit. This means that the work was below the standard that may be reasonably expected from a designated public accountant. The injured party must prove that the auditor's carelessness or unintentional behaviour caused harm and therefore breached the duty of care.

An auditor's duty of care to their client has been established and defined through case law over more than a century. In these cases, the definition of reasonable care and skill has changed over time to reflect changes in professional standards. To prove that an auditor has been negligent, a plaintiff, whether a client or a third party, must establish that an auditor did not comply with auditing standards, ethical pronouncements, or some element of the law in place at the time the auditor conducted their audit. Often-cited cases are described below.

London and General Bank Ltd. (No. 2) (1895) 2 Ch. 673

This case established that an auditor has a duty to report to the shareholders, not the directors, of the company being audited. In forming his judgement, Lord Justice Linley noted that "an auditor however is not bound to do more than exercise reasonable care and skill in making inquiries and investigations. He is not an insurer; he does not guarantee that the books do correctly show the true position of the company's affairs. What is reasonable care and skill in any particular case must depend upon the circumstances of that case." This case provided an explanation of the extent to which an auditor could be held liable for the actions of their clients.

Kingston Cotton Mill (No. 2) (1896) 2 Ch. 279

In this case, Lord Justice Lopes noted that "it is the duty of an auditor to bring to bear on the work he has to perform that skill, care and caution, which a reasonably competent, careful and cautious auditor would use. What is reasonable skill, care and caution must depend on the particular circumstances of each case. An auditor is not bound to be a detective or, as was said, to approach his work with suspicion or with a foregone conclusion that there is something wrong. He is a watchdog, but not a "bloodhound." This finding indicated that an auditor is not to *assume* that the client's accounts are materially misstated.

Pacific Acceptance (1970) 90 WN (NSW) 29

This case recognized that standards of reasonable care and skill had changed considerably since the Kingston Cotton Mill case of 1896. Justice Moffit pronounced the following in his judgement in the Pacific Acceptance case:

- Auditors have a duty to use reasonable care and skill.
- Auditors have a duty to check and see for themselves rather than rely on client management and staff.
- Auditors must closely supervise and review the work of junior staff.
- Auditors must properly document procedures used.
- Auditors have a duty to warn and inform the appropriate level of management.
- Auditors have a duty to take further action where suspicion is aroused that a misstatement may have occurred.
- Auditors should be guided by professional standards.

Negligence is any behaviour that is careless or unintentional and breaches the duty of care. In proving that an auditor has been negligent, a client or its shareholders would need to prove that the auditor had not complied with auditing standards or ethical guidelines. After establishing that the auditor owed them a duty of care and that the auditor has been in some way negligent (has breached that duty of care), the client or its shareholders would need to establish that they suffered a loss as a result of that negligence. To ascertain a causal relationship between the negligent act and the loss suffered, reasonable foreseeability must be proven. This means that the auditor must have been aware that any negligence on their part could cause a loss to the client or its shareholders.

2.4.2 Contributory negligence

Contributory negligence means that where a plaintiff (the party suing) and the defendant (the auditor) can be proven to have been negligent, each party must be held accountable in proportion to their guilt. For example, management is responsible for putting in place an adequate system of internal control. However, if management fails to do this and the auditor uncovers the weakness and reports it to management, but fails to report it to the directors when management does not repair the deficient control, management, as well as the auditor, would be found to have been negligent and to have contributed to the loss of the plaintiff.

2.4.3 Legal liability to third parties

Establishing that a duty of care is owed to third parties is not straightforward. **Third parties** include anyone other than the client and its shareholders who use the financial statements to make a decision (for example, creditors). As third parties generally do not have a contractual relationship with the auditor, they must rely on tort law. The key difficulty for third parties is establishing that a duty of care was owed to them by the auditor. If they are able to prove that such a duty is owed, third parties must provide evidence that the auditor was negligent and that the third party suffered a loss as a result of that negligence. Below is a very brief summary of the key cases that have established the legal liability of auditors to third parties.

third parties anyone other than the client and its shareholders who uses the financial statements to make a decision

Ultramares Corp v. Touche (1931) 174 N.E. 441

This is an American case that has had an impact on Canadian auditors because it resulted in what is called the Ultramares doctrine. The Ultramares doctrine establishes that auditors are not liable for ordinary negligence to parties that they do not have a privity (contractual) relationship with. In this case, Judge Cardozzo ruled that an auditor cannot have "liability in an indeterminate amount for an indeterminate time to an indeterminate class." The liability of auditors would be too great, as auditors should not be required to owe a duty of care to everyone.

Hedley Byrne & Co v. Heller and Partners Ltd. (1964) A.C. 465

This is an English case heard by the House of Lords, but the outcome has had an impact on professionals in all common law countries. It introduced the concept of foreseeable third parties. The court's ruling in this case expanded the concept of auditor liability beyond the privity (contractual) relationship. The concept of liability was extended to third parties provided the auditors knew beforehand that the third party would be relying on their opinion.[4]

Haig vs. Bamford (1977) S.C.R. 466

This is a Canadian case that narrowed the foreseeable third-party concept. In this case, the auditor prepared audited financial statements knowing that the statements were being provided to an outside investor. The investor relied on the financial statements and subsequently the company went bankrupt and the investor incurred a loss. The court ruled that although the auditors did not know the name of the investor, they knew the audited financial statements were being passed on to unidentified members of a limited class for use in a transaction of which the accountants were aware.

Hercules Management Ltd. v. Ernst & Young [1997] S.C.R. 165

In this case, potential shareholders relied on the audited financial statements and made a share investment. They then brought a suit against the auditor claiming that the financial statements were prepared negligently. The outcome of this case reversed the trend of expanding auditor legal liability. The court dismissed the negligence claim in that it ruled the audited financial statements were prepared to evaluate management stewardship, not for individuals making investment decisions. Therefore, because the plaintiffs did not rely on the financial statements for the purpose for which they were prepared, there was no duty of care.

In summary, to establish that an auditor owes a duty of care to a third party, the third party must establish that the auditor was aware that the third party was going to use the financial statements and that they relied on the financial statements for the purpose for which they were prepared. Figure 2.2 illustrates auditor liability.

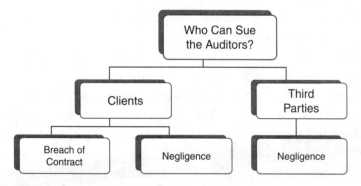

FIGURE 2.2 **Auditor liability**

PROFESSIONAL ENVIRONMENT

Litigation and audit risk in tough economic times

There are signs of a rise in the number of potential and actual claims by accountants under legal liability insurance policies in Canada. Accountants and auditors make claims against their insurance policies when they are sued by their clients.

Fraud is a megadollar problem for small businesses and a megadollar professional liability issue for chartered accountants. Our fast-paced society, advances in technology, and the growth of trade over the Internet have created an environment where the temptation to cheat has become very attractive or perhaps just that much easier to carry out. Not only are we more likely to have clients where fraud will be a major issue, but there is a growing public expectation for auditors to detect fraud. Therefore, it is common for legal action to be brought against accountants on the basis that the accountant should have "caught something as there is a growing public expectation for auditors to detect fraud." The insurer of Canadian chartered accountants, the Association of Insured Chartered Accountants (AICA), encourages the use of engagement letters to mitigate risk by specifying that the audit is conducted to primarily enable the auditor to express an opinion on the financial statements and is not specifically designed to identify all errors, fraud, or other irregularities.

Auditors are also warned to be careful about large unpaid fees. Independence requirements indicate that a self-interest threat may be created if fees due from an assurance client remain unpaid for a long time, especially if a significant part is not paid before the assurance report for the following year is issued. The unpaid fees could be regarded as equivalent to a loan to the client, potentially making it inappropriate for the audit firm to be reappointed. Auditors could be caught between loyalty to a long-term client that is facing difficulties and losing their objectivity with a client that is increasingly desperate.

Professional accounting bodies around the world highlight the importance of issues related to going concern and subsequent events during difficult economic times. Many have issued guidance to their members to help them identify and deal with going concern and other issues linked to the global financial crisis. The Auditing and Assurance Standards Board (AASB) issued a risk alert on auditing considerations in an uncertain economic environment. The bulletin emphasizes matters to consider ranging from overall decisions regarding client continuance, staffing, and the extent of supervision to detailed decisions on the nature, timing, and extent of specific audit procedures appropriate in the circumstances. The bulletin states that, "The need to exercise professional skepticism and professional judgement will also be particularly important in times of economic difficulty or uncertainty."

Sources: "Fraud Claims on the Rise," *The Chartered Accountant Risk Management Newsletter,* May 2003, Vol. XII, Issue I, www.aica.ca; AICA, 2003; "Auditing Considerations in the Current Economic Environment," Auditing and Assurance Standards Board, *AASB Risk Alert,* January 2009, www.aasb.ca.

2.4.4 Avoidance of litigation

There are a number of ways that an auditor can avoid litigation. These include:

- hiring competent staff
- training staff and updating their knowledge regularly
- ensuring compliance with ethical regulations
- ensuring compliance with auditing regulations
- implementing policies and procedures that ensure:
  - appropriate procedures are followed when accepting a new client
  - appropriate staff are allocated to clients
  - ethical and independence issues are identified and dealt with on a timely basis
  - all work is fully documented
  - adequate and appropriate evidence is gathered before forming an opinion
- meeting with a client's audit committee to discuss any significant issues identified as part of the audit

- following up on any significant weaknesses in the client's internal control procedures in a previous year's audit.

BEFORE YOU GO ON

4.1 What are the two ways a client can establish the duty of care?

4.2 What is contributory negligence?

4.3 What must be established under tort law to prove that an auditor has been negligent?

2.5 CLIENT ACCEPTANCE AND CONTINUANCE DECISIONS

The first stage of any audit is the client acceptance or continuance decision. While the decision to take on a new client is more detailed than the decision to continue with an existing client, they have much in common. CSQC 1 provides guidance on the procedures to be followed when making the client acceptance or continuance decision.

5 Identify the factors to consider in the client acceptance or continuance decision.

The first step involves the assessment of client integrity. When assessing client integrity, the auditor will consider:

- the reputation of the client, its management, directors, and key stakeholders
- the reasons provided for switching audit firms (client acceptance decision)
- the client's attitude to risk exposure and management
- the client's attitude to the implementation and maintenance of adequate internal controls to mitigate (minimize) identified risks
- the appropriateness of the client's interpretation of accounting rules
- the client's willingness to allow the auditor full access to information required to form their opinion
- the client's attitude to audit fees and its willingness to pay a fair amount for the work completed.

Information relevant to the client acceptance or continuance decision can be found through:

- communication with the previous auditor (client acceptance decision) before communicating any client details to the prospective auditor (if that permission is refused, the auditor should consider declining the appointment as auditor)
- communication with client personnel
- communication with third parties such as client bankers and lawyers
- an Internet or background search
- a review of news articles about the client
- a review of prior-period financial statements.

The code of professional conduct and the CSQC 1 deal with professional appointments. Before accepting a new client, consideration must be given to any threats to compliance with the fundamental principles of professional ethics (integrity, objectivity, professional competence and due care, confidentiality, and professional behaviour). Threats to the fundamental principles of professional ethics will occur if the prospective client is dishonest, involved in illegal activities, or aggressive in its interpretations of accounting rules. An audit firm should not accept an entity as a new client if it is concerned about any of these issues. Potential threats to compliance with the fundamental principles of professional ethics for existing clients should be considered from time to time.

To ensure professional competence and due care, an audit firm must make certain that it has the staff available at the time required to complete the audit (client acceptance decision). The audit firm must ensure that its audit staff have the knowledge and competence required to conduct the audit. The auditor must have access to independent experts if required.

To ensure that it is independent of prospective and continuing clients, the audit firm must review the threats to independence, described earlier, and make certain that safeguards are put in place to limit or remove those threats. An auditor should therefore assess independence before the client acceptance or continuance decision is made. See figure 2.3 for a sample of an independence assessment worksheet [form 410] from the *Canadian Professional Engagement Manual (C-PEM)*. It is important to note the C-PEM is not authoritative guidance, but rather it is a tool used by practitioners to assist in performing assurance and compilation engagements.

FIGURE 2.3 **Extract of independence assessment, C-PEM Form 410**
Source: CPEM Form 410

Are we satisfied there are no existing prohibitions that would preclude the firm or any staff member from performing the engagement? Address each of the following prohibitions listed below:

a) Financial interests in entity.

b) Loans and guarantees to/from client.

c) Close business relationships with client.

d) Family and personal relationships with client.

e) Future or recent employment with entity serving as officer, director, or company secretary of client.

f) Provision of non-assurance services such as corporate finance or legal services that involve dispute resolution.

g) Performance of management functions for the client.

h) Making journal entries or accounting classifications without first obtaining management's approval.

i) Acceptance of gifts or hospitality from client (other than clearly insignificant).

j) Fee quote that is considerably less than market price for the engagement.

k) Provision of legal services.

l) Preparation of source documentation.

m) Provision of corporate finance services.

Are we satisfied there are no significant "threats" to independence? Address each of the following threats in relation to the firm and any member of the engagement team:

a) Self-interest (i.e., where loss of client fees would be material).

b) Self-review (i.e., the nature and extent of bookkeeping services required or where a judgement from a previous engagement needs to be evaluated in reaching conclusions).

(continued)

FIGURE 2.3 **Extract of independence assessment, C·PEM Form 410** (continued)

---

c) Advocacy (i.e., acting as an advocate on behalf of client in litigation or in share promotion).

d) Familiarity (i.e., being too sympathetic to the client's interests).

e) Intimidation (i.e., being deterred from acting objectively and exercising professional scepticism).

Comment: Threats identified and safeguards (if any) to reduce the threat to an acceptable level:

If an independence threat appears insurmountable, an audit firm should consider declining an offer to act as an auditor of a prospective client or resign from the audit of an existing client. An example of such a threat is fee dependence, where the fees from a client would form a significant proportion of total fees earned. This can occur if a prospective client is much larger than an audit firm's current clients or if an existing client has grown significantly.

The final stage in the client acceptance and continuance decision process involves the preparation of an **engagement letter**. CAS 210 *Agreeing the Terms of Audit Engagements* provides guidance on the preparation of engagement letters. An engagement letter is prepared by an auditor and acknowledged by a client before the commencement of an audit. It is a form of contract between an auditor and the client. Engagement letters should be updated each year to remind management of the existing terms and for legal liability purposes. The purpose of the engagement letter is to set out the terms of the audit engagement to avoid any misunderstandings between the auditor and the client. The letter will confirm both the obligations of the client and the auditor.

> **engagement letter** letter that sets out the terms of the audit engagement, to avoid any misunderstandings between the auditor and their client

An engagement letter includes an explanation of the scope of the audit, summarizes the responsibilities of management and the responsibilities of the auditor, identifies the applicable financial reporting framework, and makes reference to the expected form and content of the audit report. An example of an engagement letter for statements prepared in accordance with International Financial Reporting Standards (IFRS) is provided in the appendix to CAS 210 and is reproduced in figure 2.4.

FIGURE 2.4 **Example of an engagement letter**

Source: Auditing and Assurance Standards Board 2009, CAS 210 *Agreeing the Terms of Audit Engagements*, App. 1

To the appropriate representative of management or those charged with governance of Securimax Ltd.

You have requested that we audit the financial statements of Securimax Ltd. which comprise the balance sheet as at December 31, 2011, and the income statement, statement of changes in equity, and cash flow statement for the year then ended, and a summary of significant accounting policies and other explanatory information. We are pleased to confirm our acceptance and our understanding of this audit engagement by means of this letter. Our audit will be conducted with the objective of our expressing an opinion on the financial statements.

(continued)

FIGURE 2.4 **Example of an engagement letter** (continued)

We will conduct our audit in accordance with Canadian generally accepted auditing standards. Those standards require that we comply with ethical requirements and plan and perform the audit to obtain reasonable assurance about whether the financial statements are free from material misstatement. An audit involves performing procedures to obtain audit evidence about the amounts and disclosures in the financial statements. The procedures selected depend on the auditor's judgement, including the assessment of the risks of material misstatement of the financial statements, whether due to fraud or error. An audit also includes evaluating the appropriateness of accounting policies used and the reasonableness of accounting estimates made by management, as well as evaluating the overall presentation of the financial statements.

Because of the inherent limitations of an audit, together with the inherent limitations of internal control, there is an unavoidable risk that some material misstatements may not be detected, even though the audit is properly planned and performed in accordance with Canadian generally accepted auditing standards.

In making our risk assessments, we consider internal control relevant to the entity's preparation of the financial statements in order to design audit procedures that are appropriate in the circumstances, but not for the purpose of expressing an opinion on the effectiveness of the entity's internal control. However, we will communicate to you in writing concerning any significant deficiencies in internal control relevant to the audit of the financial statements that we have identified during the audit.

Our audit will be conducted on the basis that management and, where appropriate, those charged with governance acknowledge and understand that they have responsibility:

(a) For the preparation and fair presentation of the financial statements in accordance with International Financial Reporting Standards;

(b) For such internal control as management determines is necessary to enable the preparation of financial statements that are free from material misstatement, whether due to fraud or error; and

(c) To provide us with:

   (i) Access to all information of which management is aware that is relevant to the preparation of the financial statements such as records, documentation, and other matters;

   (ii) Additional information that we may request from management for the purpose of the audit; and

   (iii) Unrestricted access to persons within the entity from whom we determine it necessary to obtain audit evidence.

As part of our audit process, we will request from management and, where appropriate, those charged with governance written confirmation concerning representations made to us in connection with the audit.

We look forward to full cooperation from your staff during our audit.

Insert: appropriate reference to the expected form and content of the auditor's report.

The form and content of our report may need to be amended in the light of our audit findings.

Please sign and return the attached copy of this letter to indicate your acknowledgement of, and agreement with, the arrangements for our audit of the financial statements, including our respective responsibilities.

Acknowledged and agreed on behalf of Securimax Ltd. by
James Reynolds, CFO
Securimax Ltd.
October 1, 2011

As indicated in the engagement letter, management is responsible for the entity's accounting process, which involves the recording of transactions and events. It is management's responsibility to ensure that the information is properly recorded, classified, and summarized at the end of the accounting period. Management is considered to be responsible for the financial statements and acknowledges this responsibility when they sign the engagement letter in which the following are outlined:

- Management is responsible for the selection and preparation of the financial statements in accordance with the appropriate financial reporting framework.
- Management is responsible for ensuring that there are adequate internal controls in place so the prepared financial statements are free from material misstatement.
- Management is responsible for providing the auditor unrestricted access to personnel and documents as needed.

By agreeing to the above, management acknowledges its understanding that the auditor does not have any responsibility for the preparation of the financial statements or for the entity's related internal controls, and that these concepts are fundamental for an independent audit.

Cloud 9

Sharon and Josh have already discussed some of the specific client acceptance issues, such as independence threats and safeguards. Sharon explains that they also have to consider the overall integrity of the client; that is, the management of Cloud 9. This means they need to perform and document procedures that are likely to provide information about the client's integrity. Josh is a little sceptical, "Do you mean that we should ask them if they are honest?" Sharon suggests that it is probably more useful to ask others, and the key people to ask are the existing auditors. Josh is still sceptical, "The existing auditors are Ellis & Associates. Are they going to help us take one of their clients from them?" Sharon says that the client must give permission first, and, if that is given, the existing auditor will usually state whether or not there were any issues that the new auditor should be aware of before accepting the work. Sharon also gives Josh the task of researching Cloud 9's press coverage, with special focus on anything that may indicate poor management integrity.

Sharon emphasizes that they must perform and document procedures to test whether W&S Partners is competent to perform the engagement and has the capabilities, time, and resources to do so. For example, they must make sure that they have audit team members who understand the clothing and footwear business. They also must have enough staff to complete the audit on time. Cloud 9 has a December 31 year end. This means that most of the audit work will be done at a time of year when enough staff may not be available.

In addition, Sharon and Josh must perform and document procedures to show that W&S Partners can comply with all parts of the ethical code, not just those that focus on independence threats and safeguards. Finally, they can draft the engagement letter to cover the contractual relationship between W&S Partners and Cloud 9.

BEFORE YOU GO ON

5.1 What will an auditor consider in assessing the integrity of a client's management, board, and other personnel?

5.2 What are the key components of an engagement letter?

5.3 Why must an auditor seek a client's permission before communicating with its prior auditor or any other relevant third party?

SUMMARY

❶ Describe the fundamental principles of professional ethics and list some of the specific rules professional accountants are required to follow.

Each of the three professional accounting bodies has a code of professional conduct and each has the same fundamental principles of professional ethics: integrity (being straightforward and honest); objectivity (not allowing personal feelings or prejudices to influence professional judgement); professional competence and due care (maintaining knowledge and skill at an appropriate level); confidentiality (not sharing information that is learned at work); and professional behaviour (upholding the reputation of the profession). There are also specific rules that incorporate the guiding ethical principles, and which are enforceable. Some of these rules concern: fees and pricing, advertising, contact with predecessor auditors, firm names, and professional contact.

❷ Define and explain auditor association and independence.

Association is the term used to indicate a public accountant's involvement with financial information. Public accountants should not be associated with anything false and misleading; therefore, they should take care to communicate the level of their involvement with the information.

Independence is the ability to make a decision that is free from bias, personal beliefs, and client pressures. An external auditor must not only be independent of their client, they must also appear to be independent of their client. Threats to auditor independence include self-interest, self-review, advocacy, familiarity, and intimidation threats. A self-interest threat can occur when an auditor has a financial interest in a client. A self-review threat can occur when an auditor must form an opinion on their own work or work done by others in their firm. An advocacy threat can occur when an auditor acts on behalf of their client. A familiarity threat can occur when there is a close relationship between the auditor and their client. An intimidation threat can occur when an auditor feels threatened by their client. Safeguards to auditor independence include the code of ethics, legislation, the establishment of audit committees by clients, client acceptance, and continuance procedures, partner rotation policies, and education within accounting firms.

❸ Explain the relationship between an auditor and key groups they have a professional link with during the audit engagement.

Auditors report to their clients' shareholders. These are the owners who rely on the audited financial statements when evaluating the performance of their company. The board of directors represents the shareholders and oversees the activities of the company and its management. It is the directors' responsibility to ensure that the financial statements being audited are fairly presented. The audit committee is responsible for liaising between the external auditor, the internal auditor, and those charged with governance to aid the board of directors in ensuring that the financial statements are fairly presented and that the external auditor has access to all records and other evidence required to form their opinion. The external auditor may use the work performed by the internal auditors after considering the function's objectivity, technical competence and due professional care, and the effectiveness of communication between internal and external auditors.

4 **Explain the auditor's legal liability to their client, contributory negligence, and the extent to which an auditor is liable to third parties.**

Contributory negligence is where a client is found to be negligent and to have contributed to the loss suffered by the plaintiff. To successfully sue an auditor, a plaintiff must prove that a duty of care was owed by the auditor, there was a breach of that duty, and a loss was suffered as a result of that breach. Several cases are discussed in the chapter in relation to an auditor's liability to third parties. To establish that an auditor owes them a duty of care, a third party must now establish that the auditor was aware that the third party was going to use the financial statements and that the users relied on the financial statements for the purpose they were prepared.

5 **Identify the factors to consider in the client acceptance or continuance decision.**

Factors to consider include the integrity of a client, such as the client's, reputation and attitude to risk, accounting policies, and internal controls. An auditor will gain an understanding of the client through communication with the client's previous auditor (in the case of a client acceptance decision), staff, management, and other relevant parties. The final stage in the client acceptance or continuance decision process involves the preparation of an engagement letter, which sets out the terms of the audit engagement to avoid any misunderstandings between the auditor and their client.

KEY TERMS

Advocacy threat, 55

Association, 53

Audit committee, 62

Board of directors, 53

Confidentiality, 51

Corporate governance, 58

Due care, 50

Engagement letter, 71

Executive director, 62

Familiarity threat, 56

Independence, 53

Independent directors, 58

Integrity, 50

Internal auditors, 63

Intimidation threat, 56

Negligence, 64

Non-executive director, 62

Objectivity, 50

Professional behaviour, 51

Professional competence, 50

Reporting issuer, 57

Self-interest threat, 54

Self-review threat, 55

Shareholders, 61

Technical competence, 63

Third parties, 66

MULTIPLE-CHOICE QUESTIONS

2.1 Professional competence and due care means that members of professional bodies must:

(a) maintain their knowledge and skill at the required level.

(b) keep up to date with changes in regulations and standards.

(c) act diligently.

(d) all of the above.

2.2 Professional behaviour means that members of professional bodies must:

(a) comply with rules and regulations.

(b) claim to possess all qualifications.

(c) question the reputation of accountants who are not members of professional bodies.

(d) provide all services clients request.

2.3 Professional independence for auditors:

(a) detracts from the ability of users to rely on the financial statements to make their decisions.

(b) is the ability to act with integrity, objectivity, and professional scepticism.

(c) is important when the auditor acts independently, and it does not matter what people believe about the auditor's independence.

(d) is only relevant to audits for new clients, not for continuing clients.

2.4 A self-interest threat arises when:

(a) the auditor owns shares in the client's business.

(b) an assurance team member has recently been a director of the client.

(c) the auditor encourages others to buy shares in the client's business.

(d) the client threatens to use a different auditor next year.

2.5 A self-review threat arises when:

(a) the auditor has a loan from the client.

(b) the auditor represents the client in negotiations with a third party.

(c) the auditor performs services for the client that are then assured.

(d) there is a long association between the auditor and its client.

2.6 Safeguards to independence:

(a) minimize the risk that a threat to independence will surface.

(b) deal with a threat when one becomes apparent.

(c) are developed by the accounting profession, legislators, regulators, clients, and accounting firms.

(d) all of the above.

2.7 Safeguards to independence:

(a) are not the responsibility of the client.

(b) are too difficult to implement by audit firms; they must be contained in legislation.

(c) include audit committees.

(d) apply only to business relationships between auditors and clients, not to social relationships.

2.8 Audit committees for listed entities per the CSA:

(a) must include the CFO if he or she is on the board of directors.

(b) can be any size.

(c) have the same chair as the board of directors.

(d) should have a formal charter.

2.9 Generally, the auditor could be legally liable:

(a) under contract law to third parties and to the client.

(b) under contract law and under the tort of negligence to the client.

(c) under contract law but not under the tort of negligence to third parties.

(d) under the tort of negligence but not contract law to the client.

2.10 If a prospective new audit client does not allow the auditor to contact its existing auditor:

(a) the auditor should contact the existing auditor anyway because it is their duty.

(b) the auditor should consider refusing to take on the prospective new client.

(c) the existing auditor should contact the new auditor to tell them all about the client.

(d) the auditor should respect the prospective client's right to privacy.

REVIEW QUESTIONS

2.1 Explain how compliance with each of the five fundamental principles in the code of professional conduct contributes to the ability of the auditor to discharge their duty to act in the public interest.

2.2 Which is more important, independence of mind or independence in appearance? Explain.

2.3 Self-interest, self-review, and familiarity threats all arise from an inappropriate close-ness between the auditor and the client. Explain how that closeness is likely to manifest in each case and why it is a problem for the value of the audit.

2.4 Explain the relationship between the auditor and the shareholders of the audited company. How realistic is it to regard the shareholders as the clients of the auditor?

2.5 Why is it so important that an audit committee not have any executive directors as members?

2.6 Some companies outsource their internal audit function to a public accounting firm. Explain how this would affect the external auditor's evaluation of the reliability of the internal audit function.

2.7 What are the three conditions that must be proven for an auditor to be found negli-gent under tort law? Based on a review of the legal cases discussed in the chapter, which conditions appear to be most difficult to prove?

2.8 Explain how an auditor would use auditing standards to avoid legal liability.

2.9 Why are there procedures governing the client acceptance or continuance decision? Explain why auditors do not accept every client.

2.10 What is the purpose of an engagement letter? Are all engagement letters the same?

PROFESSIONAL APPLICATION QUESTIONS

Basic ★   Moderate ★ ★   Challenging ★ ★ ★

2.1 Ethical principles ★

Charles is at a neighbourhood Christmas party with several of his roommates. Over a few beers, Charles gets into a conversation with a neighbour, William, about mutual acquaint-ances. Charles is a senior auditor with a large accounting firm (although he tells William that he is a partner at the firm) and William works for a large bank. During the conver-sation, Charles and William discover that they have both had professional dealings with a particular family-owned manufacturing company. William reveals that the company's line of credit is about to be cancelled because of some irregularities with the security. Charles is concerned to hear this news because he has just participated in the com-pany's financial statement audit and there was no indication of any problems with its borrowings. However, as Charles explains to William, he has his doubts about the patri-arch of the family, whom Charles believes is having an affair with his personal assistant. Charles also tells William that the family has quietly increased its shareholdings in a listed company that supplies components to the family's manufacturing company. The components manufacturing company is about to announce to the share market that it has just won a very large and very profitable contract with a Chinese company.

Required

Discuss the ethical principles that are potentially breached by Charles's behaviour at the party.

2.2 Receiving shares through inheritance ★ ★

Kerry is a senior auditor and a member of the team auditing a long-standing client, the listed public company Darcy Industries Ltd. Kerry's wife's uncle died recently and his estate is being finalized. Kerry's wife has just received a letter from the executor of her uncle's estate advising her that she will receive a large parcel of shares in Darcy Industries Ltd. from the estate, in addition to cash and other property. Kerry and his wife didn't know that her uncle had included her in the will, and they had not realized that her uncle was a large shareholder in Darcy Industries Ltd. Kerry's wife is very worried because she knows that Kerry must abide by strict rules laid down by his audit firm about holding shares in client companies. She asks him if he will be dismissed because of this.

Required

Advise Kerry's wife of the options available to Kerry to avoid any conflict of interest, and thus avoid being dismissed from the audit firm.

2.3 Provision of non-audit services to audit clients ★ ★

Elise Lauzière is the partner in charge of the audit of Hertenstein Ltd., a large listed public company. Elise took over the audit from Marjorie Szliske, who has recently retired from the audit firm. Marjorie was a very experienced auditor and the author of several reports into ethical standards in business, but Elise did not regard her highly for her ability to grow non-audit service fee revenue. Elise sees an opportunity to increase the provision of non-audit services to Hertenstein Ltd. and thus increase her reputation within the audit firm.

Required

(a) Comment on Elise's belief that increasing non-audit service fee revenue from her audit client would increase her reputation in the audit firm.

(b) Which non-audit services would you advise Elise to avoid trying to sell to Hertenstein Ltd. because of the potential ethical issues for the audit firm?

(c) Would it make any difference to your answers if Hertenstein Ltd. was a private company, not a listed public company?

2.4 Unpaid audit fees ★ ★

Linda is the managing partner of Osuji and Associates, a small audit firm. Linda's role includes managing the business affairs of the firm, and she is very worried about the amount of fees outstanding from audit clients. One client, Dreamers Ltd., has not paid its audit fees for two years despite numerous discussions between Linda, the audit partner, Bill, and the management of Dreamers Ltd. Dreamers Ltd.'s management promised the fees would be paid before the audit report for this year was issued. Linda called Bill this morning to ensure that the audit report was not issued because Dreamers Ltd. had paid only 10 percent of the outstanding account. She discovers that Bill is about to sign the audit report.

Required

Explain the ethical problem in this case. Why is it a problem? What can be done about it?

2.5 Using the work of internal auditors ★ ★

Theobald Ltd. has an internal audit department that primarily focuses on audits of the efficiency and effectiveness of its production departments. The other main role of the internal audit department is auditing compliance with various government regulations surrounding correct disposal of waste and storage of raw materials at its five factories. Theobald Ltd.'s internal audit department is run by Harry Giolti, a chartered accountant and a member of the Institute of Internal Auditors. There are three other members of the department, all of whom have experience in performance auditing and, in addition, have completed industry-run training courses in waste management and handling dangerous goods. Harry meets regularly with the chief production manager and sends monthly reports to the CEO and the board of directors. Your initial investigations suggest that Harry is highly regarded within Theobald Ltd., and his reports are often discussed at board meetings. In most cases, the board authorizes the actions recommended in Harry's reports with respect to major changes to production and logistics.

Required

Comment on the extent of reliance the external auditor should place on the work of the internal audit department at Theobald Ltd. Explain the likely impact of the internal audit department's work on the audit plan.

2.6 Legal implications of client acceptance ★ ★ ★

Godwin, Key & Associates is a small but rapidly growing audit firm. Their success is largely due to the growth of several clients that have been with the firm for more than five years. One of these clients, Carolina Company Ltd., is now listed on the TSX and must comply with additional reporting regulations. Carolina Company Ltd.'s rapid growth has meant that it is financially stretched and its accounting systems are struggling to keep up with the growth in business. The client continuance decision is about to be made for the next financial year.

The managing partner of Godwin, Key & Associates, Rebecca Haque, has recognized that the audit firm needs to make some changes to deal with the issues created by the changing circumstances of their major client and the audit firm's overall growth. She is particularly concerned that the audit firm could be legally liable if Carolina Company Ltd.'s financial situation worsens and it fails.

Required

(a) Provide guidance to Rebecca about the steps she can take to avoid the threat of litigation if Carolina Company Ltd. fails.

(b) What should Rebecca consider when making the client continuance decision for Carolina Company Ltd. for the next financial year?

2.7 Independence threats and safeguards ★ ★

Featherbed Surf & Leisure Holidays Ltd. (Featherbed) is a resort company based on Vancouver Island. Its operations include boating, surfing, fishing, and other leisure activities; a backpackers' hostel; a family hotel; and a five-star resort. Justin and Sarah Morris own the majority of the shares in the Morris Group, which controls Featherbed. Justin is the chairman of the board of directors of both Featherbed and the Morris Group, and Sarah is a director of both companies as well as the CFO of Featherbed.

In February 2012, Justin Morris approached your audit firm, KFP Partners, to carry out the Featherbed audit for the year ended June 30, 2012. Featherbed has not been audited before but this year the audit has been requested by the company's bank and a new private equity investor group that has just acquired a 20 percent share of Featherbed. You know that one of the partners at KFP went to school with Justin and has been friends with both Justin and Sarah for many years.

Source: Adapted from the Institute of Chartered Accountants Australia's CA Program's *Audit and Assurance Exam*, May 2008.

Required

(a) Identify and explain the significant threats to independence for KFP Partners in accepting the audit of Featherbed.

(b) Explain any relevant and practical safeguards that KFP could implement to reduce the threats.

2.8 Independence threats and safeguards ★ ★ ★

Securimax Limited (Securimax) has been an audit client of KFP Partners (KFP) for the past 15 years. Securimax is based in Waterloo, where it manufactures high-tech armour-plated personnel carriers. Securimax often has to go through a competitive market tender process to win large government contracts. Its main product, the small but powerful Terrain Master, is highly specialized and Securimax only does business with nations that have a recognized, democratically elected government. Securimax maintains a highly secure environment, given the sensitive and confidential nature of its vehicle designs and its clients.

Clarke Field has been the engagement partner on the Securimax audit for the last five years. Clarke is a specialist in the defence industry and intends to remain as review partner when the audit is rotated next year to a new partner (Sally Woodrow, who is to be promoted to partner to enable her to sign off on the audit).

In September 2011, Securimax installed an off-the-shelf costing system to support the highly sophisticated and cost-sensitive nature of its product designs. The new system replaced a system that had been developed in-house, as the old system could no longer keep up with the complex and detailed manufacturing costing process that provides tender costings. The old system also had difficulty with the company's broader reporting requirements.

Securimax's information technology (IT) department, together with the consultants from the software company, implemented the new manufacturing costing system. There were no customized modifications. Key operational staff and the internal audit team from Securimax were significantly engaged in the selection, testing, training, and implementation stages.

The manufacturing costing system uses all of the manufacturing unit inputs to calculate and produce a database of all product costs and recommended sales prices. It also integrates with the general ledger each time there are product inventory movements such as purchases, sales, wastage, and damaged inventory losses.

Securimax has a small internal audit department that is headed by an ex-partner of KFP, Rydell Creek. Rydell joined Securimax after leaving KFP six years ago after completing his chartered accountant's qualifications. Rydell is assisted by three junior internal auditors, all of whom are completing bachelor of commerce studies at the University of Waterloo.

Securimax's end of financial year is December 31.

Source: Adapted from the Institute of Chartered Accountants Australia's CA Program's *Audit and Assurance Exam,* May 2008.

Required

(a) Are there any threats to independence for KFP in its audit of Securimax?

(b) Can you propose any recommendations to safeguard KFP against the potential independence threats you have identified? Explain.

Questions 2.9 and 2.10 are based on the following case.

Fellowes and Associates Chartered Accountants is a successful mid-tier accounting firm with a large range of clients across Canada. During the 2011 financial year, Fellowes and Associates gained a new client, Health Care Holdings Group (HCHG), which owns 100 percent of the following entities:

· Shady Oaks Centre, a private treatment centre

· Gardens Nursing Home Ltd., a private nursing home

· Total Laser Care Limited (TLCL), a private clinic that specializes in the laser treatment of skin defects. Year end for all HCHG entities is June 30.

TLCL owns two relatively old laser machines used in therapy. Recently, staff using these machines have raised concerns that they have adverse impacts on patients.

The CEO of TCCL, Betty Raman, has approached Tania Fellowes, the audit partner responsible for the financial statement audit, about undertaking an engagement with respect to the laser machines. Betty has asked Tania to provide an opinion that the machines are fit for use. Betty pointed out that the auditor for TLCL has not been appointed for the following year and suggested Fellowes and Associates might like to take on the laser machines engagement without charging a fee as a gesture of goodwill.

Prior to the appointment for the 2011 financial year of Fellowes and Associates as the auditor for HCHG, the group that controls TLCL, some preliminary analysis by Tania Fellowes identified the following situations:

1. One of the accountants who intended to be part of the 2011 audit team owns shares in HCHG. The accountant's interest is not material to him.

2. Fellowes and Associates was previously engaged by HCHG to value its intellectual property. The consolidated balance sheet (statement of financial position) as at June 30, 2011 includes intangible assets of $30 million, which were valued by

Fellowes and Associates on March 1, 2011, following HCHG's acquisition of the subsidiary Shady Oaks Centre. The intangibles are considered material to HCHG.

Source: Adapted from the Institute of Chartered Accountants Australia's CA Program's *Audit and Assurance Exam,* December 2008.

2.9 Ethics of accepting engagements ★ ★

Required

Explain why Tania should have reservations about accepting the engagement to provide an opinion with respect to the laser machines. Make appropriate reference to fundamental ethical principles in your answer.

2.10 Independence issues in accepting engagements ★ ★ ★

Required

(a) Identify and explain the potential type of threat to Fellowes and Associates' independence in situations (1) and (2) above.

(b) What action should Fellowes and Associates take to eliminate the potential threats to independence in situations (1) and (2) above? What safeguards should be instituted to reduce the risk of similar independence threats occurring in the future?

2.11 Principles and rules of the code of professional conduct ★ ★

Required

Identify and discuss any professional conduct issues in the following independent scenarios.

(a) Adnan is a certified general accountant working for a national firm. He is at his desk when he overhears his colleague Joan having a phone conversation. She is telling the person on the other end of the call that Gupta Co., the firm's largest audit client is about to release the company's audited annual financial statements and the results are spectacular. Joan says she just bought some shares as she expects that the share price will go up.

(b) John Drake, a partner at Drake and Buetz, is meeting with a potential new client. The client recently saw the firm's TV advertisement claiming that the firm was "the premier accounting firm in western Canada." The client requires a review engagement report with its financial statements to obtain a bank loan. John advises that his fee will be 10 percent of any bank loan granted.

(c) Sue Chen, CA, is working on the audit engagement for Jones Construction, a reporting issuer. José, the accountant at Jones Construction, is unsure how to calculate the tax provision. Sue has advised José not to worry. She will prepare the tax provision and ensure that the disclosures are in accordance with generally accepted accounting principles (GAAP) so that she can issue a clean audit opinion.

(d) Sue Chen, CA, is working on the audit engagement for Jones Construction, a private entity. During the course of the audit, she prepares a number of routine journal entries. She makes the required adjustments before she releases the financial statements.

(e) Sue Chen, CA, is working on the compilation engagement for Jones Construction. The bookkeeper, Luc, processes the day-to-day transactions, but he does not prepare any closing adjusting entries. Sue prepares the year-end amortization entry and the adjustment to the shareholder account. She then reviews the financial statements with Wade Jones, the owner, and releases the financial statements.

(f) Jack Bond is a partner in a national firm. He is responsible for the audit for Canada Bank. He recently purchased a car for his daughter and took out a car loan with Canada Bank.

(g) Jack Bond is a partner in a national firm. The firm is the auditor for Canada Bank. Jack's father-in-law is the chief operating officer for Canada Bank.

(h) James Lei, CA is reviewing his firm's accounts receivables. He notices that one of his largest audit clients has not paid its fees for the last two years.

(i) Alison Kotecha, CA, is meeting with a potential new audit client, Klein Advertising. She paid Johan Smit, a former colleague, $1,000 for the referral. Although she hasn't performed any audit engagements for the last four years, she did recently take a GAAP course. During the meeting, she reads over the prior year's financial statements and tells the client she will accept the engagement. She tells the client that she will do a substantive-based audit; therefore, she is certain that the fee will be less than the fee charged by the previous auditor.

(j) Matt Green is married to Jennifer Green, who owns Muffins to Go, a small private entity. Jennifer is a baker and not an accountant. However, she needs a set of financial statements prepared to attach to her tax return. Her husband Matt tells her that he will prepare them.

2.12 Auditor legal liability ★ ★

Ahmad & Partners is a CGA firm in eastern Canada. Last year it audited Chan Corporation, a publicly traded company that manufactures automobile component parts. Although the company has been profitable for many years, Ahmad & Partners was hired by Canada Bank, which was considering extending a large loan to Chan Corp. The bank wanted the audit as Chan's expansion plans would change the company's financial structure significantly from the previous year. Ahmad & Partners conducted the audit and gave an unmodified opinion. Xing Investments Inc. purchased $750,000 of the common stock of Chan, intending to hold the stock as a long-term investment. Unfortunately, Chan went bankrupt shortly after the share purchase and Xing Investments lost all of its $750,000 investment. Canada Bank was unable to recover any of its loan to the company. Xing Investments and Canada Bank subsequently sued Ahmad & Partners to recover their losses.

Required

(a) Did Ahmad & Partners owe a duty of care to Xing Investments?

(b) What are some of the defences Ahmad & Partners could use for their defence?

Source: © CGA-Canada. Reproduced with permission.

2.13 Breaches to the principles and rules of the code of professional conduct ★ ★ ★

Required

Identify and discuss any breaches, if any, to the principles and rules of the code of professional conduct in the following independent scenarios. Explain.

(a) Susanne, a professional accountant, has agreed to audit the financial statements of a newly formed biotechnology company that is publicly traded. The company has an immaterial amount of revenues and mostly incurs research and development costs, which results in a fairly simple set of financial statements. Accordingly, Susanne charges the client a very low audit fee of $7,000 for the first year, since she expects to make a substantial amount of money in preparing the personal tax returns of the company's key executives for 2012.

(b) Aziz, a professional accountant and a partner in a public accounting firm, is discussing the audit plan for his client, a private entity. The company's unaudited financial statements show exceptional revenue growth and earnings this year, and Aziz is concerned that management may be manipulating the financial statements in anticipation of a future public offering. Accordingly, Aziz tells the senior auditor to contact him immediately if she uncovers any evidence of deliberate fraud because Aziz does not want his firm to be associated with clients who lack integrity and may resign from the engagement.

(c) Mandip, a professional accountant, has been engaged to compile the quarterly financial statements for his new client, a private company that develops and markets computer software. The owners employ a part-time bookkeeper to maintain basic accounting records but rely on Mandip to put all the information in proper form each quarter.

The statements consist of a balance sheet, income statement, and statement of cash flows, but no footnotes or other disclosures. The owners use the quarterly statements to help them manage the company. Because the company has limited resources, Mandip's fees for his services are paid in company shares. Mandip has agreed to this unusual arrangement since he knows that the owners plan a public offering of shares within the next few years, and he will then be able to sell the shares. Finally, to obtain a better knowledge of the company's operations and to make sure that the reported dollar amounts are plausible, Mandip performs a thorough ratio analysis of the compiled statements each quarter and discusses any unusual findings with management.

Source: © CGA-Canada. Reproduced with permission.

2.14 Auditor legal liability ★ ★

HHH Corporation manufactures automobile engines. In 2012, the treasurer at HHH decided to invest the company's surplus funds in the commodities market. She intended for it to be a short-term investment, as the company had $1 million in extra funds that would not be needed for three months. Unfortunately, the market price of the commodity she purchased declined sharply and in three months the investment was sold for only $500,000. The treasurer prepared documents to make the loss of the investment appear as a sale of excess inventory, so the company showed a lower profit on sales than usual, but no trading loss. The auditor audited the 2012 financial statements and issued an unmodified report, even though the amount in question exceeded the materiality threshold. HHH has always been owned privately. In 2012, all of the shares of the company were purchased by a group of engineers who had retired from the automobile industry. There were no other changes in the shareholders during 2013 or 2014.

Required

Assume that the shareholders of HHH sued the auditors. Explain how the elements of negligence would apply to this case.

Source: © CGA-Canada. Reproduced with permission.

2.15 Quality assurance ★ ★

Required

You have been working with a national chartered accounting firm for a number of years and you now feel like you are ready to start your own chartered accounting firm.

(a) Given the requirements of the code of professional conduct, what is an acceptable name for your firm?

(b) Given the requirements of the code of professional conduct, how will you market and advertise the services offered by your firm?

(c) As you plan to take on assurance work, you realize that you will need a quality assurance manual. Create the table of contents for your manual.

(d) Describe the requirements of your quality assurance manual with respect to the file quality review and monitoring.

CASES

CASE STUDY—CLOUD 9

Sharon Gallagher, Josh Thomas, and Jo Wadley are members of the audit firm W&S Partners. Sharon is the audit manager and Josh is the audit senior assisting the partner, Jo Wadley, evaluate the decision to accept the Cloud 9 Ltd. (Cloud 9) audit engagement for the year ended December 31, 2012.

Background information about the company is presented in Appendix B of this book. In addition, Josh has discovered the following facts and has requested your help to document and assess the factors that affect the client acceptance decision.

• The finance director of Cloud 9, David Collier, is married to a distant relation of P. S. Nethercott, a partner in W&S Partners' consulting department.

• The consulting department at W&S Partners has quoted on an IT installation project at Cloud 9. The fees from this project, if the tender is successful, would be twice the size of the audit fee.

• A survey of audit staff at W&S Partners has revealed that 30 percent have purchased Cloud 9's products (basketball shoes) in the past.

• Four members of the IT department at W&S Partners have shares in retailers that sell Cloud 9's products. In each case, the shareholdings were disclosed on the firm's share register, and the size of the shareholding is deemed material under W&S Partners' ethical guidelines.

• An article in a newspaper published in Canada has claimed that Cloud 9 Inc. (Cloud 9's parent company) was secretly running "third-world sweat shops." The article alleged that shoes made by other wholly owned subsidiaries of Cloud 9 Inc. in China and Brazil were using illegal child labour in factories that did not meet local health and safety rules. Cloud 9 Inc. has vehemently disputed the accuracy of the article, suggesting that it was planted by a rival company. Cloud 9 Inc. has invited international advocacy groups to visit its factories at any time.

Required

Answer the following questions based on the information presented above, in Appendix B of this book, and throughout chapters 1 and 2. Consider your answers to the case study questions in chapter 1 where relevant.

(a) Prepare a document that explains the impact, if any, of each piece of information relevant to your client acceptance decision for Cloud 9.

(b) List and explain any additional actions you would take before making your client acceptance recommendation to the partner, Jo Wadley.

(c) Assume the decision is made to accept Cloud 9 as a client. Prepare the client engagement letter.

RESEARCH QUESTION 2.1

One way of getting accounting expertise onto audit committees is to recruit ex-audit firm partners and/or employees onto the board of directors. However, appointing former audit firm partners to boards and audit committees raises independence concerns, and the Corporations Act requires that a retired partner must not take on a senior role at an audit client's firm for one year after retiring.

Naiker and Sharma provide evidence that financial statements are of higher quality when former audit partners are on the audit committee, and raise doubts about the benefits of a rule limiting their recruitment.

Required

(a) What are the arguments for and against allowing former audit firm partners and/or employees to join audit committees?

(b) Explain how these accounting experts could help or hinder the audit process and thereby have an impact on the quality of a company's internal controls and financial statements.

RESEARCH QUESTION 2.2

Each of the professional accounting bodies has its own rules of professional conduct, which may also vary from province to province.

Required

(a) Go to the website of the Certified General Accountants Association of Canada (CGA-Canada). Locate the *Independence Standard* and *Code of Ethical Principles and Rules of Conduct*.

What are the six principles listed under the Code of Ethical Principles?

What are the requirements of the Rules of Conduct for the following: rules 201, 202.4, 301, and 402?

(b) Go to the website of the Certified Management Accountants of British Columbia (CMA BC).

Click on "I am a CMA."

Click on "Policies," which will connect you to the CMA's *Rules of Professional Conduct*. What are the requirements of the rules of conduct for the following: rules 201, 211, 302, 403?

(c) Go to the website of the Institute of Chartered Accountants of Ontario (ICAO). Click on "Resources" and select "Members handbook." Here you will find the Institute's *Rules of Professional Conduct*. What are the requirements of the rules of conduct for the following: rules 102.1, 209, 303, and 402?

FURTHER READING

Certified General Accountants Association of Canada. *Independence Standard* and *Code of Ethical Principles and Rules of Conduct*. November 2010, www.cga-canada.org.

Certified Management Accountants of British Columbia. *Rules of Professional Conduct*. November 2010, www.cmabc.com.

Institute of Chartered Accountants of Ontario. *Rules of Professional Conduct*. November 2010, www.icao.on.ca.

SOLUTIONS TO MULTIPLE-CHOICE QUESTIONS

1. d, 2. a, 3. b, 4. a, 5. c, 6. d, 7. c, 8. d, 9. b, 10. b.

NOTES

1. Makkula Ethics Centre. Santa Clara University. *A Framework for Thinking Ethically.* November 2010. <www.scu.edu>
2. Canadian Institute of Chartered Accountants. *Guide to New Canadian Independence Standards*. October 2003. <www.icans.ns.ca>
3. The Free Dictionary 2009, www.legal-dictionary.thefreedictionary.com/Tort+Law.
4. Davison, Alan G. "Auditors Liability to Third Parties for Negligence," *Accounting & Business Research*, Autumn 82, Vol. 12, Issue 48, pp. 257–64.

CHAPTER 3

Audit planning I

LEARNING OBJECTIVES

After studying this chapter, you should be able to:

1. identify the different stages of an audit

2. explain the process used in gaining an understanding of the client

3. explain how related parties can impact risk

4. define fraud risk and understand audit procedures to reduce this risk

5. explain the going concern assumption

6. describe corporate governance

7. explain how a client's information technology (IT) can affect risk

8. explain how client closing procedures can affect reported results.

AUDITING AND ASSURANCE STANDARDS

CANADIAN	INTERNATIONAL
CAS 240 *The Auditor's Responsibilities Relating to Fraud in an Audit of Financial Statements*	ISA 240 *The Auditor's Responsibilities Relating to Fraud in an Audit of Financial Statements*
CAS 300 *Planning an Audit of Financial Statements*	ISA 300 *Planning an Audit of Financial Statements*
CAS 315 *Identifying and Assessing the Risks of Material Misstatement Through Understanding the Entity and Its Environment*	ISA 315 *Identifying and Assessing the Risks of Material Misstatement Through Understanding the Entity and Its Environment*
CAS 550 *Related Parties*	ISA 550 *Related Parties*
CAS 570 *Going Concern*	ISA 570 *Going Concern*

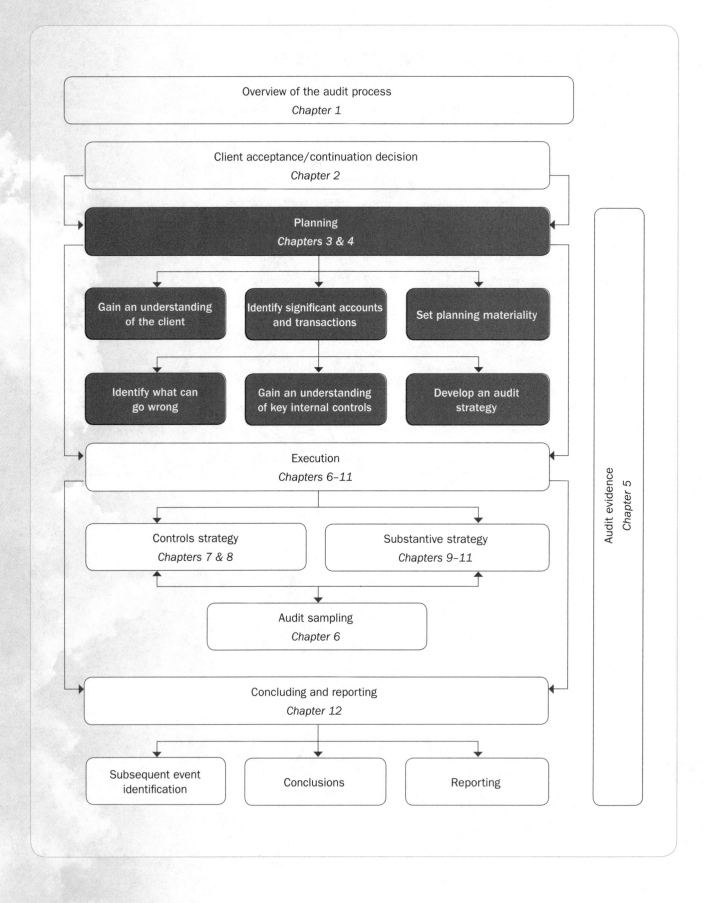

Cloud 9

"Great news!" announces Sharon Gallagher at the weekly team meeting. "We have just had word that the audit engagement letter for Cloud 9 Ltd. (Cloud 9) has been signed. We are now officially their financial statement auditors and the planning phase starts now!"

Later, at the first planning meeting, Sharon and Josh Thomas focus on assigning the tasks for gaining an understanding of Cloud 9. Ian Harper, a first-year graduate, is not happy. He grumbles to another new member of the team, Suzie Pickering, as he leaves the room, "This is such a waste of time. Why did we sign an engagement letter if we don't understand the client? Why don't we just get on with the audit? What else is there to know?"

"Oh boy, are you missing the point!" Suzie says. "If you don't spend time planning, where are you going to start 'getting on with it'?"

"The same place you always start," replies Ian. Suzie realizes that she has a big job explaining to Ian, and invites him for a coffee so that they can talk. Although Suzie is new to the team, she has audit experience with other clothing and footwear clients, and will be helping Sharon and Josh manage the Cloud 9 audit. Her first question to Ian at coffee is "What do you think could go wrong with the Cloud 9 audit?"

AUDIT PROCESS IN FOCUS

Audit planning is an important topic that we will cover in this and the next chapter. In this chapter, we begin with a discussion of the different stages (or phases) of the audit: the planning stage, the performing stage (where the detailed work is conducted), and the reporting stage (where the audit opinion is formed). At the planning and reporting stages, the auditor adopts a broad view of the client as a whole and the industry in which it operates. An understanding of the client is gained in the early stages of each audit and that knowledge drives the planning of the audit. It informs the choice of where to focus the most attention throughout the audit. When forming an opinion on the fair presentation of the financial statements, consideration is given to the evidence gathered during the performing stage of the audit, placing that information within the context of the knowledge of the client gained from the planning stage.

During the planning stage, an assessment is made of the risk that a material misstatement (significant error or fraud) could occur in the client's financial statements. By understanding where the risks are most significant, an auditor can plan their audit to spend more time where the risks are greatest. During the planning stage, an auditor will gain an understanding of their client, their client's internal controls, their client's information technology (IT) environment, their client's corporate governance environment, and their client's closing procedures. An auditor will identify any related parties, factors that may affect their client's going concern status, and significant accounts and classes of transactions that will require close audit attention to gauge the risk of material misstatement.

Each of these important elements of the planning stage of the audit is considered in this chapter. The process adopted when gaining an understanding of a client is explained in detail. That explanation is followed by a discussion of the specific audit risks associated with related party transactions and the risk that a client's financial statements are misstated due to fraud. The audit procedures used to assess the risk that a fraud has occurred and common frauds are included in the discussion. That is followed by a discussion of the processes used to assess the going concern assumption.

Corporate governance is the rules, systems, and processes within companies used to guide and control. During the planning stage, an auditor will assess the adequacy of their client's corporate governance structure in assessing the risk that the financial statements are materially misstated.

A client's IT system is used to capture, process, and report on the accounting records. During the planning stage, an auditor will assess the adequacy of their client's IT system. This process is discussed in this chapter.

The final section of this chapter includes a discussion of the procedures used by an auditor to assess their client's closing procedures. Closing procedures aim to ensure that transactions are recorded in the appropriate accounting period. An auditor will assess the adequacy of their client's closing procedures to assess the risk that a material misstatement will occur in the financial statements as a consequence.

3.1 STAGES OF AN AUDIT

1 Identify the different stages of an audit.

Before commencing our discussion of audit planning, we provide an overview of the various stages of the audit, which is represented diagrammatically in figure 3.1. The main stages of an audit are planning, performing, and reporting. Once the client acceptance or continuation decision has been made (described in chapter 2), the first stage is planning the audit. Broadly, the **planning stage** involves gaining an understanding of the client, identifying factors that may impact the risk of a material misstatement in the financial statements, performing a risk and **materiality** assessment, and developing an **audit strategy**. The risk of a material misstatement is the risk that the financial statements include a significant error or fraud. The **execution stage** (or performing stage) of the audit involves the performance of detailed testing of controls and substantive testing of transactions and accounts. The **reporting stage** involves evaluating the results of the detailed testing in light of the auditor's understanding of their client and forming an opinion on the fair presentation of the client's financial statements. An overview of each stage of the audit follows.

planning stage gaining an understanding of the client, identifying risk factors, developing an audit strategy, and assessing materiality

materiality information that impacts the decision-making process of the users of the financial statements

audit strategy a strategy that sets the scope, timing, and direction of the audit and provides the basis for developing a detailed audit plan

execution stage detailed testing of controls and substantive testing of transactions and accounts

reporting stage evaluating the results of the detailed testing in light of the auditor's understanding of their client and forming an opinion on the fair presentation of the client's financial statements

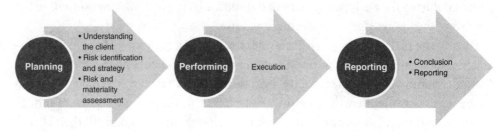

FIGURE 3.1 **Overview of the audit**

3.1.1 Planning an audit

CAS 300 *Planning an Audit of Financial Statements* requires that an auditor plan their audit to reduce audit risk to an acceptably low level. Audit risk is the risk that an auditor issues an unmodified or clean audit opinion when the financial statements are in fact materially misstated. The planning stage involves determining the audit strategy as well as identifying the nature and the timing of the procedures to be performed. This is done to optimize efficiency and effectiveness when conducting an audit. Efficiency refers to the amount of time spent gathering audit evidence. Effectiveness refers to the minimization of audit risk. A well-planned audit will ensure

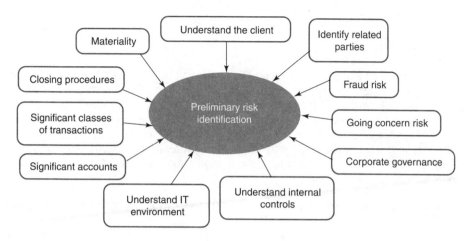

FIGURE 3.2 **Preliminary risk identification**

that **sufficient appropriate evidence** is gathered for those accounts at most risk of material misstatement. Figure 3.2 provides a graphical depiction of the preliminary risk identification process used during the planning stage of each audit.

Each element of figure 3.2 is now discussed in turn, starting with "understand the client" and proceeding clockwise. The process used by an auditor when gaining an understanding of their client is outlined in section 3.2. Part of that process includes the identification of a client's related parties to ensure that they are identified and appropriately disclosed following the relevant accounting standards. CAS 550 *Related Parties* provides audit guidance associated with related party transactions and disclosures. This is further discussed in section 3.3.

When planning an audit, an auditor will assess the risk of material misstatement due to **fraud** (CAS 240 *The Auditor's Responsibilities Relating to Fraud in an Audit of Financial Statements*) and consider whether it is appropriate to assume that their client will remain as a **going concern** (CAS 570 *Going Concern*). Fraud risk is discussed in section 3.4 and going concern is discussed in section 3.5.

A client's **corporate governance** structure is assessed when planning an audit. The Canadian Securities Administrators (CSA) have issued a policy statement for reporting issuers. This policy statement provides guidance on corporate governance practices; however, it does not prescribe any particular practices. The CSA's policy is discussed further in section 3.6.

According to CAS 315 *Identifying and Assessing the Risks of Material Misstatement Through Understanding the Entity and Its Environment*, an auditor must gain an understanding of their client's system of internal controls. Elements of control risk are discussed in chapter 4, and chapter 7 contains a discussion of the procedures used by an auditor in gaining an understanding of a client's system of internal controls. When gaining an understanding of their client's system of internal controls, an auditor will consider the impact of IT (CAS 315). IT is discussed in more detail in section 3.7.

Significant accounts and classes of transactions are identified when planning so that an auditor can structure their audit testing to ensure that adequate time is spent testing these accounts and classes of transactions. During the planning stage, an auditor will also consider the adequacy of their client's **closing procedures**. An auditor's consideration of their client's closing procedures and the associated risks are discussed in section 3.8. An important task in the early stages of every audit is to set planning materiality. This important concept is discussed in detail in chapter 4.

sufficient appropriate evidence the quantity and quality of the evidence that has been gathered

fraud an intentional act through the use of deception to obtain an unjust or illegal advantage

going concern the viability of a company to remain in business for the foreseeable future

corporate governance the rules, systems, and processes within companies used to guide and control

closing procedures processes used by a client when finalizing the books for an accounting period

Cloud 9

Ian thinks that all audits are pretty much the same and that W&S Partners must have an audit plan that they can use for the Cloud 9 audit. Suzie explains that if they tailor the plan to the client, the audit is far more likely to be efficient and effective. That is, they will get the job done without wasting time and ensure that sufficient appropriate evidence is gathered for the accounts that are most at risk of being misstated. If they can do this, W&S Partners will not only issue the right audit report, but make a profit from the audit as well. In other words, if the plan is good, performing the audit properly will be easier.

3.1.2 Performing an audit

The performance, or execution, stage of the audit involves detailed testing of controls, transactions, and balances. If an auditor plans to rely on their client's system of internal controls, they will conduct tests of control (discussed in chapter 8). An auditor will conduct detailed substantive tests of transactions throughout the year and detailed substantive tests of balances recorded at year end (discussed in chapters 9, 10, and 11). This detailed testing provides the evidence that the auditor requires to determine whether the financial statements are fairly presented (discussed in chapter 12).

3.1.3 Concluding and reporting on an audit

The final stage of the audit involves drawing conclusions based on the evidence gathered and arriving at an opinion regarding the fair presentation of the financial statements. The auditor's opinion is expressed in the audit report (see chapter 12). At this stage of the audit, an auditor will draw on their understanding of the client, their detailed knowledge of the risks faced by the client, and the conclusions drawn when testing the client's controls, transactions, and account balances.

BEFORE YOU GO ON

1.1 What are the three main stages of the audit?

1.2 List three factors that affect an auditor's preliminary risk identification.

1.3 What are related parties?

3.2 GAINING AN UNDERSTANDING OF THE CLIENT

2 Explain the process used in gaining an understanding of the client.

At the outset of every audit, an auditor must gain an understanding of their client. The purpose of this procedure is to assess the risk that the financial statements contain a material misstatement due to:

- the nature of the client's business
- the industry in which the client operates
- the level of competition within that industry
- the client's customers and suppliers
- the regulatory environment in which the client operates.

CAS 315 provides guidance on the steps to take when gaining an understanding of a client. It requires the auditor to do the following:

(a) Make inquiries of management and of others within the entity who may have information to help identify the risk of material misstatements. This includes making inquiries of both financial and non-financial staff at all levels of the organization, including those charged with governance, internal audit, sales, and operational personnel.

(b) Perform analytical procedures at the planning stage of the audit to identify any unusual or unexpected relationships that may highlight where risks exist. Analytical procedures are a study of plausible relationships between both financial and non-financial data.

(c) Perform observation and inspection procedures to corroborate the responses made by management and others within the organization. These procedures also provide information about the entity and its environment. Examples of such audit procedures include observation or inspection of the entity's operations, premises, and facilities; business plans and strategies; internal control manuals; and any reports prepared and reviewed by management (such as management reports, interim financial statements, and minutes of board of directors' meetings).

By performing these activities, the auditor will gain an understanding of the issues at the entity level, the industry level, and the economy level.

Cloud 9

Ian knows that there are many possible problems in an audit that would cause the auditor to issue the wrong type of audit report, but he is struggling to understand why the audit team will be spending time gaining an understanding of a client. How does this help? Why aren't audits all the same?

Suzie explains to Ian that issuing the wrong type of audit report is a risk the auditor always faces, but the risk varies across audits. The variation in the risk is partly related to how well the audit team performs its tasks, which is dependent on the team members' level of skill, effort, supervision, and so on. But the variation in risk is also related to the particular characteristics of the client and its environment. Some clients are more likely than others to have errors or deficiencies in their accounting and financial reporting systems, operations, or underlying data. Even within one client's business, some areas are more likely to have problems than, or will have problems different to, others. Suzie asks Ian to think about what sort of problems Cloud 9's draft financial statements are most likely to have, and why.

3.2.1 Entity level

It is important that an auditor gains a detailed knowledge of their client. Knowledge about the entity is gained through interviews with client personnel, including those charged with governance. The auditor will ask questions about what the client does, how it functions, how its ownership is structured, and what its sources of financing are. For new clients, this process is very detailed and time consuming. For a continuing client, this process is less onerous and involves updating the knowledge gained on previous audits. By gaining an understanding of the client, the auditor is in a stronger position to assess entity-level risks and the financial statement accounts that require closer examination. The following paragraphs outline some of the procedures followed by an auditor when gaining an understanding of their client at the entity level.

Major customers are identified so that the auditor may consider whether those customers have a good reputation, are on good terms with the client (that is, likely to remain a customer in future), and are likely to pay the client on a timely basis. Dissatisfied customers may withhold payment, which affects the allowance for doubtful accounts and the client's cash flow, or may decide not to purchase from the client in the future, which can affect the going concern assumption. If a client has only one or a few customers, this risk is increased. The auditor also considers the terms of any long-term contracts between their client and their client's customers.

Major suppliers are identified to determine whether they are reputable and supply quality goods on a timely basis. Consideration is given to whether significant levels of goods are returned to suppliers as faulty, and what the terms of any contracts with suppliers and the terms of payment to suppliers include. The auditor also assesses whether the client pays its suppliers on a timely basis. If the client is having trouble paying its suppliers, it may have trouble sourcing goods as suppliers may refuse to transact with a company that does not pay on time.

Whether the client is an *importer or exporter* of goods is identified. If the client trades internationally, the auditor considers the stability of the country (or countries) the client trades with, the stability of the foreign currency (or currencies) the client trades in, and the effectiveness of any risk management policies the client uses to limit exposure to currency fluctuations (such as hedging policies).

The client's *capacity to adapt to changes in technology and other trends* is assessed. If the client is not well positioned to adjust to such changes, it risks falling behind competitors and losing market share, which in the longer term can affect the going concern assumption. If the client operates in an industry subject to frequent change, it risks significant losses if it doesn't keep abreast of such changes and "move with the times." For example, if a client sells laser printers, the auditor will need to assess whether the client is up to date with changes in technology and customer demands for environmentally friendly printers.

The nature of any *warranties* provided to customers is assessed. If the client provides warranties on products sold, the auditor needs to assess the likelihood that goods will be returned and the risk that the client has underprovided for that rate of return (adequacy of the warranty provision). The auditor will pay particular attention to goods being returned for the same problem, indicating that there may be a systemic fault. For example, say a client sells quality pens and the auditor notices that a number of pens are being returned because the mechanism to twist the pen open is faulty. In this case, the auditor will assess the likelihood that other pens will be returned for the same reason, the steps being taken by the client to rectify the problem, and whether the provision for warranty is adequate in light of this issue.

The terms of *discounts* given by the client to its customers and received by the client from its suppliers are reviewed. An assessment is made of the client's bargaining power with its customers and suppliers to determine whether discounting policies are putting profit margins at risk, which may place the future viability of the client at risk.

An assessment is made of the client's *reputation* with its customers, suppliers, employees, shareholders, and the wider community. A company with a poor reputation places future profits at risk. It is also not in the best interests of the auditor to be associated with a client that has a poor reputation.

An understanding is gained of client *operations*. The auditor will note where the client operates, the number of locations it operates in, and the dispersion of these locations. The more spread out the client's operations are, the harder it is for the client to effectively control and coordinate its operations, increasing the risk of errors in the financial statements. The auditor will need to visit locations where the risk of material misstatement is greatest to assess the processes and procedures at each site. If the client has operations in other provinces or overseas, the auditor may plan for a visit to those sites by staff from affiliated offices at those locations where risk is greatest. For example, an auditor is more likely to visit client operations if the client opens a new, large site, or if the business is located in a country where there is a high rate of inflation or where there is a high risk of theft.

An understanding is gained of the *nature of employment contracts* and the client's *relations with its employees.* The auditor will consider the way employees are paid, the mix of wages and bonuses, the level of unionization among the workforce, and the attitude of staff to their employer. The more complex a payroll system, the more likely that errors can occur. When staff are unhappy, there is greater risk of industrial action, such as strikes, which disrupt client operations.

The client's *sources of financing* are reviewed. An assessment is made of a client's debt sources, the reliability of future sources of financing, the structure of debt, and the reliance on debt versus equity financing. An auditor assesses whether the client is meeting interest payments on funds borrowed and repaying funds raised when they are due. If a client has a covenant with a debt provider, the auditor will need to understand the terms of that covenant and the nature of the restrictions it places on the client. Debt covenants vary. A company may, for example, agree to limit further borrowings. It may agree to maintain a certain debt-to-equity ratio. If the client does not meet the conditions of a debt covenant, the borrower may recall the debt, placing the client's liquidity position at risk, and increasing the risk that the client may not be able to continue as a going concern.

The client's *ownership structure* is assessed. The auditor is interested in the amount of debt funding relative to equity, the use of different forms of shares, and the differing rights of shareholder groups. The client's dividend policy and its ability to meet dividend payments out of operating cash flow are also of interest.

Cloud 9

Ian is starting to think about Cloud 9 more closely. He can remember something being said about Cloud 9 importing the shoes from a production plant in China and then wholesaling them to major department stores.

"OK," says Suzie. "Let's just take that one aspect of the operations and think about the issues that could arise."

Ian realizes that the department stores would be customers of Cloud 9 (although they should check that the stores actually purchase the shoes rather than hold them on consignment). If there was a mistake or a dispute with one of the stores, or if the store was in financial difficulties, the collectability of the accounts receivable would be in doubt, so assets could be overstated. If the store disputed a sale, or a sale return was not recorded correctly, sales (and profit) could be overstated. Is Cloud 9 liable for warranty expenses if the shoes are faulty? Would the auditors need to read the terms of the contract to determine if a warranty liability should be recorded on the balance sheet? What about the balance of inventory? Do the shoes belong to Cloud 9 when they are being shipped from China, or only after they arrive at the warehouse?

Suzie points out that the answer to each of these questions could be different for Cloud 9 than for other clients because of its different circumstances. The auditors need to gain an understanding of these circumstances so that they can assess the risk that accounts receivable, sales, sales returns, inventory, and liabilities are misstated. Once they understand the risks, they are in a position to decide how they will audit Cloud 9.

3.2.2 Industry level

At the industry level, an auditor is interested in their client's position within its industry, the level of competition in that industry, and the client's size relative to competitors. The auditor evaluates the client's reputation among its peers and the level of government support for companies operating in that industry. Another consideration is the level of demand for the products sold or services supplied by companies in that industry and the factors that affect that demand. For example, a soft-drink manufacturer is affected by the weather; that is, revenue is seasonal. Also, competition is generally strong.

A comparison is made between the client and its close competitors nationally and internationally. When an auditor has a number of clients that operate in the one industry, this stage of the audit is more straightforward than if the client operates in an industry that the auditor is not already familiar with. The following paragraphs outline some of the procedures followed by auditors when gaining an understanding of their client at the industry level.

The *level of competition* in the client's industry is assessed. The more competitive the client's industry, the more pressure placed on the client's profits. In an economic downturn, the weakest companies in highly competitive industries face financial hardship and possible liquidation. A key issue for an auditor is their client's position among its competitors and its ability to withstand downturns in the economy.

An auditor also considers their client's *reputation* relative to other companies in the same industry. If the client has a poor reputation, customers and suppliers may shift their business to a competing firm, threatening their client's profits. The auditor can assess their client's reputation by reading articles in the press and industry publications.

Consideration is given to the level of *government support* for the client's industry. This issue is important if the industry faces significant competition internationally or the industry is new and requires time to become established. Support is sometimes provided to industries that produce items in line with government policy, such as manufacturers of water tanks, solar heating, and reduced-flow taps in the context of environmental policies.

An assessment is made of the impact of *government regulation* on the client and the industry in which it operates. Regulations include tariffs on goods, trade restrictions, and foreign exchange policies. Regulations can affect a client's viability and continued profitability. An auditor will consider the level of taxation imposed on companies operating in their client's industry. The auditor assesses the different taxes and charges imposed on their client and the impact these have on profits.

The level of *demand* for the goods sold or services provided by companies in the client's industry is considered. If a client's products or services are seasonal, this will affect revenue flow. If a client is an ice-cream producer, sales would be expected to increase in summer. However, if the weather is unseasonal, profits may suffer. If a client sells swimsuits, sales will fall in a cool summer. If a client sells ski equipment, sales will fall if the winter brings little snow. If a client operates in an industry subject to changing trends, such as fashion, the client risks inventory obsolescence if it does not keep up and move quickly with changing styles. When a product or process is subject to technological change, there is the risk that a client will quickly be left behind by its competitors. Either its products will become obsolete or its outdated processes will mean that it may find it difficult to compete with competitors that stay abreast of technological innovations.

3.2.3 Economy level

Finally, when gaining an understanding of a client, an auditor assesses how economy-level factors affect the client. Economic upturns and downturns, changes in interest rates, and currency fluctuations affect all companies. An auditor is concerned with a client's susceptibility to these changes and its ability to withstand economic pressures.

During an economic upturn, companies are under pressure to perform as well as or better than competitors, and shareholders expect consistent improvements in profits. When conducting the audit in this environment, more focus is given to the risk of overstatement of revenues and understatement of expenses. During an economic downturn, companies may decide to "take a bath." This means that companies may purposefully understate profits. When the economy is poor, there is a tendency to maximize write offs, as a fall in profits can easily be explained to the investment community since most companies experience a decline in earnings. A benefit of "taking a bath" is that it provides a low base from which to demonstrate an improvement in results in the following year. Conducting the audit when the economy is in recession and clients may be tempted to "take a bath" means the auditor must focus more on the risk of understatement of revenues and overstatement of expenses.

Cloud 9

Suzie explains to Ian that the partner, Jo Wadley, has asked her to join the team for this audit because she has extensive experience in the clothing and footwear industry. Wadley wants to make sure that the team's industry knowledge is very strong. Several other members of the team also have experience in auditing clients in the retail industry, including Jo Wadley and manager Sharon Gallagher. In addition, Josh is highly regarded at W&S Partners for his knowledge of sales and cash receipts systems.

Suzie has the task of assessing the industry-specific economic trends and conditions. The documentation has to include an assessment of the competitive environment, including any effects of technological changes and relevant legislation. So that Ian can appreciate how understanding the client is an important part of planning the audit, Suzie asks him to help research the product and customer and supplier elements. Then, together, they will assess the specific risks arising from the entire report, including risks at the economy level, for the Cloud 9 audit.

BEFORE YOU GO ON

2.1 What is the purpose of gaining an understanding of a client?

2.2 What will an auditor consider if their client is an importer or exporter?

2.3 What does a client risk if it operates in an industry subject to changing trends?

3.3 RELATED PARTIES

As discussed, it is the responsibility of the auditor to ensure that related parties are identified and appropriately disclosed in accordance with relevant accounting standards. Therefore, related party transactions require some specific consideration throughout the audit.

3 Explain how related parties can impact risk.

According to the CICA Handbook (IAS 24, *Related Party Disclosures*, and ASPE s. 3840), related parties include parent companies, subsidiaries, joint ventures, associates, company management, and close family members of key management. Since related parties are not independent of each other, these transactions may not be in the normal course of business and therefore, they may take place under favourable terms. As a result, related party transactions not only increase the susceptibility of the financial statements to material misstatement due to fraud and error, they may also impact the overall financial statement results. Therefore, financial statement users need sufficient information to assess the impact of these transactions on the financial statements overall. Some examples of related party transactions that require disclosure are listed below:

- purchase and sales transactions between companies under common control or when one party has significant influence over another
- rent paid from one related party to another
- loans made to shareholders or senior management
- loan guarantees provided by a shareholder of the company.

As both the International Financial Reporting Standards (IFRS) and the Accounting Standards for Private Enterprises (ASPE) include specific reporting requirements for related party transactions, the auditor must consider the risk of material misstatement throughout the audit if such relationships are not appropriately accounted for or disclosed. Therefore, CAS 550 *Related Parties* requires the auditor to do the following:

- discuss with the engagement team the susceptibility of the financial statements to material misstatement due to fraud or error that could result from the entity's related party relationships and transactions
- ask management to identity all related parties and to provide an explanation as to the nature, type, and purpose of transactions with these entities
- obtain an understanding of the processes and procedures management has in place to ensure all related party transactions are identified, authorized, accounted for, and disclosed in accordance with the chosen financial reporting framework
- remain alert when inspecting documents such as bank confirmations, unusual sales and purchase invoices, minutes of board of director and shareholder meetings, and contracts for indicators that related party transactions may not have not been identified or disclosed to the auditor
- identify and assess the risk that transactions may not be in the normal course of operations. For such transactions, inspect any underlying documents and determine the business rationale for such transactions to ensure that they are not an attempt to fraudulently misstate the financial results.

Figure 3.3 lists risk assessment procedures outlined in the *Canadian Professional Engagement Manual (C·PEM)*.

FIGURE 3.3 **Sample risk assessment procedures, *C·PEM*, Form 515**
Source: CICA, "Understanding Related Parties," *C·PEM*, Electronic Templates, Form 515, 2010-2011.

Preparation

(a) Review the entity's list of directors, managers, key staff, family members, and advisors to identify potential or existing related party transactions.
(b) Obtain or prepare a listing of related party transactions.
(c) Consider history (if any) of not disclosing related parties or transactions.

(continued)

(d) Inquire of management and document what internal controls (if any) or procedures exist to ensure that related parties are identified, approved (especially those outside the normal course of business), and accounted for in accordance with the applicable financial reporting framework. Assess the control design and implementation of any relevant internal controls.

2. Risk of unidentified transactions

(a) Identify where related party transactions could possibly occur. Consider existence of transactions designed to improve liquidity or profitability, reduce debt to equity leverage, avoid corporate or personal taxes, avoid breach of a bank covenant, shift income/expense to future periods, or conceal other financial statement manipulation or misappropriation of assets.

(b) Inquire of management, key employees, and any component auditors about the existence of:
  · Related parties not already identified and details of such transactions.
  · Agreements or loan guarantees not reflected in the financial statements.
  · Any payments (kickbacks), preferential terms, or side deals not disclosed.

(c) Review minutes of corporate meetings and other relevant documentation.

BEFORE YOU GO ON

3.1 Define related parties.

3.2 How do related parties impact risk? Why?

3.3 What are three procedures the auditor should perform regarding related parties?

3.4 FRAUD RISK

As a part of the risk identification process during the planning stage of the audit, an auditor will assess the risk of a material misstatement due to fraud (CAS 240). When assessing fraud risk, an auditor will adopt an attitude of **professional scepticism** to ensure that any indicator of a potential fraud is properly investigated. This means that the auditor must remain independent of their client, maintain a questioning attitude, and search thoroughly for corroborating evidence to validate information provided by the client. The auditor must not assume that their past experience with client management and staff is indicative of the current risk of fraud.

Fraud is an intentional act to obtain an unjust or illegal advantage through the use of deception (CAS 240, para. 11). An auditor can use red flags[1] to alert them to the possibility that a fraud may have occurred. Red flags include:

- a high turnover of key employees
- key finance personnel refusing to take leave
- overly dominant management
- poor compensation practices
- inadequate training programs
- a complex business structure
- no (or ineffective) internal auditing staff
- a high turnover of auditors
- unusual transactions
- weak internal controls.

There are two kinds of fraud. Financial reporting fraud is intentionally misstating items or omitting important facts from the financial statements. Misappropriation of assets generally involves some form of theft. Table 3.1 provides examples of financial reporting and misappropriation of assets frauds.

4 Define fraud risk and understand audit procedures to reduce this risk.

professional scepticism maintaining an attitude that includes a questioning mind, being alert to conditions that may indicate possible misstatement due to error or fraud, and a critical assessment of audit evidence

TABLE 3.1 **Examples of frauds**

Financial reporting frauds	Misappropriation of assets frauds
• Improper asset valuations • Unrecorded liabilities • Timing differences—bringing forward the recognition of revenues and delaying the recognition of expenses • Recording fictitious sales • Understating expenses • Inappropriate application of accounting principles	• Using a company credit card for personal use • Employees remaining on the payroll after ceasing employment • Unauthorized discounts or refunds to customers • Theft of inventory by employees or customers • Using a company car for unauthorized personal use

The responsibility for preventing and detecting fraud rests with those charged with governance at the client. Prevention refers to the use of controls and procedures aimed at avoiding a fraud. Detection refers to the use of controls and procedures aimed at uncovering a fraud should one occur. It is the responsibility of the auditor to assess the risk of fraud and the effectiveness of the client's attempts to prevent and detect fraud through their internal control system. When assessing the risk of fraud, an auditor can consider incentives and pressures to commit a fraud, opportunities to perpetrate a fraud, and attitudes and rationalizations used to justify committing a fraud (CAS 240, App. 1).

3.4.1 Incentives and pressures to commit a fraud

In assessing the risk of fraud, an auditor will consider incentives and pressures faced by their client to commit a fraud. While the examples provided below indicate that a client may be inclined to commit a fraud, they in no way indicate that a fraud has definitely occurred. When an auditor becomes aware of any of these risk factors, in isolation or combination, they will plan their audit to obtain evidence in relation to each risk factor.

Examples of incentives and pressures that increase the risk of a client committing fraud include:
- operation in a highly competitive industry
- a significant decline in demand for products or services
- falling profits
- a threat of takeover
- a threat of bankruptcy
- ongoing losses
- rapid growth
- poor cash flows combined with high earnings
- pressure to meet market expectations
- planning to list on a stock exchange
- planning to raise debt or renegotiate a loan
- about to enter into a significant new contract
- a significant proportion of remuneration tied to earnings (that is, bonuses, options).

3.4.2 Opportunities to perpetrate a fraud

After identifying one or more incentives or pressures to commit a fraud, an auditor will assess whether a client has an opportunity to perpetrate a fraud. An auditor will utilize their knowledge of how other frauds have been perpetrated to assess whether the same opportunities exist at the client. While the examples below of opportunities to commit a fraud suggest that a fraud may have been carried out, their existence does not mean that a fraud has definitely occurred. An auditor must use professional judgement to assess each opportunity in the context of other risk indicators and consider available evidence thoroughly.

Examples of opportunities that increase the risk that a fraud may have been perpetrated include:

- accounts that rely on estimates and judgement
- a high volume of transactions close to year end
- significant adjusting entries and reversals after year end
- significant related party transactions
- poor corporate governance mechanisms
- poor internal controls
- a high turnover of staff
- reliance on complex transactions
- transactions out of character for a business (for example, if a client leases its motor vehicles it should not have car registration expenses).

3.4.3 Attitudes and rationalization to justify a fraud

Together with the identification of incentives or pressures to commit a fraud and opportunities to perpetrate a fraud, an auditor will assess the attitudes and rationalization of client management and staff to fraud. Attitude refers to ethical beliefs about right and wrong, and rationalization refers to an ability to justify an act. While the examples below indicate that a fraud may occur in companies where these characteristics are identified, they do not mean that a fraud has occurred.

Examples of attitudes and rationalizations used to justify a fraud include:

- a poor tone at the top (that is, from senior management)
- the implementation of an effective internal control structure not seen as a priority
- an excessive focus on maximization of profits and/or share price
- a poor attitude to compliance with accounting regulations
- rationalization that other companies make the same inappropriate accounting choices.

Cloud 9

Suzie explains that fraud risk is always present and that auditors must explicitly consider it as part of their risk assessment. Being aware of the incentives and pressures, opportunities, and attitudes within the client relating to fraud helps the auditor make the assessment. Ian admits that he has a little trouble understanding the difference between incentives and attitudes; he thinks he understands the concept of opportunity. Suzie explains that incentives relate to what pushes (or pulls) a person to commit a fraud. Examples include a need for money to pay debts or gamble. Attitudes or rationalization relate to the thinking about the act of fraud. For example, a person believes it is acceptable to steal from a nasty boss; that is, the theft is justified by the boss's "nastiness."

3.4.4 Audit procedures relating to fraud

Besides assessing the fraud risk factors noted above, the following are some of the specific procedures the auditor should perform to comply with CAS 240:

1. The auditor should ask management and those charged with governance if they are aware of a known fraud or suspect there has been a fraud. If the company being audited has an internal audit department, it should also be asked this question. The results of these enquiries should be documented.

2. All members of the audit team, including the partner, should attend a team planning meeting. During this planning meeting, the significant fraud risk factors and where the financial statements may be particularly susceptible to fraud should be reviewed. This allows the more experienced team members to share their knowledge with the less experienced members.

3. The auditor should perform preliminary analytics (these are discussed in more detail in chapter 4) to identify any unusual relationships that may indicate fraud and thus require further investigation during the audit.

4. The auditor must consider the risk of management override. As management is in a position to manipulate the accounting records or override the controls designed to prevent such fraud, the auditor should test a sample of journal entries, review accounting estimates for reasonableness, contemplate the risk of earnings management (particularly in the area of revenue recognition), and carefully examine unusual business transactions to ensure that they have business substance.

If during the course of the audit, the auditor finds fraud, then they should contemplate their legal and professional responsibilities. As the auditor remains bound by confidentiality, they should seek legal advice to determine if there is a requirement to report the fraud to an outside third party. The auditor may also consider withdrawing from the engagement. Finally, the auditor must report the fraud to the level of management above that under which the fraud occurred and report the fraud to the audit committee.

BEFORE YOU GO ON

4.1 What are the responsibilities of the client and the auditor when it comes to fraud?

4.2 List four incentives and pressures that increase the risk of fraud.

4.3 What is management override and what procedures should the auditor perform to address it?

3.5 GOING CONCERN

❺ Explain the going concern assumption.

When planning an audit, performing an audit, and evaluating the results of an audit, an auditor will consider whether it is appropriate to assume that their client will remain as a going concern (CAS 570). The concept of going concern is introduced here and will appear again at various stages throughout this book. The going concern assumption is made when it is believed that a company will remain in business for the foreseeable future (CAS 570, para. 2). Under this assumption, assets are valued on the basis that they will continue to be used for the purposes of conducting a business, and liabilities are recorded and classified as current and non-current on the basis that the client will pay its debts as they fall due in the years to come. It is the responsibility of management and those charged with governance to assess whether their company is likely to remain a going concern. It is the responsibility of the auditor to obtain sufficient appropriate evidence to assess the validity of the going concern assumption made by their client's management and those charged with governance when preparing the financial statements.

3.5.1 Going concern risk—indicators

For each client, an auditor will use their professional judgement to assess whether the going concern assumption is valid. There are a number of indicators that, alone or combined, can suggest that the going concern assumption may be at risk. A comprehensive list of events and conditions that place doubt on the going concern assumption is provided in CAS 570. Indicators include:

- a significant debt-to-equity ratio
- long-term loans reaching maturity without alternative financing in place
- prolonged losses
- an inability to pay debts when they fall due
- supplier reluctance to provide goods on credit
- the loss of a significant customer
- overreliance on a few customers or suppliers
- high staff turnover
- the loss of key, long-standing personnel
- staff regularly out on strike
- uncertainty around the future availability of a key input or raw material
- rapid growth with insufficient planning
- inadequate risk management procedures
- being under investigation for non-compliance with legislation
- falling behind competitors
- significant rapid increase in competition
- prolonged drought for the agricultural sector.

If the auditor identifies risk factors that indicate that the going concern assumption is in doubt, they will undertake procedures to gather evidence regarding each risk factor. For example, if a client has lost a number of key, long-standing personnel, an auditor may assess the quality of the remaining staff and the likelihood that the client will be able to hire suitable replacements in the near future. If the auditor believes that there is an unresolved going concern issue outstanding, an assessment is made of the appropriateness of management disclosures in the notes to the financial statements regarding that issue. An auditor will assess the process used by management to evaluate the extent of the going concern risk. If a company has a history of losses and difficulties, an auditor will expect management to take a great deal of time and care in their going concern assessment. Once the auditor has an understanding of the process used by management, which may include the careful preparation of detailed cash flow projections and budgets, they will assess the adequacy of that process and conduct additional procedures if necessary.

If the auditor concludes that the going concern assumption is in doubt, further procedures are undertaken. CAS 570 provides a list of appropriate audit procedures. They include:

- assessment of cash flows
- assessment of revenue and expense items
- assessment of interim financial statements
- review of debt contracts
- review of board and other meetings
- discussions with client management and lawyers
- identification and assessment of mitigating factors.

3.5.2 Going concern risk—mitigating factors

Mitigating factors reduce the risk that the going concern assumption may be in doubt. For example, if a client is experiencing a severe cash shortage but has a letter from its bank agreeing to provide additional financing, the letter reduces (but does not remove) the risk that the going concern assumption may be invalid. Other mitigating factors include:

- a letter of guarantee from a parent company
- the availability of non-core assets, which can be sold to provide needed cash, without interrupting the company's operating capacity
- the ability to raise additional funds through the sale of shares
- the ability to raise additional funds through borrowings
- the ability to sell an unprofitable segment of the business.

Cloud 9

Going concern is another type of audit risk. When management adopts the going concern assumption, it records assets and liabilities on the basis that the entity will be able to realize its assets and discharge its liabilities in the normal course of business. If the going concern assumption is not valid, the financial statements should include adjustments to the recoverability and classification of recorded assets and liabilities. If these adjustments are not made, the auditor must express an adverse opinion.

Suzie explains that in most cases the assessment of going concern is not clear-cut. Sometimes there are questions about the going concern assumption and various circumstances that mitigate such questions. The auditor's job is to gather evidence about the issues in order to make a judgement about the nature of the uncertainties surrounding the going concern assumption and decide if, and how, these affect the audit report.

PROFESSIONAL ENVIRONMENT

Soccer as a going concern

Auditors are required to assess the ability of an entity to continue as a going concern for approximately the next 12 months. In Canada, CAS 570 requires the auditor to add a paragraph to the audit report drawing attention to any material uncertainty regarding the entity's continuation as a going concern. There is a similar requirement in the United Kingdom, and, as a result, the auditor of the parent company of Liverpool Football Club,

KPMG, warned in its 2009 audit report that there was a material uncertainty that may cast significant doubt on the company's ability to continue as a going concern.

KPMG was forced to make this statement because of uncertainty about the parent company's ability to refinance certain debts. There was no indication at the balance sheet date that the debt would definitely be refinanced, and the state of world credit markets in 2009 made it tougher for all companies to borrow large amounts.

Kop Football Holdings (KFH) purchased Liverpool FC in February 2007 using mostly borrowed funds. The company's 2008 financial statements showed that interest on this debt was £36.5 million, contributing to a loss of £42.6 million. KFH had to refinance borrowings of £350 million, which were due to expire on July 24, 2009.

Liverpool fans were reportedly angry about the situation. Liverpool FC itself is profitable, with a record turnover for the 2009 year of £159.1 million and profit of £10.2 million. This meant that any financial problems faced by the group were not due to the performance of the club itself. Some fans were so angry that they tried to end the control of their club by George Gillett and Tom Hicks, the U.S. sports tycoons behind KFH. They started a campaign to try to persuade the banks not to refinance the debt and to encourage fans to approach their local members of Parliament to urge them to stop the refinancing arrangements.

It was feared that KFH's financial problems would affect Liverpool FC's performance on the football field. Staying competitive on the field means being able to buy the right players and pay the large transfer fees. However, the U.S. backers of the club were confident that the fundamentals of the club were sound and they would continue to provide substantial personal guarantees to satisfy the banks.

Despite the personal guarantees, the company continued to struggle with its debt load. In April 2010, Hicks and Gillett put the club up for sale. After some legal wrangling with the board of directors regarding the sale of the club, it was sold in October 2010 to New England Sports Ventures (NESV), the company that also owns the Boston Red Sox. The transaction valued the club at £300 million and eliminated all of the acquisition debt placed on LFC by its previous owners, reducing the club's debt servicing obligations from £25 million–£30 million a year to £2 million–£3 million.

Sources: "KPMG Issues Going Concern Warning on Liverpool FC," *Accountancy Age*, June 5, 2009; A. Weston, "Fans React with Dismay over State of Liverpool FC's Finances," *Liverpool Echo*, June 6, 2009; P. Kelso, "Debt Hits Liverpool FC," *The Age*, June 7, 2009; "Liverpool FC Sold to NESV," Liverpoolfc.tv, October 15, 2010. (Access date: July 2011)

BEFORE YOU GO ON

5.1 What is the going concern assumption?

5.2 List three factors that indicate that the going concern assumption may be at risk.

5.3 List three factors that mitigate the risk that the going concern assumption may be in doubt.

3.6 CORPORATE GOVERNANCE

Corporate governance is the rules, systems, and processes within companies used to guide and control. Governance structures are used to monitor the actions of staff and assess the level of risk faced. Controls are designed to reduce identified risks and ensure the future viability of the company. The CSA published national policy guidelines on corporate governance to help improve performance and enhance accountability to shareholders. Figure 3.4 presents an excerpt from those guidelines. While these guidelines do provide a framework for corporate governance practices, they do

6 Describe corporate governance.

Board Composition

· The board should have a majority of independent directors.
· The chair of the board should be an independent director.

Meetings of Independent Directors

· The independent directors should hold regularly scheduled meetings at which non-independent directors and members of management are not in attendance.

Board Mandate

· The board should adopt a written mandate in which it acknowledges responsibility for the stewardship of the issuer, including responsibility for:
  (a) satisfying itself as to the integrity of senior management;
  (b) adopting a strategic planning process that takes into account the opportunities and risks of the business;
  (c) identifying the key risks to the business, and ensure there are appropriate systems in place to manage these risks;
  (d) ensuring succession planning;
  (e) adopting a communication policy;
  (f) overseeing the internal control and management information systems; and
  (g) developing the issuer's approach to corporate governance, including outlining a set of corporate governance principles and guidelines to be followed.

The written mandate of the board should also set out:
  (i) establishing methods for receiving feedback from stakeholders (whistleblowers);
  (ii) setting expectations and responsibilities of directors.

Position Descriptions

· The board should develop job descriptions for the chair of the board and the chair of each board committee.

Orientation and Continuing Education

· The board should ensure all new directors receive a comprehensive orientation so they fully understand their role and the nature and operation of the business.
· The board should provide continuing education opportunities for all directors.

Code of Business Conduct and Ethics

· The board should adopt a written code of business conduct and ethics to address conflicts of interest, protection and proper use of corporate assets, confidentiality of corporate information, fair dealing with investors, customers, suppliers, competitors and employees; compliance with laws, rules and regulations; and reporting of any illegal or unethical behaviour.
· The board should monitor compliance with this code.

FIGURE 3.4 **Excerpt from the CSA's *Corporate Governance Guidelines***

Source: CSA, *National Policy 58-201: Corporate Governance Guidelines*, June 30, 2005.

not dictate any particular requirements. However, reporting issuers must disclose their corporate governance practices and why they believe these practices are appropriate for the entity.

From an auditor's perspective, considering a client's corporate governance principles is an important part of gaining an understanding of that client. A client that does not take its corporate governance obligations seriously may not fulfill its obligation to ensure its financial statements are fairly presented.

3.7 INFORMATION TECHNOLOGY

When gaining an understanding of a client, an auditor will consider the particular risks faced by the client associated with **information technology** (IT). IT is a part of most companies' accounting processes, which include transaction initiation, recording, processing, correction as necessary, transfer to the general ledger, and compilation of the financial statements. CAS 315 requires that the auditor gain an understanding of the client's IT system and the associated risks.

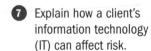 Explain how a client's information technology (IT) can affect risk.

information technology the use of computers to store and process data and other information

Risks associated with IT include unauthorized access to computers, software, and data; errors in programs; lack of backup; and loss of data. Unauthorized access to data can occur when there is insufficient security or poor password protection procedures. Unauthorized access can result in data being lost or distorted. Unauthorized access to computer programs can result in misstatements in the financial statements. Access can be limited in a number of ways, such as through the use of security (such as locked doors) and passwords.

Errors in computer programming can occur if programs are not tested thoroughly. It is important that new programs and changes to programs are tested extensively before being put into operation. Errors can also occur if mistakes are made when writing a program or if programs are deliberately changed to include errors. Deliberate changes may be made by staff or outsiders who gain unauthorized access to a client's IT system. For example, unhappy staff may purposefully change a program, causing errors to embarrass their employer. It is therefore important that access be limited to authorized staff. Errors can also occur if programming changes are not processed on a timely basis. Programs need to be changed from time to time for a variety of reasons, such as to change sales prices, update discounts being offered to customers, and so on. It is important that these changes be made by authorized personnel on a timely basis to avoid errors.

New programs can be purchased "off the shelf" from a software provider or developed internally by a client's staff. When a client purchases a general-purpose program off the shelf, there is a risk that it will require modification to suit the client's operations, which can lead to errors. An advantage of purchasing general-purpose programs from reputable companies is that they will have been tested before being made available for sale. In contrast, when a client's staff develop a program internally, the program is more likely to have the features required, but there is a risk of errors if the program is written by inexperienced staff or the program is not adequately tested before being put into operation.

When a client installs a new IT system, there are a number of risks. There is the risk that the system may not be appropriate for the client and its reporting requirements. After installation, there is the risk that data may be lost or corrupted when transferring information from an existing system to the new system. There is the risk that the new system does not process data appropriately. There is the risk that client staff are not adequately trained to use the new system effectively. It is important that a client has appropriate procedures for selecting new IT systems, changing from an old to a new system, training staff in using the new system, and ensuring that a new system includes embedded controls to minimize the risk of material misstatement.

When a client has an established IT system, an auditor will gain an understanding of the risks posed by that system as part of their assessment of the risk of a material misstatement in the client's financial statements. An auditor will assess whether their client has the processes and procedures in place required to reduce IT risk to an acceptably low level. The two broad categories of controls used to reduce IT risk are general controls and application controls.

General controls are policies and procedures that relate to many applications and support the effective functioning of application controls (CAS 315). They include procedures for purchasing, changing, and maintaining new computers; procedures for purchasing, changing, and maintaining new software; the use of passwords and other security measures to minimize the risk of unauthorized access; and procedures to ensure appropriate segregation of duties between, for example, the staff who amend and maintain the programs and the staff who use the programs.

Application controls are manual or automated procedures that typically operate at a business process level and apply to the processing of transactions by individual applications (CAS 315). These controls are designed to prevent and/or detect a material misstatement in the financial statements by ensuring all transactions are recorded only once, and rejected transactions are identified and corrected. Application controls impact procedures used for data entry, data processing and output, or reporting. They include reconciliations between input and output data and automated checks on data entered to ensure accuracy; for example, a check that a customer number entered is valid. A more detailed discussion of general and application controls is included in chapters 7 and 8.

When an auditor has identified an IT risk, they will assess the adequacy of their client's general and application controls in mitigating that risk. If an auditor believes that their client's general and application controls appear adequate, their audit strategy is to test those controls with a view to relying on the client's procedures to minimize IT risk exposure. If an auditor believes that a client's general and application controls do not appear to be adequate, their audit strategy is to rely more heavily on their own tests of the transactions and balances produced by the client's IT system.

general controls controls that apply to a company's IT system as a whole. They include policies and procedures for the purchase, maintenance, and daily operations of an IT system, security, and staff training

application controls manual or automated controls that operate at a business process level and apply to the processing of transactions by individual applications

Cloud 9

Suzie explains to Ian that her experience in the clothing and footwear industry has taught her to be very inquisitive about the systems used to manage orders. She has seen a few clothing businesses fail because they could not get their goods to retail outlets in time. Fashion is such a fickle market that even being a few weeks late means that stores run out of inventory, and, when inventory does arrive, stores have to discount it to sell it. After this situation occurs a couple of times, retailers turn to more reliable suppliers, even if the designs aren't as imaginative.

Suzie has heard that Cloud 9 is very reliant on an inventory management software program developed by their parent company. Because it is not a widely used package, she does not know anything about it and is concerned about its ability to provide reliable data. Suzie and Ian decide to allocate extra time in the audit plan to assessing the reliability of this software.

BEFORE YOU GO ON

7.1 What are some of the risks associated with the purchase of a new IT system?

7.2 What are two common sources of new computer programs?

7.3 What are application controls?

3.8 CLOSING PROCEDURES

When finalizing the financial statements, a client will close its accounts for the financial reporting period. Revenue and expense items must include all transactions that occurred during the period and exclude transactions that relate to other periods. Asset and liability balances must include all relevant items, accruals must be complete, and contingent liabilities must accurately and completely reflect potential future obligations. From an audit perspective, there is a risk that the client's closing procedures are inadequate.

An auditor is concerned that transactions and events have been recorded in the correct accounting period. This is the responsibility of those charged with governance. It is the responsibility of the auditor to ensure that their client has applied its closing procedures appropriately.

An auditor will determine the risk associated with their client's closing procedures. In addition to the annual financial statements, clients prepare monthly and quarterly financial statements for internal and/or external purposes. An auditor can check these reports to assess the accuracy of their client's closing procedures when preparing those reports. If there are significant errors, where closing procedures are inadequate and transactions are not always recorded in the appropriate reporting period, an auditor will plan on spending more time conducting detailed testing around year end.

There are a number of ways that an auditor can assess the adequacy of their client's closing procedures. Clients that report monthly are more likely to have in place well-established closing procedures than clients that only report annually. An auditor will check the accuracy of accrual calculations around year end. An auditor can look at earnings trends to assess whether the reported income is in line with similar periods (months or quarters) in prior years. For example, revenues are generally higher for an ice-cream seller in warmer months, and wages are generally higher during the months when a client holds its annual sales and extra staff are hired to help out with the increased activity.

If an auditor believes that their client is under pressure to report strong results, there is a risk that revenues earned after year end will be included in the current year's income and expenses incurred before year end will be excluded. If the auditor believes that their client is under pressure to smooth its income and not report any unexpected increases, there is a risk that revenues earned just before year end will be excluded from current income and expenses incurred after year end will be included. In both cases, the auditor will trace transactions recorded close to year end to source documentation and confirm that all transactions are recorded in the appropriate accounting period.

Figure 3.5 lists additional recommended risk assessment procedures from the *Canadian Professional Engagement Manual (C·PEM).*

8 Explain how client closing procedures can affect reported results.

FIGURE 3.5 Excerpt of risk assessment procedures, *C·PEM*, Form 435

Source: CICA, "Risk Asessment Procedures—Planning & Execution" *C·PEM*, Form 435, April 2010.

Procedure	WP	Comments	Completed by and date
OBSERVATION AND INSPECTION			
Identify potential risk factors from reading key entity documents such as the following: a) Business plans, budgets and most recent financial results. b) Minutes of directors'/audit committee meetings. c) Reports/letters, etc. from regulators or government agencies. d) Internet/magazine/newspaper articles on the entity or industry. e) Details of actual or threatened litigation including correspondence with external legal counsel. f) Significant contracts and agreements. g) Communications with staff on changes in entity-level control matters. h) Tax assessments and correspondence.			
INQUIRY			
Make inquiries of management and those responsible for financial reporting. Who Interviewed By whom Date Ask about: a) Business objectives, industry trends, management's assessment of current and potential risk factors and their planned responses. b) Major events or changes that took place during the period. Consider • economic conditions • changes in products and services • new technologies, contracts • funding • operating results • ownership • organizational structure • key personnel, bonus plans • IT infrastructure or applications • internal control processes and financial reporting. c) Any instances of alleged, suspected or actual fraud (Forms 511 and 512). d) Any performance bonuses or incentive plans. e) The identity of and nature and amount of related party transactions during the period (Form 640). f) Any going-concern events or conditions (complete Form 527 and, if necessary, Form 625). g) Transactions, events and conditions that give rise to accounting estimates (Form 635). h) Nature, extent and status of litigation/claims against the entity or key personnel. i) Whether the entity is in compliance with required filings (tax returns, etc.), declarations and other regulatory requirements.			
Where applicable, make inquiries of members of the governance board (directors and audit committee members, etc.). Who interviewed By whom Date Ask about: a) The composition, mandate and meetings of the board of directors and any audit committee. b) Any knowledge of management override, fraud or suspected fraud.			
c) Their opinion on: • The effectiveness of management oversight. • The control environment (culture, competence, attitudes, etc.). • What financial statement areas are susceptible to fraud (Form 512).			

PROFESSIONAL ENVIRONMENT

Top management compensation

Just how big are the incentives for good performance by chief executive officers (CEOs) of publicly traded Canadian companies? A survey of Canadian executives shows that they can be very big indeed. The top paid CEO in Canada in 2008, Thomas Glocer of Thomson Reuters Corp., was paid a total of $36.6 million (comprising cash and bonuses, perks, options, and equity grants). Most of Glocer's pay, $28.2 million, came from equity rather than cash.

Second on the list was Ted Rogers, head of Rogers Communications Inc., who was paid $21.5 million. Overall, the top five Canadian executives had total compensation of more than $100 million in 2008.

Academic research suggests that auditors need to be aware of the potential effects of incentives related to compensation packages. For example, Paul Healy provided evidence that when top executives are paid a bonus according to a formula incorporating minimum and maximum profit levels, profits appear to be "managed" in predictable ways. Healy's evidence suggests that if the minimum profit is not likely to be reached, managers will take action to increase accruals (such as closing entries) to reduce the current year's profit. When the over accrual reverses in the next year, there will be a boost to profit, and therefore managers will receive a bonus on the amount that they are able to "shift" into the next year. Managers take the same action to reduce profit if it is likely to be above the required maximum; therefore, deferring the profit and bonus to the following year. However, if profit is between the required minimum and maximum, managers will try to increase profit to increase their bonus.

The lesson from the academic research is that if auditors understand how the bonus arrangement works, they will be more alert to the type of profit shifting likely to be attempted by managers.

Sources: Hugh MacKenzie, "A Soft Landing, Recession and Canada's 100 Highest Paid CEO's," Canadian Centre for Policy Alternatives, January 2010; P. Healy, "The Effect of Bonus Schemes on Accounting Decisions," *Journal of Accounting and Economics*, April 1985, pp. 85–107.

Cloud 9

The partner, Jo Wadley, has learned of pressure from the parent company on Cloud 9's management to increase revenue by 3 percent this year. Jo is also aware of cost increases associated with a new store and sponsorship deals. Jo believes that this places additional pressure on Cloud 9's management to meet targets resulting in additional risks for closing procedures, and has instructed Suzie to allocate additional time to auditing closing procedures on the Cloud 9 audit.

BEFORE YOU GO ON

8.1 Explain how an auditor can assess the risk associated with their client's closing procedures.

8.2 Outline how an auditor can assess the adequacy of their client's closing procedures.

8.3 What is the particular risk when an auditor believes that their client is under pressure to report strong results?

SUMMARY

❶ Identify the different stages of an audit.

The stages of an audit include planning, performing, and reporting. During the planning stage, an auditor will gain an understanding of their client, identify risks, develop an audit strategy, and set their planning materiality. During the performing stage, an auditor will execute their detailed testing of account balances and transactions. The final stage of every audit involves reviewing all of the evidence gathered throughout the audit and arriving at a conclusion regarding the fair presentation of the client's financial statements. The auditor will then write an audit report that reflects their opinion based upon their findings.

❷ Explain the process used in gaining an understanding of the client.

An auditor will gain an understanding of their client to aid in the risk identification process. This process involves consideration of issues at the entity level, the industry level, and the broader economic level. At the entity level, an auditor will identify the client's major customers, suppliers, and stakeholders (that is, banks, shareholders, and employees). The auditor will also determine whether their client is an importer or exporter, who the client's competitors are, what the client's capacity is to adapt to changes in technology, and what the nature of any warranties provided to customers is. At the industry level, an auditor is interested in their client's position within its industry. At the economic level, an auditor will assess how well positioned the client is to cope with current and changing government policy and economic conditions.

❸ Explain how related parties can impact risk.

Related parties include parent companies, subsidiaries, joint ventures, associates, company management, and close family members of key management. Since related parties are not independent of each other, these transactions may not be in the normal course of business. This increases the risk of material misstatement and may impact the overall financial results. Therefore, related party transactions require some specific consideration throughout the audit and specific procedures should be performed and documented.

❹ Define fraud risk and understand audit procedures to reduce this risk.

Fraud is an intentional act through the use of deception to obtain an unjust or illegal advantage. The two kinds of fraud are financial reporting fraud and misappropriation of assets fraud. There are a number of techniques the auditor uses to assess the risk of fraud. The audit file must document the fraud risk assessment and procedures performed to support that assessment.

❺ Explain the going concern assumption.

The going concern assumption is made when it is believed that a company will remain in business for the foreseeable future. An auditor will consider the appropriateness of this assumption during the planning stage and then throughout the audit.

❻ Describe corporate governance.

Corporate governance is the rules, systems, and processes within companies used to guide and control. Among other things governance structures are used to assess the level of risk faced and to design controls to reduce identified risks.

7 **Explain how a client's information technology (IT) can affect risk.**

There are a number of risks associated with IT. During the planning stage of the audit, the auditor will assess the likelihood that their client's financial statements are misstated due to limitations in its IT system.

8 **Explain how client closing procedures can affect reported results.**

There are a number of risks associated with a client's closing procedures. Closing procedures are the processes used by a client at year end to ensure that transactions are recorded in the appropriate accounting period. From an audit perspective, there is a risk that the client's closing procedures are inadequate.

KEY TERMS

Application controls, 108

Audit strategy, 90

Closing procedures, 91

Corporate governance, 91

Execution stage, 90

Fraud, 91

General controls, 108

Going concern, 91

Information technology, 107

Materiality, 90

Planning stage, 90

Professional scepticism, 99

Reporting stage, 90

Sufficient appropriate evidence, 91

MULTIPLE-CHOICE QUESTIONS

3.1 When gaining an understanding of the client, the auditor will identify the geographic location of the client because:

(a) more spread-out clients are harder to control.

(b) the auditor will need to visit the various locations to assess processes and procedures at each site.

(c) the auditor will plan to use staff from affiliated offices to visit overseas locations.

(d) all of the above.

3.2 When gaining an understanding of the client's sources of financing, the auditor:

(a) is not interested in debt covenants because all debt contracts are the same.

(b) will assess if the client is meeting interest payments when they are due.

(c) will ignore the relative reliance on debt versus equity funding because that is a management decision not an audit issue.

(d) none of the above.

3.3 When gaining an understanding of the client at the industry level the auditor:

(a) will not ignore information about the client's industry.

(b) will not consider the level of demand for the goods and services provided by other companies in the client's industry.

(c) will not consider government taxes on the industry because they are out of the client's control.

(d) will not listen to bad news reports about the client firm because the client's reputation in the press is not important.

3.4 The CSA's *Corporate Governance Guidelines* are designed to help companies:

(a) improve their corporate structure.

(b) improve performance.

(c) enhance their accountability to shareholders and other interested third parties.

(d) all of the above.

3.5 An attitude of professional scepticism means:
(a) the auditor can rely on past experience to determine current risk of fraud.
(b) any indicator of fraud is properly investigated.
(c) the auditor can rely on management assertions.
(d) all of the above.

3.6 An example of an incentive or pressure that increases the risk of fraud is:
(a) the client operates in a highly competitive industry.
(b) the client has a history of making losses.
(c) a significant percentage of management remuneration is tied to earnings.
(d) all of the above.

3.7 The auditor must consider whether it is appropriate to assume that the client will remain as a going concern:
(a) because this means that assets are valued on the basis that they will continue to be used for the purposes of conducting a business.
(b) only if the client is facing bankruptcy, and long-term debt is likely to be withdrawn.
(c) only if the client is listed on a stock exchange.
(d) because mitigating circumstances are not important.

3.8 The planning stage of an audit does not include:
(a) gaining an understanding of the client.
(b) identifying factors that may affect the risk of a material misstatement in the financial statements.
(c) developing an audit strategy and a risk and materiality assessment.
(d) executing and reporting on an audit.

3.9 When gaining an understanding of the client, the auditor will consider:
(a) related party identification.
(b) the appropriateness of the client's system of internal controls to mitigate identified business risks.
(c) controls over the technology used to process and store data electronically.
(d) all of the above.

3.10 Client closing procedures:
(a) are routine transactions that do not have an impact on audit risk.
(b) are the responsibility of those charged with governance who must ensure that transactions are recorded in the correct accounting period.
(c) affect expense accounts only.
(d) all of the above.

REVIEW QUESTIONS

3.1 Explain the relationship between the planning, executing, and reporting stages of an audit. Why is risk identification in the first stage?

3.2 Explain the importance of the planning stage of a financial statement audit.

3.3 When gaining an understanding of a client, an auditor will be interested in an entity's relationships with both its suppliers and customers. What aspects of these relationships will the auditor be interested in and how would they affect the assessment of audit risk?

3.4 List and briefly explain the key factors that the auditor would consider during preliminary risk identification with respect to related parties.

3.5 In the context of fraud, explain the differences between (1) incentives and pressures, (2) opportunity, and (3) attitudes and rationalization. Why is it important for an auditor to consider client systems relevant to all three concepts?

3.6 What procedures should the auditor perform with respect to fraud?

3.7 What does it mean when we say that a business is a "going concern" or, alternatively, has "going concern issues"? Why must an auditor specifically consider evidence about the going concern assessment for each client?

3.8 What are mitigating factors in the context of the going concern assessment? Give some examples of mitigating factors for a loss-making client.

3.9 Why does an auditor need to understand a client's IT system? Explain how IT affects the financial statements.

3.10 Give an example of a client closing procedure. Using your example, explain the accounts that would be affected if the closing procedure is performed inadequately.

PROFESSIONAL APPLICATION QUESTIONS

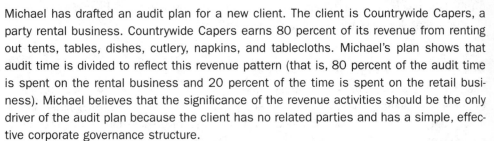

Basic ★   Moderate ★ ★   Challenging ★ ★ ★

3.1 Audit planning ★

Michael has drafted an audit plan for a new client. The client is Countrywide Capers, a party rental business. Countrywide Capers earns 80 percent of its revenue from renting out tents, tables, dishes, cutlery, napkins, and tablecloths. Michael's plan shows that audit time is divided to reflect this revenue pattern (that is, 80 percent of the audit time is spent on the rental business and 20 percent of the time is spent on the retail business). Michael believes that the significance of the revenue activities should be the only driver of the audit plan because the client has no related parties and has a simple, effective corporate governance structure.

Required

What questions would you have for Michael before accepting his audit plan?

3.2 Understanding the client and its governance ★

Ajax Ltd. is a listed company and a new client of Delaware Partners, a medium-sized audit firm. Jeffrey Nycz is the engagement partner on the audit and has asked the members of the audit team to start the process of gaining an understanding of the client in accordance with CAS 315. One audit manager is leading the group investigating the industry and economic effects, and another is helping Jeffrey consider issues at the entity level. Jeffrey is holding discussions with members of the audit committee, and his talks will cover a wide range of issues, including the company's corporate governance principles. He has a meeting arranged for next week with the four members of the audit committee, including the chair of the committee, Stella South, who, like the other members of the audit committee, is an independent director.

Required

(a) Make a list of the main factors that will be considered by each audit manager's group.

(b) What are the required disclosures related to Ajax Ltd. corporate governance practices?

3.3 Understanding the client and its risks—audit planning ★ ★

Ivy Bishnoi is preparing a report for the engagement partner of an existing client, Scooter Ltd., an importer of scooters and other low-powered motorcycles. Ivy has been investigating certain aspects of Scooter Ltd.'s business given the change in economic conditions over the past 12 months. She has found that Scooter Ltd.'s business, which experienced rapid growth over its first five years in operation, has slowed significantly during the last year. Initially, sales of scooters were boosted by good economic conditions and solid employment growth, coupled with rising gas prices. Consumers needed transport to get to work and the high gas prices made the relatively cheap running costs of scooters seem very attractive. In addition, the low purchase price of a small motorcycle or scooter, at between $3,000 and $8,000, meant that almost anyone who had a job could obtain a loan to buy one.

However, Ivy has found that the sales of small motorcycles and scooters have slowed significantly and that all importers of these products, not just Scooter Ltd., are being adversely affected. The onset of an economic recession has restricted employment growth, and those people who still have jobs are less certain of continued employment. In addition, the slowdown in the world economy has caused oil prices to fall, further reducing demand for this type of economical transport. Ivy has also discovered that, due to the global financial crisis, the finance company used by Scooter Ltd.'s customers to finance the purchase of scooters and motorcycles has announced that it will not be continuing to provide loans for any type of vehicle with a purchase price of less than $10,000.

Required

(a) Identify the issues that potentially have an impact on the audit of Scooter Ltd.

(b) Explain how each issue affects the audit plan by identifying the risks and the financial statement accounts that require closer examination.

3.4 Financial reporting fraud risk ★ ★

Vaughan Enterprises Ltd. has grown from its beginnings in the steel fabrication business to become a multinational manufacturer and supplier of all types of packaging, including metal, plastic, and paper-based products. It has also diversified into a range of other businesses, including household appliances in Europe, the United States, and Asia. The growth in the size of the business occurred gradually under the leadership of the last two CEOs, both of whom were promoted from within the business.

At the beginning of last year, the incumbent CEO died of a heart attack and the board took the opportunity to appoint a new CEO from outside the company. Despite the company's growth, returns to shareholders have been stagnant during the last decade. The new CEO has a reputation of turning around struggling businesses by making tough decisions. The new CEO has a five-year contract with generous bonuses for improvements in various performance indicators, including sales/assets, profit from continuing operations/net assets, and share price.

During the first year, the new CEO disposed of several segments of the business that were not profitable. Very large losses on the discontinued operations were recorded and most non-current assets throughout the business were written down to recognize impairment losses. These actions resulted in a large overall loss for the first year, although a profit from continuing operations was recorded. During the second year, recorded sales in the household appliances business in the United States increased dramatically, and, combined with various cost-saving measures, the company made a large profit.

The auditors have been made aware through various conversations with middle management that there is now an extreme focus on maximizing profits through boosting sales and cutting costs. The attitude toward compliance with accounting regulations has changed, with greater emphasis on pleasing the CEO than taking care to avoid breaching either internal policies or external regulations. The message is that the company has considerable ground to make up to catch up with other companies in both methods and results. Meanwhile, the share price over the first year and a half of the CEO's tenure has increased 65 percent, and the board has happily approved payment of the CEO's bonuses and granted the CEO additional options over the company's shares in recognition of the change in the company's results.

Required

(a) Discuss the incentives, pressures, and opportunities to commit financial statement fraud, and the attitudes and rationalizations to justify a fraud in the above case.

(b) What financial statement frauds would you suspect could have occurred at Vaughan?

(c) What are the procedures surrounding the fraud risk assessment that should be performed and documented?

3.5 Going concern ★★

The Wellington Plaza Hotel is located close to the main railway station in a large regional city. Its main client base is business people visiting the city for work-related purposes. The second largest group of clients consists of groups of (mainly) women visiting the city for its great shopping. All major department stores have a presence in the city and there are also lots of specialty shops and factory outlets. Another large group of clients are groups of (mainly) men visiting the city for various sports events, including several important hockey games during the winter.

Occupancy rates have been reasonable but stagnant for several years, providing a steady but unsatisfactory rate of return for the owners of the hotel. Revenues have been sufficient to cover operating costs, but no substantial progress has been made on repaying the large, long-term loans used to finance the hotel. In an effort to increase the hotel's profitability, a major renovation program was undertaken and completed earlier this year. The renovation was predicted to increase the relative attractiveness of the hotel to guests. It was also undertaken to earn additional revenue from the rent of a new coffee shop on the ground floor. The coffee shop is run by a separate company that has purchased a franchise of a major international brand.

The global financial crisis has hit the hotel business very hard this financial year. Business travel is down by 25 percent across the country. Further, discretionary retail spending is down by 40 percent. Several specialty shops in the city have already shut down and others are cutting their opening hours. In addition, the hockey series was won by the local team in four games (instead of the possible seven games). Thousands of visitors left the city early once the game was over. Just before the hockey games began, the coffee-shop owners went bankrupt and closed down, breaking their lease. The hotel owners are seeking legal advice on whether they can claim penalty fees on the broken lease.

Finally, the hotel owners' bank is warning that the short-term financing obtained for the renovations will not be renewed when it is due (one month after year end). The hotel managers had expected to repay the debt from this year's bookings and the coffee-shop lease. The hotel owners are still hopeful that the summer will bring a large lift in occupancy (and revenue) as the weather is expected to be nice. This expected summer trade is essential to meet repayments on the long-term debt and to convince the bank to extend the short-term debt.

Required

(a) Is there a going concern issue in this case? Explain.
(b) Are there mitigating factors? Explain them and how they would affect the auditor's conclusion.

3.6 Assessing the risks associated with information technology ★★

Shane Whitebone is getting to know his new client, Clarrie Potters, a large discount electrical retailer. Ben Brothers has been the engagement partner on the Clarrie Potters' audit for the past five years, but the audit partner rotation rules have meant that the engagement partner has had to change this year. Shane discovers that toward the end of last year, Clarrie Potters installed a new IT system for inventory control. The system was not operating prior to the end of the last financial year, so its testing was not included in the previous audit. The new system was built for Clarrie Potters by a Montreal-based software company, which modified another system it had designed for a furniture manufacturer and retailer.

Required

What audit risks are associated with the installation of the new inventory IT system at Clarrie Potters?

3.7 Audit planning in an EDP environment ★ ★ ★

Farm Fresh Foods Inc. (FFF) is a new food distribution company that has been profitable since the second month of operations. It has arranged with Smith LLP, a certified general accounting firm, to conduct an external audit of its first year of operations. FFF has a large electronic data processing (EDP) installation with six EDP employees, including the EDP manager, a former accountant who is taking courses to upgrade her skills in computer operations and programming. Mary Heston of Smith LLP is in charge of designing an audit plan for the EDP function, and Ahmed Khan is auditing receivables, purchases, and payroll.

Required

What information does Smith LLP need to obtain about the EDP function when developing its audit plan for FFF? State six examples.

Source: Adapted from the Certified General Accountant Canada, Auditing 1 Exam, June 2006.

3.8 Impact of closing procedures on performance ★ ★

Dunks Holdings Ltd. (Dunks) is an importer of hardware goods and distributes the goods to hardware retailers around the country. The growth in the do-it-yourself (DIY) market, which has accompanied the boom in house prices in most capital cities over the past five years, has provided consistent sales growth for both hardware retailers and wholesalers like Dunks. However, the recession that began last year has cast doubt on the ability of this sector to keep growing. Some analysts believe that the DIY market will not be affected by the recession because, in tough economic times, homeowners increase their "nesting" behaviour; that is, they spend even more on improving their homes and retreat from outside activities such as holidays, the theatre, and restaurants. This view is disputed by other analysts who believe that job losses and general pessimism in the economy will impact adversely on all company profits, including Dunks.

Dunks' share price has fallen over the last year as doubt about its ability to grow its profits in the current year spreads. The CEO and other senior management have large bonuses linked to both share prices and company profitability, and there is a mood within the company that achieving sales and profit targets this year is vital to avoid job losses at the company.

You have been brought into the audit team for Dunks this year and given the responsibility for auditing Dunks' closing procedures. Dunks has a monthly reporting system for internal management, but you notice that the reports are being issued later in the following month this year than they were last year.

Required

(a) Explain why and how the circumstances described above could affect your risk assessment.

(b) How do you plan to audit Dunks' closing procedures? What potential errors would you be most interested in?

Questions 3.9 and 3.10 are based on the following case.

Featherbed Surf & Leisure Holidays Ltd. (Featherbed) is a resort company based on Vancouver Island. Its operations include boating, surfing, diving, and other leisure activities; a backpackers' hostel; a family hotel; and a five-star resort. Justin and Sarah Morris own the majority of the shares in the Morris Group, which controls Featherbed. Justin is the chairman of the board of directors of both Featherbed and the Morris Group, and Sarah is a director of both companies as well as the CFO of Featherbed.

In February 2012, Justin Morris approached your audit firm, KFP Partners, to carry out the Featherbed audit for the year ending June 30, 2012. Featherbed has not been audited before but this year the audit has been requested by the company's bank and a new private equity investor group that has just acquired a 20 percent share of Featherbed.

Featherbed employs 30 full-time staff. These workers are employed in administration, accounting, catering, cleaning, and hotel/restaurant duties. During peak periods, Featherbed also uses part-time and casual workers.

Justin and Sarah have a fairly laid back management style. They trust their workers to work hard for the company and reward them well. The accounting staff, in particular, are very loyal to the company. Justin tells you that some of the accounting staff enjoy their jobs so much that they have never taken any holidays, and hardly any workers ever take sick leave.

There are three people currently employed as accountants, the most senior of which is Peter Pinn. Peter heads the accounting department and reports directly to Sarah. He is in his fifties and plans to retire in two or three years. Peter prides himself on his ability to delegate most of his work to his two accounts staff, Kristen and Julie. He claims he has to do this because he is very busy developing a policy and procedures manual for the accounting department. This delegated work includes opening mail, processing payments and receipts, banking funds received, performing reconciliations, posting transactions, and performing the payroll function. Julie is a recently designated chartered accountant. Kristen works part-time—coming into the office on Mondays, Wednesdays, and Fridays. Kristen is responsible for posting all journal entries into the accounting system and the payroll function. Julie does the balance of the work, but they often help each other out in busy periods.

Source: Adapted from the Institute of Chartered Accountants Australia's CA Program's Audit and Assurance Exam, May 2008.

3.9 Gaining an understanding of a new client ★ ★ ❷

You have access to the following information for Featherbed:
- prior period financial statements
- anticipated results for the current year
- industry comparisons.

Required

Explain how you would use this information to understand your new client.

3.10 Assessing fraud risk ★ ★ ❹

Required

(a) Identify and explain any significant fraud risk factors for Featherbed.
(b) For each fraud risk factor you identify, explain how the risk will affect your approach to the audit of Featherbed.

3.11 Fraud risk ★ ★ ★ ❹

Fellowes and Associates Chartered Accountants is a successful mid-tier accounting firm with a large range of clients across Canada. During 2011, Fellowes and Associates gained a new client, Health Care Holdings Group (HCHG), which owns 100 percent of the following entities:
- Shady Oaks Centre, a private treatment centre
- Gardens Nursing Home Ltd., a private nursing home
- Total Laser Care Limited, a private clinic that specializes in laser treatment of skin defects. Year end for all HCHG entities is June 30.

The audit partner for the audit of HCHG, Tania Fellowes, has discovered that two months before the end of the financial year, one of the senior nursing officers at Gardens Nursing Home was dismissed. Her employment was terminated after it was discovered that she had worked in collusion with a number of patients to reduce their fees. The nurse would then take secret payments from the patients.

The nursing officer had access to the patient database. While she was only supposed to update room-located changes for patients, she was able to reduce the patient period of stay and the value of other services provided. The fraud was detected by a fellow employee who overheard the nurse discussing the "scam" with a patient. The employee reported the matter to Gardens Nursing Home's general manager.

Required

(a) Which accounts on the balance sheet and income statement are potentially affected by the fraud?

(b) Describe how Gardens Nursing Home's business could be affected as a result of the fraud.

Source: Adapted from the Institute of Chartered Accountants Australia's CA Program's Audit and Assurance Exam, December 2008.

3.12 Motives and opportunities to commit fraud ★

Required

From the list below, identify what you would consider as

(1) a motive for fraud, and

(2) an opportunity for fraud.

    a) college or university tuition

    b) gambling debts

    c) nobody counts the inventory, so losses are not known

    d) the petty cash box is often left unattended

    e) drugs

    f) the finance vice-president has investment authority without any review

    g) alimony and child support

    h) expensive lifestyle (homes, cars, boats)

    i) business or stock speculation losses

    j) upper management considered publishing a written statement of ethics but decided not to

    k) taxation on good financial results

    l) supervisors set a bad example by taking supplies home

    m) an employee was caught and fired, but not prosecuted.

3.13 The fraud triangle ★

Francine Rideau, controller of Quatco Company, is reviewing the year-end financial statements with Tonya Kowalski, the company president. The financial statements currently report a net income of $563,480. Tonya is applying for a very substantial bank loan for a plant expansion, and thus would like to report a net income of at least $700,000.

Toward this end, Tonya suggests accruing several sales based on orders received, even though the goods will not be shipped at year end, and thus are technically sales of the following year. She said, "If we record sales revenue for these two large orders, our net income should be more than $700,000. This should not be a problem even next year, as we will never notice the loss of these sales then, since our sales revenue will dramatically increase once the expanded plant is in place."

Required

Identify the incentives or pressures to commit a fraud, the opportunity to perpetrate a fraud, and the rationalizations used to justify committing a fraud.

CASES

3.14 Cool Look Limited—Integrative Case Study ★ ★ ★

Cool Look Limited (CLL) is a high-end clothing design and manufacturing company that has been in business in Canada since 1964. CLL started as an owner-managed enterprise created and run by Hector Gauthier. Its ownership has stayed within the family, and Martin Roy, Hector's grandson, is the newly appointed president, chief executive officer, and chairman of the board of CLL.

You are a chartered accountant and the audit senior on the CLL audit for its fiscal year, which ended November 30, 2012. Today is December 9, 2012, and you are reviewing correspondence from CLL's bank. You come upon a letter dated November 1, 2012, from the bank's credit manager that causes you some concern (Exhibit I). You pull out your notes from your review of the board's minutes (Exhibit II) to clarify your thoughts.

EXHIBIT I

LETTER TO CLL FROM BANK

November 1, 2012

Dear Sir:

We have reviewed CLL's internal third-quarter financial statements, dated August 31, 2012. As a result of this review, we have determined that your financial ratios continue to decline and that you are in default of the covenants in our agreement for the second consecutive quarter.

However, since the bank and CLL have a long history, and because CLL continues to make required debt payments on time, we are willing to extend the $6,000,000 secured operating line of credit until the end of February 2013.

Based on CLL's February 28, 2012, internal financial statements, we will expect CLL to meet the following financial ratios. If this is not done, we reserve the right to call the loan at that time.

Ratios:

Current ratio no less than 1:1

Maximum debt-to-equity ratio (Debt/Debt + Equity) of 80%; debt is defined as total liabilities.

We thank you for your business.

Yours truly,

Mr. Charles Burbery
Credit Manager

EXHIBIT 2

EXCERPTS FROM NOTES TAKEN DURING REVIEW OF BOARD MINUTES

- August 7, 2012. Management presented a document discussing the temporary cash crunch at CLL. Management presented options to conserve cash until the Christmas buying season, when a new large contract with a U.S. chain of stores begins. One alternative was to delay remitting HST and employee withholdings. The board passed a resolution to temporarily delay remitting HST and employee withholdings until cash flows improved.
- September 5, 2012. The board received information from management regarding an incident at the factory. Some dirty rags had caught fire in a metal garbage can. The fire was put out quickly and no damage was done. Management and the board were quite relieved that the fire had not spread because CLL has not renewed its fire and theft insurance this year due to the need to conserve cash. For the same reason, CLL has not renewed the directors' liability insurance. The board decided that the renewals would be done immediately after cash flows improved.
- November 10, 2012. The board passed a motion to allow Martin Roy to postpone repayment of his interest-free shareholder loan by another six months to May 31, 2013. He owes CLL $500,000.

Financial facts

- The November 30, 2012, unadjusted financial statements show CLL's current ratio is 1.64:1.
- If the long-term debt is re-classified as a current liability, the current ratio would be 0.42:1.
- The $500,000 shareholder loan to Martin Roy is also classified as long term; however, if it is classified as current, the ratio would decline further.
- The debt-to-equity ratio is 85.8%.
- The company has traditionally had a history of positive earnings; however, in the last two years, it has reported a net loss.
- Cash on hand is $1,094,000.
- Accounts payable has increased by more than 100%.
- Share capital is reported on the 2012 balance sheet at $10,386, 000.
- CLL's long-term debt includes the $6,000,000 secured operating line of credit. The line of credit is a revolving loan, which the bank can call on three months' notice if certain financial covenants are not met. It had been classified as long-term debt in 2011 because the bank waived its right to call the loan before December 1, 2012.

Required

(a) What facts indicate that CL may not be a going concern? What facts indicate that CL may be a going concern? Make a conclusion on whether you believe it is appropriate to assume the company will remain a going concern.

(b) What are the risks related to the shareholder loan? What are three recommended procedures the auditor should perform related to the shareholder loan?

(c) What type of report should be issued if management refuses to disclose the shareholder loan as required by IFRS and ASPE? Why?

(d) Discuss the decisions made by the board. Are they ethical? Do they comply with the requirements of CSA's *Corporate Governance Guidelines*?

Source: Adapted from the Uniform Final Exam (UFE), The Institutes of Chartered Accountants in Canada and Bermuda, Paper 3, 2005.

CASE STUDY—CLOUD 9

You are a graduate working for W&S Partners, a Canadian accounting firm with offices located in each of Canada's major cities. W&S Partners has just been awarded the December 31, 2012, statutory audit for Cloud 9 Ltd. (Cloud 9). The audit team assigned to this client is:

- Jo Wadley, partner
- Sharon Gallagher, audit manager
- Josh Thomas and Suzie Pickering, audit seniors
- Mark Batten, IT audit manager
- Ian Harper and you, graduates.

As a part of the planning process for the new audit, the audit team needs to gain an understanding of Cloud 9's structure and its business environment. By understanding the client's business, the audit team can identify potential risks that may have a significant effect on the financial statements. This will assist the team in planning and performing the audit.

Required

Answer the following questions based on the additional information about Cloud 9 presented in the appendix to this book and in this and earlier chapters. You should also consider your answer to the case study questions in earlier chapters where relevant.

Your task is to research the retail and wholesale footwear industries and report back to the audit team. Your report will form part of the overall understanding of Cloud 9's structure and its environment.

You should concentrate your research on providing findings from those areas that have a financial reporting impact and are considered probable given Cloud 9's operations. In conducting your research, you should consider the following key market forces as they relate to Cloud 9's operations.

General and industry-specific economic trends and conditions
(a) What is the current condition of the economy?
(b) Is the business affected by developments in other countries, foreign currency fluctuations, or other global forces?
(c) If the industry is labour intensive, are there unusual or unique labour relations issues?
(d) How does the company's growth and overall financial performance compare with the industry, and what are the reasons for any significant differences?
(e) What is the volume and type of transactions in the business?
(f) Are the client's operations centralized or decentralized?
(g) Is the client's business cyclical in nature or influenced by seasonal fluctuations in the market?
(h) What is the susceptibility to fraud/theft? (Is the product something that can easily be stolen and has a sale market?)

Competitive environment
(i) What products does the client sell and have there been significant changes with respect to:
  i. major products or brands?
  ii. selling strategies?
  iii. sales/gross margin by product?
(j) Who are the client's major competitors, and what share of the market does each hold?
(k) Is there significant differentiation between the client's and competitors' merchandise?
(l) What is the effect on the client of potential new entrants into the market? Are there any significant barriers to entering the market?

Product information
(m) Is there a specific life cycle for the product?
(n) Is the product dependent on trends or styles?

Customer information
(o) Are there specific customers on whom the client is highly dependent?
(p) What is the overall profile of the client's customers? Have there been significant fluctuations in the client's customer base?

Supplier information
(q) Who are the key suppliers?
(r) Are the materials subject to significant price movements or influenced by external market forces?

Technological advances and the effect of the Internet
(s) How does the industry use technology?
(t) What technological trends are impacting the industry?

Laws and regulatory requirements
(u) Are the client's operations affected significantly by local or foreign legislation?
(v) What new laws and regulations recently enacted (or pending) may have significant effects on the company?

RESEARCH QUESTION 3.1

The auditor and the Ponzi scheme

Bernard Madoff was convicted in 2009 of running a Ponzi scheme, the biggest in U.S. history. A Ponzi scheme is essentially the process of taking money from new investors on a regular basis and using the cash to pay promised returns to existing investors. The high and steady returns received by existing investors are the attraction for new investors, but they are not real returns from investments.

As long as new investors keep contributing and existing investors do not seek redemptions, or the return of their money, the scheme continues. However, eventually, as in the Madoff situation, circumstances change, the scheme is discovered, and the remaining investors find that their capital has disappeared.

At age 71, Madoff was sentenced to prison for 150 years and will die in jail. Now that Madoff is behind bars, attention has turned to Madoff's auditor, David G. Friehling. Friehling is accused of creating false and fraudulent audited financial statements for Madoff's firm, Bernard L. Madoff Investment Securities LLC. Prosecutors allege that these fraudulent reports covered the period from the early 1990s to the end of 2008.

Required

(a) Research the progress of the case against David Friehling. Write a report explaining his alleged role in the Madoff Ponzi scheme and the current (at the time you write your report) state of the legal action against him.

(b) Friehling was subject to U.S. auditing standards and legislation. Explain if, and how, Friehling's alleged actions would violate Canadian auditing standards and professional ethics.

Sources: D. Searcey and A. Efrati, "Sins and admission: getting into top prisons," *The Wall Street Journal: Europe* 17–19, July 2009, p. 29; C. Bray and A. Efrati, "Madoff ex-auditor set to waive indictment," *The Wall Street Journal: Europe* 17–19, July 2009, p. 29.

RESEARCH QUESTION 3.2

Public company financial statements

The financial statements for public companies are available through the website SEDAR (www.sedar.com). This is the official site that provides access to information filed by public companies and investment funds with the CSA. The objective in making public this financial information is to enhance investor awareness of the business and affairs of public companies, and to promote confidence in the operation of capital markets in Canada. Achieving this objective relies heavily on the provision of accurate information on market participants.

Required

Go to www.sedar.com and select the most recent set of *audited annual* financial statements for a Canadian public company. Using this set of financial statements, answer the following:

(a) When planning the audit, the auditor needs to gain an understanding of the entity's structure and its business environment. To do this, the auditor focuses on identifying potential risks that may have a significant effect on the financial statements. Prepare a memo for the audit planning file and discuss the entity, industry, and economy-level factors that the auditor should consider to plan the audit for this entity.

(b) Review the financial statement notes. Are there any related parties? If so, who are the related parties? Are there many or just a few? What is disclosed in the related party note? What impact will this have on the auditor's preliminary risk assessment?

(c) With the information provided, discuss the entity's ability to continue as a going concern using the going concern indicators discussed in this chapter.

Source: www.sedar.com

FURTHER READING

Canadian Securities Administrators. (2005). *National Policy 58–201: Corporate Governance Guidelines.* www.osc.gov.on.ca/en/SecuritiesLaw_rule_20050617_58–201_corp-gov-guidelines.jsp

Chartered Accountants of Canada. (2011). *Canadian Professional Engagement Manual.* www.castore.ca/product/canadian-professional-engagement-manual-members/5

Wilson, J.D. & Root, S.J. (2000). *Internal Auditing Manual.* Warren, Gorham and Lamont Inc. www.knowledgeleader.com.

SOLUTIONS TO MULTIPLE-CHOICE QUESTIONS

1. d, 2. b, 3. a, 4. d, 5. b, 6. d, 7. a, 8. d, 9. d, 10. b.

NOTE

1. Wilson, J.D. & Root, J.J. *Internal Auditing Manual* 2nd ed. (1989), Warren Gorham & Lamont.

CHAPTER 4

Audit planning II

LEARNING OBJECTIVES

After studying this chapter, you should be able to:

1. define audit risk
2. describe the concept of materiality
3. describe how an auditor determines the audit strategy
4. outline how clients measure performance
5. describe how an auditor uses analytical procedures when planning an audit.

AUDITING AND ASSURANCE STANDARDS

CANADIAN	INTERNATIONAL
CAS 200 *Overall Objectives of the Independent Auditor and the Conduct of an Audit in Accordance with Canadian Auditing Standards*	ISA 200 *Overall Objectives of the Independent Auditor and the Conduct of an Audit in Accordance with International Standards on Auditing*
CAS 300 *Planning an Audit of Financial Statements*	ISA 300 *Planning an Audit of Financial Statements*
CAS 315 *Identifying and Assessing the Risks of Material Misstatement Through Understanding the Entity and Its Environment*	ISA 315 *Identifying and Assessing the Risks of Material Misstatement Through Understanding the Entity and Its Environment*
CAS 320 *Materiality in Planning and Performing an Audit*	ISA 320 *Materiality in Planning and Performing an Audit*
CAS 520 *Analytical Procedures*	ISA 520 *Analytical Procedures*

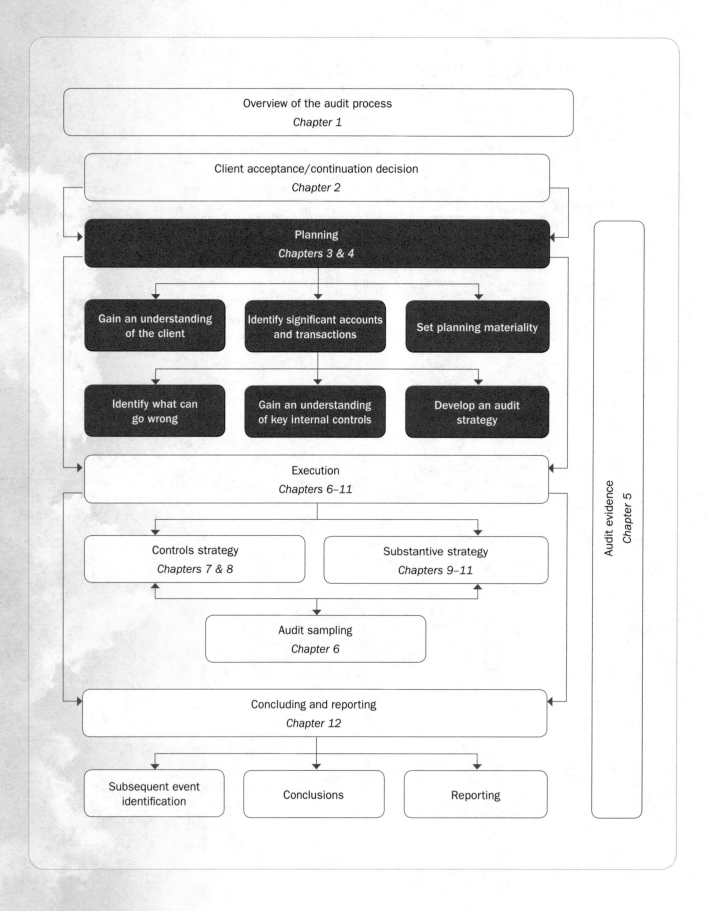

Overview of the audit process
Chapter 1

Client acceptance/continuation decision
Chapter 2

Planning
Chapters 3 & 4

Gain an understanding of the client

Identify significant accounts and transactions

Set planning materiality

Identify what can go wrong

Gain an understanding of key internal controls

Develop an audit strategy

Execution
Chapters 6–11

Controls strategy
Chapters 7 & 8

Substantive strategy
Chapters 9–11

Audit sampling
Chapter 6

Concluding and reporting
Chapter 12

Subsequent event identification

Conclusions

Reporting

Audit evidence
Chapter 5

Cloud 9

Ian Harper is still impatient. Despite his lengthy conversation with Suzie Pickering about the importance of gaining an understanding of the client in order to identify and manage audit risk, he is still not convinced that it makes a real difference to the audit. He has been with W&S Partners for only a few months, but every audit seems to him to be the same. Suzie knows that Ian has not yet seen enough audits to be able to understand the different strategies being used for different areas of the audit. How can she explain this to him?

Suzie calls Ian to her office. "I want you to work with me on the draft audit plan for Cloud 9," she tells him. "We have already started, but there is still a lot of work to do. What do you think is already in the plan?"

Ian is a bit surprised by Suzie's question, but he thinks about their previous discussions. "Well, first we have the results of the work done to assess the client before the engagement, followed by the engagement letter that sets out the work we have promised to perform. Then, after the client was accepted, we have the results of the partner's assessment of Cloud 9 Ltd.'s (Cloud 9's) corporate governance. We also have the report on the economy-wide conditions likely to affect firms in the clothing and footwear industry, plus the specific industry reports on competition, technology, and so on. I helped you with the preliminary risk assessments based on those reports, which identify the accounts most at risk. Those risk assessments are not complete, because we haven't yet done a control system evaluation. However, the preliminary risk assessments include some consideration of going concern and fraud risk.'

"That's very good," says Suzie. "So, what do you think we need to do next?"

AUDIT PROCESS IN FOCUS

In chapter 3, we began our discussion of audit planning by considering the audit as a whole. Then we focused on gaining an understanding of the client's business and identifying key risk factors that impact the audit plan. Auditors use this information to develop their audit strategy.

When developing an audit strategy, auditors consider the risks identified when gaining an understanding of their client's business. This helps them assess the risk that their audit procedures will not identify a material misstatement in the client's financial statements should one exist (audit risk). This chapter begins with a discussion of audit risk.

The process of setting planning materiality is then described. Qualitative and quantitative materiality factors are explained, as are performance and specific materiality. We then move on to describe how auditors develop their audit strategy based on their assessment of the risk of material misstatement.

The final sections of this chapter deal with performance measurement and analytical procedures. By understanding how a client assesses its own performance, an auditor gains an insight into which accounts may be at risk of material misstatement. An overview is provided of the performance measurement mechanisms used by companies that an auditor will focus on when planning their audit. The conduct of analytical procedures is a key element of the planning stage of each audit and is explained in detail in this chapter.

4.1 AUDIT RISK

1 Define audit risk.

audit risk the risk that an auditor expresses an inappropriate audit opinion when the financial statements are materially misstated

inherent risk the susceptibility of the financial statements to a material misstatement without considering internal controls

assertion statement made by management regarding the recognition, measurement, presentation, and disclosure of items included in the financial statements

significant risk an identified and assessed risk of material misstatement that, in the auditor's judgement, requires special audit consideration

control risk the risk that a client's system of internal controls will not prevent or detect a material misstatement

Audit risk is the risk that an auditor expresses an inappropriate audit opinion when the financial statements are materially misstated (CAS 200 *Overall Objectives of the Independent Auditor, and the Conduct of an Audit in Accordance with Canadian Auditing Standards*). This means that an auditor reports that in their opinion the financial statements are fairly presented when, in fact, they contain a significant error or fraud, and therefore are materially misstated. While it is impossible to eliminate audit risk altogether, an auditor will aim to reduce it to an acceptably low level. Audit risk can be reduced at the planning stage of the audit by identifying the key risks faced by the client and allocating more audit time to gathering sufficient and appropriate evidence where the risk of material misstatement is highest.

The first stage in assessing the risk of material misstatements involves an **inherent risk** assessment, where the auditor considers the risk of material misstatement before consideration of any internal controls. This is done at the financial statement level by considering such things as the nature of the business, the industry, and any previous experience with the client. Inherent risk is also assessed at the assertion level for classes of transactions, account balances, and disclosures. An **assertion** is a statement made by management regarding the recognition, measurement, presentation, and disclosure of items included in the financial statements and notes. Assertions help guide the testing conducted by an auditor. For example, if a client sells valuable goods, such as precious stones, the auditor will consider the risk of overstatement of inventory because goods may be stolen but remain recorded in the client's books. Therefore, there is a high inherent risk regarding the inventory account, as there is a risk that management's assertion about the existence of the recorded inventory may not be valid. In this example, the auditor will spend more time testing for the existence of recorded inventory than in the case of a client that sells lower valued goods.

When identifying accounts and related assertions at risk of material misstatement, some risks are classified as being more significant than others. A **significant risk** is an identified and assessed risk of material misstatement that, in the auditor's judgement, requires special audit consideration (CAS 315 *Identifying and Assessing the Risks of Material Misstatement Through Understanding the Entity and Its Environment*). When classifying risks as being significant, consideration is given to whether the risk:

- involves fraud
- is related to significant economic or accounting developments
- involves complex transactions
- involves significant related party transactions
- involves significant subjectivity in measurement of financial information
- involves significant transactions outside the client's normal course of business.

The second stage in the audit risk assessment involves an evaluation of the client's system of internal controls (**control risk**). The auditor is interested in whether the client has controls in place to minimize the risk of material misstatement in the financial statements for each account and related assertion that the auditor has identified as high risk. In the above example, if a client sells valuable goods, an auditor will assess whether the client has controls in place to reduce the risk that inventory may be stolen.

Finally, an auditor will plan to undertake detailed testing of each identified account to the extent determined necessary. This final assessment will depend upon the assessed riskiness of the account and related assertion and the deemed effectiveness of the client's system of internal controls.

Cloud 9

Ian is still struggling with the idea of risk. He knows that audit risk is the risk that the auditor issues the wrong audit report, or gives an inappropriate audit opinion, and that this risk is related to the client's circumstances. But how does that actually work in practice? What does an auditor do differently for each audit?

Suzie reminds Ian of how taking just one issue, such as how sales are made to major department stores, helped him to focus on some specific questions about accounts receivable, sales, liabilities, and inventory.

"Let's break this down," she advises. "Auditors face the risk that they issue an unmodified opinion when, in fact, the financial statements are materially misstated. So, how does a material misstatement get into the published financial statements?"

Ian works through the logic. "First, the error has to be created, either by accident or on purpose. Second, the client's control system must fail to either prevent the error from getting into the accounts or detect the error once it is in the system. And, finally, the auditor has to fail to find the error during the audit."

"Correct!" says Suzie. "Now, before we go on, I want to break down the idea of 'financial statements,' too. The financial statements are the balance sheet (statement of financial position), income statement (statement of comprehensive income), cash flow statement (statement of cash flows), statement of changes in equity, and all the notes. So when we talk of the risk of misstatements, we are referring to the risk of misstatement in every line item in each of these statements. If we focus on just one line in a balance sheet—say, accounts receivable—what are the possible misstatements that could occur?"

Ian tries to work through the logic again. "The amount could be either understated or overstated. I suppose there are lots of errors that could occur. Obviously, basic mathematical mistakes and other clerical errors could affect the total in either direction. In addition, accounts receivable would be understated if management omitted some customer accounts when calculating the total. I think the deliberate 'mistakes' are more likely those that overstate accounts receivable because they make the balance sheet look better, and probably mean that profit is overstated, too. Accounts receivable would be overstated if some of the customer accounts claimed in the total did not exist at year end, did not belong to Cloud 9, or were overvalued because bad debts were not written off, or because sales from the next period were included in the earlier period."

"Very good," says Suzie. "It is the same for every line item. Every time management prepares the financial statements it *asserts* that all of these errors did not occur—that all of the individual items in the statements are not materially misstated. The auditor has to break down the financial statements into accounts and assertions and consider the risk of misstatement for *each* assertion for *each* account. The auditor deals with the risk of material misstatement of all of the financial statements by gathering evidence at the assertion level for each account. Then all the evidence is put together so the auditor can form an overall opinion on all of the financial statements. Now, let's see how this works for Cloud 9."

4.1.1 The audit risk model and its components

Audit risk is a function of the risk of material misstatement and detection risk (CAS 200). The risk of material misstatement exists at the financial statement level and at the assertion level. At the financial statement level, the risk of material misstatement refers to risks that affect the financial statements as a whole. For example, if a client purchases a new computer system and does not adequately train staff in its use, there is a risk of errors when recording transactions used to prepare the financial statements. All accounts are at risk of material misstatement. At the assertion level, the risk of material misstatement refers to risks that affect classes of transactions, account balances, and disclosures. For example, if a client sells goods overseas, there is a risk that transactions may not be recorded correctly using appropriate exchange rates at the date of each transaction. The risk of material misstatement at the assertion level comprises inherent risk and control risk (CAS 200, para. 13).

Inherent risk is the possibility that a material misstatement could occur before consideration of the internal controls. The inherent risk assessment should incorporate the knowledge of the business as discussed in chapter 3, since many of the factors that contribute to business risks may increase inherent risk. These factors can include the competitive environment, the current economic environment, the risk of technological obsolescence, and the level of government regulation. When assessing inherent risk, it is also important to consider such factors as the nature of the entity in terms of the type of products and services offered, the size and complexity of the organization, the experience and knowledge level of employees, the pressures on management to meet earning targets, the extent of errors found in previous audits, and the accounting policies selected. For example, an organization undergoing a first-time audit will be assessed as having a higher inherent risk than an entity having a repeat audit. An organization in a highly competitive industry will have a higher inherent risk than an entity in an industry with few competitors. A geographically dispersed conglomerate will have a higher inherent risk than an organization with a single location. An entity with complex transactions, such as numerous foreign exchange transactions, will have a higher inherent risk than one with transactions only in the local currency.

Control risk is the risk that a client's system of internal controls will not prevent or detect a material misstatement. In order to determine this risk, the auditor must have an understanding of the controls in place. The auditor will consider, for example, the organization's attitudes toward controls and the control procedures implemented. If the auditor determines the controls are effective, then control risk may be assessed as lower. If control risk is assessed as lower, the auditor will plan to rely on the controls and therefore perform less detailed audit work on year-end balances. If control risk is assessed as high, where the auditor believes the controls are ineffective, the auditor will do the minimum work required on the controls and then perform more detailed work on the year-end balances.

An auditor must identify client characteristics that place the financial statements at risk of material misstatement (inherent risk, the first stage in audit risk assessment) and determine whether controls designed to limit such a risk exist and are effective (control risk, the second stage in audit risk assessment). Inherent risk and control risk are the client's risks. An auditor will determine the detection risk in response to the assessed audit risk and the client's inherent and control risk combined. **Detection risk** is the risk that the auditor's testing procedures fail to detect a material misstatement should there be one.

detection risk the risk that the auditor's testing procedures will not be effective in detecting a material misstatement

As noted in CAS 200, para. A36, audit risk can be presented in a mathematical model that indicates the relationship between its components. The model states that audit risk is inherent risk multiplied by control risk multiplied by detection risk, as shown in figure 4.1.

$$AR = IR \times CR \times DR$$

where:

AR = Audit risk

IR = Inherent risk

CR = Control risk

DR = Detection risk

FIGURE 4.1 **Audit risk**

Audit risk =	Inherent risk	Control risk	Detection risk
	High	High	Low

TABLE 4.1 **High-risk client**

The acceptable audit risk for the financial statements overall is set by the auditor at the beginning of the audit. This generally tends to be quite low (0–5 percent), and it remains constant throughout the audit. The inherent and control risks are then assessed, and the auditor determines the acceptable level of detection risk. Therefore, there is an inverse relationship between the assessed level of inherent and control risk (the risk of material misstatement) and the acceptable level of detection risk. For example, if inherent and control risk are assessed as high, the resulting detection risk will be assessed as low to bring audit risk down (see table 4.1). This means that the auditor will increase the level of reliance placed on their detailed substantive procedures, which involve intensive testing of year-end account balances and transactions from throughout the year.

Example

A client sells high-end fashion clothing and has inadequate security. Inherent risk is high for inventory as clothing may be stolen but not removed from the client's books. Control risk is high as there is inadequate security, increasing the risk of theft. The auditor cannot rely on the client's security system to reduce the risk of material misstatement associated with the existence of inventory. The auditor will set detection risk as low and spend more time checking that recorded inventory is actually on hand.

Example

A client is an importer with inexperienced clerical staff. Inherent risk is high for the accuracy of recorded purchases as they involve foreign currency translation. Control risk is high as clerical staff are inexperienced and not accustomed to recording complex foreign currency transactions. Therefore, the auditor will not test the controls. As detection risk is assessed as low, the auditor will perform more substantive testing, such as checking that purchases are recorded at appropriate amounts.

In contrast, if inherent risk and control risk are assessed as low, the auditor will assess the detection risk as high (see table 4.2). As above, there is an inverse relationship between the assessed level of inherent and control risk (the risk of material misstatement) and the auditor's acceptable level of detection risk. By assessing detection risk as high, an auditor will reduce the level of reliance placed on their detailed substantive procedures. This does not mean that the auditor is eliminating their detailed testing of year-end account balances and transactions from throughout the year. Rather, the auditor is acknowledging that the client is low risk; that is, there is a low risk of material misstatement in the client's financial statements, and extensive substantive testing is not required.

TABLE 4.2 **Low-risk client**

Audit risk =	Inherent risk	Control risk	Detection risk
	Low	Low	High

> **Example**
>
> A client sells mud bricks and has a high-voltage fence surrounding the inventory of bricks. Inherent risk is low for the existence of inventory as mud bricks are very heavy and difficult to move; thus, it is unlikely that recorded bricks do not exist. After checking that the security system is working and has been operational throughout the year, the auditor can assess control risk as low. In this case, the auditor will need to spend relatively little time checking that the recorded bricks actually exist.

> **Example**
>
> A client uses a reputable off-the-shelf computer program to record purchases of raw materials. Inherent risk is low for the accuracy of recorded purchases as the program is considered reliable; thus, purchases should be recorded accurately. After checking that the program is working properly and the transactions are recorded correctly, the auditor will verify that access to the program is limited to authorized personnel and that the program has not been tampered with. When the auditor is satisfied that the program is working well and that the client's controls are effective, the auditor can set control risk as low. In this case, the auditor will need to spend relatively little time testing that purchases are recorded accurately.

The examples provided in this section are extremes. The reality will often fall somewhere in-between, where inherent risk is high, but the client has an effective system of internal controls in place to mitigate that risk. For example, a client sells high-end fashion clothing and has adequate security, so the risk for the existence of inventory is reduced. Alternatively, inherent risk is low and the client does not consider it worthwhile investing in sophisticated control procedures (that is, any benefit is perceived to exceed the cost). For example, a client sells mud bricks and has low security, reasoning that the bricks would be very difficult to steal. In both cases, an auditor will spend a moderate amount of time testing for the existence of inventory.

Cloud 9

Cloud 9 sells customized basketball shoes. The shoes are likely to "go out of fashion" reasonably quickly, making obsolescence a big issue. These factors affect the inherent risk of inventory valuation. Based on their brief discussion of the complications surrounding transporting the shoes from the Chinese factory to the department stores in Canada, Ian can see that there is a risk of errors occurring in transactions with suppliers, which will also affect inventory balances. How high is the control risk? Much to Suzie's delight, Ian suggests that they will be able to make better assessments of both inherent and control risk for all assertions now that they have a better understanding of the client.

PROFESSIONAL ENVIRONMENT

A Canadian auditing drama

Auditors played a leading role in the dramatic accounting scandal involving the now-defunct, Toronto-based live theatre company, Livent. In one courtroom, company co-founders Garth Drabinsky and Myron Gottlieb were convicted of fraud for misstating financial results for five years. In a parallel legal drama, the firm's auditors were found guilty of professional misconduct in a case that could rewrite the standards of liability for Canadian auditors.

The Institute of Chartered Accountants of Ontario (ICAO), the self-governing body for the accounting profession in Ontario, found that the auditors failed to meet generally accepted practices of the profession. The ICAO said that the auditors suspected irregularities regarding Livent's accounting practices, even deeming the risk of financial statement error as "sky high," but they still issued a clean audit opinion of its financial statements. These actions "should have caused the (auditors) to increase their level of scepticism in conducting the audit and examining evidence," the ICAO found.

The ICAO found that the auditors questioned an agreement Livent had with a real estate company to refurbish one of its theatres. The real estate firm had the right to pull out of the redevelopment deal ahead of other investors. But Livent managers told the auditors that it cancelled the agreement because it required Livent to hold off on recording revenue from the redevelopment until later. However, the auditors discovered that the agreement was still in place, and when they asked for an explanation, Livent provided letters that were conflicting. In another instance, the auditors requested that Livent write down its production costs, which Gottlieb resisted until just days before the audit was completed when he suggested writing off $27.5 million, more than twice what the auditors were suggesting. These events should have caused the auditors to more closely scrutinize the company's books, the ICAO determined.

The auditors lost their appeal before the ICAO's appeal committee, a divisional court, and the Ontario Court of Appeal. They were slapped with more than $1.5 million in fines—the largest ICAO penalty ever, following the ICAO's longest disciplinary proceedings.

Livent, known for such productions as Phantom of the Opera, went bankrupt in 1998 after the new owners discovered accounting irregularities.

Drabinsky and Gottlieb's appeal of their criminal convictions was heard in mid-2011. Gottlieb's lawyer admitted that the two men received kickbacks from suppliers before the company went public in 1993 and that a company employee had counted the revenue as an asset on the financial statements. The lawyer said that neither Drabinsky nor Gottlieb had sophisticated accounting knowledge, and they were unaware that the company's assets were overinflated when Livent became publicly traded.

Sources: Janet McFarland, "Drabinsky Lawyer Calls for New Livent Trial," *The Globe and Mail,* May 2, 2011; Janet McFarland, "Gottlieb Not Involved in Major Livent Decisions: Lawyer," *The Globe and Mail,* May 3, 2011; "Court Reinstates Ruling Against Livent Auditors," *Toronto Star,* June 6, 2011; "Livent Auditors' Misconduct Appeal Denied," *Canadian Business,* February 18, 2009; Institute of Chartered Accountants of Ontario, Appeal Committee decision, February 13, 2009; Sandra Rubin, "Auditors Take Centre Stage," *Financial Post,* May 29, 2002.

BEFORE YOU GO ON

1.1 What are the three components of audit risk?

1.2 What is the relationship between audit risk and detection risk?

1.3 What are four factors that affect inherent risk?

4.2 MATERIALITY

Materiality is used to guide audit testing and to assess the validity of information contained in the financial statements and their notes. Information is considered material if it impacts the decision-making process of the users of the financial statements. This

 2 Describe the concept of materiality.

materiality information that impacts the decision-making process of users of the financial statements includes information that is misstated or omitted but should be disclosed. CAS 320 *Materiality in Planning and Performing an Audit* provides guidelines on materiality from an audit perspective.

Materiality is a key auditing concept and is assessed during the planning stage of every audit. This preliminary assessment of materiality guides audit planning and testing. Before explaining how an auditor arrives at their preliminary materiality assessment, it is important to understand the qualitative and quantitative factors to be considered when determining materiality.

4.2.1 Qualitative and quantitative factors

When determining materiality, the auditor needs to consider both quantitative and qualitative factors as information can be considered material because of its nature and/or its magnitude. These concepts are explained below. The auditor should also consider whether performance materiality or specific materiality are necessary. This is also explained below.

Qualitative factors

Information is considered material if it affects a user's decision-making process. This may be due to factors other than the magnitude of misstatements. For example, a misstatement due to fraud is considered to be significant due to its nature. When such a misstatement is uncovered, it is investigated further by an auditor. After gaining an understanding of the client, an auditor will ensure that all disclosures in the financial statements and the notes to the financial statements accurately reflect the auditor's understanding of the client. Therefore, when reading the notes to the financial statements, an auditor will assess accounting disclosure accuracy and compliance with any regulations and legislation, and ensure that any legal matters that should be disclosed are disclosed correctly. If any of these disclosures are inaccurate or omitted in error, an auditor will consider the potential impact on users. If an auditor believes that an inaccurate disclosure or omission will affect a user's decision-making process, the inaccuracy or omission is considered to be material, and the auditor will request that the client amends the disclosure or includes any omitted information.

Items that should be considered significant due to their nature include a change in an accounting method, related party transactions, a change in operations that affects the level of risk faced, and the danger of breaching a debt covenant.

Quantitative materiality factors

quantitative materiality information that exceeds an auditor's preliminary materiality assessment

Information is considered **quantitatively material** if it exceeds an auditor's preliminary materiality assessment. An auditor uses their professional judgement to arrive at an appropriate materiality figure for each client. The *Canadian Professional Engagement Manual (C•PEM)* suggests guidelines for this calculation, which we discuss below. Materiality is a percentage of an appropriate base. An auditor will select an appropriate base and then decide on the percentage to use depending on the client's circumstances.

In selecting an appropriate base, an auditor can choose an item from the balance sheet or income statement. Balance sheet bases are generally total assets or equity. Income statement bases are profit before tax, revenue, expenses, or gross profit. An auditor will select an appropriate base, using their professional judgement based on

- 5–10% of normalized pre-tax profit
- 0.5–2 % of total assets
- 0.5–5% of equity
- 0.5–2% of revenues or expenditures

FIGURE 4.2 **Common bases and percentages used for materiality**

their knowledge of the client and the needs of financial statement users for decision-making. For example, if a client is publicly listed, net income before tax is likely to be important as it drives dividends and return-on-investment decisions. Therefore, the base selected would be net income before tax. However, if a client is a not-for-profit organization, either assets or expenses are more likely to be chosen as a base.

Net income before tax will not be used as a base when a client is in a loss position or profits vary significantly from one year to the next. In such a case, revenue may be used as a base. For newly established companies with little or no revenue, equity or total assets are generally the preferred base. These choices depend on an auditor's knowledge of their client and on the auditor's professional judgement.

Once a base is selected, consideration should be given to whether there are any unusual or non-recurring items that may need to be "normalized" or adjusted for. Examples of such normalizing items include bonuses paid to owner managers for tax-planning purposes, unusual gains and losses, and significant repair and maintenance expenses of a non-recurrent nature. Once a selected base is normalized, an appropriate percentage is determined. The *C•PEM* provides guidelines on the percentages to use when calculating materiality (see figure 4.2). Normally, any item that is 10 percent or greater of profit before tax is considered to be material, and any item that is less than 5 percent of profit before tax is considered to be immaterial. The determination of the appropriate percentage to determine materiality of any item is a matter for professional judgement. When using total assets or revenue as a base, the percentages fall to 0.5–1 percent and when equity is the base, the percentages are .05–2 percent. Whichever base is used, there is a percentage above which items are deemed to be clearly material, a percentage below which items are deemed to be immaterial, and a range in the middle that is a matter for an auditor's professional judgement.

Performance materiality

The auditor may also determine **performance materiality**. This is an amount less than materiality, which is set by the auditor to reduce the likelihood that any uncorrected and undetected misstatements within a class of transactions, account balances, or disclosures, in aggregate, do not exceed overall materiality. For example, if an auditor assesses that there is a risk of recorded inventory not being valued appropriately, materiality when testing for the valuation of inventory may be set lower than it would when testing for other assertions. The determination of performance materiality is again a matter of professional judgement; however, the *C•PEM* suggests 60–85 percent of overall materiality may be appropriate.

Specific materiality

The third level of materiality the auditor may determine is called **specific materiality** for account balances, specific transactions, and disclosures. Specific materiality is relevant when some areas of the financial statements are expected to influence

performance materiality an amount less than materiality, which is set to reduce the likelihood that a misstatement in a particular class of transactions, account balances, or disclosures, in aggregate, do not exceed materiality for the financial statements as a whole

specific materiality information that is relevant when some areas of the financial statements are expected to influence the economic decisions made by users of the financial statements

Trudo Inc. has a December 31 year end. Although Trudo is a private company, its annual financial statements must be audited as a condition of Trudo's long-term debt agreement with Canada Bank. Extracts from the entity's financial statements are as follows:

Revenue	$10,525,000
Pre-tax profit	$1,525,000 (before bonus to owner of $200,000)
Total assets	$15,500,000

Planning materiality calculation:

1% of revenue = 1% × 10,525,000 = $105,250

1% of total assets = 1% × $15,500,000 = $155,000

5% of normalized pre-tax profits = 5% × ($1,525,000 + $200,000) = $86,250

Trudo is a profit-oriented entity and the primary user of the financial statements is the bank. Therefore, the most appropriate base for materiality is pre-tax profit. This is because the bank is primarily concerned with Trudo's ability to generate a positive net income to repay its loan in the future.

Performance materiality: To reduce the risk of an aggregate material misstatement in account balances and classes of transactions, performance materiality is 60 percent of planning materiality:

60% × $86,250 = $51,750

Specific materiality: As there is no indication that users of the financial statements will be affected by any particular account balance, specific materiality is not required.

Conclusion: Materiality for financial statements overall is $85,000 (rounded). This means total misstatements should be less than $85,000 for the auditor to issue an unmodified opinion.

Performance materiality is $50,000 (rounded). This means any error found in a specific account (that is, accounts receivables) greater than $50,000 is considered material.

However, if one error is found that exceeds performance materiality (that is, $65,000), but total errors remain below overall materiality, the auditor can conclude the financial statements are not materially misstated.

FIGURE 4.3 **Example of materiality**

the economic decisions made by users of the financial statements. For example, if an entity has a bank loan, and one of the requirements of the loan agreement is to maintain a particular current ratio, the auditor should consider the need to determine specific materiality for the accounts included in the current ratio calculation. This would be necessary if a material misstatement less than overall financial statement materiality could impact the bank's decision to continue extending the loan. Figure 4.3 shows a sample materiality calculation.

4.2.2 Materiality and audit risk

Materiality and audit risk are both considered in identifying and assessing the risk of a material misstatement. They both determine the nature, timing, and extent of the audit work performed, and they are both considered when evaluating the effect of uncorrected misstatements on the financial statements and in forming the opinion in the auditor's report.

However, when selecting a percentage within the appropriate range, the auditor should not use audit risk to make this determination. Audit risk is based on factors that relate to the entity, while materiality is based on the needs of the users of the financial statements. If materiality were assessed in terms of audit risk, a higher risk audit would have a lower materiality than a low-risk audit for a similar entity. But since the information needs of the users are the same, it is inappropriate to imply that smaller misstatements will be identified and additional audit work performed on the higher risk engagement to reduce audit risk to an acceptably low level.[1]

Cloud 9

Throughout their conversation, Suzie and Ian have been discussing "material" misstatements in financial statements. What is material for Cloud 9? Suzie explains that if they set materiality at a low level in the planning phase, they will have to plan to gather more and better quality evidence to be sure that a mistake of this low magnitude has not occurred. This will give the auditor confidence that the opinion is the appropriate one, but it will also increase the cost of the audit.

Ian is worried about getting the materiality level right. "What if we set it too low or too high?" Suzie explains that all parts of the audit plan, including the materiality decision, will be reviewed throughout the audit and changed if necessary.

BEFORE YOU GO ON

2.1 What is qualitative materiality?

2.2 What is quantitative materiality?

2.3 What is the most appropriate materiality base for a for-profit entity? Why?

4.3 AUDIT STRATEGY

3 Describe how an auditor determines the audit strategy.

audit strategy strategy that sets the scope, timing, and direction of the audit and provides the basis for developing a detailed audit plan

CAS 300 *Planning an Audit of Financial Statements* requires that an auditor establish an overall **audit strategy**, which sets the scope, timing, and direction of the audit and provides the basis for developing a detailed audit plan. The audit strategy chosen depends on the auditor's preliminary inherent and control risk assessment (that is, the auditor's overall assessment of the risk of material misstatement). Tables 4.3 and 4.4 provide examples of audit strategies for two extreme cases: a high-risk client and a low-risk client.

When inherent and control risk are assessed as high (see table 4.3), the risk of material misstatement is assessed as high and, therefore, detection risk will be low to reduce audit risk to an acceptably low level. There is an inverse relationship between audit risk (a client's inherent and control risk combined) and detection risk, as previously stated. By assessing control risk as high, an auditor has determined that the client's system of internal controls is non-existent, very poor, or unlikely to be effective in mitigating the inherent risks identified.

TABLE 4.3 **Audit strategy—high-risk client**

Audit risk	Inherent risk	Control risk	Detection risk
	High	High	Low
Audit strategy		No (or very limited) tests of controls	Increased reliance on substantive tests of transactions and account balances

For example, a client sells expensive medical testing equipment and has limited security. Not many of these pieces of equipment have to go missing or be stolen for there to be a material impact on the value of the inventory. No regular inventory counts are performed either. In this case, inherent risk is high for the inventory as it may be recorded but not actually on hand. In this case, control risk is high as there are no controls in place to mitigate (reduce) the identified risk.

By assessing control risk as high (see table 4.3), an auditor will adopt a predominantly **substantive audit strategy**. When this audit strategy is adopted, an auditor will gain the minimum necessary knowledge of the client's system of internal controls as required by the auditing standards (CAS 315), but will generally not conduct tests of those controls. If a client's system of internal controls is non-existent, very poor, or unlikely to be effective in mitigating an identified inherent risk, there is generally no point in testing the internal controls because the auditor will not be planning to rely on them. Instead, an auditor will increase their level of reliance on detailed substantive procedures, which involves intensive testing of year-end account balances and transactions from throughout the year. An exception is where an auditor has identified a significant risk. In this case, an auditor will gain an understanding of the client's controls relevant to that risk (CAS 315, para. 29). For example, if a client has significant transactions that involve estimation, an auditor will review the processes used by management to make those estimations. If a client does not have adequate controls to address significant risks, this is considered a significant deficiency in a client's system of internal controls (CAS 315, para. A126).

When assessing control risk as low (see table 4.4), an auditor will generally plan to perform a **combined audit strategy** where the auditor obtains a detailed understanding of the client's system of internal controls and plans to rely on that system to identify, prevent, and detect material misstatements.

Once an auditor has gained a detailed understanding of their client's system of internal controls, they will conduct extensive tests of those controls. When the cost of testing controls exceeds the benefit expected, an auditor may decide not to test the client's internal controls. For low-risk clients, if tests of controls are conducted and found to be effective, an auditor will plan on reducing their reliance on detailed substantive testing of transactions and account balances. However, an auditor can never completely rely on a client's system of internal controls and will always conduct some substantive procedures to gather independent evidence regarding the numbers that appear in the client's financial statements. Control risk and testing of controls are discussed further in chapters 7 and 8.

For example, a client sells nuts and bolts and conducts regular inventory counts. Inherent risk is low as a significant number of nuts and bolts would have to be stolen before there was a material impact on the amount recorded for inventory. The auditor will plan on testing the effectiveness of the inventory counts and the timeliness with which records are updated for any inventory losses.

substantive audit strategy strategy used when the auditor does not plan to rely on the client's controls and increases the reliance on detailed substantive procedures that involve intensive testing of year-end account balances and transactions from throughout the year

combined audit strategy strategy used when the auditor obtains a detailed understanding of their client's system of internal controls and plans to rely on that system to identify, prevent, and detect material misstatements

TABLE 4.4 **Audit strategy—low-risk client**

Audit risk	Inherent risk	Control risk	Detection risk
	Low	Low	High
Audit strategy		Increased reliance on tests of controls	Reduced reliance on substantive tests of transactions and account balances

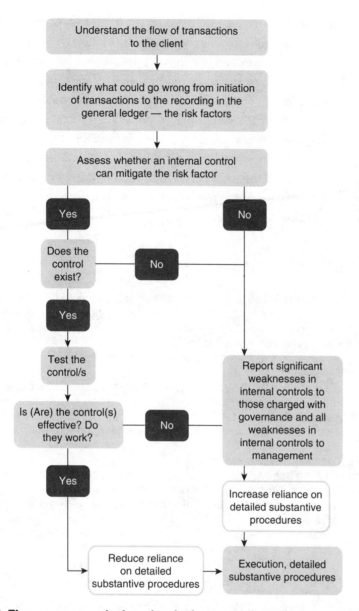

FIGURE 4.4 **The process used when developing an audit strategy for risks identified**

The example provided above is for the development of an audit strategy at the financial statement (client) level. In practice, an audit strategy is developed for each identified risk at the assertion level. Figure 4.4 shows the process used when developing an audit strategy for identified risks. Risks are identified when gaining an understanding of the client as described in chapter 3. Part of that process involves conducting a **walkthrough** for each significant class of transactions. This means that each transaction flow is traced from inception to the recording in the general ledger. When conducting a transaction walkthrough, an auditor will identify the risk factors.

For each identified risk, the first step is to assess whether an internal control could reduce the likelihood of a material misstatement occurring as a result of the risk. If the auditor believes one or more internal controls could be designed to mitigate the identified risk, the auditor will assess whether the client has controls in place; that is, do they exist?

If the client has one or more appropriate controls in place, the audit strategy is to test the effectiveness of those controls; that is, do they work? If, after testing the controls, the auditor concludes that they are effective, the auditor plans to rely on those controls

walkthrough tracing a transaction through a client's accounting system

and is able to reduce their reliance on detailed substantive procedures. However, if the auditor tests the controls and believes them to be ineffective (that is, the controls do not work), the auditor cannot rely on the controls. In this case, the auditor reports any significant deficiencies to those charged with governance, and identifies other weaknesses to management. The auditor also makes recommendations on improving the controls, and increases the reliance placed on detailed substantive procedures.

If the client does not have appropriate controls for the identified risk in place, the audit strategy is to conduct few or no tests of controls for the identified risk. In this case as well, the auditor reports the weaknesses identified to those charged with governance, makes recommendations on improving the controls, and increases the reliance placed on detailed substantive procedures.

Cloud 9

Suzie explains that Cloud 9's audit could be planned and conducted in different ways, depending on the audit strategy adopted. In fact, the overall audit strategy sets the scope, timing, and direction of the audit, and guides the development of the detailed audit plan.

"What audit strategy would be suitable for Cloud 9? Start by thinking about the scope of the audit," she prompts Ian. "The scope is about the different types of work we have to do—some audits have extra requirements."

"I suppose we should find out if Cloud 9's parent company has any special requirements. The fact that it is a Canadian public company might mean it has some additional regulations that apply," Ian suggests. "Plus, Cloud 9's statements would have to be consolidated into the parent's accounts. We would have to make sure that we plan to do the work they would need for that."

"That is a good start," says Suzie. "What else?"

"Well, I can think of a number of other things, such as whether any other auditors will be involved (including Cloud 9 Inc.'s internal auditors); whether any foreign currency translation issues exist; whether any industry-specific regulations must be followed (although I don't think this is as big an issue for clothing and footwear as it would be for banks, for example); whether any service organizations are involved, such as payroll services; and whether computer-aided audit technology is to be used."

"Very good," says Suzie. "That will do for now. What about timing issues? Are there any special considerations we should take into account for Cloud 9?"

"What date does the audit have to be finished?" asks Ian.

"Good question," says Suzie. "If we have a deadline, we obviously have to work toward it."

"Also," says Ian, "when are our staff available and when are their key people available to talk to us?"

"Yes," says Suzie. "This is all kind of basic. But if we don't ask these really important questions, we will find ourselves unable to meet the deadlines and perhaps be under pressure to cut corners. We also have to think about the timing of requests to third parties for information and so on. Now, can you think of anything to say about the direction of the audit?"

"I understand about the extra requirements and working out the timing. But I don't really know what you mean by 'direction,'" Ian says, confused.

"We have already discussed it to some extent," Suzie explains. "Remember when we spoke about the risk for Cloud 9 created by complex inventory transactions, and dealing with purchases from international suppliers? 'Direction' is about where we think there should be extra attention because of higher risk, and how we give that extra attention. We could, for example, make sure that we have suitable experts available, if required, to value the inventory. This is also where we bring in our work on materiality, both setting materiality for planning purposes and identifying the material account balances. In our plan, we need to allocate additional time to areas where there may be higher risk of material misstatement. And, one of our biggest tasks will be considering the evidence about the design and operating effectiveness of internal controls at Cloud 9, which we haven't yet considered in detail."

"I see," says Ian. "If we assess the internal controls as being strong, then we plan to do more testing of controls (to confirm our assessment), and less testing of the underlying substance of transactions and account balances. We have to put this in our plan now. But what if our first thoughts about controls are wrong? Our plan will be wrong!"

"That happens," replies Suzie. "That is why a plan is constantly changing as we gather more information about the client. Particularly, as in this case, for a new client that we don't have a lot of detailed information on yet. However, we already know what accounts are important to Cloud 9—its previous years' statements and interim results show us that. We have an understanding of the drivers of its profits and the pressure to increase profits coming from the head office. We also know about its new store opening this year (including the new debt) and the change in marketing strategy. We actually know quite a lot—certainly enough to make a start on a detailed audit plan."

BEFORE YOU GO ON

3.1 What is the purpose of developing an overall audit strategy?

3.2 What is a substantive audit strategy and when might an auditor adopt this approach?

3.3 To whom will an auditor report uncovered deficiencies in a client's system of internal controls?

4.4 CLIENT APPROACHES TO MEASURING PERFORMANCE

Part of the process used when gaining an understanding of a client involves learning how the client measures its own performance. The **key performance indicators (KPIs)** used by a client to monitor and assess its own performance and the performance of its senior staff provide an auditor with insight into the accounts that their client focuses on when compiling its financial statements and indicate which accounts are potentially at risk of material misstatement.

Some KPIs are common to many clients, such as return on assets and return on shareholder funds. Other KPIs will vary from industry to industry and client to client. For example, a client in the airline industry is concerned about revenue per passenger kilometre, a client in the retail industry is concerned about inventory turnover, and a client in the finance industry is concerned about its risk-weighted assets and interest margins. It is very important for an auditor to understand which KPIs a client is most concerned about throughout the year so that the audit can be planned around relevant accounts. It is inappropriate to assume that all clients will use the same KPIs. It is also inappropriate to assume that a client will use the same KPIs every year. Just as businesses change their focus, KPIs change to help businesses achieve new goals.

4 Outline how clients measure performance.

key performance indicators (KPIs) measurements, agreed to beforehand, that can be quantified and reflect the success factors of an organization

4.4.1 Profitability

It is common for companies to use **profitability** measures to assess their performance and that of their senior staff. Companies will track their revenue and expenses over time and assess any variability. They will compare their revenue and expenses with close competitors and assess their ability to compete, as well as provide valuable insights to management as to whether results are matching expectations based on known factors such as seasonality or economic downturns. This also provides the auditor with valuable insights into the expectations of management.

profitability the ability of a company to earn a profit

A company will track revenues from month to month to identify and explain trends. Large companies will compare revenues earned across divisions to highlight good and poor performance. Comparisons between divisions may be used to assess how well the managers of those divisions are controlling costs. Changes from one year to the next may reflect an increased cost of doing business or highlight that it may be time to source cheaper suppliers.

price-earnings (PE) ratio market price per share to earnings per share

earnings per share (EPS) profit to weighted average ordinary shares issued

Companies are concerned about their shareholders (owners). The **price-earnings (PE) ratio** (market price per share divided by earnings per share) shows how much a shareholder is willing to pay per dollar of earnings. **Earnings per share (EPS)** (profit divided by weighted average ordinary shares issued) reflects the book value of the company. When a client's PE ratio or EPS are in decline, an auditor may be concerned that management may be under pressure to manipulate earnings.

Retailers and manufacturers are generally concerned about their inventory turnover (cost of goods sold divided by inventory). An assessment of this ratio is made within the context of the industry in which a company operates. For example, a company that sells perishable goods, such as ice cream, requires a much higher turnover than a company that sells non-perishable goods, such as furniture. If a client's inventory turnover falls sharply, an auditor may be concerned that stock is overvalued.

4.4.2 Liquidity

liquidity the ability of a company to pay its debts when they fall due

Liquidity is the ability of a company to meet its needs for cash in the short and long term. It is vital for a company to have access to cash to pay its debts when they fall due. If it cannot meet these obligations, a company may go into liquidation. Companies require cash to pay their employees' wages, utility bills, supplier bills, interest payments on money lent, dividends to shareholders, and so on. In the longer term, companies need cash to repay long-term debt and undertake capital investment.

Companies enter into debt covenants with lenders when taking on significant loans. That is, they promise to maintain specified profitability, liquidity, or other financial ratios, or to seek the lender's permission before taking on new borrowings or acquiring other companies. These covenants are written into the borrowing contracts and restrict a company's activities. If a company breaches a debt covenant, it will need to renegotiate or repay the loan.

By understanding how their client measures and assesses its own performance and any restrictions implied by debt covenants, an auditor will gain a deeper understanding of the accounts potentially at risk of material misstatement. An auditor will use their own ratio calculations and trend analyses to identify any unusual fluctuations that warrant further investigation. This analysis is referred to as analytical procedures, which are explained in detail in the next section.

Cloud 9

In her discussions with the partner, Jo Wadley, Suzie learns that the senior people in the Cloud 9 finance section are entitled to participate in the company's employee stock purchase plan and also to receive stock options in the parent company if revenue targets are met. The Canadian parent company is a public company and its share price, which determines the value of the stock options, reflects market expectations about the group's future profits.

Cloud 9 has taken on additional debt this year, and costs are rising because of issues associated with its drive to increase market share. When these results are consolidated into the group, they increase debt/equity ratios and decrease profitability ratios, potentially reducing the value of the stock options. Suzie decides to allocate time in the audit plan to consider whether these pressures could impact any of the senior staff's incentives and increase audit risk.

PROFESSIONAL ENVIRONMENT

Profitability restatements help bring down Nortel

Returning to profitability is good news for any company. But when the independent auditors of Canadian telecommunications giant Nortel saw the firm posting profits in 2003 after losing money in the 2001 Internet bust, they were sceptical. The auditors informed the head of the company's audit committee that the board should re-examine how profits were determined. They felt that Nortel could not adequately justify its accounting for millions of dollars in special charges related to future liabilities for its recent downsizing, such as lawsuits and employee severance packages.

The board of directors hired a law firm with securities regulation expertise to investigate Nortel's accounting practices, and it found that the company's finance department lacked accounting expertise, internal controls, and clear accountability.

The U.S. Securities and Exchange Commission (SEC), which regulates Nortel's trading in the United States, later alleged that the company improperly reversed at least $274 million in special charges it had previously deducted from revenues, which had resulted in huge losses in 2001 and 2002. The result: instead of posting a loss of $220 million in the first quarter of 2003, Nortel reported a $54-million profit.

Over the next several quarters, Nortel continued to restate its financial numbers as more accounting errors came to light, and its share price dropped steadily. Shareholders launched class action lawsuits seeking billions of dollars in compensation. Nortel reached a deal with the SEC and Ontario Securities Commission to pay more than $20 million in fines and to regularly report on its efforts to get its accounting house in order. The company estimated that it spent more than $400 million on independent auditors and other accounting experts to revamp its accounting system and practices.

As various civil and criminal legal actions against it continued, Nortel filed for bankruptcy protection in early 2009. But the accounting scandal, along with the recession and increased competition, meant that it could not emerge solvent. Nortel's share price, peaking at $1,231 at the height of the telecom boom, had fallen to mere pennies. Later in 2009, under court supervision, Nortel began selling its assets to big-name telecommunications companies willing to spend millions to acquire its patents and other intellectual property.

What was at one point the world's biggest supplier of telecom equipment, with share values accounting for more than one-third the value of the S&P/TSX Composite Index, was auctioned off to the highest bidders.

Sources: James Bagnall, "The Beginning of the End: How an Accounting Scandal Permanently Weakened Nortel," *The Ottawa Citizen,* November 2, 2009; "Nortel Then and Now," *Canadian Business,* February 18, 2009; Andrew Wahl, "The Good, the Bad, and the Ugly: Nortel Networks," *Canadian Business,* March 30, 2009; The Canadian Press, "Nortel Sale Mediation Process Fails," *The Globe and Mail,* April 13, 2011; CBC News, "The Wild Ride of Canada's Most-Watched Stock," February 27, 2008, www.cbc.ca.

BEFORE YOU GO ON

4.1 What is a PE ratio?

4.2 Explain how internal performance reports may be used.

4.3 What is a debt covenant?

4.5 ANALYTICAL PROCEDURES

⑤ Describe how an auditor uses analytical procedures when planning an audit.

analytical procedures an evaluation of financial information by studying plausible relationships among both financial and non-financial data

execution stage detailed testing of controls and substantive testing of transactions and accounts

CAS 520 *Analytical Procedures* defines **analytical procedures** as an evaluation of financial information by studying plausible relationships among both financial and non-financial data. They involve the identification of fluctuations in accounts that are inconsistent with the auditor's expectations based upon their understanding of their client. For example, if an auditor is aware that the client has borrowed a significant amount of money in the previous financial year, a reduction in the client's debt-to-equity ratio would be unusual and would warrant further investigation. It is essential that an auditor has clear expectations about the client's results for the reporting period before conducting analytical procedures, so that unexpected fluctuations can be correctly identified and investigated. An auditor's expectations are based on their understanding of the client, the industry in which it operates, and the economy as a whole.

Analytical procedures are conducted throughout an audit. During the planning stage, analytical procedures are used to aid in the risk identification process. During the **execution stage**, analytical procedures are an efficient method of identifying differences between recorded amounts and the auditor's expected values that require further investigation (CAS 520.5d). At the final review stage, analytical procedures are used to assess whether the financial statements reflect the auditor's knowledge of their client. In this section, we will concentrate on the application of analytical procedures at the planning stage of the audit. The use of analytical procedures when conducting substantive procedures is discussed in chapters 9 to 11.

Analytical procedures are conducted at the planning stage of the audit to:
- highlight unusual fluctuations in accounts
- aid in the identification of risk
- enhance the understanding of a client
- identify the accounts at risk of material misstatement
- reduce audit risk by concentrating audit effort where the risk of material misstatement is greatest.

CAS 315 stipulates that an auditor should perform analytical procedures as part of their risk identification process. Analytical procedures include simple comparisons, trend analysis, common-size analysis, and ratio analysis. Each of these forms of analysis is now discussed, followed by a review of factors to consider when undertaking analytical procedures.

4.5.1 Comparisons

Simple comparisons are made between account balances for the current year and the previous year and for the current year and the budget. When comparing account balances from one year to the next, significant changes can be tracked and investigated further by the auditor. An auditor will assess these changes in light of their expectations based on their understanding of the client and any changes experienced over the past year. For example, if the client has opened a new retail outlet, sales may be expected to have increased since last year. When comparing account balances with budgeted amounts, an auditor is concerned with uncovering variations between actual results and those expected by the client. Significant unexpected variations are discussed with client personnel.

Figure 4.5 illustrates a comparative income statement, which shows how the auditor will calculate the dollar and percentage changes for all line items for both the income

XYZ Company
Comparative Income Statement

	Current year	Prior year	Dollar change	% change	Explanation
Revenue	1,790,000	1,630,000	160,000	9.8%	
Cost of goods sold	1,320,000	1,275,000	45,000	3.5%	
Gross margin	470,000	355,000	115,000	32.4%	
Gross margin %	26.26%	21.78%		4.5%	
Operating expenses:					
Rent	60,000	58,000	2,000	3.4%	
Wages	150,000	145,000	5,000	3.4%	
Interest	75,000	25,000	50,000	200.0%	
Amortization	64,000	64,000	0	0.0%	
	349,000	292,000	57,000	19.5%	
Net income	121,000	94,000	27,000	28.72%	

FIGURE 4.5 **Comparative income statement of XYZ Company**

statement and the balance sheet. The auditor will identify areas where the calculated results are different from expectations based on the knowledge of the business and the evidence gathered to date, and will highlight the areas that may require further audit work. For example, if the current economy is in a slowdown, is it reasonable for revenues to grow by almost 10 percent? If the auditor determines that this is a mature company in a stable industry and expects that revenues will stay relatively flat, then this is an unexpected result, indicating that more work may be needed in this area. If this is an industry with relatively stable margins, why did the gross margin increase by 4.5 percent? Why did the cost of sales not increase in the same proportion as the revenues? These results may indicate that the company is missing some expenses and this area requires further investigation.

4.5.2 Trend analysis

Trend analysis (horizontal analysis) involves a comparison of account balances over time. It is conducted by selecting a base year and then restating all accounts in subsequent years as a percentage of that base. Trend analysis allows the auditor to gain an appreciation of how various accounts have changed over time. When conducting a trend analysis, it is important for an auditor to consider significant changes in economy-wide factors, such as a recession, which may affect their interpretation of the trend. Figure 4.6 provides an example of a trend analysis.

trend analysis a comparison of account balances over time

Various accounts can be selected for inclusion in a trend analysis. Accounts that vary from one year to the next are generally the focus. In the trend analysis depicted in figure 4.6, 2008 was selected as the base year. The following years appear as a percentage increase or decrease of the 2008 amount. For example, sales in 2009 were 20 percent lower than sales in 2008; in 2010, sales were only 10 percent lower than the 2008 figure; and in 2011, sales were 20 percent higher than the 2008 amount. A trend analysis allows an auditor to assess movements in the accounts over time and to determine whether the underlying trends discovered through this type of analysis match their understanding of the client and its activities over the period under review.

	2008	2009	2010	2011
	$M	%	%	%
Income statement items				
Sales	250	(20)	(10)	20
Cost of sales	110	(10)	0	10
Interest expense	10	(30)	30	0
Wages expense	70	(20)	30	6
Rent expense	40	0	0	0
Balance sheet items				
Cash	400	20	10	25
Inventory	350	30	20	10
Trade receivables	300	(10)	5	15

FIGURE 4.6 **Trend analysis**

4.5.3 Common-size analysis

common-size analysis a
comparison of account balances to
a single line item

Common-size analysis (vertical analysis) involves a comparison of account balances to a single line item. In the balance sheet, the line item used is generally total assets. In the income statement, the line item used is generally sales or revenue. A common-size analysis allows the auditor to gain a deeper appreciation of how much each account contributes to the totals presented in the financial statements. By preparing common-size accounts for a number of years, an auditor can trace the relative contribution of various accounts through time. Figure 4.7 provides an example of a common-size analysis.

The common-size analysis depicted in figure 4.7 shows that the cost of sales grew and then reduced as a proportion of sales. This reduction may reflect a change in prices charged by suppliers, a change in prices charged to customers, or the quantity

	2008	2009	2010	2011
	%	%	%	%
Income statement items				
Sales	100	100	100	100
Cost of sales	44	50	48	40
Interest expense	4	4	6	3
Wages expense	28	28	22	25
Rent expense	16	20	18	13
Balance sheet items				
Cash	5	4	4	3
Inventory	20	27	23	23
Trade receivables	18	25	22	18
Payable	15	15	17	16
Total assets	100	100	100	100

FIGURE 4.7 **Common-size analysis**

of goods on hand. In the balance sheet, inventory levels rose and then dropped, which may indicate a buildup of inventory on hand when sales dropped in 2009.

4.5.4 Ratio analysis

Ratio analysis is conducted by an auditor to assess the relationship between various financial statement account balances. An auditor will calculate profitability, liquidity, and solvency ratios.

Profitability ratios

Profitability ratios reflect a company's ability to generate earnings and ultimately the cash flow required to pay debts, meet other obligations, and fund future expansion. Table 4.5 shows the common profitability ratios: gross profit margin, profit margin, return on assets, and return on shareholders' equity.

The gross profit and profit margins indicate the proportion of sales turned into profits. The **gross profit margin** indicates whether a seller of goods has a sufficient markup on goods sold to pay for other expenses. A markup is the difference between the selling price and cost price for goods sold. A decline in this ratio indicates that a client may be paying more for its inventory or charging less to its customers. If the gross profit margin continues to decline, the client may face making an overall loss if it is not able to cover its operating expenses.

> **gross profit margin** gross profit to net sales

The **profit margin** indicates the profitability of a company after taking into account all operating expenses. By looking at the trend in the profit margin over time, the auditor is able to identify variability in the profit-earning capacity of their client. If the profit margin is steadily falling, this may affect the future viability of the client. If the profit margin varies widely from year to year, this indicates volatility and uncertainty, which makes it difficult to assess the fair presentation of the current reported earnings without further investigation.

> **profit margin** profit to net sales

The **return on assets (ROA)** indicates the ability of a company to generate income from its average investment in total assets. The **return on equity (ROE)** indicates the ability of a company to generate income from the funds invested by its common (ordinary) shareholders. If a company is unable to generate a sufficient return on funds invested, there may be insufficient funds available to pay dividends and invest in future growth. An auditor will calculate these ratios to assess trends in profitability. If the ROA and ROE are falling, they will affect the ability of a client to generate funds to pay dividends and interest and to repay loans.

> **return on assets (ROA)** profit to average assets

> **return on equity (ROE)** profit to average equity

An auditor will make comparisons between the current year and previous years to identify trends in their client's profitability. Comparisons will also be made with budgeted results and with competitors. When comparing with budget, an auditor will assess

RATIO	DEFINITION
Gross profit margin	$\dfrac{\text{Gross profit}}{\text{Net sales}}$
Profit margin	$\dfrac{\text{Profit}}{\text{Net sales}}$
Return on assets	$\dfrac{\text{Profit}}{\text{Average assets}}$
Return on shareholders' equity	$\dfrac{\text{Profit}}{\text{Average equity}}$

TABLE 4.5 **Common profitability ratios**

how profitable the client is compared to management's expectations. An auditor will discuss any significant variance with management. When comparing the client with competitors, an auditor will assess the client's profitability relative to companies of a similar size operating in the same industry. Any significant trends that appear unusual when compared to previous years, budget, or competitors are investigated further by an auditor as they indicate that there may be a risk of a material misstatement.

Liquidity ratios

Liquidity ratios reflect a company's ability to meet its short-term debt obligations. If a company is unable to pay its debts when they fall due, the company may lose key employees, suppliers may refuse to supply goods, and lenders may recall funds borrowed. An auditor is concerned with the client's liquidity situation and will alert the client to any potential going concern issues. Table 4.6 shows a number of short-term liquidity ratios. These include the current ratio and the asset-test (quick) ratio. The inventory and receivables turnovers are used as liquidity ratios as well as indicators of managerial efficiency and client activity.

The **current ratio** indicates how well current assets cover current liabilities. A ratio that is greater than one indicates that a company should be able to meet its short-term commitments when they fall due. In reality, this will depend on the ability of a company to convert its inventory and receivables into cash on a timely basis. The **asset-test (quick) ratio** indicates how well liquid (cash or near cash) assets cover current liabilities. Liquid assets include cash, short-term investments, and receivables. Acceptable current and asset-test ratio benchmarks vary from one industry to another. An auditor will compare the trend in both ratios over time to assess whether their client's liquidity situation is improving or deteriorating. An auditor will also compare the client's ratios with the industry average to assess the client's liquidity relative to close competitors. If a client's liquidity situation is deteriorating or is poor when compared to the industry average, an auditor may be concerned about the future viability of the company.

Inventory turnover measures how many times a company sells its inventory in a year. An auditor will look at the trend in this ratio to determine whether inventory is being turned over more or less frequently from year to year. This turnover will vary widely from one industry to another. For example, the turnover for a supermarket would be expected to be much higher than for a luxury boat manufacturer. An auditor will compare the inventory turnover for their client to the industry average to determine whether their client is competitive and has as high a turnover as its rivals. If a client operates in a high-technology industry or the fashion industry, where customer preferences change quickly, a slowing down of inventory turnover may indicate that the client is not keeping up with change. When a client's inventory turnover slows, an

current ratio current assets to current liabilities

asset-test (quick) ratio liquid assets to current liabilities

inventory turnover cost of sales to average inventory

TABLE 4.6 **Short-term liquidity ratios**

RATIO	DEFINITION
Current ratio	$\dfrac{\text{Current assets}}{\text{Current liabilities}}$
Asset-test (quick) ratio	$\dfrac{\text{Cash + Short-term investments + Receivables (net)}}{\text{Current liabilities}}$
Inventory turnover	$\dfrac{\text{Cost of sales}}{\text{Average inventory}}$
Receivables turnover	$\dfrac{\text{Net credit sales}}{\text{Average net receivables}}$

auditor will spend more time testing for the valuation of inventory, as stock may need to be written down in response to slowing demand.

Receivables turnover measures how many times a year a company collects cash from its accounts receivable customers. A slowdown in this ratio may indicate that the client is making sales to customers who are unable to pay for their goods on a timely basis or that the client is not efficiently following up on customers who are late in paying. If receivables turnover falls, an auditor will spend more time considering the adequacy of the allowance for doubtful accounts.

receivables turnover net credit sales to average net receivables

Solvency ratios

Solvency ratios are used to assess the long-term viability of a company. Liquidity ratios tend to take a short-term view of a company; solvency ratios have a long-term perspective. Table 4.7 shows common solvency ratios: the debt to equity ratio and times interest earned.

RATIO	DEFINITION
Debt to equity ratio	$\dfrac{\text{Liabilities}}{\text{Equity}}$
Times interest earned	$\dfrac{\text{Profit before income taxes and interest expense}}{\text{Interest expense}}$

TABLE 4.7 **Common solvency ratios**

The **debt to equity ratio** indicates the relative proportion of total assets being funded by debt relative to equity. A high debt to equity ratio increases the risk that a client will not be able to meet interest payments to borrowers when they fall due. Companies with long-term debt are more likely to have a debt covenant with a lender, which restricts the company's activities. An auditor will consider the trend in the client's debt to equity ratio over time. An increasing ratio increases the risk that a client will not be able to repay their loans when they fall due, and the risk that a client will breach a debt covenant, as many covenants restrict the raising of additional debt. An auditor will also compare a client's debt to equity ratio with similar companies in the same industry as this ratio tends to vary across industries.

debt to equity ratio liabilities to equity

Times interest earned measures the ability of earnings to cover interest payments. A low ratio indicates that a client will have difficulty meeting its interest payments to lenders. An auditor will consider how this ratio has changed over time. A downward trend is a concern as it indicates that lenders may charge the client a higher rate of interest on future borrowings. At the extreme, lenders may recall monies lent if the client does not meet interest payments.

times interest earned profit before income taxes and interest expense

4.5.5 Factors to consider when conducting analytical procedures

There are a number of factors to consider when conducting analytical procedures. The first is the reliability of client data. If the auditor believes there is a significant risk that the client's records are unreliable due to, for example, poor internal controls, then the auditor is less likely to rely on analytical procedures. Another issue is the ability to make comparisons over time. If the client has changed accounting methods, this will reduce the comparability of the underlying data. In this case, an auditor will need to restate prior years' financial statements using the current accounting methods before making any comparisons. If past results are unaudited, they are considered less reliable for comparison purposes.

During the planning stage of an audit, an auditor may have access only to the client's interim results. In this case, an auditor will need to annualize revenue and expense items before making comparisons with the prior year. If the client earns revenues evenly throughout the year, it is appropriate to double the half-year revenues. If the client earns more revenues in some months relative to others (for example, an ice seller in warmer months), trends must be considered when annualizing interim results.

When comparing actual financial results to budgeted results, an auditor will consider the reliability of the budget. This can be assessed by comparing budget to actual results for prior years. If the client continually overestimates earnings, for example, an auditor can take this into account when comparing actual and budgeted results for the current period.

When benchmarking a client with industry data, care must be taken. If the client is significantly smaller or larger than most companies in its industry, the comparison may not be valid. If competitors do not use the same accounting methods, the comparison is problematic. If the client has very different results and ratios compared with the industry average, there may be a problem with industry data rather than with client data.

In conducting analytical procedures, the following information sources are generally considered to be reliable:

- information generated by an accounting system that has effective internal controls
- information generated by an independent reputable external source
- audited information
- information generated using consistent accounting methods
- information from a source internal to the client that has proven to be accurate in the past (for example, information used to prepare budgets).

After conducting analytical procedures, an auditor will investigate all significant unexpected fluctuations: the existence of fluctuations where none were expected and the absence of fluctuations where they were expected. An example of the former would be a significant increase in sales for no apparent reason. An example of the latter would be no significant change in inventory turnover when the auditor is aware that sales have fallen significantly.

Cloud 9

Ian volunteers to start the analysis of Cloud 9's interim results and previous period's financial data. He has previously attended a training session on the W&S Partners' software that he will use to produce reports showing unusual relationships and fluctuations. Suzie is grateful for the help but cautions Ian, "You do realize that judging what is 'unusual' is a little more complex than getting a software program to identify a change above a certain percentage? You need considerable industry experience and client knowledge to make sense of the information. For example, no change in a figure can be more suspicious than a large change, depending on the circumstances."

"Yes, I realize that," Ian says, "and I know that I don't have the experience to complete the analysis, but I am hoping that I will learn from you by seeing what you do with the data and reports that I hadn't considered doing."

BEFORE YOU GO ON

5.1 Why are liquidity ratios calculated?

5.2 Define the gross profit ratio and explain what it indicates.

5.3 What is a trend analysis and why might an auditor use this form of analysis?

SUMMARY

❶ Define audit risk.

Audit risk is the risk that an auditor expresses an inappropriate audit opinion when the financial statements are materially misstated. The three components of audit risk are inherent risk, control risk, and detection risk.

❷ Describe the concept of materiality.

Information is considered to be material if it impacts the decision-making process of users of the financial statements.

❸ Describe how an auditor determines the audit strategy.

The audit strategy is a key component of the planning stage of the audit. It sets the scope, timing, and direction of the audit and provides the basis for developing a detailed audit plan. An audit strategy will depend on the auditor's preliminary inherent and control risk assessment.

❹ Outline how clients measure performance.

By understanding how a client measures its own performance, an auditor can plan the audit to take into consideration areas where the client may be under pressure to achieve certain outcomes.

❺ Describe how an auditor uses analytical procedures when planning an audit.

Analytical procedures are conducted at the planning stage of the audit to identify unusual fluctuations, help identify risks, help when gaining an understanding of a client, identify the accounts at risk of material misstatement, and reduce audit risk by concentrating audit effort where the risk of material misstatement is greatest. There are many processes that can be used when conducting analytical procedures. The processes discussed in this chapter included simple comparisons, trend analysis, common-size analysis, and ratio analysis.

KEY TERMS

MULTIPLE-CHOICE QUESTIONS

4.1 A predominantly substantive audit strategy:

(a) is appropriate when internal controls are very strong.

(b) means that the auditor will gain the minimum necessary knowledge of the client's system of internal controls.

(c) requires the auditor to conduct extensive control testing.

(d) means that the auditor will conduct some interim testing and minimal year-end account balance testing.

4.2 A combined audit strategy:

(a) is appropriate when internal controls are minimal.

(b) means that the auditor will gain the minimum necessary knowledge of the client's system of internal controls.

(c) requires the auditor to conduct extensive control testing.

(d) means that the auditor will conduct extensive testing of year-end account balances.

4.3 Profitability ratios are used to assess performance and:

(a) companies will be interested in trends in the ratios.

(b) companies will try to have the same ratio in each month of operation.

(c) should be the same for all divisions of the company.

(d) companies will track their revenue and expenses over time and assess any variability.

4.4 Common uses of analytical procedures include:

(a) risk identification during the audit planning stage.

(b) estimation of account balances during the audit execution stage.

(c) overall assessment of the financial statements at the final review stage of the audit.

(d) all of the above.

4.5 An auditor is interested in the client's inventory turnover ratio because it helps the auditor understand:

(a) if the industry is the same as another industry.

(b) if the client is as competitive and has as high a turnover as the industry average.

(c) if the client's accounts receivable customers are paying their accounts on time.

(d) if the client is in the right industry.

4.6 Analytical procedures:

(a) cannot be performed on interim data.

(b) are not affected by different accounting methods between the client and other members of the industry.

(c) must take into account seasonal variation in the client's business.

(d) are only useful if the client's variance from budget is low.

4.7 An auditor will identify accounts and related assertions at risk of material misstatement:

(a) after testing internal controls.

(b) before writing the audit report.

(c) in order to plan the audit to focus on those accounts.

(d) to eliminate audit risk.

4.8 For an audit, the auditor can control:

(a) inherent risk.

(b) control risk.

(c) financial risk.

(d) detection risk.

4.9 An example of an item that is material is:

(a) a theft of $100.

(b) an undisclosed lawsuit for $1 million.

(c) an undisclosed related party.

(d) all of the above.

4.10 Testing controls means that:

(a) the auditor can completely rely on a client's system of internal controls.

(b) no substantive testing is required.

(c) the auditor can plan to reduce their reliance on detailed substantive testing of transactions and account balances.

(d) all of the above.

REVIEW QUESTIONS

4.1 Explain the approach adopted by auditors of identifying accounts and related assertions at risk of material misstatement. How does this approach help reduce audit risk to an acceptably low level?

4.2 How does the auditor's preliminary assessment of materiality affect audit planning? What does an auditor consider when making the preliminary assessment of materiality?

4.3 The materiality of an item is assessed relative to a particular base number. What are some of the choices for this base and what factors guide the auditor in this choice?

4.4 If an auditor adopts a predominantly substantive strategy for the audit, do they have to consider and test the client's internal controls? If an auditor adopts a combined audit strategy, do they have to perform any substantive procedures? Explain.

4.5 A client has physical controls over inventory, including a locked warehouse with access restricted to authorized personnel. Testing of these physical controls over inventory shows that they are very effective. Can the auditor conclude that the valuation assertion for inventory is not at risk? Explain.

4.6 Explain using examples how you could use analytical procedures in assessing the risk of misstatement of sales revenue.

4.7 What are some possible explanations of a change in the gross profit margin? How could the auditor investigate which of these explanations is the most likely cause of the change in the ratio?

4.8 What is the difference between liquidity and solvency? Why does this difference matter to an auditor?

4.9 Consider the following statement: "If inherent and control risk are high, the auditor will set detection risk as low, to bring audit risk down." Explain how setting detection risk as low brings down audit risk.

4.10 What is the relationship between audit risk and materiality, and evidence? Why does setting a lower materiality level affect the number of items that are material and the assessment of the sufficiency and appropriateness of audit evidence?

PROFESSIONAL APPLICATION QUESTIONS

Basic ★   Moderate ★★   Challenging ★★★

4.1 Audit risk and revenue ★   ❶

Ajax Finance Ltd. (Ajax) provides small- and medium-sized personal, car, and business loans to clients. It has been operating for more than 10 years and run throughout its life by Bill Schultz. Bill has been the public face of the finance company, appearing in most of its television and radio advertisements. He has developed a reputation as a friend of the "little person" who has been mistreated by the large finance companies and banks.

Ajax's major revenue stream is generated by obtaining large amounts on the wholesale money market and lending in small amounts to retail customers. Margins are tight, and the business is run as a "no frills" service. Offices are modestly furnished and the mobile lenders drive small, basic cars when visiting clients. Ajax prides itself on full disclosure to its clients, and all fees and services are explained in writing to clients before loans are finalized. However, although full disclosure is made, clients who do not read the documents closely can be surprised by the high exit charges when they wish to make early repayments or transfer their business elsewhere.

Ajax's mobile lenders are paid on a commission basis; they earn more when they write more loans. For example, they are encouraged to sell credit cards to any person seeking a personal loan. Ajax receives a commission payment from the credit card companies when it sells a new card and Ajax also receives a small percentage of the interest charges paid by clients on the credit card.

Required

What are the inherent and control risks for Ajax's revenue? Explain which assertions are most at risk.

4.2 Audit risk components and materiality ★ ★

Carl's Computers imports computer hardware and accessories from China, Japan, Korea, and the United States. It has branches in every capital city, and the main administration office and central warehouse is in Montreal. There is a branch manager in each store plus a number (depending on the size of the store) of permanent staff. There are also several casual staff who work on weekends—the stores are open both Saturday and Sunday. Either the branch manager or a senior member of the permanent staff is on duty at all times to supervise the casual staff. Both casual and permanent staff members are required to attend periodic company training sessions covering product knowledge and inventory and cash handling requirements.

The inventory is held after its arrival from overseas at the central warehouse and distributed to each branch on receipt of an inventory transfer request authorized by the branch manager. The value of inventory items ranges from a few cents to several thousand dollars. Competition is fierce in the computer hardware industry. New products are continuously coming onto the market, and large furniture and office supply discount retailers are heavy users of advertising and other promotions to win customers from specialists like Carl's Computers. Carl's Computers' management has faced difficulty keeping costs of supply down and has started to use new suppliers for some computer accessories such as printers and ink.

Required

(a) Explain the inherent risks for inventory for Carl's Computers. How would these risks affect the financial statement accounts?
(b) What strengths and weaknesses in the inventory control system can you identify in the above case?
(c) Comment on materiality for inventory at Carl's Computers. Is inventory likely to be a material balance? Would all items of inventory be audited in the same way? Explain how the auditor would deal with these issues.

4.3 Inherent risk assessment ★ ★

LLL Avionics Ltd. has contacted your certified general accounting firm to inquire about the cost of an external audit. The company's president explained that he feels that "the previous auditor charged too much and only issued a qualified opinion." Your firm was recommended to LLL by your bank manager. LLL has a large loan request at the bank, and the interest rate of the new loan will depend on the audit opinion. As the partner in charge of this file, you interviewed the president and controller of the company as part of your decision to accept or reject LLL as a client. You have found that the company has a new design for an aircraft and plans to borrow funds from the bank and to issue common shares to finance a prototype plane to test the design. The new funds will also greatly improve the company's balance sheet by providing the funds to bring the company's existing bank loan up-to-date. If the design is successful, more common shares will be issued for more capital.

The controller was very helpful in your discussions, and you note his high level of enthusiasm for the project as this is his first job at this level. However, the president was not so helpful and seemed annoyed with your questions.

Required

Indicate five factors in the above situation that point to high inherent risk. Explain your answer.

Source: © CGA-Canada. Reproduced with permission.

4.4 Audit risk ★★

This is the second year that your firm is auditing JJ Company, which is developing a new drug for a rare form of cancer. The company is controlled by Jack, who purchased the shares from the previous owner this year. You have been informed that the company's bank requires an audit to increase the company's operating line of credit. Jack has also informed you that he would like to convert the company into a public company next year, and sell shares on the stock exchange, as he does not expect that the company will have significant revenues for at least four years. At present, the company has two other drugs under patent, and these products produce sufficient revenues to service the debt load of the company, including anticipated new borrowing this year. However, these patents will expire in five years, so Jack is trying to plan ahead.

Required

Indicate whether you feel the overall audit assurance should be high or low in the audit of JJ. State two reasons to support your answer.

Source: © CGA-Canada. Reproduced with permission.

4.5 Materiality ★★★

Ana used 0.5–5 percent of gross profit in determining materiality of $70,000 in her audit of XYZ Inc., a company that builds replacement engines for tractors and combines. She used the $70,000 amount as her performance materiality, identifying account balances and transactions to be tested. She also used materiality as a guide when deciding on the appropriate audit opinion in her report.

Required

(a) Provide three other examples of a base (other than 0.5–5 percent of gross profit) that an auditor could use in determining materiality in a financial statement audit.
(b) Suppose Ana initially reviewed parts inventory account #102641–1 and found that none of the account transactions exceeded $45,000. Does this mean that none of these transactions should be selected for examination, based on her materiality decision of $70,000? Explain your answer.

Source: © CGA-Canada. Reproduced with permission.

4.6 Planning, performance, and specific materiality ★★★

Claytonhill Beverages Ltd. is 100 percent owned by Buzz Bottling. While the company has in the past been profitable, it incurred a loss for the year ended December 31, 2012. The parent company, Buzz Bottling, has indicated that if Claytonhill incurs another loss, it will put the subsidiary up for sale. In response, Claytonhill is looking to expand its market share and therefore its profitability by performing private labelling for a nationwide supermarket chain, ValueFoods Inc. Private labelling involves producing and packaging pop and other non-alcoholic beverages under the ValueFoods label. However, in order to proceed with this endeavour, Claytonhill needs a packaging facility dedicated exclusively to co-packing. To finance this expansion, the company has applied to the Better Business Bank for financing.

The bank has indicated that before it will approve the loan application it would like to see audited financial statements for 2012. It also wants to ensure the entity has a current ratio of 2:1.

Claytonhill Beverages has provided you, their new auditor, with the following draft (unaudited) financial statements:

Revenue

Sales	2,057,505
Cost of goods sold	1,445,450
Gross margin	612,055

Less:

General and administration costs	
(including bonuses of $100,000)	775,899
Net income before tax	(163,844)

Balance Sheet as at December 31, 2012

Assets

Current assets

Total cash	179,825
Accounts receivable, net	64,475
Prepaid expenses	3,004
Inventory	1,507,413
Total current assets	1,754,717

Capital assets

Office furniture & equipment, net	85,106
Building, net	964,224
Land	2,004,933
Total capital assets	3,054,263

Total assets	4,808,980

Liabilities

Current liabilities

Accounts payable	799,255
Other accrued expenses	44,875
Warranty provision	9,456
Current portion long-term debt	25,000
Total current liabilities	878,586

Long-term liabilities

Bank loans	2,200,000
Total long-term liabilities	2,200,000

Total liabilities	3,078,586

Equity

Common shares	248,000
Retained earnings	1,482,394
Total equity	1,730,394

Liabilities and Equity	4,808,980

FIGURE 4.8 **Unaudited financial statements for Claytonhill Beverages**

Required

(a) Identify the users of the financial statements and their needs.

(b) Given the users' needs, what is the most appropriate base for materiality?

(c) Calculate the three levels of materiality and conclude on each.

(d) What impact did audit risk have on the materiality calculation?

4.7 Determining an audit strategy ★ ★ ★

Niagara Dairy is a boutique cheese maker based in the Niagara region of Ontario. Over the years, the business has grown by supplying local retailers and, eventually, by exporting cheese products. In addition, there is a "farm-gate" shop and café located next to the main processing plant in Niagara-on-the-Lake, which serves tourists who also visit other specialist food and wine businesses in the region. Quality control over the cheese manufacturing process and storage of raw materials and finished products at Niagara Dairy is extremely high. The company is committed to high quality control because poor food-handling practices could cause a drop in cheese quality or contamination of cheese products, which would ruin the business very quickly.

The export arm has been built up to become the largest revenue earner for the business by the younger of the two brothers who have run Niagara Dairy since it was established. Jim Bannock has a natural flair for sales and marketing but is not as good at completing the associated detailed paperwork. Some of the export deals have been poorly documented, and Jim often agrees to different prices for different clients without consulting his older brother, Bob, or informing the sales department. Consequently, there are often disputes about invoices, and Jim makes frequent adjustments to accounts receivable using credit notes when clients complain about their statements. Jim sometimes falls behind in responding to customer complaints because he is very busy juggling the demands of making export sales and running his other business, Café Consulting, which provides contract staff for the café business at Niagara Dairy.

Required

(a) Identify the factors that would affect the preliminary assessment of inherent risk and control risk at Niagara Dairy.

(b) Explain how these factors would influence your choice between a predominantly substantive strategy and the combined audit strategy for sales, inventory, and accounts receivable.

4.8 Planning analytical procedures using profitability ratios ★ ★

Li Chen has calculated profitability ratios using data extracted from his client's pre-audit trial balance. He also has the values for the same ratios for the preceding two years (using audited figures). Table 4.8 presents the data for the gross profit and profit margins.

	2012	**2011**	**2010**
Gross profit margin	0.45	0.35	0.40
Profit margin	0.09	0.15	0.20

TABLE 4.8 **Gross profit and profit margin**

Li is a little confused because the profit margin shows declining profitability, but the gross profit margin has improved in the current year and is higher in 2012 than in the previous two years.

Required

(a) Make a list of possible explanations for the pattern observed in the gross profit and profit margins.

(b) Which of your explanations suggests additional audit work should be planned? For each, explain the accounts and/or transactions that would need special attention in the audit.

4.9 Analytical procedures for liquidity and solvency issues ★ ★ ★

Bright Spark Fashion has retail outlets in six large regional cities in eastern Canada. The shops are run by local managers but purchasing decisions for all stores are handled by Ray Bright, the owner of the business. Fashion is an extremely competitive business. Bright Spark Fashion sells only for cash and generates sales through a reputation of low prices for quality goods. The winter range is quite slow moving, but summer fashion sells very well, providing a disproportionate amount of the business's sales and profits. Ray is constantly monitoring cash flow, and negotiating with suppliers about payment terms and banks about interest rates and extensions of credit.

Jenna Kowalski has the tasks of assessing the liquidity and solvency of Bright Spark Fashion and identifying the audit risks arising from this aspect of the business. She discovers that a major long-term debt is due for repayment two months after the close of the financial year, but Ray is having difficulty obtaining approval from his current bank for a renewal of the debt for a further two-year term. In addition, interest rates have risen since the last fixed rate was agreed upon two years ago, adding an additional 2 percentage points to the likely rate for the new debt (if it is approved).

The seasonality of the business means that inventory levels fluctuate considerably. At the end of the financial year (December 31), Ray placed pre-paid orders for the summer fashion line, and the goods started arriving in the stores by February.

Required

(a) What liquidity and solvency issues does Bright Spark Fashion face? Explain the likely impact of each issue on the usual liquidity and solvency ratios.
(b) Advise Jenna Kowalski about the audit risks for Bright Spark Fashion and suggest how she could take these into account in the audit plan.

4.10 Risk assessment ★ ★   ❶

Featherbed Surf & Leisure Holidays Ltd. (Featherbed) is a resort company based on Vancouver Island. Its operations include boating, surfing, diving, and other leisure activities: a backpackers' hostel, a family hotel, and a five-star resort. Justin and Sarah Morris own the majority of the shares in the Morris Group, which controls Featherbed. Justin is the chairman of the board of directors of both Featherbed and the Morris Group, and Sarah is a director of both companies as well as the CFO of Featherbed.

In February 2012 Justin Morris approached your audit firm, KFP Partners, to carry out the Featherbed audit for the year ended June 30, 2012. Featherbed has not been audited before but this year the audit has been requested by the company's bank and a new private equity investor group that has just acquired a 20 percent share of Featherbed.

Featherbed employs 30 full-time staff. These workers are employed in administration, accounting, catering, cleaning, and hotel/restaurant duties. During peak periods, Featherbed also uses part-time and casual workers. These workers tend to be travellers visiting the west coast who are looking for short-term employment to help pay their travelling expenses.

Justin and Sarah have a fairly laid back management style. They trust their workers to work hard for the company and reward them well. The accounting staff, in particular, are very loyal to the company. Justin tells you that some accounting staff enjoy their jobs so much they have never taken any holidays, and hardly any workers ever take sick leave.

There are three people currently employed as the accountants, the most senior of which is Peter Pinn. Peter heads the accounting department and reports directly to Sarah. He is in his fifties and plans to retire in two or three years. Peter prides himself on his ability to delegate most of his work to his two accounting staff, Kristen and Julie. He claims he has to do this because he is very busy developing a policy and procedures manual for the accounting department. This delegated work includes opening mail, processing payments and receipts, banking funds received, performing reconciliations, posting journals, and performing the payroll function. Julie is a recently graduated chartered accountant. Kristen works part-time—coming into the office on Mondays, Wednesdays, and Fridays. Kristen is responsible for posting all journal entries into the accounting system and the payroll function. Julie does the balance of the work, but they often help each other out in busy periods.

Required

Using the factors in the above scenario assess audit risk.

Source: Adapted from the Institute of Chartered Accountants Australia's CA Program's *Audit and Assurance Exam*, May 2008.

Questions 4.11 and 4.12 are based on the following case.

Securimax Limited (Securimax) has been an audit client of KFP Partners (KFP) for the past 15 years. Securimax is based in Waterloo, where it manufactures high-tech armour-plated personnel carriers. Securimax often has to go through a competitive market tender process to win large government contracts. Its main product, the small but powerful Terrain Master, is highly specialized and Securimax only does business with nations that have a recognized, democratically elected government. Securimax maintains a highly secure environment, given the sensitive and confidential nature of its vehicle designs and its clients.

In September 2011, Securimax installed an off-the-shelf costing system to support the highly sophisticated and cost-sensitive nature of its product designs. The new system replaced a system that had been developed in-house, as the old system could no longer keep up with the complex and detailed manufacturing costing process that provides tender costings. The old system also had difficulty with the company's broader reporting requirements.

The manufacturing costing system uses all of the manufacturing unit inputs to calculate and produce a database of all product costs and recommended sales prices. It also integrates with the general ledger each time there are product inventory movements such as purchases, sales, wastage, and damaged stock losses.

Securimax's end of financial year is December 31.

Source: Adapted from the Institute of Chartered Accountants Australia's CA Program's *Audit and Assurance Exam*, May 2008.

4.11 Assessing inherent risk ★ ★ ★

Required

Based on the background information, what are the major inherent risks in the Securimax audit? Consider both industry and entity risks in your answer.

4.12 Assessing preliminary materiality ★ ★ ★

Required

Discuss the factors to consider when determining preliminary materiality for Securimax.

Questions 4.13 and 4.14 are based on the following case.

Fellowes and Associates Chartered Accountants is a successful mid-tier accounting firm with a large range of clients across Canada. During the 2011 financial year, Fellowes and Associates gained a new client, Health Care Holdings Group (HCHG), which owns 100 percent of the following entities:

- Shady Oaks Centre, a private treatment facility
- Gardens Nursing Home Ltd., a private nursing home
- Total Laser Care Limited (TLCL), a private clinic that specializes in laser treatment of skin defects.

Year end for all HCHG entities is June 30.

On April 1, 2011, Gardens Nursing Home Ltd. switched from its "home grown" patient revenue system to the HCHG's equivalent system. HCHG is confident that its "off-the-shelf" enterprise system would perform all of the functions that Gardens Nursing Home's home-grown system performed.

Gardens Nursing Home's home-grown patient revenue system comprised the following:

1. **Billing system**—a system that produced the invoice to charge the patient for services provided, such as accommodation, medications, and medical services. This software included a complex formula to calculate the patient bill allowing for government subsidies, pensioner benefits, and private medical insurance company benefits plans.
2. **Patient database**—a master file that contained personal details about the patient as well as the period of stay, services provided, and the patient's medical insurance details.
3. **Rates database**—a master file that showed all accommodation billing rates, rebate discounts, and government assistance benefits.

At the request of the board, the group's internal audit unit was involved throughout the entire conversion process. The objective of its engagement, as the board stated, was to "make sure that the conversion worked without any problems."

As part of the planning arrangement for the 2011 financial statement audit, the audit partner, Tania Fellowes, asked her team to speak with a number of Gardens Nursing Home staff about the impact of the switching to the HCHG patient revenue system. Below is an extract of the staff's comments:

- "There were some occasions where we invoiced people who were past patients. This seems to have happened when they shared the same surname as a current patient."
- "We seem to have some patient fee invoices where, for no reason, we have billed patients at a lower room rate than what we have on the rates database."
- "Lately we've had an unusually high number of complaints from recently discharged patients that the fee invoice we sent them does not line up with the agreed upon medical fund and government subsidy rates. We then found out that halfway through last month someone from the IT team made a software change to fix a bug in the billing calculation formula."
- "There was some sort of power surge last Friday, and we had to re-enter every patient invoice that we had processed in the last two weeks."

Source: Adapted from the Institute of Chartered Accountants Australia's CA Program's Audit and Assurance Exam, December 2008.

4.13 Planning in context of IT system changes ★ ★ ★

Required

Identify the audit risks associated with the installation of the new IT system for patient revenue.

4.14 Determining audit strategy ★ ★ ★

Required

Comment on the audit strategy likely to be adopted for the audit of patient revenue for Gardens Nursing Home.

4.15 Audit risk and materiality ★ ★ ★

Gold Explorers Inc. (Gold Explorers) is a major Canadian gold mining corporation. Gold Explorers has mines and development projects in Canada (Northern Ontario and British Columbia), the United States, and South America. Shares of Gold Explorers trade on three major international stock exchanges—New York, Toronto, and London. Gold Explorers is known as one of the lowest-cost producers of gold worldwide, and in the current fiscal year it achieved record gold production levels. Due to the record levels, revenues increased this year. Revenues grew from $1,357 million last year to $1,432 million in this year's draft financial statements (all dollar figures are U.S. dollars). Corresponding gross profit figures are $642 million for last year and $678 million for the current year.

Terrence, chairman and CEO of Gold Explorers, is known throughout the Canadian mining industry as a man of principle and integrity. He governs Gold Explorers in accordance with three key guiding principles, which he articulated in 1978 when he founded the company. These principles are entrepreneurial management, financial discipline, and corporate responsibility. Adherence to these principles has given Gold Explorers a stable and dedicated work force, and a strong balance sheet that includes $623 million in cash, virtually no net debt, and shareholders' equity of just over $3 billion ($3,023 million). In addition, Gold Explorers boasts an "A" credit rating and has access to a $1-billion line of credit. Gold Explorers' efforts with respect to corporate responsibility have been recognized internationally, and the company was awarded eight major awards for environmental protection in the past four years. In spite of this, however, Gold Explorers has had to expend some money on site restoration in the past in order to meet the requirements of environmental compliance orders.

Your firm has been Gold Explorers' auditors for the past eight years. In that time, there have been very few misstatements discovered during the audits, which have required adjustments to the draft financial statements. In fact, Raj, the partner in charge of the audit, and Margaret, audit manager, have found the audit to be almost routine in the past four years of their involvement with Gold Explorers. However, this year promises to be a little different. Responding to the need for consolidation in the industry, Gold Explorers merged this year in an all-share deal with a major U.S. gold company that had significant mining operations in Canada. Furthermore, immediately prior to year end, Gold Explorers reassessed the carrying value of its capital assets. The reassessment resulted in a $1.1-billion writedown of Gold Explorers' property, plant, and equipment assets to a carrying value of $3,565 million. Even with this writedown, Gold Explorers' total assets remain at a substantial $4,535 million; however, the writedown resulted in a significant net loss before taxes of $944 million in the current year, compared to net incomes before taxes of $441 million and $443 million in the preceding two years.

Required

(a) Identify eight factors that Margaret needs to consider that would affect her assessment of audit risk, inherent risk, and control risk for this year's audit of Gold Explorers. For each factor you identify, indicate which one of the three risks would be affected and state whether the factor is likely to increase or decrease Margaret's assessment of that risk relative to other companies in other industries. In addition, for each factor, explain why the risk will increase or decrease. Set up your answer in the following manner:

FACTOR	TYPE OF RISK	IMPACT (INCREASE/DECREASE)	EXPLANATION

(b) Identify the most appropriate basis for determining materiality for this year. Justify the basis of the materiality you selected and explain why other bases are not appropriate.

Source: © CGA-Canada. Reproduced with permission.

CASES

4.16 Integrative Case Study—AutoCare Ltd. ★ ★ ★

AutoCare Ltd. (ACL) is a federally incorporated public company formed in 2007 to manufacture and sell specialty auto products such as paint protection and rust proofing. By 2010, ACL's board of directors felt that the company's products had fully matured and that it needed to diversify. ACL aggressively sought out new "concepts," and in November 2011, it acquired the formula and patent for a new product—synthetic motor lubricant (Synlube).

Synlube is unlike the synthetic motor oils currently on the market. Its innovative molecular structure accounts for what management believes is its superior performance. Although Synlube is more expensive to produce and, therefore, has a higher selling price than its conventional competitors, management believes that its use will reduce maintenance costs and extend the life of the equipment in which it is used.

ACL's main competitor is a very successful multinational conglomerate that has excellent customer recognition of its products and a large distribution network. To create a market niche for Synlube, management is targeting commercial businesses in western Canada that service vehicle fleets and industrial equipment.

ACL's existing facilities were not adequate to produce Synlube in commercial quantities, so in June 2012 ACL began construction of a new blending plant in a western province. The new facilities became operational on December 1, 2012.

ACL has financed its recent expansion with a term bank loan. Management is considering a share issue later in 2013 to solve the company's cash flow problems. ACL's March 31, 2012, draft balance sheet is provided in Exhibit I.

Although they had been with the company since its inception, ACL's auditors have just resigned. It is now April 22, 2012. You and a partner meet with the CEO to discuss the services your firm can provide to ACL for the year ended March 31, 2012. During your meeting, you collect the following information:

· ACL has started a lawsuit against its major competitor for patent infringement and industrial espionage. Management has evidence that it believes will result in a successful action and wishes to record the estimated gain on settlement of $4 million. Although no court date has been set, legal correspondence shows that the competitor intends "to fight this action to the highest court in the land."

· The CEO, Jack Douglas, contacted your firm after ACL's former auditors resigned. The previous auditors informed Mr. Douglas that they disagreed with ACL's valuation of deferred development costs and believed that the balance should be reduced to a nominal amount of $1.

ACL has incurred substantial losses during the past three fiscal years, but revenue for the 2012 was $6.2 million.

EXHIBIT I

AutoCare Ltd.
DRAFT BALANCE SHEET
as at March 31 (in thousands of dollars)

Assets

	2012 (Unaudited)	2011 (Audited)
Current		
Accounts receivable	$ 213	$ 195
Inventories	1,650	615
Prepaid expenses	45	30
	1,908	840
Capital assets	2,120	716
Investment in JDP Ltd.	1	1
Deferred development costs	1,979	686
Patent	835	835
	$6,843	$3,078

Liabilities
Current

	2012	2011
Bank indebtedness	$1,225	$ 462
Accounts payable	607	476
Current portion of long term debt	400	98
Advances from shareholders	253	-
	2,485	1,036
Long-term debt	3,114	650
	$5,599	$1,686

Shareholders' Equity

	2012	2011
Capital stock	2,766	2,766
Deficit	(1,522)	(1,374)
	1,244	1,392
	$6,843	$3,078

Required

(a) List five procedures that the auditor should perform before deciding to accept ACL as a client.

(b) Evaluate four factors that impact the audit risk assessment for the current year and indicate how these factors influence audit risk (that is, increase or decrease audit risk).

(c) Conclude on overall audit risk and indicate how this will impact the audit planning.

(d) Using at least three of your calculations of materiality, calculate the range of materiality for the current year. Conclude on the most appropriate materiality and include a detailed explanation supporting your decision.

(e) Perform planning analytic procedures and identify at least three accounts with unusual fluctuations. For each of the "risky" accounts you identify, indicate a possible client error that may have caused this significant fluctuation as well as a possible business reason for the change.

CASE STUDY—CLOUD 9

PART 1 Materiality

W&S Partners commenced the planning phase of the Cloud 9 audit with procedures to gain an understanding of the client's structure and its business environment. You have completed your research on the key market forces as they relate to Cloud 9's operations. The topics you researched included the general and industry-specific economic trends and conditions; the competitive environment; product, customer, and supplier information; technological advances and the effect of the Internet; and laws and regulatory requirements. The purpose of this research is to identify the inherent risks. The auditor needs to identify which financial statement assertions may be affected by these inherent risks. Identifying the risks will help determine the nature of the audit procedures to be performed.

Management implicitly or explicitly makes assertions regarding the recognition, measurement, presentation, and disclosure of the various elements of the financial statements. Auditors use assertions for account balances to form a basis for the assessment of risks of material misstatement. That is, assertions are used to identify the types of errors that could occur in transactions that result in the account balance. Consequently, further breaking down the account into these assertions will direct the audit effort to those areas of higher risk. The auditors broadly classify assertions as existence or occurrence; completeness; valuation or allocation; rights and obligations; and presentation and disclosure.

An additional task during the planning phase is to consider the concept of materiality as it applies to the client. The auditor will design procedures in order to identify and correct errors or irregularities that would have a material effect on the financial statements and affect the decision-making of the users of the financial statements. Materiality is used in determining audit procedures and sample selections, and in evaluating differences from client records to audit results. It is the maximum amount of misstatement, individually or in aggregate, that can be accepted in the financial statements. In selecting the base figure to be used to calculate materiality, an auditor should consider the key drivers of the business and ask, "What are the end users (that is, shareholders, banks, and so on) of the accounts going to be looking at?" For example, will shareholders be interested in profit figures that can be used to pay dividends and increase share price?

W&S Partners' audit methodology dictates that one planning materiality (PM) amount is to be used for the financial statements as a whole. Further, only one basis should be selected—a blended approach or average should not be used. The basis selected is the one determined to be the key driver of the business.

W&S Partners use the percentages in table 4.9 as starting points for the various bases.

TABLE 4.9 **Starting percentages for materiality bases**

BASE	THRESHOLD (%)
Profit before tax	5.0
Revenues	0.5
Gross profit	2.0
Total assets	0.5
Equity	1.0

These starting points can be increased or decreased by taking into account qualitative client factors, such as:
• the nature of the client's business and industry (for example, rapidly changing through growth or downsizing, or because of an unstable environment)
• the client is a public company (or subsidiary of) that is subject to regulations
• the knowledge of or high risk of fraud.

Typically, profit before tax is used; however, it cannot be used if reporting a loss for the year or if profitability is not consistent.

When calculating PM based on interim figures, it may be necessary to annualize the results. This allows the auditor to plan the audit properly based on an approximate projected year-end balance. Then, at year end, the figure is adjusted, if necessary, to reflect the actual results.

Required

Answer the following questions based on the information presented for Cloud 9 in the appendix to this book and in the current and earlier chapters. You should also consider your answers to the case study questions in earlier chapters.

(a) Using the September 30, 2012 trial balance (in the appendix to this book), calculate planning materiality and include the justification for the basis that you have used for your calculation.

(b) Based on your results from researching the client and its industry in chapter 1 and chapter 2, discuss the inherent risks in the audit of Cloud 9. Identify the associated financial accounts that would be affected and provide an assessment of "high," "medium," or "low" in relation to the likelihood and materiality of the risk occurring.

PART 2 Analytical procedures

Required

Answer the following questions based on the information presented for Cloud 9 in the appendix to this book and the current and earlier chapters. You should also consider your answers to the case study questions in earlier chapters.

(a) Using analytical procedures and the information provided in the appendix, perform preliminary analytics of Cloud 9's financial position and its business risks. Discuss the ratios indicating a significant or an unexpected fluctuation.

(b) Which specific areas do you believe should receive special emphasis during your audit? Consider your discussion of the results of analytical procedures as well as your preliminary estimate of materiality. Prepare a memorandum to Suzie Pickering outlining potential problem areas (that is, where possible material misstatements in the financial report exist) and any other special concerns (for example, going concern). Specify the accounts and related assertions that would require particular attention.

RESEARCH QUESTION 4.1

Executive renumeration

Listed companies are required to make certain disclosures in their annual reports about the compensation paid to their top executives. One reason for this is to help interested stakeholders assess the performance of executives. It also helps executives and companies set appropriate compensation levels based on what other companies in the same industry and/or of the same size are paying their executives. These disclosures are audited.

Required

Obtain the annual reports of five listed Canadian companies in the same industry through the website SEDAR (www.sedar.com). You can search by industry and choose the companies whose annual reports you want to review. Extract the information on executive remuneration and describe the data using graphs and tables. Write a report addressing the following questions (justify your responses by referring to the data where appropriate).
· How are the executives paid (cash, bonuses, and so on)?
· Which companies' executives are paid the most and what is the range of pay?
· Which companies' executives' pay is most linked to the company's profit and/or share price performance? (Explain any assumptions you have to make.)
· Overall, what do you conclude about how Canadian company executives are paid and how clearly the compensation data are reported?

RESEARCH QUESTION 4.2

Public company financial statements

The financial statements for public companies are available through the website SEDAR (www.sedar.com). This is the official site that provides access to information filed by public companies and investment funds with the Canadian Securities Administrators (CSA). The objective in making public this financial information is to enhance investor awareness of the business and affairs of public companies and to promote confidence in the transparent operation of capital markets in Canada. Achieving this objective relies heavily on the provision of accurate information on market participants.

Required

Go to www.sedar.com and select the most recent set of *audited annual* financial statements for a Canadian public company. Using this set of financial statements:
(a) Assess the inherent risk of the company chosen.
(b) Calculate materiality for the engagement.
(c) Perform preliminary analytics and summarize your findings.

FURTHER READING

The Canadian Institute of Chartered Accountants. *Canadian Professional Engagement Manual* (2010). http://cica.ca/.

SOLUTIONS TO MULTIPLE-CHOICE QUESTIONS

1. b, 2. c, 3. a, 4. d, 5. b, 6. c, 7. c, 8. d, 9. d, 10. c.

NOTE

1. The Canadian Institute of Chartered Accountants. *Canadian Professional Engagement Manual* (2010). http://cica.ca/.

CHAPTER 5

Audit evidence

LEARNING OBJECTIVES

After studying this chapter you should be able to:

1 outline the audit assertions

2 identify and describe different types of audit evidence and define sufficient appropriate audit evidence

3 determine the persuasiveness of audit evidence

4 explain the issues to consider when using the work of an expert

5 explain the issues to consider when using the work of another auditor

6 describe the evidence-gathering procedures most often used by auditors

7 explain how auditors arrive at a conclusion based upon the evidence gathered

8 describe how auditors document the details of evidence gathered in working papers.

AUDITING AND ASSURANCE STANDARDS

CANADIAN	INTERNATIONAL
CAS 230 *Audit Documentation*	ISA 230 *Audit Documentation*
CAS 315 *Identifying and Assessing the Risks of Material Misstatement through Understanding the Entity and Its Environment*	ISA 315 *Identifying and Assessing the Risks of Material Misstatement through Understanding the Entity and Its Environment*
CAS 330 *The Auditor's Responses to Assessed Risks*	ISA 330 *The Auditor's Responses to Assessed Risks*
CAS 500 *Audit Evidence*	ISA 500 *Audit Evidence*
CAS 501 *Audit Evidence—Specific Considerations for Selected Items*	ISA 501 *Audit Evidence—Specific Considerations for Selected Items*
CAS 505 *External Confirmations*	ISA 505 *External Confirmations*
CAS 580 *Written Representations*	ISA 580 *Written Representations*
CAS 600 *Special Considerations—Audits of Group Financial Statements (Including the Work of Component Auditors)*	ISA 600 *Special Considerations—Audits of Group Financial Statements (Including the Work of Component Auditors)*
CAS 620 *Using the Work of an Auditor's Expert*	ISA 620 *Using the Work of an Auditor's Expert*
Rules of Professional Conduct of each Provincial Institute / Order	*Code of Ethics for Professional Accountants*
CSQC 1 *Quality Control for Firms that Perform Audits and Reviews of Historical Financial Information, and other Assurance and Related Services Engagements*	ISQC 1 *Quality Control for Firms that Perform Audits and Reviews of Historical Financial Information, and other Assurance and Related Services Engagements*

```
┌─────────────────────────────────────────────────────────┐
│                Overview of the audit process             │
│                       Chapter 1                          │
└─────────────────────────────────────────────────────────┘

┌─────────────────────────────────────────────────────────┐
│            Client acceptance/continuation decision        │
│                       Chapter 2                          │
└─────────────────────────────────────────────────────────┘

┌─────────────────────────────────────────────────────────┐
│                        Planning                          │
│                     Chapters 3 & 4                       │
└─────────────────────────────────────────────────────────┘

┌───────────────────┐  ┌───────────────────┐  ┌───────────────────┐
│ Gain an           │  │ Identify          │  │ Set planning      │
│ understanding     │  │ significant       │  │ materiality       │
│ of the client     │  │ accounts and      │  │                   │
│                   │  │ transactions      │  │                   │
└───────────────────┘  └───────────────────┘  └───────────────────┘

┌───────────────────┐  ┌───────────────────┐  ┌───────────────────┐
│ Identify what can │  │ Gain an           │  │ Develop an audit  │
│ go wrong          │  │ understanding     │  │ strategy          │
│                   │  │ of key internal   │  │                   │
│                   │  │ controls          │  │                   │
└───────────────────┘  └───────────────────┘  └───────────────────┘

┌─────────────────────────────────────────────────────────┐
│                        Execution                         │
│                     Chapters 6–11                        │
└─────────────────────────────────────────────────────────┘

┌───────────────────────────┐    ┌───────────────────────────┐
│     Controls strategy     │    │    Substantive strategy   │
│      Chapters 7 & 8       │    │      Chapters 9–11        │
└───────────────────────────┘    └───────────────────────────┘

              ┌───────────────────────────┐
              │       Audit sampling      │
              │         Chapter 6         │
              └───────────────────────────┘

┌─────────────────────────────────────────────────────────┐
│                Concluding and reporting                  │
│                       Chapter 12                         │
└─────────────────────────────────────────────────────────┘

┌───────────────────┐  ┌───────────────────┐  ┌───────────────────┐
│ Subsequent event  │  │   Conclusions     │  │    Reporting      │
│ identification    │  │                   │  │                   │
└───────────────────┘  └───────────────────┘  └───────────────────┘
```

Audit evidence
Chapter 5

Cloud 9

At the next planning meeting for the Cloud 9 Ltd. (Cloud 9) audit, Suzie Pickering presents the results of the analytical procedures performed so far and the working draft of the audit plan. The audit manager, Sharon Gallagher, and the audit senior, Josh Thomas, are also involved in the planning, with special responsibility for the internal control assessment.

The purpose of the meeting is to discuss the available sources of evidence at Cloud 9 and specify these in the detailed audit program. The team also has to make sure that they have enough evidence to conduct the audit. There are two specific issues worrying members of the team. First, there are three very large asset balances on Cloud 9's trial balance that have particular valuation issues. Suzie suggests that an expert valuator will be required for the derivatives, but they can handle the accounts receivable and inventory themselves. Second, Sharon is worried about the auditors of Cloud 9's parent company, Cloud 9 Inc.—the auditors did some audit work on the relationship between the two companies (Cloud 9 Inc. and Cloud 9 Ltd.) during the year and she hasn't been able to gain access to the confidential report yet.

The questions being considered by the team in the planning meeting include:
- What evidence is available?
- What criteria will the team use to choose between alternative sources of evidence?
- What are the implications of using the work of experts and other auditors?

AUDIT PROCESS IN FOCUS

In this chapter, we look at audit evidence. In the last two chapters, we considered audit risk and planning. A great deal of that discussion considered the importance of risk identification to aid with audit risk minimization. Once an auditor has identified the key risk factors for their client, they will plan their audit to obtain sufficient appropriate audit evidence to ensure that relevant accounts and related note disclosures are reported accurately. In the chapters that follow, we discuss the detailed testing conducted by auditors. In these chapters, the evidence-gathering procedures introduced in this chapter will be explained in more detail.

We start this chapter by defining and describing audit assertions, which are used when designing and conducting testing. We then consider the different types of evidence that an auditor will gather, including evidence gathered through confirmations, documentary evidence, representations, verbal evidence, computational evidence, physical evidence, and electronic evidence. Each form of evidence is used to substantiate the information provided by the client in its trial balance and its preliminary financial statements. Some forms of evidence are more persuasive than others: internally generated evidence is the least persuasive; externally generated evidence sent directly to the auditor is the most persuasive. Examples are provided of different types of evidence and the evidence that auditors tend to rely on most as providing the most dependable, independent proof that the amounts included in the client's financial statements are fairly presented.

After considering the relative persuasiveness of different types of evidence, we consider special types of evidence. In particular we consider evidence provided by experts and evidence provided by other auditors. Using the work of these two groups presents particular challenges for an auditor. These challenges are discussed in this chapter.

We then provide an overview of the evidence-gathering procedures used by auditors. These procedures include inspection of records and physical assets, observation of procedures used by clients where no audit trail is left, enquiry of client management and personnel, confirmation of balances with external parties, recalculation to ensure numerical accuracy, re-performance of procedures used by a client, and analytical procedures.

A discussion follows on how the auditor arrives at a conclusion regarding the fair presentation of the financial statements. This conclusion is based upon an auditor's understanding of their client, the risks identified during the planning stage of the audit, and the evidence gathered throughout the remainder of the audit when conducting detailed testing of controls, transactions, and accounts.

Auditors document the details of evidence gathered in their working papers. An auditor's working papers provide proof of audit work completed, procedures used, and evidence gathered. Each accounting firm has its own working paper format and preferences. In this chapter, we provide some examples of a typical audit file and the types of working papers it may contain.

5.1 ASSERTIONS

1 Outline the audit assertions.

assertions statements made by management regarding the recognition, measurement, presentation, and disclosure of items included in the financial statements

It is the responsibility of those charged with governance to ensure that the financial statements are prepared so as to give a fair presentation of the entity and its operations. When preparing the financial statements, management makes **assertions** about each account and related disclosures in the notes. For example, when reporting on inventory, management should ensure that the amount disclosed exists, is owned by the entity, represents a complete list of the inventory owned, and is valued appropriately. When reporting on sales, management should ensure that the amount disclosed represents sales of the entity that occurred during the accounting period. They should also ensure that sales are recorded at the correct amount, represent a complete list of all sales, and are classified correctly.

Auditors use assertions for transactions, account balances, and presentations and disclosures when assessing the risk of material misstatement and when designing their audit procedures. CAS 315 *Identifying and Assessing the Risks of Material Misstatement through Understanding the Entity and Its Environment* provides a summary of the assertions used by auditors. Transaction-based assertions focus on the transactions that took place during the period as opposed to the account balance. For example, when auditing inventory, the auditor will audit a sample of the transactions that impact the inventory account, such as purchases and sales, but they will also conduct procedures on the ending inventory balance (the account balance). Table 5.1 shows the assertions used for transactions and events, including income statement items, for an accounting period.

occurrence transactions and events that have been recorded have occurred and pertain to the entity

When testing for **occurrence**, an auditor searches for evidence to verify that a recorded transaction or event, such as a revenue or an expense item, took place and relates to the entity. This assertion is particularly important when the auditor believes that there is a risk of overstatement and that some transactions or events are recorded but did not actually occur—for example, false sales recorded to overstate revenue and profit.

completeness all transactions, events, assets, liabilities, and equity items that should have been recorded have been recorded

When testing for **completeness**, an auditor searches for transactions or events and makes sure these have been recorded. This assertion is particularly important when the auditor believes there is a risk of understatement and that some transactions or events that should have been recorded have not been recorded—for example, expenses incurred but not recorded to understate expenses and overstate profit.

Occurrence	Transactions and events that have been recorded have occurred and pertain to the entity.
Completeness	All transactions and events that should have been recorded have been recorded.
Accuracy	Amounts and other data relating to recorded transactions and events have been recorded appropriately.
Cut-off	Transactions and events have been recorded in the correct accounting period.
Classification	Transactions and events have been recorded in the proper accounts.

TABLE 5.1 **Assertions about classes of transactions and events for the period under audit**

When testing for **accuracy**, an auditor searches for evidence that transactions and events have been recorded at appropriate amounts. This assertion is particularly important when the auditor believes there is a risk that the reported amounts are not accurate—for example, when a client has complex discounting systems or foreign exchange calculations where errors can easily occur.

accuracy amounts and other data relating to recorded transactions and events have been recorded appropriately

When testing for **cut-off**, an auditor searches for evidence that transactions have been recorded in the correct accounting period. This assertion is particularly important for transactions close to year end. For example, a client may record a sale before year end that occurred after year end. Or, a client may record an expense after year end that was incurred before year end. When testing for **classification**, an auditor ensures that transactions and events have been recorded in the proper accounts.

cut-off transactions and events have been recorded in the correct accounting period

classification transactions and events have been recorded in the proper accounts

Table 5.2 shows the assertions used when testing balance sheet items. When testing for **existence**, an auditor searches for evidence to verify that asset, liability, and equity items included in the account balances that appear in the financial statements actually exist. This assertion is particularly important when the auditor believes there is a risk of overstatement.

existence recorded assets, liabilities, and equity interests exist

When testing for **rights and obligations**, an auditor searches for evidence to verify that recorded assets are owned by the entity and that recorded liabilities represent commitments of the entity. This assertion is particularly important when the auditor believes there is a risk that recorded assets or liabilities are not owned by the entity. This assertion is different from existence, as the assets and liabilities may exist but not be owned by the entity. For example, inventory held on consignment (and therefore not owned by the entity) is recorded as an asset of the entity.

rights and obligations rights to assets held or controlled by the entity, and liabilities (obligations) of the entity

When testing for completeness, an auditor searches for assets, liabilities, and equity items and ensures that they have been recorded. This assertion is particularly important when the auditor believes there is a risk of understatement and the client

Existence	Assets, liabilities, and equity interests exist.
Rights and obligations	The entity holds or controls the rights to assets, and liabilities are the obligations of the entity.
Completeness	All assets, liabilities, and equity interests that should have been recorded have been recorded.
Valuation and allocation	Assets, liabilities, and equity interests are included in the financial statements at appropriate amounts and any resulting valuation or allocation adjustments are appropriately recorded.

TABLE 5.2 **Assertions about account balances at year end**

has omitted some items from the balance sheet. For example, an auditor will search for unrecorded liabilities.

When testing for **valuation and allocation**, an auditor searches for evidence that assets, liabilities, and equity items have been recorded at appropriate amounts and allocated to the correct general ledger accounts. This assertion is particularly important when the auditor believes there is a risk of over- or undervaluation. For example:

- an auditor checks that inventory has been appropriately recorded at the lower of cost and net realizable value (risk of overstatement)
- an auditor tests for the adequacy of the allowance for doubtful accounts (risk of understatement)
- an auditor checks that transactions are allocated to the correct account when auditing research and development expenditure (risk of understatement of the expense account).

> **valuation and allocation** assets, liabilities, and equity interests are included in the financial statements at appropriate amounts and any resulting valuation or allocation adjustments are appropriately recorded

Cloud 9

Ian and Suzie have already talked in general terms about the errors that could occur in Cloud 9's accounts receivable. For example, basic mathematical or other clerical errors could affect the accounts receivable total in either direction. Suzie emphasizes that Cloud 9's management asserts that this error does not exist when they prepare the financial statements—they assert that accounts receivable are valued correctly. The auditor has to gather evidence about each assertion for each transaction class, account, and note in the financial statements. Now that Ian understands this idea better, he is able to identify the assertions that relate to the potential errors in accounts receivable that they discussed earlier:

- There are no mathematical or other clerical errors that could affect the total in either direction—valuation and allocation.
- No accounts receivable were omitted when calculating the total—completeness.
- Accounts receivable represent valid amounts owing for goods sold in the current period—existence.
- All accounts receivable belong to Cloud 9—rights and obligations.
- Bad debts are written off—valuation and allocation. Suzie confirms that there can be more than one instance of a type of assertion for an account.
- Sales from the next period are not included in the earlier period—cut-off. Ian is a bit confused about this one, because cut-off is an assertion for transactions, not assets. Suzie agrees that it is a special sort of assertion that relates to transactions or events but also gives evidence about balance sheet accounts. This is due to double entry accounting, and when auditors test cut-off for sales, they also gather evidence for the balance sheet side of the entry, which is usually accounts receivable.

Table 5.3 shows the assertions used for presentation and disclosure. An auditor ensures that all items included in the financial statements are presented and disclosed appropriately. They check that disclosed items represent events and transactions that occurred for the entity, are recorded at appropriate amounts, and are described accurately. An auditor searches to ensure that all items that should have been disclosed are included in the financial statements.

For example, required presentation and disclosures for inventory include the way inventories are measured, including the cost formula, as well as the carrying amount of inventory in total and by classification. If the cost formula was not disclosed, the inventory note would not be complete and therefore the completeness assertion over

Occurrence, rights, and obligations	Disclosed events, transactions, and other matters have occurred and pertain to the entity.
Completeness	All disclosures that should have been included in the financial statements have been included.
Classification and understandability	Financial information is appropriately presented and described, and disclosures are clearly expressed.
Accuracy and valuation	Financial and other information is disclosed fairly and at appropriate amounts.

TABLE 5.3 **Assertions about presentation and disclosure**

presentation and disclosure would not be satisfied. If the entity discloses the First in First Out method (FIFO) as its cost method but in fact it uses the weighted average cost formula, then the presentation assertion of accuracy would not be met. Lastly, if the entity does not disclose its raw material and finished goods separately, then the classification and understandability assertion would not be realized.

PROFESSIONAL ENVIRONMENT

Fraud at the audit assertion level

Details of material fraudulent transactions and other illegal acts detected by the corporate regulator in the United States are published periodically in the Securities and Exchange Commission's (SEC) Accounting and Auditing Enforcement Releases (AAERs). The companies identified in the AAERs have been found by the SEC to have misstated their financial statements. The companies, typically relatively large, publicly listed entities, have been ordered to correct their financial statements. In each case, the SEC can take action against the company, its managers, its auditors, or other parties and initiate an investigation based on news reports or anonymous tip-offs.

Wang, Radich, and Fargher investigated the AAERs from 2005 to 2008, with a focus on those that related to accounting manipulations. They sought to determine the role of management override of internal controls relating to the preparation of financial statements. The authors were interested in which audit assertions relating to transactions tend to be violated when management overrides the internal controls and issues fraudulent financial statements.

The authors examined financial statement fraud at the audit assertion level for 160 companies with 440 transactions alleged to involve accounting manipulations. They report that the assertions most at risk for revenue transactions are *occurrence*, *accuracy*, and *cut-off*, and the assertion most at risk for expense transactions is *completeness*.

Revenue fraud arose primarily from the creation of fictitious transactions such as "round-trip" and "circular" transactions. The authors provide an example of this type of revenue fraud as the series of transactions reported by a telecom company, Qwest. Qwest swapped with other telecom firms the rights to use fibre-optic strands for no legitimate business reason and immediately recognized revenue, allegedly to meet Wall Street's earnings expectations. Another common revenue fraud was the use of contingent or consignment sales to inflate revenue, where the accounts misrepresented the actual transaction, or where the underlying transaction did not even exist. These transactions violate the occurrence assertion. The cut-off assertion was violated when the companies backdated or misdated contracts to overstate revenue by recording revenue of next-period sales or services into the current year's accounts.

Wang et al. report that the majority of the fraudulent transactions in their study were non-routine transactions, which implies that they would not be detected if auditors focused solely on testing internal controls over routine transactions. They suggest that auditors need to be aware of the assertions at high risk of fraud and consider the need for additional testing to compensate for the risk of control override by management.

Sources: P. M. Dechow, W. Ge, C. R. Larson, & R. G. Sloan, "Predicting Material Accounting Misstatements," unpublished paper, University of California, Berkeley, 2009. I. Wang, R. Radich, & N. Fargher, "An Analysis of Financial Statement Fraud at the Audit Assertion Level," unpublished paper, Macquarie University, 2009.

BEFORE YOU GO ON

1.1 List the assertions for classes of transactions and account balances.

1.2 What does the accuracy assertion mean?

1.3 What is the auditor trying to ensure when conducting cut-off tests?

5.2 TYPES OF AUDIT EVIDENCE

2 Identify and describe different types of audit evidence and define sufficient appropriate audit evidence.

evidence information gathered by the auditor that is used when forming an opinion on the fair presentation of a client's financial statements

Audit **evidence** is the information that an auditor uses when arriving at their opinion on the fair presentation of their client's financial statements (CAS 500 *Audit Evidence*). It is the responsibility of management and those charged with governance of a client to ensure that the financial statements are prepared in accordance with Canadian generally accepted accounting principles (GAAP). They are also responsible for ensuring that accurate accounting records are maintained and any potential misstatements are prevented, or detected and corrected. It is the responsibility of the auditor to gather sufficient appropriate evidence to arrive at their opinion. This involves gathering evidence to support the audit assertions for the transactions and account balances. Before considering the different types of evidence that an auditor will use, we start this section with a discussion of what is meant by the term "sufficient appropriate evidence."

5.2.1 Sufficient appropriate audit evidence

sufficient appropriate evidence quantity (sufficiency) and quality (appropriateness) of audit evidence gathered

Sufficient appropriate evidence is a core concept in auditing. Sufficiency relates to the quantity and appropriateness relates to the quality of audit evidence gathered. These concepts are interrelated, as the quality of evidence gathered will affect the quantity required.

Audit risk affects the quantity and quality of evidence gathered by an auditor during the execution stage of the audit. When there is a significant risk that an account will be misstated and the client's system of internal controls is not considered to be effective at reducing that risk, detection risk is set as low and more high-quality evidence is gathered when conducting substantive tests of that account. This relationship is shown in table 5.4.

TABLE 5.4 **High-risk account**

Audit risk	Inherent risk	Control risk	Detection risk	Evidence
	High	High	Low	More

When there is a low risk that an account will be misstated and the client's system of internal controls is considered to be adequate for that account, detection risk is set as high and less high-quality evidence is gathered when conducting substantive tests of that account. This relationship is shown in table 5.5.

TABLE 5.5 **Low-risk account**

Audit risk	Inherent risk	Control risk	Detection risk	Evidence
	Low	Low	High	Less

The risk patterns illustrated in tables 5.4 and 5.5 are extremes. The risk of material misstatement associated with most accounts falls somewhere in between. As such, the sufficiency evidence gathered when conducting substantive procedures is a matter of professional judgement and will vary from account to account and client to client. Nevertheless, there is a direct relationship between the risk of material misstatement (inherent and control risk) and the amount of evidence gathered when testing transactions and balances.

The appropriateness of audit evidence refers to its relevance and reliability. Relevance of information means there is a logical connection to the audit assertions at risk. Therefore, evidence is considered **relevant** if it provides confirmation about an assertion most at risk of material misstatement. For example, if the auditor determines that the primary assertion at risk is the existence of inventory, it would not be appropriate to spend more time gathering evidence in relation to the completeness assertion than the existence assertion. By identifying the key risk areas for the client, an auditor is able to focus on gathering more (sufficient) high-quality (appropriate) evidence where the risk of material misstatement is believed to be most significant.

relevance extent to which information is logically connected to an assertion

Reliability refers to whether the evidence reflects the true state of the information. In terms of the reliability of information, the auditor should consider the following:

reliability extent to which information reflects the true state of the information

- the source of the information—It is important for the evidence to be unbiased. Information from external third parties, such as those provided from banks and other third parties is generally reliable, as the respondent or the person from whom the information is sought is independent of the organization.
- the expertise of the respondent—If the respondent does not understand what the confirmation letter is asking for, they will not provide a knowledgeable reply. For example, if a customer is asked to confirm their accounts receivable balance as at year end, but they confirm the balance outstanding at another date, the reliability of the confirmation may be in question.
- the consistency of the information—Evidence that is consistent from one source to another is more reliable than evidence that is inconsistent from one source to another. For example, if responses to enquiries of management and internal audit are not consistent, the reliability of the information will be reduced.
- the source of the information and whether it is produced where internal controls operate effectively—For example, if there are good controls over the payroll cycle, then employee time cards, cheque stubs, and journal entries will provide more reliable evidence than if the controls are not effective.

Cloud 9

Ian thinks he finally understands: in order to limit the risk of an inappropriate audit opinion for Cloud 9, the audit team will assess inherent risk and control risk at the assertion level for account balances and transactions. They make these assessments after gaining an understanding of the client because these risks are influenced by the client's circumstances.

If inherent and control risk are assessed as high, then the audit team will set detection risk as low. This means that they will need to gather more, better-quality evidence than if inherent and control risk are assessed as low. In addition, planning materiality is set based on the needs of the users. The lower the materiality level, the more sufficient and appropriate evidence needs to be gathered.

Suzie thinks the money spent on coffee has been well worth it!

The different types of audit evidence described in the remainder of this section include documentary evidence, confirmations, representations, verbal evidence, computational evidence, physical evidence, and electronic evidence.

5.2.2 External confirmations

CAS 505 *External Confirmations* provides guidance on the use of **external confirmations.** An external confirmation is sent directly by an auditor to a third party, who is asked to respond to the auditor on the matter(s) included in the confirmation letter. External confirmations can be sent to the client's bank, lawyers, lenders, and debtors, and third parties holding the client's inventory.

A **bank confirmation** is a request for information about the amount of cash held in the bank or in overdraft, details of any loans with the bank, details of any pledges of assets made to guarantee loans, and interest rates charged. This information is used to confirm that the asset "cash at bank" is recorded at the appropriate amount (valuation and allocation assertion) and is in the client's name (rights and obligations assertion) and that all loans with the bank are included in the liability section of the balance sheet (completeness assertion). The bank confirmation also requests details of interest rates paid on cash deposits and term deposits, and interest rates charged on bank overdrafts and loans. This information is used when auditing interest income and interest expense items (accuracy assertion). A sample bank confirmation letter is reproduced in Appendix A of this book.

An external confirmation may also be sent to a client's suppliers and lenders (**payable confirmation**) to confirm the details of amounts owed to creditors and significant loans. Where payable confirmations are used, vendors provide details of amounts outstanding at year end (completeness and valuation and allocation assertions) and interest rates changed on those amounts (accuracy assertion). They also confirm that the amounts owed are to be paid by the client (rights and obligations assertion). Payable confirmations can only be used if an auditor is certain that the list of vendors supplied by the client is complete, as an incomplete list will not provide evidence regarding the completeness assertion. Also, as the focus is on the completeness assertion, accounts payable confirmations are usually sent to suppliers with small or zero balances (especially if there were significant balances owing in the prior year) to ensure that there are no unrecorded payables.

External confirmations can be sent to customers with credit terms (**receivable confirmation**) to verify the receivables balance. The auditor will select the specific accounts to whom they will send confirmations. Criteria used when selecting the accounts receivable customers to be sent confirmations include materiality (large trade receivables), age (overdue accounts), and location (if customers are dispersed, a selection from various locations). The primary assertion when using receivable confirmations is existence—they provide audit evidence that the credit customers exist. They also provide some evidence on ownership (rights and obligations assertion), as credit customers confirm that they owe money to the client. As they are also asked to confirm that they owe the amount outstanding at year end, very little evidence is provided regarding the valuation and allocation assertion. Credit customers only confirm the amount owing; they do not confirm their intention to pay the amount due.

External confirmations may be used when a client owns inventory that is held on its behalf in another location; that is, the inventory is held in premises not owned by the client. In this case the auditor may send a confirmation asking the third-party owner

external confirmation evidence obtained as a direct written response to the auditor from a third party, in paper form, or by electronic or other medium

bank confirmation a letter sent directly by an auditor to their client's bank requesting information such as the amount of cash held in the bank (or overdraft), details of any loans with the bank, and interest rates charged

payable confirmation a letter sent directly by an auditor to their client's vendor or supplier requesting information about amounts owed by the client to the vendor or supplier

receivable confirmation a letter sent directly by an auditor to their client's credit customers requesting information about amounts owed to the client by the debtor

of the premises where the inventory is held to verify the description and quantity of inventory held. This type of confirmation provides audit evidence that the inventory recorded by the client exists (existence assertion), is complete (completeness assertion), and is owned by the client (rights and obligations assertion).

There are two broad types of external confirmations: positive and negative confirmations (examples can be found in Appendix A of this book). **Positive confirmations** ask the recipient to reply in all circumstances. **Negative confirmations** ask the recipient to reply only if they disagree with the information provided. If a recipient does not respond to a negative confirmation, it is assumed that they agree with the information provided. This form of request is of limited benefit when the assertion being tested is existence. A negative confirmation may be used when an auditor has conducted detailed testing for existence using alternative procedures such as inspecting signed receiving reports. In this case, the negative confirmation is used to corroborate other evidence. Positive confirmations provide superior evidence, as a non-response from a negative confirmation request may provide false reassurance. For example, a client may record fake sales to customers that do not exist close to year end to boost revenue. A non-response from a non-existent customer may be interpreted by an auditor as confirmation that the customer agrees with the amount outstanding. In this case the conclusion would be unjustified.

When an auditor sends a receivable confirmation, they ordinarily include the amount recorded in their client's records for each accounts receivable customer to confirm. There is a risk that a customer may sign and return the confirmation to the auditor without checking the balance outstanding. As the primary assertion being tested when using this audit procedure is existence, rather than valuation and allocation, the auditor will perform other procedures to provide evidence on the valuation and allocation of the trade receivables balance. If an auditor were to send a confirmation to credit customers requesting that they provide the balance outstanding, there is a risk that credit customers will not respond, as locating the amount owed takes some effort to find, which would reduce the overall response rate and the amount of evidence available for the existence assertion.

positive confirmation a letter sent directly by an auditor to a third party, who is asked to respond to the auditor on the matter(s) included in the letter in all circumstances (that is, whether they agree or disagree with the information included in the auditor's letter)

negative confirmation a letter sent directly by an auditor to a third party, who is asked to respond to the auditor on the matter(s) included in the letter only if they disagree with the information provided

PROFESSIONAL ENVIRONMENT

Updating audit confirmation standards

How has technology influenced audit practice and standards? According to Daniel Goelzer, a member of the Public Company Accounting Oversight Board (PCAOB) in the United States, it has affected practice more than standards. Goelzer believes that changes to the U.S. standard on audit confirmations (AU 330) are necessary to bring it into the 21st century. Goelzer suggests that technological innovations like the Internet and e-mail have changed confirmation practice since AU 330 was written in the early 1990s.

In the U.S., the practice of audit confirmations is essentially mandatory, unlike the situation that typically prevails in the rest of the world, where confirmations are an optional procedure—a tool available for auditors to use as part of a package of audit procedures. The U.S. requirement to use confirmations dates back to a famous fraud case, McKesson Robbins, in the 1930s. More recent scandals, such as the Madoff, Satyam, and Parmalat cases, have meant that the confirmation process is back in the spotlight.

At the time of writing, the PCAOB had issued a concept release on possible revisions to the audit confirmations standard, and was seeking public comment on whether changes are necessary, and, if they are required, how those changes would impact on a new standard.

The PCAOB believes that the new confirmation standard should take into account today's sophisticated security and encryption tools for e-mail and online transactions. Specifically, PCAOB member Steven Harris believes that the standard should address the use and reliability of confirmations received electronically: "It should address the authenticity and accuracy of direct access to online account information," he says. In addition, auditors are continually faced with disclaimers—clauses inserted into a client's customer's reply to a confirmation request disclaiming responsibility for any inaccuracy in the information provided. In a litigious society such as that in the U.S., these disclaimers are routinely used to avoid legal liability for statements made. However, the auditor is then faced with a decision: how much weight to place on a statement that is accompanied by a disclaimer? The PCAOB has included this issue in its request for public comment on the new standard.

Following the redrafting of the Canadian Auditing Standards, paragraph A12 of CAS 505 addresses the issue of validating the source of replies received in electronic format, such as e-mail. It may be possible for the auditor to establish a secure environment for electronic responses—for example, by the use of encryption, electronic digital signatures, and procedures to verify website authenticity. However, if this is not possible and the auditor has doubts about the reliability of any form of evidence obtained through the confirmation procedure, CAS 505 requires the auditor to consider alternative procedures—for example, telephone contact with the respondent (CAS 505, para. A14).

Sources: Daniel L. Goelzer, "Statement on Consideration of Concept Release on Possible Revisions to the Standard on Audit Confirmations," Public Company Accounting Oversight Board, April 14, 2009, http://pcaobus.org; WebCPA, "PCAOB Mulls Revising Audit Confirmation Standards," 14 April, 2009.

Cloud 9

Suzie explains to Ian that they can use external confirmations to gather sufficient and appropriate evidence about Cloud 9's outstanding accounts receivable balances and the existence and rights and obligations assertions. However, the confirmations will not be sufficient for valuation purposes, as a reply from a customer to confirm that the accounts receivable exists does not mean that the customer is going to be able to pay the balance owing when it is due. They will use other documents to provide evidence about the valuation assertion for accounts receivables.

Suzie also suggests that bank confirmations will be useful on the Cloud 9 audit for the rights and obligations, existence, and valuation assertions for bank accounts. Because they will also ask the banks to supply any information they have about any other bank accounts or loans, bank confirmations will also be useful for gathering evidence about the completeness assertion for these accounts. Suzie suggests that they do not rely on payable confirmations. This is because the biggest issue with these liabilities is discovering any omitted liabilities, not confirming the existence of the liabilities the client has already disclosed to them.

Suzie incorporates her ideas on confirmations into the draft audit plan.

5.2.3 Documentary evidence

documentary evidence information that provides evidence about details recorded in a client's list of transactions (for example, invoices and bank statements)

Documentary evidence includes invoices, suppliers' statements, bank statements, minutes of meetings, correspondence, and legal agreements. It may be internally generated or externally generated. Internally generated documents are produced by the client. Externally generated documents are generated by third parties. The persuasiveness of audit evidence varies depending on its source. This issue is explained in detail in the next section of this chapter.

There are a number of ways that documentary evidence can be used during an audit. An auditor can trace details recorded in a client's accounting records to supporting (external) documents to verify the amount recorded. For example, details of the price paid for inventory may be traced to a supplier's invoice to verify the amount recorded. This provides evidence on the accuracy of the purchase price (accuracy assertion).

Recorded investments may be traced to share certificates or their electronic equivalent to gain evidence that the investments exist (existence assertion) and that they are owned by the client (rights and obligations assertion).

Documents can be read and details traced to a client's accounting records and financial statements to ensure that items are included correctly (classification and understandability assertion). An auditor may ensure that all inventory confirmed as held by a third party is included in the client's records (completeness assertion). An auditor may ensure that all loans confirmed by external parties are included in the client's records (completeness assertion). Details of lease agreements can be read to ensure that leases are disclosed accurately in the body and the notes to the financial statements (classification and understandability assertion). The minutes of board meetings are read to ensure that relevant issues are adequately disclosed in the notes to the financial statements (classification and understandability assertion).

Cloud 9

An example of documentary evidence that will be useful for auditing Cloud 9's accounts receivable is cash receipts from credit customers after year end. If the customer pays the account owing at year end, there is little doubt about its valuation at year end. However, sales returns or evidence of disputes with customers during the post–year-end period provide evidence that valuation and existence are in doubt.

Also, Suzie recommends in the draft audit plan that the complex inventory transactions (importing from overseas plants with payment in U.S. dollars) can be audited through the relevant documents showing dates of shipping and arrival and details of the goods. She is particularly concerned about auditing the "goods in transit" balance using this evidence. The forward exchange contracts (used because the goods are purchased in U.S. dollars but the accounts are kept in Canadian dollars) are vital pieces of evidence that will be used to establish the correct valuation of the inventory balances, accounts payable, and cost of sales.

Sharon and Josh note in the plan that there are many other documents that will be used as evidence, including the board meeting minutes, lease agreement (for the premises), sponsorship agreements, loan agreements, and other documents supporting the accounting records.

5.2.4 Representations

CAS 501 *Audit Evidence—Specific Considerations for Selected Items* requires an auditor to gather sufficient appropriate audit evidence regarding any legal matters involving their client. Evidence is gathered from board meeting minutes, discussions with client personnel, and representation letters from the client's lawyers and management. When an auditor has reason to believe that there are legal issues that may impact the financial statements, such as the client being sued by a third party, or when a law firm is engaged by the client for the first time, a legal letter is requested from the legal firm(s) that the client deals with. An auditor will come to this conclusion after enquiries of client personnel, reading board meeting minutes, reading other documentation such as contracts and leases, reviewing legal expenses, and reading correspondence between the client and third parties.

A **legal letter** is generally sent by the client to its lawyers asking them to complete the letter and return it directly to the auditor. According to CAS 501 *Audit Evidence— Specific Considerations for Selected Items*, the legal letter can include any legal matters involving the client, and the lawyer's opinion on the client's description of any outstanding legal matters and whether the client's evaluation of those matters appears reasonable. It can include a request to provide details of any legal matters on which the

legal letter a letter sent to a client's lawyer asking them to confirm the details of legal matters outstanding identified by management

lawyer is in disagreement with the client. Schedule A of CAS 501 contains examples of a request for a legal letter from a client to its lawyer. Figure 5.1 contains an example of a legal (solicitor's) letter where there are claims or possible claims.

Sandra Carson   January 5, 2013
Jones and Jones LLP
192 Park Avenue
Suite 3500
Toronto, Ontario
MJ7 2K8

Skyward Ltd. (the "Company")

Dear Ms. Carson:

   In connection with the preparation and audit of our financial statements as of December 31, 2012 and for the year then ended, we have made the following evaluations of claims and possible claims with respect to which your firm's advice or representation has been sought:

Description	Evaluation
Always Right Inc. vs. Skyward Customer seeking damages of $1,000,000 for product that they claim was defectively manufactured and resulted in lost sales. At this point in time, no proceedings have commenced and Always Right has not been able to provide support that product was not damaged after shipment.	Likelihood that obligation exists is minimal and reliable estimate of any possible obligation or potential settlement cannot be determined.

Would you please advise us, as of February 14, 2013 on the following points:
(a) Are the claims and possible claims properly described?
(b) Do you consider that our evaluations are reasonable?
(c) Are you aware of any claims not listed above which are outstanding? If so, please include in your response letter the names of the parties and the amount claimed.

   For your purposes in providing the information requested, your response need not include any matter involving potential losses (or gains) whose expected effects on the financial statements would be less than $25,000, unless the aggregate for all such individual amounts is more than $25,000, (except for (product liability or similar) claims which may be indicative of possible further claims which could in the aggregate exceed $25,000).

   We expect to have our audit completed about February 19, 2013, so we would appreciate receiving your reply by February 15, 2013 with a specified effective date no earlier than February 14, 2013.

   This inquiry is made in accordance with the Joint Policy Statement of January 1978 approved by The Canadian Bar Association and the Auditing Standards Committee of The Canadian Institute of Chartered Accountants ("CICA") and CICA Auditing Guideline 46. Please address your reply, marked "Privileged and Confidential", to this company and send a signed copy of the reply directly to our auditors, Ernst & Young LLP, 222 Bay Street, Toronto, Ontario M5K 1J7.

Yours truly,

John Smith

c.c.: Ernst & Young LLP

FIGURE 5.1 **Example of a legal letter**
Source: Ernst & Young LLP, 2011

CAS 580 *Written Representations* requires that an auditor attempt to obtain written representations from their client's management. A **management representation letter** generally includes an acknowledgement that management is responsible for the preparation of the financial statements. Management is responsible for ensuring that the statements give a fair presentation of the company's financial position and comply with Canadian accounting standards. The letter will include written details of any verbal representations made by management during the course of the audit. As verbal evidence is weaker than written evidence, an auditor will seek written confirmation of any significant discussions in the management representation letter.

The management representation letter can also include an undertaking that laws and regulations have been complied with, that there have been no material frauds or errors that would impact the financial statements, and that the internal controls system is effective. The letter can acknowledge that the auditor was provided with access to all documents, records, and other evidence as requested. It can include an undertaking that the financial statements include the required disclosures in relation to related parties, share options, and contingent liabilities and that the company owns all assets listed. Appendix 2 of CAS 580 contains an example of a management representation letter. Figure 5.2 provides another example of a management representation letter.

management representation letter a letter from the client's management to the auditor acknowledging management's responsibility for the preparation of the financial statements and details of any verbal representations made by management during the course of the audit

FIGURE 5.2 **Example of a management representation letter**
Source: C·PEM

 FJR Construction Company

April 30, 2012 (same date as Auditor's Report)

To W&S Partners, Chartered Accountants

Dear W&S Partners:

This representation letter is provided in connection with your audit of the financial statements of **FJR Construction Company** for the period ended December 31, 2011 for the purpose of expressing an opinion as to whether the financial statements are presented fairly, in all material respects, in accordance with Canadian accounting standards for private enterprises.

We confirm that (to the best of our knowledge and belief, having made such inquiries as we considered necessary for the purpose of appropriately informing ourselves):

Financial Statements

- We have fulfilled our responsibilities, as set out in the terms of the audit engagement in accordance with Canadian accounting standards for private enterprises; in particular, the financial statements are fairly presented in accordance therewith.
- Significant assumptions used by us in making accounting estimates, including those measured at fair value, are reasonable.
- Related-party relationships and transactions have been appropriately accounted for and disclosed in accordance with the requirements of Canadian accounting standards for private enterprises.

(continued)

FIGURE 5.2 **Example of a management representation letter** (continued)
Source: C·PEM

- All events subsequent to the date of the financial statements and for which Canadian accounting standards for private enterprises require adjustment or disclosure have been adjusted or disclosed.
- The effects of uncorrected misstatements are immaterial, both individually and in the aggregate, to the financial statements as a whole.

Information Provided

- We have provided you with:
  - Access to all information of which we are aware that is relevant to the preparation of the financial statements such as records, documentation and other matters;
  - Additional information that you have requested from us for the purpose of the audit; and
  - Unrestricted access to persons within the entity from whom you determined it necessary to obtain audit evidence.

All transactions have been recorded in the accounting records and are reflected in the financial statements.
- We have disclosed to you the results of our assessment of the risk that the financial statements may be materially misstated as a result of fraud.
- We have disclosed to you all information in relation to fraud or suspected fraud that we are aware of and that affects the entity and involves:
  - Management;
  - Employees who have significant roles in internal control; or
  - Others where the fraud could have a material effect on the financial statements.
- We have disclosed to you all information in relation to allegations of fraud, or suspected fraud, affecting the entity's financial statements communicated by employees, former employees, analysts, regulators or others.
- We have disclosed to you all known instances of non-compliance or suspected non-compliance with laws and regulations whose effects should be considered when preparing financial statements.
- We have disclosed to you the identity of the entity's related parties and all the related-party relationships and transactions of which we are aware.

Yours very truly,

Jose Parra
Chief Financial Officer

Jack Green
Chief Executive Officer

Cloud 9

Sharon notes in the draft audit plan that a management representation letter will be obtained toward the end of the audit to confirm all verbal discussions held up to that point. The legal letter will also be obtained toward the end of the audit to ensure that there are no pending legal cases that would complicate matters.

5.2.5 Verbal evidence

verbal evidence responses of key client personnel to auditor enquiries throughout the course of the audit

Throughout the audit, an auditor meets with client management and staff to discuss various issues. **Verbal evidence** is used when gaining an understanding of the client and its internal controls system. It can be used to corroborate other forms of evidence.

Verbal evidence is documented in the auditor's working papers so that a record is kept of all key discussions with the client.

5.2.6 Computational evidence

Computational evidence is gathered when an auditor checks the mathematical accuracy of the numbers that appear in the financial statements (accuracy and valuation and allocation assertions). This involves re-adding the entries included in a client's journals and ledgers. It involves recomputing more complex calculations, such as foreign currency translation, employee benefits, interest of loans outstanding, and fair value modelling. When conducting complex recomputations, an auditor traces the amounts included in the calculations to externally prepared documentary evidence, where available, as well as checking that the formulae used are applied appropriately.

computational evidence evidence gathered by an auditor checking the mathematical accuracy of the numbers that appear in the financial statements

5.2.7 Physical evidence

An auditor gathers **physical evidence** through **inspection** of a client's tangible assets, such as its inventory and fixed assets. An auditor traces recorded amounts to assets to gain evidence that the assets exist (existence assertion). For example, an auditor will select inventory items from client ledgers for testing and trace the quantities recorded to the physical items, and then count the items on hand to check that the quantities recorded are accurate. This test is done to ascertain whether the quantities recorded are accurate and that assets physically exist.

physical evidence inspection of a client's tangible assets, such as its inventory and fixed assets

inspection an evidence-gathering procedure that involves checking documents and physical assets

An auditor also traces details of tangible assets on hand back to the recorded amount (completeness assertion). For example, an auditor selects physical inventory items, counts the number on hand, and traces them back to client records to make sure that the records are complete. This test is done to ascertain whether quantities on hand are accurately included in the client's records.

An auditor inspects a client's physical assets to ascertain whether machinery is functioning, inventory appear to be in good repair, and fixed assets are well looked after. This evidence is used to determine whether assets should be written down below current book value (valuation and allocation assertion). If inventory appears dusty, perhaps the client is having difficulty selling those goods. If machinery is not being used, perhaps it is obsolete or redundant. If the auditor does not have the expertise to ascertain the value of a client's assets, they may ask an independent expert for some help. The process for using the work of an expert is discussed in section 5.4 of this chapter.

Cloud 9

Suzie will head the team gathering evidence about inventory. There are some issues with Cloud 9's inventory controls, including difficulties in delivering merchandise from the warehouse to the store in a timely manner. Suzie is also concerned about the thefts at Cloud 9's retail store. Although Cloud 9's management has been very open in disclosing the thefts, Suzie is concerned about what this means for the quality of the inventory controls. She plans to inspect inventory and gather physical evidence of its existence and quality (because obsolescence is another major concern).

Sharon will also assign a team to inspect the furniture and equipment and the leasehold improvements, as there have been some major additions this year (because of the new store opening).

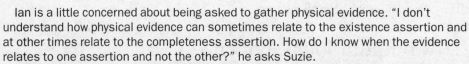

Ian is a little concerned about being asked to gather physical evidence. "I don't understand how physical evidence can sometimes relate to the existence assertion and at other times relate to the completeness assertion. How do I know when the evidence relates to one assertion and not the other?" he asks Suzie.

Suzie tries to explain that it depends on the process. If you start with the accounting records and then gather physical evidence to support the records, you are gathering evidence about existence. For example, the furniture and equipment ledger account has a record stating that Cloud 9 owns a photocopier. The record contains information about brand, size, and other details. Can you trace the records to the physical item—that is, can you find the photocopier in the office? If so, you have evidence that it exists. (You would also do separate tests for its valuation and rights and obligations.) However, if you start with the photocopier, for example, you see a photocopier in the office, and your question is then whether the item is in the accounting records—that is, are the accounting records complete? In this case you start with the physical item and trace it to the records. If the photocopier is entered in the ledger (furniture and equipment), you have evidence about the completeness of the accounting records.

5.2.8 Electronic evidence

electronic evidence data held on a client's computer, files sent by e-mail to the auditor, and items scanned and faxed

Electronic evidence includes data held on a client's computer, files sent by e-mail to the auditor, and items scanned and faxed. Transactions are commonly initiated and stored electronically. They leave no paper trail. To access the details of these transactions, an auditor must access their client's computer system, where details are kept. It is now common for companies to send their auditors copies of their accounting records and files by e-mail. The auditor then searches for corroborating evidence to verify the amounts included in those files.

If a company initiates and completes a transaction electronically, its auditor will use the electronic evidence to establish that the transaction occurred (occurrence assertion). For example, a client e-mails a supplier placing an order; the supplier replies via e-mail confirming that the order has been received; the supplier provides details regarding the estimated delivery date and the amount to be invoiced upon delivery of the goods; the client's receiving department notifies the accounts department that the goods ordered have been received; finally, the client initiates an electronic transfer of funds from its bank account to its supplier's bank account.

The extent to which an auditor can rely on electronic evidence produced by their client's computer system will depend a great deal on the internal controls in place. As discussed in chapter 3, IT creates risks within a client's accounting system. An auditor must consider those unique risks and assess the effectiveness of their client's internal controls in mitigating those risks. Chapter 8 contains a discussion of the methods used by an auditor when testing their client's internal controls, including those that protect data created and stored electronically.

Cloud 9

Josh is an expert on the computer systems Cloud 9 uses to process transactions, and the audit plan will show him as leading the team assessing the controls and performing the associated tests.

2.1 What is a bank confirmation?

2.2 List three things that may be included in a management representation letter.

2.3 Which assertion is tested when an auditor traces details of tangible assets on hand back to the recorded amount?

5.3 PERSUASIVENESS OF AUDIT EVIDENCE

As detailed earlier, when an auditor accesses their client's records, they then search for **evidence** to prove that recorded amounts are accurate. Evidence relates to each of the headings used in the previous section of this chapter. Specifically, an auditor verifies amounts recorded in their client's records using confirmations, documentary evidence, representations, verbal evidence, computational evidence, physical evidence, and electronic evidence.

There are three broad categories of corroborating evidence. Each category varies in its persuasiveness. The categories are internally generated evidence, externally generated evidence held by the client, and externally generated evidence sent directly to the auditor. Each category will now be discussed in turn.

3 Determine the persuasiveness of audit evidence.

evidence information gathered to confirm amounts recorded in client records

5.3.1 Internally generated evidence

Internally generated evidence held by the client includes records of cheques sent, copies of invoices and statements sent to customers, purchase orders, company documentation regarding policies and procedures, contracts, minutes of meetings, journals, ledgers, trial balances, spreadsheets, worksheets, reconciliations, calculations, and computations. This evidence may be held electronically (soft copy) or in paper form (hard copy). Auditors document in their working papers details of their meetings with client management and staff to gain an understanding of the client's business and system of internal controls. As previously stated, internally generated evidence is the least persuasive, as it can only be used to verify that a client has accurately converted this information into the financial statements. That is, as the client generates and holds this evidence, it is possible that evidence may be manipulated or omitted. Figure 5.3 shows common types of internally generated documents used as evidence by the auditor.

internally generated evidence information created by the client (for example, customer invoices, purchase orders)

FIGURE 5.3 **Internally generated evidence commonly used by the auditor**

The following is a list of internally generated documents frequently used by the auditor as evidence. Examples are provided in Appendix A.

Trial balance A listing of the accounts and balances at the end of the accounting period. The balances are used to prepare the financial statements.

General ledger Transaction details are posted to the general ledger, with each general ledger account reflecting the account opening balance, the transactions processed during the period, and the ending balance. The ending balance is reflected in the trial balance.

Sub-ledger Organizes accounting information by characteristic. Sub-ledgers are commonly used for accounts receivable, accounts payable, inventory, and payroll. They sort data by such things as customer, supplier, inventory classification, and employee, making it easier to organize information.

(continued)

FIGURE 5.3 **Internally generated evidence commonly used by the auditor** (continued)

For example, an accounts receivable sub-ledger will show the balance outstanding by customer and by days outstanding. The balance in the sub-ledger and the related general ledger control account should agree.

Master files Where the permanent information is maintained. For example, the accounts receivable master file includes customer names, addresses, contact details, and credit limits.

Purchase requisition A request for goods that is prepared and submitted to the purchasing department.

Purchase order Prepared once goods have been sourced, and serves as authorization for the purchase. Indicates the supplier, date, items ordered, quantity, and agreed-upon purchase price.

Receiving report Serves as proof that goods ordered were received, and notes the quantity, date, and receiver.

Invoice Indicates the amount owing for goods received.

Shipping document Sent with goods being shipped, indicating who the receiving company is, what is being shipped, and the shipping terms.

Remittance advice Sent with payment, indicating the invoice being paid.

5.3.2 Externally generated evidence held by the client

externally generated evidence
information created by a third party (for example, supplier statements, bank statements)

Externally generated evidence held by the client includes supplier invoices and statements, customer orders, bank statements, contracts, lease agreements, and tax assessments. These sources of evidence are quite persuasive, as they are produced by third parties. It is, however, possible for the client to manipulate these documents, which reduces their reliability to the auditor. Also, if the client provides the auditor with photocopies of information from these external sources, rather than originals, the reliability is reduced.

5.3.3 Externally generated evidence sent directly to the auditor

Externally generated evidence sent directly to the auditor includes bank confirmations, customers' confirmations, correspondence with the client's lawyers, including confirmations and representations, and expert valuations. These sources of evidence are considered to be the most reliable and best quality, as they are independent of the client. As this evidence is generated by third parties and sent directly to the auditor, the client does not have an opportunity to alter it. Further, externally generated evidence is considered the most persuasive when the source of that evidence is considered to be reliable, trustworthy, and independent of the client.

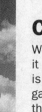

Cloud 9

Whenever Suzie's draft audit plan shows the team using enquiry (or verbal evidence), it also includes additional requirements to obtain evidence from another source. This is because the evidence obtained from the client is less persuasive than evidence gathered directly by an auditor or externally sourced evidence that has passed through the client's hands.

5.4 USING THE WORK OF AN EXPERT

It may be necessary to engage the services of an **expert** if an auditor does not have the requisite skills and knowledge to assess the validity of an account or a transaction. An expert is someone with the skills, knowledge, and experience required to aid the auditor when gathering evidence. An expert may be a member of the audit firm who is not a member of the audit team, an employee of the client, or a person independent of both the audit firm and its client. Experts commonly used by auditors include valuators for things such as real estate, works of art, collections, and jewellery, and actuaries to calculate liabilities related to employee future benefits and oil and gas reserves.

CAS 620 *Using the Work of an Auditor's Expert* provides guidelines for auditors when using the work of an expert. An auditor first assesses whether an expert is required. If it is decided that an expert is required, an auditor then determines the scope of work to be carried out. When selecting an expert to complete the work, an auditor assesses the competence and capability of the expert to do so and their objectivity. Once an expert has completed the work, an auditor assesses the work and draws conclusions based on the assessment. The ultimate responsibility for drawing conclusions based on gathered evidence rests with the auditor. Each of the stages in using an expert is now discussed.

4 Explain the issues to consider when using the work of an expert.

expert someone with the skills, knowledge, and experience required to aid the auditor when gathering sufficient appropriate evidence

5.4.1 Assessing the need to use an expert

When gathering evidence, an auditor may decide that they do not have the expertise necessary to test and evaluate the accuracy of reported information. They may decide that they require assistance in the form of an expert opinion or report to corroborate other evidence obtained. For example, an appraiser may be engaged to provide an opinion on the value of a client's property, a geologist may be engaged to evaluate the quantity and quality of mineral deposits, a vintner may be engaged to assess the quality and value of wine stocks, or an actuary may be engaged to verify insurance premiums.

The need to engage the services of an expert depends on the knowledge of the audit team, the significance and complexity of the item being assessed, and the availability of appropriate alternative corroborating evidence. If the audit team has experience with the item being audited and can draw on their knowledge from previous audits of that client or similar companies in the same industry, there is less need to use an expert. The greater the risk of material misstatement of the item under consideration, the more likely an auditor will turn to an expert for their advice. To summarize, the less knowledge an audit team has of the item under consideration, the greater the risk of material misstatement and the less corroborating evidence available, the more likely an auditor will conclude that an expert opinion is required.

5.4.2 Determining the scope of the work to be carried out

Once it has been determined that an expert opinion is required, the scope of the work to be carried out is determined by the auditor and communicated to the expert.

This involves setting the nature, timing, and extent of work to be completed by the expert. It is important for the auditor to be involved in setting the scope of the work required, as the judgement of the expert forms part of the audit evidence upon which the auditor forms their audit opinion.

Written instructions to an expert can cover the issues that the expert is to report upon, such as the market price of properties owned by the client; the details to be included in the report, such as the computations used in arriving at the expert's opinion; the sources of data to be used, such as market interest rates or market prices of shares; clarification of the way that the auditor intends to use the information included in the expert's report; and notice of the requirement that the expert's report and the data used in compiling the report must remain confidential.

5.4.3 Assessing the competence and capability of the expert

Before contacting an expert, an auditor assesses their capacity to complete the work required. This involves an evaluation of the expert's qualifications as a member of a relevant professional (or similar) body. The reputation of the expert within their field and the extent of their experience in providing the type of opinion or report sought by the auditor are also assessed. It is important that the expert's knowledge and experience be appropriate.

5.4.4 Assessing the objectivity of the expert

Objectivity refers to the ability to form an opinion or arrive at a conclusion without the influence of personal preferences. An expert is expected to be more objective if they are not associated with the client. An association will exist when the expert is an employee of the company or is connected with the client in some other way (for example, the expert is related to one of the key personnel of the client or financially linked with the client).

When an expert is an employee of the client or is in some other way connected with the client, an auditor assesses the objectivity of the expert with reference to their professional status, their reputation, and the auditor's prior experience with the expert. If an expert's opinion has proven to be accurate in the past, it increases the reliability the auditor may give the expert's opinion in the current audit. Nevertheless, the less independent the expert is from the client, the more corroborating evidence the auditor will require.

5.4.5 Assessing the expert's report

It is important that an expert's report be written in such a way that an auditor, who is not an expert in the field being reported on, can understand the technical content of the report. The report should detail each stage of the process used in arriving at the overall opinion or conclusion of the report. It should include information about the data sources or estimation models used or the calculations conducted. The auditor assesses the appropriateness of the data sources used—it is essential that the expert use data sources that are reputable and reliable. The auditor assesses the consistency of any assumptions made with those made in prior years and with other known information. The auditor assesses the consistency of information included in the expert's report with their understanding of the client. Finally, the auditor assesses the consistency of the conclusions drawn with corroborating evidence gathered by the audit team.

5.4.6 Responsibility for the conclusion

The responsibility for arriving at an overall conclusion regarding the fair presentation of a client's financial statements rests with the auditor. When an auditor decides to use an expert, that responsibility is not reduced in any way. It is the responsibility of the auditor to assess the quality of the evidence provided by an expert and determine whether it is reliable and objective. An auditor does this by following the process outlined above. They will determine the need for an expert, the scope of the expert's work, and the competence and objectivity of the expert. Finally, the auditor will assess the quality of the expert's report and the reliability of the information included in it.

Cloud 9

Suzie will take responsibility for obtaining an expert opinion on the derivatives. She knows that W&S Partners has other staff (who are not part of the audit team) who can provide additional expertise. However, because she believes the accounts are so material to the audit and derivatives have become such a big issue in audits in recent years, she deems that an external expert's opinion is also required. She has some experience using a derivatives expert on prior audits of clients in the footwear and clothing industry, and she also plans to ask Jo Wadley (the partner) to recommend a suitable expert.

Suzie plans to investigate any possible connections between the expert and Cloud 9 that could adversely impact the expert's independence before engaging him or her for this audit.

PROFESSIONAL ENVIRONMENT

Working with IT experts

Specialist IT auditors are often used in audits of clients with complex information technology (IT) environments because the effective audit of the IT systems contributes to overall audit quality. Large audit firms usually have such specialists within the firm, but smaller audit firms could be forced to engage external IT consultants for this part of a financial statement audit. In general, reliance on an IT specialist is appropriate when the financial statement auditor complies with the conditions of CAS 620, *Using the Work of an Auditor's Expert.*

If the IT expert and the financial statement auditor do not work well together, audit quality can be impaired. For this reason, researchers have investigated the factors that affect the way that financial statement auditors work with specialist IT auditors.

Brazel reviewed the research evidence and drew the following conclusions. First, responses from financial statement auditors in the United States who were surveyed about their experiences with IT auditors indicated that they believe IT auditors' competence levels vary in practice. Financial statement auditors also said that IT auditors appear to be overconfident in their abilities in some settings, and questioned the value provided by IT auditors to the financial statement audit.

Second, Brazel suggests that the research shows that both financial statement auditors' IT ability and experience and the IT auditor's competence affect how these two professions interact on an audit engagement. This indicates that audit firms need to ensure that staff training and scheduling produce appropriate combinations of financial statement auditors and IT auditors on an engagement.

Finally, Brazel argues that the research findings mean that auditors need to consider the implications of finding a balance between greater computer-assisted audit technique (CAAT) training for financial statement auditors and greater use of IT specialists for overall audit efficiency and effectiveness.

Source: J. F. Brazel, "How Do Financial Statement Auditors and IT Auditors Work Together?" *The CPA Journal,* November 2008.

BEFORE YOU GO ON

4.1 What factors may influence an auditor's decision on the need to use an expert?

4.2 How might an auditor assess the capacity of an expert?

4.3 Why is it important that an expert's report include details of data sources used?

5.5 USING THE WORK OF ANOTHER AUDITOR

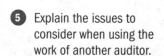

5 Explain the issues to consider when using the work of another auditor.

group engagement partner the auditor responsible for signing the audit report

component auditor an auditor who, at the request of the group engagement team, performs work on financial information related to a component for the group audit

CAS 600 *Special Considerations—Audits of Group Financial Statement (Including the Work of Component Auditors)* provides guidance when using the work of another audit firm. The auditor who is responsible for signing the audit report (the **group engagement partner**) may need to rely on evidence provided by another auditor for certain components of a client's financial statement. This occurs when a client operates in a number of locations, has divisions or subsidiaries spread around the country or the globe, or has significant assets in other locations.

When making a client acceptance or continuance decision, an auditor will consider their capacity to undertake the audit. They should also consider the proportion of the financial statements for which they will have to rely on another auditor (**component auditor**). The group engagement partner's firm should audit the majority of a client's financial statements and be knowledgeable about the components of the financial statements that they do not audit themselves. If this is not the case, the firm should not accept or continue to audit the client.

When assigning work to a component auditor, the group engagement partner will consider the capacity of the other auditor to undertake the work. The group engagement partner will also consider the reputation of the component auditor and ensure that they are a member of a reputable professional body. It is the responsibility of the group engagement partner to ensure that the work completed by a component auditor meets the group engagement partner's requirements and standards.

CAS 600 sets out the responsibilities of the group engagement partner when using the work of a component auditor. The group engagement partner determines the work to be conducted by a component auditor. The two auditors may discuss the detailed procedures to be used and the group engagement partner then reviews the main conclusions drawn in the working papers of the component auditor. The extent of review of the component auditor's work depends on a number of factors. The group engagement partner will spend more time if the component of the client's financial statements being audited by a component auditor is material and/or at risk of material misstatement. The group engagement partner will spend less time if the component auditor has a good reputation and/or has done audit work for the group engagement partner in the past.

The group engagement partner uses the evidence provided by a component auditor when drawing a final conclusion on the fair presentation of a client's financial statements.

The findings of a component auditor on a component of the financial statements will be placed in the context of the audit as a whole. If the group engagement partner is concerned about the conclusions arrived at by a component auditor, they will discuss the findings with the component auditor. They may also discuss the implications of those findings with those charged with governance at the client to gain a more complete understanding of the component of the financial statements audited by the component auditor. If the group engagement partner decides that the conclusions arrived at by the component auditor indicate a material misstatement in the component audited, and if the impact of the misstatement is material to the financial statements taken as a whole, the group engagement partner will consider issuing a modified audit opinion.

If the group engagement partner is concerned that a component auditor has not been able to gather sufficient appropriate audit evidence regarding the component of the financial statements audited, he or she will ask that further evidence be gathered. If the component auditor cannot access sufficient evidence, the engagement partner will consider issuing a modified audit opinion due to a scope limitation. This will occur when the group engagement partner is unable to obtain additional evidence on the elements of the component audited by a component auditor.

Cloud 9

Sharon knows that Cloud 9 Inc.'s auditor completed some work that was relevant to Cloud 9 before W&S Partners was appointed to the Cloud 9 audit. She has not yet seen these audit findings and does not know whether they will affect their work. She is keen to see them because she believes that some of the findings relate to the inventory management software system (Swift). Because they don't yet have enough information to make a judgement about the usefulness of the other auditor's work, Sharon decides to include in the plan some time for a discussion between the partner (Jo Wadley) and the Cloud 9 management to discuss the other auditor's findings, and whether the audit team can have access to these findings.

BEFORE YOU GO ON

5.1 Who is the group engagement partner?

5.2 What are some of the factors that a group engagement partner will consider when assigning work to a component auditor?

5.3 If the group engagement partner believes that the component auditor has not gathered sufficient appropriate audit evidence, what kind of audit report may be issued?

5.6 EVIDENCE-GATHERING PROCEDURES

The evidence-gathering procedures described in this section are carried out at various stages of the audit, when planning, gaining an understanding of the client, gaining an understanding of a client's system of internal controls, testing those controls, conducting detailed substantive testing, and drawing the final conclusions. CAS 500 provides guidelines, summarized below, on the primary evidence-gathering procedures used by auditors.

Confirmations generally provide evidence that items such as cash and accounts receivable exist (existence assertion). As previously discussed, external confirmations

6 Describe the evidence-gathering procedures most often used by auditors.

are written enquiries sent by the auditor directly to a third party, who is asked to respond to the auditor on the matter included in the confirmation letter. As confirmations are costly, they will be used when alternative evidence is limited.

Inspection involves examining records and documents and physically examining assets. An auditor will inspect records and documents for a variety of reasons. When testing controls, an auditor will inspect documents for evidence that, for example, calculations have been checked, balances have been reconciled, inputs have been agreed to outputs, and management has authorized significant purchases. Records and documents are inspected when conducting substantive testing to check, for example, the dates of transactions (cut-off assertion), that purchases were made by the client (rights and obligations assertion), and that a transaction occurred (occurrence assertion).

inspection an evidence-gathering procedure that involves examining records and documents, and physically examining assets

Tangible assets are physically inspected to provide evidence that they exist (existence assertion) and appear to be in good repair or are damaged or past their use-by date (valuation and allocation assertion). When a client conducts an inventory count, the auditor will attend and perform test counts (existence and completeness assertions).

Client staff are observed undertaking various procedures when there is no other way of establishing that a process is being used by the client. For example, an auditor will observe the opening of mail and the conduct of an inventory count to determine whether the appropriate procedures are being followed. Importantly, **observation** only provides evidence of a process at the time the auditor observes it being carried out. An auditor will need to determine whether there is evidence that the procedures observed have been applied consistently throughout the period under audit.

observation an evidence-gathering procedure that involves watching a procedure being carried out by another party

Enquiry is used when gaining an understanding of the client and to corroborate other evidence gathered throughout the audit. The results of enquiries of client personnel and third parties are documented by the auditor. If the evidence is particularly important, an auditor may document that information more formally and ask the other party to the discussion to sign an agreement that the auditor has recorded the discussion accurately.

enquiry an evidence-gathering procedure that involves asking questions verbally or in written form to gain an understanding of various matters throughout the audit

Recalculations are used to check the mathematical accuracy of client files and records. This will involve checking additions and more complex computations. Simple additions can be checked using CAATs, where client data are copied into an auditor's computer and additions are recalculated using the auditor's software package. More complex calculations will be recalculated individually.

recalculation an evidence-gathering procedure that involves checking the mathematical accuracy of client records

Re-performance means following a process used by a client. When testing controls, client procedures are re-performed to check that controls are effective. When conducting substantive testing, client estimations are re-performed to verify amounts calculated by the client. For example, when testing the allowance for doubtful accounts, an auditor will re-perform the aging of the accounts receivable to arrive at an estimated allowance amount.

re-performance an evidence-gathering procedure that involves redoing processes conducted by the client

Analytical procedures are used to appraise relationships between financial and non-financial information. During the planning stage of the audit, unusual fluctuations are identified. During the execution stage of the audit, analytical procedures are used to evaluate the information included in the financial statements (substantive analytical procedures). For example, hospital ward revenue can be estimated by counting the number of beds in the wards and then multiplying by the average occupancy rate and the amount charged per day. At the final review stage of the audit, analytical procedures are used to assess whether the financial statements reflect the auditor's understanding of the client.

analytical procedures an evaluation of financial information by studying plausible relationships among both financial and non-financial data

BEFORE YOU GO ON

6.1 Why might an auditor inspect documents when testing controls?

6.2 Provide some examples of how an auditor might use observation as part of their evidence-gathering procedures.

6.3 At which stage(s) of an audit will an auditor utilize a re-performance procedure? Explain.

5.7 DRAWING CONCLUSIONS

Sufficient appropriate audit evidence must be gathered to enable an auditor to draw a conclusion on which to base their opinion regarding the fair presentation of the client's financial statements (CAS 500). The decision as to what constitutes sufficient appropriate audit evidence is a matter of professional judgement, as it is based upon an auditor's understanding of their client and the significant risks identified when planning the audit and evidence gathered when executing the audit (CAS 315 *Identifying and Assessing the Risks of Material Misstatement through Understanding the Entity and Its Environment*; CAS 330 *The Auditor's Responses to Assessed Risks*).

7 Explain how auditors arrive at a conclusion based upon the evidence gathered.

If an auditor believes that a client has internal controls that can reduce the likelihood of a material misstatement for an identified risk, they will test those controls. This means that evidence will be gathered to establish whether the internal controls are effective. Details of tests of controls will be discussed in chapter 8. Once testing of controls is complete, an auditor will gather further evidence through their substantive testing of transactions and balances.

If an auditor decides that a client does not have in place appropriate controls for the identified risk, an auditor will adopt a predominantly substantive approach. The auditor will increase their reliance on evidence gathered through their detailed substantive tests of transactions and account balances. Details of substantive testing will be discussed in chapters 9 to 11.

After gathering all of the required evidence through their tests of controls and substantive testing, an auditor will form an opinion regarding the fair presentation of the client's financial statements. Chapter 12 includes a detailed discussion of the process used when drawing an overall conclusion at the completion of the audit.

Cloud 9

Suzie and Ian have already begun gathering evidence by performing the analytical procedures on Cloud 9's interim results and prior period's statements. Further evidence gathering at the planning stage will be performed by Josh and Sharon when they begin their assessment of the internal controls system by inspecting the relevant documents. They will also gather evidence from observing personnel performing their duties and making enquiries of members of Cloud 9's staff and management. In addition, Jo Wadley held discussions with the previous auditors (Ellis & Associates) before accepting the client. The record of these discussions, plus others that Jo Wadley has held with the Cloud 9 management, are already in the evidence files.

Ian has some questions about the evidence; in particular, why the audit team is bothering to gather verbal evidence, which has low persuasiveness. Suzie explains that all forms of evidence have their limitations. Observation is useful to see how staff perform their tasks (as opposed to what the manuals say they should be doing), but people often "behave" better when they are being watched. Documents can be lost or altered, or

misinterpreted, and not everything is written down. Electronic evidence is hard to audit if the system does not have a "hack-proof" audit trail. Signatures on documents do not mean that the author actually read the document properly; people can pre- or post-date documents. The auditor has to judge the appropriateness and sufficiency of the evidence by considering it as a whole and be prepared to follow up any problems or discrepancies until any doubts are satisfactorily resolved.

BEFORE YOU GO ON

7.1 How does an auditor decide how much evidence is sufficient?

7.2 What will an auditor do if they believe that a client has internal controls that can reduce the likelihood of a material misstatement?

7.3 What will an auditor do if they decide that a client does not have in place appropriate controls for the identified risk?

5.8 DOCUMENTATION—AUDIT WORKING PAPERS

8 Describe how auditors document the details of evidence gathered in working papers.

working papers paper or electronic documentation of the audit created by the audit team as evidence of the work completed

CAS 230 *Audit Documentation* requires an auditor to document each stage of the audit in their **working papers** to provide a record of work completed and evidence gathered in forming their audit opinion. The documentation includes the names of the preparers of the documentation, as well as the names of the reviewers of the work performed by the preparers. Documentation is cross-referenced between working papers that summarize the components of an account balance and working papers that provide details of the testing of that balance.

An auditor will document each stage of the audit and the procedures used. During the planning stage of an audit, an auditor will document their understanding of the client, the risks identified, analytical procedures used to aid in risk identification, their materiality assessment, their understanding of the client's system of internal controls, their understanding of the client's information technology, related parties identified, and any going concern matters. During the execution stage of the audit, an auditor will document their audit program, details of tests undertaken, copies of significant documents sighted, correspondence with the client's lawyers and bankers, confirmations received from accounts receivable customers, and enquiries of management.

Documentation will vary from client to client. It will depend upon, for example, the audit procedures used, the risks identified, the extent of judgement used, the persuasiveness of the evidence gathered, the nature and extent of exceptions noted, and the audit methodology utilized (CAS 230, para. A2).

An audit working paper generally includes:

- the client name
- the period under audit
- a title describing the contents of the working paper
- a file reference indicating where the working paper fits in the audit file
- initials identifying the preparer of the working paper together with the date the working paper was prepared
- initials identifying the reviewer(s) of the working paper together with the date(s) the working paper was reviewed

- cross-referencing between working papers indicating where further work and evidence is summarized elsewhere.

Working papers are used to document the details of each audit. The two main files held for each client are the permanent file and the current file. The permanent file includes documents that pertain to a client for more than one audit. The current file includes the details of work completed and evidence gathered that relate to the current audit.

5.8.1 Permanent file

The **permanent file** includes client information and documentation that apply to more than one audit. The information included in the permanent file is checked and updated at the beginning of each audit. The permanent file contains the client's head office address, other locations (where relevant), and contact details (telephone, fax, and e-mail). Key personnel are detailed, and an organizational chart will also often be included in the permanent file. A client's organizational chart includes details of key roles within the organization (such as the CEO) and the names of the people who undertake those roles. The file may also include the details of the client's bank(s) and lawyer(s).

The permanent file will include copies of long-term contracts and agreements. These documents will be used to calculate interest payable on outstanding long-term loans, and will enable the assessment of any lease obligations. Debt covenants will be included in the permanent file. An auditor can check the details of these agreements to assess their client's compliance with covenants. If a client has long-term commitments with customers and suppliers, an auditor will include the relevant documentation in the permanent file. Key long-term investments will be described, including the details of the broker used for these transactions.

The permanent file will include details of the client's board directors and its sub-committees (such as the audit committee). It will include the minutes of significant meetings held by the client, such as its board of directors meetings. It may include details of bonus and option schemes for senior client staff.

The permanent file will detail a client's principal accounting policies and methodologies. Prior financial statements and audit reports will be included. Details of prior analytical procedures will be included and added to so that the auditor can observe changing trends. Flowcharts and narratives detailing a client's system of internal controls will be included and amended as required during the planning stage of each audit.

Reports sent to the client during previous audits will be included in the permanent file. For example, management letters that detail deficiencies in internal controls identified by the auditor in previous years will be included and referred to by the auditor. An auditor will read these reports and discuss their contents with the client's management.

> **permanent file** file that contains client information that is relevant for more than one audit

Cloud 9

Cloud 9 Ltd.'s permanent file contains the basic information about the company (that is, address and key senior staff and their employment contracts) plus the copy of the engagement letter appointing W&S Partners and stating the scope of the audit. Sharon and Suzie have gathered copies of some of the relevant agreements and will add these and more (that is, those relating to leases, sponsorship, and loans) to the permanent file.

5.8.2 Current file

The **current file** includes client information and documentation that apply to the current audit. Contents of the current file will vary from client to client, depending on the accounts in the client's financial statements and the client's activities. The current file will include the details of all testing and evidence gathered in the preparation of the audit report.

The current file will also include correspondence between the auditor and the client and the client's bankers and lawyers that pertain to the current audit period. Correspondence with other auditors, experts, and relevant third parties will be included. The engagement letter will be included in the current file, along with the management letter, detailing deficiencies uncovered in the client's system of internal controls. Representation letters and confirmation letters may also be included in the current file.

The current file will include extracts from the minutes of meetings, such as the board of directors' meetings, that pertain to the current audit. The file will include details of the audit planning process and the audit program, as well as detailed descriptions of evidence gathered, testing conducted, and audit procedures performed. It will detail the analytical procedures, tests of controls, and detailed substantive testing undertaken, as well as the conclusions drawn at the completion of testing. The current file includes testing of any subsequent events and a copy of the final audit opinion.

Examples of working papers

In this section we provide some examples of working papers. While each accounting firm will have its own way of documenting evidence, to aid understanding it is worthwhile considering an example of how one firm, in this case Ernst & Young, prepares its working papers. There are many different ways of preparing working papers, although most have common elements. These are detailed later in this section of the chapter.

Working papers are prepared and stored electronically. Each audit will have a unique name, for ease of identification, which will include the client name and the year end of the financial statement being audited. Each working paper created for the audit will include the client name and year end, as well as the item being audited. In figure 5.3 the file contains the documented audit evidence for the accounts receivable account for the client, PBC Ltd., for the audit for the year ended June 30, 2010. You will see across the tabs in the worksheet that there are different types of working papers, such as a lead schedule, and supporting work papers, such as the aging analysis included in the tab "E3 AR Aging Analysis."

The notation E1, E2, E3 is the filing system used by this accounting firm. At this firm, accounts receivable are filed under E for all clients. The numbers are used for cross-referencing between worksheets within the accounts receivable, or E, file. The first worksheet or working paper in each file is referred to as the lead schedule. The lead schedule includes the summary of the account balance and typically also includes a summary of the work performed, any material issues or audit adjustments identified, and the overall conclusion relating to that account balance. The detailed testing of the elements of the account balance is documented in subsequent

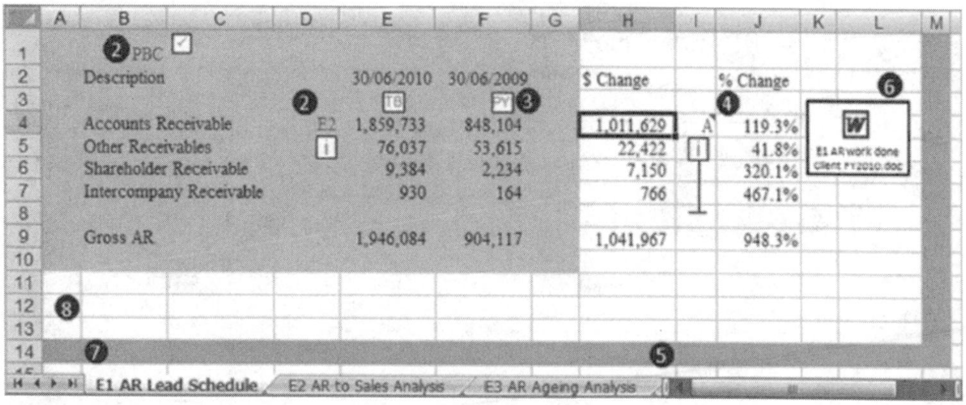

FIGURE 5.4 **Working paper example 1**
Source: Ernst & Young, 2010.

worksheets. Worksheet E2 details testing of credit sales and worksheet E3 details the accounts receivables aging analysis, which is used for testing the allowance for doubtful accounts.

The numbered elements of the example included in figure 5.4 are now described:

1. These are the formulae used to calculate the numbers included in the worksheet. These can be independently checked to ensure accuracy and consistency.
2. This shows where the work can be found for each balance listed. For example, the work performed on the $1,859,733 has been performed at E2. The $76,037 has been deemed as immaterial and marked with the "I" tickmark, which is sometimes used by firms to indicate that a balance is immaterial. A distinction is also made between the elements of the worksheet that have been prepared by the client (PBC) and the elements prepared by the audit staff. This distinction can be made by use of shading, different fonts, or different colours.
3. This column shows the balances from the prior period for comparison and analytical review purposes.
4. This column shows the movement between the current year and the prior year to assist in identifying movements that may require further investigation.
5. Each worksheet is numbered and cross-referenced to other worksheets and ultimately back to the lead schedule. Unused worksheets are deleted.
6. Word documents detailing work completed on a client are sometimes embedded in worksheets so that all relevant evidence is kept together and accounted for.
7. Shading is used to outline work completed.
8. Blank space is minimized around work completed and is often used to document any other comments or relevant factors for the reviewer(s) of the working paper.

Figure 5.5 includes another example of a working paper. This working paper details the aging analysis for accounts receivable (worksheet E3). The accounts receivable balance is broken down into amounts that are current (that is, the sale was made within the last 30 days) and amounts outstanding 31–60, 61–90, and over 90 days. The greater the number of days that an amount is outstanding, the greater the risk that the accounts receivable customer won't pay.

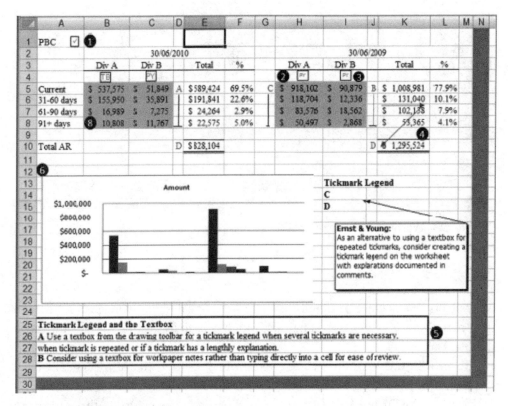

FIGURE 5.5 **Working paper example 2**
Source: Ernst & Young, 2010.

The elements of the working paper example included in figure 5.5 are now described:

1. This worksheet was prepared by the client (PBC) and the tickmark indicates that the numbers included in the worksheet have been checked by a member of the audit team.
2. This mark at the top of the column indicates that a member of the audit team has traced all numbers included in the column back to last year's audit file.
3. The letters A–D indicate the audit procedures conducted on the amounts highlighted.
4. Formulae are used within each spreadsheet to explain the relationships between numbers listed. In this case a percentage of the total is calculated for each time period outstanding.
5. Text boxes and comments are used to explain tests performed or the nature of evidence gathered.
6. Graphs are sometimes used to clarify the relationship between numbers used in tables. They highlight major shifts and unusual fluctuations.
7. Toolbars aid in working paper documentation.
8. Shading can be used to differentiate between cells where numbers have been input and cells where calculations have been input. In this case, the shaded numbers can be copied over into next year's audit file for comparative purposes.

   The working paper in figure 5.6 is an example of a Word document working paper that might be embedded in an Excel spreadsheet. In this case, the Word document is used to document the work performed, results of the work, and overall conclusion for the work performed.

EXAMPLE TEST OF CONTROL WORKING PAPER		
Client name: Indigo Ltd.	Year end: December 31, 2011	
Working paper: Cash controls testing		

Purpose of test:

The purpose of this test is to verify that the bank reconciliation control was adequately designed and implemented for the 12 months ending December 31, 2011.

Work performed:

Selected two bank reconciliations from different months, tied the balance as per the bank statement to the bank statement and bank audit certificate, tied the balance as per the general ledger to the trial balance and vouched all reconciling items between the bank statement and the trial balance greater than $50,000 to supporting documentation to ensure valid reconciling items and that the reconciliation had been performed correctly. Ensured that the reconciliation had been prepared and reviewed on a timely basis.

Findings/results of testing:

Selected bank reconciliation for the months of April and September 2011. No errors noted in the preparation of the reconciliation. Both were prepared and reviewed within four days of month end. Considered this to be on a timely basis.

Conclusion:

Based on testing performed, the bank reconciliation appears to have been designed, implemented, and operating effectively for the 12 months ended December 31, 2011.

	Prepared by: SEF	Reviewed by: FMC	Index: C1:1

FIGURE 5.6 **Working paper example 3**

The elements of the working paper example included in figure 5.6 are now described:

1. Each working paper includes the name of the client, the working paper reference, the balance being tested, and the client year end. These details are entered at the top of the working paper.
2. At the bottom of each working paper there are spaces for the initials and date for the working paper preparer and reviewer. The index refers to the working paper index code.
3. The body of the working paper includes details of the work done. In this case, the working paper provides details of a test of controls and outlines the purpose of the test, the work performed, the findings, and the overall conclusion.

Cloud 9

The first major item in the current file for Cloud 9 is the audit plan. In addition, every task that is performed during the audit will be documented. Ian and the other junior staff are still struggling with how to correctly complete the papers. They often forget to complete all the relevant fields and Sharon, Suzie, and Josh are continually sending papers back to them with requests to clarify some of their comments. However, embedding the working papers in Excel has made life easier than in the past, when everything was paper-based, because an error message will be generated if certain key fields are not completed.

BEFORE YOU GO ON

8.1 What is a current file?

8.2 What is a permanent file?

8.3 What will an auditor document during the planning stage of the audit?

SUMMARY

1 **Outline the audit assertions.**

When preparing the financial statements, management will make assertions about each account and related disclosures in the notes. Auditors use these assertions to assess the risk of material misstatement and design audit procedures. The assertions used when testing transactions and events, including income statement items, are occurrence, completeness, accuracy, cut-off, and classification. The assertions used when testing balance sheet items are existence, rights and obligations, completeness, and valuation and allocation.

2 **Identify and describe different types of audit evidence and define sufficient appropriate audit evidence.**

The different types of audit evidence include external confirmations, documentary evidence, representations, verbal evidence, computational evidence, physical evidence, and electronic evidence. External confirmations are sent directly by an auditor to a third party. Documentary evidence may be generated internally by the client or externally by third parties. Representation letters are requested from a client's lawyers or management. Verbal evidence is the discussions between the auditor and client personnel or third parties. Computational evidence is gathered when an auditor checks the mathematical accuracy of figures included in the financial statements. Physical evidence involves the inspection of tangible assets. Electronic evidence includes data held on a client's computer, files sent by e-mail to the auditor, and items scanned and faxed.

Sufficiency refers to the quantity of evidence gathered. Appropriateness refers to the relevance and reliability of audit evidence gathered.

3 **Determine the persuasiveness of audit evidence.**

The persuasiveness of evidence used to corroborate the details included in a client's accounts varies. Internally generated evidence held by the client is the least persuasive, as the client can alter or hide this evidence. Externally generated evidence held by the client is more persuasive, as it is created by an independent third party. Externally generated evidence sent directly to the auditor is the most persuasive, as the client does not handle this evidence.

4 **Explain the issues to consider when using the work of an expert.**

When an auditor decides to use the work of an expert, the report produced by the expert forms part of the evidence used by an auditor when forming their audit opinion. An expert is someone with the skills, knowledge, and experience required to help an auditor. The auditor determines the scope of the work to be carried out, and assesses the capability of the expert, the objectivity of the expert, and the expert's report.

⑤ Explain the issues to consider when using the work of another auditor.

An auditor may need to use the work of another auditor when their client operates in a number of locations, has divisions or subsidiaries spread around the country or the globe, or has significant assets in other places. When this is the case, the principal auditor may need to rely on evidence provided by another auditor for certain components of the client's financial statements.

⑥ Describe the evidence-gathering procedures most often used by auditors.

An auditor will inspect records, documentation, and tangible assets. They will observe client staff undertaking various procedures. An auditor will make enquiries of client personnel and third parties. Confirmations are sent to third parties, including banks, lawyers, lenders, and debtors. An auditor will recalculate numbers appearing in client files and records to check mathematical accuracy. They will re-perform some processes used by the client to check the effectiveness of internal controls and the validity of amounts estimated by client personnel. Analytical procedures are used throughout the audit to appraise the relationships between financial and non-financial information.

⑦ Explain how auditors arrive at a conclusion based upon the evidence gathered.

The final audit procedure is to assess the evidence gathered throughout the audit and draw a conclusion on the fair presentation of a client's financial statements.

⑧ Describe how auditors document the details of evidence gathered in working papers.

Audit evidence is documented in an auditor's working papers. Audit working papers include the client's name, the period under audit, a title describing the contents of the working paper, a file reference indicating where the working paper fits in the audit file, the initials of the preparer of the working paper together with the date the working paper was prepared, the initials of the reviewer(s) of the working paper together with the date(s) the working paper was reviewed, and cross-referencing between working papers indicating where further work and evidence are summarized elsewhere. Working papers are stored in either the permanent file or the current file. The permanent file includes client information and documentation that apply to more than one audit. The current file includes client information and documentation that apply to the current audit.

KEY TERMS

MULTIPLE-CHOICE QUESTIONS

5.1   The auditor is responsible for:

(a) ensuring that the financial statements are prepared in accordance with accounting standards and the law.

(b) ensuring that accurate accounting records are maintained.

(c) ensuring that any potential mis-statements are prevented or detected and corrected.

(d) gathering sufficient appropriate evidence to support an opinion regarding the fair presenta-tion of the client's financial statements.

5.2   The quantity of evidence that an auditor will gather:

(a) varies with audit risk.

(b) is the same for all audits because it has to be appropriate.

(c) depends on the size of the audit team.

(d) all of the above.

5.3   An external confirmation sent to a bank:

(a) requests information about the bank balances and loan amounts.

(b) requests information about interest rates paid on deposits and charged on loans.

(c) is relevant to the audit of interest revenue and expense.

(d) all of the above.

5.4   When an auditor gathers documen-tary evidence or physical evidence to support an entry in the client's records, the auditor is gathering evidence to support the:

(a) completeness assertion.

(b) existence assertion.

(c) both (a) and (b).

(d) neither (a) nor (b).

5.5   When an auditor inspects tangible assets on hand and traces the details to the details recorded in the client's records, the auditor is gathering evidence to support the:

(a) completeness assertion.

(b) existence assertion.

(c) both (a) and (b).

(d) neither (a) nor (b).

5.6   Generally the most persuasive form of evidence is:

(a) internally generated evidence.

(b) externally generated evidence held by the client.

(c) externally generated evidence sent directly to the auditor.

(d) none of the above; they are equally persuasive.

5.7   If an expert is engaged to assist with the audit:

(a) it means the auditor does not have the requisite skill and knowledge to assess the item.

(b) it means the auditor should not have taken on the audit because they are not qualified.

(c) CICA must be contacted and permission obtained before the expert starts work.

(d) the auditor does not have to take responsibility for the fair presentation of the item in the financial statements.

5.8 **Inspecting documents, such as an invoice for the purchase of fixed assets, provides the auditor with evidence relevant to the:**

(a) rights and obligations assertion, because the document will show the client's name as the purchaser.

(b) occurrence assertion, because the document will show that the transaction took place on the specified date.

(c) accuracy assertion, because the document will show the purchase amounts.

(d) all of the above.

5.9 **Analytical procedures are used to gather evidence:**

(a) at the planning stage to gain an understanding of a client.

(b) at the execution stage to evaluate information included in the financial statements.

(c) at the final review stage to assess whether the financial statements reflect the auditor's understanding of their client.

(d) all of the above.

5.10 **The working papers for a client contain both a permanent and a current file. The difference between the two files is that:**

(a) the permanent file is kept by the audit partner in charge and cannot be altered after the first audit engagement is completed, but the current file can be updated.

(b) the permanent file is provided to the client and the current file is not.

(c) the permanent file includes documents that relate to the client and are relevant for more than one audit, and the current file includes the details of work completed and evidence gathered that relate to the current audit.

(d) all of the above.

REVIEW QUESTIONS

5.1 Explain why the quality of audit evidence is determined by the choice of the audit procedure and the assertion at risk of material misstatement.

5.2 What is a legal letter? What external parties could an auditor send a confirmation to? What other parties provide representation letters to an auditor?

5.3 Explain how gathering physical evidence by inspecting a client's tangible assets assists in the audit of the completeness and existence assertions.

5.4 Discuss the impact of electronic processing of transactions on the audit.

5.5 Why does an auditor have to consider the persuasiveness of corroborating evidence? Explain.

5.6 If an auditor does not have sufficient knowledge and skill in an area, the auditor can ask for the assistance of an expert. This creates a problem—how does an auditor know if the expert's work is correct if the auditor is not also an expert? Explain.

5.7 Under what circumstances does an auditor use the work of a component auditor? Why doesn't the group engagement partner do all of the work?

5.8 What are the evidence-gathering procedures an auditor might use? At which stages of the audit are these procedures appropriate? How do the procedures relate to the types of evidence an auditor can rely upon?

5.9 What is the difference between recalculation and re-performance? Explain using examples.

5.10 Review the examples of working papers provided in the chapter. What advantages are there for the auditor in writing working papers in spreadsheets and word documents?

PROFESSIONAL APPLICATION QUESTIONS

Basic ★   Moderate ★★   Challenging ★★★

5.1 Identifying audit assertions ★

Required

For each of the following items, identify the related assertion:

(a) Inventory is recorded at the lower of cost and net realizable value.

(b) All delivery vans recorded in the accounting records are owned by the entity.

(c) All payroll-related accruals at year end are recorded.

(d) The accounts receivable sub-ledger agrees to the general ledger control account.

(e) All sales were recorded in the correct period.

(f) There is no inventory on consignment.

(g) Purchases made after year end were recorded in the prior year.

(h) There is no impairment of goodwill.

(i) There are 10 delivery vans in the parking lot.

(j) There are no undisclosed contingent liabilities.

5.2 Confirmations ★★

The following are *independent* questions.

Required

(a) List *four* factors that make audit evidence more reliable.

(b) Explain the difference between positive and negative confirmations for accounts receivable.

Source: © CGA-Canada. Reproduced with permission.

5.3 Types and persuasiveness of audit evidence ★

Jenna is working on the audit of a client's accounts receivable. During the last few weeks she has conducted interviews with the accounts receivable manager, the CFO and staff working in the accounts receivable department. She has also overseen the external confirmations of accounts receivable, 30 percent of which required the recipient to respond as to whether or not the amount stated was correct. Jenna also conducted a review of subsequent cash receipts from the client's customers. She vouched a sample of accounts receivable balances back to the underlying invoices, cash receipts, and sales returns, and traced a sample of these documents to the accounts receivable ledger.

Required

(a) List the types of audit evidence gathered by Jenna and comment on the persuasiveness of each type.

(b) Link each type of evidence to the relevant accounts receivable assertions.

5.4 Communication with lawyers ★

Conversations between the board of directors of Acme Ltd. and the engagement partner of the financial audit, Angelo Del Santo, have revealed that Acme uses three legal firms. Ball and Partners performs all legal work related to property transfers, mortgages, and planning applications. Brown and Associates handle all employment matters, such as claims for unfair dismissal and complex employment contracts. Zimmerman and Co. are retained for all other matters, such as agreements relating to products and suppliers and any international matters.

Required

(a) What type of communication should Angelo and his audit team have with each legal firm? Explain.

(b) What procedures could Angelo perform to find out whether any other legal firms have performed work for Acme during the financial year?

5.5 Bank reconciliations ★

Mohammad Amed is responsible for preparing bank reconciliation statements at Ajax Ltd. Ajax Ltd. has many bank accounts, including separate accounts for each major branch, imprest accounts for salaries and dividends, and accounts kept in foreign currency for overseas divisions. Mohammad maintains records including bank statements and weekly bank reconciliations for each account. In addition, there are files containing correspondence with banks about disputed transactions, dishonoured cheques from Ajax Ltd.'s customers, and other bank-initiated transactions such as fees and interest.

Required

(a) Comment on the persuasiveness of the evidence in Mohammad's files for Ajax Ltd.'s financial statement audit.
(b) Explain how an auditor would obtain more persuasive evidence for the relevant assertions for the bank accounts at Ajax Ltd.

5.6 Using an expert ★★

SolarTubeGen is a start-up company in the renewable energy sector. The founder, Fritz Herzberg, has developed cutting-edge technology to convert the energy in the sun's rays to electricity via a novel system of mirrors designed to focus the sun's rays onto tubes containing a patented type of gas, which then heats and expands to drive turbines. KKK Partners has won the contract for the first statutory audit of SolarTubeGen on the basis of its expertise in the energy sector. However, the lead partner, Ken Kennedy, recognizes that the success of the audit is dependent on the correct assessment of the technology being used at SolarTubeGen. Ken specified in the successful tender documents that the audit will use an external expert to help with valuation of the company's assets.

Fritz Herzberg is very protective of his company's intellectual property and is resistant to Ken's first suggested expert, Manfred Hamburg. Fritz believes that Manfred Hamburg is hostile toward him because they clashed when they both worked for a German company making photovoltaic cells in the 1990s. Fritz has suggested another expert, Lily Beilherz, with whom he has had good working relations over the last 20 years.

Required

Advise Ken Kennedy about the choice of an expert for the audit of SolarTubeGen. What must he consider when making his choice?

5.7 Gathering evidence ★★

Max Crowe is a junior auditor who has just started with the team conducting the audit of a new client in the construction industry. Max is "shadowing" Susan Wong, an experienced auditor. Susan is showing Max how to be a member of an audit team and is trying to teach Max about the benefits of getting to know the client. Susan is also trying to help Max develop experience in picking up subtle signals about the client's problems and what the client might be trying to hide from the auditor.

Max is getting a little frustrated with the "shadowing" assignment. He can't understand why Susan is spending so much time talking to the client's staff and touring the various construction sites and offices. When Susan is not doing this, she is working on a spreadsheet of the client's previous financial statements and unaudited interim data. Max wants to know when they are going to do some "real" work and start gathering audit evidence. Susan tells Max that they have already started.

Required

(a) Discuss Susan's comment that they have already started the audit. What evidence have they gathered so far?

(b) Explain what work is being done with the spreadsheets of financial data. Give some specific examples for this client. How is this type of work relevant to all stages of the audit?

5.8 Documentation ★ ★

Jennifer Daoust is reading the documents prepared by the members of the team working on the audit of receivables for a large client. Jennifer is the senior manager assisting the engagement partner, Ruby Rogers. Jennifer and Ruby have worked together on many audits and Jennifer knows the types of questions that Ruby will ask about the working papers if they are not up to the standard required by CAS 230. Jennifer is trying to make sure that all documents are up to the required standard before Ruby sees them tomorrow.

Jennifer is particularly concerned about the documents relating to the receivable confirmations. This is because the audit assistant who wrote up the confirmation results said that no further work was required. On review of the results, Jennifer discovered that the audit assistant had incorrectly treated "no reply" results as acceptable for a positive confirmation, when they are acceptable only for a negative confirmation. Jennifer had ordered further work be done to follow up these "no reply" results.

Required

(a) What is the minimum standard that the audit documentation must meet?

(b) How would you treat the corrections made to the audit assistant's recommendations and the additional work on receivable confirmations in the working papers? Explain. Refer to both CAS 505 and CAS 230 in your answer.

5.9 Documenting the audit ★ ★

Featherbed Surf & Leisure Holidays Ltd. (Featherbed) is a resort company based on Vancouver Island. Its operations include boating, surfing, diving, and other leisure activities; a backpackers' hostel; a family hotel; and a five-star resort. Justin and Sarah Morris own the majority of the shares in the Morris Group, which controls Featherbed. Justin is the chairman of the board of directors of both Featherbed and the Morris Group, and Sarah is a director of both companies as well as the CFO of Featherbed.

While performing the Featherbed audit you discover that the Wave Travel Agency, which specializes in group travel to Vancouver Island, has an account with Featherbed. The review of the aging of the accounts receivable balance shows that Wave Travel Agency's balance is large and material and is now more than 60 days overdue. However, no allowance has been made for the outstanding debt. You consult Featherbed's accounting staff, Julie and Kristen, about the account and they mention that there are rumours that the Wave Travel Agency is suffering financial difficulties.

You are aware that CAS 230 has specific requirements about documenting audit work. In particular, paragraph 9 states:

In documenting the nature, timing and extent of audit procedures performed, the auditor shall record:

(a) The identifying characteristics of the specific items or matters tested;

(b) Who performed the audit work and the date such work was completed

(c) Who reviewed the audit work performed and the date and extent of such review.

In addition, paragraph 10 states:

The auditor shall document discussions of significant matters with management, those charged with governance, and others, including the nature of the significant matters discussed and when and with whom the discussions took place.

Required

Explain how you would apply the mandatory requirements of the above paragraphs of CAS 230 in relation to the potential bad debt.

Source: Adapted from the Institute of Chartered Accountants Australia's CA Program's Audit and Assurance exam, May 2008.

5.10 Considering the work of other auditors ★ ★ ★

Securimax Limited (Securimax) has been an audit client of KFP Partners (KFP) for the past 15 years. Securimax is based in Waterloo, where it manufactures high-tech armour-plated personnel carriers. Securimax often has to go through a competitive market tender process to win large government contracts. Its main product, the small but powerful Terrain Master, is highly specialized and Securimax only does business with nations that have a recognized, democratically elected government. Securimax maintains a highly secure environment, given the sensitive and confidential nature of its vehicle designs and its clients.

Clarke Field has been the engagement partner on the Securimax audit for the last five years. Clarke is a specialist in the defence industry and intends to remain as review partner when the audit is rotated next year to a new partner (Sally Woodrow, who is to be promoted to partner to enable her to sign off on the audit).

Securimax has a small internal audit department that is headed by an ex-partner of KFP, Rydell Crow. Rydell joined Securimax six years ago, after leaving KFP and completing his Chartered Accountant qualifications. Rydell is assisted by three junior internal auditors, all of whom are completing Bachelor of Accounting and Financial Management studies at the University of Waterloo.

Securimax's fiscal year end is December 31.

Required

Discuss the effect, if any, of CAS 600 on Clarke Field's consideration of Securimax's internal audit department for the financial statement audit.

Source: Adapted from the Institute of Chartered Accountants Australia's CA Program's Audit & Assurance Exam, May 2008.

Questions 5.11 and 5.12 are based on the following case.

Fellowes and Associates Chartered Accountants is a successful mid-tier accounting firm with a large range of clients across Canada. In 2011, Fellowes and Associates gained a new client, Health Care Holdings Group (HCHG), which owns 100 percent of the following entities:
- Shady Oaks Centre, a private treatment centre
- Gardens Nursing Home Ltd., a private nursing home
- Total Laser Care Limited (TLCL), a private clinic that specializes in the laser treatment of skin defects.

Year end for all HCHG entities is June 30.

You are performing the audit field work for the 2011 year for Shady Oaks Centre. The field work must be completed in time for the audit report to be signed on August 21, 2011. You have been asked to circulate the receivable confirmations. Shady Oaks Centre's trade receivables arise from the use of clinic facilities (including the provision of medical professionals, treatment rooms, and supplies) by medical practitioners in private practice. The trade receivables balance was $3,974,569 as at June 30, 2011, and was considered material.

The centre's payment terms are 14 days from the date of the invoice. Sixty percent of the balance is represented by invoices outstanding from five different medical practitioners. The remaining 40 percent is made up of numerous smaller amounts, most of which have been outstanding for more than 60 days. Any allowance for doubtful accounts is taken directly against the trade receivables account and not shown separately.

Source: Adapted from the Institute of Chartered Accountants Australia's CA Program's *Audit & Assurance Exam,* December 2008.

5.11 Confirmation evidence ★★

Required

Discuss the strength and weaknesses of accounts receivable confirmations as audit evidence for HCHG.

5.12 Adequacy of documentation and audit evidence ★★★

Required

Is it possible for Fellowes and Associates to use accounts receivable confirmations only as audit evidence and adhere to the mandatory requirements in CAS 230? Explain your answer.

5.13 Identifying assertions and supporting evidence ★★

You are engaged to examine the financial statements of Lauzon Inc. for the year ended December 31.

On October 1, Lauzon Inc. borrowed $250,000 from a local bank to finance a plant expansion. The loan agreement provided for the annual payment of principal and interest over three years. Lauzon's existing plant was pledged as security for the loan.

Unfortunately, Lauzon ran into some difficulties in acquiring the new plant site. Thus, the plant expansion was delayed. Lauzon then proceeded to "plan B," which was to invest the borrowed funds in stocks and bonds. As a result, on October 20, the entire amount borrowed was invested in securities.

Required

Identify the assertions applicable to the above, and describe the relevant evidence that needs to be obtained to support them for the audit of investments in securities at December 31.

5.14 Identifying types of audit evidence ★★

Required

Identify the type of audit evidence being used in each situation described below:

(a) The auditor tests cash remittance advices to ensure that allowances and discounts are appropriate and that receipts are posted to the correct customer accounts in the right amounts. In addition, the auditor reviews the documents supporting unusual discounts and allowances.

(b) The auditor examines vehicle insurance policies and checks insurance expense for the year. In addition, the auditor reviews the expense with respect to changes and ending balances in capital asset accounts.

(c) The auditor observes the auditee taking a physical inventory count. In addition, a letter is received from a public storage facility stating the amounts of the auditee's inventory stored in it. The company uses a weighted average cost flow assumption, which is tested by the auditor's computer software program.

(d) Using audit software, an auditor selects vendors' accounts payable with debit balances from the client's computer screen and compares these amounts and their calculation with cash disbursements and vendor credit memos.

CASES

5.15 IndaCar—Integrative Case Study ★★★

IndaCar Inc. (IC) operates a high-end car rental agency that specializes in the rental of unique vehicles and is located next to Lester B. Pearson International Airport in Toronto. IC is a private Canadian company that is wholly owned by Jake Bouvier.

Daytona Lemans LLP, Chartered Accountants (DL), has reviewed IC's annual financial statements since IC was founded five years ago and has experienced no significant problems when performing the previous review engagements. You just found out you are the manager on the job for this year.

As a result of IC's success in Toronto, Jake is exploring the possibility of expanding IC's operations to include the Vancouver and Calgary airports. Jake expects that he will be using IC's fiscal 2012 financial statements to attract equity investors to partially finance this expansion.

To maximize IC's share value attractiveness to potential investors, Jake is wondering if he should have the financial statements audited.

Jake commented that he received a tip from one of the employees at the Pearson location that the manager is stealing cash. He wants to know if the regular audit engagement is likely to identify whether cash is being stolen and what procedures the auditor is likely to perform in this risk area.

You have reviewed the fiscal 2011 engagement file in order to familiarize yourself with the client and to review the planning documentation prepared for the previous year's engagement.

IndaCar Inc.
As at December 31
(in thousands of dollars)

	2012 (unaudited)	2011 (audited)
Assets		
Cash	$ 1,453	$ 162
Accounts receivable	1,142	130
Inventory	1,270	1,140
Prepaid expenses	112	3
	3,977	1,435
Property, plant, and equipment (net)	20,657	14,465
Investments	2,000	
	22,657	14,465
	$26,634	$15,900
Liabilities		
Bank operating loan	$ 90	$ 100
Accounts payable and accrued liabilities	1,225	166
	1,315	266
Long-term debt	1,260	200
	2,575	466
Shareholders' Equity		
Common shares	100	100
Retained earnings	23,959	15,334
	24,059	15,434
	$26,634	$15,900

EXCERPTS FROM THE INCOME STATEMENT
For the years ended December 31
(in thousands of dollars)

	2012	2011
	(unaudited)	(audited)
Revenues		
Car rentals	$22,710	$14,300
Investment income	6,085	4,485
	28,795	18,785
Expenses		
Vehicle operations, including amortization	10,670	8,870
Rent and administration	995	810
Wages and salaries	7,200	6,675
Total expenses	18,865	16,355
Income before income tax	9,930	2,430
Income tax	1,305	780
Net income	$ 8,625	$ 1,650

Required

(a) Advise Jake on the costs and benefits of upgrading from a review engagement to an audit engagement.

(b) In planning the audit, the auditor must consider audit risk. Using the above case facts, make an inherent risk assessment.

(c) If the auditor decides that control risk is high, what type of audit will DL perform? How will this impact the amount of audit work?

(d) Calculate and conclude on the most appropriate planning materiality, and include a detailed explanation supporting your decision.

(e) For the following accounts, what assertions will the auditor be most concerned with? What evidence should the auditor gather to verify the management assertions?

   1. Accounts receivable
   2. Property, plant, and equipment
   3. Accounts payable
   4. Long-term debt
   5. Car rental sales

Source: (Adapted and) reprinted with the permission of the Institute of Chartered Accountants of Ontario, copyright ICAO. Any changes to the original material are the sole responsibility of the author (and or the publisher) and have not been reviewed or endorsed by the ICAO.

CASE STUDY—CLOUD 9

W&S Partners will need the assistance of auditors in China and the United States and derivatives experts to complete the Cloud 9 audit.

The other auditors will be asked to provide evidence about the inventory shipped to Canada from the production plants in these countries. Although the inventory is shipped FOB (free on board), there have been several occasions where the shipping agent was unable to place the inventory on a ship. In these cases, the inventory is stored in the shipping agent's warehouse until a vessel is made available. Suzie has some concerns about the quality of the warehouses, because if the goods are damaged they could become worthless and the value of "goods in transit" will be overstated.

In addition, Suzie has asked Jo Wadley for help in choosing an expert to help with valuation aspects of the audit of the derivatives. Jo has provided her with three names of experts in the field, but she has had no personal experience with any of them. Suzie must make a choice and engage the expert soon in order to be sure that the expert opinion will be received in time to complete the audit.

Answer the following questions based on the information presented for Cloud 9 in the appendix at the end of this book and the current and earlier chapters. You should also consider your answers to the case study questions in earlier chapters.

Required

(a) Explain the procedures for engaging component auditors to perform the work on the inventory in China and the United States.

(b) Advise Suzie on engaging the derivatives expert. Discuss the qualities the expert must possess. What procedures must Suzie perform? What should she tell the expert about the engagement? What must the expert give to Suzie so that she can be sure she has sufficient appropriate evidence about the derivatives? Can the expert do all the work on derivatives, or must Suzie perform any other procedures?

(c) Assume you are engaging the component auditors and the derivatives expert. Create a working paper for each task.

RESEARCH QUESTION 5.1

Obtain the latest annual report of a large multinational Canadian company (for example, one of the large banks or mining companies).

Required

(a) What information is given in the annual report about the use of any component auditors, other than the Canadian audit firm issuing the audit report? If any other auditors are mentioned, what work do you think these auditors performed?

(b) Is there any information given in the annual report about the auditor's use of an expert? What sort of work would an expert have performed for the audit of your chosen company?

SOLUTIONS TO MULTIPLE-CHOICE QUESTIONS

1. d, 2. a, 3. d, 4. b, 5. a, 6. c, 7. a, 8. d, 9. d, 10. c.

CHAPTER 6

Overview of tests of controls, substantive procedures, and sampling

LEARNING OBJECTIVES

After studying this chapter, you should be able to:

1 understand the difference between tests of controls and substantive tests

2 explain the factors that impact the nature, timing, and extent of audit testing

3 explain how audit sampling is used in an audit

4 understand the difference between sampling and non-sampling risk

5 differentiate between statistical and non-statistical sampling

6 describe sampling methods and the factors to be considered when choosing a sample.

7 determine the factors that influence the sample size when testing controls

8 determine the factors that influence the sample size when substantive testing

9 outline how to evaluate the results of tests conducted on a sample.

AUDITING AND ASSURANCE STANDARDS

CANADIAN	INTERNATIONAL
CAS 200 *Overall Objectives of the Independent Auditor and the Conduct of an Audit in Accordance with Canadian Auditing Standards*	ISA 200 *Overall Objectives of the Independent Auditor and the Conduct of an Audit in Accordance with International Standards on Auditing*
CAS 300 *Planning an Audit of Financial Statements*	ISA 300 *Planning an Audit of Financial Statements*
CAS 330 *The Auditor's Responses to Assessed Risks*	ISA 330 *The Auditor's Responses to Assessed Risks*
CAS 530 *Audit Sampling*	ISA 530 *Audit Sampling*

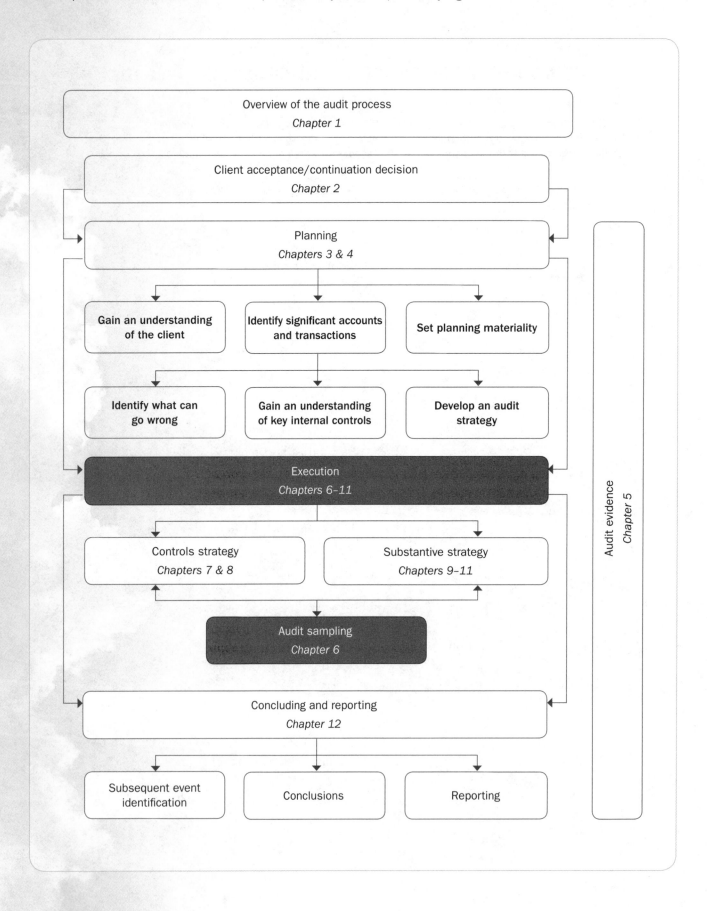

Cloud 9

Another issue that arises at the Cloud 9 Ltd. (Cloud 9) audit planning meeting is the appropriate scheduling of the control and substantive tests and the sampling criteria. After the meeting finishes, Ian Harper asks Suzie Pickering to coffee again. He wants her to explain how they can plan these tests and write a detailed audit program, including instructions on how to select the sample, when the results of one set of tests will influence the work on other tests. It all seems a bit circular to him, and he is finding it difficult to grasp.

Suzie is happy to drink more coffee and meets Ian that afternoon at their local café. "The sort of tests we have to do, and when and how we do them, depends on the quality of the client's accounting records. How likely do you think it is that Cloud 9's trial balance contains errors?" she asks Ian.

"Well that depends," replies Ian. "On what?" asks Suzie. "On whether they made any mistakes, I suppose." "Well, how likely is that?" persists Suzie. Ian is a bit confused. He wants to know about control and substantive tests and what sampling involves, but Suzie is not telling him.

Suzie tries another approach. "What can the client do to prevent mistakes getting into its accounts, or detect and correct mistakes that do enter the records?'

AUDIT PROCESS IN FOCUS

The purpose of this chapter is to introduce, compare, and contrast tests of controls and substantive testing and to provide an overview of audit sampling. When planning an audit, an auditor will develop an audit strategy based on their inherent and control risk assessment. We start this chapter with a brief reminder of how an auditor develops an audit strategy. The strategy will determine the extent of tests of controls and substantive procedures to be undertaken by the audit team. An overview is provided of the difference between these two types of procedures. Once a strategy has been developed, an audit program is written detailing the nature, timing, and extent of audit procedures to be conducted by audit staff. These terms are defined and explained in this chapter.

Audit sampling involves the selection of transactions or accounts within a balance for testing. It is used when the auditor plans on testing less than the entire population of transactions or accounts in a balance available for testing. When selecting a sample, it is important that the items chosen for testing are representative of the entire population of transactions and accounts available for testing. Sampling risk is the risk that the sample chosen is unsuitable and, as a consequence, the auditor arrives at an inappropriate conclusion after testing the sample. Non-sampling risk refers to other factors that result in an auditor arriving at an inappropriate conclusion. Both sampling and non-sampling risk are explained in this chapter.

Sampling can be conducted using statistical or non-statistical methods. These terms are explained and the benefits and drawbacks of each group of techniques are discussed in this chapter. We then provide an overview of different techniques that are used to select a sample during an audit.

The sample size chosen will be affected by a range of factors. Those factors will be different if the sample is selected for tests of controls or for substantive procedures. The factors that influence the final sample size when testing controls or conducting substantive tests are explained in this chapter. Finally, we explain how the results of testing are evaluated when a sample is used. It is vital that an appropriate assessment method is used to generalize the findings for a sample to the entire population.

6.1 TESTS OF CONTROLS AND SUBSTANTIVE PROCEDURES

❶ Understand the difference between tests of controls and substantive tests.

audit strategy strategy that sets the scope, timing, and direction of the audit and provides the basis for developing a detailed audit plan

audit plan plan that details the audit procedures to be used when testing controls and when conducting detailed substantive audit procedures

substantive audit procedures procedures used when the auditor plans to get a minimum knowledge of the client's controls and conducts extensive substantive procedures that involve intensive testing of year-end account balances and transactions from throughout the year

inherent risk the susceptibility of the financial statements to a material misstatement without considering internal controls

control risk the risk that a client's system of internal controls will not prevent or detect a material misstatement

audit risk the risk that an auditor expresses an inappropriate audit opinion when the financial statements are materially misstated

tests of controls (controls testing) the audit procedures designed to evaluate the operating effectiveness of controls in preventing or detecting and correcting material misstatements at the assertion level

A key task during the planning stage of every audit involves the development of an **audit strategy**. CAS 300 *Planning an Audit of Financial Statements* requires that an auditor establish an overall audit strategy, as described in chapter 4. The audit strategy provides the basis for a detailed **audit plan**. An audit plan includes the audit procedures to be used when testing controls and when conducting detailed **substantive audit procedures**.

An audit strategy is developed after gaining an understanding of a client's business and its internal control structure. Once an auditor has a thorough knowledge of their client's business, they can determine the overall level of **inherent risk** (the risk that a material misstatement could occur without considering any internal controls). Once an auditor has a thorough understanding of the client's controls, they can assess the **control risk** (the risk that a client's system of internal controls will not prevent or detect a material misstatement), which affect **audit risk** (the risk that an auditor expresses an inappropriate audit opinion when the financial statements are materially misstated). Table 6.1 contains an overview of the link between audit risk and audit strategy. When control risk is assessed as being high (top section of table 6.1), an auditor will adopt a predominantly substantive approach. This means that the audit strategy is to gain a minimum knowledge of the client's system of internal controls, conduct limited or no **tests of controls** (or **controls testing),** and conduct extensive detailed substantive procedures.

When control risk is assessed as or at medium to low (bottom section of table 6.1), an auditor may adopt a combined audit strategy**.** This means that the audit strategy is to gain a detailed understanding of the client's system of internal controls, conduct extensive tests of controls, and, if those controls prove effective, conduct less detailed substantive procedures.

Audit risk =	Inherent risk	Control risk	Detection risk
High	High	High	Low
Predominantly substantive audit strategy		No tests of controls	Increased reliance on substantive tests of transactions and account balances
Low	Low	Low	High
Lower assessed level of control risk leading to a combined audit strategy		Increased reliance on tests of controls	Reduced reliance on substantive tests of transactions and account balances

TABLE 6.1 **Audit risk and audit strategy**

Cloud 9

Ian is starting to understand. Suzie has already explained the idea of inherent, control, and detection risk to him, but until now he did not realize the practical implications. He can now answer Suzie's question: he is able to explain that the client is responsible for creating a system of internal controls to stop or detect mistakes entering the accounts. A strong system of internal controls means lower control risk. Tests of controls are designed to gather evidence about the strength of the system of internal controls and to justify the auditor's decision about how much reliance to place on the system. Greater reliance on a strong system of internal controls will allow the auditor to rely less on substantive procedures. This is the combined audit strategy. The other strategy, a predominantly substantive audit strategy, means low (or no) reliance on the system of internal controls and greater reliance on substantive procedures. But Ian is still worried—how do you actually make these assessments?

6.1.1 Tests of controls

Later in this book, we will provide a detailed overview of tests of controls (see chapter 8). The purpose of this brief discussion is to introduce those tests and highlight how they differ from substantive tests. When testing controls, an auditor is interested in assessing the effectiveness of internal controls identified when gaining an understanding of their client's system of internal controls during the planning stage of the audit. When making a preliminary assessment that control risk is medium or low (bottom section of table 6.1), an auditor is basing that assessment on their knowledge of the significant risks faced by the client and the suitability of the client's internal controls to mitigate those risks.

Before an auditor can conclude that control risk is medium or low, they test the controls to check their effectiveness. If the controls prove effective, the auditor can reduce their reliance on detailed substantive procedures. If the controls prove ineffective, the auditor reassesses control risk as higher than before and increases their reliance on detailed substantive procedures (that is, moves toward the top section of table 6.1).

Tests of controls are conducted to establish that controls:

- operate effectively, meaning that the rate of deviation from prescribed control procedures are minimized and controls effectively prevent and detect material misstatements, and
- operate consistently throughout the accounting period.

From chapter 5, we know that the main evidence-gathering procedures used by an auditor include inspection, observation, enquiry, confirmation, recalculation, re-performance, and analytical procedures. When testing controls, the procedures commonly used include:

- inspection of documents for evidence of authorization
- inspection of documents for evidence that details included have been checked by appropriate client personnel
- observation of client personnel performing various tasks, such as preparing bank deposits and conducting an inventory count
- enquiry of client personnel about how they perform their tasks
- re-performing control procedures to test their effectiveness.

Cloud 9

Suzie explains that control testing means, for example, that the auditor inspects documents, observes personnel, makes enquiries, re-performs certain controls, or conducts other tests that suit that particular client's systems. Suzie gives examples of the control tests that they intend to perform for Cloud 9: read the policies and procedures manuals, check for evidence of supervisors' reviews of cash receipts, observe staff in the shipping department handling dispatches, talk to the financial controller about the inventory management system, and re-perform a sample of bank reconciliations.

All of these control tests (plus others) have to be scheduled in the audit plan. Ian is still confused about how they can schedule substantive tests before they do the control tests. "What if the test results reveal poor controls?" he asks. Suzie explains that they have an initial assessment of control system strength and plan their substantive tests based on that assessment. "Remember," she adds, "we have already done some enquiries at a high level, plus we have the results of the analytical procedures. We have a pretty good idea of where the problems will arise. However, if our expectations are not met, we simply adjust the plan as we go along."

6.1.2 Substantive procedures

Later in this book, we will provide a detailed overview of substantive testing procedures (see chapters 9 to 11). The purpose of this brief discussion is to introduce those tests and highlight how they differ from tests of controls. The three types of substantive procedures include substantive tests of transactions, substantive tests of balances, and analytical procedures.

When an auditor assesses inherent and control risk as low for a client and tests of controls confirm their effectiveness (bottom section of table 6.1), an auditor will reduce the amount of planned detailed substantive procedures. This means that an auditor will rely to some extent on the client's internal control procedures to prevent and detect material misstatements. As a consequence, an auditor can rely more on their analytical procedures, which are more efficient than substantive testing of details, and place greater reliance on the client's accounting records.

When an auditor assesses inherent and control risk as high for a client and decides that the client's internal controls are unlikely to effectively reduce identified inherent risks (top section of table 6.1), an auditor will adopt a predominantly substantive approach to their testing. This means that an auditor will not place too much reliance on the client's system of internal controls to prevent and detect material misstatements and will instead conduct detailed substantive procedures of their own to reduce audit risk to an acceptably low level. Recall that audit risk is the risk that an auditor expresses an inappropriate audit opinion when the financial statements are materially misstated (CAS 200 *Overall Objectives of the Independent Auditor and the Conduct of an Audit in Accordance with Canadian Auditing Standards*). When control risk is high, an auditor will not rely too heavily on their analytical procedures and will instead conduct more time-consuming and costly substantive testing of transactions and balances.

When conducting detailed **substantive procedures** (also called **substantive testing** or **tests of details**), an auditor searches for evidence that recorded transactions occurred and relate to the client (**occurrence** assertion), that all transactions have

---

substantive procedures (substantive testing or **tests of details)** audit procedures designed to detect material misstatements at the assertion level

occurrence assertion that transactions and events that have been recorded have occurred and pertain to the entity

been recorded (**completeness** assertion), that all transactions have been recorded at appropriate carrying amounts (**accuracy** assertion), that all transactions have been recorded in the correct accounting period (**cut-off** assertion), and that all transactions have been recorded in the correct accounts (**classification** assertion). When gathering this evidence, an auditor uses a variety of audit procedures. Here are a few examples:

- receiving confirmation from the client's bank regarding interest rates charged on amounts borrowed by the client during the accounting period (accuracy assertion)
- recalculating an interest expense using the confirmed interest rates (accuracy assertion)
- inspecting documents to verify the date of transactions around year end (cut-off assertion)
- inspecting suppliers' invoices to verify amounts purchased (completeness assertion).

When conducting detailed substantive procedures, an auditor searches for evidence that recorded accounts such as assets, liabilities, and equity accounts exist (**existence** assertion), that all accounts that should have been recorded have been recorded (completeness assertion), that recorded accounts represent items owned by the client or amounts owed by the client to third parties (**rights and obligations** assertion), and that recorded accounts appear at appropriate carrying amounts (**valuation and allocation** assertion). When gathering this evidence, an auditor uses a variety of audit procedures. Here are a few examples:

- receiving confirmation from a selection of accounts receivable accounts of amounts owed to the client (existence assertion)
- recalculating the wages payable amount (valuation and allocation assertion)
- inspecting inventory and counting amounts on hand (existence and completeness assertions)
- inspecting supplier statements for amounts outstanding at year end (completeness and valuation and allocation assertions)
- inspecting title deeds to verify that property is owned by the client (rights and obligations assertion).

An auditor can use analytical procedures when testing transactions and account balances. Analytical procedures can be used to:

- estimate depreciation expense by multiplying the average depreciation rate on a class of assets by the balance at the beginning of the year (accuracy assertion)
- compare the wages expense month by month for this year and last year (completeness and occurrence assertions)
- compare inventory balances for this year and last year (existence, completeness, and valuation and allocation assertions)
- compare accounts payable balances for last year and this year (completeness, existence, and valuation and allocation assertions)
- discuss unusual fluctuations with client personnel (occurrence, completeness, and valuation and allocation assertions)
- estimate revenue for a movie theatre, for example, by multiplying the average price of a ticket by the number of seats in the theatre, by the average proportion of seats sold per session, by the average number of sessions per week, by the number of weeks per year (occurrence and accuracy assertions).

completeness assertion that all transactions, events assets, liabilities, and equity items that should have been recorded have been recorded

accuracy assertion that amounts and other data relating to recorded transactions and events have been recorded appropriately

cut-off assertion that transactions and events have been recorded in the correct accounting period

classification assertion that transactions and events have been recorded in the proper accounts

existence assertion that recorded assets, liabilities, and equity interests exist

rights and obligations assertion that the entity holds or controls the rights to assets, and liabilities are the obligations of the entity

valuation and allocation assertion that assets, liabilities, and equity interests are included in the financial statements at appropriate amounts and any resulting valuation or allocation adjustments are appropriately recorded

Cloud 9

Ian confesses to Suzie that he has a problem understanding the difference between control and substantive tests. "For example, at Cloud 9, a supervisor is supposed to check and authorize cash receipts deposited to the bank account. Suppose I find that the amount of the bank deposit is correct but that the supervisor forgot to sign the authorization. Is that an error?"

Suzie replies, "You performed a test of the control that the supervisor authorizes the transaction and found an error or a deviation from the correct performance of the control. However, you then performed an alternate substantive test and found that there was no error in the actual deposit. You have found evidence to substantiate the accuracy and occurrence assertions for that transaction. We would then consider all the other relevant evidence we have gathered about the controls over cash receipts. For example, how often do we find this type of control deviation for cash deposits? If we find significant problems with the controls, we could adjust our control risk assessment for cash receipts."

BEFORE YOU GO ON

1.1 What will be an auditor's strategy when control risk is assessed as high?

1.2 What are the two broad purposes of tests of controls?

1.3 What are the main objectives when conducting substantive tests of account balances?

PROFESSIONAL ENVIRONMENT

When auditing is critical to health

Audit work doesn't just involve financial issues—sometimes it's a matter of survival. In hospitals, internal and external auditors investigate whether medical staff follow proper procedures and controls to provide adequate patient care.

The Office of the Auditor General of Ontario audited hospital emergency departments in 2010. Among other things, it found that procedures for triage—prioritizing patients based on the severity of their illness or injury—were not met at the three emergency departments it visited. National guidelines recommend that patients be triaged within 15 minutes of arriving in the emergency department, yet some patients waited more than an hour in the hospitals the Office visited.

Hospitals assign senior nurses to perform triage audits to monitor whether patients are accurately assessed when they arrive. The Office found that in about half the files internal auditors checked, the triage nurses who assessed the patient upon arrival had underestimated the severity of the patient's condition. In some cases, people suspected of having a heart attack were assigned lower priority when they should have been given the highest priority, the triage auditors found. In about 20 percent of audited files, however, there was no documentation of patient data, such as vital signs and lists of allergies, which made it impossible to determine whether their triage assessment was appropriate.

The audit report did not mention any known cases where delays led to death, but it did document a case where a patient with chest pain waited three hours for an emergency room bed and there was no record of any reassessment in that time. Thirty minutes after getting a bed, the patient went into cardiac arrest and a doctor had to perform cardiopulmonary resuscitation.

Ontario hospitals are trying to reduce emergency room wait times, but it's difficult to measure progress without accurate data. The Office found that ambulance paramedics and emergency departments maintained separate databases and recorded different times as to when a patient was accepted at hospital. Publicly reported wait times only state how long a patient waits for treatment after they're triaged, but the Office found that some patients wait over an hour before triage.

The audit report demonstrates that even auditors can be audited to ensure they follow recommended procedures and controls. The Office of the Auditor General of Ontario examined emergency department triage audit procedures and found that one hospital had not done any triage audits for more than three years. Another stated that it did them regularly but could not provide any documentation to show it actually performed triage audits.

Source: Office of the Auditor General of Ontario, *2010 Annual Report*: Chapter 3, Section 3.05: Hospital Emergency Departments.

6.2 NATURE, TIMING, AND EXTENT OF AUDIT TESTING

The nature, timing, and extent of audit testing are crucial factors in every audit. An auditor uses their professional judgement when determining the nature, timing, and extent of audit procedures to use for each client. The audit plan details the procedures to be completed by the audit team. The nature, timing, and extent of audit procedures used on each audit varies depending on the audit strategy adopted and the type of testing relied on; that is, tests of controls or detailed substantive procedures (CAS 330 *The Auditor's Responses to Assessed Risks*).

2 Explain the factors that impact the nature, timing, and extent of audit testing.

6.2.1 Nature of audit testing

The **nature of audit testing** refers to the purpose of the test (that is, to test controls, transactions, or account balances) and the procedure used (that is, inspection, observation, enquiry, confirmation, recalculation, re-performance, or analytical procedures). The nature of an audit procedure will also depend on the assertion being tested. The higher the risk of material misstatement, the greater the use of audit procedures that access the most persuasive audit evidence.

nature of audit testing the purpose of the test and the procedure used

As described above, tests of controls are quite different from substantive procedures. Tests of controls are concerned with providing evidence that an internal control procedure exists and is effective. The nature of these controls tests is to re-perform certain procedures, inspect documents for evidence of procedures carried out by client personnel, and observe client personnel performing control procedures. Controls can also be tested by purposefully trying to trip them up. For example, transactions can be created by an auditor to test controls embedded in the client's computer programs also referred to as application controls. Such transactions (referred to as test data) can include valid and invalid items. Valid data are traced to ensure that appropriate accounts are updated when the transactions are processed. If a client's internal controls are effective, invalid data should be identified and rejected by the program. For example, if a sales program includes a procedure to check the customer number against an approved customer listing before processing a credit sale, an auditor could include a sale to a fictitious credit customer to test that the control is working. If the program processes the sale to a fictitious customer created by the auditor, the control procedure cannot be relied on as it has not operated effectively during this instance and there is a risk that some sales have been processed by the client that did not occur (occurrence assertion).

As described above, substantive procedures include detailed tests of transactions, balances, and analytical procedures. The lower the risk of material misstatement and the more effective the controls, the more reliance is placed on more efficient, less costly, analytical procedures. For these tests to be effective, it is important that an auditor plans to spend time testing all the assertions but more persuasive evidence is required for the assertions most at risk of material misstatement for each transaction class and account balance. For assertions most at risk, an auditor endeavours to gather the most persuasive evidence.

6.2.2 Timing of audit testing

timing of audit testing the stage of the audit when procedures are performed and the date, such as within or outside the accounting period, that audit evidence relates to

Timing of audit testing refers to the stage of the audit when procedures are performed and the date, such as within or outside the accounting period, that audit evidence relates to. Tests of controls are designed to provide evidence that a control was effective throughout the accounting period. As such, tests of controls can be conducted during the interim stage of the audit and then extended to the end of the year when conducting the year-end audit. The interim stage of the audit is the initial visit to a client, before year end, where planning takes place. It is common for audit planning to begin before year end to aid in efficiency and to free up time at year end. After gaining an understanding of the client and its internal controls, an auditor can begin tests of controls during the interim period. Substantive testing of transactions, which also occur throughout the year, can also begin during the interim audit.

For low-risk accounts, it is common to conduct more work during the interim audit, including testing controls and conducting substantive tests of transactions. If, after conducting these preliminary tests, the auditor concludes that the risk of material misstatements matches their initial low- to moderate-level assessment, detection risk will be set as high to medium and less reliance will be placed on detailed substantive testing at year end. If, after conducting preliminary tests of controls, the auditor concludes that control risk is higher than initially estimated because, for example, the rate of deviation in controls from the client's prescribed procedures is above the expected rate for a low-risk account, the auditor will increase their reliance on detailed substantive testing at year end.

For high-risk accounts, the timing of most audit procedures will be at, or after, year end. When there is a high risk of material misstatement in the amounts appearing in the financial statements, an auditor will spend most time conducting detailed substantive tests of those account balances. Analytical procedures may be used to aid in the identification of those accounts most at risk of material misstatement, but these procedures will not be relied on as the only audit evidence obtained.

Some assertions, such as cut-off, can only be conducted on transactions around year end. For example, as inventory counts are generally conducted on, or close to, year end, audit procedures used to assess the effectiveness of the count can only be conducted around year end. Some audit procedures are conducted throughout an accounting period (tests of controls and substantive tests of transactions), while others are predominantly conducted at year end (substantive tests of account balances). The higher the risk of material misstatement, the greater the reliance on testing conducted close to year end.

6.2.3 Extent of audit testing

extent of audit testing the amount of audit evidence gathered when testing controls and conducting detailed substantive procedures

The **extent of audit testing** refers to the amount (quantity) of audit evidence gathered when testing controls and conducting detailed substantive procedures. When control risk is low (bottom section of table 6.1), the audit strategy is to increase reliance on tests of controls and reduce reliance on substantive testing of transactions and account balances. This means that the auditor will increase the extent of their testing of controls to gain evidence that their client's system of internal controls is effective in preventing and detecting material misstatements. If that extensive testing confirms the auditor's belief that their client's system of internal controls is indeed effective, the auditor will reduce the extent of substantive testing of transactions and balances and increase the extent of their reliance on more efficient analytical procedures.

When control risk is high (top section of table 6.1), the audit strategy is to do little or no tests of controls and to increase reliance on substantive testing of transactions and account balances. This means that the auditor will not rely on their client's system of internal controls to prevent and detect material misstatements. Instead, the auditor must rely on their own extensive substantive procedures to uncover any material misstatements. In the next section of this chapter, we will discuss how an auditor selects an appropriate sample for testing controls and conducting substantive procedures.

Cloud 9

Suzie emphasizes to Ian that the detailed audit program section of the audit plan must specify three things about every test—nature, timing, and extent. That is, which tests will be performed, when they will be performed and to which period the data belong to, and how many times the tests will be performed. The "how many" part relates to the size of the sample. The population from which a sample is drawn could be documents, inventory items, people (to talk to or observe), and so on.

Because W&S Partners has been appointed before year end, it can test interim data and spread the testing over the available time before the audit report deadline. However, timing is not just about convenience. If controls are weak, more tests have to be scheduled around year end. Control risk has a very pervasive effect on testing because weaker controls mean that the auditor must perform tests that will produce more persuasive evidence and select larger samples.

BEFORE YOU GO ON

2.1 What are the three main categories of substantive procedures?

2.2 What are the two most common types of testing that can be started during the interim audit?

2.3 What does the extent of audit testing refer to?

6.3 AUDIT SAMPLING

CAS 530 *Audit Sampling* provides guidance on **audit sampling**. When creating an audit plan and designing audit procedures, an auditor also decides how to select appropriate items for testing. When an audit procedure is tested on an entire group of transactions (for example, the purchase of machinery) or all items within an account balance (for example, motor vehicles), sampling is not required. However, when there are

3 Explain how audit sampling is used in an audit.

audit sampling the application of audit procedures to less than 100 percent of items within a population

numerous transactions or items within an account balance available for testing, an auditor must decide how best to select a sample that is representative of the entire population of items available for testing.

BEFORE YOU GO ON

3.1 What is audit sampling?

3.2 When is it appropriate to use audit sampling?

3.3 How does audit sampling relate to audit risk?

6.4 SAMPLING AND NON-SAMPLING RISK

4 Understand the difference between sampling and non-sampling risk.

sampling risk the risk that the sample chosen by the auditor is not representative of the population available for testing and, as a consequence, the auditor arrives at an inappropriate conclusion

Sampling risk is the risk that the sample chosen by the auditor is not representative of the population of transactions or items within an account balance available for testing and, as a consequence, the auditor arrives at an inappropriate conclusion (CAS 530). There are two consequences of sampling risk: the risk that the audit will be ineffective and the risk that the audit will be inefficient.

6.4.1 Sampling risk and tests of controls

When testing controls, sampling risk is the risk that an auditor relies on their client's system of internal controls when they should not do so (that is, the auditor concludes that the client's internal controls are effective when they are ineffective), and the risk that an auditor concludes that the client's internal controls are less reliable than they really are (that is, the auditor concludes that the client's internal controls are ineffective when they are effective). Table 6.2 provides details of sampling risk when testing controls and the implications of that risk for the audit.

In the top section of table 6.2 the auditor has tested their client's system of internal controls and concluded that the system is effective when it is ineffective at preventing and detecting potential material misstatements. Another way of stating this risk is that an auditor has concluded that the client's system of internal controls is *more* effective than it is. As a consequence, the auditor places too much reliance on the client's system of internal controls to identify and rectify material misstatements. This can happen when the items selected for testing the effectiveness of the internal controls are not representative of all items available for testing. For example, a manager is away on vacation for two weeks during the year and another member of the client's personnel acts as manager during their absence. The auditor selects items for testing throughout the year, but the sample does not include transactions processed while the manager was on vacation. There is a risk that the auditor concludes that the controls that involve the manager's supervision and authorization are effective

TABLE 6.2 **Sampling risk when testing controls**

SAMPLING RISK	IMPLICATIONS FOR THE AUDIT
The risk that the auditor concludes that the client's system of internal controls is effective when it is ineffective	An increased audit risk (that is, the risk that the auditor will issue an inappropriate audit conclusion)
The risk that the auditor concludes that the client's system of internal controls is ineffective when it is effective	An increase in audit effort when not required (that is, there is a risk that the audit will be inefficient)

throughout the year, when they may not have worked effectively during the two-week vacation period.

From the audit risk model discussed in chapter 4, we know that when an auditor concludes that their client's system of internal controls is effective at preventing and detecting material misstatements, control risk will be assessed as low and the audit strategy will be to reduce reliance on detailed substantive testing of transactions and balances (refer to the bottom section of table 6.1). By conducting fewer substantive procedures, there is an increased risk that the auditor's detailed substantive procedures will not detect a material misstatement (that is, there is a risk that the audit will be ineffective if the auditor's original risk assessment was wrong).

In the bottom section of table 6.2, the auditor has tested their client's system of internal controls and concluded that the system is ineffective when it is, in fact, effective at preventing and detecting potential material misstatements. Another way of stating this risk is that an auditor has concluded that the client's system of internal controls is *less* effective than it is. As a consequence, the auditor does not place sufficient reliance on the client's system of internal controls. This can happen when the items selected for testing the effectiveness of the internal controls is not representative of all items available for testing. For example, a client has a control procedure requiring authorization of purchases in excess of $200,000. The auditor selected purchase orders from one division of the company. The auditor has found the control to be ineffective because the manager has not signed all purchase orders selected. In this example, the auditor runs the risk of placing less reliance on this control than strictly necessary because they did not select the sample from across all divisions, where the control may be working more effectively.

From the audit risk model, we know that when an auditor concludes that their client's system of internal controls is ineffective at preventing and detecting potential material misstatements, control risk will be assessed as high and the audit strategy will be to increase reliance on detailed substantive testing of transactions and balances (refer to the top section of table 6.1). By conducting more substantive procedures when control risk is lower than assessed, the audit will be inefficient as the auditor will spend more time conducting substantive procedures than is necessary.

6.4.2 Sampling risk and substantive procedures

When conducting substantive tests, sampling risk is the risk that an auditor concludes that a material misstatement does not exist when it does or an auditor concludes that a material misstatement exists when it does not. Table 6.3 provides details of sampling risk when conducting substantive tests and the implications of that risk for the audit.

SAMPLING RISK	IMPLICATIONS FOR THE AUDIT
The risk that the auditor concludes that a material misstatement does not exist when it does	An increased audit risk (that is, the risk that the auditor will issue an inappropriate audit conclusion)
The risk that the auditor concludes that a material misstatement exists when it does not	An increase in audit effort when not required (that is, there is a risk that the audit will be inefficient)

TABLE 6.3 **Sampling risk when conducting substantive tests**

In the top section of table 6.3, the auditor has conducted substantive procedures on a sample and concluded that there is no material misstatement when there is a material misstatement. As a consequence, the auditor will conclude that the financial statements are fairly presented when they contain a material misstatement (that is, the audit is ineffective). For example, a client has warehouses in four major cities. The auditor has selected a sample of inventory items for testing. The entire sample of inventory selected for testing is located in the one warehouse near the client's head office. The auditor has not tested material inventory items held at the other three warehouses. As a consequence, the auditor has not detected a significant error in valuing inventory at one of the warehouses. If the auditor had selected a sample for testing from each warehouse, the risk of arriving at an incorrect conclusion would have been reduced, though not eliminated (that is, sampling risk can be reduced though it can never be removed).

In the bottom section of table 6.3, the auditor has conducted substantive procedures on a sample and concluded that there is a material misstatement when there is no material misstatement. As a consequence, the auditor will conduct more extensive testing believing that there is a material misstatement reducing audit efficiency. For example, an error occurred when processing credit sales and a customer was charged twice for the same item by mistake. The auditor detects this error and concludes that if this error was to be repeated throughout the remainder of the population of credit sales, trade receivables would be materially misstated. As a consequence, the auditor increases testing to uncover the cause of the error. If the error is an anomaly and not repeated throughout the population, the audit will be inefficient.

6.4.3 Non-sampling risk

non-sampling risk the risk that the auditor reaches an inappropriate conclusion for any reason not related to sampling risk

Non-sampling risk is the risk that an auditor arrives at an inappropriate conclusion for a reason unrelated to sampling issues. This can occur when an auditor uses an inappropriate audit procedure, relies too heavily on unreliable evidence, or spends too little time testing the accounts most at risk of material misstatement.

When testing controls, non-sampling risk is the risk that an auditor designs tests that are ineffective and do not provide evidence that a control is operating properly. For example, a client uses passwords to restrict access to its computer programs. To test that the passwords are operating effectively, an auditor observes client personnel accessing programs using their passwords. This test is not effective in assessing whether the client's programs prevent access to users with invalid passwords, since the test is focused on users with valid passwords. An effective test would be to enter invalid passwords to see if access is denied. In another example, an auditor is aware that the client has a new credit policy, which places more restrictions on sales to credit customers with amounts overdue. To test the new policy, the auditor reads the client's policy manual, finds the details of the policy change, and concludes that the internal control procedure is effective. Reading the policy manual is not a test of the control. The auditor would need to select some overdue accounts receivable and check that the new policy had been enforced.

When conducting substantive procedures, there are a number of non-sampling risks. One non-sampling risk is the risk that an auditor relies too heavily on less persuasive evidence. For example, an auditor may rely too heavily on management representations without gathering independent corroborating evidence. Non-sampling risk is also the risk that an auditor spends most of their time testing assertions where the risk of material misstatement is low and ignores or spends insufficient time testing assertions most at risk of material misstatement. For example, a client sells pearls. There is a significant risk that recorded inventory does not exist, yet the auditor spends more time testing for completeness.

Cloud 9

Ian is a bit disappointed. "I thought that if you took a random sample and did not find any errors, you could conclude that there was definitely no error in the overall population. But you are saying that there is still a risk that the population has errors."

"That's right," says Suzie." 'Unless you test every item in the population, you will still have a statistical chance of making the wrong conclusion simply because you took a sample. Also, if you take a sample in a way that is biased, it is difficult to conclude that the sample results say anything at all about the population. That's why it is so important that junior staff don't just take the nearest, or most convenient, box of documents to test. Another big trap is that some part of the accounting period has different conditions, such as a key member of the client's staff is on holidays. The auditor has to recognize this and make sure that the relevant period is included in the sample. We know that Cloud 9 opened its new Toronto store on the first of June. Obviously, inventory levels will be different around this time, so we have to plan to handle these different conditions with our sampling."

BEFORE YOU GO ON

4.1 What is sampling risk?

4.2 How does sampling risk relate to tests of controls and substantive testing?

4.3 What is non-sampling risk?

6.5 STATISTICAL AND NON-STATISTICAL SAMPLING

According to CAS 530, **statistical sampling** involves random selection and probability theory to determine the sample size and evaluate the results, including sampling risk. Any sample selection method that does not incorporate random selection and probability theory is not statistical sampling; for example, when an auditor uses judgement alone to select the sample size and the items to include in the sample for testing. An advantage of statistical sampling is that it allows an auditor to measure sampling risk; that is, the risk that the sample chosen by the auditor is not representative. Sometimes a disadvantage of statistical sampling is the cost involved in using this technique.

Non-statistical sampling is easier to use than statistical sampling, is lower cost, and allows an auditor to select a sample that they believe is appropriate. Most audit firms use a combination of statistical and non-statistical sampling as both methods provide appropriate audit evidence and allow the auditor to form a conclusion on the items being tested. The next section of this chapter includes a discussion of various statistical and non-statistical sampling techniques.

 **5** Differentiate between statistical and non-statistical sampling.

statistical sampling an approach to sampling where random selection is used to select a sample and probability theory is used to evaluate the sample results

non-statistical sampling any sample selection method that does not have the characteristics of statistical sampling

BEFORE YOU GO ON

5.1 What is statistical sampling?

5.2 What is non-statistical sampling?

5.3 What are the advantages and disadvantages of statistical and non-statistical sampling?

6.6 SAMPLING TECHNIQUES AND FACTORS AFFECTING SAMPLING

6 Describe sampling methods and the factors to be considered when choosing a sample.

In this section, we discuss a range of sampling techniques available to auditors. They include random selection, systematic selection, haphazard selection, block selection, and judgement selection.

Random selection

random selection process whereby a sample is selected free from bias and each item in a population has an equal chance of selection

As explained earlier, statistical sampling requires that a sample be selected randomly and the results of the test evaluated using probability theory. **Random selection** requires that the person selecting the sample does not influence the choice of items selected. The resulting sample is then free from bias and each item within the population has an equal chance of being selected for testing. Random number generators can be used to select a sample (see figure 6.1).

stratification the process of dividing a population into groups of sampling units with similar characteristics

Stratification can be used ahead of random selection to improve audit efficiency. This means that an auditor partitions a population ahead of sampling by identifying sub populations with similar characteristics. For example, for accounts receivable, the auditor may stratify high-dollar items or balances that are overdue. After stratifying a population, items can be randomly selected within each stratum. Thus, stratification can be used to ensure that the sample includes items that have the characteristics required by the auditor, such as material or risky items, and remain a statistical sampling technique when items are randomly selected. Stratification is explained in more detail in section 6.6.1.

Systematic selection

systematic selection the selection of a sample for testing by dividing the number of items in a population by the sample size, giving the sampling interval (n) and then selecting every nth item in the population

Systematic selection involves the selection of a sample for testing by dividing the number of items in a population by the sample size, resulting in the sampling interval (n). Once the sampling interval has been determined, a starting point is selected, which is an item in the population below the sampling interval. Then the sample is selected by selecting the first item and then every nth item after that.

For example, a client has 600 creditors. The auditor has decided that the sample size when testing creditors is 20. To determine the sampling interval, the following formula is used.

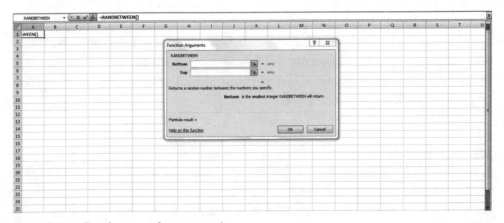

FIGURE 6.1 **Random number generator**

$$\text{Sampling interval} = \frac{\text{Population size}}{\text{Sample size}}$$

$$= \frac{600}{200}$$

$$= 30$$

This means that every 30th item will be selected for testing. An item within the first 30 in the list of creditors is selected as the starting point. From then on, every 30th item is selected for testing. If the first item selected is 15, then the following items will be tested: 15, 45, 75, 105, 135, 165, 195, 225, 255, 285, 315, 345, 375, 405, 435, 465, 495, 525, 555, and 585. If the starting item is selected randomly and the population is not arranged in any particular order, systematic selection can be considered a statistical sampling technique.

The risk in using systematic selection is that items will be listed in such a way that by selecting every nth item, the auditor is selecting items that are related in some way. For example, if the sampling interval is 7 and items in the population represent the daily sales of a particular product, then the auditor will select sales made on the same day each week. This risk can be reduced by reviewing the items in a population before calculating the sampling interval.

Haphazard selection

Haphazard selection involves the selection of a sample by an auditor without using a methodical technique. While this technique appears to have much in common with random selection, there is a risk that an auditor will avoid selecting some items or ensure other items are included in the sample. For example, an item that is going to be difficult to test because the documentation is held in another location may be purposefully omitted by the auditor, while an item that looks large or unusual and catches the auditor's eye may be purposefully included. This is a non-statistical technique as human bias may impact the sample selected, and therefore prevent the sample from being a true random sample.

haphazard selection the selection of a sample without use of a methodical technique

Cloud 9

"We are going to use haphazard selection for sales invoices and cash receipts at Cloud 9," Suzie tells Ian. "We will select our sample from the entire year because we do not expect different conditions in sales made to department stores during different times of the year. We have a well-tried system that virtually eliminates any potential bias."

Block selection

Block selection involves the selection of items that are grouped together within the population of items available. This is a non-statistical technique as many populations of items are sorted in a sequence, which makes the selection of groups of items in a block inappropriate. For example, transactions are generally grouped in date order. By using block selection, the items selected will not be representative of transactions made throughout the year.

block selection the selection of items that are grouped together within the population of items available

For example, a client has 600 creditors. They are listed alphabetically. The auditor has decided that the sample size when testing creditors is 20. Using block selection, the auditor selects the first creditor starting with D and includes the next 20 creditors in the sample.

Judgemental selection

judgemental selection the selection of items that an auditor believes should be included in the sample for testing

Judgemental selection involves the selection of items that an auditor believes should be included in the sample for testing. When testing controls, judgement may be used to ensure that transactions processed when a new computer is installed are included in the sample. When conducting substantive testing, judgement may be used to include in the sample large or unusual items. This is a non-statistical sampling technique.

PROFESSIONAL ENVIRONMENT

Sampling in practice

How do auditors use sampling in practice? Hall et al. conducted a survey of U.S. accountants in public practice, industry, and government to find the answer to this question. Although their study was conducted in 1997 and the results are not necessarily representative of today's practices, their discussion on the advantages and disadvantages of statistical and non-statistical sampling and their impact on the risk of an inappropriate audit opinion still applies.

The researchers asked auditors how they determined sample sizes, selected samples, and evaluated these samples. The auditors were asked if they used statistical selection techniques (such as simple random, stratified, and systematic dollar-unit as described below) and non-statistical selection techniques (such as haphazard, block, and systematic).

The results showed that auditors use non-statistical selection methods 85 percent of the time and only 15 percent of the selections were made using statistical methods. The most common non-statistical sample selection method was haphazard selection. This is a technique where the sample is selected without a method. The choice of items is not supposed to be based on its characteristics, such as colour, size, or convenience of location. However, very few of the auditors reported receiving any training in methods to counter the bias introduced by non-statistical sampling and none reported using any bias-reducing techniques. The results suggest that auditors might not fully understand the influence of sample selection bias on their audit conclusions.

The most common statistical sample selection method according to the study is dollar-unit sampling. This is an approach where the unit sampled is not the transaction or document but the individual dollars making up the transaction or balance. The dollar-unit sampling method means that the auditor samples the dollars in the transactions rather than the transactions themselves. Dollar-unit sampling gives large transactions a greater chance of being sampled than small transactions.

Consider the following example of sales transactions reported by a client:

#1	$2
#2	$2,000
#3	$20,000

The auditor wants to take a random sample and inspect the underlying documents. If the unit of sampling is the sales transaction, the $20,000 transaction has the same chance of being selected as the $2 transaction. However, if dollar-unit sampling is used, then every sales dollar has the same chance of being selected. The chance of the $20,000 transaction being selected is 10,000 times greater than the $2 transaction. Given that auditors are typically concerned about overstatement of sales, dollar-unit sampling has the advantage of being more likely to select potentially overstated transactions.

Source: T.W. Hall, J.E. Hunton, and B.J. Pierce, 2002, "Sampling Practices of Auditors in Public Accounting, Industry, and Government," *Accounting Horizons,* vol. 16, no. 2, June 2002, pp. 125–36.

6.6.2 Factors to consider when selecting a sample

There are a number of factors to consider when selecting a sample. The factors discussed in this section are common to all sampling methods. When selecting a sample, an auditor will use their judgement and knowledge of the client to determine control risk, detection risk, and planning materiality, all of which impact the sample size. The lower the control risk, the smaller the sample size when testing controls. The lower the detection risk, the larger the sample size when conducting detailed substantive procedures.

An auditor uses their professional judgement when selecting the population from which a sample is drawn. This decision is determined by the audit procedure undertaken, which, in turn, is determined by the assertion being tested. When testing the existence of inventory, it is appropriate to select a sample from the client's inventory listing (that is, the population from which a sample is selected is the client's complete list of inventory), whereas when testing the completeness of inventory, it is appropriate to select a sample of physical inventory (that is, the population from which a sample is selected is the client's physical inventory).

An auditor may decide to stratify the population before selecting a sample from it. Stratification improves audit efficiency by dividing the population into groups and then selecting items from each group. For example, a population may be divided into months of the year. When testing controls, it is important to ensure effectiveness throughout the year. By dividing items into months of the year and selecting from each month, an auditor can efficiently ensure that the whole year is covered by their test. If stratification were not used in this example, the sample chosen would likely be much larger to ensure each month is included in the sample. In another example, a population may be divided into different characteristics so that riskier items have an appropriate chance of being selected for testing. Credit sales are riskier than cash sales, so sales may be divided into credit and cash before a sample is selected.

An auditor will also use their professional judgement when considering what would be considered an error within the population tested. When testing controls, an auditor will define what represents a deviation from a prescribed control procedure. For example, if a client has a control procedure that requires a manager to authorize purchases greater than $20,000, a deviation will be evidence of unauthorized purchases greater than $20,000. When conducting substantive procedures, an auditor will define what represents a misstatement in transactions or account balances. For example, if an auditor conducts receivable confirmations to test the existence of accounts receivables, a non-reply would be considered a potential error and would require further audit work. If an auditor conducts a test of the accuracy of the depreciation expense by recalculating selected items, and some items are significantly different from the

tolerable misstatement the maximum error an auditor is willing to accept within the population tested

client's depreciation amounts, those differences would be considered potential errors that would require further audit testing.

An auditor will use their professional judgement to determine the **tolerable misstatement** and required level of confidence. The tolerable misstatement is the maximum error an auditor is willing to accept within the population tested (CAS 530). When testing controls, this is the tolerable rate of deviation that an auditor is willing to accept before concluding that a control is ineffective. When conducting substantive procedures, tolerable error relates to auditor-assessed materiality. If an error is considered material, an auditor will conclude that the account is materially misstated.

The required level of confidence is a function of control risk when testing controls and of detection risk when conducting substantive procedures. When control risk is initially assessed as low, based on an auditor's understanding of the client's system of internal controls, an auditor will require a high level of confidence that the controls are effective before concluding that control risk is low. In this situation, an auditor will increase the sample size when testing controls to reduce the risk that the client's system of internal controls is believed to be effective when it is ineffective (refer to the top section of table 6.2).

When detection risk is determined to be low, an auditor will require a high level of confidence that the transactions and accounts are not materially misstated. Recall that by determining a low detection risk, the auditor believes that inherent risk and control risk are high; that is, the transactions and accounts are at risk of material misstatement and the client's internal controls are believed to be ineffective. In this situation, the auditor will increase the sample size when conducting substantive tests of transactions and balances to reduce the risk that the auditor concludes that a material misstatement does not exist when it does (refer to the top section of table 6.3).

To summarize, before selecting a sample, an auditor will use their professional judgement to assess control and detection risk, set planning materiality, select an appropriate population for testing, define what is to be considered to be an error within the population to be tested, set the tolerable error rate, and set the required level of confidence. Once these parameters are set, an auditor will select the sample using a statistical or non-statistical sampling technique.

BEFORE YOU GO ON

6.1 What is the difference between random and haphazard sample selection?

6.2 What is the risk in using systematic sample selection?

6.3 What factors should be considered when selecting a sample?

6.7 FACTORS THAT INFLUENCE THE SAMPLE SIZE—TESTING CONTROLS

7 Determine the factors that influence the sample size when testing controls.

There are a number of factors that will influence the sample size when testing controls. These are summarized in table 6.4, which comes from CAS 530.

The first factor listed in table 6.4 is an increase in the extent to which the risk of material misstatement is reduced by the operating effectiveness of controls. If an auditor believes that a control will be effective in reducing an identified risk of material misstatement, their audit strategy will be to increase testing of that control to ensure

FACTOR	EFFECT ON SAMPLE SIZE
1. An increase in the extent to which the auditor's risk assessment takes into account relevant controls	Increase
2. An increase in the tolerable rate of deviation	Decrease
3. An increase in the expected rate of deviation of the population to be tested	Increase
4. An increase in the auditor's desired level of assurance that the tolerable rate of deviation is not exceeded by the actual rate of deviation in the population	Increase
5. An increase in the number of sampling units in the population	Negligible

TABLE 6.4 **Factors that influence the sample size when testing controls**

Source: Auditing and Assurance Standards Board 2010, CAS 530 *Audit Sampling*, App. 2, pp. 21–2.

it is effective (refer to the bottom section of table 6.1). When concluding that a control is effective, an auditor will rely on that control to prevent and detect a material misstatement, and reduce their detailed substantive procedures.

The second factor listed in table 6.4 is an increase in the **rate of deviation** from the prescribed control activity that the auditor is willing to accept. As described previously, an auditor will use their professional judgement to determine the tolerable rate of deviation that is acceptable. There is an inverse relationship between the tolerable rate of deviation and sample size. If an auditor intends to rely on a control to prevent and detect a material misstatement, a lower tolerable error rate will be set, and the sample size will be increased to provide the auditor with the evidence required to demonstrate that the control is effective. If an auditor expects to place relatively more reliance on their substantive procedures and reduce their reliance on an internal control, they will increase the tolerable rate of deviation and reduce the sample size when testing the control.

rate of deviation when testing controls, the proportion of items tested that did not conform to the client's prescribed control procedure

The third factor listed in table 6.4 is an increase in the rate of deviation from the prescribed control activity that the auditor expects to find in the population. If an auditor believes that the rate of deviation has increased when compared to prior audits, they will increase the sample size to accurately evaluate the impact of the changed circumstances. For example, the rate of deviation could increase if the client has new staff, if the client has significantly changed a computer program, or if the client has changed its internal control procedures.

The fourth factor listed in table 6.4 is an increase in the auditor's required confidence level. When control risk is assessed as low (refer to the bottom section of table 6.1) for a risk factor, an auditor's required level of confidence in the effectiveness of their client's internal control is higher than when control risk is assessed as medium to high (refer to the top section of table 6.1). If an auditor is to rely on the client's internal control procedures to prevent or detect an identified material misstatement, their required confidence level in that control increases and they will increase the sample size when testing that control.

The fifth and final factor listed in table 6.4 is an increase in the number of sampling units in the population. When a population is large and fairly homogenous, there is little benefit from continuing to increase the sample size as the results from continued testing should confirm early findings. For example, an auditor may test control procedures surrounding the processing of sales. When all sales are processed using the same procedure, there will be little difference in the sample size if the population of sales was to vary from one year to the next.

BEFORE YOU GO ON

7.1 What are the factors that influence sample size when testing controls?

7.2 What is the relationship between the tolerable rate of deviation and sample size?

7.3 How is the auditor's required confidence level influenced by control risk?

6.8 FACTORS THAT INFLUENCE THE SAMPLE SIZE—SUBSTANTIVE TESTING

8 Determine the factors that influence the sample size when substantive testing.

There are a number of factors that will influence the sample size when testing transactions and balances. These are summarized in table 6.5, which comes from CAS 530.

The first factor listed in table 6.5 is an increase in the auditor's assessment of the risk of material misstatement. This risk is influenced by the auditor's assessment of inherent and control risk. The higher the inherent and control risk, the greater the risk that a material misstatement exists in a client's financial statements, and the more an auditor must rely on their substantive tests of transactions and balances to identify potential material misstatements (refer to the top section of table 6.1). When an auditor decides to increase their reliance on their substantive procedures, they will increase the substantive testing sample size.

The second factor listed in table 6.5 is an increase in the use of other substantive procedures directed toward the same assertion. When testing transactions and balances, an auditor will use a number of audit procedures. The more procedures that are directed to the same audit assertion, the less an auditor will need to rely on the evidence provided by one test alone and the smaller the sample size required. For example, when testing the valuation of inventory, a number of procedures can be used. They include inspecting inventory on hand for evidence of damage, recalculating cost

TABLE 6.5 **Factors that influence the sample size when testing transactions and balances**

FACTOR	EFFECT ON SAMPLE SIZE
1. An increase in the auditor's assessment of the risk of material misstatement	Increase
2. An increase in the use of other substantive procedures directed at the same assertion	Decrease
3. An increase in the auditor's desired level of assurance that tolerable misstatement is not exceeded by actual misstatement in the population	Increase
4. An increase in tolerable misstatement	Decrease
5. An increase in the amount of misstatement the auditor expects to find in the population	Increase
6. Stratification of the population when appropriate	Decrease
7. The number of sampling units in the population	Negligible

Source: Auditing and Assurance Standards Board 2010, CAS 530 Audit Sampling, App. 3, pp. 23–5.

multiplied by quantity on hand, tracing of cost to supplier invoices, and testing for the lower of cost and net realizable value.

The third factor listed in table 6.5 is an increase in the auditor's required confidence level. This factor is also related to the level of inherent and control risk. The greater the inherent and control risk, the lower the detection risk established by the auditor, and the greater the confidence level required when conducting substantive tests of transactions and balances (refer to the top section of table 6.1). When an auditor requires more confidence from the results of their testing, they will increase the sample size.

The fourth factor listed in table 6.5 is an increase in the total error that the auditor is willing to accept. When an auditor increases the tolerable error, they are indicating that they are not relying on that particular test to provide all of the evidence required for a particular assertion. In that case, the auditor will reduce the sample size. The tolerable error is equal to or less than the materiality level set for the class of transactions or balances being tested.

The fifth factor listed in table 6.5 is an increase in the amount of error the auditor expects to find in the population. When an auditor believes that there is likely to be a material misstatement in the population of transactions or amounts making up an account balance, they will increase the sample size to gain a better estimate of the actual misstatement in the population. This will occur when an account is at risk of material misstatement, such as when it requires estimation (for example, the allowance for doubtful accounts); when it requires complex calculations (for example, foreign exchange translations); or when it requires difficult valuation techniques (for example, fair values). This will also occur when the auditor has assessed that control risk is high and the client's control procedures are inadequate.

The sixth factor listed in table 6.5 is stratification of the population. As described previously, stratification of the population will result in more efficient sampling and reduce the sample required. The seventh and final factor listed in table 6.5 is the number of sampling units in the population. As described previously for tests of controls, when a population is large and fairly homogenous, there is little benefit from continuing to increase the sample size, as the results from continued testing should confirm early findings.

BEFORE YOU GO ON

8.1 What are the factors that influence sample size when conducting substantive procedures?

8.2 What influences an increase in the auditor's assessment of the risk of material misstatement?

8.3 What could occur to increase the amount of error an auditor expects to find in a population?

6.9 EVALUATING SAMPLE TEST RESULTS

After an auditor has completed their audit testing, the next stage is to evaluate the results. When testing controls, an auditor will consider whether the results of the tests applied to a sample provide evidence that the control tested is effective within the entire population. When testing transactions and balances, an auditor will

9 Outline how to evaluate the results of tests conducted on a sample.

consider whether the results of the tests applied to a sample provide evidence that the class of transactions or account balance tested is fairly stated (that is, does not contain a material misstatement).

If an auditor discovers departures from prescribed controls when testing controls, they will calculate a deviation rate. The deviation rate is the proportion of departures within the sample. For example, if an auditor finds three departures from a prescribed control when testing a sample of 30 items, the deviation rate is 10 percent (3/30). If the sample is representative of the population, the auditor will compare this deviation rate with their tolerable rate of deviation. If the rate of deviation exceeds the tolerable rate, the auditor will extend their testing (particularly when the auditor is concerned that their sample may not be representative) and gather further evidence of other controls that may be aimed at reducing the identified risk of material misstatement. If, after conducting more testing, the auditor finds that the rate of deviation remains consistent with their initial findings and other controls are similarly ineffective, the auditor will conclude that the client's system of internal controls cannot be relied on to prevent or detect a potential material misstatement and the auditor will increase their reliance on their substantive tests of the account tested.

If an auditor discovers errors when testing transactions or account balances, the auditor will need to project the error to the population being tested provided that the sample is representative of the population (CAS 530). First, an auditor will consider whether an error is considered to be an anomaly and not likely to be repeated throughout the population being tested. If an error is considered to be an anomaly, it will be removed before projecting remaining errors to the population. Second, an auditor will consider whether the population was stratified before being sampled. If so, errors are projected within each stratum and then totalled together with any unique errors identified. An auditor will consider the impact of **projected errors** on the class of transactions or account balance being tested to determine whether a material misstatement has occurred.

projected error extrapolation of the errors detected when testing a sample to the population from which the sample was drawn

For example, an auditor has conducted substantive testing on an account balance, which has been split into three strata. The results of that test are summarized in table 6.6. The first column contains the stratum number, the second column the error found for each stratum, the third column the dollar value of the sample tested, the fourth column the dollar value of the entire stratum available for testing, and the final column the calculation of the projected error for each stratum.

The net total error for the sample is $2,649. It would be incorrect to compare that amount to the tolerable error rate as the error in the sample underestimates the error in the entire population. The errors found are projected to the population in the final column in table 6.6, providing a total net error of $4,134. That error is

TABLE 6.6 **Evaluation of results of substantive testing**

STRATUM (1)	ERROR (2)	SAMPLE (3)	STRATUM (4)	PROJECTED ERROR (2)/(3) × (4)
1	$1,586	$20,235	$25,732	$ 2,017
2	$ (658)	$ 8,398	$15,367	$(1,204)
3	$1,605	$12,886	$26,667	$ 3,321
Total	$2,533	$41,519	$67,766	$ 4,134

compared to the tolerable error rate for that account balance. If the tolerable error rate was set conservatively at $3,500, the auditor would conclude that the errors uncovered are material and further work is required. This may involve increasing the sample size and/or conducting other tests aimed at the assertion being tested. If the tolerable error rate was set at $7,500, the auditor would conclude that the errors uncovered are not material. As the total net error is close to the tolerable error rate, some additional testing within the sample may be considered to confirm that conclusion.

BEFORE YOU GO ON

9.1 What will an auditor consider when evaluating test results?

9.2 What is the rate of deviation and when will an auditor calculate this?

9.3 What will an auditor do if the rate of deviation exceeds the tolerable rate?

SUMMARY

❶ Understand the difference between tests of controls and substantive tests.

The purpose of tests of controls is to assess the effectiveness of a client's system of internal controls throughout the accounting period being audited. The purpose of substantive testing is to gather direct evidence that the financial statements are free from material misstatement.

❷ Explain the factors that impact the nature, timing, and extent of audit testing.

The nature of audit testing refers to the purpose of the test and the procedure used. The timing of audit testing refers to the stage of the audit when procedures are performed and the date, such as within or outside the accounting period, that audit evidence relates to. The extent of audit testing refers to the amount of audit evidence gathered when testing controls and conducting detailed substantive procedures.

❸ Explain how audit sampling is used in an audit.

When creating an audit plan and designing audit procedures, an auditor also decides how to select appropriate items for testing. When there are numerous transactions or items within an account balance available for testing, an auditor must decide how best to select a sample that is representative of the entire population of items available for testing.

❹ Understand the difference between sampling and non-sampling risk.

Sampling risk is the risk that the sample chosen by the auditor is not representative of the population of transactions or items within an account balance available for testing and, as a consequence, the auditor arrives at an inappropriate conclusion. Non-sampling risk is the risk that an auditor arrives at an inappropriate conclusion for a reason unrelated to sampling issues, such as an auditor using an inappropriate audit procedure.

❺ Differentiate between statistical and non-statistical sampling.

Statistical sampling involves random selection and probability theory to evaluate the results. Non-statistical sampling is any sample selection method that does not have these characteristics.

❻ Describe sampling methods and the factors to be considered when choosing a sample.

Sampling methods include random selection, systematic selection, haphazard selection, block selection, and judgemental selection. Before selecting a sample, an auditor will set parameters pertaining to control and detection risk, planning materiality, population, tolerable error rate, and the required level of confidence. Once these parameters are set, an auditor may select a sample using a statistical or non-statistical sampling technique.

❼ Determine the factors that influence the sample size when testing controls.

When testing controls, the factors that influence the sample size include the extent to which the risk of material misstatement is reduced by the operating effectiveness of controls, the rate of deviation from the prescribed control activity that the auditor is willing to accept, the rate of deviation from the prescribed control activity that the auditor expects to find in the population, the auditor's required confidence level, and the number of sampling units in the population.

8 **Determine the factors that influence the sample size when substantive testing.**

When conducting substantive testing of transactions and balances, the factors that influence the sample size include the auditor's assessment of the risk of material misstatement, the use of other substantive procedures directed at the same assertion, the auditor's required confidence level, the tolerable error, the amount of error the auditor expects to find in the population, the stratification of the population, and the number of sampling units in the population.

9 **Outline how to evaluate the results of tests conducted on a sample.**

When testing controls, the auditor will compare the rate of deviation with the tolerable rate of deviation and determine whether they believe that the control tested is effective in preventing and/or detecting a material misstatement. When testing transactions and balances, the error in the sample will be projected onto the population and then compared to the tolerable error rate. The auditor will then determine whether the class of transactions or account balance being tested appears to be materially misstated.

KEY TERMS

Accuracy, 221
Audit plan, 218
Audit risk, 218
Audit sampling, 225
Audit strategy, 218
Block selection, 231
Classification, 221
Completeness, 221
Control risk, 218
Cut-off, 221
Existence, 221
Extent of audit testing, 224
Haphazard selection, 231
Inherent risk, 218
Judgemental selection, 232
Nature of audit testing, 223
Non-sampling risk, 228

Non-statistical sampling, 229
Occurrence, 220
Projected error, 238
Random selection, 230
Rate of deviation, 235
Rights and obligations, 221
Sampling risk, 226
Statistical sampling, 229
Stratification, 230
Substantive audit procedures, 218
Substantive procedures, 220
Systematic selection, 230
Tests of controls, 218
Timing of audit testing, 224
Tolerable misstatement, 234
Valuation and allocation, 221

MULTIPLE-CHOICE QUESTIONS

6.1 A detailed audit plan:
  (a) is based on the overall audit strategy.
  (b) contains a description of the control testing procedures.
  (c) lists the audit procedures to be used in substantive testing.
  (d) all of the above.

6.2 When testing controls the auditor:
  (a) is interested in assessing the effectiveness of controls.
  (b) gathers evidence about the balances of the main accounts.
  (c) does not have to have any prior knowledge of the client's

inherent risks and how the controls address those risks.

(d) all of the above.

6.3 Deviations:

(a) are errors that affect account balances by a material amount.

(b) occur when controls do not operate as intended.

(c) are relevant only when they occur consistently throughout the accounting period.

(d) are caused by auditors choosing incorrect audit procedures.

6.4 Analytical procedures:

(a) are less efficient than substantive testing of details.

(b) place less reliance on the client's accounting records than substantive testing of details.

(c) are relied on to a greater extent when a client's internal controls are effective.

(d) are most useful when inherent and control risk are high.

6.5 The relationship between audit risk, reliance on substantive testing, and evidence persuasiveness is:

(a) high audit risk, low reliance on substantive testing, low evidence persuasiveness required.

(b) low audit risk, high reliance on substantive testing, low evidence persuasiveness required.

(c) high audit risk, high reliance on substantive testing, high evidence persuasiveness required.

(d) low audit risk, low reliance on substantive testing, high evidence persuasiveness required.

6.6 If preliminary testing of controls reveals that the rate of deviation in controls is above the expected rate, the auditor will:

(a) reduce detection risk and increase reliance on detailed substantive testing at year-end.

(b) increase detection risk and increase reliance on detailed substantive testing at year-end.

(c) reduce detection risk and decrease reliance on detailed substantive testing at year-end.

(d) increase detection risk and decrease reliance on detailed substantive testing at year-end.

6.7 Sampling risk:

(a) is the risk that the results of the test will be misinterpreted by the auditor.

(b) is the risk that the sample chosen by the auditor is not representative of the population of transactions.

(c) can be eliminated by taking a random sample.

(d) applies only to samples for substantive testing.

6.8 Non-sampling risk:

(a) occurs only if you test every member of the population.

(b) applies only to samples taken for the purposes of control testing.

(c) is the risk that an auditor arrives at an inappropriate conclusion for a reason unrelated to sampling issues.

(d) does not occur if an auditor relies on unreliable evidence.

6.9 Tolerable error:

(a) is the maximum error an auditor is willing to accept within the population.

(b) is positively related to sample size.

(c) relates only to control testing.

(d) is an amount prescribed by CAS 530.

6.10 The auditor has discovered errors when conducting substantive testing on a sample of invoices. If the total error discovered is $3,442, the dollar value of the sample is $25,136, and the population dollar value is $64,912, then the projected error is:

(a) $3,442.

(b) $8,889.

(c) $1,885.

(d) $1,369.

REVIEW QUESTIONS

6.1 Explain the difference between tests of controls and substantive procedures. How are the results of tests of controls related to decisions about the nature, timing, and extent of substantive procedures?

6.2 Explain how analytical procedures could be used for control testing and substantive testing. Give examples of each.

6.3 How is test data used to gather evidence about the effectiveness of controls? Why is using test data likely to be a more effective audit test than reading client procedure manuals?

6.4 Why are audit tests more likely to be conducted at or after year end for high-risk clients than for low-risk clients? Explain.

6.5 Explain the difference between the two types of sampling risk for controls: overreliance on an ineffective system of internal controls, and underreliance on an effective system of internal controls. What are the errors' different implications for the audit? Which is the more serious risk? Explain.

6.6 Why does non-sampling risk exist for all types of tests in all audits? Explain.

6.7 Describe the main non-statistical sampling methods. What are the advantages of non-statistical sampling?

6.8 Explain the relationship between the sample size for controls testing and each of the following factors: (1) the likely effectiveness of a control; (2) the acceptable rate of deviation; (3) the expected rate of deviation; (4) the required level of confidence in the effectiveness of the client's system of internal controls; and (5) the number of units in the population.

6.9 How does stratification of the population reduce the required sample size? Give an example of substantive testing where stratification would be appropriate.

6.10 Assume an auditor finds total errors of $25,300 in a sample of sales invoices. Why is it not appropriate to conclude that sales are misstated by $25,300? How would you determine the estimate of misstatement in sales?

PROFESSIONAL APPLICATION QUESTIONS

Basic ★   Moderate ★★   Challenging ★★★

6.1 Testing accounts receivable ★

Emma Maltz has been appointed as audit senior of the accounts receivable area in the audit of Fantastic Cruises, a company operating leisure cruises from ports in eastern Canada. Fantastic Cruises sells cruises to individuals (via its website) and to travel agents for resale to customers. All cruises are paid in advance, with a 10 percent deposit on booking, and the remainder collected at least four weeks prior to sailing. Travel agents collect money from their customers, deduct their commission, and forward the remainder to the cruise company before the deadline. Emma has made a preliminary assessment that the client is a low control risk and plans to conduct extensive testing of controls in the accounts receivable area to support her assessment.

Required

(a) What is Emma's objective in testing of controls over accounts receivable?

(b) Assuming Emma achieves her objective, discuss the implications for the nature, timing, and extent of substantive testing of accounts receivable.

6.2 Sample selection in practice ★

Rahim, a first-year auditor, is asked to select a sample of invoices to audit the utility expense account. Below is the account detail.

The audit program asks to select a sample of four items.

Month	Balance
January	15,245
February	12,973
March	11,359
April	9,326
May	6,380
June	4,558
July	2,901
August	2,837
September	3,690
October	5,890
November	9,823
December	14,906

Required

(a) Using a random number generator in Excel, determine which months will be selected.

(b) Using systematic selection, determine which four months will be selected.

(c) Using haphazard selection, determine which four months will be selected.

(d) Using block selection, determine which four months will be selected.

6.3 Sampling and non-sampling risk for control testing ★ ★

Fred Saros is auditing cash payments for OGA, a large supermarket. OGA deals with several very large corporate suppliers who expect payment by electronic funds transfer within three business days of delivery. Other large suppliers will accept cheques or electronic funds transfer on terms of 14 days, and small suppliers receive cheques with payment terms of 30 days. Other regular, large cash payments include wages (paid weekly by electronic funds transfer from a wages imprest account), utilities (electricity accounts are paid monthly by cheque), cleaning (paid monthly by cheque), and rent (paid monthly by electronic funds transfer). In addition, there are irregular payments for items such as maintenance, fixtures purchase and lease, and vehicle running costs.

All cash payments are processed in the central office after the required set of documents has been assembled and checked by two junior accounts staff. Payments are authorized by a senior accountant, and electronic funds transfer authorities and cheques are countersigned by the chief accountant (except if he is on leave when another member of the accounting staff performs this task). Journals and ledgers are maintained by staff not involved in cash payment processing.

Fred needs to test controls over cash payments and has planned to make extensive use of sampling.

Required

(a) What population(s) would be relevant to Fred's control testing?

(b) Explain the potential implications of sampling risk for the audit of cash payments.

(c) What possible non-sampling risks exist in this case?

6.4 Sampling methods ★ ★

Bob Downe is auditing Red Gum Home Furniture (RGHF), a manufacturer and retailer of boutique home furniture. RGHF was founded 25 years ago by a husband and wife team and has grown rapidly in the last five years as solid, environmentally friendly, wooden furniture has grown in popularity. However, although RGHF's owners have attempted to expand the administration department to keep pace with the growth in sales, some systems are not operating as effectively as they should. This is partly due to difficulty in attracting and retaining accounting staff with appropriate experience and skills.

RGHF's owners have recently realized that they need to increase pay and improve conditions for the accounting staff to avoid having periods with unqualified staff, particularly for sales invoice processing. The staff shortages have resulted in sluggish performance in processing invoices, sending out customer statements, and collecting cash from account customers. In addition, there have been numerous mistakes in processing sales invoices, some of which have been discovered after customer complaints.

Bob is selecting a sample of sales invoices for substantive testing. All documents relating to sales invoices for the last five years are stored in boxes in the shed behind the office. The shed is very small and the boxes are stacked on top of each other because the shelves are full. Due to the damp conditions some labels have peeled from the boxes, so it is not clear which boxes relate to the current year.

Required

(a) Describe the population(s) that would be relevant to Bob's sample selection.

(b) Which sample selection methods would be appropriate for choosing sales invoices for substantive testing at RGHF? Explain the factors that would influence your choice.

6.5 Determining sample size for control testing ★ ★

Alice Pang is planning the control testing of the accounts payable function in the hardware retailer Bunns and Major. Alice is attempting to determine the appropriate sample size for her tests and is writing a report to the engagement partner of the audit justifying her choices. She has had the opportunity to talk to management at Bunns and Major and tour the facilities. She has also reviewed the working papers from the previous audits and identified factors that have changed from previous years. She notes that the number of accounts payable has increased by 50 percent since last year because Bunns and Major has changed some of its suppliers from large corporate wholesalers to dealing directly with manufacturers.

Overall, Alice believes that the controls in accounts payable are likely to be operating more effectively than in previous years, and she expects a reduction in control deviations. This situation is likely because of the appointment of an additional staff member in the accounts payable department three months after the start of the fiscal year. However, she is recommending that a lower rate of deviation would be acceptable this year because of the increased importance of accounts payable to Bunns and Major's solvency situation in the current economic climate. In addition, she is recommending that substantive testing of accounts payable be less extensive than in past years.

Required

Explain how the factors mentioned above would impact the sample size for control testing of accounts payable.

6.6 Evaluating substantive testing results ★ ★

The results of substantive testing of sales invoices at City Electronics are shown in table 6.7.

The three strata correspond to different departments and the overall tolerable error is set at $40,000.

Required

(a) Project the errors for each stratum and calculate the total projected error. Is the projected error material? What difference would it make if the tolerable error was set at $30,000? Explain.

(b) Discuss the implications for the substantive testing if it was discovered that the permanent staff member in the department corresponding to stratum 3 was on long-term leave for three months of the fiscal year.

TABLE 6.7 **Substantive testing results of City Electronics' sales invoices**

STRATUM	ERROR FOUND	SAMPLE TOTAL VALUE	STRATUM TOTAL VALUE	PROJECTED ERROR
1	$ 7,930	$101,170	$128,660	
2	$ 3,290	$ 41,990	$ 76,830	
3	$ 8,600	$ 62,840	$162,280	
Total	$19,820	$206,000	$367,770	

Questions 6.7 and 6.8 are based on the following case.

Fabrication Holdings Ltd. (FH) has been a client of KFP Partners for many years. You are an audit senior and have been assigned to the FH audit for the first time for the fiscal year ended December 31, 2012. You are completing the audit planning for the property, plant, and equipment (PPE) account class, which is one of FH's most material balances. You are also aware that FH has made a large investment in a new manufacturing process to place itself in a more competitive position. Your analytical procedures indicate an increase in acquisitions of PPE.

You are testing the appropriateness of the depreciation rate assigned to PPE, and whether it is consistent with the present condition and expected use of the assets over their remaining life. You have sampled 35 PPE items, with a total dollar value of $1,145,000. The results show that for the sample items, some depreciation rates were too low and/or the remaining useful life of the equipment was overstated by management. Together, these issues produce an error in the sample of $48,500. FH has a profit before tax for the current year of $1,875,000, and a PPE account balance at the end of the year of $11,345,000.

Source: Adapted from the Institute of Chartered Accountants Australia's CA Program's *Audit and Assurance Exam*, May 2008.

6.7 Sampling methods and risk ★★

Required
Discuss the appropriate method of sampling PPE for the planned tests of depreciation. Define the population. What assertions are most at risk?

6.8 Projecting errors for PPE ★★

Required
What conclusion would you draw about "valuation and allocation" of PPE from the above information? Justify your conclusion.

Questions 6.9 and 6.10 are based on the following case.

Fellowes and Associates Chartered Accountants is a successful mid-tier accounting firm with a large range of clients across Canada. During the financial year 2011, Fellowes and Associates gained a new client, Health Care Holdings Group (HCHG), which owns 100 percent of the following entities:
- Shady Oaks Centre, a private treatment centre
- Gardens Nursing Home Ltd., a private nursing home
- Total Laser Care Limited (TLCL), a private clinic that specializes in the laser treatment of skin defects. Year end for all HCHG entities is June 30.

During the 2011 financial year, Shady Oaks released its own line of treatment supplies, such as orthotics, massage oils, and exercise discs and balls, which are sold by direct marketing by a sales team employed by the centre. The sales team receives a base salary and a bonus component, which is based on the dollar value of sales it generates. You recognize that the team's main motivation is to maximize its bonuses. You select a sample of payments received by the centre post year end and trace the payments back to the general ledger and customer account balance.

TEST	RESULT	CONCLUSION
1	A number of suppliers were selected from the list of trade creditors at year end and balances traced to supplier invoices and goods received notes to ensure that goods were received prior to the year end. For two creditors out of 15 tested, the balance was only marginally overstated.	Accepted as no material errors were found
2	A number of suppliers' invoices were selected and checked to ensure that the pricing and discount terms were reviewed and authorized by the purchase manager. Three out of 20 invoices tested had not been authorized and incorrect discounts were recorded for these invoices. A follow-up of the three samples with deviations did not highlight a pattern or specific reason for the errors.	Accepted as the errors in discounts taken were immaterial

TABLE 6.8 **Testing results of Gardens Nursing Home's accounts payable**

In addition, you are reviewing the results of a number of tests in relation to accounts payable at Gardens Nursing Home as shown in table 6.8.

Source: Adapted from the Institute of Chartered Accountants Australia's CA Program's *Audit and Assurance Exam*, December 2008.

6.9 Substantive testing and assertions ★★

Required
(a) Identify the key account balance at risk because of the remuneration of the sales team at Shady Oaks. Identify and explain the key assertion at risk.
(b) Identify the key account balance and key assertion being tested using the substantive procedure. Given the bonus structure in place for the sales team, justify your answer.

6.10 Substantive testing versus control testing ★★★

Required
For each of the test results for Gardens Nursing Home:
(a) Identify whether this is a test of controls or a substantive test of detail.
(b) Determine the key assertion addressed by the test procedure.
(c) Explain why the conclusion reached is appropriate or inappropriate.
(d) Outline the key additional procedure that you believe needs to be performed.

6.11 Interpreting sampling documentation ★★★

Min-Li is auditing RRR Services Inc. and has designed the following tests:

Test A
1. Select 150 cancelled cheques (8 percent of the total number of cheques) at random from the purchases journal for the year.
2. Ignore any cheques with a recorded value of less than $1,000.
3. Examine the cancelled cheques to verify if they have been approved by the accounting supervisor (indicated by her initials on the cheque).
4. Compare the percentage of cheques (of the sample) that lacks the accounting supervisor's initials to a pre-determined percentage of 5 percent.

Test B
1. Select 150 cancelled cheques (8 percent of the total number of cheques) at random from the purchases journal for the year.
2. Compare the amount of each cheque to the amount recorded in the purchases journal.
3. Total the net overstatement or understatement for all cheques examined and project this amount to obtain an estimate for the population.
4. Compare the population estimate from step 3 to a predetermined amount of $8,000.

Required

(a) Identify the attribute being tested in the test of controls.

(b) Can the results in Test B be used to project a value for the population? Explain your answer.

(c) Can the results in Test A be used to project a value for the population of cancelled cheques for the year? Explain your answer.

(d) Explain sampling risk in substantive testing (in one or two sentences).

Source: © CGA-Canada. Reproduced with permission.

6.12 Types of audit sampling and sampling risk ★

Match the numbered situations below with one of the following types of audit sampling or sampling risk:

(a) Statistical sampling

(b) Non-statistical sampling

(c) Sampling risk

(d) Non-sampling risk

1. Rather than looking only for authorized signatures, an auditor checked to see if there were any signatures in the credit approval box on a sample of sales orders.

2. An auditor concluded that, based on a statistical sample, the client's control system was working acceptably when, in fact, the population deviation rate was unacceptable.

3. Using the laws of probability, an auditor selected a sample and evaluated the results of her sample.

6.13 Benefits of statistical sampling ★

You are an audit senior, and your manager, Monique Lauzon, feels that non-statistical sampling is the best method to use on the audit of Konway Corporation. However, you believe that statistical sampling is much superior, and you have a great deal of training in the proper use of sampling techniques.

Required

Which arguments could you use to convince Monique that statistical sampling should be used?

6.14 Potential impact of sampling risk ★ ★

Your friend, Alexei Antropov, has recently began working for an auditing firm and he wants your advice regarding some tests of sales transactions that he is currently undertaking with respect to one of his clients. He has been careful not to disclose to you the name of his client so as not to breach confidentiality.

Alexei selected a haphazard sample of 30 sales with a total book value of $150,000. In his sample, he found a total of $1,000 in net overstatement errors. The total sales balance per books is $20 million. Overall materiality for the engagement is $600,000. Tolerable error for sales is $140,000. The sample results indicate that Alexei's best estimate of total misstatement in sales is $70,000.

Required

Could Alexei safely conclude that no additional audit work is needed in this area? Support your answer.

6.15 Sample size selection ★

Patrizia Montani is considering the sample size needed for a selection of sales invoices relating to the test of internal controls of the Caistor Company. She is determining the acceptable risk and deviation rates, and is considering two possible scenarios as shown in table 6.9.

RISK OR DEVIATION RATE	CASE A	CASE B
Acceptable risk of underreliance	High	Low
Acceptable risk of overreliance	High	Low
Tolerable deviation rate	High	Low
Expected population deviation rate	Low	High

TABLE 6.9 **Risk or deviation rate for sample scenarios**

Required

In which of the two cases should Patrizia select a larger sample size?

CASE

CASE STUDY—CLOUD 9

Answer the following questions based on the information for Cloud 9 presented in Appendix B of this book and in the current and earlier chapters. You should also consider your answers to the case study questions in earlier chapters.

Required

(a) Consider and explain the effects that the opening of Cloud 9's first retail store would have on its accounting.
(b) Describe how this business change would affect the components of audit risk.
(c) What changes would you expect to see in inventory transactions and balances as Cloud 9 changes from a wholesale-only business to a retail and wholesale business? Be specific in your answer.
(d) Which inventory balance and transaction assertions would be most affected? Explain.
(e) Describe the population(s) and suggest a sampling approach for controls and substantive testing for inventory.

RESEARCH QUESTION 6.1

McKesson & Robbins was a company at the centre of a famous fraud in the United States in the 1930s.

Required

(a) Research the facts of the McKesson & Robbins fraud and write a short description of the case.
(b) Make a list of the defects in the company's system of internal controls that are relevant to the fraud and suggest audit tests that would have revealed these problems.

SOLUTIONS TO MULTIPLE-CHOICE QUESTIONS

1. d, 2. a, 3. b, 4. c, 5. c, 6. a, 7. b, 8. c, 9. a, 10. b.

CHAPTER 7

Gaining an understanding of the client's system of internal controls

LEARNING OBJECTIVES

After studying this chapter, you should be able to:

1. define internal control

2. explain the seven generally accepted objectives of internal control activities

3. understand and describe the elements of internal control at the entity level

4. understand and describe the elements of internal control at the transaction level, and apply them to the sales, purchases, and payroll cycles

5. explain the different techniques used to document internal controls

6. explain the importance of identifying strengths and weaknesses in a system of internal controls

7. explain how to communicate internal control strengths and weaknesses to those charged with governance.

AUDITING AND ASSURANCE STANDARDS

CANADIAN	INTERNATIONAL
CAS 260 *Communication with Those Charged with Governance*	ISA 260 *Communication with Those Charged with Governance*
CAS 265 *Communicating Deficiencies in Internal Control to Those Charged with Governance and Management*	ISA 265 *Communicating Deficiencies in Internal Control to Those Charged with Governance and Management*
CAS 315 *Identifying and Assessing the Risks of Material Misstatement Through Understanding the Entity and its Environment*	ISA 315 *Identifying and Assessing the Risks of Material Misstatement Through Understanding the Entity and its Environment*

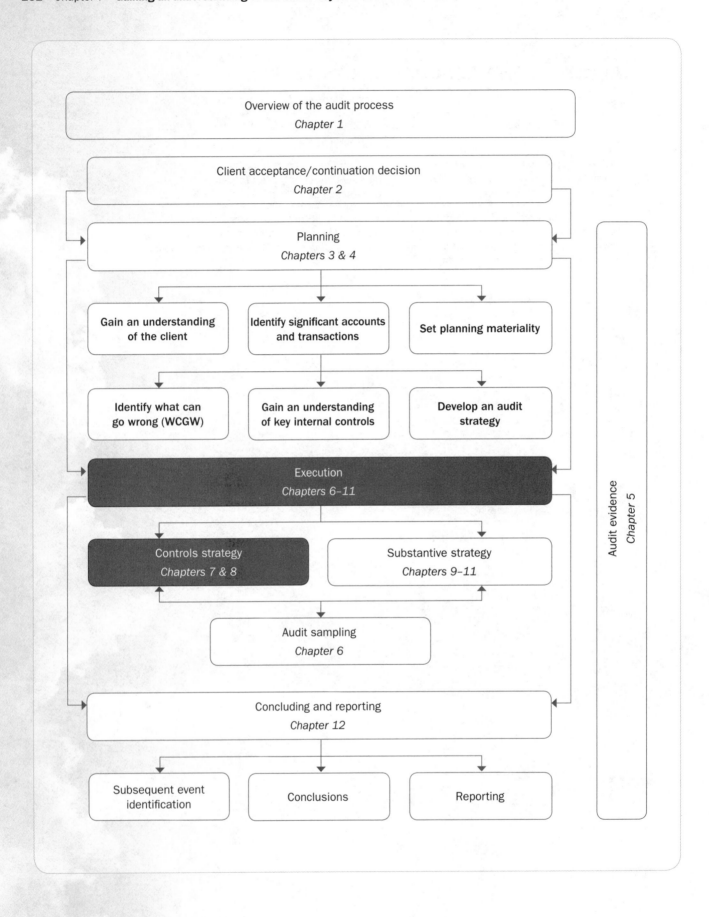

Cloud 9

Sharon Gallagher and Josh Thomas are working on the draft of their internal control assessment report for Cloud 9 Ltd. (Cloud 9). They met with the Cloud 9 finance director, David Collier, to gain an understanding of the internal controls at the entity level. The interview covered issues such as management integrity, policies and procedures, and monitoring of control activities. Sharon asks Josh to write up the results of the interview and make an assessment about the effectiveness of entity-level controls. Does the company demonstrate an environment where potential material misstatements are prevented or detected?

Sharon also wants Josh to document in detail an understanding of the controls at the transaction level. Sharon emphasizes to Josh that their description of Cloud 9's system of internal controls is part of the evidence for the audit, and their assessment of the system's strengths and weaknesses will influence the remainder of the planning process. They must understand when, where, and how potential material misstatements can occur.

How will Josh complete his tasks?

AUDIT PROCESS IN FOCUS

The purpose of this chapter is to assist in understanding the client's system of internal controls as it relates to the audit of the financial statements. This involves understanding the term "internal control," being aware of the objectives of the internal controls put in place by management and the components of these controls (particularly at the entity level), and obtaining an understanding of a client's system of internal controls.

This chapter will also discuss the importance of evaluating how the design and implementation of controls will prevent material misstatements from occurring, or how they will detect and correct material misstatements after they have occurred. The chapter will also discuss the implications of an absence of internal controls and provide a description of how strengths and weaknesses in a system of internal controls are communicated to both management and those charged with governance.

7.1 INTERNAL CONTROL DEFINED

Why is understanding the internal controls of an organization important? Because when controls are effective, the organization is more likely to achieve its strategic and operating objectives. Internal control is a very broad concept and encompasses all of the elements of an organization—its resources, systems, processes, culture, structure, and tasks. When these elements are taken together, they support the organization to achieve its objectives. For the purposes of this chapter, we will focus on the components of internal control that have a direct impact on the financial reporting. We will focus on the safeguards put in place by management to prevent and detect errors including misappropriation of assets and human errors. **Internal control** is defined in the auditing standards as:

> The process designed, implemented and maintained by those charged with governance, management and other personnel to provide reasonable assurance about the achievement of the entity's objectives with regard to reliability of its financial reporting, effectiveness and efficiency of operations, and compliance with applicable laws and regulations. The term "controls" refers to any aspect of one or more of the components of internal control. (CAS 315)

1 Define internal control.

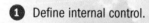

internal control the process designed, implemented, and maintained by those charged with governance, management, and other personnel to provide reasonable assurance about the achievement of the entity's objectives with regard to reliability of financial reporting, effectiveness and efficiency of operations, and compliance with applicable laws and regulations

audit risk the risk that an auditor expresses an inappropriate audit opinion when the financial statements are materially misstated

As discussed in chapter 6, understanding internal control is a key component of the overall **audit risk** assessment and provides evidence that influences the resulting strategy developed by the auditor. Also, CAS 315 *Identifying and Assessing the Risks of Material Misstatement Through Understanding the Entity and its Environment* requires the auditor to obtain an understanding of internal control on all audit engagements.

Frameworks for internal controls have been developed such as the *Internal control—integrated framework* developed by the Committee of Sponsoring Organizations of the Treadway Commission (COSO) and the *Guidance on Controls* issued by the Criteria of Control Board of the CICA. These frameworks provide a structure that allows the auditor to assess the internal controls of an organization as compared to a theoretical model. Therefore, where internal controls put in place by management agree closely with the theoretical framework, the internal controls may be described as strong. However, where internal controls do not agree closely with the theoretical framework, they may be described as weak.

While we will not discuss these frameworks specifically, the general principles are consistent with the objectives and components of internal control discussed in more detail in this chapter and included in CAS 315.

BEFORE YOU GO ON

1.1 What is an internal control?

1.2 Why is it important to understand (and assess) internal controls?

1.3 Name a generally accepted framework used to describe internal controls.

7.2 OBJECTIVES OF INTERNAL CONTROLS

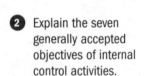 Explain the seven generally accepted objectives of internal control activities.

There are seven generally accepted objectives of internal controls. Internal controls are designed and implemented to ensure that transactions are real, recorded, correctly valued, classified, summarized, and posted on a timely basis. When the system of internal controls meets its objectives as these relate to the recording of transactions and balances, management assertions are also likely to be valid. The internal control objectives are matched with the relevant assertions as follows:

1. Real—there are controls in place to ensure that fictitious or duplicate transactions are not included in the books and records of the organization (occurrence, rights and obligations, and existence assertions).
2. Recorded—there are controls in place that will prevent or detect the omission of transactions from the books and records of the organization (accuracy, completeness, and valuation and allocation assertions).
3. Valued—there are controls in place to ensure that the correct amounts are assigned to the transactions (accuracy, and valuation and allocation assertions).
4. Classified—there are controls in place to ensure that transactions are charged and allocated to the correct general ledger account (accuracy, classification, and valuation and allocation assertions).
5. Summarized—there are controls in place to ensure that the transactions in the books and records are summarized and totalled correctly (accuracy and valuation and allocation assertions).

6. Posted—there are controls in place to ensure that the accumulated totals in the transaction file are correctly transferred to the general ledger and subsidiary ledgers (accuracy, classification, and valuation and allocation assertions).
7. Timely—there are controls in place to ensure that transactions are recorded in the correct accounting period (cut-off and completeness assertions).

The assertion relating to classification and understandability, which is a presentation and disclosure assertion, is not specifically addressed by these internal control objectives. An entity may still design controls over this assertion. The auditor performs procedures based on the controls the entity has in place. The auditor usually ensures this assertion is met by substantively testing the draft financial statements. An example of how this is often done is by using a disclosure checklist. These checklists typically include all of the disclosures required by the accounting standards. They assist the auditor in ensuring that all of the required material disclosures have been made.

When the auditor gains an understanding of the client's system of internal controls and how the client uses internal controls to manage risks in the business, it is important for the auditor to remember each of these objectives. By focusing on each of these objectives, the auditor will be able to select the appropriate controls to test to gain the greatest level of assurance possible that the client's system of internal controls is operating effectively.

The concept of testing and assessing controls is discussed in more detail in chapter 8. It is worth mentioning here that when the objectives of internal controls are not met, it is considered to be a deficiency in internal control. The auditor then considers whether the weakness has a significant impact on their risk assessment for the relevant account balances and transactions. This is discussed in further detail later in this chapter.

Internal control, no matter how effective, can only provide an entity with reasonable assurance in achieving its financial reporting objectives. There are inherent limitations of internal control. These include:

- human error that results in a breakdown in internal control
- ineffective understanding of the purpose of a control
- collusion by two or more individuals to circumvent a control
- a control within a software program being overridden or disabled.

An example of a limitation is an internal control that may be designed appropriately but never implemented by management. The control, therefore, has no ability to mitigate risks. These limitations of internal controls are often mitigated by other controls (often referred to as compensating controls). If there are no other controls mitigating the weaknesses or limitations, the risks are addressed by the auditor performing extensive substantive procedures. This concept is discussed further in chapters 8 and 9.

Cloud 9

Josh knows that as he writes his report he has to think about the whole system of internal controls at Cloud 9 and how effective it is in helping the company achieve its objectives. However, as the auditor, he has to focus mostly on the controls that relate to the integrity of the company's financial statements. Which controls are keeping transactions real, recorded, correctly valued, classified, summarized, and posted on a timely basis? Also, which controls are protecting assets and ensuring that the company complies with relevant laws and regulations? The better these controls, the more likely W&S Partners can adopt a combined audit approach to the audit.

BEFORE YOU GO ON

2.1 What are the seven generally accepted objectives of internal controls as related to the recording of transactions?

2.2 Why are internal controls important to an organization?

2.3 Why are internal controls important to an auditor?

7.3 ENTITY-LEVEL INTERNAL CONTROLS

3   Understand and describe the elements of internal control at the entity level.

As set out in CAS 315, internal control consists of five components:

1. the control environment
2. the entity's risk assessment process
3. the information system, including the related business processes, relevant to financial reporting, and communication
4. control activities
5. monitoring of controls.

These internal control components, when collectively assessed, are often referred to as **entity-level controls** because each exists at an organizational or entity level rather than at a more detailed transactional level. For example, a control ensuring that sales are recorded in the sales ledger is a transaction-level control. A control such as the internal audit function of a company is an entity-level control. The different types of controls are discussed further in chapter 8.

entity-level controls the collective assessment of the client's control environment, risk assessment process, information system, control activities, and monitoring of controls

Gaining an understanding of the entity-level internal control components helps in establishing the appropriate level of professional scepticism, gaining an understanding of the client's business and financial statement risks, and making assessments of inherent risk, control risk, and the combined risk of material misstatement, which, in turn, determines the nature, timing, and extent of audit procedures (as discussed in chapters 4, 6, 8, and 9).

7.3.1 The control environment

The control environment sets the tone of an entity and influences the control consciousness of its people. It is the foundation for all other components of internal control and is often thought of as a combination of the culture, structure, and discipline of an organization. It reflects the overall attitude, awareness, and actions of management, the board of directors, others charged with governance, and the owners concerning the importance of controls and the emphasis given to controls in determining the organization's policies, processes, and organizational structure. Therefore, the control environment is sometimes referred to as the "tone at the top."

control environment the attitudes, awareness, and actions of management and those charged with governance concerning the entity's internal control and its importance in the entity

The **control environment** also sets the foundation for effective internal control, providing discipline and structure, and includes the following elements.

- *Communication and enforcement of integrity and ethical values.* Integrity and ethical values are essential elements of the control environment, affecting the design, administration, and monitoring of key processes. Integrity and ethical behaviour are the products of the organization's ethical and behavioural standards, how they are communicated, and how they are monitored and enforced in its business activities. Control activities include management's actions to remove or reduce incentives, pressures, and opportunities that might prompt personnel to engage in dishonest, illegal, or unethical acts. Other control activities also include the communication of the organization's values and behavioural standards to personnel through policy statements and codes of conduct, and the examples set by management.

For example, management may state in its code of conduct that employees are not allowed to accept gifts from suppliers valued above a certain price and that all offers of gifts (whether accepted or not) are to be reported in a gift register (or something similar). Although a code of conduct does not guarantee that employees will act ethically when it comes to gifts, it does indicate that management communicates standards of behaviour that it expects employees to adhere to. Coupled with other procedures, such actions may demonstrate an effective control environment. It is also important that management is seen to comply with its own policies.

- *Commitment to competence.* Management's commitment to competence refers to considering the skill levels required for particular positions within the organization and making sure that staff with the required skills are hired and matched to the right jobs. Among the factors that management may consider are the nature and degree of judgement to be applied to a specific job and the extent of supervision required. Auditors use professional judgement to determine whether they believe management and employees appear to be competent to carry out their assigned roles and receive adequate supervision where required.

  For example, do employees have the knowledge and expertise necessary to understand and execute the requirements of the generally accepted reporting framework, the International Financial Reporting Standards (IFRS) or the Canadian Accounting Standards for Private Enterprises (ASPE)?

- *Participation by those charged with governance.* The organization's control environment is influenced significantly by its board of directors and others charged with governance of the entity: for example, by the audit committee members or the CEO if they are charged with responsibility for governance and are members of management. Those charged with governance are responsible for overseeing the entity's accounting and financial reporting policies and procedures. As a result, those charged with governance have an obligation to be concerned with the entity's financial reporting to shareholders and the investing public, and to monitor the entity's accounting policies and the internal and independent (external) audit processes.

  In determining the effectiveness of the participation of those charged with governance, in particular the board of directors, auditors consider the board's independence from management, the experience of its members, the extent of its involvement and scrutiny of management's day-to-day activities, and its interactions with the internal and/or external auditors. For example, if the board has regular and open communications with its auditors, management may be more willing to inform the board of issues arising in the business on a timely basis (to avoid "surprises").

- *Management's philosophy and operating style.* Obtaining an understanding of management's philosophy and operating style is necessary to identify the factors that influence management's attitudes toward internal control. This understanding affects the auditor's assessment of how management makes judgements and accounting estimates, and provides an insight into the competence and motivations of management. The more confidence an auditor gains regarding management's abilities and integrity, the more reliance the auditor can place on the information, explanations, and representations provided by management. Alternatively, doubts about management's ability and integrity will increase the level of corroborating evidence required for representations made by management. An understanding of management's operating style is therefore a fundamental input into assessing audit risk.

- *Organizational structure.* The client's organizational structure provides the framework within which its activities for achieving entity-wide objectives are planned, executed, controlled, and monitored. Establishing an organizational structure includes considering the key areas of authority and responsibility as well as the appropriateness of the lines of reporting.

  The size and complexity of the organization together with management's business and operating philosophies significantly affect the organizational structure and the need for formal organization charts, job descriptions, and policy statements. In addition to the formal organizational structure, an informal structure may also exist that affects the control environment. An auditor will gain an understanding of their client's organizational structure and the suitability of its policies and procedures in light of its size and complexity.

  The information technology (IT) environment is also an important aspect of the auditor's review of the organizational structure. Consideration needs to be given to whether the IT deployed by the entity allows clear assignment of responsibilities. This should include the assignment of authorization to initiate and/or change transactions and programs as well as ensuring that there is appropriate segregation of duties related to the programming, administration, operation, and use of IT. Segregation of duties is explained further in sections 7.3.4 and 7.3.6.

- *Assignment of authority and responsibility.* Assignment of authority and responsibility includes how authority and responsibility for operating activities are assigned, and how reporting relationships and authorization hierarchies are established. It includes policies relating to appropriate business practices, knowledge, experience of key personnel, and resources provided for carrying out duties. Assignment of authority and responsibility also includes policies and communications directed toward ensuring that all employees understand the organization's objectives, know how their individual roles and actions contribute to those objectives, and recognize how they will be held accountable for their actions.

- *Human resource policies and practices.* Human resource policies and practices relate to hiring, inducting, training, evaluating, counselling, promoting, and compensating employees. As discussed above, the competence and integrity of an entity's employees are essential elements of its control environment. The organization's ability to recruit and retain competent and responsible employees is therefore dependent to a large extent on its human resource policies and practices.

For example, standards are often set for hiring qualified individuals, focusing on educational background, prior work experience, past accomplishments, and evidence of a cultural fit with the employer organization (values and ethics). These standards show the organization's commitment to employing only competent and trustworthy people. Often job descriptions illustrate the expected levels of performance and behaviour.

When gaining an understanding of the control environment, the auditor considers each of the above elements and their interrelationships. In particular, the auditor needs to understand whether there are any significant deficiencies in any one element, as these deficiencies may have an impact on the effectiveness of the other elements. For example, management may establish a formal code of conduct but then act in a manner that condones breaches of that code.

The assessment of internal controls, as well as the impact of weaknesses in or exceptions to internal controls, is discussed in more detail in chapter 8.

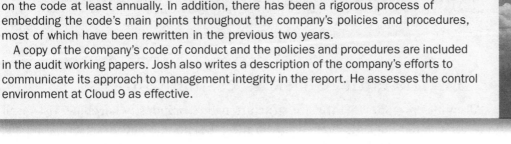

Cloud 9

During the interview Josh and Sharon held with David Collier, they learned a lot about the tone at the top at Cloud 9. Top-level management at the company is bound by a code of conduct based on a similar document adopted by the parent company, Cloud 9 Inc. The parent company has adopted a very strict approach to management integrity. Cloud 9's board members and senior managers attend training and awareness sessions on the code at least annually. In addition, there has been a rigorous process of embedding the code's main points throughout the company's policies and procedures, most of which have been rewritten in the previous two years.

A copy of the company's code of conduct and the policies and procedures are included in the audit working papers. Josh also writes a description of the company's efforts to communicate its approach to management integrity in the report. He assesses the control environment at Cloud 9 as effective.

PROFESSIONAL ENVIRONMENT

Human risks

What are the big risks for businesses? According to a report published by Ernst & Young (EY), human resource (HR) issues rank among the top five business issues impacting a company's results. Human resource issues are perennial because they are among the most difficult to define, control, and manage.

The EY report contains the results from surveying senior finance, accounting, risk, and HR executives at 150 Fortune 1000 companies. The executives were asked to rank the HR issues that they perceive as having a high impact and likelihood of occurrence within a global organization. The top five HR issues were:
1. talent management and succession planning
2. ethics/tone at the top
3. regulatory compliance
4. pay and performance alignment
5. employee training and development.

The executives were also asked about the methods used to monitor these risks. The results show that 41 percent of executives surveyed admit to reviewing these risks on an ad hoc basis or never. This result reinforces the view that HR issues are not managed effectively enough in many organizations.

One aspect of HR risk that is closely related to financial statement auditing is the effect of HR policies on promoting and communicating ethical values throughout the organization and ensuring that the appropriate "tone at the top" trickles down through the organization. The EY survey revealed that these issues have become more visible and significant in recent years, possibly as a result of adverse publicity about corporate ethics. However, although ethics is becoming more significant as an HR risk, the executives responding to the survey rated the likelihood of ethical problems arising throughout the organization as low. The survey's authors suggest HR executives should pay more attention to the alignment between values espoused by company management in public arenas and actual practices by employees at all levels within the organization.

Recent publicity on alignment of pay and performance seems to support EY's contentions. A recent report by the Canadian Centre for Policy Alternatives on Canada's top-paid executives questions the link between executive compensation and performance, which governments and citizens criticized in 2008 amid the corporate financial crisis. During this time, many CEOs were paid astronomical salaries and bonuses at the same time they were responsible for wiping out billions of dollars of shareholder value. The report points out that while remuneration of company executives is out of line with what the community expects, Canadian businesses often must pay high salaries so that they can compete for talent in a global market.

The report questions the association of pay with "performance," suggesting that some incentive pay packages have inappropriate performance hurdles, leading to substantial pay rises for "good luck." Auditors need to pay attention to such remuneration packages in order to understand the risks they create for the integrity of the client's accounts and the financial statements.

Sources: Ernst & Young, *2008 Global Human Resources (HR) Risk: From the Danger Zone to the Value Zone: Accelerating Business Improvement by Navigating HR Risk*, 2008, www.ey.com; S. Steffee, "HR Risks Are Largely Ignored," *Internal Auditor*, 65, no. 6 (December 2008): pp. 14–5; Canadian Centre for Policy Alternatives, "A Soft Landing: Recession and Canada's 100 Highest Paid CEO's," January 2010, www.policyalternatives.ca.

7.3.2 The entity's risk assessment process

All entities, regardless of their size, structure, nature, or industry, encounter risks at all levels within the organization. Risks will affect the entity's ability to survive, compete, grow, and improve the quality of its products, services, and people. It is not possible to reduce these risks to zero; however, management (in conjunction with those charged with governance) needs to determine how much risk is acceptable to the organization. Some organizations have a risk committee, which is responsible for ensuring that all of these risks are identified, managed, and reported to the board of directors.

The entity's risk assessment process is its method for identifying and responding to business risks. For financial reporting purposes, the entity's **risk assessment process** includes how management identifies risks relevant to the preparation of the financial statements to ensure a fair presentation in accordance with the entity's applicable financial reporting framework. For identified risks, management estimates their significance, assesses the likelihood of their occurrence, and decides upon actions to manage them.

Risks relevant to financial reporting include external and internal events and circumstances that may occur and adversely affect an entity's ability to initiate, record, process, and report financial data consistent with the assertions of management in the financial statements. For example, new accounting pronouncements and significant changes to the financial reporting standards (such as the change from local accounting standards to IFRS) are externally created risks relevant to the entity's financial reporting. Corporate restructurings that result in reduced employee levels may weaken the segregation of duties, and the internal control structure is an internally generated risk relevant to an entity's financial reporting. An organization's risk assessment process is different from the auditor's consideration of risk. The purpose of the entity's risk assessment process is to identify, analyze, and manage the risks that affect its ability to achieve its operational effectiveness. In an audit, the purpose is to assess the combined **inherent**, **control**, and **detection risks** to evaluate the likelihood that material misstatements could occur in the financial statements.

An entity's risk assessment for financial reporting purposes is its identification, analysis, and management of the risks relevant to the preparation of the financial

risk assessment process the entity's process for identifying and responding to business risks

inherent risk the susceptibility of the financial statements to a material misstatement without considering the internal controls

control risk the risk that a client's system of internal controls will not prevent or detect a material misstatement

detection risk the risk that the auditor's testing procedures will not be effective in detecting a material misstatement

statements that are fairly presented in compliance with the accounting framework (for example, IFRS or ASPE). Once risks are identified, management will ordinarily initiate plans, programs, or other actions to address the risks. Alternatively, management may decide to accept the risk without addressing it. Usually, this decision is made on the basis of the cost versus the benefit of managing the risk.

Risks can arise or be transformed as a result of changes to the organization and the environment it operates within. These include changes in the operating environment, new personnel, new technology, rapid growth, business restructuring, and new accounting pronouncements as discussed above. It is important for the auditor to understand the risks identified by the entity as this will assist the auditor in considering where (and if) a material misstatement in the financial statements might exist. The overall potential for risks to have a material impact on the financial statements is increased when management appears willing to accept unusually high risks when making business decisions, when entering into major commitments without sufficient consideration of the risks, and when failing to closely monitor and control the risks associated with commitments entered into.

Cloud 9

In their interview, Josh and Sharon ask David Collier about Cloud 9's risk assessment process. They want to know which risks management has identified so that they can consider whether those risks could cause a material misstatement in the financial statements. They also want to know about the company's methods of responding to the identified risks. David Collier tells them that Cloud 9's management continually monitors its competitors' activities. It also considers the risk of interruption to supplies because of shipping problems and labour disputes at production plants or transport companies.

Another example of risks that could have a major impact on the financial statements is the use of forward exchange contracts to control the risks caused by purchasing in foreign currencies. Management is also very aware of risks associated with the just-in-time inventory system, which has had some problems lately, and has planned some changes to deal with those problems.

Management is monitoring the risks of using a hockey player as a spokesman for the brand, plus the broader risks arising from sponsorship of the hockey team because there has been a lot of adverse publicity about hockey players' behaviour over the past year. Such adverse publicity could impact negatively on sales. Cloud 9's management ensures that the hockey team's management keeps the company's management informed of players' activities, where appropriate.

Josh concludes from the interview that Cloud 9 has an effective system of risk assessment because it actively searches out and considers potential risks to the business and has developed action plans to deal with each risk, depending on its likely occurrence.

7.3.3 Information systems and communication

The role of information systems is to capture and exchange the information needed to conduct, manage, and control an entity's operations. The quality of information and communication affects management's ability to make appropriate decisions in controlling the organization's activities and to prepare reliable financial statements. Information and communication involves capturing and providing information to management and employees so that they can carry out their responsibilities, including providing an understanding of individual roles and responsibilities as they relate to internal controls over financial reporting.

Information is needed at all levels of the entity to run the business and to assist in the achievement of financial reporting, operating, and compliance objectives. An array of information is used. Financial information, for instance, is used not only in developing financial statements for external dissemination; it may also be used for operational decisions, such as monitoring performance and allocating resources. Similarly, operating information (for example, airborne particle emissions and personnel data) may be needed to achieve compliance and financial reporting objectives as well as operating objectives. However, certain operating information (for example, purchases and sales data) is essential for developing the financial statements. As such, information developed from internal and external sources, both financial and non-financial, is relevant to all three objectives.

Information is identified, captured, processed, and reported by information systems. Information systems may be computerized, manual, or a combination thereof. The term "information systems" is frequently used in the context of processing internally generated data relating to transactions (for example, sales) and internal operating activities (for example, production processes). However, information systems as they relate to internal controls are much broader. That is, information systems also deal with information about external events, activities, and conditions.

Auditors are most interested in the information systems that are relevant to the financial reporting objective; that is, the systems responsible for initiating and recording transactions, balances, and events that will ultimately be reflected in the financial statements. These systems consist of the procedures, whether automated or manual, and records established to initiate, authorize, record, process, and report transactions (as well as events and conditions) and to maintain accountability for the related assets, liabilities, and equity. They include the client's asset safeguarding controls and the process for authorizing transactions, including adequate segregation of incompatible duties. The quality of system-generated information affects management's ability to make appropriate decisions in managing and controlling the entity's activities and to prepare reliable financial statements.

The information systems that are relevant to the financial reporting objective encompass methods that ensure transactions and disclosures are real, recorded, valued, classified, summarized, and posted on a timely basis (refer to section 7.2 for discussion of the seven generally accepted objectives of internal controls).

Communication is the process by which information is provided to those who need it on a timely basis. For example, a monthly management reporting package contains information about the company's financial performance and is used by many companies as the major way of communicating this information to executives and directors.

Cloud 9

Josh is an expert on information systems and based on the interview with David Collier, which covered the information systems at a high level, he can conclude that the entity-level controls in this area are effective. Josh will gather further information in an interview with Cloud 9's financial controller, Carla Johnson. Based on this second interview and a review of the company's documents, he will write a description of his understanding of the processes used in each of the major transaction cycles.

7.3.4 Control activities

Control activities are policies and procedures that help ensure that management's directives are carried out. They help guarantee that necessary actions are taken to address risks affecting the achievement of the organization's objectives. Control activities, whether automated or manual, have various objectives and are applied at various organizational and functional levels. Generally, control activities that may be relevant to an audit may be categorized as policies and procedures pertaining to the following:

- *Performance reviews.* These control activities include reviews of actual performance versus budgets, forecasts, and prior-period performance. Performance reviews compare different sets of data (operating or financial), analyzing these relationships and investigative and corrective actions. They also include reviews of functional or activity performance, such as, at a bank, a consumer loan manager's review of reports by branch, region, and loan type for loan approvals and collections. By investigating unexpected results or unusual trends, management identifies circumstances where the underlying activity objectives are in danger of not being achieved.
- *Information processing.* A variety of controls are performed to check accuracy, completeness, and authorization of transactions within information processing environments. Information processing controls can be manual controls; automated controls (that is, application dependent); manual controls dependent on an automated process (that is, IT dependent); or IT general controls (ITGCs). These concepts are discussed further in chapter 8.
- *Authorization controls.* These control activities define who can approve the various transactions within the organization. There is typically an approval hierarchy indicating authorization levels within the organization. The approval level generally increases as management responsibility increases. Approval should be required before any expenditure is made, including the hiring of employees, the ordering of goods and services, and the ability to extend credit.
- *Account reconciliations.* Reconciliations involve the preparation and review of account reconciliations on a timely basis. Bank accounts, intercompany accounts, and any clearing and suspense accounts should be reconciled on a regular basis. Sub-ledgers should be reconciled to the general ledger accounts. Reconciling items should be investigated and corrected promptly.
- *Physical controls.* These control activities encompass the physical security of assets, including adequate safeguards over access to assets and records (such as secured facilities and authorization for access to computer programs and data files) and periodic counting and comparison with amounts shown on control records. The extent to which physical controls intended to prevent theft of assets are relevant to the success of the business and the reliability of the financial statement preparation and, therefore, the audit, depends on the circumstances, such as if assets are highly susceptible to misappropriation.
- *Segregation of incompatible duties.* This control activity encompasses the concept that no one employee or group of employees should be in a position to both perpetrate and hide errors or fraud in the normal course of their duties. In general, the principle duties that are incompatible and should be segregated are:
  - custody of assets
  - authorization or approval of transactions affecting assets
  - recording or reporting of transactions.

control activities policies and procedures that help ensure that management directives are carried out. Control activities are a component of internal control.

In addition, a control over the processing of a transaction should not be performed by the same person who is responsible for actually recording or reporting the transaction.

Assigning different people the responsibilities of authorizing transactions, recording transactions, and maintaining custody of assets reduces the opportunity for an individual to both carry out and hide errors (whether intentional or not) or commit fraud in the normal course of his or her duties. Adequate segregation of duties is an important consideration in determining whether a client's controls are effective, as it reduces the likelihood that errors (intentional or not) will remain undetected. When IT is used in an information system, segregation of incompatible duties is often achieved by implementing system-based controls (referred to as logical access controls).

In understanding the client's control activities at the entity level, consideration is given to factors such as:

- the extent to which performance of control activities relies on IT
- whether the necessary policies and procedures exist with respect to each of the entity's activities, including IT security and system development
- the extent to which controls included in the organization's policies are being applied
- whether management has clear objectives in terms of budget, profit, and other financial and operating goals, and whether these objectives are clearly written, communicated throughout the entity, and actively monitored
- whether planning and reporting systems are in place to identify variances from planned performance and communicate such variances to the appropriate level of management
- whether the appropriate level of management investigates variances and takes appropriate and timely corrective actions
- to what extent duties are divided or segregated among different people to reduce the risk of errors, fraud, or manipulation of results
- whether software is used to control access to data and programs and, if so, the extent to which segregation of incompatible duties is achieved by implementing these software controls
- whether periodic comparisons are made of amounts recorded in the accounting system with physical assets
- whether adequate safeguards are in place to prevent unauthorized access to or destruction of documents, records, and assets.

The auditor finds these controls the easiest to test when compared to other types of entity-level controls as their operation is readily verifiable. For example, the controls surrounding the segregation of duties can be observed, while management integrity is not observable or easily verified. This concept is covered in more detail in chapter 8.

7.3.5 Monitoring of controls

After establishing and maintaining internal controls, another important responsibility of management is to monitor the controls to assess whether they are operating as intended and are modified for changes in conditions on a timely basis. Over time, systems of internal controls change and the way controls are applied may evolve. Also, the circumstances for which the system of internal controls was originally designed may change, causing it to be less effective in warning management of risks brought about by new conditions. Accordingly, management needs to determine whether its internal controls continue to be relevant and able to address new risks.

Monitoring is a process of assessing the quality of internal control performance over time, considering whether controls are operating as intended, and making sure controls are modified as appropriate for changes in conditions. It involves assessing the design and implementation of controls on a regular basis and taking necessary corrective actions. This process is accomplished through ongoing activities and separate evaluations, or through a combination of the two.

Ongoing monitoring procedures are built into the normal recurring activities of the entity and include regular management and supervisory activities. For example, managers of sales, purchasing, and production at divisional and corporate levels should understand the entity's operations and question the accuracy of reports that differ significantly from their knowledge of operations. Monitoring activities may include using information obtained from communications with external parties. For example, customers ordinarily verify and corroborate a client's billing data by paying their invoices or by complaining about overcharging.

Much of the information used in monitoring is produced by the entity's information systems. If management assumes that data used for monitoring is accurate without having a basis for the assumption, errors may exist in the information, potentially leading management to incorrect conclusions from its monitoring activities.

One of the most common monitoring activities is the internal audit function. In many organizations, internal auditors (or personnel performing similar functions) contribute to the monitoring of the client's activities through separate evaluations. They regularly provide information about the functioning of internal controls, focusing considerable attention on the evaluation of the design and implementation of controls. They communicate information about strengths and weaknesses and make recommendations for improving internal control. The importance that a company places on its internal audit function also provides evidence about its overall commitment to internal control.

As discussed in chapter 6, when evaluating the effectiveness of the internal audit function, factors to consider include independence, reporting lines, adequacy of staffing, adherence to applicable professional standards, scope of activities, adequacy of work performed, and conclusions reached.

The internal audit activities most relevant to the audit include those that provide evidence about the design and effectiveness of internal controls or that provide substantive evidence about potential material misstatements in the financial statements.

Finally, when gaining an understanding of the client's monitoring processes at the entity level, factors such as the following are ordinarily considered:
- whether periodic evaluations of internal control are made
- the extent to which personnel, in carrying out their regular duties, obtain evidence as to whether the system of internal controls continues to function
- the extent to which communications from external parties corroborate internally generated information, or indicate problems
- whether management implements internal control recommendations made by internal and external auditors

- whether management's approach to correcting known significant deficiencies is on a timely basis
- whether management's approach to dealing with reports and recommendations from regulators is effective
- whether an internal audit function exists that management uses to assist in its monitoring activities
- whether evaluations or observations are made by the external auditors.

Cloud 9

In the interview with David Collier, Sharon and Josh ask questions about both the control activities and the monitoring of those activities at Cloud 9. Sharon and Josh are particularly interested in the systems used at the company to make sure that information about management's plans and orders is transmitted throughout the organization and that there are policies and procedures to ensure that the appropriate actions are taken and reviewed.

In addition to asking David Collier about these matters, Josh reads the policy and procedures manuals and he and Sharon tour the offices and other facilities. For example, Cloud 9 has a tightly structured system of performance reviews. Managers at each level must report financial and operating performance against budget at regular intervals. Higher-level managers are able to access information about activities within their area of responsibility for monitoring purposes through the information system. Although there have been some issues with theft of goods from the retail store, the losses have been contained following the installation of additional security, including cameras. Josh and Sharon are particularly impressed with the thorough approach to segregation of incompatible duties.

Josh is able to conclude that at an entity level, there is sufficient evidence that these controls are effective. He plans to review the specific controls that affect transaction cycles in more detail so that he can document his understanding of these processes.

7.3.6 Internal control in small entities

In smaller entities, there are often limitations surrounding the entity's ability to put effective internal controls in place. This is due to the small number of employees, which, in turn, impacts the ability of the organization to segregate duties. Also, it is often not practical for smaller organizations to create an appropriate paper trail of documentation that allows an assessment of internal controls to be made.

However, despite the size limitations of these entities, internal controls still exist. Ordinarily, in smaller businesses, there is an owner-manager who is heavily involved in the day-to-day running of the business. This can be seen as both a strength and a weakness. It is a strength (assuming that the individual is competent) because the owner-manager is so closely involved in the business and day-to-day operations, including the selling of goods and services and the daily cash management of the operations. Therefore, it is unlikely that material errors that might occur would not be detected by the owner-manager. It is also a weakness because the same owner-manager is in a position to be able to override internal controls.

The risk of management override can be reduced by establishing documented policies and procedures. However, if no such procedures or controls are in place, the risk of management override will need to be reduced from an audit perspective by the performance of additional audit procedures (through an increase in substantive procedures).

7.3.7 Concluding on entity-level controls

Having gained an understanding of each of the components of internal control at the entity level, tested them to ensure they are designed effectively and implemented properly, and ensured that there are no factors relating to the five components of entity-level control that indicate ineffective controls, the conclusion is made that the client's internal control environment at the entity level is considered to be supportive of the prevention or detection and correction of material misstatements whether due to fraud or error. If one or more factors exist that indicate poor internal control, this does not automatically mean that internal control at the entity level is ineffective. The evaluation of the factors is often highly subjective and requires considerable professional judgement. There are no formulas or other explicit indicators that tell us when internal control at the entity level is ineffective. This means that it is critical that the more experienced audit personnel (including the engagement partner) make this overall assessment. In reaching their conclusion, they will consider the size, complexity, and ownership of the client. This is because the importance of many of the factors considered in reaching the conclusion is affected by these three characteristics (size, complexity, and ownership). For example, a small company may not have a written code of conduct but through the active involvement of management in the day-to-day activities of the business, it may have cultivated a culture that emphasizes the importance of integrity and ethical behaviour. That is, the lack of a formal document may not be a concern. However, for a larger more complex group of companies with multiple overseas locations, a similar lack of documentation may indicate an area for concern.

BEFORE YOU GO ON

3.1 What are the five components of internal control?

3.2 Why is segregation of duties important when understanding internal control?

3.3 How does management's attitude and control consciousness affect the internal control environment of an organization?

7.4 TRANSACTION-LEVEL INTERNAL CONTROLS

Now that we have discussed entity-level controls, we will briefly overview transaction-level controls. These are discussed in more detail in chapter 8. As explained previously, entity-level internal controls are at the entity-wide or whole-of-organization level and have the potential to impact all of the processes management puts in place for the entire organization. This includes controls that may not have a direct impact on the financial statements. See table 7.1 for a listing of common transaction-level controls.

As its name suggests, **transaction-level controls** are controls that affect a particular transaction or group of transactions. Transactions in this sense refer to transactions that are ordinarily recorded in the general ledger for the client and span from initiation of the transaction through to the reporting of the transaction in the financial statements. Transaction-level controls respond to things that can go wrong with transactions. They must be sensitive enough to either prevent an error from occurring or to detect the error, report it, and have it rectified on a timely basis. These controls are referred to as preventative and detective controls and are explained further in chapter 8.

4 Understand and describe the elements of internal control at the transaction level, and apply them to the sales, purchases, and payroll cycles.

---

transaction-level controls controls that affect a particular transaction or group of transactions

7.4.1 Example transaction flows—sales process

The transaction flow in a client's sales process affects a number of the financial statement accounts, including accounts receivable, allowance for doubtful accounts, bad debt expense, sales, sales returns and allowances, and cash. Generally, an auditor is most concerned with the overstatement of sales and assets, and, therefore, audit procedures for this cycle tend to focus on existence (occurrence) and valuation (accuracy) assertions. See Appendix A for sample documents associated with these activities.

A typical sales process for a client that sells goods includes the following activities:

1. *Accepting and processing orders*—Customer orders should be received by sales staff. The details of the order are agreed upon, such as the quantity required, the selling price, and the shipping terms. These details are documented on the sales order form. When the order is received, the availability of the goods in inventory should be verified.

2. *Authorizing credit*—Before a customer order is forwarded to the warehouse, a credit check should be performed. A credit check should be required for both new and existing customers. New customers should complete a credit application, and sales staff should obtain a credit report from a credit rating agency. If the customer is determined to be creditworthy, the credit manager approves the credit application. The customer is then set up in the accounts receivable master file with the established credit limit. For existing customers with credit terms, the credit available should be checked to prevent customers from exceeding their predetermined credit limit. If the customer's order exceeds the credit limit, the order should not be processed until the credit manager grants special approval.

   In order to ensure the appropriate segregation of duties, the sales staff should not be responsible for approving credit. Otherwise, they may accept sales from customers that are not creditworthy to boost sales. Therefore, the credit department should have responsibility for approving credit.

3. *Shipping goods*—Once credit has been granted, a copy of the approved sales order is sent to the warehouse, so the order can be assembled and shipped to the customer. To ensure the appropriate segregation of duties, order assembly and shipping should not be done by the person who approved the order.

   When the order is compiled, a pre-numbered shipping document (also called a bill of lading or a dispatch document) is prepared indicating the date and quantity of the goods sent out. A copy of the shipping document accompanies the goods; a copy is kept in the shipping department; and a copy is sent to the accounting department.

4. *Invoicing customers*—The receipt of the shipping document in the accounting department serves as verification that the goods have been shipped and triggers the creation of a sequential sales invoice. The invoice is created based on the quantity of goods ordered and shipped per the shipping documents, and on the agreed upon price per the sales order form or pre-approved price list. Once the invoice is prepared, it should be reviewed by an independent person for accuracy.

5. *Recording sales and trade receivables*—Once the invoice has been created and sent to the customer, it should be posted to the appropriate account in the sales journal and in the accounts receivable sub-ledger in the appropriate accounting period. This updates the accounting records and records the earned revenue. The sub-ledger should be reconciled to the general ledger at the end of each accounting period. The sales journal should be reconciled to the related general ledger accounts. Accounts receivable statements should be sent to customers on a regular basis so discrepancies can be dealt with.

6. *Processing cash receipts*—Once invoiced, collection of the cash is expected within the credit period. Cheques received by mail should be prelisted and endorsed for deposit only to the specific account. The cheques should then be sent to the cashier for prompt deposit to the bank. A copy of the pre-listing and the remittance advice is sent to the accounts receivable department for posting to the customer's account. The cashier should reconcile the pre-list, the duplicate bank deposit slip, and the cash receipts journal. To ensure an appropriate segregation of duties, the person responsible for receiving the cash should have no involvement in the recording of the cash collections within the accounting system.

7. *Writing off uncollectable accounts and providing for bad debts*—A review of the accounts receivable aging should be performed regularly by a person independent of the sales and cash receipts functions. Collection activities should be employed over aging accounts. Once an account is determined to be uncollectable, the approval to write off the account should be performed by someone independent of the cash receipt function. Otherwise, a sale could be recorded, the cash collected and stolen, and the related accounts receivable written off as uncollectable.

The transaction flows for a client that sells and/or performs services is the same as for a client that sells goods. In this chapter, we will use sales in the context of a client that sells goods. Table 7.1 shows examples of risks and controls that can be put in place for the sales process.

TABLE 7.1 **Sales process example risks and controls**

TRANSACTION	RISKS (WHAT CAN GO WRONG)	EXAMPLE CONTROL
Processing orders	Orders are processed to the wrong customer	Review of orders processed each day by an independent staff member (for example, a salesperson)
		Three-way match of order, shipping document, and invoice before dispatch of goods
	Orders are accepted from customers with no approved credit history or credit limit	Application control that will only allow orders to be processed for existing approved customers with enough unused credit
Approving credit	Credit is approved for customers unable to pay	Credit manager review and authorization of credit application
	Credit limits are set too high or too low	Credit manager review of credit limits on a quarterly basis
	Credit limits are exceeded	Application control requires approval for exceeding credit limits (orders are not processed until exception report generated, reviewed, and approved by credit manager)
Shipping goods	Products are shipped without shipping documents being generated	Application control generates shipping and delivery documentation when order is processed
		Three-way match of order, shipping document, and invoice before dispatch of goods
	Unauthorized shipments may be made	Person dispatching is not the same as person filling the order (segregation of duties)

(*continued*)

TABLE 7.1 **Sales process example risks and controls** (continued)	TRANSACTION	RISKS (WHAT CAN GO WRONG)	EXAMPLE CONTROL
			Three-way match of order, shipping document, and invoice
			Access to shipping area is limited to authorized personnel
		Goods are shipped to the wrong customer	Warehouse staff review delivery address against customer master file
	Invoicing customers	Invoices are not correct as to the quantities of goods shipped	Quantities per shipping document marked as correct when picked by warehouse staff
			Three-way match of order, shipping document, and invoice
			Invoices automatically generated from order and dispatch document
		Invoices are raised twice (or more) for the same order, or fictitious invoices are created	Three-way match of order, shipping document, and invoice
			All orders are assigned a sequential number. System prevents duplicate numbers from being used.
		Shipments are made but never invoiced	Three-way match of order, shipping document, and invoice.
			Review shipping documents that have not been matched with an invoice
		Wrong unit prices are used on the invoices	Approved master price list automatically used by application as source for invoice pricing.
			Access to update master price list is restricted to only authorized personnel.
		Quantity times price is incorrectly calculated	Application is programmed to calculate correctly
		Discounts (such as volume rebates) are incorrectly applied	Sales manager approves all discounts
		Invoices do not add correctly	Application is programmed to calculate correctly
		Shipping documents and invoices do not reflect correct transaction dates	Application cannot be modified as to date of transaction (set by calendar) without approval.
	Recording sales and trade receivables	Sales are recorded in the wrong period	Date recorded is set by date of transaction in software; therefore, invoice dates cannot be changed without approval
		Sales tax, GST, HST, discounts, rebates, and other invoice adjustments are coded to the wrong general ledger account	Application control (driven by approved chart of accounts) within the accounting software used
		Invoices are posted to the wrong customer account	Accounts receivable statements are sent to customers monthly and issues promptly resolved
		Fictitious sales are posted	Three-way match of order, shipping document, and invoice.

(continued)

TRANSACTION	RISKS (WHAT CAN GO WRONG)	EXAMPLE CONTROL
		Review of journal entries and supporting documentation for any journal entries posted to the sales account
	Sales are not recorded in the sales subsidiary ledger	Application control within the accounting software used
	Total recorded sales in the sales subsidiary ledger is not recorded in the general ledger	Application control within the accounting software used
		Monthly sales and trade receivables reconciliation between the subsidiary ledgers and general ledger
	There are duplicate postings	Monthly sales and trade receivables reconciliation between the subsidiary ledger and general ledger
Processing cash receipts	Missing cash receipts due to loss or theft	Cheque pre-listing prepared
		Cheques endorsed immediately when received
		Cheque pre-list is reconciled to the cash receipts
		Accounts receivable statements are sent to customers monthly and issues promptly resolved
	Cash receipts are recorded at incorrect amount	Preparation and review of the monthly bank reconciliation
	Cash receipts posted to wrong customer account	Accounts receivable statements are sent to customers monthly and issues promptly resolved

7.4.2 Example transaction flows—purchasing and payables process

The transaction flow in the cost of sales process affects a number of the financial statement accounts, including accounts payable, inventory (for a manufacturing environment), cost of goods sold, various asset and expense accounts and cash. Generally, an auditor is most concerned with the understatement of expenses and liabilities, and, therefore, audit procedures for this cycle tend to focus on the completeness assertion.

A typical purchasing and payables cycle includes the several activities. See Appendix A for sample documents associated with these activities.

1. *Requisition*—once a need for goods or services has been identified, a request should be made by an authorized individual in the form of a requisition. The request for goods or services should be documented on a pre-numbered purchase requisition indicating the item and quantity required. This request should be forwarded to the person or department responsible for purchasing.

2. *Purchasing*—the purchase requisition is sent to the purchasing department, where the orders from various departments are compiled. The purchasing department is responsible for acquiring the right quantity and quality of goods at the best possible price. This is usually done by obtaining at least three quotes from approved suppliers. Once a supplier is selected, the order is placed, and a sequential purchase

order is assigned to the order. A copy of the purchase order is sent to the supplier indicating the specific product and quantity ordered, as well as the agreed upon price and the expected delivery date. A copy of the purchase order is also sent to the accounts payable department.

3. *Receiving*—when the goods arrive, the person responsible for receiving counts and inspects the goods. The quantity received is documented on the pre-numbered receiving report. A copy of the receiving report is sent to accounting. Goods received should be promptly moved to a secured location until required. Access to the receiving area should be restricted to authorized personnel only.

4. *Invoice processing*—the accounts payable department processes the invoices for payment. This involves performing the three-way match in which the purchase order and the receiving report are compared to the invoices for terms, quantities, prices, and extensions. This ensures that the accounts payable department pays for only goods that were authorized, received, and properly priced. Outstanding unmatched purchase orders and receiving reports should be reviewed periodically and investigated on a timely basis as they may indicate unrecorded liabilities.

5. *Recording purchases and payables*—once the invoice has been "matched" it should be posted to update the accounting records. Posting involves updating the purchase journal and the accounts payable sub-ledger in the appropriate accounting period. At the end of each accounting period, the accounts payable sub-ledger should be reconciled to the general ledger, and the purchase journal should be reconciled to the general ledger accounts.

6. *Disbursements*—once the invoices are processed, the cheques are prepared and signed. Cheques should be signed by two authorized individuals. The supporting documentation should be reviewed before the cheque is signed. Once an invoice has been paid, it should be stamped "paid" to ensure that it is not paid twice.

Table 7.2 shows examples of risks and controls that can be put in place for the purchasing process.

TABLE 7.2 **Purchasing process example risks and controls**

TRANSACTION	RISKS (WHAT CAN GO WRONG)	EXAMPLE CONTROL
Purchase requisition	Unauthorized purchases are made	Purchase requisitions are prepared by authorized person
		Spending limits are set based on level of authority
Purchasing	Purchases are made but they are not recorded in the general ledger for inventory, assets, expenses, or payables	Three-way match between purchase order, receiving report, and invoice
		Supplier statements reconciled monthly
	Purchases are recorded in the general ledger but the goods are never received	Three-way match between purchase order, receiving report and invoice
		Regular inventory counts
	Purchases of unwanted goods are made	All purchase orders are approved by purchasing manager
Receiving	Goods are received that were not ordered	Three-way match between purchase order, receiving report, and invoice
	Goods are damaged when they are received into the warehouse	Damaged goods are rejected by warehouse manager, and payables clerk and purchasing officer are notified

(*continued*)

TRANSACTION	RISKS (WHAT CAN GO WRONG)	EXAMPLE CONTROL
Invoicing	The wrong price is charged on the purchase invoice by the supplier	Invoice prices are checked against approved purchase orders and master price lists
	The wrong amount is paid against an invoice	All relevant documentation (invoice and cheque) is reviewed and approved by two people
		Supplier statements reconciled monthly
Recording purchases and related items	Purchases are recorded in the wrong period	Date recorded is set by date of transaction in software; therefore, invoice dates cannot be changed without approval
	Sales tax, HST, discounts, rebates, and other invoice adjustments are posted to the wrong general ledger account	Application control (driven by approved chart of accounts) within the accounting software used
	Purchases are not recorded in the purchase journal	Application control within the accounting software used
	Total recorded purchases in the payables subsidiary ledger is not recorded in the general ledger	Application control within the accounting software used
		Monthly purchases journal reconciled to the accounts payable sub-ledger
	There are duplicate postings	Monthly purchases and trade payables reconciliation between the subsidiary ledger and general ledger
Cash disbursements	Cash disbursements are made but not recorded	Use and review of sequential cheques
	Cash disbursements are recorded but not made	Supplier statements reconciled monthly
		Preparation and review of the monthly bank reconciliation
	Cash disbursements are recorded at incorrect amounts	Cash disbursement journal reconciled to total of cheques issued
		Vendor statement reconciliations
		Preparation and review of the monthly bank reconciliation
	Cash disbursements are posted to wrong vendor account	Supplier statements reconciled monthly

7.4.3 Example transaction flows—payroll process

The transaction flow of the payroll process affects a number of financial statement accounts, including salaries and wage expenses, payroll liabilities, and payroll-related accruals. Payroll tends to be one of the largest expenses for most organizations, and, therefore, the auditor usually gives it some specific consideration. From an audit perspective, the risk with payroll generally tends to be overstatement, as employees ensure underpayments are corrected on a timely basis.

A typical payroll process for a client includes the following activities:

1. *Hiring of personnel*—hiring occurs with the identification and approval of a suitable candidate. All new hires should have a personnel file. All documentation relating to an employee should be kept in this file, including the job application, references, offer of employment, performance reviews, authorized pay rates, and tax forms. These documents should be kept in a secure location for privacy purposes. Once an employee is hired, the employee's payroll information should be sent to the payroll department, where, after it is authorized, the employee is set up in the payroll master file.

2. *Timekeeping*—there should be a mechanism to track the hours worked by employee. This may be in the form of as, for example, sign-in sheets, punch clocks, and finger scans. Actual hours worked should be based on an employee schedule. At the end of the pay period, the departmental manager or supervisor should approve the actual hours worked.

3. *Compilation of the payroll*—once the departmental manager approves the actual hours worked, this information is forwarded to the payroll department. The payroll department will apply the appropriate wage rates to the hours worked, thus compiling the dollar amount to be paid by employee and in total. The payroll manager should review the payroll for accuracy and reasonableness before processing. Access to the approved wage rates should be restricted to prevent unauthorized increases from being made.

4. *Payroll processing*—once the payroll is compiled and approved, the actual payment may be made by cheque or electronic funds transfer. Wages paid for the period and year to date by employee and in total are maintained in the payroll register. The details from the payroll register are journalized into the general ledger to record the payroll expense and related liabilities. Therefore, the total payroll expense should reconcile to the payroll register by pay period and year to date.

Table 7.3 shows examples of risks and controls that can be put in place for the payroll process.

TABLE 7.3 **Payroll process example risks and controls**

TRANSACTION	RISKS (WHAT CAN GO WRONG)	EXAMPLE CONTROL
Hiring of personnel	Fictitious employees are added to the payroll	Restrict access to payroll master file
		Only authorized employees added to payroll master
Timekeeping	Employees may be paid for hours not worked	Hours worked tracked by time clock
		Departmental manager approves hours worked
Compilation of the payroll	Payroll data may be incorrect due to the use of incorrect wage rates	Review payroll expenses to budget
		Approved wage rates in payroll master file compared to approved wage rate per employee file
	Payroll data not calculated correctly	Application is programmed to calculate correctly
	Payroll benefits and withholding taxes not calculated correctly	Application is programmed to calculate correctly

(*continued*)

TRANSACTION	RISKS (WHAT CAN GO WRONG)	EXAMPLE CONTROL
Payroll processing	Journal entry is not recorded	Review payroll expenses to budget
		Reconcile payroll register to general ledger
		Reconcile tax remittances to tax filings
	Incorrect journal entry is recorded	Review payroll expenses to budget
		Journal entry is reviewed before posted

In addition to the controls identified above, the appropriate segregation of duties is required for the each of the above cycles to ensure that one person is not in the position to make errors or commit fraud and cover them up.

Cloud 9

Josh will document his understanding of the processes for the various transaction cycles. This document will allow the audit team to identify the points within the accounting process where errors or fraud can occur. These points are more likely where information is changed, there is significant human involvement, or access to systems is not restricted. In essence, these points are where something in the process can go wrong. The auditors will concentrate on the points that have an impact on the financial statements.

Once the types of potential material misstatements are understood, the audit team will consider the magnitude and likelihood of the misstatement in the financial statements. This will help narrow the risk assessment and determine what audit procedures should be performed. In addition, the audit team considers how errors in each financial statement assertion might occur.

This analysis will guide the audit planning for additional substantive testing. Sharon and the audit partner can also decide if there are any deficiencies that should be included in the management letter and/or significant deficiencies that should be communicated to the Audit Committee.

Josh knows that documenting his understanding of the processes is necessary for the team to identify control strengths that can be relied on to justify reduced substantive testing. Substantive testing will be reduced if tests of those controls confirm that these design strengths are reflected in the actual performance of the control system. Josh thinks that he will need to discuss his assessment of control strengths and weaknesses with Sharon before finalizing the audit plan. He needs her to help him determine if some control weaknesses are compensated for by other strengths. They will also identify the most important controls to test. Some controls are actually redundant; that is, another control exists that performs the same function.

BEFORE YOU GO ON

4.1 What is the difference between entity-level controls and transaction controls?

4.2 Name two risks and corresponding controls to address those risks for sales transactions.

4.3 Name two risks and corresponding controls to address those risks for cost of sales transactions.

7.5 DOCUMENTING INTERNAL CONTROLS

⑤ Explain the different techniques used to document internal controls.

Before the auditor tests the internal controls, they need to document their understanding of them. The most common forms of documentation include the following:

- *Narratives*—this is the most common form of documentation, particularly in smaller environments where accounting and internal control activities are simple or where a particular flow of a transaction is relatively simple and straightforward. It involves the auditor describing (in words) each step of the flow of transaction from start to finish (that is, from initiation to reporting in the financial statements). Refer to figure 7.1 for an example.
- *Flowcharts*—this form of documentation is used in larger and more complex environments. It involves the auditor summarizing (in flowcharts/boxes) each step of the flow of a transaction from start to finish (that is, from initiation to reporting in the general ledger). While a flowchart may take longer to prepare, it provides a visual representation of the flow of the transaction and the key controls throughout the flow that is often simpler for the reader or reviewer to understand. The key to a good flowchart is to keep it as simple as possible, with as few words as possible so as not to overload the reader with information. Refer to figure 7.2 for an example.
- *Combinations of narratives and flowcharts*—this form of documenting internal controls is typically a page divided into two sections with the process flowchart on the left-hand side (or the top side) and the narrative describing each step in the flow on the right-hand side (or the bottom half of the page). The flowchart side highlights the key activities from initiation to reporting, while the narrative column contains the details about what happens in the flow of the transaction. Refer to figure 7.3 for an example.
- *Checklists and preformatted questionnaires*—an internal control checklist or questionnaire is another technique used to systematically identify the most common types of internal control procedures that should be present. This is particularly helpful in industries that the auditor may not personally be familiar with auditing, or when less experienced auditors find it difficult to identify which are the critical controls (for example, when documenting entity-level controls). Refer to figure 7.4 for an example.

Sales order is received by fax or email. Check customer details against customer account balance to see if the customer has exceeded its credit limit. If the customer has exceeded its limit, refer the sales order to the credit manager (S. Fitzpatrick) for approval. If approval is denied, refer the order back to the sales manager to notify or discuss with the customer and notify customer. If customer has not exceeded its credit limit or the credit manager (S. Fitzpatrick) has provided an approval to exceed the limit, process the sale in the sales ledger.

FIGURE 7.1 **Example narrative for documenting credit sales process**

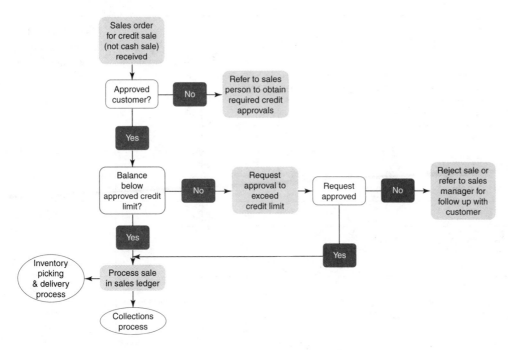

FIGURE 7.2 **Example flowchart for credit sales process**

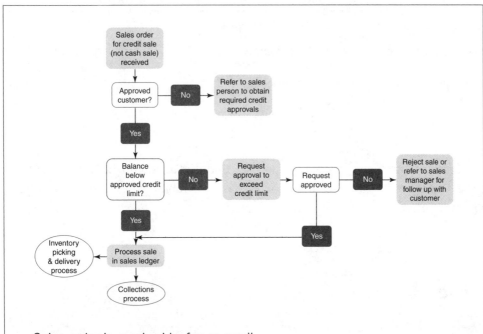

- Sales order is received by fax or email.
- Check customer details against customer account balance to see if the customer has exceeded its credit limit.
- If customer has exceeded its limit, refer the sales order to the credit manager (S. Fitzpatrick) for approval. If approval is denied, refer the order back to the sales manager to notify or discuss with the customer.
- If customer has not exceeded its credit limit or the credit manager (S. Fitzpatrick) has provided an approval to exceed the limit, process the sale in the sales ledger.

FIGURE 7.3 **Example combination documentation for credit sales process**

Process step	Performed by	IT/reliance on electronic data Yes/No?
Customer places sales order and order is input into sales order program		
Credit and/or credit terms approved		
Order filled and prepared for shipment		
Shipping/delivery documents prepared		
Order shipped/delivered to or picked up by customer		
Sales invoice prepared		
Prices (or deviations from standard prices) approved		
Invoice reviewed for accuracy and mailed/delivered to customer		
Sales journal produced		
Sales journal summarized and posted to general ledger and trade receivables detail		
Provide any other details that are necessary to understand the initiation, processing, recording, and reporting of the transactions:		
Briefly describe the client's **revenue recognition policy,** *including* **standard billing** *and* **collection terms:**		
Briefly describe the client's **credit terms** *and* **credit authorization procedures:**		
Briefly describe the client's procedures for **sales returns and allowances** *and the issuance of* **credit memos:**		

FIGURE 7.4 **Example checklist for documenting a credit sales process**
Source: Ernst & Young 2010.

Regardless of which of the above approaches is used to document internal controls, the extent of the documentation will increase as the complexity of the client, its systems, and its internal controls increases.

Cloud 9

Josh will prepare a flowchart or narrative to document his understanding of the different transaction cycles. This will help him understand the stages at which the errors can occur. He will include the entire process from the initiation of the transaction through to recording in the general ledger. Where appropriate, he will link several accounting processes together into one seamless flow of transactions. For example, he has made a simple diagram of the flow of transactions from initiation of a purchase order through to the cash payment to the supplier (see figure 7.5). The process comprises three smaller processes: Initiating a purchase order through to receipting the goods as they arrive; receiving the purchase invoice from the supplier through to entering the invoice in the general ledger; and requesting cash payment and recording the payment to the supplier. Once the transaction cycles are documented, Josh will perform walk throughs. That is, he will walk one transaction from its inception to when it is recorded in the books to ensure his understanding of the processes are correct.

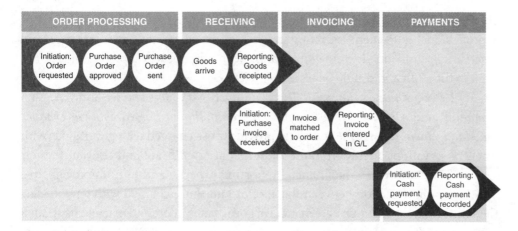

FIGURE 7.5 **Cloud 9 flow of transaction—order to payment**

BEFORE YOU GO ON

5.1 Explain the different techniques used to document internal controls.

5.2 What is the difference between a narrative and a flowchart?

5.3 When would it be more appropriate to use a flowchart instead of a narrative to document internal controls?

7.6 IDENTIFYING STRENGTHS AND WEAKNESSES IN A SYSTEM OF INTERNAL CONTROLS

Another important outcome of understanding the system of internal controls that a client puts in place is the ability to make observations, draw conclusions, and offer recommendations regarding the strengths and weaknesses observed. Strengths and weaknesses in internal control are usually noted by the auditor when performing tests of controls as part of the control risk assessment. An internal control strength is when a control is in place and working as intended; therefore, it is effective in preventing and detecting a material misstatement in the financial statements. Weaknesses in internal controls exist when an internal control is unable to prevent, detect, and correct material misstatements. While clients will often be interested in obtaining feedback from external auditors as to the relative strengths of their internal controls, focus is ordinarily on the areas of weakness identified. This is because it is the weaknesses that increase the risk of material misstatements being undetected by management's processes and controls, and, thus, it is on the areas of weakness that the auditor typically performs additional substantive testing to quantify the (potential) material misstatements. The link between these **internal control exceptions** (the observations that controls being tested did not operate as intended) and the level of substantive procedures required to address these exceptions is explained further by way of examples in chapter 8.

Some observations made by the auditor will relate to controls that are not directly relevant to the audit. As discussed previously, some controls within the system of internal controls have a financial reporting impact, whereas other controls are implemented to assist the entity in meeting its organizational and compliance objectives. For example, a bank reconciliation is a control that has a financial reporting impact, whereas an approved supplier list is a control that ensures inventory is only purchased

6 Explain the importance of identifying strengths and weaknesses in a system of internal controls.

internal control exception
an observed condition that provides evidence that the control being tested did not operate as intended

from reputable sources but has no direct financial reporting impact. Significant levels of professional judgement are required when deciding whether an internal control observation (individually or in combination with other observations) is, in fact, relevant to the audit and should be tested.

CAS 260 *Communication with Those Charged with Governance* and CAS 265 *Communicating Deficiencies in Internal Control to Those Charged with Governance and Management* require the auditor to provide those charged with governance with timely observations arising from the audit that are significant and relevant to their responsibility to oversee the financial reporting process, and to promote effective two-way communication between the auditor and those charged with governance. The auditor should communicate matters of governance interest to management, such as significant (or material) weaknesses in the design or implementation of internal control, as soon as practicable, and at an appropriate level of responsibility. Examples of significant deficiencies include the following:

- evidence of an ineffective control environment, such as identification of management fraud
- absence of a risk assessment process within the entity
- evidence of an ineffective entity risk assessment process
- evidence of an ineffective response to identified significant
- misstatements that were not prevented or detected by the entity's internal control
- evidence of management's inability to oversee the preparation of the financial statements.

It is for these key reasons that the auditor prepares what is often called a management letter.

BEFORE YOU GO ON

6.1 Why is it important to identify both the strengths and weaknesses in a system of internal controls?

6.2 Does the auditor provide feedback on strengths in internal controls or just weaknesses? Explain.

6.3 What obligations does the auditor have regarding communicating strengths or weaknesses in internal controls?

7.7 MANAGEMENT LETTERS

 7 Explain how to communicate internal control strengths and weaknesses to those charged with governance.

management letter a document prepared by the audit team and provided to the client that discusses internal control weaknesses and other matters discovered during the course of the audit

A **management letter** is a deliverable prepared by the audit team and provided to management and those charged with governance. The management letter discusses internal control weaknesses and other matters discovered during the course of the audit. The purpose of the management letter is to inform the client of the auditor's recommendations for improving its internal controls.

The example management letter shown in figure 7.6 demonstrates that the combination of the auditor's experience in auditing various businesses, and the thorough understanding they gain while conducting an audit, places them in a unique position for communicating insights about the system of internal controls designed and monitored by those charged with governance. The management letter also enables the auditor to provide timely feedback to management on the implementation of internal controls.

FIGURE 7.6 **Example management letter**

Ernst & Young LLP
Chartered Accountants
Ernst & Young Tower
222 Bay Street, P.O. Box 251
Toronto, Ontario M5K 1J7

Tel: 416 864 1234
Fax: 416 864 1174
ey.com/ca

To the Management Team of Skyward Ltd.:   15 March 2013

Our audit of the financial statements as at and for the year ended 31 December 2012 has been completed. In performing our audit procedures at Skyward, we noted certain items that may be of interest to you and your team.

Our procedures were designed to express an opinion on the financial statements of Skyward Ltd. and were not designed to evaluate the adequacy of individual internal controls. Accordingly our audit would not necessarily discover all conditions requiring your attention or all opportunities to improve internal controls. Furthermore, the observations below should not be considered to be the sole matters to be addressed by management.

Our observations are as follows:

A. Internal Controls Over Cash Disbursements

Observation - We noted that user access to the online banking system was granted to many individuals and certain of these individuals did not require such access for their day-to-day activities.

Implication - Without proper controls over cash disbursements, fictitious payments may be issued without detection from management.

Recommendation - Management should adopt a formalized review process for access to the online banking system. Stronger controls in this area can prevent any potential loss arising from inappropriate access to Skyward's online banking portal. In particular, management should consider those parties who require access to the online bank account, including which users require the ability to execute transactions versus read-only access. Access for personnel not requiring access should be removed.

B. Review of bank reconciliation

Observation – While executing our testing of controls over the cash disbursement and cash receipts processes, we noted some instances where there was a lack of documentation of the review process for bank reconciliations by appropriate individuals.

Implication - The lack of formalized review and approval of bank reconciliations could lead to undetected misappropriation of cash or unreconciled items that are not resolved on a timely basis. Timely preparation and review of bank reconciliations is a critical control activity, that when properly conducted, can lead to the detection and correction errors in account balances or improvements in other related processes.

(continued)

FIGURE 7.6 **Example management letter** (continued)

Ernst & Young LLP
Chartered Accountants
Ernst & Young Tower
222 Bay Street, P.O. Box 251
Toronto, Ontario M5K 1J7

Tel: 416 864 1234
Fax: 416 864 1174
ey.com/ca

Recommendations - We recommend that management ensure that a timely and thorough review and approval process for bank reconciliations is adhered to on a monthly basis.

C. No Formal Analysis of Leases

Observation - We noted that management does not perform a formal analysis of new lease agreements as they are entered into.

Implication - Without a formalized process for analyzing new leases on a timely basis, the accounting for leases could be materially misstated.

Recommendations - Management should establish a formalized process by which all new leases are analyzed based on the finance lease criteria. This analysis should be maintained for all leases that are in use at the current time and the conclusions reached should be supported by the contracts associated with the lease.

We would like to take this opportunity to thank the employees and management of Skyward for the excellent cooperation given to us throughout the audit.

This letter is intended solely for the information and use of Skyward's Management and its Audit Committee and Board of Directors and is not intended to be and should not be used by anyone other than these specified parties.

Sincerely,

Audit Partner, Ernst & Young LLP

Source: Ernst & Young LLP, 2011

---

professional judgement the auditor's professional characteristics such as their expertise, experience, knowledge, and training

Significant **professional judgement** is necessary in deciding whether a weakness identified is significant enough to warrant communicating to management and to those charged with governance. When the auditor identifies risks of material misstatement that the entity has not controlled (or has not adequately controlled), or if in the auditor's judgement there is a significant deficiency in the entity's design or implementation of internal control, the auditor is required to communicate these deficiencies as soon as practicable to those charged with governance. Deciding whether an observation should be reported to those charged with governance is often a matter of consultation and discussion among the audit team. As discussed in chapter 2, various cases have demonstrated that in the past some auditors have observed significant deficiencies but failed to communicate them. As a result of these cases, auditors often report all matters observed, irrespective of whether they are considered material or not. Some of the most recent and high-profile corporate collapses globally led to the creation of the U.S. Public Company Accounting Oversight Board (PCAOB) by the U.S. Securities and Exchange Commission and the Sarbanes-Oxley Act (2002), which contains explicit provisions for internal control reporting.

The auditor may also identify and communicate internal control deficiencies not considered significant but still worthy of management's attention. While it is not mandatory to provide this feedback in writing, the auditor ordinarily prefers to provide their recommendations in the form of a letter or report to avoid any ambiguity or confusion as to what observations, conclusions, and recommendations they have made. Responding to a management letter also provides a simple way for management to document the actions they have taken in response to the issues raised and to share these actions (and the progress toward the resolution of the issues) with those charged with governance. Such a response also provides the auditor with valuable insights into management's attitude toward the importance of internal controls by being able to evaluate what management has done in response to the recommendations made in the previous year at the start of each audit. Depending on the size of the engagement and the timing of when control weaknesses are identified relative to the final audit visit, teams will sometimes prepare an interim management letter at the end of planning and interim procedures, with a final management letter issued at the completion of the audit.

Cloud 9

Josh provides his documented understanding of Cloud 9's system of internal controls and his preliminary assessment of the system's strengths and weaknesses to Jo Wadley, the engagement partner of the audit. The audit team will gather additional evidence about the system of internal controls during the audit, and at the completion of the audit the senior members of the audit team will make a final assessment of Cloud 9's internal controls and write a management letter. Providing a management letter, including recommendations for future changes to the system of internal controls, is an important part of the auditor's role. The management letter not only discharges the audit team's responsibilities to the client, but helps the client improve its systems. In turn, this will likely increase the quality of the client's financial reporting in the future and improve the efficiency and effectiveness of future financial statement audits.

PROFESSIONAL ENVIRONMENT

How regulation can change the audit process

Audit processes change as new techniques are developed, and auditors are influenced by developments in technology and auditing standards. Another influence on audit processes is a sudden change in a country's laws or regulations. When the country making the changes is economically powerful, these changes can affect audit processes around the world. In the early 2000s, the United States changed its laws through the introduction of the Sarbanes-Oxley Act (2002), which is also known as SOX.

Section 404 of SOX requires U.S. public companies to report on the effectiveness of their internal control over financial reporting. Management is required to assess the effectiveness of internal control and the independent auditor then reports on management's assessment and on the effectiveness of the company's internal controls over financial reporting. The auditor's report on internal controls required by SOX is in addition to the independent auditor's report on the company's financial statements.

If one or more material weaknesses exist in the company's internal controls at year end, the auditor cannot conclude that internal control over financial reporting is effective. The U.S. PCAOB defines a material weakness as a "significant control deficiency, or a combination of deficiencies, that results in more than a remote likelihood that material misstatement of the annual or interim financial statements will not be prevented or detected." In other words, a material weakness does not mean that a material misstatement has occurred or will occur, but that it could occur.

The introduction of SOX in 2002 created additional work for auditors because an understanding of internal controls as required to express an opinion on the financial statements is not sufficient for the auditor to be able to offer an opinion on the controls themselves. Auditors of companies affected by SOX, including foreign subsidiaries of U.S. companies and foreign companies raising capital in the United States, had to design and implement new procedures in order to satisfy the new internal control reporting obligations. For example, prior to 2002, auditors often focused on testing controls in some of the entity's transaction cycles while performing minimal testing to confirm the absence of control changes in the remaining cycles, and rotating through these cycles each year. The requirement in SOX to report comprehensively on the effectiveness of internal controls means that such a cycle rotation approach is no longer acceptable for companies affected by SOX.

Sources: Deloitte and Touche LLP, Ernst & Young LLP, KPMG LLP, and PricewaterhouseCoopers LLP, *Internal Control Over Financial Reporting: An Investor Resource*, December 2004, www.aicpa.org, pp. 2 and 3; D.K. McConnell and G.Y. Banks, "How Sarbanes-Oxley Will Change the Audit Process," *Journal of Accountancy*, September 2003, www.journalofaccountancy.com.

BEFORE YOU GO ON

7.1 Do we always communicate weaknesses in internal controls to those charged with governance? Explain your answer.

7.2 Can the content ordinarily included in a management letter be delivered verbally to those charged with governance? Explain your answer.

7.3 Why is it preferred that most communications with those charged with governance be done in writing?

SUMMARY

① Define internal control.

Internal control is the process designed, implemented, and maintained by those charged with governance, management, and other personnel to provide reasonable assurance about the achievement of the entity's objectives with regard to reliability of financial reporting, effectiveness and efficiency of operations, and compliance with applicable laws and regulations. The term "controls" refers to any aspects of one or more of the components of internal control. Controls include entity-level controls and transaction-level controls.

② Explain the seven generally accepted objectives of internal control activities.

Internal controls are designed and implemented to ensure that transactions are real, recorded, correctly valued, classified, summarized, and posted, and timely.

③ Understand and describe the elements of internal control at the entity level.

The elements of internal control at the entity level are the control environment, the entity's risk assessment process, the entity's information system and communications, control activities, and monitoring. Internal control also includes how the controls are implemented, such as through appropriate segregation of duties.

④ Understand and describe the elements of internal control at the transaction level, and apply them to the sales, purchases, and payroll cycles.

Transaction-level controls are controls that impact a particular transaction or group of transactions. Transactions in this sense refer to transactions that are ordinarily recorded in the general ledger for the client and span from initiation of the transaction through to the reporting of the transaction in the financial statements. Transaction-level controls are those controls that respond to things that can go wrong with transactions.

⑤ Explain the different techniques used to document internal controls.

The most common forms of documentation are narratives, flowcharts, combinations of narratives and flowcharts, and checklists and preformatted questionnaires.

⑥ Explain the importance of identifying strengths and weaknesses in a system of internal controls.

An important outcome of understanding a client's system of internal controls is the ability to make observations, draw conclusions, and offer recommendations regarding the strengths and weaknesses observed. CAS 260 and CAS 265 require auditors to provide those charged with governance with timely observations arising from the audit. This is generally done through a management letter.

⑦ Explain how to communicate internal control strengths and weaknesses to those charged with governance.

A management letter (sometimes also referred to as a letter of recommendations) is a deliverable prepared by the audit team and provided to the client (including those charged with governance). It informs the client of the auditor's recommendations for improving its internal controls.

KEY TERMS

Audit risk, 254

Control activities, 263

Control environment, 256

Control risk, 260

Detection risk, 260

Entity-level controls, 256

Inherent risk, 260

Internal control, 253

Internal control exception, 279

Management letter, 282

Professional judgement, 280

Risk assessment process, 260

Transaction-level controls, 267

MULTIPLE-CHOICE QUESTIONS

7.1 Internal control is a process:

(a) designed to provide reasonable assurance about the achievement of the entity's objectives with regard to reliability of financial reporting, effectiveness and efficiency of operations, and compliance with applicable laws and regulations.

(b) that is the responsibility of those charged with governance.

(c) that is designed and implemented to address identified business risks that threaten the achievement of the entity's objectives.

(d) all of the above.

7.2 The objectives of internal controls include:

(a) that fictitious transactions are not included in the organization's records.

(b) that correct amounts are assigned to transactions.

(c) that transactions are recorded in the correct accounting period.

(d) all of the above.

7.3 The control environment:

(a) is the economic environment in which the organization operates.

(b) is the combination of the culture, structure, and discipline of an organization.

(c) applies only to listed companies.

(d) all of the above.

7.4 An entity's risk assessment process:

(a) is the entity's process for identifying and responding to business risks and the results thereof.

(b) is established only if the entity is subject to unusually high risk.

(c) is designed to help an entity think about risk in the same way that an auditor thinks about risk.

(d) never allows management of an entity to decide to accept a risk without taking any action.

7.5 Auditors are interested in an entity's information systems:

(a) because they consist of procedures and records to deal with transactions and maintain accountability for related assets, liabilities, and equity.

(b) because their quality affects management's ability to make appropriate decisions and prepare reliable financial statements.

(c) even if they are purely manual systems.

(d) all of the above.

7.6 Performance reviews:

(a) are not relevant to internal controls.

(b) are applicable only to the chief executive officer in an organization.

(c) are part of control activities.

(d) can include financial data only.

7.7 Segregation of incompatible duties:

(a) is a guarantee that fraud cannot occur.

(b) is the same as performance review by a supervisor.

(c) means that different people are assigned responsibilities for authorizing transactions, recording transactions, and maintaining custody of assets.

(d) all of the above.

7.8 Internal control in small entities:

(a) is always stronger because the owner-manager can supervise every activity.

(b) is likely to be less formal than in a larger entity.

(c) does not have the risk of management override.

(d) always results in an auditor placing a greater emphasis on testing internal controls.

7.9 Documenting internal controls:

(a) is always handled through the use of checklists and preformatted questionnaires.

(b) is done after internal controls are tested so that the results can be included in the documentation.

(c) can be handled with a combination of narratives and flowcharts.

(d) is not done for smaller clients because of the risk of management override.

7.10 A management letter:

(a) contains recommendations for improving internal control and discusses other issues discovered during the course of the audit.

(b) is written by management to the auditor at the start of the audit.

(c) lists only the significant deficiencies discovered during the audit.

(d) all of the above.

REVIEW QUESTIONS

7.1 If an auditor does not intend to rely on internal controls in the audit, does the auditor need to obtain an understanding of internal control? Explain.

7.2 Explain the difference between entity-level controls and transaction-level controls. Is an auditor interested in both?

7.3 Discuss the contention that the control environment is the most important part of a system of internal controls because it provides the foundation.

7.4 What sorts of risks would an entity's risk assessment process consider? Give some examples for a retailer. Which of these risks would be relevant to financial reporting? Explain.

7.5 Explain the importance of segregation of incompatible duties. What sorts of duties would be segregated within the sales process? Why?

7.6 Why would an auditor be interested in a client's control monitoring processes?

7.7 List three steps in the sales process. For each step selected, also identify a WCGW and an example control that should be incorporated in the step to mitigate that risk.

7.8 List the steps of the cost of sales process and give an example control that should be incorporated into each step.

7.9 Four approaches to internal control documentation are discussed in the chapter. Assess the advantages and disadvantages of each. How would documentation assist the auditor to identify strengths and weaknesses of an entity's system of internal controls?

7.10 Why do auditors prepare management letters?

PROFESSIONAL APPLICATION QUESTIONS

Basic ★   Moderate ★★   Challenging ★★★

7.1 Importance of internal control ★   ❶

Powersys is an electricity distribution company based in a large capital city. Its business is to manage the electricity assets, including poles, wires, and other equipment, that are used to deliver electricity to more than 500,000 retail and business customers in the city. Pole, wire, and substation maintenance and improvements are a large part of the company's operations, and teams of highly trained technicians are used for both planned work and emergency response activities. Emergency response is required when storms or fires bring down power lines, the power must be turned off at the direction of police, or the electricity supply fails for any reason.

Each team has several vehicles (vans and trucks) and uses additional heavy equipment, such as cherry pickers, cranes, and diggers, as required. Each vehicle carries a core set of specialized parts and tools, and additional items are obtained as required from the stores, which are located in a large warehouse in the northern suburbs. The warehouse is staffed on a 24-hour basis to assist night maintenance (designed to minimize disruption to business customers) and emergency response.

Required

(a) Make a list of the potential problems that could occur in Powersys' maintenance and improvements program.
(b) Suggest ways that good internal control over parts, equipment, and labour could help Powersys avoid these problems.

7.2 Objectives of internal control ★ ★

Carmel Harrison runs Emerald Spa, a business providing women-only hairdressing, beauty, relaxation massage, and counselling services in a small tourist town. Ninety percent of the clients using the beauty and massage services at Emerald Spa are weekend visitors to the town, but 80 percent of the hairdressing and counselling clients are locals. The masseuse and counsellor have formal qualifications and are registered with the medical authorities, allowing clients to claim the cost of the service with their private health insurer if an appropriate receipt is provided when the client pays.

Emerald Spa has just opened another branch of the business in a town 100 kilometres away, and there are plans for a third branch to be opened next year. Carmel has been very busy establishing each new branch and relies on staff in each office to run the day-to-day operations, including ordering supplies and banking receipts. In addition, the branch manager organizes the staff and authorizes their time sheets. Carmel makes the payments for rent, power, salaries, and large items of expenditure, such as furniture purchases.

Required

(a) Give examples of transactions that would occur at Emerald Spa.
(b) Explain what could go wrong with these transactions if the system of internal controls could not meet any of the seven generally accepted objectives of internal controls.

7.3 Control environment at a large company ★ ★

International Bank is experiencing bad publicity surrounding huge fraud losses in its foreign currency department. Accusations are being made in the press that the rogue trader blamed for the losses was operating outside the official guidelines with the tacit approval of senior management in the department because of the large profits made by this trader in previous years. The press claims that it was common knowledge in the foreign currency department that strict policies and procedures surrounding the size of trades and the processes for balancing out trades at the end of each day were not to be followed if the trader had verbally informed his supervisor of the trade. The press is also suggesting that the problems are not confined to the foreign currency department, and that poor attitudes are prevalent throughout all commercial departments at International Bank.

Required

Discuss the control environment at International Bank, assuming the press reports are correct. Which parts appear to be most deficient?

7.4 Segregation of duties in a small business ★

Big Town Computers has premises in the main street of a large regional city. The business is owned by Max and Betty Waldup, who purchased it three years ago. Betty has an extensive background in IT and has a talent for diagnosing and solving problems with computers that are brought in for repair. Max also has an IT background and oversees the sales and administration staff. There are three staff in the business: a computer technician who assists Betty; a part-timer who helps with sales; and a junior trainee, Sally, who does other tasks, such as banking. Sally is also responsible for issuing invoices and statements to clients who have a service contract with the business. These clients are generally other businesses who ask Betty to visit their premises for routine and emergency repairs, and who purchase software and hardware from the business.

Max and Betty have worked very hard over the last three years, but they have cash flow problems. Their bank manager has requested a meeting to discuss the business' growing overdraft. The bank manager asks Max and Betty to prepare for the meeting by analyzing their accounts receivable and customer receipts. Max and Betty review the accounts receivable ledger and find that it is not up to date. They also discover that client statements have not been issued for four months. They are also unable to identify from the cash receipts journal which clients have paid their accounts.

Required

(a) Discuss the attitude and control consciousness of Big Town Computers' management.
(b) Which duties should be segregated in this business? Recommend an appropriate allocation of duties for the staff at Big Town Computers.

7.5 Segregation of duties and documentation ★ ★

Lise Couture is documenting the purchasing and cash payments processes at Hardies Wholesaling. Hardies Wholesaling imports garden and landscaping items, such as pots, furniture, fountains, mirrors, and sculpture, from suppliers in Southeast Asia. All items are non-perishable, are made from materials such as stone, concrete, metal, and wood, and are distributed to retailers throughout the country.

Purchases are denominated in U.S. dollars, which the company acquires under forward exchange contracts. The purchasing department initiates a purchase order when inventory levels reach reorder points or sales staff notify the department of large customer orders that need to be specially filled. The purchase order is approved and sent to suppliers selected from an approved supplier list. Goods are transported from Southeast Asia by ship and are delivered by truck to Hardies Wholesaling's central warehouse. A receiving report is generated by the receiving department and forwarded to the accounts department for matching with the copy of the original purchase order and the supplier's invoice. When the package of documents is completed, the purchase order and invoice are entered into the general ledger. The cash payments department initiates a voucher to request payment of the invoice according to the supplier's payment terms. The payment is approved and the cash payment is made.

Required

(a) Create a flowchart to represent the flow of transactions from the initiation of a purchase order to cash payment.
(b) Which duties in the above process should be segregated?

7.6 Categories of controls ★

There are several categories of control activities listed in this chapter. They include performance reviews, authorization controls, account reconciliations, physical controls, and segregation of duties.

Required

For each of the following, identify the type of control:

(a) Petty cash is kept in a safe.

(b) All invoices are stamped "paid" after processing.

(c) Cheques received are pre-listed by the receptionist and recorded in the books by the accounts receivable clerk.

(d) Accounts receivable sub-ledger is agreed to the general ledger at each month end.

(e) Passwords are required before journal entries may be posted.

(f) Monthly results are compared to budget, and unexpected results are investigated.

(g) Overtime must be approved by a supervisor.

(h) Pre-numbered purchase orders are required before an invoice will be paid.

(i) Employee payroll records are kept in a locked filing cabinet.

(j) The person responsible for shipping and receiving goods does not perform the related billing.

(k) Monthly results are sent to divisional managers for review.

7.7 Transaction-level controls over financial reporting ★ ★ ★

Closing the books is critical for ensuring that an entity's financial statements are complete and accurate. This process involves recording adjusting journal entries Since the recorded entries have an impact on the resulting financial statements, an auditor should consider the controls over the financial reporting process.

Required

List five possible errors that could result if the controls over the financial reporting process with respect to journal entries are not effective. Identify a control that management could implement to mitigate this risk.

7.8 Controls at a small start-up company ★ ★

Two of your friends from high school will soon realize their lifetime dream of opening an English-style pub. They recently spoke with their accountant who indicated that they should ensure that they implement some strong controls. They have no idea what the accountant was talking about. They know you are studying accounting and they have come to you for advice about what their accountant meant.

Required

(a) Explain the concept of internal controls.

(b) List four things your friends should do to ensure that they create a strong control environment.

(c) List eight control activities they should have in place. Describe how each activity is relevant to their business.

Source: © CGA-Canada. Reproduced with permission.

7.9 Strengths and weaknesses of controls ★ ★ ★

GGG Electronics builds short-wave radios. Its manufacturing plant is also a warehouse. When parts are received, the receiver compares the type of goods and quantity to a copy of the purchase order available online. If the quantity received differs from the quantity on the purchase order, the receiver adjusts the purchase order amount online. When the goods are checked by the receiver, she sends an e-mail to the accounting department, recording the type of goods, quantity, and date received. The accounting department uses the e-mail to create a receiver's report, and the purchase order is then printed and filed in the accounting department. The online system allows the company to reduce paper, as a hard copy is not needed until the goods are actually received. The company's order-entry and tracking system automatically assigns the next number in a series to the purchase order just before printing.

Inventory is physically moved to the warehousing area, which is located in a locked-up area at the end of the plant. There is a stores department in a separate area for supplies such as gloves, wire, and adhesives, all of which are used in significant quantities on a regular basis. When an assembly line worker requires supplies, the supervisor fills out a serially pre-numbered requisition card, signs it, and gives it to the worker, who then takes it to the stores department to obtain the needed items. Each supervisor has a stock of requisition cards. When the supplier's invoice is received by the purchasing department, one of the purchasing department staff sends an e-mail to the accounting department, noting the invoice amount, supplier name, date of shipment, and type of goods. The accounting department then matches these items to the purchase order and receiving report, and prepares a cheque for the controller to sign.

The controller does not sign the cheque until she also receives an e-mail from the accounting staff indicating that the purchase order, receiving report, and invoice have been matched.

Required

(a) List four internal controls that appear to be effective in GGG's system.

(b) List three examples of weak internal controls in GGG's system. Explain why each of your examples would be a weak control.

Source: © CGA-Canada. Reproduced with permission.

7.10 Control weaknesses ★ ★ ★

WWW Corp. sells its products to clients ranging from proprietorships to medium-sized entities. WWW is controlled by two family members, and most of the employees are casual staff employed during the busy seasons (November 1 through January 15, and May 1 through July 15). The company's managers feel that on-the-job training is adequate for their needs and that the labour savings from using temporary staff are reflected in the profits that WWW has earned for the family each year.

The company has made a niche in its market by guaranteeing excellent and quick customer service. When a customer order is received, either by phone or by fax, the customer service clerk (CSC) who takes the order checks that WWW has the goods in stock and the correct price by checking an online database of inventory on hand. If the goods are available, the clerk then personally phones the customer to verify the order, including both quantity and price for each item and the extension for the entire order. The clerk then prepares a sales invoice and faxes a copy to the customer. WWW's policy is for the sales invoice to show a shipping date of one day from the order date. The clerk then walks to the warehouse (adjacent to the sales office), selects the goods, and takes them to shipping.

The company has a shipping staff of four people, and the shipping department will not ship any goods without a sales invoice initialled by the CSC. The shipping department is determined to reduce the number of shipping errors. This year, only nine shipments have occurred in which there was no sales invoice initialled and attached to the shipping bill. One of these turned out to be an urgent shipment to a long-time customer that was sent on the manager's verbal instructions. In that case, the shipping clerk noted that the manager had provided a sales invoice within one day for the shipping records. Another shipment resulted in the CSC being fired for fraud when it was discovered that he had sent a shipment of goods to a friend at below cost. Therefore, only the other seven shipments were considered to be true errors. If the sales invoice does not indicate who is to pay the shipping costs, then WWW sends the goods FOB shipping point. When a shipment occasionally is delivered to an incorrect address, it is the CSC's job to contact the customer and obtain the correct information. If the account is unpaid after the due date (30 days), the receptionist mails a reminder invoice to the customer. If the account remains unpaid after 60 days, the receptionist pulls the sales invoice and gives it to the CSC who made the sale. The CSC then is responsible for contacting the customer by phone to determine if there is a problem.

Required

Identify five different types of weaknesses or problems in WWW's internal controls.

Source: © CGA-Canada. Reproduced with permission.

Questions 7.11 and 7.12 are based on the following case.

Featherbed Surf & Leisure Holidays Ltd. (Featherbed) is a resort company based on Vancouver Island. Its operations include boating, surfing, diving, and other leisure activities; a backpackers' hostel; a family hotel; and a five-star resort. Justin and Sarah Morris own the majority of the shares in the Morris Group, which controls Featherbed. Justin is the chairman of the board of directors of both Featherbed and the Morris Group, and Sarah is a director of both companies as well as the CFO of Featherbed.

Justin and Sarah have a fairly laid-back management style. They trust their workers to work hard for the company and reward them well. The accounting staff, in particular, are very loyal to the company. Justin tells you that some accounting staff enjoy their jobs so much they have never taken holidays, and they rarely take sick leave. Justin and Sarah have not bothered much in the past with formal procedures and policies, but they have requested that the accounting staff start documenting the more common procedures. Justin and Sarah do not conduct formal performance reviews; they rely on their staff to tell them when there is a problem.

There are three people currently employed in the accounting department, the most senior of which is Peter Pinn. Peter heads the accounts department and reports directly to Sarah. He is in his fifties and plans to retire in two or three years. Peter prides himself on his ability to delegate most of his work to his two staff members, Kristen and Julie. He claims he has to do this because he is very busy developing the policy and procedures manual for the accounting department. The delegated work includes opening mail, processing payments and receipts, banking funds received, performing reconciliations, posting journals, and performing the payroll function. Julie is a recently graduated chartered accountant. Kristen works part-time—coming into the office on Mondays, Wednesdays, and Fridays. Kristen is responsible for posting all journal entries into the accounting system and the payroll function. Julie does the balance of the work, but they often help each other out in busy periods. Kristen authorizes Julie's transactions, and Julie returns the favour by authorizing Kristen's transactions. Together, they usually make the accounts balance.

Source: Adapted from the Institute of Chartered Accountants Australia's CA Program's *Audit and Assurance Exam*, May 2008.

7.11 Internal control components ★★★   ❸ ❹

Required

(a) Explain how the internal control components are usually adjusted to meet the needs of small entities. What advantages and disadvantages does this bring?

(b) Assess the internal controls at Featherbed. What changes would you recommend?

7.12 Communication with management ★★   ❼

Required

Write a management letter to Justin and Sarah Morris.

7.13 Components of internal control ★★★

Securimax Limited (Securimax) has been an audit client of KFP Partners (KFP) for the past 15 years. Securimax is based in Waterloo, Ontario, where it manufactures high-tech armour-plated personnel carriers. Securimax often has to go through a competitive market tender process to win large government contracts. Its main product, the small but powerful Terrain Master, is highly specialized and Securimax only does business with nations that have a recognized, democratically elected government. Securimax maintains a highly secure environment, given the sensitive and confidential nature of its vehicle designs and its clients.

In September 2011, Securimax installed an off-the-shelf costing system to support the highly sophisticated and cost-sensitive nature of its product designs. The new system replaced a system that had been developed in-house, as the old system could no longer keep up with the complex and detailed manufacturing costing process that provides tender cost-ings. The old system also had difficulty with the company's broader reporting requirements.

Securimax's IT department, together with the consultants from the software company, implemented the new manufacturing costing system. There were no customized modifications. Key operational staff and the internal audit team from Securimax were significantly engaged in the selection, testing, training, and implementation stages.

The manufacturing costing system uses all of the manufacturing unit inputs to calculate and produce a database of all product costs and recommended sales prices. It also integrates with the general ledger each time there are product inventory movements such as purchases, sales, wastage, and damaged inventory losses.

It is now October 2011 and you are beginning the audit planning for the December 31, 2011 annual financial statement audit. You are assigned to assess Securimax's IT controls with particular emphasis on the recent implementation of the new manufacturing costing system.

Source: Adapted from the Institute of Chartered Accountants Australia's CA Program's *Audit and Assurance Exam,* May 2008.

Required

Select two components of internal control. Explain how the roles of the internal and external audits would differ when assessing these components in relation to the new manufacturing costing system.

Questions 7.14 and 7.15 are based on the following case.

Fellowes and Associates Chartered Accountants is a successful mid-tier accounting firm with a large range of clients across Canada. During the financial year 2011, Fellowes and Associates gained a new client, Health Care Holdings Group (HCHG), which owns 100 percent of the following entities:

· Shady Oaks Centre, a private treatment centre
· Gardens Nursing Home Ltd., a private nursing home
· Total Laser Care Limited (TLCL), a private clinic that specializes in the laser treatment of skin defects.

Year end for all HCHG entities is June 30.

During the financial year 2011, HCHG released its own line of treatment supplies, such as orthotics, weights, and other equipment, which are sold by direct marketing by a sales team employed by the centre. The sales team receives a base salary and a bonus component, which is based on the dollar value of sales it generates. You recognize that the team's main motivation is to maximize its bonuses.

On April 1, 2011, Gardens Nursing Home Ltd. switched from its "home-grown" patient revenue system to HCHG's equivalent system. HCHG is confident that its "off-the-shelf" enterprise system would perform all of the functions that Gardens Nursing Home's home-grown system performed.

Gardens Nursing Home's home-grown patient revenue system comprised the following:

1. **Billing system**—a system that produced the invoice to charge the patient for services provided, such as accommodation, medications, and medical services. This software included a complex formula to calculate the patient bill allowing for government subsidies, pensioner benefits, and benefits from private medical insurance benefit plans.

2. **Patient database**—a master file that contained personal details about the patient as well as the period of stay, services provided, and the patient's medical insurance details.
3. **Rates database**—a master file that showed all accommodation billing rates, rebate discounts, and government assistance benefits.

At the request of the board, the group's internal audit unit was involved throughout the entire conversion process. The objective of its engagement, as the board stated, was to "make sure that the conversion worked without any problems."

Source: Adapted from the Institute of Chartered Accountants Australia's CA Program's *Audit and Assurance Exam,* March 2009.

7.14 Control environment ★ ★ ★

Required

Discuss the implications of the sales bonus system for the control environment within HCHG. What special factors would management have to consider?

7.15 Control risks in new IT systems ★ ★ ★

Required

With reference to the control activities component of internal control, formulate one question that the internal audit team and the external auditteam will ask regarding the conversion of the patient revenue systems by Gardens Nursing Home.

7.16 Transaction-level controls over the payroll cycle ★ ★ ★

TTT Ltd. has had strong growth over the past three years. The company is involved in mining in northern Canada. While revenues have been increasing, the costs of mining at its remote locations have also increased. An investigation revealed that the controller had added a fictitious employee and had defrauded TTT by collecting and cashing false payroll cheques. The CEO fired the controller and, instead, hired a new accountant with a mandate to cut costs. The accountant eliminated a number of administrative staff because these employees did not contribute to the income-earning process. Under the new office structure, only the personnel manager can authorize the hiring of new employees and their pay rate, and only the accountant can prepare and distribute the payroll cheques.

Required

Does the new accountant's plan provide strong internal controls over payroll? Justify your answer by stating the strength(s) and weakness(es) of the new plan.

Source: © CGA-Canada. Reproduced with permission.

CASES

7.17 Integrative Case Study—Harlan Venture Inc.

Harlan Venture Inc. (HV) operates a restaurant named Harlan's, which is located in Toronto. The shareholder, Taufiq Noorani, is concerned whether the system and controls in place at the restaurant are appropriate for monitoring and controlling its operations and for ensuring that employees don't steal. He provides the following information:

Restaurant operations
The restaurant manager's duties include looking after reservations, seating customers, and managing the restaurant's operations.

Servers take customers' orders and enter them into a system that uses off-the-shelf restaurant software that HV purchased. Each order is temporarily stored in the "orders placed file" and is transmitted to the kitchen staff who receive a printed order. This order is the basis for preparing the meal. The kitchen staff throw out the order forms when the meals are picked up by the servers.

The server instructs the system to prepare a customer's bill. Customers pay by cash or by credit card (HV accepts Visa, MasterCard, American Express, and Diners Club). The server enters the payment amount and method of payment into the system. The amount of the tip is entered as a separate item for both cash payments and credit card payments. The order in the "orders placed file" is transferred to the "orders completed file" only when the server enters the customer's payment information.

At the end of the day, the restaurant manager prepares cash envelopes that contain the tips for the servers and kitchen staff based on the amount of the tips recorded in the system. The cash in the tip envelopes is taken from the cash payments made by customers. The restaurant manager then clears the system for any orders that remain in the "orders placed file."

The system generates a daily report of revenue recorded by method of payment, and HST collected. This report is used by the part-time accountant to make the entries in the general ledger. The restaurant manager prepares the daily bank deposit, which includes the credit card vouchers and the cash to be deposited. A cash float of $250 is maintained in the sales register. He takes the deposit home and makes the bank deposit first thing the next morning.

HV receives monthly statements from the credit card entities that report the amount of the credit card sales processed by the entity and the fee charged by the entity. The bookkeeper enters these expenses in the general ledger.

The bartender is responsible for all sales of wine and liquor. He provides wine (by the glass or by bottle) and drinks to the servers who are not allowed access to these items. The on-site wine is stored behind the bar and expensive wines are stored in the basement wine cellar. He takes inventory of the wines and liquor weekly and places the appropriate purchase orders.

Catering services

HV provides both in-restaurant special function catering and out-of-restaurant special function catering (for example, at a private residence). The price of the function is based on the menu cost plus a markup of 60 percent. The customer is billed in full for the function after it is completed and when the customer indicates satisfaction with HV's performance by sending in the "customer satisfaction form." Revenue is recognized at the time of billing. Discounts are authorized by the restaurant manager if the customer deems HV's performance to be less than satisfactory. The amount of discounts given to date has been minimal. Billings are often made as much as 60 days after the date of the function. As of May 31, 2012, 10 functions with a contract value of $50,000 have been completed and as yet not billed. Forty functions have been billed.

Required

Based on the above, identify five control weaknesses. For each weakness, state the implication and make an appropriate recommendation to improve the control weakness.

Source: (Adapted and) reprinted with the permission of the Institute of Chartered Accountants of Ontario, copyright ICAO. Any changes to the original material are the sole responsibility of the author (and or the publisher) and have not been reviewed or endorsed by the ICAO.

7.18 Integrative Case Study—Integrated Measurement Systems Inc.

Integrated Measurement Systems Inc. (IMS) is a Canadian public company that manufactures high-end measuring devices used primarily in the oil and natural gas industries.

Ted Pollock, CEO of IMS, is a proponent of strong corporate governance. He has spent the last year strengthening IMS's internal control environment. He believes that organizations that demonstrate good corporate governance practices will be perceived favourably by the markets.

Ted has some concerns regarding the purchasing process. He has provided you with a description of the purchasing process in Exhibit 1.

EXHIBIT I

Control objectives that relate to the purchasing process:
1. proper approval of all transactions
2. safeguarding of company assets
3. prevention and detection of errors and irregularities
4. accuracy and completeness of books and records.
5. appropriate use of information

PURCHASING PROCESS DOCUMENTATION

The purchasing process has four major components, namely:
1. vendor prequalification
2. purchase of goods and/or services
3. receipt of goods
4. settlement.

Process description

The purchasing process begins when there is a requirement for goods or services. A manually completed purchase request form is sent from the operating department (for example, sales, marketing, manufacturing, and so on) to the purchasing department. The purchasing clerk numbers these documents and reviews each purchase request form to verify that a signature is present. Purchase request forms must be authorized by the signature of a person with the appropriate level of authority. The amount of the expenditure determines the level of authority required, and the expenditure authorization levels are organized in tiers. Because there are so many possible combinations of departments and authorization levels, the operating departments are responsible for ensuring that their purchase request forms are signed by individuals with the appropriate level of authority. This requirement eliminates the need for the purchasing clerk to check the specifics of the signatures.

The purchasing clerk sends the purchase requests to the purchasing manager for review and approval. The approved purchase request is then sent to the buyer, who sources the purchase. If the amount is below $5,000, selection of the vendor is left up to the buyer. For purchases in excess of $5,000 but less than $25,000, a vendor from the prequalification listing is selected, again at the discretion of the buyer. For purchases in excess of $25,000, a formal bidding process is performed. However, at the discretion of the buyer, the bid process can be waived if deemed to be cost inefficient.

Upon selection of the vendor, the buyer inputs the purchase request information into a purchase order form. The purchase order is forwarded to the purchasing manager for review and a photocopy is made and filed, in numerical order, with the appropriate photocopy of the purchase request. The original purchase order is then sent back to the buyer, who delivers it to the vendor.

All goods are received in the warehouse. All employees have access to the warehouse. The goods are checked against the packing slip and are examined for damage and so on. If the goods are acceptable, the bill of lading is signed off by the receiver. A copy of the signed bill of lading is then forwarded to the purchasing clerk, who matches it to the file copy of the purchase request and purchase order. If there are differences in the details (over/under shipment, wrong product, and so on), the bill of lading is forwarded to the buyer for resolution with the vendor. If no problems are noted, copies of the three documents are sent to the payables group for settlement.

The receiver, Ali Jenoubi (who was hired six months ago), sends the goods to the user department that made the original purchase request along with a photocopy of the bill of lading. The user department agrees the quantities noted by the receiver and files the bill of lading. User departments have noted that, recently, there have been an increasing number of manual adjustments to the quantities shipped versus those received. Any unmatched purchase requests and purchase orders that remain outstanding for over 90 days are returned by the purchasing clerk to the user department that originally ordered the goods on the assumption that the goods have been received. It is then the responsibility of the user department to follow up and forward the paperwork to the payables group for settlement.

If a signed bill of lading is forwarded to the purchasing clerk for which there is no source documentation (that is, no purchase request or purchase order exists), the purchasing clerk follows up with the buyer to understand the nature of the receipt. At the same time, a copy of the bill of lading is also sent to the payables group.

Required

(a) Identify the existing key internal controls within the purchasing process and relate each to the appropriate control objective.
(b) Identify the internal control weaknesses within the purchasing process and recommend improvements.
(c) To further strengthen the control environment, Ted is considering creating an internal audit department. Outline the kinds of activities this group could be involved in.

Source: Simulation 1 from the Uniform Evaluation (UFE), Paper III, 2004.

CASE STUDY—CLOUD 9

Answer the following questions based on the information presented for Cloud 9 in Appendix B to this book and in the current and earlier chapters. You should also consider your answers to the case study questions in earlier chapters.

Sharon Gallagher and Josh Thomas have assessed the internal controls at Cloud 9 as being effective at an entity level. This means that, at a high level, the company demonstrates an environment where potential material misstatements are prevented or detected.

Required

You have been assigned the task of documenting the understanding of the process for recording sales, trade receivables, and cash receipt transactions for wholesale customers. In your absence, Josh met with the Cloud 9 financial controller, Carla Johnson, and received permission to tape the interview, which is provided as a transcript (see Appendix B to this book). Using this interview transcript and other information presented in the case, you are asked to:

(a) Prepare a flowchart or narrative documenting your understanding of the sales to cash receipts process for wholesale sales.
(b) Identify any follow-up questions you would like to ask the client if aspects of the process are not adequately explained. You could address such questions to Carla Johnson or any other employee you deem appropriate.
(c) Identify the potential material misstatement that could occur in the sales to cash receipts process for wholesale sales.

(d) Identify, for the material misstatements in (c), the financial statement assertion that is affected.

To answer (c) and (d), draw up a worksheet using the following format. Use as many rows as you need. Use the first three columns to present your findings. (You will complete the fourth column in the next chapter.)

SIGNIFICANT PROCESS	POTENTIAL MATERIAL MISSTATEMENT	ASSERTIONS	TRANSACTION-LEVEL INTERNAL CONTROLS

RESEARCH QUESTION 7.1

Concerns have been raised over how quickly the Alberta oil sands are being developed. Amid the international concern of global warming, the oil sands have emerged as Canada's fastest growing source of greenhouse gas pollution. Other ecosystem impacts include toxic waste, strip mining, and species loss. Assume you are a member of senior management at a large property development company.

Required

Write a report identifying the main risks to your company that you believe should be considered at the next meeting of the risk assessment committee. Include risks to the company's operations and assets, finances, and personnel.

Source: Environmental Defence, The Pembina Institute, and Equiterre. *Duty Calls: Federal Responsibility in Canada's Oil Sands*, 2010, www.pembina.org.

SOLUTIONS TO MULTIPLE-CHOICE QUESTIONS

1. d, 2. d, 3. b, 4. a, 5. d, 6. c, 7. c, 8. b, 9. c, 10. a.

CHAPTER 8

Execution of the audit–testing of controls

LEARNING OBJECTIVES

After studying this chapter, you should be able to:

1 identify the different types of controls

2 understand the different techniques for testing controls

3 explain how to select and design tests of controls

4 understand how to interpret the results of testing of controls

5 explain how to document tests of controls.

AUDITING AND ASSURANCE STANDARDS

CANADIAN	INTERNATIONAL
CAS 230 *Audit Documentation*	ISA 230 *Audit Documentation*
CAS 260 *Communication with Those Charged with Governance*	ISA 260 *Communication with Those Charged with Governance*
CAS 265 *Communicating Deficiencies in Internal Control to those Charged with Governance and Management*	ISA 265 *Communicating Deficiencies in Internal Control to those Charged with Governance and Management*
CAS 315 *Identifying and Assessing the Risks of Material Misstatement Through Understanding the Entity and Its Environment*	ISA 315 *Identifying and Assessing the Risks of Material Misstatement Through Understanding the Entity and Its Environment*

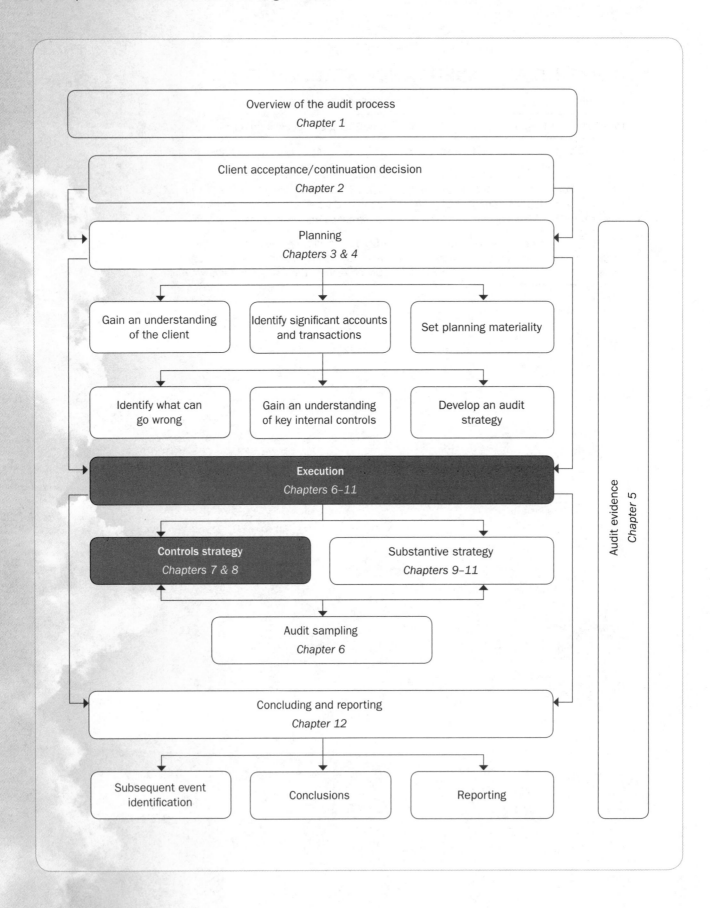

Cloud 9

Cloud 9 Ltd. (Cloud 9) has effective internal controls at the entity level. Sharon Gallagher, the audit manager, believes that when considered at a high level, the company has an environment where potential misstatements are preventive or detective. Sharon has instructed the audit team to turn its attention to considering the controls at the transaction level.

Josh and his group begin by documenting the various accounting processes at Cloud 9. For each process, they identify the potential misstatements that could occur. In other words, they make a list of possible problems for major areas of the accounts. These possible problems are commonly referred to within the audit the firm as WCGWs ("what can go wrong"). Then, for each WCGW, they identify the financial statement assertion that would be affected.

Weijing Fei, a new member of Josh's group, needs some help. Josh has asked her to identify the controls that Cloud 9 uses to either prevent or detect the types of misstatements they have identified so far. Weijing does not understand the difference between preventive and detective controls. Also, Josh tells Weijing that he needs the results of her work so that he can design the control testing for Cloud 9. He wants to focus the testing on the critical controls. Weijing is confused. She thought a lower assessed control risk approach to an audit required the auditors to test all the controls.

How can they justify testing only some controls? Which are the critical controls?

AUDIT PROCESS IN FOCUS

As discussed in chapter 4, assessing audit risk involves assessing the inherent and control risk and determining the detection risk for each significant account and assertion. The assessment of control risk is performed on the client's system of internal controls (see chapters 4 and 7). The auditor is interested in whether the client has controls in place that are designed to minimize the risk of material misstatement for each account and related assertion identified as being high risk by the auditor. When the controls appear to have been designed and implemented appropriately, the audit team can decide to test controls, as the team will expect to be able to assess control risk as low. This will then reduce the need to perform significant amounts of substantive testing. As control risk decreases, detection risk increases, and therefore the amount of substantive testing decreases. After controls have been found effective, control risk is assessed as low. This combined approach reduces the auditor's reliance on detailed substantive testing.

When the auditor decides to include controls testing in their audit strategy, they select those controls that will provide the most efficient and effective audit evidence (that is, they will provide the assurance required that the controls are working). Also, the auditor will test only those controls they believe are critical to their opinion. That is, they select those controls that are extensive and sensitive enough to provide reasonable assurance that the controls operated effectively throughout the period of reliance (that is, the reporting period).

Deciding which controls to test will be influenced by the type of control, the frequency with which the control is performed, and the level of assurance the auditor wants to gain from the control being designed and implemented effectively.

There are many techniques available to test the controls identified when planning the audit, and in this chapter we will provide an overview of several of the more typical testing techniques. This overview will include examples of the extent of controls testing to perform (depending on the type of control being tested) and how this extent of testing will influence the level of assurance we obtain toward the overall audit conclusion or opinion.

Finally, we will discuss what the auditor's response should be to any exceptions or errors found in their testing of controls, as well as how the auditor should document the results of their testing. In the discussion of the results we will also include examples of how these affect the overall risk assessment and the resulting substantive audit procedures performed.

8.1 TYPES OF CONTROLS

① Identify the different types of controls.

As described in chapter 7, there are two types of internal **controls: entity-level controls** and **transaction-level controls.** This chapter will focus on transaction-level controls. Transaction-level controls relate to one of the five components of entity-level **internal control** as set out in CAS 315 *Identifying and Assessing the Risks of Material Misstatement Through Understanding the Entity and Its Environment* (the five components are the control environment, the client's risk assessment process, information and communication, **control activities,** and monitoring). Transaction-level controls are implemented by businesses to reduce the risk of misstatement due to error or fraud as well as to ensure that processes are operating effectively. Controls can include any procedure the client uses and relies on to prevent errors from occurring during the processing of transactions, or to detect and correct errors that may occur in these transactions.

Controls have two main objectives: to prevent or detect misstatements in the financial statements, or to support the automated parts of the business in the functioning of the controls in place. Preventive controls are those applied to each transaction that prevent fraud or errors from occurring. Detective controls are those applied after transactions have been processed to identify whether fraud or errors have occurred. These concepts will be explained in more detail in section 8.1.1.

Controls are classified as one of four types:

1. manual
2. automated (otherwise known as application controls)
3. information technology (IT) general controls (ITGCs) (the overall controls put in place to manage changes to applications and programs, as well as to limit access to appropriate users of those IT applications only)
4. a combination of control types referred to as IT-dependent manual controls.

Figure 8.1 illustrates the types of controls and how they interrelate. As the figure also shows, each type of control has the potential to be a preventive or a detective control. Each of these control types is discussed in more detail in section 8.1.1.

The reason controls are classified is to assist the auditor in understanding the type of risks each control addresses, how the control addresses those risks, and the potential audit evidence that a control provides. Also, the classification assists in considering the nature, timing, and extent of the tests of controls and in determining the skills needed to perform the tests. It is not important what these controls are labelled; what is important is whether the control can be tested, is effective, and can be relied on to provide audit evidence.

controls (referring to control activities) the terms "internal control," "control(s)," "system of internal controls," and "components of internal control" may be used to refer to the same process

entity-level controls the collective assessment of the client's control environment, risk assessment process, information system, control activities, and monitoring of controls

transaction-level controls controls that affect a particular transaction or group of transactions

internal control the process designed, implemented, and maintained by those charged with governance, by management, and by other personnel to provide reasonable assurance about the achievement of the entity's objectives with regard to reliability of financial reporting, effectiveness and efficiency of operations, and compliance with applicable laws and regulations

control activities policies and procedures that help ensure that management directives are carried out. Control activities are a component of internal control

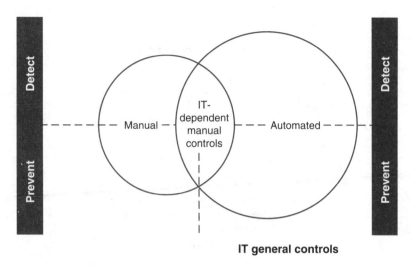

FIGURE 8.1 **Types of controls**

8.1.1 Preventive and detective controls

Tests of controls (or **controls testing**) are the audit procedures performed to test the operating effectiveness of controls in preventing, or detecting and correcting, material misstatements at the assertion level. The controls are tested to determine if they are properly applied throughout the entire period. Remember, this testing is required if the auditor plans to rely on the controls to reduce the amount of substantive work to be performed.

Preventive controls

Preventive controls can be applied to each transaction during normal processing to avoid errors occurring. Preventing errors during processing is an important objective of every accounting system. To be effective, controls over transactions should ideally include both preventive and detective controls. This is because without the underlying preventive controls, detective controls may not be sufficiently sensitive to identify and correct misstatements. This concept is discussed further in the detective controls section below.

When designing controls, consider what can go wrong with the transaction (that is, what is the risk of material misstatement) that would result in an error. These are sometimes referred to as **WCGWs** (what can go wrongs). Effective preventive controls should prevent the WCGWs from occurring. If they do occur, detective controls should ensure that the errors are detected and corrected as quickly as possible.

Table 8.1 shows examples of preventive controls and some of the WCGWs each control is designed to prevent.

Preventive controls do not always produce physical evidence indicating whether the control was performed, who performed it, or how well it was performed. In other cases, there may be evidence that the control was performed, but evidence as to the effectiveness of the control may not be available. For example, the signature of the warehouse receiver on a receiving report or a bill of lading indicates that the receiver agreed that goods were physically received into the warehouse, but it does not guarantee that the person carefully reviewed the shipment or checked that the quantities of each item matched the quantities on the bill of lading. The

tests of controls (controls testing) the audit procedures designed to evaluate the operating effectiveness of controls in preventing, or detecting and correcting, material misstatements at the assertion level

WCGWs areas where material misstatements due to error or fraud could occur in a flow of transactions or in the sourcing and preparation of information that affects a relevant financial statement assertion

TABLE 8.1 **Examples of preventive controls**

WCGW	PREVENTIVE CONTROL
Sales occur that are not collectable.	The computerized accounting program will not allow a sale to be processed if a customer has exceeded its credit limit.
Fictitious employees are paid.	Amounts cannot be paid to employees without first matching a valid social insurance number to the employee master file.
Sales are recorded at the wrong amount.	Sales invoices are automatically priced using a master pricing file.
Transactions are classified and coded to incorrect accounts.	The account coding on each purchase order is checked by the computer using a table of valid account numbers, and then various logic tests are performed by the computer.

documentation may have been signed based on a quick glance or without any review at all. Thus, goods may be recorded that do not exist, excess goods may have been received but not recorded, or the goods received may not match the goods ordered and recorded. Therefore, in this example, the quality of the evidence that the control will prevent one of these errors from occurring is not persuasive enough for the auditor to conclude that the control operated effectively throughout the reporting period. This concept is discussed further in the section on techniques for testing controls.

A lack of effective preventive controls increases the risk that errors will occur or that fraud may occur and therefore increases the need for controls that are sensitive enough to detect these errors should they occur.

Detective controls

The purpose of detective controls is to discover fraud or errors that may have occurred during transaction processing (in spite of any preventive controls) and to rectify those errors. As discussed earlier, companies put detective controls in place to help management ensure that WCGWs do not occur and that the business is functioning as planned through the design and implementation of its business processes.

Generally, detective controls are not applied to each transaction during the normal flow of processing. Instead, they are applied outside the normal flow of individual transactions to groups of transactions that have been fully or partially processed. For example, often when payables are paid, a cheque run is processed to print the cheques, but the transaction is not completed: the debit is not recorded to the payables account and credit is not recorded to the cash account. Instead, the transaction is only partially processed and then "held" by the system. Once the cheques have been signed as approved for payment, the payables clerk will process the rest of the transaction by "releasing" the payments and recognizing the debit to payables and credit to cash.

Detective controls vary from client to client to a greater extent than preventive controls. Detective controls can depend on the nature of the client's business and on the competence, preferences, and imagination of the people who perform the controls. Detective controls may be formally established procedures, such as the preparation of a monthly reconciliation and the subsequent follow-up of reconciling or unusual items. Or they may be procedures that employees regularly perform and typically document, even though they are not formally required to do so by the company. For example, the financial accountant may keep a list of standard month-end journals to use as the basis for checking the entries each month as they are made, following up on any exceptions. Detective controls are often "unofficial" procedures similar to this example, which client personnel perform to make sure that the information they are responsible for is accurate.

It is important that detective controls:

1. completely and accurately capture all relevant data
2. identify all potentially significant errors
3. are performed consistently and regularly
4. include timely follow-up and correction for any misstatements or issues detected.

There are many examples of detective controls, including the following:

- Management-level reviews are made of actual performance versus budgets, forecasts, prior periods, competitors (if available), and industry averages (if available). Management's actions in analyzing and following up on unexpected variances is a detective control. For example, the financial controller may review the monthly results and compare the number of days' sales outstanding to previous periods to ensure any allowance for doubtful accounts is reasonable.

- Performance indicators relate different sets of data, operating or financial, to each other. These indicators, together with an analysis of the relationships and the subsequent follow-up of anomalies, are also control activities. The auditor needs to understand whether the client uses the information for operational purposes only (that is, to assist in making operating decisions), or whether the client also uses the information to follow up on unexpected results in the financial reporting system. If the information is only used for operational purposes, it is unlikely that the auditor will gather a significant amount of audit evidence to assist them in the financial statement audit. Performance indicators include, for example, purchase price variances, stock ordered but not yet manufactured, and percentage of sales returned compared to total sales orders. By investigating unexpected results or unusual trends, the client may identify issues in the underlying procurement and manufacturing processes.

- Reconciliations are prepared, reconciling or unusual items are then investigated, and issues are resolved or corrections made, if necessary. The performance of reconciliations without following up on reconciling or unusual items is not a control. The control is the follow-up. Typical reconciliations are performed between the general ledger and some other form of external evidence or a subsidiary ledger. For example, the bank reconciliation reconciles the bank statement to the cash recorded in the general ledger. The accounts receivable reconciliation reconciles sales recorded in the trade receivables subsidiary ledger (via the sales ledger) to the trade receivables recorded in the general ledger.

- Reports are automatically produced showing transactions/groups of transactions that fall outside a set of parameters selected by the client. These exception reports are then reviewed and followed up (if necessary). For example, a report may be produced that shows all sales made to a customer that has exceeded its credit limit. The credit manager then follows up these sales with the salesperson to ensure no further sales are made until the balance is brought below the credit limit. Alternatively,

TABLE 8.2 **Examples of detective controls**

WCGW	DETECTIVE CONTROL
Cash is received but not recorded in the general ledger, payments are made but not recorded, cash receipts or cash payments are not real or not recorded on a timely basis.	Bank reconciliation and follow-up of unexpected outstanding items (e.g., unexpected or large deposits not yet cleared by the bank, cheques presented by the bank but not recorded in the general ledger).
Shipments are not billed and recorded, or billings are not related to actual shipments of product.	The computer performs a daily comparison of quantities shipped to quantities billed. If differences are revealed, a report is generated for review and follow-up by the billing supervisor.
Unrecorded billings and errors in classifying sales or cash receipts.	Quarterly reviews of credit balances in accounts receivable to determine their causes.
Errors in the number of units or unit prices being calculated or applied incorrectly.	The sales manager reviews daily shipments, total sales, and sales per unit shipped.

if necessary, a re-evaluation of the customer's credit limit is performed and the limit is increased (if appropriate).

Table 8.2 shows examples of detective controls and some of the WCGWs each control is designed to prevent.

As illustrated in this section, detective controls are often accompanied by physical evidence, such as a monthly reconciliation. This is in direct contrast to preventive controls, which are often driven by the programming of the particular software used by the company, and therefore produce no physical evidence of the control.

When assessing detective controls, it is not necessary for the auditor to re-perform all of the steps in, for example, preparing a reconciliation to gain sufficient evidence that the control is operating effectively. It is normally enough to examine evidence that the reconciliation was properly completed and that the appropriate reviews and follow-ups were carried out by the client in a timely manner.

Preventive and detective controls compared

Preventive controls may be dependent on IT (that is, they are IT-dependent manual controls). Specialist IT skills are required to audit IT-dependent manual controls, depending on how sophisticated the client's IT system is. It is important to note, however, that detective controls are only effective, and therefore only provide audit assurance, when the underlying data and transactions (and therefore preventive controls) can be relied on. Therefore, it is important to gain an understanding of (and possibly test) the preventive controls in addition to the detective controls to which they relate.

For example, the review and follow-up of a monthly management report that compares actual results to budget results would be ineffective if there is no evidence available to show that the budgeted amounts are the approved amounts and the actual amounts are the total of the transactions recorded in the general ledger. In addition, the auditor needs to obtain evidence that the underlying transactions are captured and recorded properly. This is ordinarily done via the identification and testing of the underlying preventive controls. Also, the monthly comparison needs to be at an information level that is detailed enough to identify material misstatements, and the review and follow-up needs to be timely.

Because detective controls can be applied to groups of transactions rather than on a transaction-by-transaction basis, they are ordinarily performed less frequently than preventive controls. Therefore, if detective controls operate effectively throughout the period, a high degree of reliance can be obtained by examining a relatively small amount of evidence.

As noted earlier, this does not mean that the auditor will forego tests of controls over individual transactions. Performing tests of transactions allows the auditor to satisfy themselves that a preventive control was in use and functioned as intended. The auditor also performs tests of transactions to confirm that their understanding of the flow of transactions from initiation to reporting is correct (as described in chapter 4). In computerized environments, preventive controls can often be tested just as effectively and efficiently as detective controls. This is because preventive controls are accompanied by direct evidence (for example, review and follow-up of exception reports) as to the effectiveness of their operation. As well, the auditor is able to re-perform the control to ensure it is operating effectively. This is discussed in more detail in the section on automated controls.

Cloud 9

Weijing asks Josh about the types of controls that are normally used in a company like Cloud 9. Josh explains that it is useful to start by classifying controls as automated, manual, IT-dependent manual, or IT general controls. However, he says that Weijing's focus should be on considering whether each of these controls prevents an error occurring in the first place, or whether each is designed to detect an error that has already occurred so it can be brought to someone's attention.

Josh gives Weijing an example of a preventive control at Cloud 9. Based on his conversation with Carla Johnson, the financial controller, he has discovered that the computerized credit checking system at Cloud 9 will not allow a sale to be processed if a customer has exceeded its credit limit. This control prevents a customer order becoming a sale unless the client has been assessed as being able to pay the amount. It also helps prevent some clerical errors, such as 10 units being entered incorrectly as 1,000 units (because this would usually take a customer's order over the customer's credit limit). This control is designed to operate for every order, but there does not seem to be anything in Cloud 9's system to show if and when it is done, so it is not easy to know if the control is operating effectively.

Josh also gives Weijing an example of a detective control at Cloud 9. Carla Johnson performs a monthly bank reconciliation that is reviewed and approved by David Collier, the financial director. However, Josh explains to Weijing that he does not know yet if there is any follow-up on unusual items discovered during the reconciliation and review. If this follow-up is being done, then the control should detect errors in the bank account.

8.1.2 Manual and automated controls

In this section we consider manual and automated controls, as well as ITGCs and application controls (subsets of automated controls), and IT-dependent manual controls (which combine the characteristics of manual and automated controls).

Manual controls

Purely manual controls are those that do not rely on the client's IT environment for their operation. An example is a locked safe for cash to which only a few authorized staff have access. However, manual controls may use IT-produced information from third parties. For example, a client may reconcile the amount of consignment inventory that was manually counted during its inventory count to the amounts listed in the third party's computer-generated consignment inventory listing.

There are very few, if any, companies that do not use some form of IT to assist in transaction processing, and most controls rely on IT in some way (refer to the section on IT-dependent manual controls).

Automated controls

Controls generally rely on the client's IT applications (or software) in some way. It is important to identify how much a control is automated in order to determine how IT will affect the evaluation of controls. The key consideration is to determine whether or not the client has effective ITGCs.

IT general controls (ITGCs)

ITGCs are the client's controls over the hardware and software it uses, including acquisition and maintenance of equipment, backup and recovery procedures, and the organization of the IT department to ensure the appropriate segregation of duties.

These ITGCs support the ongoing functioning of the automated (that is, programmed) aspects of preventive and detective controls and also provide the auditor with a basis for relying on electronic audit evidence. The auditor needs to identify, understand, walk through, test, and evaluate the ITGCs that have been implemented for computer applications they plan to rely on, as they do for any other type of control.

Ordinarily, an entity has three types of ITGCs in place:

1. program change controls—only appropriately authorized, tested, and approved changes are made to applications, interfaces, databases, and operating systems. All changes are documented so systems documentation is up to date.
2. logical access controls—only authorized personnel have access to IT equipment, data files, programs, and applications, and these personnel can perform only authorized tasks and functions. For example, the accounts receivable clerk does not have access to or authorization to use the cash payments application; the payroll manager may have access to the electronic funds transfer application but is unable to process any pay runs without the additional approval (and use of passwords) of the financial controller.
3. other ITGCs (including IT operations)—often difficult to identify in smaller organizations, these include controls such as ensuring regular and timely backups of data, following up and resolving program faults and errors regularly, following up any deviations from scheduled processing on a timely basis, and planning regular upgrades to programs and applications, as well as ensuring the existence of a disaster recovery plan.

Table 8.3 provides a more complete list of common general IT controls.

TABLE 8.3 **Common general IT controls**

Source: Based on CICA C·PEM form 532 "General IT controls—Design/implementation," in C·PEM Forms—Audits, April 2010

CONTROLS TO ENSURE THE EFFECTIVE MANAGEMENT OF THE IT DEPARTMENT

- Specific job descriptions exist for the IT manager and support staff (or person(s) assigned IT responsibilities).
- The data access and span of control exercised by IT staff is limited, where possible, through access cards, passwords, and segregation of duties.
- Contracts are signed with qualified third-party service providers that address the expectations, risks, security controls, and procedures/controls for information processing (for example, payroll).
- Job performance of IT staff is periodically evaluated and reviewed with the employee, and appropriate action is taken.

CONTROLS TO ENSURE THE ACCURATE PROCESSING OF DATA

- Entity uses mainstream accounting and other software packages with no modification.
- Access to applications is restricted by passwords, etc., to authorized personnel.
- Staff that uses or enters data into software applications has been suitably trained.
- Only authorized software is permitted for use by employees.
- Custom software is subject to an appropriate level of testing before being implemented.
- Program changes are subject to formal change management procedures.

CONTROLS TO PREVENT UNAUTHORIZED ACCESS TO DATA (including destruction of data, improper changes, unauthorized or non-existent transactions, or inaccurate recording of transactions)

- Networks, servers, firewalls, routers, and switches are properly configured to prevent unauthorized access.
- Management protects data in storage and during transmission against unauthorized access or modification.
- Data files and critical applications are regularly backed up and stored in offsite locations.
- Access to IT facilities, equipment, and applications (including remote access) is restricted to authorized personnel.
- Passwords are changed regularly.
- Policies exist to ensure departing employees are denied access to software programs and databases.
- Procedures exist to protect against computer viruses.

ITGCs are important because they impact the effectiveness of both application controls and IT-dependent manual controls, as well as potentially affecting the reliability of electronic audit evidence the auditor may wish to rely on during the audit. For example, if a client relies on an application that records a sale and then automatically records and updates the accounts receivable ledger for that particular customer, the client also relies on its IT program change procedures and security to verify that the program and this specific control are not changed without appropriate approval and testing.

Examples of tests of controls over program changes and access to data files include:

- program change controls—examine documentation for evidence (for example, signatures on the program change forms) that the changes were authorized, tested, documented, and approved by appropriate personnel (for example, users, programmers, the IT manager)

- access controls—check whether the access control software options in effect are properly approved and whether the options selected are reasonable; test or observe attempts to log on to terminals and access files using unauthorized user IDs; review the related access violation or exception reports to determine whether all of the attempts are properly recorded.

Application controls

Application controls are the fully automated controls that apply to the processing of individual transactions. They are the controls that are driven by the particular software application being used, hence the name "application" controls. These are the controls that ensure transactions are processed correctly. There are generally three categories of application controls:

1. Input controls are the controls designed to detect and prevent errors during the data input stage. Examples of input controls include:
   - verification controls to check input to previously entered data such as the master file
   - missing data checks to ensure all required data has been input and no data is missing
   - check digits to prevent input errors by applying a mathematical formula.
2. Processing controls are the controls in place to ensure the data is processed as intended and no data is lost, added, duplicated, or altered during processing. Examples of processing controls include:
   - control totals ensure that input totals are balanced and reconciled
   - reasonable checks compare actual data to expected data and ensure they are reasonable
   - sequence tests review sequential data and produce exception reports for missing numbers.
3. Output controls ensure that the processed results are correct and that only authorized personnel have access to the output. Examples of output controls include:
   - reconciling totals to ensure that input totals agree with the output totals
   - uploading output to a secure server location in read-only format
   - printing output on a secure printer with limited access.

Application controls may also be important in enforcing the segregation of incompatible duties, particularly in large organizations.

It is usually difficult for smaller organizations to implement effective application controls unless there are enough employees to make sure that the physical segregation of duties is mirrored by appropriate access restrictions for particular applications.

IT-dependent manual controls

In many situations, the auditor identifies preventive or detective controls that have both manual and automated aspects. These are referred to as IT-dependent manual controls, and consideration must be given to both their manual and automated aspects. For example, suppose management reviews a monthly variance report and follows up on significant variances. Because management relies on the computer-generated report to identify the variances, the auditor also needs to check that there are controls in place to ensure that the variance report is complete and accurate.

When evaluating the completeness and accuracy of computer-produced information, before the auditor can rely on the information, they need to identify the source and the controls that ensure the information is complete and accurate. As illustrated earlier, the client often relies on both application and IT general controls to make sure that any computer-produced information is complete and accurate. If the auditor does not test both the application controls and the ITGCs and determine that the controls are effective (as they relate to particular reports or data), they run the risk of placing undue reliance on reports or data produced by the client's IT system. Auditors need to ensure any evidence they plan to rely on (even if it is in the form of an internal system-generated report) is accurate, complete, and can be relied on. This testing can either be performed directly on the report in question or, alternatively, can be performed on the overall application that produces the report and the relevant ITGCs, which then removes the need to test the actual report.

BEFORE YOU GO ON

1.1 What are the different types of controls?

1.2 What is the difference between an application control and an IT general control?

1.3 Which type of control, preventive or detective, is usually a more efficient control type to test?

PROFESSIONAL ENVIRONMENT

Monitoring a system of internal controls

All companies benefit from an effective system of internal controls because such controls help organizations achieve their goals. They also ensure that if a company is subject to an external financial statement audit, the audit will be carried out more efficiently and effectively.

The Committee of Sponsoring Organizations (COSO) of the Treadway Commission produced an integrated framework on internal control in 1992 following the release of the Treadway Commission's recommendations. The framework provides principles-based guidance for designing and implementing effective internal controls. It is now the most widely used internal control framework in the United States and is adopted by numerous countries and businesses around the world.

COSO recently released further guidance on internal controls, specifically addressing the issue of effective monitoring of a system of internal controls. COSO provided the guidance because it believed some companies were not effectively monitoring their system of internal controls, which meant their auditors needed to do additional testing of the systems at year end.

Companies that monitor their internal controls can identify and correct problems on a timely basis. This means that rather than reacting to problems identified by auditors, company management can be proactive in maintaining the quality of internal controls, potentially avoiding inefficiencies and reducing auditing costs.

Monitoring procedures identified by COSO include:

· periodic evaluation and testing of controls by internal audit
· program of continuous monitoring built into information systems
· analysis of, and appropriate follow-up on, operating reports or metrics that might identify anomalies indicative of a control failure
· supervisory reviews of controls, such as reconciliation reviews, as a normal part of processing
· self-assessments by boards and management regarding the tone they set in the organization and the effectiveness of their oversight functions

- audit committee enquiries of internal and external auditors
- quality assurance reviews of the internal audit department.

Source: Committee of Sponsoring Organizations of the Treadway Commission (COSO) 2010, www.coso.org; COSO, *Guidance on Monitoring Internal Control Systems,* January 2009.

8.2 TECHNIQUES FOR TESTING CONTROLS

2 Understand the different techniques for testing controls.

Tests of controls, described in this section, include enquiry, observation, inspection of physical evidence, and re-performance. Ordinarily, a combination of these testing techniques provides the evidence that the control operated as intended throughout the period in which the auditor wishes to place reliance on it.

Enquiry

This technique involves the auditor asking questions to determine how the control is performed and whether it appears to have been carried out properly and on a timely basis. For example, the auditor may ask the employees who prepare the sales invoices how they determine when to prepare the invoice and how they ensure that the revenue is recorded on a timely basis. They may also ask management how it makes sure revenue is reported correctly and completely at year end.

Observation

This technique involves the auditor observing the actual control being performed. For example, they may observe the preparation of an invoice to determine if the related shipping report has been received. The limitation with this technique is that employees may perform the procedures more diligently when they know they are being observed. Therefore, the evidence gathered applies only to the point of time of the observation.

Inspection of physical evidence

This technique relies on the auditor testing the physical evidence to verify that a control has been performed properly. For example, the auditor may select a sample of invoices to determine if the related shipping document is attached. Also, they may review a sequential listing of invoices and shipping documents issued during the period to determine whether the control routinely detected missing invoices and whether explanations were documented to ensure the exceptions were dealt with appropriately.

Re-performance

This technique involves the auditor re-performing the control to test its effectiveness. For example, the auditor may test the application controls for accessing the billing module to ensure an unauthorized employee is unable to generate invoices (and that an unauthorized attempt to do so is recorded on an exception report).

Cloud 9

Weijing can see that there are several possible tests they could use to test the bank reconciliation and follow-up controls at Cloud 9. In addition to observing Carla and David perform their duties, the auditors could ask them about the process, with particular reference to how they follow up on unusual items. The auditors could inspect the completed bank reconciliation, and they could re-perform the reconciliation. These latter tests would be the most reliable and will be used if Josh decides the bank reconciliation and follow-up of unusual items is a critical control.

Weijing is less sure about how they could test the credit limit checking that is performed within the inventory and sales management system. However, because the process at Cloud 9 is fully automated, Josh explains that one possible test is to feed dummy data into the system to see if sales over a client's credit limit are rejected. Also, they can use computerized audit techniques to interrogate the client's programs and produce reports to diagnose the performance of that part of the program.

BEFORE YOU GO ON

2.1 When would an auditor most likely perform observation and enquiry procedures on a control?

2.2 Name the four different techniques for testing controls.

2.3 Give an example of a situation when inspection of physical evidence might be used to test a control.

8.3 SELECTING AND DESIGNING TESTS OF CONTROLS

The auditor must decide which controls should be selected for testing and how much audit testing must be performed. Both decisions require the auditor to apply a large degree of professional judgement, and the considerations that must be taken into account are explained in the following sections.

3 Explain how to select and design tests of controls.

8.3.1 Which controls should be selected for testing?

As explained above, controls are put in place to prevent or detect errors occurring (or a WCGW from actually going wrong). When the auditor decides to include controls testing in the audit approach, they select those controls that will provide the most efficient and effective audit evidence (that is, evidence that will provide the assurance required that the controls are working). To improve efficiency, the auditor will test only those controls that they believe are critical to their opinion. In other words, they must decide which controls identified for each assertion are likely to be most effective at preventing the WCGWs from occurring or detecting them if they do occur (see table 8.4). The auditor also considers which controls provide reasonable assurance that the controls operated effectively throughout the period of reliance. Deciding which controls to test will be influenced by the types of controls, the frequency at which the controls are performed, and the level of assurance the auditor wants to gain from the controls being designed and implemented effectively. As a general rule, the best controls to test are those that address the WCGWs most effectively with the least amount of testing required (this is an efficient testing strategy). If one control addresses multiple WCGWs, it stands to reason that this control would be selected instead of testing several different controls that each address one of the WCGWs to obtain the same level of assurance that a WCGW had not occurred.

TABLE 8.4 **Identification of WCGW with related assertion and control testing selection**

WCGW	RELATED ASSERTION	CONTROL HAS BEEN IMPLEMENTED	WHAT CONTROL TO TEST
Goods are shipped but not invoiced	C	Use of sequential shipping documents. Monthly reconciliations of missing shipping documents performed.	*Review sequence of shipping documents and reconciliations.*
		Three-way match of order, shipping document, and invoice.	*Trace a sample of shipping documents to the invoice.*
Fictitious sales recorded in accounts.	CE	Approved sales order and shipping document required before invoicing.	*Match invoices and shipping documents to approved sales orders.*
Goods are shipped/ services provided to customers that are a bad credit risk.	V	Credit approval required for all new customers before order forwarded to shipping.	*Select a sample of new customers and review the credit file for evidence of review of credit history and approval.*
		Customer credit limits checked for existing customers before order forwarded to shipping.	*Review aging receivables for customers exceeding credit limits. Review file to determine if special approval documented.*
Receipts are only partially or not at all deposited.	CA	Independent verification of pre-listing of cash and cheques to deposit slip.	*Select a sample and verify pre-listing to deposit slip.*
Cash receipts are credited to the wrong account (fraud or error).	A	Statements are mailed to customers each month.	*Observe mailing of monthly statements to credit customers.*
Errors are made when recording cash receipts.	CEA	Preparation of monthly bank reconciliations.	*Examine bank reconciliations and follow up on reconciling items.*

C = Completeness

E = Existence

A = Accuracy

V = Valuation

Source: Based on CICA C·PEM form 545 "Control design / implementation — Revenues, receivables, receipts," in C·PEM Forms—Audits, April 2010.

8.3.2 How much testing does the auditor need to do?

Once the controls have been selected for testing, the auditor must decide how much testing is to be performed, a decision that is driven by the frequency of the control in question. For example, is the control operating daily, weekly, monthly, or for every transaction processed?

When testing controls, either statistically based sampling techniques (as described in chapter 6) or professional judgement can be used to determine the extent of testing. There are a number of factors to consider. The more assurance the auditor wants from the performance of the controls, the more testing they need to do. That is, if they are intending to reduce control risk to the lowest level possible, they perform more testing than if they are planning to obtain only limited assurance from their testing (and reducing control risk by only a limited amount). The factors to consider when deciding the extent of testing include the following:

- How often the control is performed. The less frequently a control is performed (for example, a control applied monthly compared to a control applied daily), the fewer instances of the control there are to test and therefore the less testing the auditor needs to perform to be satisfied the control is operating effectively.
- The degree to which the auditor intends to rely on the control as a basis for limiting their substantive tests. The greater the degree of intended reliance (that is, the more they intend to rely on the particular control and thereby limit their substantive procedures), the more they test that control to provide the required assurance.
- The persuasiveness of the evidence produced by the control. As discussed earlier, if the performance of a control results in little or no direct evidence that the control operated effectively, the tests of that control—no matter how extensive—may not provide the necessary assurance required. Conversely, if direct evidence of the effective operation of a control is available, the auditor might decide that they need to examine a limited amount of that evidence to be satisfied that it is operating effectively.
- The need to be satisfied that the control operated as intended throughout the period of reliance. When planning audit procedures to test the effective operation of a control, the auditor must consider whether they need evidence from different times during the period of reliance. For some controls they may only need evidence at year end, whereas for most controls they need evidence that the control operated throughout the year.
- The existence of a combination of controls that may reduce the level of assurance needed from any one of the controls. When other controls related to a particular objective or WCGW are also in place and are tested, the level of assurance that might be needed from any one control is not as high as it would be if the auditors were relying solely on a single control.
- The relative importance of the "what could go wrong" questions or statements being considered. Considering the WCGWs and the level of assurance needed to address the WCGWs is a matter of professional judgement and requires the consideration of a number of issues. These include the inherent risk of the transactions or account, the audit assertion being addressed, the volume of transactions subject to the control, the complexity of the transactions, and the materiality of the transactions being processed.

- Other factors that relate to the likelihood that a control operated as intended. In determining the extent of tests of a control, the auditor considers several other factors that affect the auditor's perception of the likelihood that a control operated as intended throughout the period of reliance, including:
  - The competence and integrity of the employee performing the control, the employee's independence from the related processing procedures, the degree to which the employee is supervised, and the extent of employee turnover all contribute to the perception of whether the control operated as intended.
  - The quality of the control environment. The extent of testing is affected by the quality of the control environment, with consideration being given to:
    - the likelihood that a control is bypassed during peak processing periods
    - the potential for management to override a control
    - the extent to which the internal auditors have performed similar or related tests during the year
    - the likelihood in a good control environment that a control will continue to operate as intended throughout the period of reliance.
  - Changes in the accounting system. Where there have been changes in the accounting system, the auditor considers whether a control may have been less effective during the period when the changes were being implemented, and whether the control is still applicable to the new accounting system.
  - Unexplained changes in related account balances. When the client cannot provide satisfactory explanations for fluctuations (or for the absence of expected fluctuations) in the related account balances, the auditor considers whether they need to revise the extent of their tests of controls.
  - The auditor's prior-period experiences with the engagement. The results of the tests in prior audits and the current audit to date affect the perception of risk. If tests in prior audits indicated that a particular control was ineffective, and if there have been no improvements in the control, tests of that control in the current audit are not likely to be useful. Similarly, if in prior audits the tests showed that the control was effective, the expectation of errors would be reduced and, therefore, the tests of controls might be less extensive. The auditor also considers whether the changes in the types or volume of transactions could affect the auditor's expectations.

Even though the factors listed above may reduce the expectation of errors, the auditor's tests of a control need to be sufficiently extensive to provide reasonable assurance that the control operated effectively throughout the period of reliance.

When the control is applied every month, the auditor may decide to test the application of the control in detail for two months and review the remaining 10 months for unusual items. If the control is applied more frequently (say, weekly or daily), the auditor might test more than one application of the control in detail and review a sample of the remaining applications for unusual items.

Tests of preventive controls that are accompanied only by inferential (rather than physical) evidence of their effective operation include, for example, reviewing documents for an initial or signature and re-performing the checking routine itself (for example, if the signature signifies that the price, extensions, and additions have been checked, the auditor checks the price, extensions, and additions). The extent of such tests is a matter of professional judgement, but, generally speaking, large sample sizes are not necessary. Under normal circumstances, a random sample of, say, 25 to 30 items, assuming no control exceptions (that is, deviations) are observed, when combined with the evidence obtained from other audit procedures performed on the related accounts, provides evidence that controls operated as intended (that is, the control was effective). This sample size has been calculated using audit risk tables and a technique called **attribute sampling**, a sampling technique used to reach a conclusion about a population in terms of a rate (frequency) of occurrence. For instance, a sample of cash payments can be examined for signatures that are required as evidence of proper approvals. The number of missing signatures (that is, exceptions) is then used to estimate the overall rate of exceptions for the entire file of payments. Each sample item provides one of only two possible outcomes: the attribute being tested (for example, a signature, price, or recorded balance) is correct or incorrect, present or absent, valid or not valid.

attribute sampling a sampling technique used to reach a conclusion about a population in terms of a rate (frequency) of occurrence

Normally, attribute sampling by itself does not provide a direct estimate of dollar values, such as the dollar amounts of exceptions. That is why attribute sampling is most often used for tests of controls (rather than as a substantive test of account balances). However, by using this sampling technique, the auditor is able to determine with a certain level of confidence (90 percent or more) that the error rate for **control exceptions** is acceptably low; that is, they may not need to perform additional controls testing to reduce control risk further. If the audit objective is to obtain evidence directly about a dollar amount being examined, the auditor generally uses a different sampling technique (such as systematic selection).

control exception an observed condition that provides evidence that the control being tested did not operate as intended

There may be circumstances where more or less testing is carried out. Regardless of the size of the sample, all control exceptions (deviations) (including those that are accompanied by errors) are investigated by the auditor (see section 8.4). The auditor is careful not to dismiss an observed control exception as a random, non-systematic occurrence. Therefore, the detection of one control exception results in the auditor extending the sample size (when the auditor anticipates no further control exceptions will be found), amending the decision to rely on that control, and/or considering whether another control is available that can be substituted for the control being tested (often referred to as a compensating control).

Cloud 9

Talking with Josh about the factors that have to be considered when deciding how much control testing to do helps Weijing appreciate her task. She realizes that her previous understanding of a combined audit strategy was too simple. Gathering evidence about the effectiveness of controls in order to reduce the reliance on substantive testing does not mean that the auditor has to test every control in the same way.

Weijing realizes that if the evidence that would be produced from testing a control is not very persuasive, there is little point in devoting a lot of effort to testing that control. For example, a preventive control that requires a supervisor to authorize a transaction only produces evidence of the presence or absence of a signature, not evidence of whether the supervisor was performing the task of reviewing the transaction effectively. Obtaining plenty of evidence that the supervisor's signature was on the appropriate form will not provide much assurance by itself about the effectiveness of the control.

Also, Weijing is now starting to understand what Josh means by "critical control." Josh wants to know which of the controls identified for each assertion are likely to be the most effective at preventing the WCGWs from occurring or detecting them if they do occur. Josh would like to focus testing on these controls and gather sufficient, appropriate evidence to justify reduced substantive testing.

For example, there are usually several controls designed to prevent or detect errors and misstatements in inventory and sales. In the wholesale sales area at Cloud 9, these controls include signed delivery receipts, policies requiring undelivered goods to be returned to the warehouse at night, and use of a locked shipping cage. Other controls include the use of electronic scanners and matching and authorizing documents in the dispatch and invoicing process. However, despite all these controls, Josh has also identified from his conversation with Carla Johnson that unless the controls over the inventory management software system are tested thoroughly, they will not be able to justify reduced substantive testing. This is because so much of the document matching and authorization depends on the correct operation of the programs.

Application controls

The auditor may decide to rely on application controls identified and evaluated earlier in the audit. The functioning of the application control is tested to determine whether it can be relied on as an effective control. The auditor also tests the operating effectiveness of the control over the period of reliance by one or both of the following methods.

1. Focusing on manual follow-up procedures that support the application control. For example, if the computer prices the invoices using data in the price master file, the application control is a computer-generated exception report listing all sales orders entered for which there are no prices on the master file. The auditor may choose to focus on how the client follows up on these exceptions.

2. Testing controls over program changes and/or access to data files. Here the auditor is testing the ITGCs (as discussed previously). Using the example in (1) above, the auditor may choose to test controls to ensure that all additions, deletions, and changes to the pricing master file are approved.

If these testing strategies are not feasible, the auditor can still rely on application controls by testing them throughout the period of reliance. Using the price master file example above, the auditor may choose to select a sample of invoices from throughout the period and compare the prices to the approved price list instead of just testing at a single point in time.

When the client relies on controls over program changes and/or access to data files (ITGCs), it is efficient for the auditor to test these controls, as they may support reliance on several other application controls. For example, the auditor may decide to do a system-wide test of access to data files for controls that apply to more than one control objective or application.

Regardless of which testing strategy is selected, the auditor establishes a basis for concluding that the underlying processing of data is complete and accurate. The techniques to test controls over program changes and/or access to data files are similar to those used to test manual controls. They usually involve enquiry, observation, and examination of physical evidence. The testing applies to the specific applications of interest (for example, a test of program changes is limited to changes to the sales application only) if it is possible and efficient to do so.

Recognizing that application controls operate in a systematic manner, the auditor may be able to limit their testing of those controls to the significant transaction types. For example, a computerized interest calculation may consistently use the same formula (principal multiplied by an interest rate from a rate master file). Or a computerized edit check will not allow the finalization of payments greater than $100,000 without appropriate authorization. In these examples, the auditor could limit their testing to a "test of one" per transaction type (that is, test one interest calculation or attempt to process a cheque request in excess of $100,000) rather than testing a sample using audit risk tables. This test of one may have been performed as part of the walkthrough, which took place when the auditor gained an understanding of the transaction, the WCGWs, and the controls.

Benchmarking

Benchmarking is an audit testing strategy that can be used to carry forward the benefit of certain application controls testing into future audit periods. It can also assist in reducing or eliminating certain substantive audit procedures in the current and following audit periods.

Benchmarking is based on the premise that a computer will continue to perform any given procedure in exactly the same way until such time as the program (or application) is changed. If the auditor can verify that a given program that executes a process or control has not changed since last tested, they may decide not to repeat certain audit procedures in a subsequent period. This period might extend, for example, from interim through to year end and beyond into future audit periods.

The auditor establishes their benchmark as at a point in time (for example, at an interim date) by performing a test of the application control using normal audit procedures. Then, at a later point in time, they determine that the application has not been changed or modified since they performed their test of the application control. In order to verify that there have been no changes, it may be necessary for the audit team to use a team member with specialist IT assurance skills.

Benchmarking is appropriate when:

- a programmed control can be matched to a defined program within an application (for example, the auditor may be able to benchmark the specific program that performs the invoice extension calculation or interest computation)
- the application is stable (that is, few changes have happened or are expected to happen from period to period)
- a reliable trail of program changes exists (refer to the previous discussion on ITGCs). This record or trail of program changes is used to identify each change that has been made to the application and how these changes might impact the audit approach.

It is a matter of professional judgement as to when it is necessary to re-benchmark an application. Factors to consider in making this assessment are the effectiveness of the ITGCs, the nature and timing of other related tests, and the consequences of errors associated with application controls that are benchmarked. In some cases, the auditor may choose to rely on benchmarked controls from year to year; in other instances, they may choose only to rely on benchmarked controls between interim and year end.

It is worth noting that benchmarking may not be an efficient strategy if the complexity of the application makes it difficult to easily identify and test the function or application the auditor wants to test and rely on. For example, a warranty provision may be based on a calculation performed by an application, which is reliant on many interrelated applications, and the client may not be able to help the auditor identify which application(s) actually performs the calculation. In this situation, it may be more efficient to retest the underlying data or information in the following audit period.

Timing of tests of controls

Tests of controls will usually be carried out at an interim date (that is, before year end). It is preferable to test entity-level controls and ITGCs early in the audit process because the results of this testing could affect the nature and extent of other procedures the auditor plans to perform. For example, if it is found that the ITGCs are not effective and cannot, therefore, be relied on, more extensive testing of application controls will need to be performed if the auditor is planning to rely on applications and computer-generated audit evidence.

The auditor updates their evaluation of controls from the time of their interim procedures through to the year-end date. They update their evaluation by identifying changes, if any, in the control environment and in the controls themselves. If changes are identified, consideration is given to the effect of such changes on their evaluation of the controls. This update is often done via enquiry, observation, and, in some cases, testing the control again at year end. In most cases, a client will not have made significant changes in the control environment or controls between completion of the interim work and year end. When this is the case, and the auditor has noted an effective control environment, they satisfy themselves by enquiry and observation that controls continued to function throughout the remainder of the period without the need for additional detailed tests of controls.

Figure 8.2 illustrates the timing of substantive testing depending on the level of assurance to be obtained from controls testing. As can be seen from the figure, if a large amount of assurance is being gained from controls testing, the work tends to be performed much earlier in the audit process (up to six months before year end). If little or no assurance is being obtained from controls testing, any testing that is being performed will be done at or near year end.

Summary of extent of testing

Table 8.5 suggests how many tests of each control might be performed depending on the frequency of use for the control in question. For example, if it is a monthly control and the auditor wants to obtain a reasonable level of assurance from the controls testing, two controls (for example, a monthly bank reconciliation) would

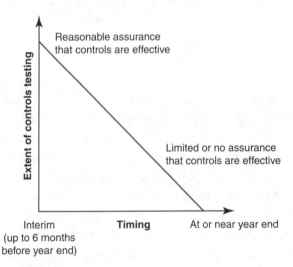

FIGURE 8.2 **Timing of testing**

FREQUENCY	REASONABLE ASSURANCE FROM TESTS OF CONTROLS	LIMITED ASSURANCE FROM TESTS OF CONTROLS
> 1,000 instances	25–30	10–15
Daily	25–30	10–15
Weekly	5	2
Monthly	2	1
Quarterly	2	1
Annually	1	1
Other	Professional judgement	Professional judgement
Application control (effective ITGCs)	1	1
Application control (ineffective ITGCs)	25–30	25–30

TABLE 8.5 **Suggested extent of testing**

be tested from throughout the year. If, however, only a limited level of assurance from the controls testing is required, only one control would be tested from throughout the year.

A limited level of assurance may be planned for when additional evidence from other testing is already available to the auditor (such as evidence from **substantive procedures**— also called **substantive testing** or **tests of details**—which are audit procedures performed to detect material misstatements at the assertion level), or where it may be an efficient strategy to test some controls and to perform some additional substantive procedures. Reasonable assurance may be planned for when there is no additional audit evidence available from other testing, or when it is more efficient to test and rely on controls without performing a significant amount of substantive testing. This is an area that requires a significant level of professional judgement. However, the limited approach is rarely used in practice. Many auditors feel if you are going to perform some tests of controls, you should test as many as necessary to reduce control risk to the lowest level. If the auditor is testing controls, they will want to get as much benefit from it as possible.

substantive procedures (substantive testing or **tests of details)** audit procedures designed to detect material misstatements at the assertion level

Cloud 9

Making sure that testing covers the critical controls and provides sufficient, appropriate evidence of the effectiveness of the controls allows the auditor to reduce the control risk of the related financial statement assertion. Josh and Weijing have a discussion about how they can design their control tests so that they can conclude that each control:
• operated as it was understood to operate
• was applied throughout the period of intended reliance
• was applied on a timely basis
• encompassed all applicable transactions
• was based on reliable information
• resulted in timely correction of any errors that were identified.
   Josh explains that if they can satisfy the above objectives in their design, and no exceptions are found when they perform their tests, the control will be deemed to be effective. If any exceptions are found, they need to perform additional procedures to obtain sufficient assurance, or reduce their reliance on the control. This latter action might require additional testing of another compensating control or increased substantive testing.

8.4 RESULTS OF THE AUDITOR'S TESTING

4   Understand how to interpret the results of testing of controls.

Before the auditor tests the controls, they should review the internal control documentation (as described in chapter 7). This will ordinarily be in the form of narratives, flowcharts, checklists, a questionnaire, or a combination of these. This review should be used to validate the controls testing strategy.

If the tests of controls confirm the auditor's preliminary evaluation of controls (and control risk), the planned substantive audit procedures are not modified. If the test results do not confirm their preliminary evaluation of controls (and control risk), the auditor revises the overall audit risk assessment for the related account and the planned audit strategy (that is, they increase the level of substantive procedures). For example, if the tests of controls indicate that certain controls are not as effective as originally believed or have not functioned as prescribed, and if mitigative (compensating) controls are not available or were not effective, the auditor revises their audit risk assessment (increases control risk), reduces or eliminates the intended reliance, and reduces detection risk by designing more extensive substantive audit procedures (which are intended to detect and estimate the effect of errors in the related significant account balances). As mentioned previously, when a control has not performed as it was intended, it is referred to as a control exception (deviation).

Figure 8.3 illustrates the decision tree or thought process an auditor goes through when assessing the results of their controls testing.

The auditor needs to investigate any control exceptions (deviations) they identify during their testing to find out, to the extent practical, the causes (for example, whether the exceptions may be indicative of a pattern of similar exceptions), the amounts involved, the financial statement accounts affected, and the potential effect on other audit procedures. The auditor is required to document the resolution of any

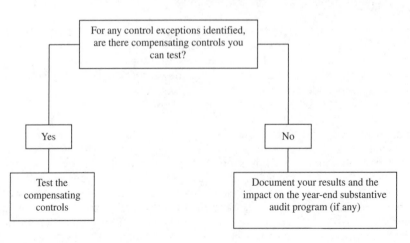

FIGURE 8.3 **Results of testing**

control exceptions (including the impact on the remaining audit approach) and report the control exceptions in a management letter to those charged with governance, as they are considered matters of governance interest in accordance with CAS 260 *Communication with Those Charged with Governance* and CAS 265 *Communicating Deficiencies in Internal Control to those charged with Governance and Management*. (Refer to figure 7.6 in chapter 7.)

If the auditor extends their testing and another control exception is identified, they should change their decision to rely on that control. If another (compensating) control is not available to be substituted for the control being tested, or if it is not considered efficient to continue testing controls, the auditor should update (and potentially increase) the nature, timing, and extent of the planned substantive procedures. That is, the audit strategy is altered and detection risk is reduced. Therefore, if tests of controls indicate the controls are not operating effectively, then control risk must be assessed as high for that assertion. It is not possible to moderate control risk if the controls are only effective some of the time.

In trying to determine whether there is a need for additional detailed tests of controls, the following factors are considered.

- *Results of enquiries and observations.* If, during their enquiries or observations later in the audit process, the auditor identifies that significant changes to processes and controls have occurred, their previous tests of controls may no longer provide a basis for relying on those controls. Therefore, they may need to identify and test other controls, perform additional tests of controls, or increase the level of substantive testing performed at year end. Changes to processes or controls are only significant if they have implications for the continued functioning and effectiveness of controls on which the auditor is relying in the first place.

- *Evidence provided by other tests.* Tests of account balances (substantive testing) can often provide evidence about the continued functioning of controls. For example, when the auditor examines vendors' invoices in support of year-end creditors and expense account balances, they learn whether controls relating to the recording of these transactions continue to function. To the extent that their other audit procedures provide evidence of the effectiveness of controls from the date of interim work to the end of the period under audit, additional tests that otherwise might be necessary can be reduced.

- *Changes in the overall control environment.* An effective entity-level control environment may allow the auditor to limit their tests of controls to enquiry and observation during the period between when they tested the controls (interim) and year end. If they become aware of adverse changes in the overall control environment of the entity, such as a loss of employees and key management who perform key controls and who provide evidence as to the effectiveness of the overall entity control environment, additional tests of controls may be necessary.

BEFORE YOU GO ON

4.1 What does the auditor do when they identify control exceptions?

4.2 Why does the auditor consider the entity's overall control environment when performing controls testing?

4.3 Why does the auditor always investigate control exceptions?

8.5 DOCUMENTING CONCLUSIONS

5 Explain how to document tests of controls.

Once controls have been tested, the auditor documents their work in a working paper. In this working paper, the auditor would ordinarily set out the purpose of the tests of the controls identified. This assists in carrying out the testing by reminding the auditor of their overall purpose in testing the controls. If the auditor identifies any exceptions or issues, they are able to decide if there is an impact on their testing strategy by considering whether the control exception means that the control no longer meets the objective of the test. For example, assume that the control selected for testing is a bank reconciliation, and the objective of the test is to verify that a review by the financial controller occurred on a timely basis. When performing the testing, however, it was noted that while there was evidence of the review (a signature), there was no date, so timeliness could not be verified. Therefore, the auditor is able to conclude that the control operated, but they are not able to conclude that it operated on a timely basis. The auditor would need to determine whether a compensating control should be tested, or whether the timeliness of the review is not critical to the auditor's ability to rely on the bank reconciliation as audit evidence.

The auditor also documents the test performed, the actual controls selected for testing, and the results of the testing. There must be enough detail regarding the controls selected to allow another auditor to review the working paper, re-perform the steps (if necessary), and reach the same conclusion as the auditor who prepared the working paper. The results are often set out in a table to make it easier to review and identify quickly what (if any) exceptions were identified during the testing. Before an overall conclusion is reached for each section of work performed, the results table also assists the person reviewing the working paper to determine if enough work has been performed and if the right conclusion regarding the controls testing has been reached. The working paper should also include a conclusion specific to whether the test results support the overall purpose of the test. This is the documentation standard that is required by CAS 230 *Audit Documentation*.

Regardless of how they prepare their working papers and document their results, the extent of the auditor's documentation will increase as the complexity of the client's operations, systems, and controls increases. Also, the more complex the client's operations and its internal controls, the more experienced the auditor who performs the work needs to be.

Figure 8.4 is an example of a working paper relating to controls testing (this was also included in Chapter 5).

The first part of figure 8.5 overleaf illustrates in a table format the impact of controls testing on the subsequent amount of substantive testing required to be performed. For example, if inherent risk is low and a reasonable level of assurance has been gained from controls testing (that is, controls are operating effectively), the auditor can rely on his or her original control risk assessment and continue to perform a combined audit. This means that the controls tested can be relied on, and less substantive work is required. Therefore, potentially only overall analytical review procedures would need to be performed to reduce detection risk (and audit risk) to an acceptable level to be able to make a conclusion about the significant account assertion. If, however, the auditor has found control deviations, the cause of the deviations and the number need to be assessed. If the number of deviations exceeds a predetermined tolerable rate, the auditor may conclude that no assurance has been obtained from the

FIGURE 8.4 **Example test of control working paper**

EXAMPLE TEST OF CONTROL WORKING PAPER							
Client name: Indigo Ltd.					Year end: December 31, 2011		
Working paper: Cash controls testing							

Purpose of test:

The purpose of this test is to verify that the bank reconciliation control was adequately designed and implemented for the 12 months ending December 31, 2011.

Work performed:

Selected two bank reconciliations from different months, tied the balance as per the bank statement to the bank statement and bank confirmation, tied the balance as per the general ledger to the trial balance, and vouched all reconciling items between the bank statement and the trial balance greater than $50,000 to supporting documentation to ensure valid reconciling items and that the reconciliation had been performed correctly. Ensured the reconciliation had been prepared and reviewed on a timely basis.

Findings/results of testing:

Selected bank reconciliations for the months of April and September 2011. No errors noted in the preparation of the reconciliation. Both were prepared and reviewed within four days of month end. Considered this to be on a timely basis.

Month tested	Balance agreed to bank statement and bank confirmation	Balance agreed to general ledger and trial balance	Vouched deposits >$50,000 to stamped deposit slips and cut-off bank statement	Vouched outstanding cheques >$50,000 to cheque register, cancelled cheque, and cut-off bank statement	Vouched all other outstanding items >$50,000 to supporting documentation	Verified mathematical accuracy	Date prepared and reviewed
April	Y	Y	Y	Y	NA	Y	Prepared May 2, reviewed May 4
September	Y	Y	Y	Y	NA	Y	Prepared October 3, reviewed October 4

Conclusion:

Based on testing performed, the bank reconciliation appears to have been designed, implemented, and operating effectively for the 12 months ended December 31, 2011.

	Prepared by: SEF	Reviewed by: FMC	Index: CI:I

controls testing. In this case, control risk will be assessed as higher than originally planned and the audit strategy may be revised to a primarily substantive approach. This means extensive substantive procedures designed to estimate the dollar value of any error in the balance would need to be performed The second part of figure 8.5 illustrates the same information in a graph format. That is, the higher the level of confidence gained from controls testing, the lower the level of assurance required to be obtained from the substantive procedures in order to form conclusions (a combined audit strategy).

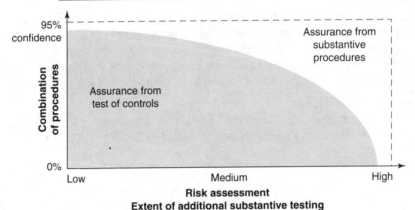

Inherent risk assessment		Reasonable level of assurance from controls testing	Limited level of assurance from controls testing	No assurance obtained from controls testing
	Low	Overall analytical review	Some substantive procedures	Considerable testing
	High	Some substantive procedures	Considerable testing	Extensive procedures focused on estimating errors in the balance

FIGURE 8.5 **Impact Of Controls Testing On Level Of Substantive Testing**

Cloud 9

Josh and the rest of the audit team have finished testing and assessing the controls at Cloud 9. Where necessary, they performed additional testing to investigate the deviations or exceptions discovered during initial testing. They sent their completed working papers to Sharon Gallagher, the audit manager, and Jo Wadley, the partner. The more senior members of the audit team must review the results of the controls testing and judge whether there is sufficient and appropriate evidence to support the decision to continue to use a lower assessed level of control risk approach to the audit.

Josh has been busy over the last few days answering questions from Sharon and the partner about particular aspects of the controls testing, but it now seems that all problems and issues have been resolved satisfactorily. Although the audit team has been concentrating on controls testing, the plans for substantive testing are well advanced and attention now turns to this phase of the audit.

PROFESSIONAL ENVIRONMENT

Audit quality and fees

Who audits the auditors? National Instrument #52-108, issued by the Canadian Securities Administrators, requires the auditors of publicly listed entities to be registered with the Canadian Public Accountability Board (CPAB). It also requires CPAB to inspect these audit firms' compliance with audit quality and auditor independence requirements. Firms with 100 or more reporting issuer clients are inspected annually, those with between 50 and 99 reporting issuer clients are inspected at least once every two years, and those with fewer than 50 reporting issuer clients are inspected at least once every three years. CPAB also reports on the inspection program to better inform firms, the investing public, companies, audit committees, and other interested stakeholders.

Each year, CPAB publishes the results of its most recent inspection program of Canadian audit firms. In its 2010 inspection report, CPAB noted that the current business environment may not be conducive to improving audit quality. This is due to a number of factors, including fee pressure on firms, the uncertain economic outlook, and the transition to new standards. CPAB urges audit firms to maintain their focus on high-quality audits as they address these issues.

CPAB warns that viewing the audit as a commodity, differentiated primarily based on price, has the potential to negatively impact audit quality and the audit profession. Increasing complexity in financial reporting, and the speed with which standards are changing, suggests that more audit effort is required, not less. The demands that certain audit committees are putting on firms to reduce audit fees is also of concern, given the committees' important role in oversight and corporate governance and in helping to ensure the integrity of financial reporting. One of an audit committee's key priorities should be to obtain high-quality auditing services as a means of ensuring that it is effectively executing its responsibilities.

Increased audit fee pressures may also cause firms to reduce their investment in audit quality, including recruiting, training, and retaining senior staff. Looking forward, in five to 10 years, this could result in a shortage of senior, experienced auditors and audit managers who have a sufficient knowledge of business, auditing, accounting, and tax. Furthermore, some firms are choosing to have more routine aspects of the audit done offshore, thereby denying their own staff the opportunity to learn. This, too, has the potential to adversely impact audit quality in the future, as staff will not have been exposed to necessary learning opportunities.

Source: Canadian Public Accountability Board, "Enhancing Audit Quality: Report on the 2010 Inspections of the Quality of Audits Conducted by Public Accounting Firms Subject to CPAB Inspections," April 2011, www.cpab-ccrc.ca/.

BEFORE YOU GO ON

5.1 What level of detail does the auditor need to include in the audit working papers when documenting the results of their controls testing?

5.2 Which auditing standard sets the minimum level of documentation required in the working papers stored in the audit files?

5.3 What is the impact on the extent of required substantive testing if inherent risk is high and no assurance has been obtained from controls testing?

SUMMARY

❶ Identify the different types of controls.

There are four different types of controls: manual, automated (otherwise known as application controls), IT general controls (ITGCs), or a combination of control types referred to as IT-dependent manual controls. Each of these types can be described as either a preventive control or a detective control. Preventive controls, as the name suggests, prevent errors from occurring. Detective controls detect the error after it has occurred and rectify the error on a timely basis.

❷ Understand the different techniques for testing controls.

There are four key techniques used for testing controls: enquiry (questions are asked regarding the operation of the control), observation (the operation of the control is observed to be occurring), inspection (of physical evidence resulting from the performance of the control), and re-performance (when the auditor re-performs the control to test its effectiveness).

❸ Explain how to select and design tests of controls.

The selection of which controls to test is a matter of professional judgement. Deciding which controls to test will be influenced by the control objective, the type of control, the frequency at which the control is performed, and the level of assurance the auditor plans to gain from determining the control is designed and implemented effectively. As a general rule, the best controls to test are those that address the WCGWs most effectively with the least amount of testing required.

The extent of testing of controls (that is, deciding how many to test) is also a matter of professional judgement, although there are sampling techniques available (discussed in chapter 6). The extent of testing is affected by many factors, including how often the control is performed, the degree to which reliance will be placed on the control as part of the audit, the persuasiveness of the evidence produced by the control, the need to be satisfied that the control operated as intended throughout the period of reliance, the existence of a combination of controls that may reduce the level of assurance that might be needed from any one control, the relative importance of the WCGW questions or statements being considered, and any other factors such as the competence of the person carrying out the control, the quality of the control environment, and any changes in the accounting system.

❹ Understand how to interpret the results of testing of controls.

If the controls tested are considered to be effective and can be relied on for the purposes of reducing overall audit risk for a particular significant account and assertion, the level of additional substantive testing required is reduced. If the controls tested are considered to be ineffective and are not able to provide any audit evidence that reduces overall audit risk for a particular significant account and assertion, the level of additional substantive testing that is required is increased.

❺ Explain how to document tests of controls.

The purpose of the test of controls, the selection of controls to test, the results of the controls testing performed, and the conclusion regarding the design and implementation of the controls are all documented in the audit working papers. The working papers are then reviewed by more experienced auditors to determine if sufficient work was performed and if the appropriate conclusion was reached.

KEY TERMS

Attribute sampling, 319

Control activities, 304

Control exception, 319

Controls, 304

Entity-level controls, 304

Internal control, 304

Substantive procedures (substantive testing or tests of details), 323

Tests of controls (controls testing), 305

Transaction-level controls, 304

WCGWs, 305

MULTIPLE-CHOICE QUESTIONS

8.1 The auditor decides which controls to test by considering:
(a) the type of control.
(b) the frequency of the control being performed.
(c) the level of assurance the auditor wishes to gain.
(d) all of the above.

8.2 The purpose of controls is to:
(a) prevent misstatements in the financial statements.
(b) detect misstatements in the financial statements.
(c) support automated parts of a business in the functioning of the controls.
(d) all of the above.

8.3 Which is not a type of control?
(a) automated controls.
(b) substantive controls.
(c) manual controls.
(d) IT-dependent manual controls.

8.4 Detective controls do not include:
(a) management level reviews.
(b) performance indicators.
(c) account coding.
(d) reconciliations.

8.5 ITGCs are important because they:
(a) prevent authorized personnel from having access to data and applications.
(b) impact the effectiveness of both application controls and IT-dependent manual controls.
(c) prevent the reliability of electronic audit evidence.
(d) allow client staff to change computer programs without needing to receive authorization for the change.

8.6 Examples of application controls include:
(a) edit checks.
(b) validations.
(c) calculations.
(d) all of the above.

8.7 Inspection of physical evidence is a control test used by auditors. It:
(a) relies on questioning skills.
(b) is subject to a limitation because employees may be more diligent when they know they are being observed.
(c) relies on testing the physical evidence.
(d) requires the auditor to re-perform the control.

8.8 Which of the following would require the auditor to increase the level of control testing for a particular control?
(a) The control is performed monthly instead of daily.
(b) There are several controls relating to a particular audit objective.
(c) The WCGW addressed by the control is not very important.
(d) A high degree of reliance is to be placed on the control to limit the amount of substantive testing required.

8.9 A major change in the accounting system has taken place during the year. The effect on control testing is that:
(a) the auditor should ensure controls testing is performed for periods both before and after the accounting change became effective.
(b) the auditor can assume the accounting system change was

necessary and has improved the client's controls, so should only test the period following the change.

(c) the auditor can assume the accounting system change was necessary and has improved the client's controls, so should only test the period before the change.

(d) the auditor will not conduct controls testing because obviously the client has thought about making sure the accounting system works well.

8.10 Working papers:

(a) document the purpose of the test of the control identified and the results of the test, including a specific conclusion about whether the test results supported the overall purpose of the test.

(b) are necessary for the junior auditor to keep track of the daily work but are not important to the overall audit.

(c) document the results of the tests but not the purpose of the control selected for testing.

(d) document the purpose of the control selected for testing and the conclusion made by the auditor but not the results of the test.

REVIEW QUESTIONS

8.1 Explain the purpose of (a) preventive controls and (b) detective controls. Why would it be important for an entity to have both types of controls?

8.2 Explain the difference between automated and manual controls.

8.3 Explain the three types of ITGCs. Why are they "general" controls? Why are they important controls?

8.4 What are the four types of tests of controls? Explain them and comment on the reliability of the evidence obtained from each.

8.5 Does an auditor have to test every control? Explain.

8.6 What factors do auditors consider when deciding how much control testing to do?

8.7 Explain the concept of benchmarking and its benefits to the auditor.

8.8 Discuss the concepts of nature, timing, and extent as they relate to controls testing.

8.9 What is the relationship between the results of tests of controls and substantive testing?

8.10 Explain the process of documenting the auditor's conclusions. What must be documented?

PROFESSIONAL APPLICATION QUESTIONS

Basic ★   Moderate ★★   Challenging ★★★

8.1 Performance indicators ★

The audit assistant has been assigned to review performance indicators in the purchasing department of Kentucky Kapers, a manufacturing audit client. The assistant reports to you that he has obtained a copy of reports used by the supervisor in the purchasing department to assess the performance of the purchasing team. The reports include details of orders processed each day, any backlog of orders and the time taken to clear the backlog each week, and overtime requests by staff in the department. The assistant also reports that his discussions with the supervisor reveal that the performance indicators are used to manage the department but are not used for follow-up on unexpected results in the financial reporting system.

Required

Are the performance indicators in the report useful as audit evidence for the financial statement audit? Explain.

8.2 Preventive controls ★★

Alabama Industries manufactures and wholesales small tools. It sells the tools to a large group of regular customers and makes most sales by telephone to this group. Additionally, it receives orders online from its sales team, who sign up new customers within the sales area. In the past, Alabama Industries has had trouble with customers who do not pay their accounts on time. Despite instructing the sales team not to make sales to customers before their creditworthiness has been assessed, sales are still being made to new customers before their limits have been set and to existing customers beyond their credit limit. Also, the economic situation has started to impact Alabama's customers, and management is concerned about the possibility of increasing bad debts.

Required

(a) What sort of preventive control could be used to deal with the problems faced by Alabama Industries? Explain how the control would work.
(b) Assume the preventive control is implemented, and during this year there have been no sales to customers that have taken any customer beyond its credit limit. What are two possible explanations for this that the auditor must consider?
(c) If an auditor finds two sales transactions during the year that are in excess of a customer's credit limit at the time of the sale, what conclusion would the auditor draw from this evidence? What other evidence could the auditor consider before concluding that the preventive control has failed?

8.3 Testing bank reconciliation controls ★★

You are testing the controls over bank accounts for your audit client, Manitoba Ltd. You note that the responsibility for bank reconciliations has changed due to a corporate reorganization halfway through the current financial year. Both the staff member performing the bank reconciliations and the supervisor have changed. You are only able to talk to the current staff member and supervisor because the other staff took voluntary retirement and left the client's employment three months ago.

Required

(a) What techniques are available to you to gather evidence about the bank reconciliations? Explain how you would use each technique and comment on the quality of the evidence obtained from each.
(b) When you ask the employees responsible for bank reconciliations about how they perform the reconciliations, there is a possibility that they will not tell the whole truth about their performance of the reconciliations. Given this, will you bother to ask them? Explain.
(c) Explain the impact of the staff changes on your controls testing program.

8.4 Inventory program controls ★★

Ontario Drapers supplies custom-fitted curtains and blinds to retail customers. It has recently expanded to offer a wide variety of home decorating products through its six stores across the province. After some initial problems with inventory control, it installed a new automated inventory system in April this year. The system replaced another automated system that had been modified so often over the years that the auditor had advised Ontario's management that they did not regard it as reliable. That is, the auditor was unable to rely on the old system sufficiently to assess control risk for inventory as anything less than high.

Required

(a) Explain the normal process an auditor would expect to find in the client's systems governing changes to computer programs. Why is an auditor concerned about program changes?

(b) Ontario Drapers' financial year end is December 31. Does the auditor need to obtain evidence about the performance of the inventory control system from every month in the year or from a sample of months? Explain.

(c) If the auditor conducts tests of the inventory controls at an interim date, is it appropriate to conclude that the controls are still in place at the end-of-period date? Why?

8.5 Control testing results and documentation ★★★

Arne Adams, the audit senior, is reviewing the working papers written by the audit assistant on the audit of Quebec Creepers, a garden nursery and retailer of garden accessories. Arne reads the following description of the results of testing of inventory controls written by the audit assistant:

> The Inventory Manager advises that no changes have been made to the inventory programs during the current financial year. There are no documents on file authorizing program changes, so I conclude the Inventory Manager's statement is true.
>
> The Inventory Manager also advises that management did not attempt to override any controls relating to inventory. There are no memoranda or e-mails from management on file instructing the Inventory Manager to go against procedures, so I conclude the Inventory Manager's statement is true.

The audit assistant concludes that the inventory controls have not been changed or overridden during the financial year, so the results of the interim testing of controls can be relied on.

Required

(a) Examine the statements by the audit assistant. What deficiencies in the testing can you identify?

(b) If the results of testing one control show that the control is not effective, does the auditor have to increase substantive testing? What other options are available to the auditor?

(c) Explain why it is important for the working papers to be completed with sufficient detail for another auditor to understand what has been done. Make a list of the parties who might review the documents.

8.6 Techniques for testing computerized controls ★★★

The sales transactions at Alberta Park, a new audit client, are handled by a software application that is not supported by very detailed documentation. The audit partner requests that the team re-perform some controls to ensure that the software application controls are working as described by Alberta Park's management. The audit software used by the audit team can access the data on the client's files, allowing the use of standard audit procedures.

Required

Provide a list of possible audit procedures that could be used by the audit team to test the controls in the client's sales software application.

Questions 8.7 and 8.8 are based on the following case.

Securimax Limited (Securimax) has been an audit client of KFP Partners (KFP) for the past 15 years. Securimax is based in Waterloo, Ontario, where it manufactures high-tech armour-plated personnel carriers. Securimax often has to go through a competitive market tender process to win large government contracts. Its main product, the small but powerful Terrain Master, is highly specialized, and Securimax does business only with nations that have a recognized, democratically elected government. Securimax maintains a highly secure environment, given the sensitive and confidential nature of its vehicle designs and its clients.

In September 2011, Securimax installed an off-the-shelf costing system to support the highly sophisticated and cost-sensitive nature of its product designs. The new system replaced a system that had been developed in-house, as the old system could no longer keep up with the complex and detailed manufacturing costing process that provides tender costings. The old system also had difficulty with the company's broader reporting requirements.

Securimax's IT department, together with the consultants from the software company, implemented the new manufacturing costing system. There were no customized modifications. Key operational staff and the internal audit team from Securimax were significantly engaged in the selection, testing, training, and implementation stages.

The manufacturing costing system uses all of the manufacturing unit inputs to calculate and produce a database of all product costs and recommended sales prices. It also integrates with the general ledger each time there are product inventory movements such as purchases, sales, wastage, and damaged stock losses.

Securimax's financial year end is December 31.

Source: Adapted from the Institute of Chartered Accountants Australia's CA Program's *Audit and Assurance Exam,* May 2008.

8.7 Understanding types of controls ★★

Required

In relation to the new manufacturing costing system, describe two automated application controls that you would expect to find.

8.8 Assessing control testing results ★★

Required

Discuss the implications of finding evidence that the controls identified in question 8.7 are (a) effective or (b) not effective.

Questions 8.9 and 8.10 are based on the following case.

Fellowes and Associates Chartered Accountants is a successful mid-tier accounting firm with a large range of clients across Canada. During 2011, Fellowes and Associates gained a new client, Health Care Holdings Group (HCHG), which owns 100 percent of the following entities:

- Shady Oaks Centre, a private treatment centre
- Gardens Nursing Home Ltd., a private nursing home
- Total Laser Care Limited (TLCL), a private clinic that specializes in the laser treatment of skin defects

Year end for all HCHG entities is June 30.

You are an audit senior on the Shady Oaks Hospital engagement. Your initial review of the business has highlighted the following significant risks.

1. Payroll expense. Shady Oaks employs, in addition to its full-time staff, a significant number of casual professional, cleaning, and administrative staff. Overtime is often worked on weekends and night shifts due to a shortage of staff. Payment at overtime rates for standard weekend and night shifts has been a common occurrence.
2. Accounts payable. Shady Oaks also has a large number of suppliers for various medical supplies. Paying the supplier twice for the same purchase has been a continuing problem.

8.9 Preventive and detective controls ★★★

Required

For each of the accounts (1 and 2 above) identified to be a significant risk:

(a) determine the key assertion at risk

(b) describe a practical preventive internal control that would directly address the risk

(c) describe a practical detective internal control that Shady Oaks could implement in relation to the risk.

You may wish to present your answer in the form of a table, as follows.

Account at risk	a. Key assertion at risk	b. Preventive internal control	c. Detective internal control
A. Payroll expense: overpayment of overtime			
B. Accounts payable: payments made twice to the same supplier			

8.10 Preventive controls ★ ★ ★

In addition, your business risk assessment procedures indicate there is a risk that payments to suppliers are made prior to goods being received. As part of your evaluation of the potential mitigating internal controls, you note that accounting staff perform the following procedures:

1. A pre-numbered cheque requisition is prepared for all payments.
2. The details on the supplier's invoice are matched to the appropriate receiving report.
3. The details on the supplier's invoice and receiving report are matched to an authorized purchase order.
4. The cheque requisition is stapled to the authorized purchase order, receiving report, and supplier's invoice and forwarded to the appropriate senior staff member for review and authorization.
5. The authorized cheque requisition, together with the supporting documents, is passed to accounts payable for payment.

Required

(a) Identify the key assertion at risk for payables in relation to payments made prior to receipt of goods.
(b) For the control procedures (1) to (5) above for payables:
   (i) Identify the key preventive internal control that directly addresses the risk of payments being made by Shady Oaks to its suppliers before the goods are received.
   (ii) Outline how your choice of the internal control in (i) will prevent payment to suppliers prior to receipt of goods.
   (iii) Design and describe in detail an appropriate test of control that you would use to satisfy yourself that this internal control is effective.

Source: Adapted from the Institute of Chartered Accountants Australia's CA Program's *Audit and Assurance Exam,* December 2008 and March 2009.

8.11 Transaction-level controls over purchases ★ ★ ★

The following procedures are used for EGO Company:

· EGO's purchasing manager approves all purchases above $250. This allows the administrative staff to use the petty cash system to purchase minor items that are needed for the office and the manufacturing plant.
· When a supplier invoice is received, the accounting department matches it to the corresponding purchase invoice and prepares a voucher containing the two documents.
· Vouchers are then reviewed against the outstanding unmatched receiving reports. When the clerk can match a receiving report to a purchase order and a supplier invoice, the voucher is given to the accountant for entry into the purchases journal.
· If there is no receiving report on file, the voucher with supplier invoice and purchase order remains in the unmatched supplier invoice file.
· The purchase order contains a description of the goods, the vendor name, the date of the purchase approval, whether the goods were purchased FOB destination or FOB shipper, and the purchase manager's initials showing her authorization for the purchase.

- When the company receives goods, the receiver prepares a receiving report and forwards it to the accounting department. The accounting department checks the unmatched supplier invoice file, and if there is no corresponding supplier invoice on hand, the receiving report is placed in the unmatched receiving report file.
- The company's accounting system maintains a purchases journal and sub-ledger accounts for all authorized suppliers.

You are conducting an external audit of the company's financial statements and are working at the auditee's office two weeks after year end.

Required

(a) Design a test with *two* audit procedures, using the unmatched supplier invoice file to test at least *one* internal control objective. Specify which objective(s) you are testing, which documents and any other financial records you are using besides the unmatched supplier invoice file, and how your test would verify the objective(s). Do *not* use any analytical procedures.

(b) Design a test with *two* audit procedures, in addition to sample selection, using the unmatched receiving report file to test at least *one* internal control objective. Specify which objective(s) you are testing, which documents and any other financial records you are using besides the unmatched receiving report file, and how your test would verify the objective(s). Do *not* use any analytical procedures.

Source: © CGA-Canada. Reproduced with permission.

8.12 Transaction-level controls over purchases ★ ★ ★

ABC is a company that purchases ski equipment from a European manufacturer and then sells the equipment to stores in eastern Canada. The company's records include pre-numbered shipping and purchasing invoices, a sales journal, a purchases journal, and sub-ledgers for both payables and receivables.

All customers have a predetermined credit limit that is noted in their files. If a customer's order exceeds the authorized credit limit, the credit manager must approve the sale; otherwise, the sales clerk enters and approves the order for processing. Access to the company's order-entry system requires a password so that all entries can be tracked. Approved orders are received in the warehouse by one of the shipping supervisors, who assigns each order to one of the 10 shipping clerks. The shipping clerk then selects the merchandise and packages it for shipping. The clerk also prepares the shipping order, which is checked by the shipping supervisor before the merchandise is loaded into a delivery truck. The shipping supervisor enters the shipments at the end of each day so that the sales department can track the orders in case of customer queries. The accounting department receives a report each day of goods shipped and purchased goods received.

Required

For each of the following questions, specify which audit procedure you intend to use, such as tracing, vouching, observing, scanning, and so on.

(a) Design an audit program of *three* specific procedures to test that all purchases have been recorded.

(b) Design an audit program of *three* specific procedures to test that all receivables are real. Do not use confirmations.

Source: © CGA-Canada. Reproduced with permission.

8.13 Transaction-level controls over sales ★ ★ ★

Jintian Clothing Ltd. manufactures sportswear and sells it to large department stores in western Canada. The company records sales in a sales journal. When a customer orders merchandise, a sales clerk prepares a sales invoice. The credit manager must approve all sales to new customers, and a record is kept of all approved customers with their credit limit, as established by the credit manager. The company manufactures several styles of sportswear, and each item is listed in a catalogue with the price updated quarterly.

Sales are not recorded until the goods are shipped. When the goods are shipped, the shipping clerk prepares a bill of lading in triplicate, with one part retained in shipping, one part accompanying the shipment, and one part forwarded to accounting. The accounting department matches the bill of lading to the sales invoice, records the sale, and adjusts the inventory records. All documents are pre-numbered.

Required

(a) Prepare an audit plan with two audit procedures, other than sample selection, to test that all sales at Jintian Clothing have been recorded. Do not use analytical procedures.

(b) Prepare an audit plan with two audit procedures, other than sample selection, to test that the sales at Jintian clothing are correctly valued at Jintian Clothing. Do not use analytical procedures.

(c) Prepare an audit plan with two audit procedures, other than sample selection, to test that sales at Jintian clothing are real. Do not use analytical procedures. State the objective being tested.

Source: © CGA-Canada. Reproduced with permission.

8.14 Identifying preventive and detective controls ★ ★   ❶

Required

For each of the following controls:

(a) identify whether it is preventive or detective, and

(b) indicate whether it relates to the control objective of authorization.

1. The computerized accounting program will not allow a sale to be processed if a customer has exceeded its credit limit.

2. The computer checks the account coding on each purchase order against a table of valid account numbers, and then performs various logic tests.

3. Bank reconciliation and follow-up is conducted of unexpected outstanding items (such as unexpected or large deposits not yet cleared by the bank and cheques presented by the bank but not recorded in the general ledger).

4. Sales invoices are automatically priced using a master pricing file.

5. The computer performs a daily comparison of quantities shipped to quantities billed. If differences are revealed, a report is generated for review and follow-up by the billing supervisor.

6. Amounts cannot be paid to employees without first matching a valid social insurance number to the employee master file.

7. Quarterly reviews are conducted of credit balances in accounts receivable to determine their causes.

8. The sales manager reviews daily shipments, total sales, and sales per unit shipped.

Cases

8.15 Integrative Case Study—Farmco ★ ★ ★

Farmco is in the agricultural industry and has five branches located in Saskatchewan. Farmco's year end is June 30. Farmco is well established and has been profitable for many years. It is privately owned, and its inventory and receivables turnovers and debt to equity ratio are all comparable to industry averages.

Half of Farmco's revenue is derived from the sale of animal feed supplements and animal health products. This revenue is earned fairly evenly throughout the year. The products are purchased from 20 regular suppliers, and another 20 suppliers are used on an occasional basis. Sales are roughly equal at Farmco's five locations, and each location normally keeps one month's inventory of these products on hand. The credit terms that the feed division's suppliers allow Farmco are varied, but most suppliers require payment from Farmco in 30 days, with some offering small discounts for early payment. The credit terms Farmco offers its feed division customers are net 30, 2/10. The other half of Farmco's revenue is from the sale of fertilizer and herbicides. This revenue is very seasonal, with most fertilizer sales occurring between mid-March and mid-May, and most herbicide sales in May and June.

The fertilizer is delivered directly from the manufacturer to the customer by Farmco trucks, so no inventory is kept on hand, except for the occasional truckload of product in transit. By year end (June 30), fertilizer sales are complete. Farmco purchases all fertilizer from one supplier. Any herbicides that remain unsold at the end of the season cannot be kept for the next year because they expire, so any amounts on hand on June 15 are returned to the supplier. This is the normal industry procedure.

The herbicides are purchased from three different suppliers. The credit terms for the fertilizer and herbicide division's customers are quite different from the credit terms for the feed division's customers. Fertilizer and herbicide customers can get a substantial discount for placing and paying for orders early. However, many customers prefer to take advantage of another option Farmco offers, which is to pay interest on unpaid balances and then pay for their purchases in October, after crops have been harvested. Farmco receives the same credit terms from its fertilizer and herbicide suppliers, and pays them when cash is received from its own customers.

The five branch managers and one company sales representative report to the general manager. The general manager reports to the president of Farmco's parent company, who lives in Regina. Management team meetings, attended by the parent company's president, are held quarterly, and branch revenue and profits are compared in detail. The managers receive an annual bonus based on the net income before taxes of their branch, and the general manager and the controller receive bonuses based on Farmco's overall net income.

The accounting system—acquisitions and expenditures cycle

At Farmco's head office, the full-time accounting staff consists of the following people:

- Joan (the controller)
- Ernesto (full-time senior accountant)
- Wendy (a temporary accounting assistant who is hired from March to August to deal with the extra work required by the seasonal sales of fertilizers and herbicides)

Each of the five branches also has one office administrator, who handles mainly accounts receivable and general office duties.

All purchases are made using a purchase order system. Branch managers order products directly from the approved suppliers using pre-numbered purchase orders, one copy of which is sent to the head office when the order is placed. Ernesto files these purchase orders numerically until the supplier's invoice is received.

When goods are received, the branch's warehouse supervisor prepares a pre-numbered receiving report, signs it, and sends it with any delivery documents to head office, where Ernesto files it numerically. Once a month, Ernesto reviews the purchase orders and receiving report files, and follows up on any missing numbers.

Suppliers' invoices are normally sent directly to head office, where Ernesto matches them with the signed purchase order and receiving report, checking the supplier's calculations and initialling the invoice to note that he has done so. He then posts the payable invoice. The accounts payable system requires that the due date and any discounts available are entered when the invoice is posted. Once a week, Ernesto runs a cheque requisition listing, which is a list of payables due that week. Joan reviews the listing and initials all that are to be paid. Ernesto then prepares the cheques, attaching the supplier's invoice, purchase order, and receiving report to each cheque. During the busy months, Wendy helps out with all of these tasks, mainly focusing on the fertilizer and herbicide accounts, but available to help wherever asked to.

The cheques, together with the supporting documentation, are routed to Joan and the general manager for signing. Joan initials each supplier invoice before signing the cheque. The general manager double-checks the purchase order for price and for branch manager approval, then initials the purchase order before signing the cheque.

Each month, Joan prepares the bank reconciliation, which is reviewed and initialled by the general manager. Accrued liabilities are recorded only at year end, and Ernesto and Joan have divided responsibility for these calculations and entries.

Required

(a) Identify *four* specific factors that would either increase or decrease the inherent risk for Farmco's accounts payable and/or accrued liabilities. State whether the factor would create an increase or decrease.

(b) State your conclusion on the risk level.

(c) Identify *four* internal control objectives that appear to be met for the acquisition and expenditure cycle; describe *one* specific control procedure to meet each of the objectives identified; and indicate how the auditor would test the control(s).

Source: © CGA-Canada. Reproduced with permission.

CASE STUDY—CLOUD 9

Answer the following questions based on the information presented for Cloud 9 in Appendix B of this book and in the current and earlier chapters. You should also consider your answers to the case study questions in earlier chapters.

Effective internal controls at the transaction level are designed to prevent or detect material misstatements that could occur within the flow of transactions. In the case study assignment in chapter 7, you were required to identify potential misstatements and affected financial statement assertions within the sales to cash receipts process for wholesale sales.

Required

(a) Use your worksheet from the case study assignment in chapter 7 to complete this part of the assignment. In column four, include the transaction-level internal controls Cloud 9 has implemented to prevent and/or detect potential errors.

(b) In designing the audit strategy, auditors should consider the effectiveness of the client's internal control structure, thereby determining the control risk. An auditor should perform a preliminary assessment of control risk in order to be confident that they can use a controls-based approach to the audit strategy. A controls-based strategy is one in which the internal controls of a significant process are tested and proven to be effective, which means they can be relied on to reduce the level of substantive testing needed.

If internal controls are tested and proven to be operating effectively, the auditor can reduce the control risk of the related financial statement assertion. This method of testing controls can reduce the number of substantive procedures to be performed or can allow substantive testing to be performed prior to year end.

When designing control tests, consider whether there will be sufficient evidence that the control:

· operated as it was understood to operate

· was applied throughout the period of intended reliance

· was applied on a timely basis

· encompassed all applicable transactions

· was based on reliable information

· resulted in timely correction of any errors that were identified.

Based on the preliminary assessment of Cloud 9's control environment obtained in earlier procedures, the audit team has decided to test controls over the sales to cash receipts process. It is expected that there will be no deficiencies in the transaction-level internal controls.

Josh has partially completed the testing for selected controls over the sales/receivables and cash receipts processes. He has asked you to complete the testing for him. All information has been provided by the client (refer to Appendix B of this book). Document your findings on the workpapers Josh has started (see tables 8.6 and 8.7), and then conclude with your assessment on the overall effectiveness of the controls tested.

TABLE 8.6 **Cloud 9 controls testing—sales/receivables process as at December 31, 2012**

	SALES INVOICE #	DATE	CUSTOMER NAME	SALE AMOUNT (EXCL. HST)	INVOICE MATCHES SHIPPING NOTE (A)	SHIPPING NOTE #	SHIPPING SUPERVISOR AUTHORIZATION (B)
1	124874	1/14/2012	David Jones—Moose Jaw	645.87	✔	D00124874	✔
2	125048	1/23/2012	Foot Locker—Ottawa	745.21	✔	D00125048	✔
3	125324	2/7/2012	Rebel Sport—Vancouver Island	905.46	✔	D00125324	✔
4	125542	2/16/2012	Rebel Sport—Sunshine Coast	517.32	✔	D00125542	✔
5	125987	3/2/2012	Myer—Moncton	675.28	✔	D00125987	✔
6	126067	3/10/2012	Dick's Sports—St. John's	367.96	✔	D00126067	✔
7	126845	4/8/2012	Foot Locker—Regina	781.62	✔	D00126845	✔
8	127111	4/27/2012	Running Shop—Calgary	457.24	✔	D00127111	✔
20							
21							
22							
23							
24							
25							

Note: For the purposes of this case study, sample tests 9 to 19 have been removed. There were no exceptions noted in the results.

Aim: To test selected controls over the sales and receivables process.

Sample: We randomly selected 25 sales invoices from the entire year.

(a) To complete this test, we matched the sales invoice to the shipping note, ensuring it was signed by the customer.

(b) We used the shipping note reference number in order to recall the online authorization screen. We noted the passcode entered by the shipping supervisors, which agreed with the passcode listings obtained by the IT manager.

TABLE 8.7 **Cloud 9 controls testing—cash receipts process as at December 31, 2012**

	DATE	TOTAL POSTED TO TRADE RECEIVABLES	TOTAL BANK DEPOSIT	EVIDENCE OF REVIEW
1	1/8/2012	10,548.45	10,548.45	✔
2	1/18/2012	9,587.37	9,587.37	✔
3	2/15/2012	11,486.82	11,486.82	✔
4	2/27/2012	7,456.24	7,456.24	✔
5	3/11/2012	5,836.08	5,836.08	✔
6	3/19/2012	8,012.74	8,012.74	✔
7	4/4/2012	8,753.91	8,753.91	✔
8	4/22/2012	9,687.45	9,687.45	✔
20				
21				
22				
23				
24				
25				

Note: For the purposes of this case study, sample tests 9 to 19 have been removed. There were no exceptions noted in the results.

Aim: To test selected controls over the cash receipts process.

Sample: We randomly selected 25 working days from the entire year in order to test the reconciliation of daily bank receipts to trade receivables.

Document the conclusion of the controls testing.

Using the results of your controls testing, assess the control risk for the following assertions and write your conclusions in the worksheet in table 8.8. Use the information you provided in the worksheet completed for part (a) to focus your controls testing on the significant assertions.

TABLE 8.8 **Cloud 9 controls testing conclusions**

ACCOUNT ASSERTION	CONTROL RISK	EXPLANATION
Sales—occurrence		
Sales—completeness		
Sales—measurement		
Trade receivables—existence		
Trade receivables—completeness		
Trade receivables—valuation		
Cash—existence		
Cash—completeness		

RESEARCH QUESTION 8.1

Explain the differences between an audit of internal controls as required by section 404 of the U.S. Sarbanes–Oxley Act 2002 and the testing of internal controls for the purposes of expressing an opinion on the financial statements as mandated by CAS 315. Refer to the standard and legislation in your answer.

SOLUTIONS TO MULTIPLE-CHOICE QUESTIONS

1. d, 2. d, 3. b, 4. c, 5. b, 6. d, 7. c, 8. d, 9. a, 10. a.

CHAPTER 9

Execution of the audit–performing substantive procedures

LEARNING OBJECTIVES

After studying this chapter you should be able to:

1 define substantive audit procedures

2 understand the link between the audit risk model and the nature, timing, and extent of substantive procedures

3 provide examples of different substantive audit procedures

4 explain the different levels of audit evidence obtained when performing substantive procedures

5 describe the documentation of the conclusions reached as a result of performing substantive procedures.

AUDITING AND ASSURANCE STANDARDS

CANADIAN	INTERNATIONAL
CAS 200 *Overall Objectives of the Independent Auditor and the Conduct of an Audit in Accordance with Canadian Auditing Standards*	ISA 200 *Overall Objectives of the Independent Auditor and the Conduct of an Audit in Accordance with International Standards on Auditing*
CAS 240 *The Auditor's Responsibilities Relating to Fraud in an Audit of Financial Statements*	ISA 240 *The Auditor's Responsibilities Relating to Fraud in an Audit of Financial Statements*
CAS 315 *Identifying and Assessing the Risks of Material Misstatement Through Understanding the Entity and Its Environment*	ISA 315 *Identifying and Assessing the Risks of Material Misstatement Through Understanding the Entity and Its Environment*
CAS 500 *Audit Evidence*	ISA 500 *Audit Evidence*
CAS 501 *Audit Evidence—Specific Consideration for Selected Items*	ISA 501 *Audit Evidence—Specific Considerations for Selected Items*
CAS 505 *External Confirmations*	ISA 505 *External Confirmations*
CAS 520 *Analytical Procedures*	ISA 520 *Analytical Procedures*
CAS 530 *Audit Sampling*	ISA 530 *Audit Sampling*

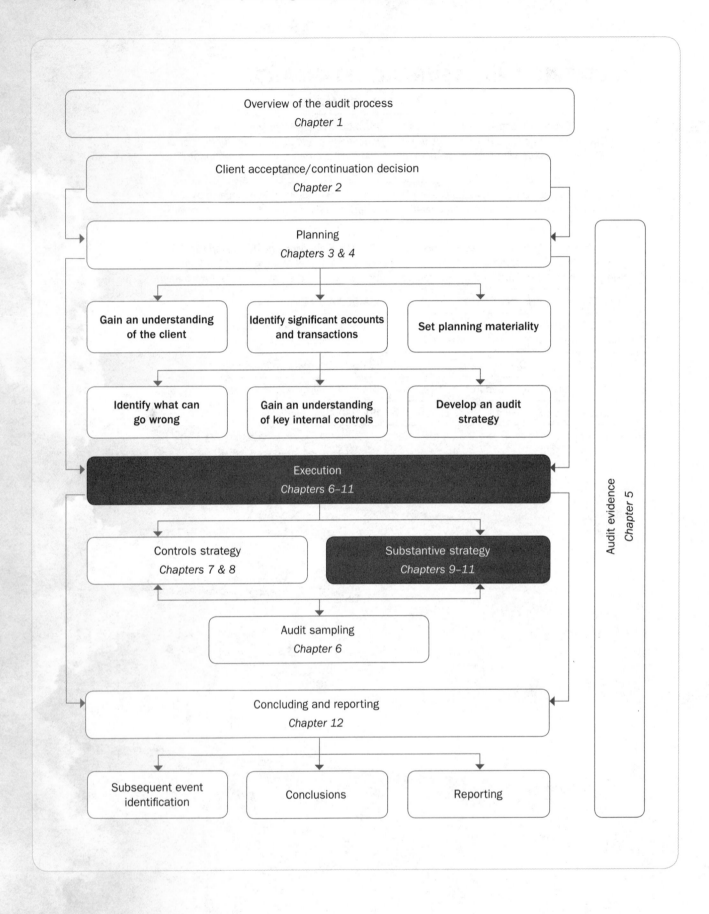

Cloud 9

Suzie Pickering is the clothing and retail industry specialist on the Cloud 9 Ltd. (Cloud 9) audit. Suzie is mentoring Ian Harper, a junior member of the audit team, and they are working together on the detailed substantive audit program.

Ian remembers that Suzie used analytical procedures in the early planning phase and that she explained to him how useful they could also be in the testing phase. Ian suggests that they plan to rely extensively on analytical procedures for Cloud 9's substantive tests. He is very enthusiastic and wants to put analytical procedures in the plan for all transaction cycles and major balances because he believes that analytical procedures will help keep the cost down and help the team bring the audit in on budget. Suzie is more cautious. Although she definitely plans to use some analytical procedures, she knows they will also need other types of tests.

"Why?" asks Ian. "How will I know when to use only analytical procedures? What other tests do we need?"

AUDIT PROCESS IN FOCUS

Finding an appropriate combination of audit procedures to minimize an engagement's audit risk at an acceptable cost to the auditor is a constant challenge. The purpose of this chapter is to describe the audit execution process, often referred to as "performing substantive procedures." The overall objective of substantive procedures is to supplement controls testing the auditor may have performed in order to determine that the underlying accounting records are materially correct and reconcile to the financial statements on which the auditor will ultimately form an opinion (further discussion on the overall conclusion of the audit is in chapter 12).

The types of substantive procedures discussed in this chapter include analytical procedures, tests of key items, representative sampling, tests of underlying transactions and data, and the use of computers to assist in performing substantive procedures.

We will explain the link between the audit risk model and the nature, timing, and extent of substantive procedures. This link helps in the preparation of the audit program. We will also describe the levels of audit evidence the auditor can obtain from the various substantive procedures they have available to select from, and we will explain how to conclude that the overall account balance or disclosure being audited is not materially misstated.

9.1 OVERVIEW OF SUBSTANTIVE PROCEDURES

In this section we discuss the link between audit risk, assertions, and substantive procedures, and we define substantive procedures in detail.

9.1.1 Substantive procedures and assertions

As discussed in previous chapters, the nature, timing, and extent of audit procedures are determined in response to the risk assessment for each **significant account** and assertion using the formula for **audit risk** (that is, the risk that an auditor expresses an inappropriate audit opinion when the financial statements are materially misstated).

❶ Define substantive audit procedures.

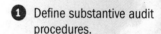

significant account an account or group of accounts that could contain material misstatements based on their materiality and/or relationship to identified inherent and financial statement risks

$$AR = IR \times CR \times DR$$

where:

AR = Audit risk

IR = Inherent risk

CR = Control risk

DR = Detection risk

FIGURE 9.1 **Audit risk model**

audit risk the risk that an auditor expresses an inappropriate audit opinion when the financial statements are materially misstated

professional judgement the auditor's professional characteristics such as their expertise, experience, knowledge, and training

inherent risk the susceptibility of the financial statements to a material misstatement without considering the internal controls

control risk the risk that a client's system of internal controls will not prevent or detect a material misstatement

detection risk the risk that the auditor's testing procedures will not be effective in detecting a material misstatement

This determination requires the use of **professional judgement**. Figure 9.1 contains the audit risk model introduced in chapter 4.

Inherent risk is the risk of a misstatement occurring irrespective of any controls management may put in place. These risks tend to be driven by the nature of the significant account or business that the client is in. There is no way for the auditor to influence the inherent risk of an account or assertion.

Control risk is assessed as high when there are no internal controls that the auditor can test or rely on (or when there are internal controls but they cannot be tested and relied on). Control risk is assessed as low when there are good internal controls in place that have been designed and implemented effectively to reduce an identified risk, and when the auditor has been able to test the controls and verify their operating effectiveness throughout the period subject to audit. (Control risk and controls testing were discussed in detail in chapter 8.)

The combination of inherent risk and control risk, the risk of material misstatement as described in CAS 200 *Overall Objectives of the Independent Auditor and the Conduct of an Audit in Accordance with Canadian Auditing Standards)* determines the level of **detection risk** (that is, the risk that the auditor's testing procedures will not detect a material misstatement) that the auditor is willing to accept to be able to conclude that the financial statements are not materially misstated. There is an inverse relation between the auditor's assessed risk of material misstatement and detection risk. Detection risk is reduced or increased in direct proportion to the amount of substantive testing performed. For example, if the combined inherent risk and control risk is high (that is, the client is in a high-risk industry and a particular assertion of a significant account has a higher chance of being materially misstated because there are no controls in place and no controls have been tested), the amount of detection risk the auditor is likely to accept will be low, so significant substantive procedures will be necessary to reduce the detection risk. If the combined inherent risk and control risk are low (that is, the client is in a low-risk industry and a particular assertion of a significant account has a lower chance of being materially misstated because there are controls in place), the auditor will likely accept a higher amount of detection risk, and only a small number of substantive procedures will be necessary to reduce the detection risk.

Figure 9.2 shows how the assessment of inherent risk and control risk impacts on the amount of substantive testing required to reduce detection risk to an acceptable level.

As discussed in previous chapters, the risk assessments discussed in this section must be performed at the assertion level as well as at the financial statement level.

Control risk assessment

		Low	Medium	High
		Controls tested extensively and able to be relied on	Limited controls testing, and they are not to be relied on	No controls tested and no assurance from controls
Inherent risk assessment / Low	Lower risk of material errors if no controls in place	Few substantive procedures required	Some substantive procedures required	Considerable substantive procedures required
Inherent risk assessment / High	Higher risk of material errors if no controls in place	Some substantive procedures required	Considerable substantive procedures required	Extensive substantive procedures required

FIGURE 9.2 **Linkage between inherent risk, control risk, and detection risk**

Figure 9.3 gives an example of this risk assessment by assertion using accounts receivable. Chapter 5 introduced and defined each of the audit assertions, as outlined in CAS 315 *Identifying and Assessing the Risks of Material Misstatement Through Understanding the Entity and Its Environment*. They are reproduced in table 9.1 and grouped to show the assertions that have common objectives.

Table 9.1 illustrates how the objective of each assertion relates to the particular type of account or disclosure. For example, the auditor needs to verify that sales transactions recorded in the income statement occurred and relate to the entity (the occurrence assertion). Those same sales transactions flow through to the trade receivables balance in the balance sheet, and the auditor needs to verify that the balance of trade receivables as at year end exists and that the client holds the rights to those receivables (the existence assertion, and the rights and obligations assertion). The auditor then needs to verify that the balances disclosed in the financial statements as sales revenue and trade receivables occurred and relate to the entity

TABLE 9.1 **Audit assertions**

ASSERTIONS ABOUT CLASSES OF TRANSACTIONS AND EVENTS	ASSERTIONS ABOUT ACCOUNT BALANCES AT YEAR END	ASSERTIONS ABOUT PRESENTATION AND DISCLOSURE
Typically *income statement* accounts	Typically *balance sheet* accounts	*Disclosures* made in the financial statements
Occurrence	Existence	Occurrence
	Rights and obligations	Rights and obligations
Completeness	Completeness	*Completeness*
Cut-off		
Accuracy		Accuracy and valuation
Classification	*Valuation and allocation*	Classification and understandability

ACCOUNT ASSERTION	INHERENT RISK	CONTROL RISK	OVERALL RISK ASSESSMENT	DETECTION RISK	AUDIT APPROACH
Accounts receivable—valuation	High	High	High	Low	Substantive approach
Accounts receivable—rights and obligations	Low	Low	Low	High	Combined audit approach
Accounts receivable—completeness	Low	Low	Low	High	Combined audit approach

FIGURE 9.3 **Example of accounts receivable risk assessment**

(the occurrence assertion, and the rights and obligations assertion). Figure 9.3 gives an example of an assessment by assertion of inherent and control risk for accounts receivable.

It is clear from Table 9.1 that testing performed on sales revenue transactions will also provide evidence on trade receivables in the balance sheet and in the financial statements disclosures; however, additional testing will still be needed on the trade receivables balance regarding the other assertions not addressed by this example (such as testing the valuation assertion).

Do not assume that audit assertions across all three categories are the same. For example, "classification" in the income statement is not exactly the same as "classification and understandability" in the financial statements. Classification as it relates to transactions requires verification that transactions and events have been recorded in the proper accounts (that is, within the general ledger). Classification and understandability as they relate to the financial statement disclosures require verification that financial information included in the financial statements is appropriately presented and described, and that disclosures are clearly expressed. This is slightly different from the first audit assertion discussed, as the first assertion is focused on the transaction being captured in the correct general ledger account. The second assertion discussed focused on the information being presented, described in the notes, and disclosed correctly and clearly. To ensure that this audit assertion is met, the auditor must ensure that the right account(s) in the general ledger are summarized, presented, described in the notes to the accounts, and disclosed in the financial statements in accordance with an applicable accounting framework (such as International Financial Reporting Standards or ASPE).

It is also important to note that when determining the substantive procedures to be performed, the auditor will consider the nature of the account, and the key assertions at risk. For example, usually the auditor is concerned with an overstatement of the asset accounts; therefore, the procedures performed will generally focus on whether the assets exist and if they are appropriately valued. Conversely, for liability accounts, the auditor is most concerned with an understatement, so the auditor focuses on the completeness assertion, to ensure that all liabilities have been recorded.

Cloud 9

Suzie emphasizes to Ian that their testing must respond to the risk of material misstatement at the assertion level. For each assertion, the audit team determines the level of detection risk, which is based on the inherent risk assessment and the results of the control testing, which is used to establish the level of control risk. The auditors also have to consider a range of practical factors, such as constraints on timing and the complexity of the client's systems.

"Analytical procedures are always useful, but the decision to use analytical procedures and/or other substantive procedures must consider risk and practical factors," she says. "We have to decide what an acceptable level of detection risk is, and how to achieve it, for every assertion about transactions, account balances, and disclosures."

9.1.2 Definition of substantive procedures

Substantive procedures are designed to obtain direct evidence of the completeness, accuracy, and validity of data, and the reasonableness of the estimates and other information contained in the financial statements. Substantive procedures include inspection, observation, enquiry, confirmation, recalculation, re-performance, and analytical reviews. These procedures were introduced in chapter 5. They are also referred to as **substantive testing** or **tests of details**.

The number of substantive tests performed, and their timing, are influenced by several factors. The most important factor, described in section 9.1.1, is the overall risk assessment for the item being tested. Before making this assessment, the auditor will have performed planning procedures and controls testing (including testing of any controls that the auditor has identified and intends to rely on). The results of these planning and interim procedures allow the auditor to make an overall assessment as to how much detection risk still exists before any substantive testing is performed. The auditor then designs what they believe are appropriate substantive audit procedures that will allow material errors and exceptions to be identified and rectified before an overall conclusion is made. These procedures are documented in what is usually referred to as the **audit program**. The audit program typically includes a detailed listing of the audit procedures to be performed during the planning, interim, and year-end stages. The program should include enough detail to enable the auditor to understand the nature, timing, and extent (or scope) of testing required. It describes the controls testing (as detailed in chapter 8) as well as the resulting substantive procedures (as detailed in this chapter). Examples of typical substantive procedures for common significant accounts are included in chapters 10 (balance sheet accounts) and 11 (income statement accounts).

There are several other factors (over and above the audit risk assessment) that influence how much (extent) and when (timing) substantive procedures are performed. These include the following.

- The nature of the test. Some tests lend themselves more easily to testing during the year-end visit as opposed to during the interim audit visit(s). For example, it is easy to vouch prepayment amounts to their supporting documentation (that is, the invoices that were paid during the year) before year end; in contrast, verifying the calculation of the split between the amount to be recognized as a prepayment and the amount to be expensed in the income statement is easier to do at or after year end.

substantive procedures (substantive testing *or* tests of details) audit procedures designed to detect material misstatements at the assertion level

audit program a detailed listing of the audit procedures to be performed, with enough detail to enable the auditor to understand the nature, timing, and extent of testing required

- The level of assurance necessary. If you want reasonable assurance, rather than just moderate assurance, you will have to obtain more evidence from substantive procedures in order to reach a conclusion.
- The type of evidence required. For example, are the procedures designed to provide persuasive, corroborative, or minimal audit evidence? (These concepts are discussed further in section 9.4).
- The complexity of the client's data capturing systems. The more complex the systems, the more complex and sophisticated the substantive audit procedures need to be.

It is ordinarily more efficient to test and rely on controls than to carry out substantive procedures; however, there are situations when this may not be possible or practicable. In these situations, the auditor will need to perform extensive substantive procedures to provide sufficient audit evidence to reach a conclusion. This is often the case when auditing smaller businesses that do not have appropriate segregation of duties, or that may not have internal controls in place for the entire period of reliance.

The types of procedures used to reduce detection risk to an acceptable level consist of key item testing, representative samples, other tests of details, and analytical procedures. These are described in more detail in section 9.3.1. When controls are tested and determined to be effective, the auditor may address any residual detection risk by using substantive analytical procedures. These are described in more detail in section 9.3.2.

The auditor must use professional judgement to decide whether the substantive audit procedures start with analytical procedures and are then supplemented with additional procedures as necessary, or whether to begin with tests of details, including key item testing, and to use analytical procedures after enough other substantive procedures have been performed.

By using a combination of techniques, the auditor is able to perform substantive procedures that, when coupled with any other audit evidence obtained during the planning and interim phases of the audit, will provide sufficient and appropriate audit evidence to enable the auditor to conclude both at the significant account level and overall at the financial statement level.

It is worth noting that there are certain substantive procedures that are normally performed. These include sending bank confirmations, observing inventory counts (CAS 501 *Audit Evidence—Specific Consideration for Selected Items*), confirming receivables balances (CAS 505 *External Confirmations*), and examining material journal entries and other adjustments of audit importance during the course of preparing the financial statements (CAS 240 *Auditor's Responsibilities Relating to Fraud in an Audit of Financial Statements*).

Cloud 9

Ian is starting to realize that the standards of professional practice would not allow him to rely exclusively on analytical procedures. Cloud 9 has significant inventory balances (around 25 percent of total assets) and receivables (more than 40 percent of total assets), so the auditors will need to gather persuasive evidence about the existence, valuation, and rights and obligations assertions for these accounts. Procedures such as confirming receivables balances and observing inventory counts are definitely going to be included in the detailed audit program.

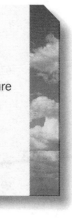

Suzie warns Ian that it is not always the size of the account that determines the use of analytical procedures or other procedures. For example, in Cloud 9's trial balance there is a liability called "Loans with directors." The balance of this account at September 30 is $149,354, less than 1 percent of total assets, but the accounting standard covering related party transactions (IAS 24 *Related Party Transactions)* creates additional disclosure requirements for these accounts, increasing the significance of the account and the amount of testing required.

"Auditors also have to be particularly careful in assessing the materiality of any liability balance," Suzie explains. "This is because we are usually more worried about understatement than overstatement of liabilities, so the assertion most at risk is completeness, not existence."

BEFORE YOU GO ON

1.1 Describe why audit assertions are important in the determination of audit risk.

1.2 Define substantive procedures.

1.3 Are there any audits where the auditor would perform no substantive audit procedures? Explain your answer.

9.2 RELATIONSHIP BETWEEN RISK ASSESSMENT AND THE NATURE, TIMING, AND EXTENT OF SUBSTANTIVE PROCEDURES

The nature of substantive procedures varies from account to account and ordinarily consists of one or a combination of the following techniques:

- key item testing
- representative sampling
- other tests of transactions/underlying data
- analytical procedures.

These techniques are described in more detail in section 9.3.

The appropriate mix of substantive procedures depends on factors such as the nature of the account balance (that is, balance sheet versus income statement account) and the risk assessment for both the specific account and the client overall (that is, at the account level and at the financial statement level).

The nature, timing, and extent of substantive procedures are responsively related to the risk assessments for each of the relevant sources of information affecting a significant account. In the case of an accounting estimate, the auditor may conclude, for example, that the likelihood of material misstatement is lower in measuring the provision for warranty claims, but there is a risk that not all such claims are identified, as there may be a management bias to minimize warranty expense. In this case, extensive tests are directed at determining whether all claims have been identified (completeness assertion), while less extensive tests are directed at determining whether the amounts already recognized as claims are appropriate (existence assertion, valuation and allocation assertions). Risk assessments not only affect the extent of the tests but can also affect the nature and timing. For example, in the situation described above, the auditor would likely test the completeness of claims at or near year end; however,

2 Understand the link between the audit risk model and the nature, timing, and extent of substantive procedures.

the tests of the valuation for individual claims by product type could be carried out before year end.

Similarly, the auditor may have agreed with the client that, based on the risk assessment, it is appropriate for the client to carry out a physical inventory count prior to year end (existence assertion). However, it is not appropriate for the auditor to test the client's valuation (pricing) of its inventory at that date. Rather, the auditor would perform tests of inventory pricing at a date nearer to or at year end.

Significant professional judgement is therefore required in relating the risk assessment to the nature, timing, and extent of the tests in order to hold overall audit risk to an acceptable level.

9.2.1 Timing of substantive procedures

As can be seen from figure 9.4, the timing of substantive procedures is directly influenced by the level of control risk (that is, how much assurance has already been gained from the controls testing performed). Typically, substantive testing tends to be performed at or near year end, with controls testing performed during visits before year end (interim). The timing of substantive procedures is described in more detail in section 9.3.

For accounts that accumulate transactions that, for the most part, will remain in the account balance at year end, the auditor can normally perform effective procedures before year end. For example, they could test additions and disposals to the fixed asset register or vouching of individually material expense items, such as severance expenses. Since these transactions accumulate during the year and, for the most part, remain in the account balance at the end of the year, the auditor's decision to perform procedures prior to year end does not generally depend on the effectiveness of controls or the likelihood of material misstatement. Rather, the timing of such procedures is a matter of convenience and whether it is expected to contribute to audit efficiencies. It is normal for an auditor to perform as much audit testing as possible before the client's year end due to the large number of clients needing their audits completed by the same date. The more work the auditor performs prior to the year-end visit, the less year-end work they will need to perform during the audit firm's "busy season," which will allow more flexibility when performing audits.

For other accounts, the auditor's ability to perform substantive audit procedures at an interim date generally depends on the existence of an effective control environment

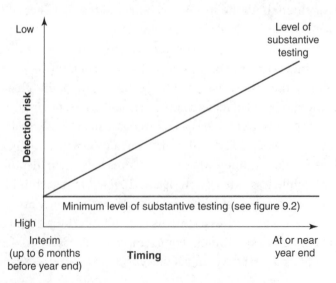

FIGURE 9.4 **Timing of substantive procedures**

and the effectiveness of controls. When the control environment is ineffective or there are specific ineffective controls, the auditor considers whether or not it is appropriate to perform substantive procedures at an interim date.

The timing of the substantive procedures is most flexible when controls have been assessed as effective and tested to confirm this assessment. In these circumstances, the substantive procedures may be performed earlier in the year (for example, six months before year end). When controls are assessed as effective but not tested, the substantive procedures may still be performed at an interim date (for example, two or three months before year end).

Whenever substantive procedures are performed prior to year end, the auditor performs **roll-forward procedures** to update their audit findings from the time of the interim procedures through to year end. The nature and extent of these roll-forward procedures are matters of judgement and are responsive to the risk assessment. For example, when the entity's control environment has been assessed as effective, controls have been tested, and no significant changes in the control environment and controls have occurred, limited roll-forward procedures such as analytical procedures or limited testing of intervening transactions may be all that is necessary.

The auditor might also perform substantive procedures prior to year end because of a client reporting requirement. For example, the auditor may be requested to confirm receivables and observe the counting of inventory before year end so the client is able to close its books promptly.

In the absence of specific effective controls, it may be acceptable for the auditor to perform substantive procedures prior to year end when they are able to conclude overall that the client's control environment is effective and the likelihood of errors is not high, or when they can perform sufficient procedures both at an interim date and during the intervening period (often referred to as the "roll-forward period"). The nature of the roll-forward procedures performed is responsive to the risk associated with the absence of controls and the timing of substantive procedures.

roll-forward procedures procedures performed during the period between an interim date and year end (the roll-forward period) to provide sufficient and appropriate audit evidence to base conclusions on as at year end when substantive procedures are performed at an interim date

Cloud 9

Suzie asks Ian to consider Cloud 9's warranty provision. Cloud 9 has a provision at September 30 of $91,456, which is slightly higher than the provision for the previous financial year of $85,597. What is the likelihood that the provision is understated? Are there any reasons to believe there are unidentified claims, and how would the auditors detect such claims?

Ian does not know of any change in manufacturing conditions that would affect the quality of Cloud 9's product and, by extension, the obligation under the warranty program. However, there was a new product introduced at the start of the previous year. "Because sales of the new 'Heavenly 456' walking shoe are now 20 percent of total sales," he notes, "we should consider any possible effects on the warranty provision. I recommend specific work be done to assess the claims from this product.

"However, if we remove this product from the analysis, the relationship between the warranty provision and sales is likely to be similar to past years. Because warranties apply to products, the amount of the warranty liability is determined by sales volume and product quality. Therefore, if conditions affecting product quality have not changed, and there is no change to the warranty program, analytical procedures are a useful way of testing the reasonableness of the provision.

"Finally," Ian concludes, "relying on analytical procedures to test the warranty provision is more justified if control testing suggests that Cloud 9 has effective controls over warranty claim identification and processing."

9.3 SUBSTANTIVE AUDIT PROCEDURES

❸ Provide examples of different substantive audit procedures.

In this section we explore the types of substantive procedures, including tests of details (key item testing, representative sampling, and other tests of transactions/underlying data) and analytical procedures. We also consider using computer-assisted audit techniques in performing substantive testing.

9.3.1 Tests of details

Substantive procedures that are not analytical procedures are referred to as "tests of details"; they may include tests of details of transactions or tests of details of accounts balances. **Tests of details of transactions** are predominantly designed to verify a balance or a transaction back to supporting documentation (called "vouching" or "tracing").

tests of details of transactions tests predominantly designed to verify a balance or a transaction back to supporting documentation; therefore, they usually include vouching and tracing

Vouching is when a balance or transaction is taken from the underlying accounting records and verified by agreeing the details to supporting evidence outside the accounting records of the company (typically, the details are agreed to external third-party information such as a supplier invoice or delivery documentation). Because vouching involves testing and verifying information already recorded in the accounting records, the primary purpose of the testing is to ensure that the balances or transactions are not overstated (for example, existence and occurrence assertions). **Tracing** is when a source document is traced back to the underlying accounting records. Because tracing involves testing and verifying information outside the accounting records that is not necessarily recorded (for instance, it does not appear on a source document such as an invoice), the primary purpose of the testing is to ensure that the balances are not understated (for example, completeness assertion).

vouching taking a balance or transaction from the underlying accounting records and verifying it by agreeing the details to supporting evidence outside the accounting records of the company

tracing tracking a source document back to the underlying accounting records

Sometimes, tests of details of transactions are **dual purpose tests** in that the procedures performed provide evidence of a control's effectiveness (test of controls) and also indicate if an item is being recorded properly (substantive test). An example of a dual purpose test is when the auditor tests the postings of the totals in the sales ledger to the general ledger and the sub-ledger. This is a test of control in that it provides evidence there are controls in place to ensure that totals are transferred correctly from the general ledger to the subsidiary ledger (point). It is also a substantive procedure that provides evidence for the completeness audit assertion because if the balances do not agree, it indicates something is missing.

dual purpose tests procedures that provide evidence for both tests of controls and substantive procedures

Tests of details of balances are tests that support the ending general ledger balance of an account. An example of this type of test is when the auditor sends out accounts receivable confirmations, as this provides evidence that the accounts receivable ending balance exists.

tests of details of balances tests that support the correctness of an account ending balance

When agreeing a balance or transaction to supporting documentation, the auditor must consider the type of evidence that is available. As noted in CAS 500 *Audit*

Evidence, evidence that is external to the client is ordinarily considered more relevant and reliable audit evidence than evidence generated internally by the client. For this reason, appropriate external evidence (or "third-party" evidence), when it is available, is preferred when performing these types of tests.

Auditors do not ordinarily audit an entire balance or class of transactions. Auditing requires that professional judgement be applied when determining how much testing to apply to a balance. For this reason, an auditor uses **audit sampling** (CAS 530 *Audit Sampling*). Audit sampling was defined and described in detail in chapter 6 and is a valid way of performing audit procedures. The auditor is not required (nor are they able) to perform audit procedures on 100 percent of the balances and disclosures within the financial statements. Instead, they select transactions, balances, and disclosures that are more likely to contain material errors. Further, the nature, timing, and extent of testing are based on the application of professional judgement in assessing the risks of material misstatement in the financial statements.

audit sampling the application of audit procedures to less than 100 percent of items within a population

The three main types of tests of details, which are also techniques applied when deciding how much of a balance to test, are (1) key item testing, (2) representative sampling, and (3) other tests of transactions/underlying data. Each of these is discussed in the following sections.

Key item testing

When conducting substantive testing, the auditor uses either a statistical basis or professional judgement to identify and test key items within a balance. Their focus is on selecting the largest transactions within a balance to obtain "coverage" over the total. That is, by selecting the largest transactions to test, the auditor is able to conclude over the entire balance based on the conclusions they reached by testing the largest transactions within a balance.

For example, an auditor is testing accounts receivable existence using accounts receivable confirmations. The total receivables are $3 million, with two key item trade receivables due from customers totalling $2.75 million of the balance. By selecting these two accounts and sending confirmation requests to them, assuming they reply, the auditor is able to conclude that because 91.7 percent of accounts receivables exist as at the confirmation date ($2.75 million / $3 million), it is reasonable that total accounts receivables of $3 million exist as at the confirmation date.

Some audit firms have software that assists in determining whether key items selected will provide enough of a basis to conclude that the audit assertion being tested has been met (within the confines of materiality). These software tools use a variety of methods to assess the approach planned and ordinarily take into consideration the total population (the account balance being audited), the materiality for the audit, and the other procedures that might be planned that will provide evidence to the auditor about the assertion being tested. The more persuasive the evidence from other procedures, the less coverage these key items need to address. The less persuasive the evidence from other audit procedures, the more coverage is generally necessary from these key items.

Representative sampling

After key items have been segregated, there may remain a large population of items that are individually unimportant but significant in total. These populations can consist of either transactions through a point in time (for example, sales) or items within an account balance at a point in time (for example, year-end finished goods inventory on hand). If risk assessments indicate the results of key item testing do not provide sufficient evidence to conclude that the population is free from material errors, the auditor obtains additional required evidence by sampling from the remainder of the population (after excluding the key items). When sampling from the remainder of the population, the sample items are selected, either statistically or non-statistically, in such a way that the sample is expected to be representative of that remaining population. This is referred to as representative sampling.

When a representative sampling approach is appropriate, the sample should be large enough to achieve the audit objective. The auditor also attempts to ensure that every item in the population has an equal chance of selection and that there is no conscious or inappropriate bias in the selection of items.

When the auditor applies representative sampling, there are three common sampling strategies applied, depending on the auditor's expectations of error and their overall audit objective (that is, identifying overstatement or understatement of the amount being audited). The following are the three sampling strategies.

1. *Representative sampling using audit risk tables.* The auditor uses this technique when they do not expect errors or they expect a low number of errors; that is, the risk of material misstatement has been assessed as low, and their primary concern is with the overstatement in an account balance. This is a common technique used to obtain "coverage" of a total balance as at year end and can be used to calculate errors that can then be extrapolated across a total balance. Many firms have software tools that assist in the calculation of representative samples; the audit risk tables are embedded within the tool and will calculate the sample size, depending on the input of other considerations, such as materiality, total key items already tested, and audit evidence obtained from other substantive procedures. The technique is generally not used for accounts where the key concern is understatement, as the technique will sample (and therefore test) items that are in the balance. It will not, however, select a sample of items that may be missing from the balance. In these cases, the auditor may supplement the testing of the balance with extensive cut-off and completeness substantive tests (for example, testing a sample of transactions after year end to determine if any of the transactions should have been recorded in the period subject to audit).

2. *Variables estimation sampling.* The auditor uses this technique if they expect more than a few errors in an account balance. This technique differs from representative sampling in that it can be used when the concern is both understatement and overstatement. Variables estimation sampling is usually applied to detect misstatements of the book values (carrying amounts or recorded values) of populations. The sample items selected are examined to determine their audited value (that is, the true or estimated amounts at which they should be carried). The differences between the book and audited values are then projected to estimate the error in the population. This technique evaluates selected characteristics of a population on the basis of a sample of the items constituting the population. The design of a variables estimation sampling approach involves mathematical calculations that tend to be complex and difficult to apply manually. Because of this, most audit firms use a specialized tool as well as a sampling specialist to assist them in applying this technique.

3. *Attribute sampling.* The auditor uses this technique to supplement other substantive procedures to obtain audit assurance related to tests of transactions when they do not expect errors (or when they expect a low number of errors). Attribute sampling is used to obtain a level of confidence, based on a statistically valid sample of transactions, that key attributes in existence for the sample tested can be inferred to be in existence for the entire population. Attribute sampling does not ordinarily lend itself to calculating a precise error that can be extrapolated across the entire balance.

Sampling is a complex area that requires the use of mathematically relevant, statistically valid techniques as well as a high degree of professional judgement to determine the nature, timing, and extent of testing.

Another key factor impacting the nature, timing, and extent of testing is the auditor's ability (or inability) to rely on computer-generated data or reports. When the auditor is unable to rely on the IT general controls or application controls of a client, control risk is assessed as high; in this case, the sample size when conducting substantive testing is likely to be larger and will be subject to a higher level of precision or confidence in the test results. When the client has strong controls and these have been tested to provide a basis for reliance, control risk is assessed as low, the sample size when conducting substantive testing is likely to be smaller, and the auditor would ordinarily accept a lower level of precision or confidence in the test results.

Other tests of transactions/underlying data

In addition to substantive procedures related to key items and representative sampling, the auditor often performs other tests of transactions or underlying data. Some common examples of these other tests are:

- tests of client-prepared schedules for mathematical accuracy
- tests using confirmations for such things as bank balances, accounts receivables, accounts payable, and various types of debt and share capital
- tests that inspect the physical existence of items such as inventory and capital assets
- tests to agree sub-ledger balances to general ledger balances for completeness
- tests to agree individual customer account balances to control account balances for completeness
- tests to confirm items are recorded in the correct period to ensure cut-off
- tests performed at an interim date and then roll-forward procedures performed on the intervening period between the interim date and year end
- tests of underlying data to be used as part of the analytical procedures (refer to section 9.3.2)
- tests of income statement accounts for account classification
- tests of individual transactions by vouching/agreeing to supporting documentation.

A decision on the amount of testing to perform (the extent of testing) is a matter of professional judgement. Testing needs to be sufficient to allow the auditor to conclude that the underlying data is free from material misstatement (material error).

If the auditor identifies errors when performing these tests, they request the client to investigate the reason for the errors. The reason the client provides will help the auditor determine the impact these errors may have on their risk assessment and the resultant change to the auditor's planned audit approach (this change is ordinarily to perform additional audit work).

Cloud 9

During their conversation about Cloud 9's warranty provision, Suzie asks Ian how they would use other substantive procedures to obtain evidence about the completeness assertion for the liability balance. "For example," Suzie asks, "would vouching and tracing be useful and, if so, how would you use them?" Ian is still keen on using analytical procedures, but he considers the question carefully. "I think we would use vouching to get evidence about transactions or balances that are recorded as warranty claims by Cloud 9. However, it might be more useful to consider tracing, because this would allow us to start with the documents and get evidence about how and whether the transactions are recorded in the accounts. If we find a warranty claim has been incorrectly recorded as another type of expense, we would be concerned that the liability is understated, or not complete. Additionally, we would like to examine transactions around the balance sheet date and make sure they are recorded in the correct accounting period. This evidence relates to the cut-off assertion, and is part of considering completeness."

9.3.2 Analytical procedures

analytical procedures evaluations of financial information made by a study of plausible relationships among both financial and non-financial data. Analytical procedures also encompass the investigation of identified fluctuations and relationships that are inconsistent with other relevant information or deviate significantly from predicted amounts

The fourth type of substantive procedures, **analytical procedures**, may be used:

- as primary (persuasive) tests of a balance
- as corroborative tests in combination with other procedures
- to provide at least some minimal level of support for the conclusion.

As outlined in CAS 520 *Analytical Procedures*, properly designed and executed analytical procedures provide an efficient alternative to tests of details of account balances and, in some cases, may provide the most effective test of the appropriateness of account balances (for example, management's estimate of the allowance for doubtful accounts or accrual for warranty costs). In other cases, analytical procedures may provide the only method of testing. For example, if the client does not maintain an effective costing system, overheads in the closing inventory might be estimated by relating actual overheads for the year to actual direct labour (assuming reliable direct labour reporting and reliable overhead expense records). It is expected that overall analytical procedures at the financial statement level will be performed on every audit engagement, irrespective of the audit approach planned for a client.

Therefore, when planning the audit approach, the auditor should consider what analytical procedures are available. The extent to which analytical procedures can reduce the extent of, or eliminate, other substantive procedures will depend on the risk assessment and the level of assurance provided by the analytical procedures.

Types of analytical procedures

There are a number of techniques that can be used to perform analytical procedures as a substantive test. As discussed in chapter 4, the objective is to select the most appropriate technique (or combination of techniques) to provide the necessary levels of assurance and precision. The techniques or types of analytical procedures include:

- absolute data comparisons (comparing current year to previous year, budgets and forecasts)
- ratio analysis (activity, liquidity, profitability, and leverage ratios)
- trend analysis (comparing certain data for several accounting periods)
- preparing common-size financial statements
- break-even analysis

- pattern analysis and regression analysis (sophisticated techniques not often used on audits).

Testing the reliability of underlying data

The biggest risk when performing analytical procedures is that the results will lead the auditor to accept an account balance as materially correct when, in fact, it contains material misstatements. The key way to minimize this risk is to evaluate the relevance of the information used in the analytical procedure and to ensure that the financial and non-financial data used in the analytical procedure are reliable.

The following are examples of points the auditor should consider when evaluating the relevance of the information used in the analytical procedure:

- Analytical procedures may not be useful when they are used on a company with significantly diverse operations and geographical segments. In order to be useful, consolidated balances need to be broken down by geography, nature, etc. to facilitate a meaningful analysis.
- The analytical procedure is adversely affected if the industry data is unreliable or is not comparable to the client's data. Industry ratios that are no longer meaningful because of rapidly changing economic conditions may be misleading.
- For entities with operations in inflationary economies, the extent to which increases in, say, costs or prices have been affected by inflation should be considered before performing analytical procedures and relying on the results.
- The comparison of budget to actual results is meaningful only if the client's budget process is well controlled. In some cases it may be necessary to expand the understanding of the process beyond that obtained during the planning phase of the audit (as described earlier).

The auditor also needs to be satisfied, when using an analytical procedure, that the financial and non-financial data used are reliable, especially when the analytical procedure is used as a persuasive substantive procedure. When using analytical procedures as part of an overall financial statements analysis, it is not necessary to test the underlying data, because an overall financial statements analysis is performed to increase the understanding of the client's business, provide a basis for developing the scope of the audit, and identify areas requiring further investigation. However, when the analytical procedures are to be persuasive and the primary (and potentially only) substantive test of a balance, it is necessary to test the reliability of the data being used. For example, if the auditor uses an aging report to support the reasonableness of the allowance for doubtful accounts, they ordinarily first test the accuracy of the aging.

The extent to which the auditor needs to test the underlying data is driven by the extent to which they have been able to test and form a basis for reliance on the controls surrounding the data. Primarily, this means assessing the overall control environment at the company (is it effective?), the IT general controls (are they effective?), and the application controls (have they been tested and can they be relied on?). The more effective the controls over the data that the auditor intends to use in an analytical procedure, the more the analytical procedure can be relied on as a substantive procedure. Conversely, the less effective the client's controls over the data, the less reliable the analytical procedure is likely to be, although it still may be useful in identifying areas for further investigation.

Another factor to consider is that often client-produced non-financial data used in analytical procedures (such as the tonnage of product produced in a particular location) are not subject to the same type of controls as the client's financial data. As a result, the auditor may not be able to draw a conclusion about the reliability of the non-financial data without performing tests of that data. On the other hand, if such data is used as a key indicator of performance in running the business, the auditor may take comfort in the fact (in the absence of evidence to the contrary) that the client finds the data reliable for such purposes.

In summary, the auditor tests the reliability of underlying data when the analytical procedure is to provide persuasive assurance; they use judgement to determine the need for, and extent of, tests of underlying data when the analytical procedure provides corroborative assurance; and they need not test underlying data when the analytical procedure provides minimal assurance (refer to section 9.4 for a discussion of each of these levels of assurance or evidence).

Substantive analytical procedures—summary

When the auditor performs analytical procedures, the steps they take can be summarized as follows:

1. Identify the computation, comparison, or relationship to be made or to be investigated.
2. Assess the reliability of any data to be used.
3. Estimate the probable balance in the account or the probable outcome of the computation.
4. Make whatever computations are needed using data in the client's records or data from reliable outside sources.
5. Compare the estimated amount with the computed or recorded amount and evaluate whether the difference, if any, is significant.
6. Determine appropriate procedures for investigating the reasons for the difference if it is significant.
7. Perform the procedures.
8. Draw conclusions.

9.3.3 Performing substantive testing using computers

As clients have become more sophisticated and complex over time, the auditor's audit procedures and techniques have needed to respond to these complexities and have also become more sophisticated. One such development is the use of computers to assist the auditor with their testing. This is often referred to as "computer-assisted audit techniques" (CAATs).

There are two main categories of CAATs. The first type is software used to interrogate and examine client data files. Whenever computers are used to maintain or process accounting data, CAAT software can be used to perform procedures such as calculations (for example, the re-adding of a report) and logic tests (for example, sorting or comparing current year amounts with those from the previous year), and to select and print key items and representative samples for testing.

Using CAAT software makes the audit (1) more comprehensive, because each item in a file can be examined and subjected to a variety of tests; and (2) more efficient, because the computer can handle large volumes of data, thereby reducing time-consuming clerical tasks. Using software will also allow the auditor to concentrate on designing the test criteria and on evaluating and interpreting the results, rather than on performing the detailed audit procedures. Available software ranges from large, highly sophisticated products through to basic electronic spreadsheets and financial statement packages. Software does not necessarily have to be designed specifically for audit purposes.

The second type of CAAT is software that individual firms have either purchased or developed that is designed to plan, perform, and evaluate audit procedures, regardless of whether the client is automated or not.

The main considerations in deciding whether to use CAATs are the completeness of the records and the reliability of the data. As with any audit procedure, the nature and extent of the procedures performed with a CAAT will largely depend on the evaluation of the effectiveness of the client's control environment, IT general controls, and application controls.

Cloud 9

Ian and Suzie continue their discussion about using analytical procedures. Ian is starting to feel more confident and suggests that there are some factors to consider about the Cloud 9 audit that would affect the use of the various procedures. "We could use all of the usual techniques in the Cloud 9 audit, although we have to be careful in making comparisons across years for a couple of reasons. We have only just taken over the audit, so although prior-year data was audited, we are still building up our level of familiarity with the data and don't really understand all the conditions that applied to the previous years. Also, the changes at Cloud 9, in particular the opening of the retail store and the additional borrowing to finance the purchase of the delivery trucks that we discovered during our preliminary work, will impact the data, and we will have to think through these impacts before using the data in our tests."

BEFORE YOU GO ON

3.1 Name two common sampling strategies.

3.2 How do the control environment and results of control testing influence the timing of the substantive audit procedures?

3.3 Why is it important to test the reliability of the underlying data used in analytical procedures?

9.4 LEVELS OF EVIDENCE

Several different levels of evidence can be obtained when performing substantive procedures, depending on the type of substantive procedure performed. Evidence can be persuasive, corroborative, minimal, or general. Each of these levels is described below, illustrated by an example of substantive analytical procedures. Examples of the different types of evidence show that analytical procedures performed for planning purposes (as outlined in chapter 4) are quite different from those used for substantive testing purposes.

 **4** Explain the different levels of audit evidence obtained when performing substantive procedures.

9.4.1 Persuasive

Analytical procedures can be the primary test of a balance (that is, the primary basis for the conclusion) if they provide persuasive evidence. This would be the case when the procedures generate an amount that the auditor believes is a reasonable estimate of what the balance should be, thus enabling them to conclude that the account balance is free from material errors. If an analytical review procedure is classified as persuasive, it means that no further substantive procedures need to be performed on the related account balance, even in moderate risk situations. Accordingly, the auditor must give careful consideration to the quality of evidence provided by the particular analytical procedure before they conclude that the analytical procedure is persuasive. Table 9.2 includes examples of analytical procedures that may provide persuasive evidence.

TABLE 9.2 **Examples of analytical procedures that provide persuasive evidence**

EVIDENCE	ANALYTICAL PROCEDURE
Material content of work in progress and finished goods	Relate raw materials put into production and quantities sold to normal yield factors
Overheads in closing inventory	Relate actual overheads for the period to actual direct labour, production volumes, or another appropriate measure
Finished goods pricing	Refer to selling prices less selling costs and "normal" gross margin
Charges for depreciation	Refer to asset balance, effect of additions and disposals, and average depreciation rate
Payroll expense	Refer to days accrued and average daily payroll or subsequent period's gross payroll
Commission expense	Refer to commission rates and related sales
Accruals for commissions or royalties	Refer to terms of agreements and payment dates
Accrued warranty costs for established products	Refer to applicable payroll and previous year's contribution rate
Scrap income	Relate standard cost scrap factor to weight of material processed and apply the result to published scrap prices
Interest expense and related accrual	Refer to the average debt outstanding, weighted average interest rate, and payment dates
Investment income	Relate average amounts invested to an average interest rate or yield
Total revenue for a school	Relate school fee per each year level by number of students in each respective level

9.4.2 Corroborative

An analytical procedure provides corroborative evidence if it (1) confirms audit findings from other procedures and (2) supports management representations or otherwise decreases the level of audit scepticism. For example, year-to-year detailed comparisons by product line of inventory levels and other key relationships such as turnover, gross margin, percentage composition of materials, labour, and overheads provide some evidence of the reasonableness of the inventory balance, but do not provide sufficient evidence by themselves to allow us to conclude that the account is free from material misstatement.

A corroborative analytical procedure includes comparisons of account balances to expectations developed and documented earlier in the audit. These comparisons generally provide corroborative evidence about an account balance and enable the auditor to limit the extent of other procedures in that area. In these cases, the auditor's understanding of the client's business should help confirm the reasonableness of a balance. For example, an auditor expects general administrative expense for the year to be approximately $10 million based on their review of the client's budget and the trend in the relationship of those expenses to sales. If actual general and administrative expenses fall within a reasonable range of the expected balance, a comparison of the recorded balance with the expected balance would provide corroborative evidence about the reasonableness of the balance. In addition, this supports the auditor's plan to reduce the extent of or eliminate other substantive testing of general administrative expenses. However, if an unexpected fluctuation is noted (for example, if general administrative expenses are less than, or exceed, the auditor's expectation by a significant amount), the auditor would expand other substantive audit procedures to obtain an explanation for the fluctuation and to provide additional evidence that would allow them to conclude that the balance was free from material misstatement. For example, they may review a listing of accounts comprising general and administrative expenses for individual account balance fluctuations, and investigate those with significant or unexpected fluctuations. Table 9.3 includes examples of analytical procedures that may provide corroborative evidence.

EVIDENCE	ANALYTICAL PROCEDURE
Trade receivables, sales, going concern	Review the volatility of the customer base (e.g., new customers as a percentage of existing customers) and compare with expectations
Trade receivables	Compare the current period's receivables as a percentage of net sales with prior-periods' percentages, and consider the reasonableness of the current period's percentage in relation to current economic conditions, credit policies, collectability
Prepayments	Compare the prepayment account balances with those of prior periods and investigate any unexpected changes (or the absence of expected changes)
Property, plant, and equipment	Review the reasonableness of the depreciation expense by referring to the previous year's balance and the effects of acquisitions and disposals
Sales, commissions expense	Compare sales commissions or bonuses with related sales
Payroll expense	Compare payroll tax expenses to the annual payroll times the statutory tax rates

TABLE 9.3 **Examples of analytical procedures that provide corroborative evidence**

9.4.3 Minimal

Analytical procedures that do not provide persuasive or corroborative evidence contribute minimal support for the conclusion. In deciding whether a particular analytical procedure or combination of procedures provides corroborative evidence or only minimal support for the conclusion, the auditor evaluates both the extent of their analytical procedures and the quality of the evidence they expect to obtain. For example, they may simply compare a current-year overall balance (for example, inventory) to the prior-year balance to help identify potential problems or trends, and not to reduce the extent of other substantive procedures. If they do not supplement that comparison with any other analytical procedures (for example, product-line comparisons of turnover, gross margin, or percentage composition of materials, labour, and overhead), they obtain only minimal support for the conclusion. Table 9.4 includes examples of analytical procedures that provide minimal evidence.

9.4.4 General

Analytical procedures might provide persuasive evidence in one circumstance but not in another. To illustrate, the risk assessment related to investments might indicate a low likelihood of material misstatement related to recording investment income. If a client has a relatively stable investment portfolio, a comparison of the average amount invested to an average market rate of interest or yield may provide the auditor with persuasive evidence to conclude that the amount of investment income recorded for the year is free from material misstatement. On the other hand, another client's portfolio might be more diversified, with rapid turnover. In that case, the auditor may need to expand the analytical review by segmenting the client's portfolio and applying the average yield test to the various segments. If that is not feasible, they may find it necessary to perform a test of details of investment income.

TABLE 9.4 **Examples of analytical procedures that provide minimal evidence**

EVIDENCE	ANALYTICAL PROCEDURE
Trade receivables	Understand the reason for any large credit transactions/balances on the ledger
Trade receivables	Compare the number and amounts of credit notes issued with those of prior periods
Property, plant, and equipment	Review the property, plant, and equipment and related accounts in the general ledger for unusual items
Trade payables	Compare the number of days purchases in trade payables with those of prior years
Equity	Compare the equity account balance with that of prior years and investigate any unexpected changes (or the absence of expected changes)
Payroll expense, cost of sales	Compare the relationship between direct labour costs and number of employees with those of prior periods

Cloud 9

Suzie agrees with Ian's assessment of the usefulness of analytical procedures and the possibility of using other techniques for testing the warranty provision at Cloud 9. "Using analytical procedures as the only substantive procedure is appropriate if we can find a close relationship between the underlying activity data and the account balance," she says. "The weaker or less consistent the relationship between the account balance and the other data, the more likely it is that we will have to perform other substantive procedures in order to obtain sufficient and appropriate evidence."

Ian suddenly has a thought. "I have just realized that when we are using prior-year data, we know it is audited, but the trial balance is unaudited. This means that we need to recognize that there could be errors in those figures. Also, as we do the audit and we find and correct misstatements, we should have another look at our analytical procedures—the change in the underlying data might change our conclusions."

"That's right," says Suzie. "We might also discover a change in conditions, such as operational changes, that could affect our interpretation of the data. We have to be aware of how everything is connected and review our conclusions and decisions as we go through the audit."

"If we can get persuasive evidence from using analytical procedures," Suzie concludes, "we can reduce the reliance on the other substantive tests."

BEFORE YOU GO ON

4.1 What is persuasive audit evidence? Give an example.

4.2 When does an analytical procedure provide corroborative audit evidence?

4.3 When does an analytical procedure provide minimal audit evidence?

9.5 EVALUATING AND DOCUMENTING SUBSTANTIVE ANALYTICAL PROCEDURES RESULTS

The auditor's understanding of the client's business and industry alerts the auditor to likely fluctuations in the financial data when they are planning the audit. These fluctuations may be caused by trends, seasonal patterns, cyclical patterns, dependent relationships, specific business decisions taken, or external decisions directly impacting the business. For example, if management and the union representing the workforce have negotiated a 3 percent pay rise over the next two years, the auditor would expect the analytical procedures performed on average wages and salaries per employee to confirm this increase. Also, if the federal government enacted a law to collect an additional 1 percent in payroll tax, the auditor would expect the analytical procedure to confirm this increase in payroll tax expense.

The lack of a significant change from one year to the next does not necessarily mean that the auditor can assume that the balance is reasonable. Whether and to what extent they investigate the lack of change in a balance depends on the auditor's understanding of the client's business, the relevant controls, and the industry in which the client operates.

5 Describe the documentation of the conclusions reached as a result of performing substantive procedures.

PROFESSIONAL ENVIRONMENT

Interpreting the results of analytical procedures

Before they can complete an audit, auditors need to evaluate the causes of any unexpected fluctuations in a client's financial statements detected by the use of analytical procedures. Auditors have to consider possible causes of the fluctuation, search for additional information about these possible causes, evaluate the alternatives, and decide which possible cause of the fluctuation is the correct one. As part of this process, auditors can make inquiries of management to obtain their explanations of the fluctuation's cause. Management could provide the correct explanation because of their superior knowledge of the situation. However, it is possible that management will give the auditor an incorrect explanation, deliberately or not.

Wendy Green conducted an experiment to investigate whether receiving an incorrect management explanation affected auditors' performance in determining the correct explanation for financial data fluctuations. The subjects in the experiment were 61 auditors from one large accounting firm, with an average of almost four years' experience. The subjects were required to complete a computerized experimental task involving analytical procedures relating to an error in cost of sales. The subjects in a control group did not receive a management explanation while the other auditors received a management explanation either before or after considering their own alternative explanations.

Green found that only 15 of the 61 auditors selected the correct cause of the data fluctuation, with the remainder selecting either management's explanation or another cause considered a possibility by the auditor. Although 47 of the auditors actually considered the correct cause, 32 dismissed it in favour of another alternative. The data showed that 14 auditors never even considered the correct cause as a possibility during their investigations.

Overall, Green concluded that receiving an incorrect explanation from management affected the auditors' performance by influencing them to judge it as the correct cause. None of the auditors in the control group, who did not receive the management explanation, judged that explanation to be the correct one. Green suggests that audit firms could consider offering more guidance to auditors to prompt their consideration of more alternatives. In addition, auditor training could focus more on the evaluation of evidence, particularly in relation to management explanations. However, it is possible that, in practice, more experienced auditors, such as partners, would not be so easily distracted by management's explanations.

Source: Wendy Green, "Are Auditors' Analytical Procedures Judgements Affected by Receiving Management Explanations?" *Australian Accounting Review* 15, no. 3 (2005), pp. 67–74.

Cloud 9

Ian and Suzie have decided that analytical procedures will not be sufficient for all accounts. For each major transaction cycle and account balance, they will also conduct tests of details. For the vouching tests, the auditors will sample transactions and balances in the accounting records and go to the underlying documentation (or physical assets) to confirm the recorded details. For example, for sales recorded as being made prior to the financial year end, they will examine the invoices and shipping documents to gather evidence on the date, amount, and other details of the transactions. If they find a sales invoice with a January date has been included in the sales for the year ended December 31, they will have evidence of a misstatement in the occurrence and cut-off assertions for sales.

They will also trace the details in a sample of documents through to Cloud 9's accounting records. This means that they will start with the documents and then test how that transaction (or asset or liability) is recorded in the client's accounts. For example, if they find a sales invoice with a December date that is *not* included in the sales for the year, they

will have evidence of a misstatement in the completeness and cut-off assertions for sales. Suzie advises Ian that the sample sizes and approach to sampling are determined by the results of the controls testing and the resulting expectations for errors.

Suzie also asks Ian to include tests of schedules, such as trade receivables and property, plant, and equipment (PPE), in the detailed audit plan. Where the risk is low, such as PPE, they will perform these tests at an interim date.

Finally, Suzie informs Ian that the IT audit manager, Mark Batten, is writing a CAAT program.

9.5.1 Evaluating errors identified in testing

As the auditor executes their substantive procedures, they may identify misstatements or errors. When they identify differences they did not expect, they reconsider their evaluation of the effectiveness of controls and overall risk assessments made in planning to determine whether additional procedures need to be performed. When a **misstatement** (either an error—including fraud—or a difference between the auditor's professional judgement and the client's as to whether a balance is correct) is identified, it is captured centrally in the audit working papers. This will allow the auditor to assess the overall impact of all misstatements at the financial statements level during the completion phase of the audit.

As mentioned, there are two key types of misstatements ordinarily identified during the audit procedures: errors (including fraud) and judgemental misstatements. Errors may arise from a one-off event or may systematically arise as the result of a breakdown in controls. The auditor may have identified these errors as part of controls testing or as part of their substantive testing. They may have been specifically identified as a result of the testing performed, or they may have been extrapolated from a statistically valid sample. Errors do not ordinarily have any element of judgement to them and are often considered by those charged with governance as just wrong; they may therefore be corrected by management irrespective of their size or potential effect on the financial statements.

Judgemental misstatements, however, often arise due to a difference between the auditor's and management's interpretation or application of an accounting policy or standard. These differences tend to be the focus of discussions held with those charged with governance and are often round numbers or a possible error "range" rather than an exact number.

The identification and resolution of misstatements is one of the auditor's most important responsibilities in an audit and is a critical step in the formulation of their opinion on the fairness of the client's financial statements. This is discussed in greater detail in chapter 12.

misstatement a difference between the amount, classification, presentation, or disclosure of a reported financial statement item and the amount, classification, presentation, or disclosure that is required for the item to be in accordance with the applicable financial reporting framework. Misstatements can arise from error or fraud

9.5.2 Concluding and documenting the results of substantive procedures

As discussed earlier, the nature, timing, and extent of the audit procedures are influenced by a range of factors, including the type of balance or disclosure being tested, the level of detection risk remaining after the planning procedures and controls testing is complete, and the audit assertion addressed by the test. Once the auditor has determined the nature, timing, and extent of the substantive procedures, these are documented in the audit program. This program then serves as the instructions for the audit team members to complete the required testing.

When reaching their conclusion on the results of substantive procedures, the auditor considers the results of all of their testing related to the account balance or disclosure being audited, the responses to inquiries made during the performance of the procedures, and the resolution of any misstatements identified during the audit testing. With respect to all substantive procedures, the auditor documents the conclusion statement for each significant account (including the execution of the relevant audit program steps), the results, and any significant findings, including any misstatements. They also document that the financial statements reconcile to the underlying accounting records.

Overall conclusion statements are usually prepared for each audit program step completed, as well as for each significant account and significant assertion. These overall significant account conclusion statements are captured on what are often referred to as "lead sheets."

Cloud 9

Suzie asks Ian to set up the working papers for the tests they will perform. The priorities for Ian are to ensure that each test is described in sufficient detail in the audit program so the audit staff can perform the test correctly and identify any misstatements. The working papers also have to provide for comments to be included as the work is completed and by senior staff when they review the test results and form their conclusions on each account's assertions.

PROFESSIONAL ENVIRONMENT

Assessing materiality of errors

When auditors detect an omission or misstatement as a result of their substantive testing, they must decide whether or not the error is material, both as an individual error and in aggregate with all other errors. Auditors must take both the size of the error (its quantity) and its qualitative characteristics into account when making the materiality decision. Their final conclusion is that the error is either material or not material.

Rosner, Comunale, and Sexton argue that the binary choice (material or not) over-simplifies the situation and leads to auditors focusing only on the size of the misstate-ment, ignoring its qualitative characteristics. They propose that a "fuzzy logic" approach is useful in materiality assessments. Fuzzy logic allows "omissions and misstatement to possess a degree of value—that is, each omission or misstatement is material to a greater or lesser degree, measured on a scale from 0 to 1."

The concept of fuzzy logic can be used to construct a rule-based expert system. An initial materiality assessment is made for each aspect of materiality, quantitative and qualitative, for the relevant omission or misstatement. The initial assessment is a number between 0 and 1, with 1 meaning the omission or misstatement is material on that attribute, and 0 meaning that it is not material. A validity value must then be assigned for each rule, where more important attributes of materiality are assigned greater validity values. The authors give the example of a modest 0.35 validity value for the rule relating to the size of the misstatement, with a greater 0.85 validity value for the rule relating to whether the misstatement increases management compensation.

The authors suggest that the final materiality value could be the highest value for the product of the initial materiality assessment value and the validity value across the materiality attributes. Alternatively, the auditor could determine the misstatement is material if any one of the materiality assessments indicated that the misstatement was material (for example, above 0.5). Finally, an auditor could create their own policy for converting the fuzzy materiality values into rules for further audit action. Whichever decision rule is adopted, the authors argue that using a formal model structure requires that the auditor evaluate each quantitative and qualitative factor explicitly. This will encourage better communication between the audit team and the client and will enhance consistency across auditors, engagements, and years.

Source: R.L. Rosner, C.L. Comunale, and T.R. Sexton, "Assessing Materiality: A New 'Fuzzy Logic' Approach," *The CPA Journal* (June 2006), pp. 26–28.

BEFORE YOU GO ON

5.1 What is a misstatement?

5.2 What is the difference between an error and a judgemental misstatement?

5.3 What is an audit program?

SUMMARY

① Define substantive audit procedures.

Substantive audit procedures are procedures designed to obtain direct evidence of the completeness, accuracy, and validity of data, and the reasonableness of the estimates and other information contained in the financial statements. Substantive procedures include inspection, observation, enquiry, confirmation, recalculation, re-performance, analyses of many types, and analytical reviews.

② Understand the link between the audit risk model and the nature, timing, and extent of substantive procedures.

The combination of inherent risk and control risk determines the level of detection risk the auditor is willing to accept that will still allow them to conclude that the financial statements are not materially misstated. Detection risk is reduced or increased in direct proportion to the amount of substantive testing performed. There are several factors that influence how much substantive testing must be performed, including the nature of the test, the level of assurance necessary, the type of evidence required, and the complexity of the client's data capturing systems. The timing of substantive procedures is most flexible when controls have been tested and assessed as effective. In that case, the procedures can be performed up to six months before year end. When controls are not tested or are not assessed as effective, the timing of substantive procedures is at or near year end.

③ Provide examples of different substantive audit procedures.

The different types of substantive procedures are key items testing, representative sampling (including representative sampling using audit tables, variables estimation sampling, and attribute or discovery sampling), other tests of transactions/underlying data, and analytical procedures. Different analytical procedures include absolute data comparisons, ratio analysis, trend analysis, common-size financial statements, break-even analysis, and pattern and regression analysis. Substantive analytical procedures are different from those analytical procedures used during the planning phase of the audit.

④ Explain the different levels of audit evidence obtained when performing substantive procedures.

The different levels of audit evidence obtained when performing substantive procedures include persuasive, corroborative, minimal, and general audit evidence.

⑤ Describe the documentation of the conclusions reached as a result of performing substantive procedures.

Conclusion statements are documented for each significant account (including the execution of the relevant audit program steps), the results, and any significant findings, including any misstatements. The auditor also documents that the financial statements reconcile to the underlying accounting records. Overall conclusions are usually prepared for each audit program step completed, as well as for each significant account and significant assertion.

KEY TERMS

MULTIPLE-CHOICE QUESTIONS

9.1 Designing substantive procedures responds to:

(a) the risk of material misstatement at the entity level.

(b) the risk of material misstatement at the assertion level.

(c) the risk of all types of misstatements at the assertion level.

(d) the risk of all types of misstatements at the entity level.

9.2 The following factor(s) influences how much and when substantive procedures are performed:

(a) the nature of the test.

(b) the level of assurance necessary.

(c) the type of evidence required.

(d) All of the above.

9.3 Analytical procedures:

(a) are used to test controls and are not substantive procedures.

(b) are substantive procedures and cannot be used at any other stage of the audit.

(c) are used at planning and substantive testing stages of the audit.

(d) can be used as substantive tests but cannot be used as primary tests of a balance.

9.4 We can conclude that analytical procedures provide persuasive evidence:

(a) always.

(b) never.

(c) if they do not provide sufficient evidence by themselves to allow us to conclude that the account is free of material errors.

(d) if we are able to conclude that no further substantive tests need to be performed on the related account balance.

9.5 The following conditions make absolute data comparisons relatively less useful:

(a) multiple years of financial data available.

(b) single-location clients.

(c) changes in production methods.

(d) budgets that are carefully prepared.

9.6 The reliability of data used for analytical procedures:

(a) affects the persuasiveness of the evidence from analytical procedures.

(b) is more useful on a consolidated basis than an individual business segment basis.

(c) is unaffected by inflation.

(d) is never affected by the strength of controls over the client's budgetary processes.

9.7 Vouching is:

(a) not a useful audit procedure.

(b) agreeing a balance or transaction to supporting documentation.

(c) the main audit procedure used to gather evidence on the completeness assertion.

(d) not designed to be used as a substantive audit procedure.

9.8 The primary advantage of selecting the largest transactions within a balance to test is:

(a) it is an example of random sampling.

(b) it is more interesting for the auditor because they see the most important transactions in detail.

(c) that the auditor is able to draw a conclusion about the entire balance based on the conclusions they reached by testing the largest transactions.

(d) all of the above.

9.9 Roll-forward procedures:

(a) need to be responsive to the control risk assessment.

(b) are procedures done during the month after year end.

(c) have no effect on audit efficiency.

(d) none of the above.

9.10 Misstatements:

(a) are documented in the audit working papers.

(b) can be categorized as errors or judgemental misstatements.

(c) must be considered for their effect on the financial statements both individually and in aggregate.

(d) all of the above.

REVIEW QUESTIONS

9.1 Explain how the nature of a substantive test could affect decisions about when and how much substantive testing is performed. How do these decisions relate to the overall risk assessment for the item being tested?

9.2 What are substantive procedures designed to obtain evidence about? What are the main types of substantive procedures?

9.3 What are analytical procedures? Describe how they can be used as substantive tests in an audit.

9.4 What conditions must be satisfied before we can regard evidence from analytical procedures as persuasive rather than corroborative or minimal? Why are these conditions important?

9.5 Why is it important to consider the quality of the data used in analytical procedures? How important to this question are client controls over financial data?

9.6 Vouching transactions and balances back to supporting documentation would ordinarily provide evidence about which assertions? Which assertions would vouching be least likely to provide evidence about?

9.7 Explain the differences between key items testing and representative sampling using audit risk tables. How would software to select each type of sample be used?

9.8 Explain the two main types of CAATs. What are the advantages of using software to interrogate and examine client data files? Does using CAATs remove the need to test client control systems?

9.9 Which accounts and/or clients are more suitable for interim substantive testing?

9.10 Provide an example of (1) an error and (2) a judgemental misstatement that could affect the balance of property, plant, and equipment.

PROFESSIONAL APPLICATION QUESTIONS

 Basic ★　　Moderate ★★　　Challenging ★★★

9.1 Designing substantive procedures ★

Carla has been asked to join the team responsible for designing the audit program for a new client, Gaskin Industries Ltd. (Gaskin), a manufacturing and wholesaling firm. Gaskin recently went public and is now listed on the Toronto Stock Exchange. Carla has worked for the audit firm for a year and received a very high performance rating from her supervisors on the previous year's audit of Bryson Ltd. (Bryson), a firm that provides marketing and other consulting services. Gaskin and Bryson have total revenue of approximately the same amount, so Carla feels confident that she can apply her knowledge to the new audit. She takes a copy of the audit program for Bryson to the first meeting, intending to suggest they use it as the basis for the audit program for Gaskin. Carla thinks that the Gaskin audit program could use the same substantive procedures they used on the Bryson audit.

Required

List some of the problems with Carla's idea of using Bryson's audit program as a basis for designing substantive procedures for Gaskin.

9.2 Data for analytical procedures ★ ★

North West Paper Ltd. (North West) provides cardboard, paper, and plastic packaging materials to a large number of manufacturers and distributors in all provinces. The cardboard and paper division is a well-established business, but North West has been providing plastic products only since it took over Plastic Products Ltd. 18 months ago. The takeover doubled North West's revenue and caused changes in its management structure, adding another two divisional managers. These new divisional managers are in charge of plastic product sales to different areas of the country—Plastic (Eastern) and Plastic (Western)—and they join the Paper (Eastern) and Paper (Western) division managers in reporting directly to the CEO.

All internal operating reports are now structured along the four divisional reporting lines, although external financial statements continue to be produced for the whole business. All purchasing and billing systems are fully integrated, although it is possible to extract data along divisional lines and by province (as before). North West purchases bulk supplies of raw plastic and paper and makes boxes, rolls, and sheets of these materials to fill customer orders. Production processes in the paper divisions have not changed, and North West has made minimal changes to the production processes used by Plastic Products Ltd.

Required

List and discuss the factors that would increase or decrease the reliability of data used in analytical procedures at North West.

9.3 Persuasiveness of evidence from analytical procedures ★ ★

Mathieu has the task of reviewing the evidence from analytical procedures conducted by the audit juniors on the audit of Soleil Services Ltd. The audit juniors have reported the results of these analytical procedures:

1. Comparison of depreciation expense with the closing balance of each depreciable asset class in property, plant, and equipment.
2. Recalculation of sales commission expenses using the standard sales commission rate and total sales.
3. Comparison of payroll expense with previous year payroll.

Required

(a) What questions would Mathieu ask about each analytical procedure?
(b) If all questions could be answered satisfactorily, explain whether the evidence from each analytical procedure would be persuasive, corroborative, minimal, or general. What are the implications of this judgement for further substantive testing?

9.4 Tests of details ★ ★

Marty has to audit the sales transactions of Okawa Ltd., which supplies tools to the mining industry. Okawa Ltd. carries a large number of different makes and models of standard mining tools. It also designs and manufactures tools for special purposes and for miners operating in difficult conditions. The custom-designed tools are made only after a contract has been signed and a deposit received, while standard tools are supplied to regular customers on receipt of a telephone order. Okawa Ltd.'s sales transactions vary from a few dollars to millions of dollars depending on the number of items sold, whether the individual items are large or small tools, and whether the tools are standard items or custom designed.

Marty is instructed to gather evidence about the sales transactions using sampling and vouching. This is explained in detail in the audit program.

Required

(a) What would you expect to see in the audit program given to Marty about (1) the sample selection and (2) the vouching procedures? Explain.

(b) How could Marty use CAATs to help gather the evidence?

9.5 Timing of substantive tests ★ ★ ★

Connie is the recently appointed engagement partner of the audit of Camel Ltd. She has just taken over the audit from Kar-Ming Leo, who rotated off the audit after a seven-year period as the engagement partner. Kar-Ming had a small portfolio of clients and was able to complete most substantive testing for Camel at year end. Connie is unable to do this because she is facing difficulties with two of her other large clients. These clients have just been advised that their financing arrangements with U.S.-based banks may not be renewed, raising doubts about their ability to continue as going concerns. The U.S. banks will make their financing decisions very close to the clients' year ends, forcing Connie to spend considerable time in this period with these clients.

The financing problems of Connie's existing clients have created demands on her audit team that she must resolve. The audit firm cannot provide her with the additional staff she has requested for the year-end period because the clients of several other partners are also facing financing difficulties due to the credit crisis in the United States.

The audit firm's ethical rules do not allow Kar-Ming to remain as the auditor of Camel, and it is too late to find new partners for any of her other clients, so Connie must find a way to continue with the audit and still meet all professional and legal standards. So far, the audit team has conducted the preliminary risk assessment for Camel, and the results of early control testing confirm that Camel has excellent controls.

Connie calls a meeting with her senior audit team members to discuss the issue.

Required

Explain how Connie could vary the timing of the substantive testing at Camel to help her meet her audit obligations. Specifically:

(a) give examples of substantive procedures that could be performed prior to year end

(b) explain how Connie will use roll-forward procedures to complete the audit

(c) explain any other considerations that would affect the timing of substantive procedures for Camel.

9.6 Evaluating substantive testing results ★ ★

The following items are documented in the audit working papers:

1. Sales transaction included in the year ended December 31, 2012, but evidence from the cut-off procedure suggests that the sale should be dated January 2, 2013 ($1,250,000).

2. Warranty expenses in the trial balance for the year to December 31, 2012, total $150,000; the provision for warranty claims as at December 31, 2011, was $100,000. Evaluation of correspondence suggests that an additional $200,000 in warranty claims could result from ongoing disputes with customers. No provision for these claims has been made. Management has made a warranty provision for 2012 of $120,000.

3. Severance expenses related to reorganization of head office administration were incorrectly charged to rental expenses ($578,920).

4. Management has not recorded an impairment for assets. A drought-induced recession has adversely impacted property values in regional cities where seven branch offices are located (head office and two branch offices are located in the capital city). Total land and buildings in the trial balance is $5,500,000.

Required

(a) Evaluate each item above and explain whether it is an error or a judgemental misstatement. What action do you recommend for each?

(b) Which accounts would be affected, and how, if an adjustment is made for each item?

Questions 9.7–9.10 are based on the following case.

Fellowes and Associates Chartered Accountants is a successful mid-tier accounting firm with a large range of clients across Canada. During 2011, Fellowes and Associates gained a new client, Health Care Holdings Group (HCHG), which owns 100 percent of the following entities:

- Shady Oaks Centre, a private treatment centre
- Gardens Nursing Home Ltd., a private nursing home
- Total Laser Care Ltd. (TLCL), a private clinic that specializes in the laser treatment of skin defects. Year end for all HCHG entities is June 30.

You are a senior auditor working on the Shady Oaks Centre engagement for 2011 and are currently in the planning stage of the audit. In discussions with management, you discover that Shady Oaks has recently acquired two new full-body scanning machines. These machines use the latest technology and cost the company more than $10 million each. Although they are more than 50 percent more likely to detect abnormalities, new academic studies suggest there may be potential long-term side effects for patients scanned by these machines. However, because the machines are new, the evidence about long-term effects will not be known for many more years. Despite this, there has been some bad press for Shady Oaks highlighting the potential risks to patients.

Shady Oaks charges a premium price for patients using the scanning machines, and there is extremely high demand. To manage the demand, Shady Oaks requires that all patients pay for their scans in full at the time of booking, and the payments are immediately recognized as revenue by the centre. Shady Oaks has taken bookings for four months in advance—although it is only April 2011, the centre has bookings for July and August 2011.

The Canadian Medical Association is currently reviewing the use of the scanning machines and is considering banning their use within Canada until the issue is resolved. A decision is expected on August 1, 2011, and managers tell you that they believe there is an 80 percent chance the scanners will be approved.

Source: Adapted from the Institute of Chartered Accountants Australia's CA Program's *Audit and Assurance Exam*, December 2008 and March 2009.

9.7 Substantive testing for specific assertions at risk ★★★

Required

(a) Identify two key account balances likely to be affected by the above information.

(b) For each account balance identified in (a), identify and explain the key assertions most at risk.

(c) For each assertion identified in (b), identify specific substantive tests of detail that would be responsive to the identified risk.

9.8 Using analytical procedures ★ ★

Your assurance services manager has requested you use substantive analytical procedures to calculate Shady Oaks' estimated revenue for patients staying in the centre, excluding medical procedures and ancillary costs such as medication.

Required

Based on the background provided, describe all the key information required to estimate Shady Oaks' revenue for patients staying in the centre.

9.9 Planning substantive tests ★ ★ ★

Inventory of various medical supplies and drugs is a material account on the Shady Oaks Centre audit engagement. You are planning to adopt a combined audit approach for existence of inventory and rely heavily on preventative control procedures (for example, access to the dispensary and the store room being limited to a few authorized staff) to ensure the physical security of inventory.

You have just completed your tests of controls in relation to physical security procedures. Your projected error rate, based on the results of your already large sample size, is higher than the tolerable error. You are satisfied that the sample is representative and the errors occurred throughout the period audited.

Required

(a) Briefly outline the impact of the projected error rate on your planned substantive audit procedures.
(b) Assume that all of the deviations from the internal control procedures tested (that is, all the errors in the sample) relate to a three-week period when a senior staff member was on annual vacation. Discuss how this would affect your planned substantive tests of detail.

9.10 Persuasiveness of evidence ★ ★

Required

Review your answers to the previous questions. Comment on the persuasiveness of evidence from each test. Explain any factors that would affect your assessment.

9.11 Analytical procedures ★ ★

Analysis is a substantive audit procedure that auditors use when they are performing financial statement audits.

Required

(a) Distinguish between analysis and analytical procedures.
(b) Identify the three stages in the audit process at which analysis can be performed.
(c) For each stage identified in part (b), state the auditor's objective in using analysis.
(d) Briefly describe *three* ways in which auditors can ensure that the data they use in their analytical procedures is reliable.

Source: © CGA-Canada. Reproduced with permission.

CASE STUDY—CLOUD 9

Answer the following questions based on the information presented for Cloud 9 in Appendix B and in the current and earlier chapters. You should also consider your answers to the case study questions in earlier chapters.

Required

(a) Based on your conclusions from the case study questions in previous chapters (particularly chapters 4 and 8), complete the following worksheet to determine the overall risk assessment (ORA) and the acceptable detection risk (DR).

ACCOUNT ASSERTION	INHERENT RISK	CONTROL RISK	OVERALL RISK ASSESSMENT	DETECTION RISK
Sales— occurrence				
Sales— completeness				
Trade receivables— existence				
Trade receivables— completeness				
Cash— existence				

(b) Prepare common-size statements for Cloud 9. Use total assets as the basis for the balance sheet, and revenue as the basis for the income statement. Comment on any audit implications revealed by your statements.

RESEARCH QUESTION 9.1

Economic conditions and financial markets have been significantly affected by the global financial crisis (GFC) that swept around the world in 2008. Love and Lawson identified a series of specific issues flowing from the GFC that must be considered by financial statement auditors and that may affect the procedures used in conducting an audit.

Required

Explain the impact of the GFC on decisions about the nature, timing, and extent of substantive testing. Give some specific examples of the GFC's impact on analytical procedures, and explain how auditors would adjust their audit programs to ensure that overall audit risk remains acceptable.

Source: V.J. Love and C. Lawson, "Auditing in Turbulent Economic Times," *The CPA Journal* (May 2009), pp. 30–35.

SOLUTIONS TO MULTIPLE-CHOICE QUESTIONS

1. b, 2. d, 3. c, 4. d, 5. c, 6. a, 7. b, 8. c, 9. a, 10. d.

CHAPTER 10

Substantive testing and balance sheet accounts

LEARNING OBJECTIVES

After studying this chapter, you should be able to:

1 explain the relationship between the overall risk assessment for a significant account and the extent and timing of substantive procedures

2 design and understand how to execute substantive procedures to address audit risk related to cash

3 design and understand how to execute substantive procedures to address audit risk related to trade receivables

4 design and understand how to execute substantive procedures to address audit risk related to inventory

5 design and understand how to execute substantive procedures to address audit risk related to property, plant, and equipment

6 design and understand how to execute substantive procedures to address audit risk related to payables

7 understand how substantive testing is used for other balance sheet accounts

8 understand how to assess the results of substantive procedures to determine whether additional substantive tests are necessary.

AUDITING AND ASSURANCE STANDARDS

CANADIAN	INTERNATIONAL
CAS 500 *Audit Evidence*	ISA 500 *Audit Evidence*
CAS 501 *Audit Evidence—Specific Consideration for Selected Items*	ISA 501 *Audit Evidence—Specific Considerations for Selected Items*
CAS 505 *External Confirmations*	ISA 505 *External Confirmations*
CAS 610 *Using the Work of Internal Auditors*	ISA 610 *Using the Work of Internal Auditors*
IFRS 7 *Financial Instruments: Disclosures*	IFRS 7 *Financial Instruments: Disclosures*
IAS 2 *Inventories*	IAS 2 *Inventories*
IAS 16 *Property, Plant and Equipment*	IAS 16 *Property, Plant and Equipment*

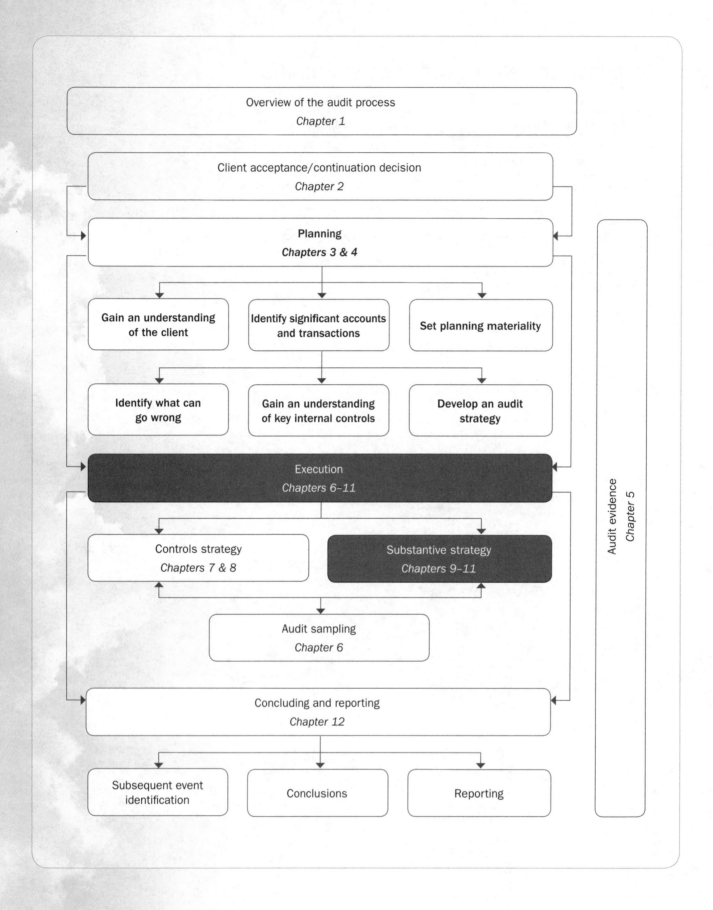

Cloud 9

Suzie and Ian are continuing their work on the substantive audit testing program for the Cloud 9 Ltd. (Cloud 9) audit. Suzie has convinced Ian that analytical procedures are not the only substantive tests they will need. They will also have to consider how audit risk and other factors impact the usefulness of analytical procedures for each area of the audit, and will have to include other substantive tests where required.

Today, they are focusing on assets and liability accounts. Significant accounts on Cloud 9's trial balance include cash; trade receivables (also known as accounts receivable inventory); property, plant, and equipment (PPE) (mainly furniture and equipment and leasehold improvements); and several different types of payables and loans. There is also a large balance in derivative financial assets.

Suzie asks Ian to suggest the key factors that they will have to consider when designing the substantive test program for each of these accounts. What will affect the design decisions? Which tests will they choose to include in the program?

AUDIT PROCESS IN FOCUS

Finding an appropriate combination of audit procedures to reduce an engagement's audit risk at an acceptable cost is a constant challenge facing most audit teams. In this chapter we discuss the objectives of substantive testing; the factors that affect the nature, timing, and extent of procedures; the processes that impact significant accounts in the balance sheet; and illustrative procedures for auditing these significant accounts.

This chapter also illustrates how the type, or nature, of substantive procedures is often the same for each significant account or disclosure, irrespective of the type of business being audited. It is instead the timing and extent of testing that are tailored to each client's circumstances.

10.1 RELATIONSHIP BETWEEN RISK ASSESSMENT AND SUBSTANTIVE PROCEDURES

This section discusses the extent, timing, and other matters to consider when designing **substantive procedures** (also called **substantive testing** or **tests of details**) to detect material misstatements at the assertion level and thereby obtain audit evidence to draw reasonable conclusions on which to base the auditor's opinion (see CAS 500 *Audit Evidence*).

 **1** Explain the relationship between the overall risk assessment for a significant account and the extent and timing of substantive procedures.

substantive procedures (substantive testing or **tests of details)** audit procedures designed to detect material misstatements at the assertion level

10.1.1 Extent of substantive procedures

The auditor decides the extent of substantive procedures needed by determining the risk assessment for each significant account. Not every account or disclosure is necessarily audited in accordance with the approach outlined in this chapter. Accounts that are clearly trivial or immaterial are usually ignored or only subjected to **analytical procedures**. The auditor must exercise **professional judgement** to determine which account balances and disclosures are material to the overall conclusion the auditor forms on the financial statements. Professional judgement is influenced

analytical procedures evaluations of financial information made by a study of plausible relationships among both financial and non-financial data. Analytical procedures also encompass the investigation of identified fluctuations and relationships that are inconsistent with other relevant information or deviate significantly from predicted amounts

professional judgement the auditor's professional characteristics, such as their expertise, experience, knowledge, and training

audit risk the risk that an auditor expresses an inappropriate audit opinion when the financial statements are materially misstated

inherent risk the susceptibility of an assertion to a misstatement that could be material, either individually or when aggregated with other misstatements, regardless of any internal controls

control risk the risk that a client's system of internal controls will not prevent or detect a material misstatement

detection risk the risk that the auditor's testing procedures will not be effective in detecting a material misstatement

tests of controls (controls testing) the audit procedures designed to evaluate the operating effectiveness of controls in preventing, or detecting and correcting, material misstatements at the assertion level

$$AR = IR \times CR \times DR$$

where:

AR = Audit risk

IR = Inherent risk

CR = Control risk

DR = Detection risk

FIGURE 10.1 **Audit risk model**

by many factors, but mainly by the following factors: materiality, the nature of the account balance or disclosure, and the risks identified.

As discussed in chapter 4, a risk assessment on each significant account or disclosure is performed using the risk assessment determined by the **audit risk** model formula in figure 10.1.

When the assessment of **inherent risk** and **control risk** is high, there are no controls tested or relied on and, therefore, the amount of substantive testing required to reduce the detection risk to an acceptable level is significant. When the assessment of inherent and control risk is low, it means there are many controls that have been tested and found to be effective; therefore, the extent of substantive procedures required to address any remaining **detection risk** is limited. It then follows that when the assessment of inherent and control risk is medium, some audit evidence will be obtained from **tests of controls** (or **controls testing**) and some from substantive testing.

10.1.2 Timing of substantive procedures

Figure 10.2 illustrates the relationship between the timing of substantive procedures and levels of assurance.

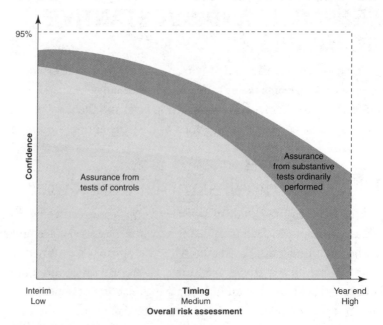

FIGURE 10.2 **Timing of substantive procedures**

As can be seen from figure 10.2, the timing of substantive testing depends on the risk assessment of the **significant account** or disclosure in question. Because most entities are audited at or around the same year end, the timing of audit procedures has a significant impact on the resources of audit firms wishing to ensure that they are able to complete all the statutory audits necessary prior to entities' reporting deadlines. As described in previous chapters, the risk assessment of an account impacts the timing of the procedures. The higher the detection risk for an account, the less work will need to be performed, and the greater the amount of audit evidence relating to the account that can be obtained through controls testing performed before year end. The lower the detection risk, the more work will need to be performed, with the majority of evidence being obtained by performing substantive procedures near or at year end. Apart from the risk assessment of the significant accounts, there are additional opportunities for influencing the timing of the work performed. These include reviewing events occurring prior to year end, reviewing activity in the period to date, performing general audit procedures prior to year end, reviewing provisions prior to year end, and leveraging off the activities of the internal audit function. Each of these methods will now be discussed.

significant account an account or group of accounts that could contain material misstatements based on their materiality and/or relationship to identified inherent and financial statement risks

Reviewing events occurring prior to year end

It is possible (and efficient) to perform audit procedures prior to year end for balance sheet and income statement accounts that accumulate transactions that, for the most part, will remain in the account balance at year end. These may include major business acquisitions or disposals, and key charges to expense accounts—for example, payroll bonuses or major fixed asset additions/disposals likely to represent significant items at year end that would ordinarily be audited substantively.

Reviewing activity in the period to date

When the year-end test is to review activity over the entire accounting period (for example, a monthly review of the aging of trade receivables), it is often possible to prepare, review, and understand the activity as part of the interim audit visit. The year-end visit will then concentrate on updating this review for the period since the interim audit visit.

Performing general audit procedures prior to year end

On all audit engagements, there are a range of audit procedures that ordinarily always need to be performed. These often involve an accumulation of knowledge throughout the year—for example, a review of board minutes, journal entries, and legal correspondence. Some of these procedures can be performed at an interim date, with an update being performed at year end.

Reviewing provisions prior to year end

Where a provision is based on a system-generated assessment as a basis for the overall calculation, audit teams often take the opportunity to review these processes prior to year end and bring forward the audit procedures at year end. This includes familiarization with the approach taken by management prior to year end, so that the auditor can begin to develop an expectation of the balances in advance of the year-end visit. As discussed in chapter 4, it is important, when performing analytical procedures, to have an expectation of the results of the procedure prior to performing it.

Leverage off internal audit

While planning the audit, an understanding of internal audit activities is gained to assess whether any audit procedures may be reduced as a result of these activities. For example, information generated by an internal audit may allow a reduction in the overall level of work performed in establishing control risk assessments and can help update the auditor's understanding of controls more efficiently at year end. CAS 610 *Using the Work of Internal Auditors* establishes the auditor's responsibilities relative to the work of internal auditors when the auditor determines that the internal audit function is likely to be relevant to the audit.

Cloud 9

Ian and Suzie have already decided that analytical procedures are to be supplemented with tests of details except where there is low inherent and control risk. If both inherent and control risk are low, allowable detection risk is high, and analytical procedures are likely to provide sufficient and appropriate evidence in some cases. In addition, when allowable detection risk is high, Ian and Suzie can plan to perform tests of details at interim dates.

Ian suggests that because their control testing has shown that internal controls over property, plant, and equipment (PPE) at Cloud 9 are reasonably effective, tests of details for PPE can be scheduled for interim dates. He suggests that they can inspect physical assets in the balance of furniture and equipment and leasehold improvements prior to the end of the financial year and then vouch acquisitions and trace disposals for the period between the interim date and the end of the financial year. The main focus of these tests would be on the existence, valuation, and rights and obligations assertions for new assets and the completeness assertion for disposals. Cloud 9's trial balance does not contain a separate maintenance and repairs expense account, and Ian is concerned about the possibility that any expenditure has been inappropriately capitalized. He suggests that for PPE, analytical procedures are most useful for testing depreciation expense.

10.1.3 Matters to consider when designing substantive procedures

Some specific issues to consider when designing substantive procedures are discussed in this section, including ensuring that substantive procedures respond to specific risks, taking credit for work already undertaken, and setting appropriate testing thresholds.

Ensure that substantive procedures respond to specific risks

When deciding on the nature of tests to perform, it is essential to understand the key assertions most at risk. For example, for most asset accounts, the primary risk is an overstatement of the account balance. Therefore, the auditor will design tests that focus on the existence, occurrence, and valuation assertions. For most liability accounts, however, the greatest risk relates to the understatement of the account balance; therefore, the substantive tests performed will primarily focus on the completeness assertion.

It is also important for the auditor to consider the specific risks driving the risk assessment for that account assertion. For example, if one client has significant overseas accounts receivable customers, the inherent risk for the valuation of receivables may be increased; however, if controls testing indicates that control risk is low for this assertion, substantive testing can be reduced. Another client may have trade receivables where the inherent risk over valuation has been assessed as low because the balance is made up of a significant number of very small accounts receivable customers, but there is a higher control risk due to poor controls being in place. Both overall risk assessments are the same, but the audit strategy for each will be different due to the controls risk assessment made.

Take credit for work already undertaken

Before the auditor begins their year-end work, it is important to remember that procedures have already been performed to assess control and inherent risks. Interim substantive procedures may also have been completed. The auditor needs to ensure that they take credit for this work. They must also ensure that the "mindset" with which they approach their year-end work is appropriate and fully reflects their risk assessment and expectation of the likelihood of material misstatements occurring.

Set appropriate testing thresholds

The threshold for what the auditor considers important will vary depending on the overall risk assessment and the context in which they make the judgement. Thresholds should be challenged in the context of the client and the overall risk assessment, and they should be set with the agreement of the engagement executives to ensure that the audit team is performing the right level of testing for each significant account. Determining the extent of testing prior to year end will allow more time during the year-end visit to focus on performing the required procedures.

Cloud 9

Ian identifies prepayments as an account that is not significant. In the absence of any other indicators suggesting high risk, he recommends that the account balances be substantiated using analytical procedures only. Analytical procedures can be very effective for prepaid rent and insurance because the balance is a mathematical derivation of the contracted amount for rent and insurance.

Accrued expenses on the September trial balance are larger than prepayments, so there is a greater risk they are overstated. However, the greater concern is whether the accrued expenses are understated (that is, the completeness assertion). Some provisions can be confirmed through recalculation (for example, annual leave provision), but others involve more judgement (for example, warranty and loyalty program provisions). Ian recommends using analytical procedures for both types of liabilities. He also recommends additional tests of details for the provisions, including examination of the documents relating to claims. Cloud 9's loyalty program is new and will therefore require the involvement of a senior member of the audit team to test the assumptions used to calculate the liability (some of this work has already been done during the planning phase).

BEFORE YOU GO ON

1.1 Describe two influences on the timing of substantive procedures apart from the risk assessment of the account in question.

1.2 How can an internal audit influence the timing of the external auditor's procedures?

1.3 Why is it important to understand the overall risk assessment for a significant account?

10.2 SUBSTANTIVE TESTING OF CASH

② Design and understand how to execute substantive procedures to address audit risk related to cash.

cash equivalents highly liquid investments that may be quickly converted to cash

imprest payroll account account established for processing payroll disbursements only

pledge something delivered as security for the payment of a debt or the fulfillment of a promise, which is forfeited if there is failure to pay or to fulfill the promise

While cash is presented as a single line item on the balance sheet, this balance at the end of the year may consist of cash on hand, cash in the bank, and cash equivalents. **Cash equivalents** are highly liquid investments that may be quickly converted to cash. Some clients also have **imprest payroll accounts**. These accounts are established for processing payroll disbursements only. The funds required to cover the payroll are transferred to this account as needed. As the issued payroll cheques clear the bank, the balance is drawn down to zero. Sometimes the cash balance on the balance sheet is presented as a liability under the caption "bank indebtedness." This happens when an entity has access to a bank overdraft facility and has spent more cash than it has on hand.

When cash is a significant account on an entity's balance sheet, the auditor must ensure that sufficient and appropriate audit evidence has been gathered on which to conclude that there are no material misstatements in cash at year end. Three audit assertions that are particularly important to enable the auditor to achieve this objective are existence, completeness, and classification.

First, the existence of cash is usually verified by the receipt of a confirmation from the client's bank. The bank should also confirm whether there are any additional bank accounts, loans, **pledges,** lease facilities, or other banking facilities. CAS 505 *External Confirmations* provides further guidance on the enquiry and confirmation methods of obtaining audit evidence.

The second significant assertion is completeness, with a particular focus on whether the balance completely reflects all cash transactions. Substantive tests usually focus on testing the client's bank reconciliation as well as the cut-off of cash transactions. The auditor tests the bank reconciliation by vouching any differences between cash as per the bank statement and cash as per the general ledger to supporting documentary evidence. The differences between the bank statement and the general ledger are often the result of cheques that have been issued but have not yet cleared the bank, as well as deposits in transit, bank fees, and sometimes small amounts of interest. Most of these items can be vouched to a bank statement after year end, providing evidence that the cheques have been honoured and the deposits have been recognized by the bank. Any fees or interest the bank charged should be vouched to the general ledger as evidence the client has recognized these reconciling items.

The third significant assertion is classification. Classification is important because of the additional information related to the cash account that is required to be disclosed in the financial statements, including unused credit facilities and other information that is part of the statement of cash flow disclosure requirements.

For certain clients, a fourth audit assertion—rights and obligations—is significant, as the client may have pledged assets such as cash, which means the use of cash by the company is restricted. That is important information not only for the auditor to understand, but also for the users of the financial statements. Valuation and allocation is not often a significant assertion, although it is very important when the client has cash balances that are held in a foreign currency.

10.2.1 Principal objectives in auditing cash

The principal objectives in auditing cash are described in table 10.1.

It is worth noting that the classification (Cl) assertion and the classification and understandability (C&U) assertion are different. Classification relates to transactions

OBJECTIVE	ASSERTION
All cash on the balance sheet is held by the entity or by others (for example, a bank) for the entity.	Existence (E)
All cash owned by the entity at year end is included in the balance sheet.	Completeness (C)
Cash is stated at its realizable value.	Valuation and allocation (V&A)
The entity owns, or has legal rights to, all the cash on the balance sheet at year end. All cash is free from restrictions on use, **liens**, or other security interests, or, if it is not free, that such restrictions, liens, or other security interests are identified.	Rights and obligations (R&O)
Cash is properly classified, described, and disclosed in the financial statements, including the notes, and disclosures of any of the above-mentioned restrictions on use, etc., are made as required by application of an appropriate accounting framework (for example, International Financial Reporting Standards or Accounting Standards for Private Enterprises).	Classification (CI), classification and understandability (C&U)

TABLE 10.1 **Objectives in auditing cash**

liens legal claims of one person on the property of another person to secure the payment of a debt or the satisfaction of an obligation

and events that occur throughout the year (for example, how they are recorded in the income statement and whether they are in the right expense account). Classification and understandability relates to presentation and disclosure in the financial statements.

10.2.2 Factors impacting the audit of cash

Prior to performing tests of details, the auditor should assess any audit evidence obtained from the testing they performed at an interim stage on significant transactions, including tests of controls over cash receipts and disbursements (for example, appropriate approvals of cash payments made). If the auditor has performed controls testing and concluded that the controls in these areas are effective and can be relied on, it is unlikely that any additional tests of controls related to the cash receipts or cash payments processes would be performed. Instead, the auditor would perform substantive tests to audit the cash balance at year end with no additional process- or control-related testing required. This is because the auditor has concluded that the controls are effective in ensuring that the "what could go wrongs" (WCGWs) identified during planning are unlikely to occur.

The auditor usually does some testing over cash even when the cash balance itself is not material. This is because most transactions flow through the cash account at some point; therefore, cash is qualitatively material. Furthermore, cash tends to have a high inherent risk if an organization has a large number of cash transactions during the year, as cash is one of the easiest assets to steal. While the audit of most account balances includes some analytics, analytics over the cash accounts are generally not very meaningful. This is because cash balances are generally unstable or "lumpy," and therefore trends and account relationships are not very informative.

Table 10.2 illustrates substantive tests of transactions the auditor may perform during the testing of significant transactions related to cash. Some of these procedures may be performed during the controls testing of the cash receipts and cash payments processes; they are dual purpose tests in that they provide evidence for both tests of controls and substantive tests. These procedures would likely be performed even when the auditor was able to test and rely on controls (that is, the controls were effective). In this case, however, the extent of testing could be reduced. There are many tests that would need to be performed over a large proportion of the transactions flowing through these significant accounting processes if a fully substantive approach were to be taken. It is therefore normally more efficient and effective to perform at least some controls testing, if possible.

Note that each substantive test illustrated in this chapter addresses a number of audit assertions. This is because many tests of transactions are designed to address multiple assertions in both the balance sheet and the income statement. Only key assertions addressed are specifically identified for the examples in this chapter.

TABLE 10.2 **Example substantive tests of transactions—cash**

CASH RECEIPTS PROCESS	CASH PAYMENTS PROCESS
Perform a proof of cash by reconciling activity per the client records to activity per the bank. Also, correlate these transactions to the activity in the sales and trade receivables ledgers. This procedure is limited to less complex engagements that have a limited number of transactions. (C, A)	Account for the numerical sequence of cheques issued during a specified period. (CO, C)
Compare remittance advices or lists of cash receipts with entries in the cash receipts journal as to date, remitter, amount, and account classification. (CI, C)	Compare paid cheques and supporting documents with the cash disbursement journal as to date, payee, amount, and account classification; determine whether supporting documents indicate the item has been paid. (C)
Compare the details of duplicate deposit slips with the entries in the cash receipts journal. Investigate abnormal delays in depositing cash receipts. (C)	Compare entries in the cash disbursement journal with the paid cheques and supporting documents as to date, payee, amount, and account classification; determine whether supporting documents indicate the item has been paid. (O)
Compare the total amounts of daily deposits shown on the bank statement with the totals of the daily cash receipts shown in the cash receipts journal. Investigate unusual delays in depositing cash receipts and any splitting of daily cash receipts into separate deposits. (C)	Test the account classifications of cash payments. (CI)
Agree invoice amounts to cash received for cash sales transactions. Agree cash collected to the recorded cash balance and supporting documents. (C)	Test the mathematical accuracy of the cash disbursement journal. (V&A)
Test the recording of miscellaneous receipts (that is, receipts not usually recorded in trade receivables, such as proceeds on disposal of assets or royalties); consider whether the recorded amounts are reasonable. (A)	Test the postings of the totals in the cash disbursement journal to the general ledger and subsidiary ledgers. (C)

(*continued*)

CASH RECEIPTS PROCESS	CASH PAYMENTS PROCESS
Compare entries in the cash receipts journal (for example, date, remitter, amount, and account classification) with the remittance advices, lists of cash receipts, bank deposit slips, and bank statements. (O)	Test the posting of individual cash payments from the cash disbursement journal to the appropriate accounts in the subsidiary ledgers. (CI)
Test the accounting classifications of cash receipts. (CI, V&A)	Determine whether the signatures on paid cheques are authorized. (A)
Test the mathematical accuracy of the cash receipts journal. (A)	
Test the postings (processing) of the totals in the cash receipts journal to the general ledger and other subsidiary ledgers. (C)	
Test the authorization of credits, discounts, and allowances in the cash receipts journal. (O, E)	
Test the posting of individual cash receipts from the cash receipts journal and supporting documents to the trade receivables sub-ledger. (CI, C)	

E—existence; C—completeness; V&A—valuation and allocation; R&O—rights and obligations; CI—classification; C&U—classification and understandability; CO—cut-off; A—accuracy; O—occurrence

10.2.3 Illustrative procedures for auditing cash

An almost limitless number of substantive procedures can be designed for the testing of account balances. Table 10.3 illustrates substantive procedures an auditor may perform when substantively auditing cash. Generally, the focus of the tests of account balances is on the audit of the bank reconciliation, which starts with the balance per the bank and identifies anything that causes the book balance to differ. See Appendix A for a sample of an audited bank reconciliation.

TABLE 10.3 **Example substantive tests of account balances—cash**

EXAMPLE TESTS ALWAYS PERFORMED
Confirm cash held by others (for example, bank balances and/or overdrafts) and cash on hand, if significant. (E, R&O)
Examine the client's bank reconciliations. (C, V&A) • Foot the bank reconciliation to ensure mathematical accuracy. • Trace the book balance to the general ledger. • Agree confirmed balance with the bank balance per the reconciliation. • Obtain cut-off bank statement. • Determine whether outstanding cheques have subsequently cleared and whether deposits in transit have been recorded by the bank. • Verify the appropriateness of reconciling items.
Test cut-off of cash receipts, cash payments, and transfers as at year end. (C, V&A)
EXAMPLE ANALYTICAL PROCEDURES
Compare the listing of cash accounts with the prior period's and investigate any unexpected changes (for example, credit balances, unusually large balances, new accounts, closed accounts) or the absence of expected changes. (E, C, V&A, CI)
Review interest received and/or paid in relation to the average cash balances and/or bank overdrafts (accuracy of interest income in the income statement). (O, A)

(continued)

TABLE 10.3 **Example substantive tests of account balances—cash** (continued)

EXAMPLE OTHER GENERAL PROCEDURES
Review the cash accounts in the general ledger for unusual items. (C, V&A)
Review bank confirmations, minutes of meetings, loan agreements, and other documents for evidence of restrictions on the use of cash or liens on cash. (C&U)
Recalculate any foreign currency–denominated bank accounts using the appropriate foreign exchange rate. (V)
Prepare a schedule of cash transfers between accounts before and after year end, ensuring that transfers are recorded in the correct period. (E, C)
Count cash on hand. (E)

Cloud 9

Suzie reminds Ian that they have conducted extensive testing of Cloud 9's controls over cash receipts and payments, and many of these tests were dual purpose. This means that the substantive and control tests were done at the same time. While examining the documents, the audit assistant completed tasks designed to detect control deviations and substantive errors. These tests included vouching cash payments and receipts (including transaction approvals and posting) to the underlying documents.

The testing already completed shows that controls over cash are reasonably strong, and they can justify focusing on the bank reconciliation at the balance sheet date. The bank confirmation will gather evidence about the existence and valuation assertions, plus rights and obligations (that is, it will reveal liens or claims over bank accounts). The cut-off bank statement will provide evidence for the outstanding items. They will include testing the cut-off of cash receipts and payment at this time. Ian notices that the savings account balance has changed significantly from $1,200,000 at the end of the previous year to $60,000 at the September interim date. This is probably due to payment of the costs associated with the new store, trucks, and marketing campaign, but it could also be a seasonal fluctuation. They will ask the finance director about the fluctuating cash balance, and compare the account balance and cash flows with budgeted figures.

BEFORE YOU GO ON

2.1 Name two assertions that are ordinarily significant for cash, and describe why they are important.

2.2 What is the impact on the level of substantive audit procedures necessary for the cash receipts process if controls are not tested and found to be effective?

2.3 Describe two substantive audit procedures ordinarily always performed for cash.

10.3 SUBSTANTIVE TESTING OF TRADE RECEIVABLES

3 Design and understand how to execute substantive procedures to address audit risk related to trade receivables.

When accounts receivable (or receivables) is a significant account in an entity's balance sheet, there are two audit assertions that are considered most important to ensure that the auditor has gained sufficient and appropriate audit evidence on which to conclude that there are no material misstatements in the balance as at year end. They are the existence assertion and the valuation and allocation assertion.

Existence of trade receivables is usually verified by sending confirmations to the client's customers. This is referred to as a positive confirmation, as the auditor requires a response to the confirmation request from the customer before concluding that the customer (trade receivable) exists. A negative confirmation is generally not used as an audit technique due to the limited level of assurance it provides. It is referred to as a negative confirmation as the auditor only requires a response if the customer disputes the balance included on the confirmation. See Appendix A for a completed trade receivables confirmation.

There can be confusion as to whether a trade receivables confirmation (as described in CAS 505 *External Confirmations*) provides assurance over the existence assertion, the valuation and allocation assertion, or both. A positive confirmation really only provides audit evidence as to the existence of the balance owing. That is, the receivable is real and goods or services were provided to the customer to the value recorded in the trade receivables subsidiary ledger. It does not, however, provide any assurance as to whether the client will recover all of the balance. For example, a customer may confirm that a balance is due and payable, but the auditor may be unable to determine whether the customer has the ability to pay the amount. The best way to ensure that the balance is valued correctly is by the full receipt of the cash by the client after year end.

The second significant assertion is valuation and allocation of trade receivables. As explained previously, the confirmation procedure does not provide assurance over the valuation and allocation assertion; instead, additional tests are required. The most common test is referred to as subsequent receipts. This is when a sample of trade receivables at year end is vouched to the subsequent receipt of cash from the customer. This procedure is also used as evidence for the existence assertion when the auditor has not received the confirmation back from the accounts receivable customer. This is based on the fact that if the supporting documentation indicates an appropriate cut-off, and the customer paid the account after year end, then the balance outstanding must have existed. The valuation assertion is further tested when the allowance for doubtful accounts is reviewed and recalculated. The auditor will identify significant accounts past due and discuss the likelihood of collection with management. Additional analytical procedures can also be performed to corroborate the results of the valuation testing. These include tests such as comparing the aging of trade receivables to the prior period, and calculating the number of days it takes to convert trade receivables to cash for the current and prior period. Other assertions may also be important in the audit of trade receivables for a client. The classification assertion is important because of the additional information related to trade receivables that is required to be disclosed in the financial statements. This information includes related party disclosures as well as the disclosures required by Canadian Accounting Standard IFRS 7 *Financial Instruments: Disclosures*. For certain clients, rights and obligations are a significant assertion, as the client may have restrictions on trade terms as part of its conditions of sale. For example, some clients sell inventory that is on consignment from a third party, and therefore the inventory is not recorded as owned by the client. Completeness is also important; however, the audit procedures to verify that trade receivables are complete are relatively simple and consist of performing cut-off procedures at year end. Example cut-off procedures are included in table 10.6.

10.3.1 A note on confirmations

While there is no specific requirement for the auditor to confirm accounts receivable, this is a frequently used procedure as it provides third-party external evidence over the existence assertion. However, when confirmations are used, the auditor must assess the reliability of the confirmation, as it may be compromised if the respondent is not independent of the client, does not understand what is being requested, or replies without verifying the information being requested.

Confirmations are usually sent to the customers with the largest and oldest balances outstanding, as the auditor looks to get sufficient coverage of the total balance. If the client has a number of smaller accounts receivable balances outstanding, the auditor may also select a sample of these accounts to confirm. However, the auditor may decide not to use confirmations if the accounts receivable balance is not material, past history of using confirmations indicates there is a low response rate, the assessed risk over the accounts receivable account is low, and sufficient and appropriate evidence can be obtained through other procedures.

The information being requested in the confirmation is considered confidential; therefore, the auditor must obtain the client's consent before sending out confirmations. Per CAS 505, if management refuses to give the auditor this consent, then there is a potential scope limitation. If this is the case, the auditor is required to find out the reasons for the limitation. Commonly, the client may have an existing legal dispute with the confirming party, and the client may feel the confirmation request could affect the resolution of the dispute. The auditor must obtain evidence as to the validity and reasonableness of management's reasons to ensure that they are not preventing access to evidence that might reveal fraud or error.

While the auditor requires the client's permission to send out confirmations, the auditor must maintain control over the confirmation process. It is the auditor's responsibility to pick the sample to be confirmed, to mail the confirmations, and to ensure that they are sent back directly to the auditor.

10.3.2 Principal objectives in auditing trade receivables

The principal objectives in auditing trade receivables are described in table 10.4.

TABLE 10.4 **Objectives in auditing trade receivables**

OBJECTIVE	ASSERTION
All receivables on the balance sheet are real claims of the entity.	Existence (E)
All real claims of the entity for amounts receivable are included on the balance sheet.	Completeness (C)
Receivables are carried at their net realizable (collectable) value (that is, the gross receivables are properly stated with appropriate allowances provided for uncollectable accounts, discounts, returns, warranties, and similar items).	Valuation and allocation (V&A)
The entity owns, or has legal right to, all the receivables on the balance sheet at year end. All receivables are free from liens, pledges, or other security interests or, if not, such liens, pledges, or other security interests are identified.	Rights and obligations (R&O)
Receivables are properly classified, described, and disclosed in the financial statements, including the notes, in conformity with prescribed accounting principles (IFRS and ASPE).	Classification (Cl), classification and understandability (C&U)

10.3.3 Processes impacting on trade receivables

Table 10.5 illustrates procedures the auditor may perform during the testing of transactions related to trade receivables. There are three important types of transactions that impact the balance: sales, sales returns and allowances (credit memos), and cash receipts. These procedures would likely be performed even when the auditor was able to test and rely on controls (that is, where the controls were effective). In this case, however, the extent of testing could be reduced.

TABLE 10.5 **Example substantive tests of transactions—trade receivables**

SALES PROCESS	SALES RETURNS AND ALLOWANCES (CREDIT MEMOS) PROCESS	CASH RECEIPTS PROCESS
Account for the numerical sequence of sales invoices, sales orders, and shipping documents during a specified period. Reconcile billings with shipping documents for substantial portion of the period. (C, CO)	Compare credit memos and supporting documents with the sales returns and allowances ledger as to dates, customers, products, quantities, prices, and amounts. (O)	Compare remittance advices or lists of cash receipts with the entries in the cash receipts journal as to date, remitter, amount, and account classification. (C)
Test the records of products ordered and shipped to the sales records; agree dates, customers, products, quantities, prices, and amounts. (O)	Account for the numerical sequence of credit memos during a specified period. (C)	Compare the details of duplicate deposit slips with the entries in the cash receipts ledger. Investigate abnormal delays in depositing cash receipts. (C)
Trace individual sales invoices to the sales journal and to the trade receivables sub-ledger. (CI)	Test the posting of individual credit memos to the sales returns and allowances ledger and to the trade receivables sub-ledger. (CI)	Compare the total amounts of the daily deposits shown on the bank statements with the totals of the daily cash receipts shown in the cash receipts journal. Investigate unusual delays in depositing cash receipts and any splitting of daily cash receipts into separate deposits. (C)
Test recorded sales to the records of products ordered and shipped; agree dates, customer, products, quantities, and amounts. (O)	Compare recorded credit memos with the documents supporting returns and allowances as to dates, customers, products, quantities, prices, and amounts. (O)	Compare entries in the cash receipts journal (for example, date, remitter, amount, and account classification) with the remittance advices, lists of cash receipts, duplicate deposit slips, and bank statements. (O)
Review the listing of accounts receivable and investigate unusual balances, credit balances, and accounts that may not be properly classified as accounts receivable. (V&A, CI)	Test credit postings in the trade receivables sub-ledger to the cash receipts journal or approved credit. (C)	Test the accounting classifications of cash receipts. (CI)
	Test the authorization of credits, discounts, and allowances shown in the cash receipts journal. (A)	

(continued)

TABLE 10.5 **Example substantive tests of transactions—trade receivables** (continued)

SALES PROCESS	SALES RETURNS AND ALLOWANCES (CREDIT MEMOS) PROCESS	CASH RECEIPTS PROCESS
Investigate large or unusual credit memos issued subsequent to year end. (V&A)	Test the pricing, mathematical accuracy, and authorization of credit memos (for example, trace information to terms and recording of original sales). (A)	Test the mathematical accuracy of the cash receipts journal. (A)
Test the pricing and mathematical accuracy of sales invoices. (A)	Test the cut-off in processing credits and allowances granted to customers by examining credit memos issued and recorded before and after year end. (CO)	Test the postings of the totals in the cash receipts journal to the general ledger, trade receivables sub-ledger, and other subsidiary ledgers. (C)
Test the accounting classification of sales transactions. (Cl)	Test the timeliness with which credits granted to customers are processed. (A)	Test the posting of individual cash receipts from the cash receipts journal and supporting documents to the trade receivables sub-ledger. (Cl, C)
Review the trade receivables, sales and sales returns, and allowances accounts in the general ledger for unusual items. (V&A)	Test the accounting classification of credit memos. (Cl)	Examine the client's bank reconciliations. When appropriate (for example, to determine whether receipts of payments are recorded on a timely basis, or to verify the appropriateness of reconciling items), obtain cut-off bank statements. (CO)
Test the mathematical accuracy of the sales ledger. (A)	Test the mathematical accuracy of the sales returns and allowances ledger. (A)	Test cut-off of cash receipts, disbursements, and transfers at year end. (C)
Trace the accounts receivable to the trade receivables sub-ledger (detailed customer aged trial balance) and investigate reconciling items. (A)	Test the postings of the totals in the sales returns and allowances ledger to the general ledger and trade receivables sub-ledger. (C)	
Test the postings of the totals in the sales ledger to the general ledger and the sub-ledger. (C)		

10.3.4 Illustrative procedures for auditing trade receivables

There is an almost limitless number of substantive procedures that can be designed for the testing of account balances. Table 10.6 illustrates example substantive procedures when auditing trade receivables. Some of the procedures are always performed (irrespective of the risk assessment the auditor reaches for the significant account), while others are additionally selected in response to the risk assessment to address any remaining detection risk that is still evident after controls testing has been performed.

EXAMPLE TESTS ALWAYS PERFORMED

Confirm accounts receivable.
- If accounts are confirmed at an interim date, review the roll-forward of activity from the confirmation date to year end and compare the level of activity with the prior period. (E)
- Investigate unusual items; consider confirming (at year end) significant new accounts and those accounts with significant increases or decreases between the confirmation date and year end. (E)
- Examine subsequent cash receipts, shipping records, sales contracts, and other evidence to verify the validity of accounts receivable for which replies to confirmation requests were unsatisfactory or were not obtained as part of supporting year-end receivables balances. (E)

Test the cut-off by inspecting the sales ledger, billings, shipping documents, and other supporting documents immediately before and after the cut-off date and determine that the transactions were recorded in the proper period; compare the receivables cut-off to cut-offs in related areas (for example, sales and inventory). (C)

Evaluate the adequacy of the allowances for doubtful accounts. See the example procedures that may be performed under other general procedures below. (V&A)

Scan the general ledger and sub-ledgers for unusual balances and unusual entries. (E)

Investigate all exceptions noted on the confirmations. (E)

EXAMPLE ANALYTICAL PROCEDURES

Allowances for doubtful accounts

Compare the aged listing of accounts receivable with the prior period's and note any significant changes (for example, changes in major customers or in major trade receivables balances overdue). (V&A)

Compare the current period's accounts written off and the allowance for doubtful accounts as percentages of accounts receivable and sales with the prior period's percentages. Evaluate the trends in light of current economic conditions and what you know about the client and the industry in which it operates. (V&A)

Compare the current year's to the prior year's allowance for doubtful accounts as a percentage of receivables and sales. (V&A)

Compare the current period's receivables as a percentage of net sales with the prior period's percentages and consider the reasonableness of the current period's percentage in relation to current economic conditions, credit policies, and collectability. (V&A)

Compare the current period's accounts receivable turnover and number of days' sales outstanding with prior amounts and consider the reasonableness of the current period's amounts in relation to current economic conditions, credit policies, and collectability. (V&A)

Compare the aging with the client's and with the industry's collection practices (if known). (V&A)

Compare the current period's sales returns and sales discounts as percentages of sales by product line with prior period percentages. Investigate significant or unusual fluctuations. (V&A)

Compare the number and amounts of sales credit notes issued with those of the prior period. (V&A)

TABLE 10.6 **Example substantive tests of account balances—trade receivables**

(continued)

TABLE 10.6 **Example substantive tests of account balances—trade receivables** (continued)

EXAMPLE OTHER GENERAL PROCEDURES
Trace the totals of accounts receivable in the trade receivables sub-ledger to the general ledger control accounts or accounts receivable summary. (V&A, C)
Allowance for doubtful accounts
Understand and document the rights of return offered to customers under the terms of sales agreements or as a matter of practice. (V&A)
Review analysis of activity in the allowance for uncollectable accounts and bad debts expense accounts during the period. (V&A)
Evaluate the adequacy of the allowance for doubtful accounts at year end. (V&A)
Review analysis of activity in the allowances for discounts, returns, warranties, and similar items during the period. (V&A)
Evaluate the adequacy of the allowances for discounts, returns, warranties, and similar items at year end. (V&A)
Test the accuracy of the accounts receivable aging by tracing details to and from the trade receivables sub-ledger or supporting documentation. Test aging for clerical accuracy. (V&A)
Evaluate the adequacy of any collateral and guarantees on any receivables balances. (V&A)
Review payments received subsequent to year end or confirmation date. (V&A)
Other
Test the timing and amount of year-end revenue recognition by tracing to long-term contracts, service agreements, licence agreements, or other appropriate documentation to detect errors and/or estimate amount of incorrect revenue recorded. (E, V&A, CI)
Examine details of accounts receivable from related parties; investigate unusual items as well as significant reductions or increases at year end; determine that necessary disclosures are made. (C&U)
Review minutes, loan agreements, and other documents for evidence of liens, pledges, or other security interests in receivables; determine that necessary disclosures are made. (R&O)

Cloud 9

Ian suggests that the controls testing over the sales and accounts receivables process and the cash receipts has provided some evidence about receivables. Dual testing has been built into the controls testing program in these areas, which means that additional substantive testing can focus on specific, more risky areas. Accounts receivable confirmations are a key substantive technique that Ian recommends be undertaken. Year-end testing will also include cut-off testing and subsequent receipts testing. Receipts from accounts receivable customers in the month following year end provide persuasive evidence about the collectability of receivables at year end. Senior members of the audit team will be involved in assessing the adequacy of the allowance for doubtful accounts.

Suzie suggests that they also consider the receivables from the Cloud 9 Inc. parent company when planning substantive tests in this area. The receivable from the parent gives rise to special disclosure requirements and is therefore an area of additional risk, even though the amount of the asset is not large.

PROFESSIONAL ENVIRONMENT

Fraud in trade receivables

A famous case that involves questions about asset values in audited financial statements is that of WorldCom, a U.S. company that filed for bankruptcy in 2002. WorldCom was a telecommunications company that had grown primarily through acquiring other companies. After WorldCom's collapse, commentators questioned the company's financial reporting practices. For example, Eichenwald claimed that when new assets were acquired in an acquisition, they were immediately written down in value, and "included in this charge against earnings [was] the cost of company expenses expected in the future. The result was bigger losses in the current quarter but smaller ones in future quarters, so that its profit picture would seem to be improving."

WorldCom also had some issues with its trade receivables, particularly relating to its acquisition of MCI Communications. Walter Pavlo was a senior manager in billing and collections at WorldCom. In January 2001, he was given a 41-month sentence for offences relating to money laundering, wire fraud, and obstruction of justice. Walter Pavlo's responsibilities were to bill customers, collect money, post the customer payments and credits, and perform account reconciliations. In a video made for the American Institute of CPAs and the Association of Certified Fraud Examiners, he described the pressure employees of the company were under to grow the business consistently, and the great incentives for growth provided by stock options, which he was given "by the thousands."

Pavlo also explained that, initially, the attempts to conceal uncollectable accounts felt more like "a little white lie" that could be fixed up in the next quarter, when more cash was collected. They knew exactly where the numbers had to be to meet analysts' expectations each quarter, and they worked toward this target. He said that he didn't have the feeling at the time that his actions were unethical. He described "learning" to find ways to conceal the problems. It was an evolutionary process rather than specific instructions to "fix the books." However, it was also known at the company that senior executive Bernie Ebbers, subsequently convicted of other offences related to the WorldCom collapse, saw the company's code of conduct as a "colossal waste of time."

The auditor for WorldCom was Arthur Andersen, which was facing big problems at the time relating to its audit of Enron. Andersen did not appear to realize the depth of the problems with asset values at WorldCom. Finally, the alarm was raised when an internal auditor, Cynthia Cooper, brought the matter to the attention of WorldCom's audit committee.

Sources: K. Eichenwald, "For WorldCom, Acquisitions Were Behind Its Rise and Fall," *The New York Times*, August 8, 2002, www.nytimes.com; American Institute of Certified Public Accountants (AICPA) and Association of Certified Fraud Examiners (ACFE), *Fraud and the Tone at the Top* (video), 2009, www.acfe.com; S. Pelliam and D. Solomon, "Uncooking the Books: How Three Unlikely Sleuths Discovered Fraud at WorldCom," *The Wall Street Journal*, October 30, 2002.

BEFORE YOU GO ON

3.1 Name two assertions that are ordinarily significant for trade receivables, and describe why they are important.

3.2 What is the impact on the level of substantive audit procedures necessary for the sales process if controls are not tested and found to be effective?

3.3 Describe two substantive audit procedures ordinarily always performed for trade receivables.

10.4 SUBSTANTIVE TESTING OF INVENTORY

An inventory listing is a list of all the items of inventory that a company has. It is used to capture purchases and sales of inventory, and it is the basis in calculating any provision for slow-moving or obsolete items. An inventory listing is essentially

4 Design and understand how to execute substantive procedures to address audit risk related to inventory.

the inventory sub-ledger that is reconciled to the general ledger account for inventory. CAS 501 *Audit Evidence—Specific Consideration for Selected Items* contains the requirements for obtaining sufficient appropriate audit evidence relating to inventory. The two key assertions for inventory are existence, and valuation and allocation.

Existence is important because the inventory the company has recorded in its inventory listing (which flows into the general ledger and finally into the financial statements) needs to actually exist. Auditors test for existence by physically observing the inventory count held by the client. Some clients conduct inventory counts once a year, while other clients perform inventory counts on a cyclical basis, counting a small number of items on multiple days throughout the year. The better a company controls its inventory, the easier it is to implement cycle counting (to test the perpetual stock records to the physical records) on a regular basis throughout the year. If the controls are not strong, or if it is physically difficult to count the inventory, often only an annual inventory count is held (usually close to or on the final day of the reporting period).

It is important to physically view inventory periodically, as this provides insight into not only whether the items exist in the quantities recorded but also whether there appear to be any items that may be slow-moving, damaged, obsolete, impaired, or excess to the client's needs, providing important evidence for the valuation and allocation assertion.

Valuation and allocation is the other significant assertion tested by auditors in relation to inventory, as it is important that inventory is recorded at the appropriate carrying value (or "fair value," as it is described and defined by the IFRS IAS 2 *Inventories*). Valuation becomes very important when companies change products, as the decisions made by management and those charged with governance will impact the values that items of inventory should be carried at. For example, if an entity decides to stop making or selling a particular product, and instead replaces it with a new one, it is likely that the value of the old inventory will be impaired and may need to be written down to its fair value (or nil).

Typical substantive procedures to test valuation focus on the initial cost recorded (by vouching to supporting invoices), the value recovered for any sales (by vouching to sales invoices), and any provision for impairment calculations for excess, slow-moving, or obsolete stock on hand at year end.

Completeness of inventory is ordinarily not a major issue for most entities as the auditor is typically most concerned with the overstatement of assets, and completeness tests tend to focus on the potential understatement of inventory on hand. However, for some clients, it is a significant assertion. For example, for clients selling to retail outlets, the retailer often does not take ownership or title of the goods held in-store until the goods are actually sold. It is not until the sale has occurred that the supplier (our client in this example) is able to recognize the sale. That is important information not only for the auditor to understand but also for the users of the financial statements to be aware of, as it gives information about the risks of whether the client is likely to receive the cash (in the example given, this is highly dependent on the customer's ability to sell the goods rather than on anything the client can necessarily do). It also represents the type of inventory that may be inadvertently omitted from the balance.

Rights and obligations is tested for particular types of rights that attach to the inventory held by a client. For example, if inventory is owned by the client as soon as it is shipped from the manufacturer, the goods in transit need to be recognized as inventory before they are actually received into the client's warehouse. Ownership of inventory is subject to a high risk of error only at a very few, very specific types of companies that purchase or sell goods with specific rights attached to the items.

Classification is generally addressed by testing the inventory listing. Therefore, verifying the amounts included in the disclosures in the financial statements is relatively straightforward, as the disclosures are often found within the listing (that is, the split of total inventory between raw materials, work in progress [WIP], and finished goods).

10.4.1 Principal objectives in auditing inventory

The principal objectives in auditing inventory are described in table 10.7.

OBJECTIVE	ASSERTION
All inventory on the inventory listing is included in the financial statements.	Existence (E)
All inventory owned by the entity at year end is included on the balance sheet.	Completeness (C)
Inventory is carried at the lower of cost or net realizable value. Ensure that the cost and net realizable value determinations are appropriate, including adequate provisions for excess, slow-moving, obsolete, and damaged goods, and for losses on purchase and sale commitments.	Valuation and allocation (V&A)
The entity owns, or has legal right to, all of the inventory on the balance sheet. All inventory is free of liens, pledges, and other security interests or, if not, such liens, pledges, or other security interests are identified.	Rights and obligations (R&O)
Inventory is properly classified, described, and disclosed in the financial statements, including the notes, in conformity with prescribed accounting principles (IFRS).	Classification (Cl), classification and understandability (C&U)

TABLE 10.7 **Objectives in auditing inventory**

10.4.2 Processes impacting inventory

Table 10.8 illustrates procedures the auditor may perform during their testing of transactions related to inventory. There are three important types of transactions that impact the inventory balance: purchasing, cash payments, and inventory processes.

PURCHASES PROCESS	CASH PAYMENTS PROCESS	INVENTORY PROCESS
Test the records of goods and services ordered by comparing purchase requisitions and purchase orders to vendors' invoices. (O)	Examine the client's bank reconciliations where appropriate—for example, to determine whether receipts or payments are recorded on a timely basis or to verify the appropriateness of reconciling items. Perform bank reconciliation cut-off procedures. (CO)	Test the posting of purchases, production, transfers, and shipments of inventory to the perpetual (or other) inventory records. (C, Cl)

TABLE 10.8 **Example substantive tests of transactions—inventory**

(continued)

TABLE 10.8 **Example substantive tests of transactions— inventory** (continued)	**PURCHASES PROCESS**	**CASH PAYMENTS PROCESS**	**INVENTORY PROCESS**
	Test the recording of goods and services received by comparing receiving documents to vendors' invoices. (C)	Account for the numerical sequence of cheques issued during a specific period. (C, CO)	Test the recording of acquisitions, transfers, and disposals of inventory to the general ledger accounts. (O,C)
	Test vendors' invoices to the purchase journal. (C)	Test the comparability of paid cheques and supporting documents with the cash disbursement journal as to date, payee, amount, and account distribution. Determine whether supporting documents indicate the item has been paid. (C)	Test transactions recorded in the perpetual (or other) inventory records to supporting documentation. (O)
	Test the records of goods and services purchased to the records of goods and services ordered and received by comparing vendors' invoices to purchase orders and requisitions, receiving documents or evidence of receipt of services. (O)	Test creditor/supplier invoices to the cash disbursement journal. (C)	Test transactions recorded in the general ledger inventory accounts to supporting documentation. (O)
	Consider the reasonableness of the quantities and the business purposes of the items purchased. (V&A)	Compare goods and services ordered (purchase orders and purchase requisitions) to supplier invoices. (O)	
	Test the mathematical accuracy of invoices. (A)	Compare evidence of goods received to the supplier invoices. (O)	
	Test the timely recording of purchases to the date of the purchase order. (C)	Test the comparability of entries in the cash disbursement journal with the paid cheques and supporting documents as to date, payee, amount, and account distribution. Determine whether supporting documents indicate the item has been paid. (C, A)	
	Test the posting of individual purchases in the purchase journal to the creditors' account as to the proper vendor, invoice number, date, and amount. (O)	Test the cash disbursement journal to supplier invoices. (O)	
	Test the mathematical accuracy of the purchase journal. (A)	Examine creditor/supplier invoices, receiving reports, or other documents supporting the account balances. (E)	
	Test the postings of the totals in the purchases journal to the general ledger and subsidiary ledgers. (C)	Compare invoices to purchase orders and purchase requisitions, and receiving reports. (C)	

(continued)

PURCHASES PROCESS	CASH PAYMENTS PROCESS	INVENTORY PROCESS
		Consider the reasonableness of the quantities and the business purposes of the items purchased. (V&A) Compare the prices on purchase orders and supplier invoices with those in vendor catalogues. (V&A) Test the mathematical accuracy of invoices. (V&A) Test cut-off of payments and transfers at year end. (CO) Test the postings of the totals in the cash disbursement journal to the sub-ledger and to the general ledger. (C)

These procedures would likely be performed even when the auditor was able to test and rely on controls (that is, where the controls were effective). In this case, however, the extent of testing could be reduced.

10.4.3 Illustrative procedures for auditing inventory

As mentioned previously, there is an almost limitless number of substantive procedures that can be designed for the testing of account balances, and this is particularly true for inventory. Table 10.9 provides example substantive procedures that can be used when auditing inventory. Some of the procedures are always performed (irrespective of the risk assessment the auditor reaches for the significant account), while others are additionally selected in response to the risk assessment to address any remaining detection risks that are still evident after controls testing has been performed. See Appendix A for an example of an inventory working paper.

TABLE 10.9 **Example substantive tests of account balances—inventory**

EXAMPLE TESTS ALWAYS PERFORMED

Observe the counting of physical inventory to establish that:
- the client's personnel are complying with the inventory count instructions (E, C, V)
- items belonging to the client, or belonging to others but for which the client is responsible, are accurately counted and recorded (R)
- items to be excluded from inventory (no-value items, non-inventory items, items belonging to others) are either subject to satisfactory control and excluded from the counting process or are accurately counted and recorded, including a clear description of their non-inventory status
- count tags, sheets, or cards are properly controlled. (C)

(continued)

TABLE 10.9 **Example substantive tests of account balances—inventory** (continued)

EXAMPLE TESTS ALWAYS PERFORMED

Perform inventory tests counts as follows:
- Select and count a sample of items from the floor and agree to the inventory records. This tests for the completeness of the inventory as the auditor determines there are no inventory items on hand missing from the records. (C)
- Select a sample of items from the inventory listing and count the number of items on hand. Agree the counted number to the recorded number. This tests for existence in that the auditor ensures that all items listed actually exist. (E)
- Record sufficient information to be able to trace the test counts into the inventory compilation at a later date; record selected information concerning the tags, sheets, or cards that are used, partially used, unused, and voided. (C)

Inspect shipping, receiving, and transfer documents and the related inventory items, when appropriate, to establish the numbers of the last documents used and other information needed for subsequently verifying cut-off in the accounting records. (E)

Review the physical inventory compilation:
- Trace test counts, confirmations, and, if necessary, records of the count prepared by the client (for example, count tags, sheets, or cards) to the compiled inventory listing. Determine that the unit of measure used in the physical inventory listing is consistent with the unit of measure used during the physical count.
- Trace items on the final inventory listing to the physical inventory tags. Determine that the unit of measure used in the physical inventory compilation is consistent with the unit of measure used during the physical count.
- Verify that the information gathered during the physical observation regarding the tags, sheets, or cards that were used, partially used, unused, and voided is accurately reflected in the inventory compilation.
- Trace the cut-off information obtained during the physical observation to the accounting records of sales and purchases. (E)

Test the valuation of inventory. Example procedures that may be performed are discussed below under "Example Analytical Procedures." (V&A)

Review the reconciliation of the physical inventory compilation with the general ledger account balances and, if applicable, the perpetual inventory records:
- Investigate large and unusual differences.
- Ensure that the book to physical adjustment is recorded. (V&A)

EXAMPLE ANALYTICAL PROCEDURES

General

Compare the current period's inventory turnover, based either on cost or on units sold or produced, with the prior period's turnover. (V&A, C)

Compare inventory quantities and/or costs by location, by type, and by product with prior period's amounts. (V&A, C)

Compare the current period's inventory turnover based either on cost or on units sold or produced with prior period's turnovers. (V&A)

Compare inventory quantities by product with units sold or used. (V&A)

Compare the current period's gross profit ratios (by month, by location, and by product line) with those of the prior period and/or industry averages. (V&A)

Compare the current year's cost of sales accounts to the prior year's and to the current year's budget (in value or percentages), and investigate any large or unusual fluctuations or the absence of expected fluctuations. (V&A)

Compare the current year's payroll expense accounts to the prior year's and to budgets by classification, and investigate any large/unusual fluctuations or the absence of expected fluctuations. (V&A)

(continued)

EXAMPLE ANALYTICAL PROCEDURES

Compare with the prior period the relationship of payroll expense to cost of sales and sales. (V&A)

Compare budgeted usage of raw materials with the actual usage. (V&A)

Compare production reports with the recorded warehouse receipts of finished products. (V&A)

Compare the relationships of material, direct labour, and overhead costs to cost of sales with the same relationships from the prior period. Investigate significant unusual fluctuations or the absence of expected fluctuations. (V&A)

Valuation

Compare the average actual unit cost charged to cost of sales during the year by product line with the costs used to price year-end inventory. (V&A)

Compare unit prices for inventory items with those of the prior period and investigate significant changes and/or unusual trends in pricing. (V&A)

Compare the relationship between actual labour and overhead costs to materials put into production with the same relationship in ending inventory. Compare with the prior period. (V&A)

Review product line operating statements and overall profitability to determine if costs are being recovered through selling prices. (V&A)

Obsolete and excess inventory

Compare quantities estimated to be sold with forecasts of industry sales. (V&A)

Compare the quantities the entity is committed to purchase and has in hand to the quantities required for future production and/or to forecast sales. (V&A)

Compare inventory quantities with production and storage capacities. (V&A)

Compare current year to the prior year's excess and obsolete reserve, write-offs, and related expenses as a percentage of inventory and cost of sales. (V&A)

Compare current year to the prior year's number of days' cost of sales in inventory by inventory category and product line. (V&A)

Compare monthly/annual amounts sold (by product/product line) for current year and prior year. (V&A)

Compare monthly/annual amounts purchased and/or production (by product/product line) for current year and prior year. (V&A)

Compare excess and obsolete experience to patterns in client's industry. (V&A)

EXAMPLE OTHER GENERAL PROCEDURES

Determine that the costing method used is consistent with the client's policy and with the method used in the prior year. (V&A)

Review the raw materials, WIP, and finished goods inventory accounts and the cost of sales accounts in the general ledger and subsidiary ledgers for unusual items. (V&A)

Review the nature of items included in non-inventory and cost of sales accounts in the general ledger for amounts that should be included in inventory. (V&A, C)

Verify the calculations of inter- and intra-company profits in inventory, and verify that such profits have been eliminated. (V&A)

Enquire as to the existence of damaged, slow-moving, excess, out-of-style, and obsolete inventory and of commitments of additional quantities of similar items. Make note of such items during inventory observations, review of perpetual records, price tests, and review of gross margins. (V&A)

Review and test the procedures for identifying obsolete, damaged, excess, and slow-moving inventory. Review the values assigned to such items. (V&A)

(continued)

TABLE 10.9 **Example substantive tests of account balances—inventory** (continued)

EXAMPLE OTHER GENERAL PROCEDURES
Investigate any sales and purchase commitments, back orders, or sales options to determine whether any losses are likely to be realized in the course of fulfilling the commitments. Verify the reasonableness of the allowances for such unrealized losses. (V&A, R&O)
Review minutes, contracts, and other documents for evidence of liens, pledges, or other security interests in inventory; determine that the necessary disclosures are made. (R&O)
Review the raw materials, WIP, and finished goods inventory accounts not tested in detail for unusual items. (V&A)
Review the reasonableness of the costs applied to the inventory accounts not tested in detail. (V&A)
Investigate significant price variance accounts. High variances may indicate incorrect standard costs. Review for reasonableness the allocation of variances between cost of sales and year-end inventory. (V&A)
Compare costs of inventory items with current replacement costs per vendor invoices, open purchase orders, current price lists, quotes, or published market prices. Consider the effect of lower current costs on materials and purchased-parts content of inventory and on commitments for additional quantities of similar items. (V&A)
Compare costs of WIP and finished goods with selling prices as shown by recent sales invoices, current price lists (adjusted for discounts), and other sources to determine whether there is sufficient margin to cover costs to complete and dispose. (V&A)
Physical inventory procedures
General procedures
Review and determine the adequacy of the instructions and other written materials concerning the counting of inventory and the recording of inventory transactions near the count date. (E)
If the physical inventory is taken on a staggered basis throughout the period, determine the extent of the client's counts during the period; observe one or more of the inventory counts; test the recording of the adjustments resulting from the counts to the inventory records; test count the quantities recorded in the inventory records; and test the recording of the adjustments in the general ledger accounts. (E)
If the physical inventory is taken at an interim date or on a staggered basis during the year, review the roll-forward of activity from the date of the physical inventory to year end and investigate unusual items; consider counting (at year end) significant new items and those items with significant increases or decreases between the physical inventory date and year end. (E)
Review for reasonableness any adjustments to the compiled inventory. (E, V&A)
Procedures for unobserved locations
Obtain a copy of the physical inventory compilation and review it for reasonableness (large and/or unusual items). (E, V&A)
Obtain client records of the physical count and review the results and details of any exceptions/problems noted. (E, V&A)
Review the activity in the inventory account since the last physical count was undertaken for reasonableness (large and/or unusual items). (E, V&A)
Vouch activity in the inventory account since the last physical count was undertaken to supporting documents. (E, V&A)
Perform analytical procedures such as comparing current year balance to prior year and budget. (E, V&A)

Cloud 9

Suzie and Ian spend a considerable amount of time discussing the substantive procedures they will include in the audit program for Cloud 9's inventory. Cloud 9's core business is importing and wholesaling inventory; in addition, the company has now established a retail store. The importance of inventory to the business's success means that Cloud 9's senior managers are very aware of the issues surrounding good inventory systems and handling procedures. The audit team has already recognized the importance of these systems by focusing much attention on the controls relating to inventory. However, Suzie and Ian have some concerns about their ability to gather sufficient appropriate evidence about Cloud 9's inventory management system. They know that if inventory is misstated in the financial statements, it is unlikely that the report will provide a fair presentation of the company's financial position and performance.

Suzie and Ian decide that they will gather substantive evidence from the inventory counts at Cloud 9 to add to the evidence gathered from analytical procedures and vouching of inventory transactions. Suzie also decides to take charge of writing the program for gathering evidence on the contracts surrounding the inventory transactions between Cloud 9 and the overseas manufacturers. She wants to be sure that the accounts appropriately reflect the terms of these contracts with respect to transfer of inventory ownership. She asks Ian to take charge of reviewing Cloud 9's procedures for identifying damaged, slow-moving, excess, out-of-style, and obsolete inventory.

BEFORE YOU GO ON

4.1 Name two assertions that are ordinarily significant for inventory, and describe why they are important.

4.2 What is the impact on the level of substantive audit procedures necessary for the cash payments, purchasing, and inventory processes if controls are not tested and found to be effective?

4.3 Describe two substantive audit procedures ordinarily always performed for inventory.

10.5 SUBSTANTIVE TESTING OF PROPERTY, PLANT, AND EQUIPMENT

The two key significant assertions for property, plant, and equipment (PPE) are existence, and valuation and allocation. PPE are often referred to as fixed assets. A fixed asset register or a continuity schedule is a register or listing of all the items of PPE that a company has. See Appendix A for an illustration of this schedule. It is used to capture additions and disposals, as well as to calculate the depreciation and to track the cost and written-down value of each item. The fixed asset register is essentially the sub-ledger that is reconciled to the general ledger for fixed assets.

5 Design and understand how to execute substantive procedures to address audit risk related to property, plant, and equipment.

Existence is important because the assets the company has recorded in its fixed assets register (which flows into the general ledger and finally into the financial statements) need to actually exist. Auditors usually test for existence by physically looking at the assets listed in the fixed asset register in the first year that a client is audited. In subsequent years, the existence procedures tend to focus on additions to, and disposals from, the fixed asset register. It is important to physically look at the fixed assets on a periodic basis as this provides insights into not only whether the asset exists but also whether there appear to be any assets that may be damaged, obsolete, impaired, or excess to the client's needs, providing important evidence for the valuation and allocation assertion.

Valuation and allocation is the other significant assertion tested by auditors in relation to PPE, as it is important that assets are recorded at the appropriate carrying value (or "fair value," as it is described and defined by IFRS, in particular IAS 16 *Property, Plant and Equipment* and IAS 36 *Impairment of Assets*). Valuation also becomes very important when a company changes processes or structures, as the decisions made by management and those charged with governance will often impact the values at which items of PPE should be carried. For example, if an entity decides to close down a factory, it is likely that the value of the fixed assets at that factory will be impaired and may need to be written down to their fair value (or nil).

Typical substantive procedures to test valuation focus on the initial cost recorded (by vouching to supporting invoices), the value recovered for any disposals (by vouching to cash received or trade-in amounts obtained), and depreciation and impairment calculations for each asset, including whether there are any additional writedown or depreciation amounts required for the period. Procedures to test depreciation include performing reasonableness testing of the depreciation charge compared to the cost base of the assets, assessing the useful lives of the assets and comparing these to the depreciation rate used, and, in the case of property, having an external valuation performed.

Completeness is usually not a major issue for most entities as the auditor is typically most concerned with the overstatement of assets, and completeness tests tend to focus on the potential understatement of fixed assets.

The rights and obligations assertion is tested during the first-year audit procedures and then again periodically depending on the type of assets in the fixed asset register. Property is easily verified by reviewing the titles related to each property. Fixed assets also comprise items of equipment, plant and machinery, vehicles, and office equipment. Ownership of these items is not subject to a high risk of error unless there are items that are leased (rather than owned). Owned items can be verified to either registration papers or original purchase invoices, which will have been tested as part of the valuation assertion. Leased items will be verified to leasing documentation signed by the business when it entered into the lease. While not always specifically testing for rights and obligations, the risk has already been addressed when testing for valuation and allocation.

Classification is generally addressed by testing the fixed asset register. Therefore, verifying the amounts included in the disclosures in the financial statements is relatively straightforward, as the disclosures are found within the fixed asset register (the key one being depreciation).

10.5.1 Principal objectives in auditing property, plant, and equipment

The principal objectives in auditing PPE are described in table 10.10.

TABLE 10.10 **Objectives in auditing PPE**

OBJECTIVE	ASSERTION
All PPE on the balance sheet (including assets leased under finance leases) are held by the entity or by others for the entity.	Existence (E)
All PPE owned or leased under finance (capital) leases by the entity at year end are included on the balance sheet.	Completeness (C)

(continued)

OBJECTIVE	ASSERTION
PPE are carried at the appropriate amount (taking into account accumulated depreciation, amortization, or impairment). The cost of the plant and equipment is allocated to the appropriate accounting periods in a systematic and rational manner. The written-down value of the PPE is expected to be recoverable through future use. PPE assets held for disposal are carried at the appropriate value.	Valuation and allocation (V&A)
The entity owns, or has legal right to, all the PPE on the balance sheet at year end. All PPE assets are free from liens, pledges, security interests, and restrictions or, if not, such liens, pledges, security interests, and restrictions are identified and disclosed (if necessary).	Rights and obligations (R&O)
PPE and related accounts are properly classified, described, and disclosed in the financial statements, including the notes.	Classification (Cl), classification and understandability (C&U)

10.5.2 Processes impacting on property, plant, and equipment

Table 10.11 illustrates procedures the auditor may perform during their testing of transactions related to PPE. There are three important types of transactions that impact the balance: cash receipts, cash payments, and purchasing. Depreciation is calculated as a monthly or year-end journal and therefore does not form part of these three processes. These procedures would likely be performed even when the auditor was able to test and rely on controls (that is, where the controls were effective). In this case, however, the extent of testing could be reduced.

CASH RECEIPTS, CASH PAYMENTS, AND PURCHASING PROCESSES
Test the cut-off of the additions to PPE, including, when applicable, transfers from construction in progress or work in progress. (CO)
For sales and disposals of capital assets: • Inspect authorizations and other data supporting retirements, sales, and other disposals. • Recalculate any resulting gains and losses. • Ensure that sold or disposed-of assets and the related accumulated depreciation have been removed from the accounts. (E, V&A) • Vouch cash receipts to verify the proceeds of the sale were received, recorded, and deposited. (E, V&A)
Review the cash receipts sub-ledger for sales of PPE. (E, V&A)
For purchases of capital assets: • Agree suppliers' invoices to the initial amount capitalized (that is, the cost recorded in the fixed asset register). (E, V&A) • Compare the actual costs of additions with the authorized or estimated amounts; investigate the reasons for any significant differences. (E, V&A) • Compare the payment made for the acquisition of the fixed asset to the supporting invoices. (V&A)

TABLE 10.11 **Example substantive tests of transactions PPE**

(continued)

TABLE 10.11 **Example substantive tests of transactions PPE** (continued)

CASH RECEIPTS, CASH PAYMENTS, AND PURCHASING PROCESSES
Scan the repairs and maintenance expense account for the period, identifying significant expenditures. Examine the supporting documents for significant expenditures to determine if they should be capitalized as PPE. (E, V&A)
Compare the actual costs of additions with the authorized or estimated amounts; investigate the reasons for any significant differences. (E, V&A)
Examine support for rentals under operating leases and for significant charges to repairs, maintenance, and other expense accounts to determine if they should be capitalized as PPE. (E, V&A)
Visually inspect selected assets and trace them to the fixed asset register to determine that they were recorded. (E, C)
Verify the physical existence of recorded fixed assets by selecting items from the fixed asset register or from the schedule of additions for the year and visually inspecting the assets. (E)
Compare the payment made for the acquisition of the fixed asset to the supporting invoices. (V&A)
Consider the reasonableness of the quantities and the business purposes of the items purchased. (V&A)
Agree the detailed records of PPE and of the related depreciation, amortization, or impairment with the appropriate profit and loss accounts. (V&A)
Test the mathematical accuracy of the fixed assets register. (V&A)

10.5.3 Illustrative procedures for auditing property, plant, and equipment

As previously discussed, there is an almost limitless number of substantive procedures that can be designed for the testing of account balances, in this case PPE. Table 10.12 provides example substantive procedures to be performed when auditing PPE. Some of the procedures are always performed (irrespective of the risk assessment the auditor reaches for the significant account), while others are additionally selected in response to the risk assessment to address any remaining detection risks that are still evident after controls testing has been performed. See Appendix A for an example working paper completed for the PPE section.

TABLE 10.12 **Example substantive tests of account balances—PPE**

EXAMPLE TESTS ALWAYS PERFORMED
Examine invoices, capital expenditure authorizations, and other data supporting additions and disposals to PPE during the period. (E, V&A)
Review and, when appropriate, examine supporting documents for significant charges to repairs, maintenance, and other expense accounts to determine if they should be capitalized as PPE. (V&A, C)
Recalculate depreciation and amortization calculations for accuracy. Also review if acceptable amortization methods and appropriate lives (or other bases for allocating costs) are being used, and if they are consistent with the methods and lives used in the prior period. (V&A)

(continued)

EXAMPLE ANALYTICAL REVIEW PROCEDURES

Review the summary of PPE by classification and location that indicates acquisitions or disposals during the period; compare with the prior period and approved capital expenditure budgets. (C&U, V&A)

Review reasonableness of depreciation expense with reference to prior year expense and the effects of additions and disposals (accuracy of depreciation expense in the income statement). (V&A, CI, accuracy of depreciation expense in income statement])

EXAMPLE OTHER GENERAL PROCEDURES

Test calculations of capitalized interest to determine if the appropriate rates, amounts, and capitalization periods have been used. (V&A)

Determine the tax basis of accounting for PPE transactions and verify that any book-tax differences have been accounted for properly. (V&A)

Examine lease agreements to determine whether leases are appropriately classified as finance (capital) or operating; determine whether the proper accounting has been performed; determine whether appropriate disclosures have been made. (CI, C&U)

Review the PPE and related accounts in the general ledger for unusual items. (E, V&A)

Ascertain the business reasons for unusual additions or disposals. (V&A)

Inspect evidence of ownership (for example, deeds, titles, registration papers) or rights to use the PPE (for example, finance leases). Obtain direct confirmation of ownership if the deeds are held by a custodian. (R&O, E)

Review the minutes, agreements, legal filings, and other documents (for example, bank confirmations and loan agreements) for evidence of liens, pledges, security interests, and restrictions on PPE. (R&O)

Review minutes, agreements, capital expenditure budgets, and subsequent appropriations for evidence of plans of commitments for future additions, disposals, or impairment (including finance leases). (V&A, C)

Physically look at assets. (E)

Inquire as to the existence of, and review detailed records for, major items of PPE that are not in service. Consider the likelihood that PPE will become idle in the foreseeable future (due to a significant drop in production, a change in product lines, or technical obsolescence). (V&A)

Determine that PPE that is being held for sale or that is no longer being used is carried at the appropriate amount (fair value after any impairment amount has been recorded). (V&A)

If evidence indicates that the undepreciated cost of major facilities in service (that is, facilities being used and not held for sale) is not expected to be recovered, determine that such items have been written down to the appropriate amount. (V&A)

Cloud 9

Ian and Suzie have already discussed their approach to PPE acquisitions and disposals, as well as using analytical procedures for depreciation expense testing. Suzie reminds Ian that they need to design substantive procedures to assess asset values. Asset impairments must be recognized under the accounting standards (IAS 36 *Impairment of Assets*), and the auditors will need to gather evidence about Cloud 9's processes for identifying and recognizing asset impairments. Suzie will discuss with Sharon Gallagher, the audit manager, whether they need to obtain expert opinions on substantive values.

PROFESSIONAL ENVIRONMENT

Reliability of asset revaluations

Valuation and allocation is a key assertion for PPE. When assets are carried at depreciated cost, auditing procedures focus on vouching the initial cost and re-performing depreciation calculations. However, if there is a question about the recoverable value of the asset, or if the asset has been revalued or carried at fair value instead of cost, the auditor needs to consider the reliability of the asset valuations.

In Australia, upward asset revaluations were very common before the introduction there of IFRS in 2005. The previous accounting standards allowed certain assets to be revalued to their fair value where this exceeded the carrying value based on historical cost. By contrast, upward asset revaluations were not permitted in Canada or the United States during this period. The ban on upward revaluations (downward revaluations are common) is thought to be based on a concern that restated values are not reliable.

Cotter and Richardson examined the Australian data on asset revaluations from 1981 to 1999 to investigate the reliability of asset revaluations performed by independent valuators and company directors. The evidence shows that independent valuators are more likely to be used to value property such as land and buildings, and directors are more likely to value investments, plant and equipment, and intangible assets. The authors believe that this pattern is explained by the fact that the values of investments, plant and equipment, and intangible assets are more dependent on their specific characteristics and situation. This means that a valuator of these assets must have detailed knowledge of the specific circumstances of the current use of the asset. By contrast, land and buildings are widely traded, and their values are less dependent on the specific characteristics of the current owner. As a result, directors of the company are more likely than external valuators to understand the value of the investments, plant and equipment, and intangible assets.

Cotter and Richardson also found evidence that where the directors of the company are less independent, they are more likely to use independent valuators to value all assets. This evidence implies that directors appear to be aware of the limitations caused by their lack of independence, and that external auditors require independent valuations to be provided in these cases. Finally, Cotter and Richardson found very little evidence of differences in reliability between the two types of valuations. This suggests that directors do not appear to bias their valuations, and that auditors are aware of the limitations of directors' valuations and ensure that they are sufficiently reliable.

Source: J. Cotter and S. Richardson, "Reliability of Asset Revaluations: The Impact of Appraiser Independence," *Review of Accounting Studies*, 7, no. 4 (December 2002), pp. 435–57.

BEFORE YOU GO ON

5.1 Name two assertions that are ordinarily significant for PPE, and describe why they are important.

5.2 What is the impact on the level of substantive audit procedures necessary for the cash receipts, cash payments, and purchasing processes if controls are not tested and found to be effective?

5.3 Describe two substantive audit procedures ordinarily always performed for PPE.

10.6 SUBSTANTIVE TESTING OF PAYABLES

6 Design and understand how to execute substantive procedures to address audit risk related to payables.

The key assertions for payables are completeness, and valuation and allocation. Completeness is critical because, as with any liability account balance, the risk is that the balance is understated. While it is relatively simple to audit the balance recorded, the bigger risk is that the client has omitted amounts from the balance, and it is therefore understated because it is not complete. The typical procedures performed are often referred to as subsequent payments testing and cut-off testing to search for unrecorded payables.

Subsequent payments testing involves vouching a sample of payments made after year end to supporting invoices to ensure that if the amount relates to invoices dated prior to year end, they have been correctly included in payables at that date. If the amount paid relates to invoices after year end, the testing is to ensure that they have been correctly excluded from payables at year end.

Cut-off testing involves selecting a sample of purchases made on either side of year end and verifying that each has been correctly included or excluded from payables based on the invoice date. This testing involves testing a sample of invoices on hand but not yet processed by the client to ensure that the client is not "holding back" invoices that should be recorded in payables at year end.

Existence, and rights and obligations are not usually significant assertions for payables. It is highly unlikely that a client will record payables that do not exist or that it does not have the obligation to pay. Classification is only important if there are related party transactions and balances, lease commitments, loan facilities, debt agreements, or other forms of finance included within the payables balance.

Payables can include the account referred to as accruals. Accruals are those amounts that the client may not have received the invoice for, but that they know they have incurred an obligation to pay as at year end. Accruals are tested in the same way as payables—that is, by subsequent payments testing. If the amount has not been paid before the audit testing is performed, another test to verify the amount as materially correct is to vouch the accrual amount to the invoices received.

10.6.1 Principal objectives in auditing payables

The principal objectives in auditing payables are described in table 10.13.

OBJECTIVE	ASSERTION
All accounts payable on the balance sheet are real debts that are payable to suppliers or other creditors of the entity for goods received or services performed.	Existence (E)
All accounts payable owed by the entity at year end are included on the balance sheet.	Completeness (C)
Accounts payable are stated at the amounts owed at year end.	Valuation and allocation (V&A)
The accounts payable on the balance sheet represent obligations of the entity at year end. The accounts payable are not secured by liens on assets, security interests, or other collateral unless otherwise indicated.	Rights and obligations (R&O)
Accounts payable are properly classified, described, and disclosed in the financial statements, including the notes.	Classification (Cl), classification and understandability (C&U)

TABLE 10.13 **Objectives in auditing payables**

10.6.2 Processes impacting on payables

Table 10.14 illustrates procedures the auditor may perform during their testing of transactions related to payables. There are two important types of processes that impact the balance: cash payments and purchasing. These procedures would likely be performed even when the auditor was able to test and rely on controls (that is, where the controls were effective). In this case, however, the extent of testing could be reduced.

TABLE 10.14 **Example substantive tests of transactions—payables**

CASH PAYMENTS PROCESS	PURCHASING PROCESS
Test cut-off of cash payments and transfers at year end. (CO)	Compare goods and services ordered (purchase orders) to vendors' invoices. (O)
Account for the numerical sequence of cheques issued during a specified period. (C, CO)	Compare evidence of goods and services received to vendors' invoices. (O,A)
Compare paid cheques and supporting documents with the cash disbursement journal as to date, payee, amount, and account classification; determine whether supporting documents have been marked to prevent reuse. (C)	Compare vendors' invoices to the initial record of entry (purchase journal). (C)
Confirm accounts payable. (E)	Examine vendors' invoices, shipping documents, or other documents supporting the account balances. (O)
Obtain the listing of accounts payable and trace the details to the purchase journal, accounts payable sub-ledger, accounts payable vendor statements, or other record of detailed accounts; investigate debit balances and other unusual items. (E)	Compare the accounts payable sub-ledger to the vendors' invoices. (O)
Compare entries in the cash disbursement journal with the paid cheques and supporting documents as to date, payee, amount, and account classification; determine whether supporting documents indicate the item has been paid. (E)	Compare vendors' invoices to purchase orders and purchase requisitions, shipping documents, or evidence of receipt of services. (C)
Determine whether the signatures on paid cheques are authorized. (A)	Test the mathematical accuracy of invoices. (A)
Examine payments of balances subsequent to year end to verify recorded payables. (C)	Review the accounts payable account in the general ledger for unusual items. (A)
Test the account classifications of cash payments. (CI)	Review the accounts payable sub-ledger and cash disbursement journal for unusual items; investigate any such items observed. (A)
Test the posting of individual cash payments from the cash disbursement journal to the appropriate accounts in the subsidiary ledgers. (C)	Test the posting of individual purchases in the purchases journal to the accounts payable sub-ledger as to the proper creditor, invoice number, date, and amount. (C)

(continued)

CASH PAYMENTS PROCESS	PURCHASING PROCESS
Test the mathematical accuracy of the cash disbursement journal. (A)	Test the mathematical accuracy of the cash disbursement journal. (A)
Test the postings of the totals in the cash disbursement journal to the general ledger and subsidiary ledgers. (C)	Test the posting of the totals in the cash disbursement journal and the accounts payable subsidiary ledgers. (C)

10.6.3 Illustrative procedures for auditing payables

There are many types of substantive procedures that can be designed for testing liability account balances. Table 10.15 provides example substantive procedures that can be performed when auditing payables. Some of the procedures are always performed (irrespective of the risk assessment the auditor reaches for the significant account) while others are additionally selected in response to the risk assessment to address any remaining detection risk that is still evident after controls testing has been performed. Appendix A shows a completed search for unrecorded liabilities.

EXAMPLE TESTS ALWAYS PERFORMED
Examine the client's bank reconciliations. When appropriate (for example, to determine whether cash receipts of payments are recorded on a timely basis, or to verify the appropriateness of reconciling items), perform bank reconciliation cut-off procedures. (C)
Test the cut-off by inspecting the cash disbursement journal, receiving reports, suppliers' invoices, and other supporting documents immediately before and after the cut-off date to determine that the transactions were recorded in the proper period; compare payables cut-off to cut-off in related areas (for example, inventory). (C, V&A)
Perform a search for unrecorded liabilities at year end by selecting subsequent payments, unpaid invoices, and invoices on hand but not yet recorded in the ledger. (C)
EXAMPLE ANALYTICAL REVIEW PROCEDURES
Compare the list of payables with the prior period and investigate any unexpected changes (for example, changes in major suppliers, in the proportion of debit balances, in the aging of the accounts) or the absence of expected changes. (C, V&A)
Compare the number of days' purchases in accounts payable with the prior year. (C, V&A)
EXAMPLE OTHER GENERAL PROCEDURES
Test the account classifications in the cash disbursement journal by comparing the nature of the goods or services purchased with the descriptions of the accounts. (V&A)
Trace the total of the detailed listing of accounts payable in the accounts payable sub-ledger to the total in the general ledger. (C, V&A)
Identify security interests and assets pledged as collateral for accounts payable by confirming with creditors and/or by inspecting public records and reviewing minutes and other documents. (R&O, C&U, V&A)
Review debit memos and other similar adjustments after year end. (C, V&A)

TABLE 10.15 **Example substantive tests of account balances—payables**

Cloud 9

Ian and Suzie review their plans for substantive testing of liabilities. The controls testing over the payables process, including related cash payments, has revealed reasonably strong controls at Cloud 9. Once again, the dual testing conducted in this area has provided some substantive evidence about the balance of payables (including accruals). The scheduled analytical procedures are particularly useful for accruals and also provide some evidence about loans (through analysis of interest expense).

The bank confirmations will provide additional evidence about the completeness assertion for liabilities (by potentially revealing information about other loans), and communication with Cloud 9's solicitors will provide evidence about any other undisclosed liabilities, including contingencies. The audit manager will read the company's significant contracts, and the audit senior will review the board meeting minutes for information that could relate to other obligations. Tests relating to warranty, loyalty program, and vacation and other employee-related provisions are already in the plan.

Suzie and Ian include a final step in the substantive testing program: a senior member of the audit team will review the liabilities as a whole for any other issues, including significant disclosures required by the accounting standards.

BEFORE YOU GO ON

6.1 Name two assertions that are ordinarily significant for payables, and describe why they are important.

6.2 What is the impact on the level of substantive audit procedures necessary for the cash payments and purchasing processes if controls are not tested and found to be effective?

6.3 Describe two substantive audit procedures ordinarily always performed for payables.

10.7 SPECIAL CONSIDERATIONS FOR AUDITING OTHER BALANCE SHEET ACCOUNTS

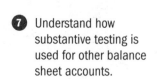

7 Understand how substantive testing is used for other balance sheet accounts.

There are several other common balance sheet account balances that have not been specifically discussed in this chapter, such as prepayments, investments, inter-company, taxation, provisions, leases, long-term liabilities, and equity. Each of these accounts is typically audited fully substantively (with limited or no controls testing), as they tend to be easier to audit substantively at year end. For example, prepayments are audited by vouching the balance to the supporting invoices and ensuring that the split between what has been expensed and what remains in the balance sheet is correctly calculated.

Investments can be vouched either to supporting external documentation, such as investment statements (from a bank), to share prices per the stock exchange (for listed investments), or to supporting financial statements (for investments in subsidiaries or associates). These sorts of investments (in subsidiaries) can also be supported by the testing performed on the subsidiary's trial balance (among other tests), and so may in fact be reliant on controls testing of the subsidiary.

Inter-company balances are vouched to the related entity or to inter-company confirmations. In addition, the auditor needs to ensure that the inter-company balances eliminate on consolidation to the extent owned by the parent entity.

Taxation balances are generally audited substantively due to the need to verify the underlying tax balance sheet (to determine the deferred tax balances as well as the provision to pay tax and the income tax expense). Also, due to the complexities of taxation law, it is common to have tax specialists as part of the audit team to assist in auditing tax calculations.

Provisions are difficult to audit using controls testing alone. They tend to be heavily reliant on transactions that are subject to management estimation processes. The only exception is payroll-related accruals for such things as vacation pay and pension benefits. These balances are reliant on the routine transactions that the payroll system records, which then form the basis for the estimation process (calculation) to ensure that the accruals for payroll-related liabilities are in accordance with the employment contracts, any relevant employment law, and accounting standards.

Leases are either finance (capital) or operating leases. Finance leases are audited substantively by vouching the lease agreement terms (for example, the monthly payments, interest, term of the lease, balloon payments) to the calculation or spreadsheet that the client uses to calculate its finance lease liabilities and commitments. As well as the risk of misstatement, the other risk that the auditor focuses on is the split between current and non-current lease liabilities. Again, this information is obtained from the lease schedule and is easily verified to the terms of the lease agreement. Operating leases are those that are not "on balance sheet"; instead, they typically relate to leased buildings or premises. This is currently a disclosure item only (that is, one that is not recognized on the balance sheet) and again is typically calculated by the client using a spreadsheet to record the number and amount of remaining lease payments. This is easily vouched to supporting operating lease documentation.

Long-term liabilities are generally audited substantively for efficiency purposes, as long-term liabilities tend to be material, but new transactions tend to be infrequent. If new debt has been issued during the year, the auditor reviews the board of director minutes for evidence of authorization. A copy of the executed debt agreement is obtained and reviewed to identify the key terms and features that require note disclosure. Receipt of the disbursement of the funds is verified by vouching to the cash receipts journal, the deposit slip, and the bank statement. For both new and existing long-term liabilities, the auditor confirms the year-end balance outstanding with all creditors. This is usually obtained with the bank confirmation, as the bank confirmation asks the bank to also confirm any loans that have been issued to the entity. Interest and principle payments are vouched to the cash disbursements journal and the bank statement. Interest expense is recalculated for reasonableness, and any covenants are recalculated. If the ratios or limits set in these covenants are breached, there are often quite serious consequences for the client, which can include making all loans immediately due and payable (that is, current liabilities).

Equity typically does not move much in any given year as it comprises share capital (which only moves when shares are issued or cancelled) and retained earnings (last year's retained earnings plus the current year's profit after income tax). Retained earnings is a simple calculation, and any shares issued or cancelled can be verified to the share register, cancelled share script, or the deposit of capital for any new shares issued.

10.8 ASSESSING THE RESULTS OF SUBSTANTIVE PROCEDURES

8 Understand how to assess the results of substantive procedures to determine whether additional substantive tests are necessary.

When performing substantive procedures, the key objective is to determine whether there are material misstatements within the balance being investigated and to quantify the amount of any errors if they exist. When tests performed identify errors or exceptions, the first response is to understand why the exception or error has arisen. Unless the auditor is able to quantify the total error in the balance without performing additional testing, an increase in the sample size may be required to ensure that there are no other errors. Additional testing (using the example substantive tests provided above) may also be an appropriate response to confirm and quantify the errors. When errors are identified, it is important to continue testing until the error can be accurately quantified or until the balance has been fully tested to an extent that proves a material error can no longer exist within the balance. This concept will be discussed in more detail in chapter 12.

SUMMARY

❶ Explain the relationship between the overall risk assessment for a significant account and the extent and timing of substantive procedures.

The higher the overall risk of error or misstatement, the higher the level of substantive procedures required, assuming that no controls have been tested or that controls cannot be relied on. When controls are effective and the overall risk assessment is therefore lower, limited substantive testing is ordinarily required to be performed. The timing of substantive procedures is affected by the detection risk—the lower the detection risk, the more work will need to be done nearer to year end.

❷ Design and understand how to execute substantive procedures to address audit risk related to cash.

The most important audit assertions in the audit of cash are existence, completeness, and classification. The transactions that form the basis of the cash balance are cash receipts and cash payments, and if controls are tested and found to be effective, it is unlikely that significant additional tests related to these transactions would be performed. The auditor would perform the minimum substantive tests for the cash balance at year end.

❸ Design and understand how to execute substantive procedures to address audit risk related to trade receivables.

The most important assertions for the audit of trade receivables are existence, and valuation and allocation. Positive confirmations are usually used to test for existence, but they do not provide audit evidence as to the valuation and allocation assertion. Subsequent receipts are the most common procedure to test valuation and allocation, supplemented by analytical procedures such as comparing the aging of trade receivables to the prior period. The three important transactions that affect the balance of trade receivables are sales, sales returns and allowances, and cash receipts.

❹ Design and understand how to execute substantive procedures to address audit risk related to inventory.

The two key assertions for inventory are existence, and valuation and allocation. Testing of client inventory counts is an important procedure for gathering evidence about existence. Such testing can also help inform tests of valuation and allocation through observation of the condition of inventory. Rights and obligations can be an important assertion where specific rights are attached to the items. Inventory balances are affected by purchases, cash payments, and inventory processes.

❺ Design and understand how to execute substantive procedures to address audit risk related to property, plant, and equipment.

Property, plant, and equipment (PPE) are also known as fixed assets. Key assertions for PPE are existence, and valuation and allocation. The auditor usually tests for existence by looking at the physical assets and testing additions to, and disposals from, the fixed asset register. The auditor also considers whether management decisions have affected the values of PPE items. Analytical procedures are useful in testing depreciation expense, and rights and obligations are usually tested by reviewing purchase or leasing documentation.

6 **Design and understand how to execute substantive procedures to address audit risk related to payables.**

The key assertions for payables are usually completeness, and valuation and allocation. Completeness is critical because the risk is that the balance is understated, so the auditor usually uses subsequent payments testing and cut-off testing to search for unrecorded payables. The transactions impacting the payables balance are cash payments and purchasing.

7 **Understand how substantive testing is used for other balance sheet accounts.**

Other balance sheet account balances include prepayments, investments, inter-company, taxation, provisions, leases, long-term liabilities, and equity. It is usually easier to test these balances fully substantively, with limited or no controls testing.

8 **Understand how to assess the results of substantive procedures to determine whether additional substantive tests are necessary.**

When procedures performed identify errors or exceptions, it is important to continue testing, either until the error can be accurately quantified or until the balance has been fully tested to an extent that it proves a material error can no longer exist within the balance.

KEY TERMS

Analytical procedures, 384

Audit risk, 384

Cash equivalents, 388

Control risk, 384

Detection risk, 384

Imprest payroll account, 388

Inherent risk, 384

Liens, 389

Pledge, 388

Professional judgement, 384

Significant account, 385

Substantive procedures (substantive testing or tests of details), 383

Tests of controls (controls testing), 384

MULTIPLE-CHOICE QUESTIONS

10.1 The timing of substantive procedures is influenced by:

(a) work done to obtain an understanding of internal audit activities.

(b) a review of processes to generate estimates of provisions.

(c) interim reviews of activities such as monthly reviews of gross margins.

(d) all of the above.

10.2 A major assertion for the cash account is:

(a) existence.

(b) completeness.

(c) classification.

(d) all of the above.

10.3 Valuation and allocation is a significant assertion for cash:

(a) always.

(b) never.

(c) when the client has cash balances that are held in a foreign currency.

(d) none of the above.

10.4 An auditor compares remittance advices or lists of cash receipts with entries in the cash receipts journal *and* entries in the cash receipts journal with the remittance advices or lists of cash receipts because:

(a) the first provides evidence about the completeness of entries in the cash receipts ledger and the second provides evidence about the existence of cash receipts ledger entries.

(b) you can't test for existence unless you compare in both directions.

(c) it gives junior staff training in comparing records.

(d) there are usually many thousands of cash receipts in a year.

10.5 An accounts receivable positive confirmation:

(a) provides evidence about the classification assertion.

(b) provides evidence about the existence of the accounts receivable.

(c) provides evidence that the accounts receivable will definitely be collected.

(d) is not as useful as a negative confirmation.

10.6 Auditing cash receipts:

(a) can provide evidence about the balance of accounts receivable.

(b) could reveal unusual delays in posting credits to debtors' accounts.

(c) can reveal cut-off problems.

(d) all of the above.

10.7 Physical inspection of PPE:

(a) is a useful technique to gather evidence about the completeness of PPE on the balance sheet.

(b) is always done for every asset every year because PPE is a very significant balance sheet account.

(c) can reveal insights into whether there are damaged, obsolete, impaired, or excess assets.

(d) provides positive evidence about rights and obligations of PPE.

10.8 Additions and disposals of PPE:

(a) are usually minor amounts so are not audited.

(b) are usually tested for cut-off.

(c) can be easily audited through analytical procedures so no other tests are required.

(d) none of the above.

10.9 Auditing payables usually focuses most heavily on:

(a) completeness, and valuation and allocation.

(b) existence.

(c) rights and obligations.

(d) existence, and rights and obligations.

10.10 Subsequent payments testing is:

(a) vouching a sample of payments made after year end to supporting invoices to ensure that amounts related to invoices dated prior to year end have been included in payables.

(b) vouching a sample of cash receipts received after year end to supporting invoices to ensure that amounts related to invoices dated prior to year end have been included in payables.

(c) not required because the client would want to make sure that all payables are included as liabilities on the balance sheet.

(d) not required because the client would not pay an invoice that was not properly recorded.

REVIEW QUESTIONS

10.1 Explain why an audit team cannot use the same combination of audit procedures for every audit.

10.2 Explain the relationship between the timing of substantive procedures and the risk assessment of the significant account in question. What options does an auditor have for performing some of the substantive procedures prior to year end? Explain.

10.3 How can an auditor use results from procedures performed during the control risk assessment phase to affect the nature of substantive testing?

10.4 Explain the difference between the audit of the processes impacting cash and the substantive testing of the cash balance. How is audit testing for each affected by the outcome of controls testing?

10.5 How would an auditor test the cut-off of inventory movements at year end?

10.6   Explain the difference between year-end and cyclical inventory counts. What conditions should exist at a client that conducts cyclical inventory counts?

10.7   What are subsequent receipts tests? Why do they provide useful evidence about accounts receivable valuations?

10.8   Explain the relationship between the repairs and maintenance expense account and the PPE asset account. Why is the auditor interested in examining debits to both accounts when auditing PPE? Explain your answer with reference to the assertions at risk.

10.9   Why is an auditor interested in PPE that is not currently being used or that could become idle in the near future? Why would an auditor review directors' board minutes to gather information about assets that could be sold or become idle in the future?

10.10   Explain why completeness is a more critical assertion for payables than for cash, receivables, inventory, or PPE. What procedures are primarily designed to address the completeness assertion for payables?

PROFESSIONAL APPLICATION QUESTIONS

Basic ★   Moderate ★ ★   Challenging ★ ★ ★

10.1 Designing audit procedures for cash ★   **1** **2**

Julie is designing the audit program for cash for her client Onslow Services Ltd. (Onslow). Onslow is a property management services company. It deals with six major clients and several smaller clients, each with a number of properties for rent in the central business district of the city. Onslow finds tenants, conducts credit checks, negotiates tenancy agreements, and arranges cleaning and maintenance services for each property. It has a staff of 15 and operates from an office in the city. Other than a small petty cash amount, no cash is kept on the premises because rents are directly deposited by the tenants to Onslow's bank account. After the relevant fees are deducted, Onslow remits the rents monthly to the property owners. These transactions pass through a bank account kept solely for this purpose. In addition, Onslow maintains a trust account (for any client moneys held on trust) and a general operating account (for salaries and other expenses).

Required

(a) Advise Julie about the controls over cash that should be maintained by Onslow.

(b) Assuming these controls are present and operating effectively, suggest the appropriate substantive procedures for Onslow's cash balance.

10.2 Accounts receivable confirmation ★ ★ ★   **1** **3**

Albert Enterprises (Albert) is a large importer of goods from China. Albert deals with thousands of suppliers in China and sells the goods to discount stores in Canada. The discount stores include some of the major department store retailers, franchise "Lo-Cost" chains, and independent dollar and variety stores. The focus of the business is on cheap, mass-produced items that sell for prices from less than a dollar to around $50. Both Albert and the discount retailers operate on a business model of high volumes and low margins. The discount stores sell for cash or on credit card only, but Albert trades on credit. In the past, Albert tried to protect its cash flow by requiring a security deposit from the smaller retailers and refusing to advance credit until a satisfactory credit check was performed on each retailer. In addition, terms of payment were seven days, which meant that the retailer had to pay almost as soon as the goods were received.

Albert has faced increasingly stiff competition over the last two years. Some of the Chinese suppliers are negotiating better deals with Albert's competitors, and retailers are also starting to use more than one importer. In an effort to retain business, Albert's management has decided to relax credit terms for retailers. Six months ago, the terms of payment were renegotiated with all larger retailers and some smaller retailers from 7 days to 30 days. In addition, security deposits are no longer required from smaller retailers, although credit checks are still performed.

Required

(a) Explain the potential impact of the change in credit terms on the accounts and the associated audit risk.

(b) What changes to the audit program for accounts receivable would you recommend this year, given the change in credit terms?

(c) How would you select a sample of Albert's accounts receivable customers for accounts receivable confirmation letters?

10.3 Accounts receivable ledger ★★★   ❶❸❽

Victoria is overseeing the accounts receivable ledger. Her main focus is the posting of entries for sales and sales returns to the control account and the individual accounts receivable accounts. The members of her team have each been given specific tasks, which are detailed in the audit program. A predominantly substantive approach is being taken to the audit of accounts receivables for this client because, although controls at the company are generally good, the accounts receivables area is not significant enough to justify extensive controls testing.

Due to staff shortages this year, Victoria has been assigned a group of inexperienced audit assistants. Therefore, she has to be very careful when evaluating the results of the testing. In some cases, the working papers are not completed with sufficient detail; in others she has to ask the audit assistants to redo the work.

Required

(a) Help Victoria explain to her audit assistants the reasons why they must account for the numerical sequence of sales invoices, credit (sales returns) memos, sales orders, and shipping documents.

(b) One of the audit assistants is checking credit memos. The task is to compare the dates, products, quantities, prices, and amounts on credit memos and supporting documents with the entries to customer accounts for sales returns and allowances. The assistant checks all memos with dates up to and including December 31 (year end) and reports that he finds nothing unusual. Why would Victoria send the assistant back to examine credit memos with January dates? Explain.

(c) Why is it important for Victoria to undertake some procedures herself, such as reviewing the accounts for unusual items, instead of assigning the tasks to the assistants? What types of things would she be looking for when performing these procedures? What other procedures would be best performed by a more senior auditor?

10.4 Valuation of PPE, additions, and disposals ★★   ❶❺

Metalinc Ltd. is a mining company based in eastern Canada. Metalinc has 10 open-cut mines, most of which primarily extract iron ore. When the iron ore is extracted, a small amount of other minerals is produced as a by-product. Iron ore is sold on forward contracts to companies in other countries. The ore is shipped, unprocessed, in bulk by ship, with payment due when the ship leaves the Canadian port. Other minerals are sold on the spot market to both domestic and overseas customers.

The world market for minerals is highly dependent on economic conditions. In addition, payment is made by the foreign companies in a foreign currency, usually U.S. dollars. These conditions create major issues for Metalinc in terms of both foreign exchange volatility (which is partially hedged) and sales revenue volatility. When conditions are very adverse, Metalinc "mothballs" one or more of its mines. Mothballing is a process of closing down all operations except essential maintenance and safety operations; staff are dismissed or transferred to another mine if possible, and machinery is left idle.

Machinery is not normally transferred between mines because of the great distances between the mines. This means that depreciation is calculated over the life of the mine if that is shorter than the usual life of the machinery. Some machinery is leased, and other machinery is purchased outright. All purchase and disposal or scrapping decisions are made by the board of directors, although authority to make these decisions is granted to the mine manager for items of lesser value, in accordance with specified company policy.

Required

(a) Explain the implications of "mothballing" for auditing PPE.

(b) Design the audit procedures for PPE for Metalinc. Discuss the audit risks and their effect on your approach.

10.5 Inventory ★ ★

Brompton Hardware runs a network of small hardware retail outlets across the province. All sales are made for cash or on credit card and processed through electronic tills. A wide range of goods is stocked by the stores, meaning that the business deals with a large number of suppliers. All goods are purchased on credit with varying terms, depending on the supplier. Invoices are paid by cheque after a package of documents is collated and approved for payment. Ordering of goods and subsequent payments are processed by the central office, with delivery direct from supplier to the stores—no central warehouse is used. Brompton uses a perpetual inventory system and conducts test counts at regular periods throughout the year.

Required

(a) What controls would you expect to see over inventory movements at the local store level and at the central office?

(b) Explain how you would audit the inventory count for Brompton Hardware. What details would you focus on most?

10.6 Payables cut-off testing ★ ★

The accounts payable clerk at Hyde Ltd. has been away sick for most of the last three months. During this time, the remaining staff in the accounts department have tried to cover for his absence, as well as continuing to do their own jobs. As a result of this disruption, the audit manager has assessed control risk as high for accounts payable and has adopted a predominantly substantive approach. He has decided to do extensive subsequent payments testing and cut-off testing.

Required

(a) Which assertions are most at risk for accounts payable at Hyde Ltd.? Explain.

(b) What is "subsequent payments" testing? How would you select the transactions to examine?

(c) How does cut-off testing differ from subsequent payments testing?

10.7 Substantive testing of inventory ★ ★

Securimax Limited (Securimax) has been an audit client of KFP Partners (KFP) for the past 15 years. Securimax is based in Waterloo, Ontario, where it manufactures high-tech armour-plated personnel carriers. Securimax often has to go through a competitive market tender process to win large government contracts. Its main product, the small but powerful Terrain Master, is highly specialized, and Securimax does business only with nations that have a recognized, democratically elected government. Securimax maintains a highly secure environment, given the sensitive and confidential nature of its vehicle designs and its clients.

In September 2011, Securimax installed an off-the-shelf costing system to support the highly sophisticated and cost-sensitive nature of its product designs. The new system replaced a system that had been developed in-house, as the old system could no longer keep up with the complex and detailed manufacturing costing process that provides tender costings. The old system also had difficulty with the company's broader reporting requirements.

The manufacturing costing system uses all of the manufacturing unit inputs to calculate and produce a database of all product costs and recommended sales prices. It also integrates with the general ledger each time there are product inventory movements such as purchases, sales, wastage, and damaged inventory.

Securimax's end of financial year is December 31.

Source: Adapted from the Institute of Chartered Accountants Australia's CA Program's *Audit and Assurance Exam,* May 2008.

Required

(a) What inventory items would you expect to see in Securimax's accounts? How would the cost of each item be calculated?

(b) Suggest some substantive procedures that you would use in the audit of inventory for Securimax. Justify your choices with respect to the risk assessment.

10.8 Substantive testing of PPE ★ ★

Fabrication Holdings Ltd. (FH) has been a client of KFP Partners for many years. You are an audit senior and have been assigned to the FH audit for the first time for the financial year ending December 31, 2012. During September 2012 you are completing the audit planning for PPE, which is one of FH's most material accounts. You are also aware that FH has made a large investment in a new manufacturing process to place itself in a more competitive position. Your analytical procedures indicate an increase in acquisitions of PPE.

Source: Adapted from the Institute of Chartered Accountants Australia's CA Program's *Audit and Assurance Exam,* May 2008.

Required

(a) What is the key assertion at risk for the PPE additions? Why is it at risk? Explain.

(b) Identify the relevant substantive tests of details that would be appropriate to address the assertion at risk identified in (a) above.

(c) How would your answers to the previous questions change if the PPE additions had been manufactured in-house by FH's engineers and toolmakers, rather than purchased?

Questions 10.9 and 10.10 are based on the following case.

Fellowes and Associates Chartered Accountants is a successful mid-tier accounting firm with a large range of clients across Canada. In 2011, Fellowes and Associates gained a new client, Health Care Holdings Group (HCHG), which owns 100 percent of the following entities:

- Shady Oaks Centre, a private treatment centre
- Gardens Nursing Home Ltd., a private nursing home
- Total Laser Care Limited (TLCL), a private clinic that specializes in the laser treatment of skin defects.

Year end for all HCHG entities is June 30.

You are performing the audit field work for Shady Oaks Centre for 2011. The field work must be completed in time for the audit report to be signed on August 21, 2011. You have been asked to send accounts receivable confirmations. Shady Oaks Centre's accounts receivable arise from the use of centre facilities (including the provision of physiotherapists, occupational therapists, and massage therapists). The accounts receivables balance was $3,974,569 as at June 30, 2011 and was considered material.

The centre's payment terms are 14 days from the date of the invoice. Sixty percent of the balance is represented by invoices outstanding from five different practitioners.

The remaining 40 percent is made up of numerous smaller amounts, most of which have been outstanding for more than 60 days. Any allowance for doubtful accounts is taken directly against the accounts receivable account and not shown separately.

Source: Adapted from the Institute of Chartered Accountants Australia's CA Program's *Audit and Assurance Exam,* December 2008 and March 2009.

10.9 Accounts receivable confirmations ★ ★ ★

Required

(a) Explain how you would select the sample of accounts receivable for confirmation.

(b) Only one in four of the accounts receivable confirmations are returned. Explain the additional audit procedures you could carry out in order to provide sufficient appropriate audit evidence on the accounts receivable balance for the existence assertion.

10.10 Payables' confirmations ★ ★

Assume that you are completing field work on payables for Shady Oaks. The payables relate to purchases of medical and therapy supplies, employee-related provisions, other accruals, and loans from banks and directors. Each account is individually material.

Required

(a) Would you use payables' confirmations? Explain.

(b) Provide a list of substantive procedures that would address the completeness and valuation assertions for each account.

10.11 Substantive procedures ★ ★ ★

Your client is a medium-sized company and is a leader in its small industry of producing replica vehicles of classic automobiles. Customers are either very wealthy individuals or from the entertainment industry (for example, movie production studios that require automobiles typical of a certain era).

The company uses a proprietary accounting software package that includes a purchases journal, perpetual inventory account, and sub-ledgers for both accounts receivable and accounts payable. Purchases are recognized on receipt of goods, and receiving reports are matched to the purchase order from the unmatched purchase order file. Records and source documents include bank statements, cancelled cheques, purchase orders, sales invoices, shipping records, and time records for employees. There are 27 employees, most of whom are long-term staff. The company is privately owned by three individuals, and the audit is required in order to comply with a covenant in a lending agreement with a large institutional investor (a venture capital fund).

Required

For each of the following management assertions, design a substantive audit program (one or two procedures, such as reconciling, tracing, and listing). Do not include selecting a sample as one of your procedures.

(a) Existence or occurrence of sales

(b) Completeness of accounts payable

(c) Valuations or measurement of accounts receivable

Source: © CGA-Canada. Reproduced with permission.

10.12 Substantive procedures ★ ★ ★

The CGA firm that you work for has audited AAA Manufacturing for several years, although this is your first year to be assigned to the audit. In familiarizing yourself with the client, you note that repairs and maintenance is one of the larger items on the income statement for this year and for prior years. It has increased by 10 percent this year, which is much more than the increase in other expenses. The dollar value of new equipment purchased in the audit year also increased. The permanent file kept in your firm's working papers for the client includes a note that AAA tends to replace its equipment long before it is worn out, in the belief that newer equipment will have lower repair costs and thus improve net profit.

Required

(a) Identify the audit procedure you should use to obtain evidence for the existence assertion for the new fixed assets.

(b) Design an audit program to verify the management assertions of completeness and ownership for AAA's fixed assets. Include *three* procedures for each assertion, not including sample selection, and explain how the evidence that your procedures provide would relate to the assertion being tested.

Source: © CGA-Canada. Reproduced with permission.

10.13 Substantive procedures to achieve audit objectives ★★★

The auditor determines that each of the following objectives will be part of your audit of Farmington Inc:

1. Establish that the client has rights to the recorded inventories.
2. Establish the accuracy of cost amounts of inventories.
3. Determine that the presentation and disclosure of inventories and cost of goods sold is adequate.
4. Establish the existence of ending inventory.
5. Establish the completeness of inventories.

Required

For each audit objective, select a substantive procedure from the list below that would help to achieve that objective. Each of the procedures may be used once, more than once, or not at all.

(a) Examine current vendors' price lists.
(b) Review drafts of the financial statements.
(c) Select a sample of items during the physical inventory count and determine that they have been included on count sheets.
(d) Select a sample of recorded items and examine supporting vendors' invoices and contracts.
(e) Select a sample of recorded items on count sheets during the physical inventory count and determine that items are on hand.

10.14 Identifying assertions ★★

The test of controls for purchases, cash disbursements, and accounts payable include the following audit procedures.

1. Vouch a sample of receiving reports to related purchase orders.
2. Select a sample of open accounts payable and vouch to supporting documents of purchase.
3. Trace debits arising from accounts payable transactions for proper account.
4. Trace a sample of voucher debits to general and subsidiary ledger accounts.
5. Select a sample of receiving reports and trace to inventory record posting of additions.

Required

For each of the procedures above, indicate the related transaction assertion.

CASES

10.15 Integrative Case Study—Floral Impressions Ltd.

You are a CA employed at B & B, Chartered Accountants. On November 20, 2012, the partner in your firm sends you the following e-mail:

Our firm has been reappointed auditors of Floral Impressions Ltd. (FIL) for the year ending December 31, 2012. I met with the president and major shareholder of FIL, Liz Yamani, last week, and I toured the Vancouver warehouse and head office. I have prepared the following background information on FIL for you to review:

- FIL, a small public company listed on a Canadian stock exchange, is a wholesaler of silk plants with three warehouses located in Ontario, Alberta, and British Columbia. It imports its inventory of silk flowers and accessories from Indonesia. FIL employees arrange bouquets, trees, wreaths, and decorative floral products for sale in Canada to flower shops, grocery stores, and other retailers. The silk-plant concept was novel when FIL was incorporated in 2001. For the first three fiscal years, sales grew at approximately 40 percent per year, and FIL expanded to meet the demand. However, increased competition resulted in declining sales and operating losses over the next six years.

- Liz inherited the shares of the company in 2010. She had just completed a marketing course and was very excited about becoming involved in the business and applying her new skills. The fiscal year ended December 31, 2011, brought a return to higher sales levels and a modest net income. Liz's management contract, which was renegotiated in 2011, provides for stock options to be granted to her each year based on the percentage increase of FIL's revenue from one year to the next. On October 31, 2012, Liz was granted stock options for the first time. She received 4,500 stock options at $2.25 each, the market price on that date.

- To gain greater exposure on the Internet, FIL is developing its own website. FIL will pay for the costs of running the site by selling advertising spots on the site to home-decorating companies. So far, FIL has pre-sold 10 spots for $200 each. The advertisements are to run for one month. Unfortunately, the site delays have caused some advertisers to cancel their contracts. Others are threatening to cancel their contracts unless FIL gets the site up and running within the next month. The controller has recorded the advertising revenue as sales.

- Craig Olthuis was hired by FIL in September 2012 as the controller. FIL's previous controller resigned in June 2012 due to illness, and the position was temporarily filled by the accounts payable clerk. Craig anticipates that he will have all year-end information ready for our audit team by March 15, 2013.

- Historically, FIL's sales are highest during February and March, and from August to October. Accounts receivable consist of a large number of small-dollar-value accounts, with the exception of five large chain store customers that account for approximately 40 percent of the total accounts receivable. The allowance for returns typically has been 1 percent of fourth-quarter sales.

- During the year, management negotiated an operating line of credit with a new financial institution. The amount authorized is limited to 75 percent of accounts receivable under 90 days old and 50 percent of inventory, to a maximum of $2 million. The loan bears interest at prime plus 3 percent. Under this agreement, FIL is required to provide audited financial statements within 90 days of its fiscal year end.

Required

(a) Evaluate *three* factors that have changed over the prior year that impact the audit risk assessment for the current year. Indicate how these factors influence audit risk (that is, how they increase or decrease audit risk) and draw a conclusion on overall audit risk.

(b) What are the two primary audit assertions B & B, Chartered Accountants, should be concerned with regarding the accounts receivable of FIL?

(c) Design a substantive audit program of at least five procedures for B & B over the accounts receivable.

(d) Design a substantive audit program for B & B of at least five procedures relating to the new line of credit.

CASE STUDY—CLOUD 9

Answer the following questions based on the information presented for Cloud 9 in Appendix B of this book and in the current and earlier chapters. You should also consider your answers to the case study questions in earlier chapters.

The worksheet you completed for the case study question in chapter 9 includes your estimates of the overall risk assessment (ORA) and the acceptable detection risk (DR) in the sales to cash receipts process.

Required

Based on your ORA and DR estimates, design substantive audit procedures for Cloud 9 that would address the DR for the following accounts: (1) accounts receivables (do not include the allowance for doubtful accounts) and (2) cash.

RESEARCH QUESTION 10.1

Management applies accounting standards in the preparation of financial statements, and auditors assess the fair application of those accounting standards. The current trend is to use fair value for certain assets and liabilities.

Required

Discuss the implications for auditors of these accounting standards and the associated questioning of the use of fair values in financial accounting. In particular, you should address the following issues in your answer:
- How do auditors audit fair values?
- Would it be easier for auditors if financial statements contained more or less fair value accounting?
- Are there different implications for auditors when fair values are rising versus when they are falling?

Source: L. Gettler, "Standard Setters Rendered Toothless by G20," *The Age,* April 15, 2009, www.theage.com.au; G. Kessler, "Accounting Standards Wilt under Pressure," *Washington Post,* December 27, 2008, www.washingtonpost.com; C. Patterson, "Tweedie: IASB Yielded to Political Pressures," *CPA Blog* (New York State Society of CPAs), January 2009, www.nysscpa.org.

SOLUTIONS TO MULTIPLE-CHOICE QUESTIONS

1. d, 2. d, 3. c, 4. a, 5. b, 6. d, 7. c, 8. b, 9. a, 10. a.

CHAPTER 11

Substantive testing and income statement accounts

LEARNING OBJECTIVES

After studying this chapter, you should be able to:

1 explain the relationship between the overall risk assessment for a significant account and the extent and timing of substantive procedures, and the differences between auditing income statement and balance sheet accounts

2 design and understand how to execute substantive procedures to address audit risk related to revenue

3 design and understand how to execute substantive procedures to address audit risk related to cost of sales and other significant expenses

4 understand how to assess the results of the substantive procedures to determine whether additional substantive tests are necessary.

AUDITING AND ASSURANCE STANDARDS

CANADIAN	INTERNATIONAL
CAS 330 *The Auditor's Responses to Assessed Risks*	ISA 330 *The Auditor's Responses to Assessed Risks*
CAS 500 *Audit Evidence*	ISA 500 *Audit Evidence*
CAS 520 *Analytical Procedures*	ISA 520 *Analytical Procedures*
CAS 530 *Audit Sampling*	ISA 530 *Audit Sampling*
IAS 38 *Intangible Assets*	IAS 38 *Intangible Assets*

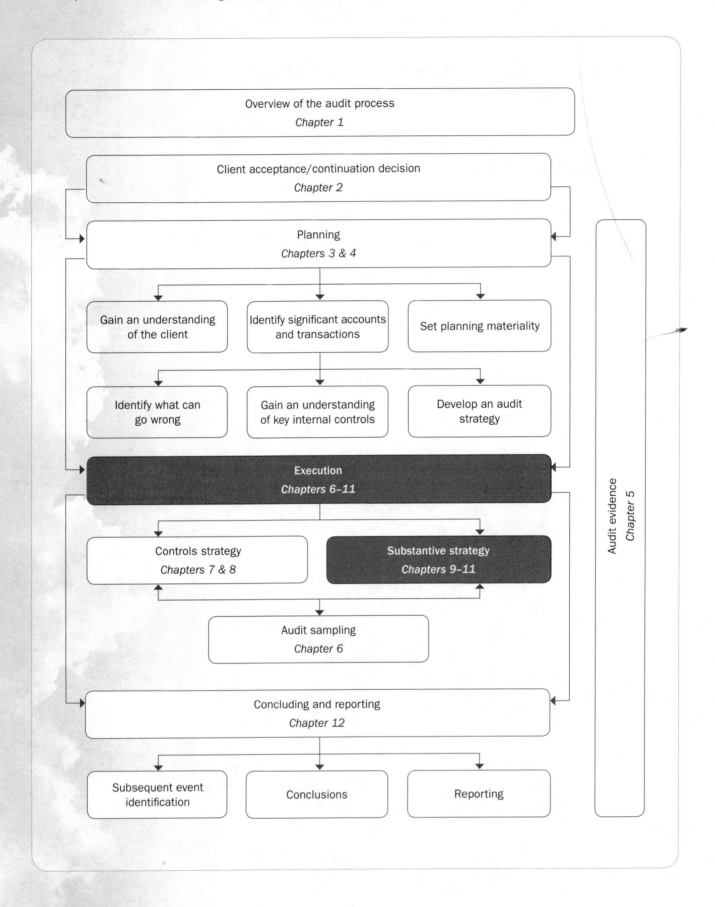

Overview of the audit process
Chapter 1

Client acceptance/continuation decision
Chapter 2

Planning
Chapters 3 & 4

Gain an understanding of the client

Identify significant accounts and transactions

Set planning materiality

Identify what can go wrong

Gain an understanding of key internal controls

Develop an audit strategy

Execution
Chapters 6–11

Controls strategy
Chapters 7 & 8

Substantive strategy
Chapters 9–11

Audit sampling
Chapter 6

Concluding and reporting
Chapter 12

Subsequent event identification

Conclusions

Reporting

Audit evidence
Chapter 5

Cloud 9

Suzie Pickering and Ian Harper are continuing their work on the audit program for Cloud 9 Ltd. (Cloud 9). The audit program contains the detailed audit procedures that will be completed during the remainder of the fieldwork on the audit. So far, they have considered the analytical procedures and other substantive tests for the main asset and liability accounts.

Ian does not understand why Suzie does not want to rely extensively on analytical procedures when testing the asset and liability accounts, although such procedures are definitely included in the audit program. However, Suzie explains that they need to vouch certain asset and liability balances and transactions back to the supporting documentation.

"How do you think substantive testing for the revenue and expense accounts differs from the testing for assets and liabilities?" Suzie asks Ian. "What factors do we have to consider for our audit program at Cloud 9 for these accounts?"

AUDIT PROCESS IN FOCUS

As discussed in chapter 10, finding an appropriate combination of audit procedures to cover an engagement's audit risk at an acceptable cost is a challenge for audit teams. This chapter illustrates the differences between substantively auditing balance sheet accounts and significant income statement accounts. This chapter will also describe the objectives of substantive testing for income statement account balances (including a brief reminder of the factors that affect the nature, timing, and extent of procedures), the processes that impact certain significant accounts in the income statement, and the procedures for auditing these significant accounts.

This chapter will also illustrate (as was done in chapter 10) how the types of substantive procedures are often the same for each significant account or disclosure, irrespective of the type of business being audited. It is instead the timing and extent of testing that are tailored to each client's circumstances.

11.1 RELATIONSHIP BETWEEN RISK ASSESSMENT AND SUBSTANTIVE PROCEDURES

This section discusses the extent, timing, and other matters to consider when designing **substantive procedures** (also called **substantive testing** or **tests of details**) to detect material misstatements at the assertion level.

11.1.1 Differences between auditing income statement and balance sheet accounts

Typically, substantive procedures for balance sheet accounts, as outlined in chapter 10, include the use of confirmations, vouching of balances back to third-party supporting evidence, and tests for completeness and cut-off of the balances on either side of year end. Many significant accounts in the balance sheet are typically made up of a portion of the income statement transactions, or are one-off transactions within the balance sheet only. For example, a loan balance is ordinarily a one-off transaction in which

1 Explain the relationship between the overall risk assessment for a significant account and the extent and timing of substantive procedures, and the differences between auditing income statement and balance sheet accounts.

substantive procedures (substantive testing or tests of details) audit procedures designed to detect material misstatements at the assertion level

TABLE 11.1 **Income statement accounts audited with the related balance sheet accounts**

BALANCE SHEET ACCOUNT	INCOME STATEMENT ACCOUNT
Accounts receivable	Sales Bad debts expense
Inventory	Cost of goods sold
Property, plant, and equipment	Amortization expense Gain/loss on sale Repairs and maintenance
Long-term debt	Interest expense
Payroll liabilities	Wage and salaries expense

cash was received and a loan payable was created (a balance sheet only transaction). For trade receivables, payables, and inventory balances, the account is typically made up of the last 30 to 60 days of sales (trade receivables), purchases (payables and inventory), and expenses (payables).

Many income statement accounts are audited when the related balance sheet accounts are audited, as listed in table 11.1. This is because each balance sheet account is linked to one or more income statement accounts due to the double-entry system of accounting. By focusing on auditing the balance sheet accounts, the auditor is also gathering evidence over the related income statement accounts.

It therefore follows that the nature of the tests required to audit income statement accounts is different from those required to audit balance sheet accounts. Instead of using techniques such as confirmations, the auditor will ordinarily use substantive **analytical procedures** (as per CAS 520 *Analytical Procedures*), coupled with some tests of details (that is, vouching back to supporting documentation) and verification of expense classification. This allows the auditor to use such techniques as trend analysis and the analysis of relationships compared to expectations to obtain audit assurance over 12 months of transaction flows.

As explained in chapter 10, there are certain substantive procedures that are required to be performed for each material class of transactions, account balance, and disclosure (particularly for balance sheet accounts such as trade receivables and inventory). These procedures are required irrespective of the assessed risks of material misstatement or the effectiveness of the control environment (CAS 330 *The Auditor's Responses to Assessed Risks*). These required procedures are not discussed extensively in this chapter as there are few required procedures for income statement account balances.

11.1.2 Extent of substantive procedures

As discussed in chapter 10, the extent of substantive procedures is determined primarily in response to the risk assessment for each **significant account** determined by the **audit risk** model formula in figure 11.1.

When the assessment of **inherent risk** and **control risk** is high, there are no controls tested or relied on and, therefore, the amount of substantive testing required to reduce the detection risk to an acceptable level is significant. This means the auditor will need to gather more evidence by selecting a larger sample for testing. When the assessment of inherent and control risk is low, it means there are lots of controls that have been tested and found to be effective; the auditor can rely on them to ensure

---

analytical procedures evaluations of financial information made by a study of plausible relationships among both financial and non-financial data. Analytical procedures also encompass the investigation of identified fluctuations and relationships that are inconsistent with other relevant information or deviate significantly from predicted amounts

significant account an account or group of accounts that could contain material misstatements based on their materiality and/or relationship to identified inherent and financial statement risks

audit risk the risk that an auditor expresses an inappropriate audit opinion when the financial statements are materially misstated

inherent risk the susceptibility of an assertion to a misstatement that could be material, either individually or when aggregated with other misstatements, assuming there are no related controls

control risk the risk that a client's system of internal controls will not prevent or detect a material misstatement

$$AR = IR \times CR \times DR$$

where:

AR = Audit risk

IR = Inherent risk

CR = Control risk

DR = Detection risk

FIGURE 11.1 **Audit risk model**

that material misstatements do not occur. Therefore, the number of substantive procedures required to address any remaining **detection risk** is reduced, and the auditor can select a smaller sample to test. It follows that when the inherent and control risk assessment is medium, there is some audit evidence obtained from **tests of controls** (or **controls testing**) and some from substantive testing.

detection risk the risk that the auditor's testing procedures will not be effective in detecting a material misstatement

tests of controls (controls testing) the audit procedures designed to evaluate the operating effectiveness of controls in preventing, or detecting and correcting, material misstatements at the assertion level

11.1.3 Timing of substantive procedures

As illustrated in chapter 10, the timing of substantive testing depends largely on the risk assessment of the significant account in question. Apart from the risk assessment of the significant account, some additional considerations that influence the timing of substantive testing include performing procedures on events that occurred prior to year end, performing procedures on activities in the period to date, performing general audit procedures prior to year end, and leveraging off an internal audit.

Cloud 9

Suzie explains to Ian that it is easier to understand financial statement auditing if he remembers the relationship between transactions and account balances. An account balance is the result of the transactions that have been posted to that account. Assets and liabilities are "permanent" accounts, and revenues and expenses are "temporary." This means that asset and liability balances reflect transactions over the life of the account, which could be many accounting periods. However, revenue and expense balances reflect transactions for the current financial period only, because they are closed at the end of each year. The work they do auditing the balance of an asset and liability account in one year carries through to the next year. In some cases, an asset or liability balance does not even change during the current year; in this situation, the auditor concentrates on substantiating the lack of change. In other cases, there are transactions to substantiate.

The other distinguishing feature of most revenue and expense accounts compared to balance sheet accounts is that they have only one type of transaction posted to them. Some revenue and expense accounts, such as sales and purchases, contain many (perhaps millions) of transactions of the same type. The client usually has good controls over these repetitive transactions, so the auditor can increase their reliance on controls testing for this part of the audit.

"The good news," she tells Ian, "is that you can rely on analytical procedures for revenues and expenses if the initial risk assessment suggests it is appropriate, and controls testing provides evidence to support low inherent and control risk. We use tests of details to supplement the analytical procedures where inherent or control risk is higher."

BEFORE YOU GO ON

1.1 Describe why substantively auditing balance sheet accounts is different from auditing income statement accounts.

1.2 Other than the nature of the test, what else affects the substantive procedures that are designed by auditors?

1.3 According to the audit risk model, when is some audit evidence obtained from tests of controls and some from substantive testing?

11.2 SUBSTANTIVE TESTING OF REVENUE

2 Design and understand how to execute substantive procedures to address audit risk related to revenue.

Sales revenue is generally a significant account for an entity (unless it is, for example, a start-up company or a junior explorer in the mining industry). Sales revenue is typically significant due to its size (material), the volume of transactions that flow through the account (high), and the overall high inherent risk associated with revenue. In particular, there is a risk of manipulation of sales revenue (through the use of journal entries) and of fraud due to the focus that most organizations place on results. For example, an easy way to meet profit targets expected by shareholders is to manipulate revenue (usually by increasing reported revenue). Because of this increased risk, auditors will either audit the account balance by using only substantive testing techniques (such as tests of details and sophisticated analytical procedures) or will use a controls testing approach, supplemented by some high-level analytical procedures (such as comparing last year's sales revenue by month to the current year's sales revenue and budgeted sales revenue).

There are three audit assertions that are important to ensure that the auditor has gained sufficient and appropriate audit evidence for sales revenue. First, occurrence of the sales is important. Testing needs to ensure that the sales recorded in the general ledger are in fact bona fide sales and have "occurred." Some of this testing can be performed when testing accounts receivable for existence.

The second significant assertion is accuracy. Substantive tests focus on ensuring that the sales have been recorded at the correct amount (or value) and have not been overstated.

The third significant assertion is cut-off. Cut-off is important because there is a risk that an entity will record sales that occur after year end in the year being audited. The pressure to achieve sales targets and budgets can lead to companies recording sales that occur after year end in the results prior to year end. As a result, procedures are designed to test material transactions on either side of year end, or all sales in the last week before year end, to ensure that all sales are recorded in the correct period. A simple way of testing which period a sale should be recorded in is to vouch the sale to the delivery documentation for the sale of goods and understanding the client's shipping terms (FOB shipping point or FOB destination). If the delivery date (out of the client's warehouse and to the customer) is before year end, it should be included in sales. If the delivery occurred after year end, it is unlikely it should be recorded as a sale. It is important to understand the client's billing/sales revenue process, as this will influence the testing performed for cut-off and will provide an expectation of when sales transactions should be recorded in the trade receivables and sales sub-ledgers.

Completeness is generally not a significant assertion, as the risk with sales revenue is that the client has overstated the balance. Completeness testing focuses on ensuring that all sales revenue that occurred has been recorded, in order to ensure that sales revenue has not been understated. Understatement of sales revenue is not a risk for most clients; however, in certain industries and circumstances, this may be a key concern and may, therefore, require that substantive procedures be developed to address this risk. For example, sometimes entities that have already achieved their budgeted results (and therefore may have earned substantial bonuses) may defer the recognition of sales until after year end to give them a "head start" on meeting the following year's budgeted sales. In this instance, testing is performed to ensure that revenue in the current year is not understated. During difficult economic times, however, this risk is low.

Total revenue in the income statement is made up of a number of items. Typically, the two significant revenue accounts are sales revenue (described above) and interest or dividend income (often referred to as "other income"). When sales revenue is generated from selling services (as opposed to goods), the testing changes in that the auditor typically tests projects delivering services that may not yet have been fully delivered to the customer. Also, with these sorts of service contracts, progress billings are common, meaning the auditor needs to test that the percentage of completion for the project and the remaining costs to complete the project are accurate, in order to ensure that the service (sales) revenue, related costs, and resulting profit are correctly recognized in the right reporting period.

The substantive audit of interest income may be performed by a recalculation of expected interest income based on the average cash balances for the year and interest rates in place for the past 12 months. This calculation is then compared to the actual interest income. If there are unexpected or significant differences between the expected interest income and the actual interest income, these are investigated to ensure that the amount recorded is materially correct. Dividend income is tested by vouching the dividends back to dividend statements and the bank account (as a cash receipt if the dividend is received prior to year end).

Other revenue accounts tend to be insignificant or immaterial, and therefore only general analytical procedures are usually performed on these balances.

11.2.1 Principal objectives in auditing revenue

The principal objectives in auditing revenue are described in table 11.2.

As described in chapter 10, the classification (Cl) assertion is different from the classification and understandability (C&U) assertion. Classification relates to transactions

TABLE 11.2 **Objectives in auditing revenue**

OBJECTIVE	ASSERTION
All sales included in the income statement represent the exchange of goods or services with customers for cash or other consideration during the period.	Occurrence (O)
All other revenues included in the income statement for the period have accrued to the entity at year end.	
Revenues applicable for future periods have been deferred.	
All sales and other revenues that accrued to the entity during the period are included in the income statement.	Completeness (C)
Sales and other revenues are stated at the appropriate amounts.	Accuracy and cut-off (A&CO)
Sales and other revenues are properly classified, described, and disclosed in the financial statements, including the notes.	Classification (Cl), classification and understandability (C&U)

and events that occur throughout the year (that is, how they are recorded in the income statement and whether they are in the right expense account). Classification and understandability relates to presentation and disclosure in the financial statements.

11.2.2 Processes impacting on sales revenue

Before performing tests of details or analytical procedures, the auditor should assess any audit evidence obtained from the interim testing they have performed on the significant processes and flows of transactions, including tests of controls.

Table 11.3 illustrates procedures that may be performed during the testing of the sales and accounts receivable cycle. The two significant accounting processes that impact the sales revenue balance are sales and sales returns and allowances. Some of these procedures may be performed even when the auditor is able to test and rely on controls (that is, where the controls are effective). In this case, however, the extent of testing can be reduced. If a fully substantive approach were taken, many tests would have to be performed over a large sample of the transactions flowing through these significant accounting processes. It is therefore more efficient and effective to perform at least some controls testing if possible.

TABLE 11.3 **Example substantive tests of transactions—sales**

SALES PROCESS	SALES RETURNS AND ALLOWANCES (CREDIT MEMOS) PROCESS
Perform a proof of cash by reconciling the activity per the client records to activity per the bank. Correlate activity with the recorded sales for the year and the change in trade receivables balance. (Effectiveness of procedures is limited to less complex engagements.) (O, A)	Compare credit memos and supporting documents with the sales returns and allowances ledger as to dates, customers, products, quantities, prices, and amounts. (C)
Test the records of products ordered and shipped to the sales records. Agree dates, customers, products, quantities, prices, and amounts. (C, A)	Account for the numerical sequence of credit memos during a specified period. (C)
Test the posting of individual sales invoices to the sales ledger and to the trade receivables sub-ledger. (C)	Test the posting of individual credit memos to the sales returns and allowances ledger and to the trade receivables sub-ledger. (C, A)
Account for the numerical sequence of sales invoices, sales orders, and shipping documents during a specific period. (C)	Compare credit memos with the documents supporting returns and allowances as to dates, customers, products, quantities, prices, and amounts. (C, A)
Test recorded sales to the records of products shipped. Agree dates, customers, products, quantities, prices, and amounts. (O, A)	Test the authorization of credits, discounts, and allowances. (A)
Investigate large or unusual credit memos issued subsequent to year end. (O)	Test the pricing and mathematical accuracy of credit memos. (A)
	Test the cut-off in processing credits and allowances granted to customers. (CO)

(continued)

SALES PROCESS	SALES RETURNS AND ALLOWANCES (CREDIT MEMOS) PROCESS
Review the sales ledger, the sales returns and allowances ledger, and the cash receipts ledger for unusual items. Investigate any such items observed. (A)	Test the timeliness with which credits granted to customers are processed. (A)
Test the pricing and mathematical accuracy of sales invoices. (A)	Test the accounting classification of credit memos. (CI)
Test the accounting classification of sales transactions. (CI)	Test the mathematical accuracy of the sales returns and allowances ledger. (A)
Test the mathematical accuracy of the sales ledger. (A)	Test the postings of the totals in the sales returns and allowance ledger to the general ledger and the trade receivables sub-ledger. (A)
Trace accounts receivable to the trade receivables sub-ledger (debtors' trial balance). Investigate reconciling items. (C)	Test and evaluate the procedures for approving customer credit and for collecting past due accounts. (A)
Test the postings of the sales ledger to the general ledger and the trade receivables sub-ledger. (C)	Test and evaluate the procedures for approving credit and allowances granted to customers. (A)

E—existence; C—completeness; V&A—valuation and allocation; R&O—rights and obligations; CI—classification; C&U—classification and understandability; CO—cut-off; A—accuracy; O—occurrence

Note that each example substantive test illustrated in this chapter addresses a number of audit assertions. This is because many tests of transactions are designed to address multiple assertions in both the balance sheet and the income statement. Only the key assertions addressed are specifically identified for the examples in this chapter.

11.2.3 Illustrative procedures for auditing revenue

An almost limitless number of substantive procedures can be designed for testing account balances. Table 11.4 illustrates example procedures an auditor may use when substantively auditing sales revenue. Some of these procedures are always performed (irrespective of the risk assessment the auditor reaches for the significant account), while others are additionally selected in response to the risk assessment to address any remaining detection risks that are still evident after controls testing has been performed.

EXAMPLE TESTS ALWAYS PERFORMED

Compare the monthly income statements to the budget and/or prior year statements and investigate any unexpected fluctuations or the absence of expected fluctuations. (C, A, CI)

Test the cut-off of revenues by inspecting the sales ledger, billings, shipping documents, and other supporting documents immediately before and after the cut-off date to determine that the transactions were recorded in the proper period. Compare the cut-offs of revenue with cut-offs in related areas—for example, accounts receivable and inventory. (CO)

EXAMPLE ANALYTICAL PROCEDURES

General

Review the client's comparison of budgeted and actual revenues by month or by quarter. Corroborate some of the reasons identified by the client for important

TABLE 11.4 **Example substantive procedures in auditing revenue**

(continued)

TABLE 11.4 **Example substantive procedures in auditing revenue** (continued)

EXAMPLE TESTS ALWAYS PERFORMED

variations. Investigate any unexpected variations or the absence of expected variations that were not identified by the client. (C, A, CI)

Sales

Compare sales to the current year's budget and to the prior period's actual sales by product line or geographic area. (C, A, CI)

Compare sales volume to industry output in total or by geographic area (if available). (C, A, CI)

Compare gross profits with those of the prior period by product line or geographic area. Compare other operating relationships, both sales and cost of sales, to units shipped with prior periods. (C, A, CI)

Compare sales for several days prior to and after year end to the average daily sales for the year. (C, A, CI)

Compare the current period's sales returns and the allowance for sales returns as percentages of sales by product line with prior period percentages. (A)

Compare the number and amounts of credits issued with those of prior periods. (A)

Review the relationships between sales and cost of sales, such as gross margin analysis, comparison of standards and actual costs, and reconciliation between cost of sales and outgoing shipments. (C, A, CI)

Review the relationships between certain types of expenses and sales—for example, freight out to units billed, and sales bonuses to sales. (A, CI)

Other revenue

Perform an overall test of revenue—for example, compare published fee rates for a school multiplied by the number of students by classification/year level. (A)

Perform an overall test of interest and dividend income on investments and receivables by, for example, multiplying the average amounts invested by interest rate or dividend yields. (A)

EXAMPLE OTHER GENERAL PROCEDURES

Sales

Enquire about management, sales personnel, or other parties who may be receiving products without billing or payment. (O, A)

Determine rights of return offered to customers under the terms of sale agreement or as a matter of practice. (O)

Other revenue

Obtain detailed analysis of selected revenue accounts and trace the details to the source data. (CI)

Review the marketable securities and related accounts—for example, interest and dividend income in the general ledger—for unusual items. (A)

Test accrued interest and interest earned during the period to average interest rates and cash balances. (A)

Verify interest and dividend income on marketable securities, investments, and equity in earnings of investees by calculating interest earned or by referring to published records of dividends paid or to the financial statements of investees. (A)

Inspect authorizations and other data supporting sales and other disposals of property, plant, and equipment, and test the computations of the resulting gains and losses. (A)

Identify and examine items that may require separate disclosure in the financial statements, including the notes; for example, discontinued operations, segment information, and gains or losses on foreign currency transactions. (C&U, V&A)

Review minutes, agreements, union contracts, budgets, and plans for evidence of new sources of revenues that may have been earned. Investigate significant items noted. (C, CI)

Figure 11.2 shows CPEM Form 705 that outlines Audit Procedures for revenue.

FIGURE 11.2 **Revenues—Audit procedures CPEM Form 705**

Procedure	WP Ref	Completed
1. Analytical procedures Develop and document expectations for revenue balance(s) based on risk factors identified and other information obtained from understanding the entity. Investigate significant changes or trends in the following: • Industry trends, profitability, the impact of new technologies or competitors, etc. that may have an impact on revenue. • Total sales with prior periods(s). • Monthly sales or sales by product line and/or geographic location with prior period(s) or budgeted amounts. • Sales by month (% of total sales) for month(s) before and after period end to the previous period. • Sales composition (%) by customer with prior period(s). Relate sales volume to productive capacity and customer capacity/past usage. (Consider the existence of economic dependence.) • The following ratios and percentages: – The ratio of sales returns and allowances to total sales to prior periods. – The ratio of sales commissions to total sales to prior periods. – Gross profit to prior periods. Document and obtain explanations for significant or unusual changes.		
2. Revenue—completeness Select a sample of shipping documents or packing slips, etc. and agree details to sales invoices.		

3. Revenue—existence and accuracy
 	
a) Review the appropriateness of the revenue recognition policy.
b) Select any large and unusual transactions during the period plus a sample of sales invoices from the sales journal.
 	
  • Agree details to supporting documentation such as packing slip, shipping advice, cash receipt, etc.
  • Determine that the revenue recognition policy has been consistently applied throughout the period. Obtain explanations for any of the following:
  – Bill and hold transactions.
  – Sales recorded before goods are shipped or services are provided.
  – Large volume of sales transactions around period end.
  – Unusual or long payment terms.
  – Buyer conditions which must be met in order to complete the sale.
  – Side transactions with customers that negate or change any of the standard terms of sale.
c) Ensure that the revenue recognition policy has been disclosed in the financial statements and that it addresses all significant revenue sources.		

4. Sales journal Scan sales journal for period for large and unusual items and ascertain propriety of such items.		

(*continued*)

FIGURE 11.2 **Revenues—Audit procedures CPEM Form 705** (continued)

Procedure	WP Ref	Completed
5. Revenue—cut-off Document: a) The entity's cut-off procedures for revenue. b) Audit procedures performed to ensure that transactions were recorded in the appropriate period. c) Check a block of selected sales invoices and credit notes to ensure that the numerical sequence of pre-numbered sales invoices and credit notes has been properly accounted for and that unused cancelled copies are on file.		
6. Component entities and related parties Ensure that all revenue from components and related parties has been identified and profits/losses between the group components have been eliminated.		

Cloud 9

Ian reviews Cloud 9's trial balance to remind himself of the main revenue accounts. "The most important revenue accounts are Revenue—Stores and Revenue—Wholesale. The stores revenue account is less than 3 percent of the size of the wholesale revenue account for the nine months to September, which implies that wholesale revenue is the most crucial to substantiate. However, the store's revenue account is new this year because of the opening of the retail store in Toronto. There are only four months of sales in the interim figures, and it is possible that controls are not yet working fully. So this implies greater risk. The remaining revenue accounts are small and include interest from banks, foreign currency gains, and 'other.'"

Suzie agrees. She adds that other relevant key risk areas identified so far in the audit include whether wholesale sales are being billed correctly by the Swift inventory management system; pressure on management to meet increased revenue targets; effects on sales from establishing the loyalty program; and the change in the product mix (due to the introduction of the "Heavenly 456" walking shoe). She asks Ian to design the substantive audit procedures for revenue, with a particular focus on the occurrence and accuracy assertions (including a focus on cut-off), and to document how each of the risk areas affects both the use of analytical procedures and tests of details.

PROFESSIONAL ENVIRONMENT

"Chainsaw Al" and Sunbeam

Sunbeam, an appliance maker based in the United States, is a household name in Canada, where many homes have a Sunbeam toaster, kettle, or iron. During the 1990s, Sunbeam was struggling to maintain its profitability, so the board appointed a new chief executive. They chose Al Dunlap, who had a reputation for turning around companies and was popularly known as "Chainsaw Al," presumably because he was fearless in trimming "dead wood" from companies.

Initially, appointing Al Dunlap appeared to work: Sunbeam's reported profit for 1997 was a record-breaking U.S.$189 million. However, the good news did not last long. The U.S. Securities and Exchange Commission (SEC) alleged that U.S.$60 million of the profit was the result of accounting fraud, and Sunbeam was forced to restate its earnings from the fourth quarter of 1996 to the first quarter of 1998. The alleged fraud involved moving merchandise from the company to distributors and retailers, using discounts and other inducements. The problem was that the company appeared to have met its target sales, but the merchandise was either sold at a very heavy discount or likely to be returned to the company because of the terms of the sale.

The SEC alleged that Sunbeam was involved with a premature revenue recognition scheme, sometimes known as channel stuffing, parking, or bill-and-hold. Companies desperate to meet sales targets take action at the end of a period by shipping goods to a buyer who is not ready for the purchase (channel stuffing) or by shifting goods to an intermediary who holds them (parking), recording a sale even though the goods are still in the selling company's warehouse (bill-and-hold). To detect this type of fraud, auditors can investigate whether sales are initiated at the request of a customer, or initiated by the selling company. Also, auditors should consider whether a customer has a legitimate business reason for requesting delayed delivery, and whether the seller has segregated the goods from other merchandise. Attention to these indicators will help auditors decide whether revenue exists.

Sources: J. Gray, "Hide and Seek," *Canadian Business*, 75, no. 6, April 1, 2002, pp. 28–32; L. Stallworth and D. Digregorio, "Improper Revenue Recognition," *Internal Auditor*, 61, no. 3, June 2004, pp. 53–56.

BEFORE YOU GO ON

2.1 Name two assertions that are ordinarily significant for sales revenue, and describe why they are important.

2.2 What is the impact on the level of substantive audit procedures necessary for the sales revenue process if controls are not tested and found to be effective?

2.3 Describe one substantive audit procedure ordinarily always performed for sales revenue.

11.3 SUBSTANTIVE TESTING OF COST OF SALES AND OTHER SIGNIFICANT EXPENSES

Cost of sales and expenses ("costs and expenses") are generally significant accounts in an entity's income statement; key audit assertions are accuracy, completeness, and cut-off. Accuracy is verified by vouching recorded amounts to supporting (third-party) documentation (for example, supplier invoices) or by reference to the significant balance sheet account that has determined the expense (as indicated in table 11.1). For example, depreciation is tested as part of the testing of the valuation of property, plant, and equipment in the balance sheet. Bad debts expense is ordinarily tested as part of the testing of the valuation of trade receivables. Opening inventory is tested as part of inventory testing in the prior year; purchases are tested as part of the testing of inventory and payables; and closing inventory is tested as part of inventory at year end. Purchases tend to be the element of total cost of sales subject to additional testing over and above testing already performed as part of balance sheet testing. Purchases testing is performed most efficiently via the use of controls testing. When this testing cannot to be performed or relied on, a large number of purchases will be vouched back to supplier documentation, unless other sophisticated or predictive analytical procedures can be used. For example, a cement supplier who purchases its raw materials (cement) at a contracted price can predict the total purchase amount for the year based on total purchases and movements established in the inventory testing.

The other significant assertion is the combination of two assertions: completeness and cut-off. Testing completeness and cut-off is important to ensure that the client has not understated its costs and expenses by deferring costs into the period after year

3 Design and understand how to execute substantive procedures to address audit risk related to cost of sales and other significant expenses.

end. There is often an incentive to reach a particular profit result for the period, which may lead to the recognition of purchases or expenses incurred before year end being deferred to the period after year end.

Classification may be important because of specific disclosure requirements related to certain costs and expenses. For example, depreciation; loss on sale of property, plant and equipment; superannuation costs; and interest expense (borrowing costs) are all required to be disclosed in accordance with the applicable financial reporting framework.

Occurrence is not typically a significant assertion, as the primary objective in testing for occurrence is to ensure that costs and expenses are not overstated. It is unlikely for most entities that there is any incentive to overstate costs and expenses. Should the client be in a situation where there is such an incentive, however, specific testing to address the risk of occurrence should be performed.

11.3.1 Principal objectives in auditing costs and expenses

The principal objectives in auditing costs and expenses are described in table 11.5.

TABLE 11.5 **Objectives in auditing costs and expenses**

OBJECTIVE	ASSERTION
All costs and expenses in the income statement are properly supported as charges against the entity in the period. Costs and expenses applicable to future periods are carried forward as inventory, prepaid expenses, deferred charges, or property, plant, and equipment.	Occurrence (O)
All costs related to the current period's revenues, and all expenses of the current period, are included in the income statement.	Completeness (C)
Costs and expenses are stated in the income statement at the appropriate amounts.	Accuracy, cut-off (A, CO)
Costs and expenses are properly classified, described, and disclosed in the financial statements, including the notes.	Classification, classification and understandability (CI, C&U)

11.3.2 Processes impacting on costs and expenses

Tables 11.6 and 11.8 illustrate procedures the auditor may perform during their testing of significant processes related to costs and expenses. In the case of costs and expenses, there are typically two important types of transactions that affect the costs and expenses balances: purchases and payroll (covered in section 11.3.4). Some of these procedures may be performed even when the auditor is able to test and rely on controls (that is, where the controls are effective). In this case, however, the extent of testing can be reduced. Alternatively, the auditor may determine that it is more efficient to test the balance substantively.

PURCHASES PROCESS

Confirm accounts payable (not often performed). (E, V&A)
Test the cut-off by inspecting the purchases journal, inventory receiving records, creditor/supplier invoices, and other supporting documents immediately before and after the cut-off date. Determine that the transactions were recorded in the proper period. Compare payables cut-off to cut-off in related areas—for example, accounts payable and inventory. (CO)
Perform a search for unrecorded liabilities as of the inventory date and/or year end by selecting subsequent payments, unmatched invoices, and receiving reports and ensuring that they are recorded in the correct period. (C)
Compare supplier/creditor invoices to the initial record of entry. (C)
Examine payments of balances subsequent to year end to verify recorded payables. (C, CO)
Compare entries in the payables sub-ledger to the supplier/creditor invoices. (O)
Test the account postings of purchases within the general ledger by comparing the nature of the goods or services purchased with the description of the accounts and the account name to which the transaction was posted. (A, Cl)
Test the mathematical accuracy of the payables sub-ledger. (A)
Test the posting of items in the payables sub-ledger to supporting documentation. (O)
Test the posting of the totals in the payables sub-ledger to the general ledger. (C)

TABLE 11.6 **Example substantive test of transactions—purchases and other expenses**

11.3.3 Illustrative procedures for auditing costs and expenses

An almost limitless number of substantive procedures can be designed for testing account balances. Table 11.7 illustrates example procedures the auditor may use when substantively auditing costs and expenses. Some of the procedures are always performed (irrespective of the risk assessment the auditor reaches for the significant account), while others are additionally selected in response to the risk assessment to address any remaining detection risks that are still evident after controls testing has been performed.

EXAMPLE TESTS ALWAYS PERFORMED

Obtain detailed analysis of selected costs and expense accounts and trace the details to the source data. (O, A)
Compare the current year's expenses to the prior year's actual amount and the current year's budgeted amount (in absolute dollars and/or as a percentage of sales). Investigate any unexpected changes or absence of expected changes. If expenses are audited at an interim date, review the roll-forward of activity from interim to year end and compare it to the activity in the equivalent period of the prior year. Investigate any unexpected changes or the absence of expected changes. Consider the need to test interim transactions. (C, A, Cl)
Review interim financial statements and investigate fluctuations or the absence of expected changes. (C, A)
Scan the repairs and maintenance account. Select a sample of invoices and review the details to ensure that they are not items that should have been capitalized. (C, E, A)
Compare the current year balance to that of the prior year. Investigate any unexpected fluctuations. Review the details of the legal expense account, the legal invoices, and correspondence files to ensure that no contingent liabilities exist of which the auditor is unaware. (C)

TABLE 11.7 **Example substantive tests of account balances—costs and expenses**

(continued)

TABLE 11.7 Example substantive tests of account balances—costs and expenses (continued)

EXAMPLE ANALYTICAL PROCEDURES

Cost of sales

Compare the current period's gross profit ratios by month, by location, by product, and by geographic area with those of prior periods and with budgeted amounts. Investigate any large or unusual variations or the absence of expected variations. (C, A)

Review the relationship with respect to the flow of goods such as gross profit analysis, comparison of standard and actual costs, and the review of the reconciliation between cost of sales and shipments. (C, A)

Compare the relationships of materials cost, direct labour cost, and overhead cost to the cost of sales with the same relationships in prior periods. Investigate significant fluctuations or the absence of expected fluctuations. (C, A)

Compare the relationship of overhead costs in cost of sales to direct labour, hours, and/or dollars with the same relationships in prior years. (C, A)

Compare units purchased to units sold. Investigate significant or unusual differences. Ensure that any differences noted are accounted for in the change in inventory during the year. (C, A)

Compare the relationship of direct labour costs to number of employees with the same relationship in prior periods. Investigate significant fluctuations. (C, A)

Compare average production and average compensation per employee with the same figures in prior years. Investigate significant fluctuations or the absence of expected fluctuations. (C, A)

Expenses

Review the client's comparison of budgeted and actual costs and expenses by month or by quarter. Corroborate the reasons identified by the client for important variations. Investigate any unexpected variations or the absence of expected variations not identified by the client. (C, A)

Compare royalty expenses with the related sales. (C, A)

Perform an overall test of interest expense by multiplying the average debt outstanding by the weighted average interest rate. (C, A)

Compare the current period's depreciation with that of the prior period, with budgeted amounts, and with property, plant, and equipment balances. (C, A)

EXAMPLE OTHER GENERAL PROCEDURES

Review the expense accounts in the general ledger for unusual items. Investigate any such items observed. (O, C, A)

Review components of significant prepaid and accrual accounts for reasonableness. If not significant, compare prepaid expense and accrued liability balances with those of prior periods. Investigate significant fluctuations or the absence of expected fluctuations. (C, A)

Review minutes, agreements, union contracts, budgets, and plans for evidence of new types of expenses that may have been incurred. Investigate significant items noted. (C, A)

Identify and examine items that may require separate disclosure in the financial statements, including the notes—for example, discontinued operations and segment information. (C, A, CI, C&U)

Review journal entries on a test basis for unusual items. Investigate any such items observed. (A)

Review the payables sub-ledger for unusual items. Investigate significant items noted. (A)

Review the allocation of expenses to cost centres for reasonableness. (A, CI)

Trace a sample of sales transactions to corresponding commissions or other sales expenses. (A)

Cloud 9

Ian is not sure how to start identifying the most significant expense accounts. He could rely on the trial balance to identify significant revenue accounts, but he is aware that the biggest risk with expenses is that they are understated on, or even omitted from, the trial balance. Suzie reminds him that the audit team has already done the planning at the entity level. As a part of this process, the team has identified the key risks, processes, and accounts.

"For example, we know that certain types of expenses will be incurred by a business that imports, wholesales, and retails footwear. Those accounts should be on the trial balance. Do the amounts look reasonable? Also, we know that the business has recently established a new store; bought delivery trucks; expanded its marketing through promotions, sponsorship, and loyalty programs; and introduced new products. Are all those activities reflected in the accounts in the way we expect?"

Ian knows that the controls testing has already produced some evidence about expenses. He suggests they use analytical procedures to focus on the key relationships between the expense accounts and various activity measures (such as employees) and other accounts (such as sales). As part of the controls testing, the audit assistants have vouched expenses, such as purchases, to the underlying documentation. He recommends they perform more tests of details of inventory movements around year end to gather evidence about cut-off and completeness of expenses. In addition, they will substantiate cash payments during the period following year end to identify unrecorded liabilities and expenses. Tracing payments to the ledger posting will help substantiate classification, particularly for items such as maintenance, which is often misclassified as an asset. He also recommends that they include specific procedures wherever there are additional disclosure requirements, such as related party transactions.

11.3.4 Processes impacting payroll and related expenses

Payroll is generally one of the most significant expenses of the income statement; therefore, the auditor may give it special consideration. Usually the auditor will test the controls over the payroll cycle and then perform substantive analytical procedures over the related expense accounts. This strategy is commonly employed due to the nature of the payroll cycle, which encompasses the following characteristics: (1) A significant number of payroll transactions may be processed during the period, but as they are generally processed the same way, they are considered routine in nature. (2) Controls over the payroll cycle tend to be good, as balances may be audited by tax authorities. (3) The risk of understatement is minimal, as employees insist on corrections when there has been an underpayment.

Many entities outsource the payroll function to a service organization. Where the payroll is outsourced, the auditor is still responsible for auditing payroll-related balances and ensuring that sufficient and appropriate evidence is documented in the audit file to support the audit opinion. To help achieve this objective, many service organizations will issue an audit report on their operations, which the auditor can rely on, thereby eliminating the need for the auditor to test the controls at the service organization directly. Requirements for relying on a service organization are dealt with in CAS 402 *Audit Considerations Relating to an Entity Using a Service Organization*. When using a service organization, the auditor is responsible for understanding the user entity, including its internal controls relevant to the audit, as the auditor must still identify and assess the risks of material misstatement and design audit procedures responsive to those risks.

TABLE 11.8 **Example substantive test of transactions—payroll**

PAYROLL PROCESS
Compare the payroll at the beginning and end of the period to identify changes in employees and in pay rates. (A)
Compare hours paid with the record of hours worked—for example, timecards. (A)
Trace the payroll payments to the payroll clearing account. (O, A)
Agree the record of hours charged—for example, timecards or job tickets—to the payroll ledger/payroll software used to record and calculate payroll. (C, A)
Obtain from a source other than the payroll department a list of employees who left during the period, and determine that the former employees were removed from the payroll on a timely basis. (A)
Compare employee data (that is, name, identification number, department, employee status or group, location, wage rate, and deductions) to authorizations on file (for example, hiring records, personnel files on wage rates and reductions, union contracts, and tax file numbers). (O, A)
Compare the names, net pay, and other data in the payroll ledger to the amount recorded in the pay run (which is then processed through the payroll clearing account). (E, A)
Test the extensions of wage rates multiplied by the hours worked. (A)
Review that the hours on the record of labour performed—for example, timecards—are recorded in the payroll ledger in the correct period. (CO)
Reconcile the accrued payroll balance to the amount in the payroll ledger for the corresponding balance. (A)
Examine payments of accrued payroll liabilities and/or payroll disbursements subsequent to the end of the period. (C, CO)
Test the postings of totals in the payroll ledger to the general ledger. (C)

Tables 11.8 and 11.9 illustrate procedures the auditor may perform during their testing of the payroll process. Some of these procedures may be performed even when it is possible to test and rely on controls (that is, where the controls were effective). In this case, however, the extent of testing can be reduced. Alternatively, the auditor may determine that it is more efficient to test the balance substantively.

TABLE 11.9 **Example substantive tests of account balances—payroll**

Review the client's comparison of budgeted and actual costs and expenses by month or by quarter. Corroborate the reasons identified by the client for important variations. Investigate any unexpected variations or the absence of expected variations not identified by the client. (C, A)
Compare sales commissions or bonuses with the related sales. (C, A)
Compare the current period's relationship of administrative payroll to direct labour with the same relationship in prior years. Investigate any unexpected variations or the absence of expected variations. (C, A)
Compare the current period's relationship of employee benefits to payroll, hours worked, or number of employees with the same relationship in prior years. Investigate any unexpected variations or the absence of expected variations. (C, A)
Compare the current period's superannuation contribution with that of prior years. Investigate any unexpected variations or the absence of expected variations. (C, A)
Compare the payroll tax expenses to the annual payroll multiplied by the statutory tax rate. (C, A)

PROFESSIONAL ENVIRONMENT

Four ways to cheat with expenses

Auditors should watch out for ways in which companies can skew their expenses to give the impression of more or less favourable results, depending on the situation. One way is with "cookie jar reserves," which are created in good years by debiting expenses and crediting a provision. In the year the entry is made, accounting profit is reduced, but this is acceptable to company management in a good year because it helps smooth the profit trend. In bad years, the entry is reversed with a debit to the provision and a credit to expenses. Accounting profit is increased in the otherwise bad year, which potentially allows the company to avoid awkward questions from analysts and other users of its financial statements. It is not always true that companies will try to understate expenses—auditors need to be alert to overstated expenses to prevent a company's setting up these so-called reserves.

Another problem of overstated expenses is "big bath accounting." This variation usually occurs when new management takes over a company, or when a company is being restructured. In such a situation, some assets need to be impaired and/or losses must be recognized on asset disposals. Management may take the opportunity to write down everything it can for as much as it can. The motive is that investors will hear all the bad news at once, and in future periods, lower depreciation expenses and impairment charges will cause profits to rise quickly. Once again, auditors need to test for the validity of expenses rather than simply assuming that management will only ever try to understate them.

Another technique used to create the impression of good performance is reclassifying expenses. Company managers are aware that analysts do not just focus on the bottom line—they also analyze line items. For example, analysts are interested in managers' performance at trading merchandise for high markups. Knowing this, a retailer might try to understate cost of sales by transferring some expenses into general administrative expenses. Reclassifying cost of sales expenses into other line items might get past an auditor, because the item is still recorded in the right period for the right amount. Auditors need to be alert to account classification, not just the amount and date of the expense.

Finally, auditors need to pay attention to deferrals. When management claims that a debit should be recorded as an asset instead of as an expense, auditors should ask whether the accounting standard requirements have been met. For example, IAS 38 *Intangible Assets* requires amounts spent on research to be expensed, and amounts spent on development to be deferred, only if it is probable that future economic benefits attributable to the asset will flow to the enterprise, and if the cost of the asset can be measured reliably.

BEFORE YOU GO ON

3.1 Name two assertions that are ordinarily significant for costs and expenses, and describe why they are important.

3.2 Describe two substantive audit procedures ordinarily always performed for costs and expenses.

3.3 Describe three possible analytic procedures the auditor may perform over payroll expenses.

11.4 ASSESSING THE RESULTS OF SUBSTANTIVE PROCEDURES

In the substantive tests available for ensuring that costs and expenses are materially correct, described above, the focus was on cost of sales (also referred to as cost of goods sold) and other significant expenses. Significant expenses are often items that have specific disclosure requirements. However, there may be significant costs or expense accounts other than those discussed in this chapter, including administration

4 Understand how to assess the results of the substantive procedures to determine whether additional substantive tests are necessary.

costs, selling expenses, audit fees, advertising and marketing costs, and impairment charges, to name a few. It is important to ensure that appropriate substantive procedures are designed to test all significant accounts. The example substantive procedures in tables 11.6 and 11.8 provide a good reference for designing the required procedures for other significant accounts. The nature of the testing is likely to be consistent with the example procedures described above, and the auditor then uses their **professional judgement**, knowledge of the client, and risk assessment for each significant account to determine the timing and extent of testing.

As noted in chapter 10, when the auditor performs substantive testing, the key objective is to determine whether there are material misstatements within the account balance and to quantify the amount of any misstatement if it exists. When tests performed identify errors or exceptions, the first response is to understand why the exception or error has arisen. The auditor may need to increase the sample size (as per CAS 530 *Audit Sampling*) to ensure that there are no other errors in the balance, unless the total error in the balance can be quantified without performing additional testing (as per CAS 330 *The Auditor's Responses to Assessed Risks* and CAS 500 *Audit Evidence*).

Additional testing (using the example substantive tests provided in this chapter) may also be an appropriate response to confirm and quantify the misstatement. When errors are identified, it is important to continue testing until the error can be accurately quantified or until the balance has been fully tested to an extent that proves a material error can no longer exist within the balance. This concept will be discussed in more detail in chapter 12.

professional judgement the auditor's professional characteristics, such as their expertise, experience, knowledge, and training

Cloud 9

Suzie is very happy with Ian's recommendations. They complete the audit program and send it to the audit manager, who reviews and approves it. Substantive testing begins, and the results start to arrive. Suzie, Josh Thomas, and Sharon Gallagher meet regularly to discuss progress and respond to the errors and exceptions as they arise. They also begin to prepare for the audit tasks that must be performed close to, or after, the client's year end. The final phase of Cloud 9's audit is about to begin.

BEFORE YOU GO ON

4.1 Provide three examples of costs or expenses that may be significant accounts in addition to cost of sales, purchases, depreciation, and bad debts expense.

4.2 What is the first response when testing identifies errors or exceptions?

4.3 Describe the consequences of finding errors or exceptions when performing substantive testing.

SUMMARY

❶ Explain the relationship between the overall risk assessment for a significant account and the extent and timing of substantive procedures, and the differences between auditing income statement and balance sheet accounts.

The higher the overall risk of error or misstatement, the higher the level of substantive procedures required, assuming that no controls have been tested or can be relied on. When controls are effective and the overall risk assessment is therefore lower, limited substantive testing is ordinarily required. Revenue and expense account balances reflect the entire reporting period, and auditors typically use substantive analytical procedures coupled with some tests of details.

❷ Design and understand how to execute substantive procedures to address audit risk related to revenue.

Sales revenue is typically significant due to its size, volume of transactions, and high inherent risk. The most important audit assertions for revenue are occurrence, accuracy, and cut-off. The two significant accounting processes that impact on the sales revenue account balance are sales and sales returns and allowances. It is normally efficient and effective to perform at least some controls testing over these processes.

❸ Design and understand how to execute substantive procedures to address audit risk related to cost of sales and other significant expenses.

Cost of sales and expenses are generally significant accounts. The key audit assertions for these accounts are accuracy, completeness, and cut-off. Typical procedures include vouching recorded amounts to supporting documentation, and testing of depreciation expense as part of the testing of property, plant, and equipment on the balance sheet. Opening and closing inventory is part of inventory testing. Purchases testing is most efficiently tested as part of controls testing. Incentives to achieve particular levels of profit could lead to a company deferring the recognition of expenses incurred before year end to the following period. Special consideration may be given to the payroll balances.

❹ Understand how to assess the results of the substantive procedures to determine whether additional substantive tests are necessary.

When tests performed identify errors or exceptions, it is important to continue testing until the error can be accurately quantified or until the balance has been fully tested to an extent that it proves a material error can no longer exist within the balance.

KEY TERMS

Analytical procedures, 434

Audit risk, 434

Control risk, 434

Detection risk, 435

Inherent risk, 434

Professional judgement, 450

Significant account, 434

Substantive procedures (substantive testing or tests of details), 433

Tests of controls (controls testing), 435

MULTIPLE-CHOICE QUESTIONS

11.1 A key difference between auditing balance sheet accounts and income statement accounts is that:
(a) balance sheet accounts always have larger totals.
(b) balance sheet accounts are always more significant accounts.
(c) income statement accounts reflect the entire 12 months of transactions.
(d) income statement accounts rely on audit techniques such as confirmations.

11.2 Sales revenue is a significant account for an entity:
(a) because of the high volume of transactions that flow through the account.
(b) because of the overall inherent risk associated with revenue.
(c) except for a start-up company.
(d) all of the above.

11.3 Delivery documentation for the sale of goods:
(a) is important because it provides evidence supporting the date of sale.
(b) is not important to audit because the invoice date is always the correct date of sale.
(c) is important because it shows how hard the personnel in the warehouse are working.
(d) is not important because the only thing that matters is whether the debtor pays the account.

11.4 The important assertion(s) for revenue is (are):
(a) occurrence, because testing needs to ensure that recorded sales are genuine.
(b) never completeness, because a company would never want to understate its revenue.
(c) completeness when there could be pressure to defer sales recognition to give the company a head start on meeting the next year's target.
(d) both (a) and (c).

11.5 Classification is an important assertion for expenses because:
(a) there is often an incentive to overstate expenses.
(b) some expenses are subject to specific disclosure requirements.
(c) vouching is a useful audit technique for expenses.
(d) auditing assets gives no evidence about certain expenses.

11.6 Comparing the relationship of overhead costs in cost of sales to direct labour is an example of this type of auditing technique:
(a) vouching to original documents.
(b) tracing posting of original documents to the ledger.
(c) analytical procedures.
(d) confirmation.

11.7 The following account is not an expense account that is ordinarily tested as part of the testing of asset balances:
(a) bad debts expense.
(b) purchases.
(c) interest received.
(d) depreciation.

11.8 Searching for unrecorded liabilities:
(a) is not an important audit procedure.
(b) can be done by examining subsequent payments or unmatched invoices.
(c) is always performed by confirming accounts payable.
(d) is part of testing the mathematical accuracy of the payables sub-ledger.

11.9 When testing payroll, the auditor:
(a) reviews that the hours on timecards are recorded in the payroll ledger in the correct period.
(b) uses only the number of employees at the end of the period as the predictor of total payroll expense.

(c) uses the list of employees who left during the period, as recorded by the payroll department, to check that former employees were removed from the payroll on a timely basis.

(d) does not examine overtime records as these are always insubstantial.

11.10 When an audit test reveals an error or exception, the auditor should:

(a) try to understand why the error or exception has occurred.

(b) consider increasing the sample size.

(c) consider additional testing.

(d) all of the above.

REVIEW QUESTIONS

11.1 How do the key differences between balance sheet accounts and income statement accounts affect the nature, timing, and extent of substantive testing of each?

11.2 What are the most important assertions for sales revenue? Compare these with the most important assertions for other revenue. Are they different? Explain.

11.3 Explain the techniques clients might deliberately use to violate the cut-off assertion because of pressure to meet sales targets. How might an auditor detect these actions?

11.4 Why is substantive testing of the processes impacting sales revenue usually kept to a minimum? How does the auditor gain sufficient assurance about these processes?

11.5 Auditors often use client budgets for revenue and expenses as part of their substantive testing. Explain how and why this is done.

11.6 Do analytical procedures use only financial data based on transactions and balances for the current period? Explain using examples.

11.7 Which assertions are violated if a client includes labour expense related to manufacturing processes as a general expense rather than in cost of sales?

11.8 Discuss the usefulness of examining subsequent payments as an evidence-gathering technique. If an auditor was to use this technique, what would they be looking for?

11.9 What is the purpose of examining the records of employees who left the client during the year? Where should the auditor obtain the information about departed employees?

11.10 Explain the process of "roll forward." When is it used?

PROFESSIONAL APPLICATION QUESTIONS

Basic ★   Moderate ★★   Challenging ★★★

11.1 Internal audit and substantive testing ★

Pedro is the engagement partner on the audit of Lynch Brothers, a public company selling small kitchen appliances. The appliances are made in China and imported and sold to retail outlets by Lynch Brothers. Lynch Brothers has a small internal audit team that was established after the business was accused of "channel stuffing" five years ago. The internal audit team reports directly to the audit committee, which has four independent directors.

After the problems of five years ago, the entire senior management team changed, and the company became extremely committed to promoting good corporate ethics. Remuneration packages for all senior staff include incentive payments for achieving targets based on governance indicators, staff satisfaction scores, peer reviews, and performance appraisals, as well as sales targets.

Pedro has audited Lynch Brothers for four years and has been impressed throughout this time with both the quality of the company's accounts and the internal audit team, which is highly qualified and effective.

Required

What approach would you recommend Pedro take to the audit of Lynch Brothers' income statement accounts? Why?

11.2 Auditing an Internet business ★ ★

Search.com is an Internet-based dating agency. Its business model is that anyone can search its website and review for free the profiles of people looking for friends or partners, but if anyone wants to post their profile or a message, or make contact with another person, they must pay a fee. In addition, it charges advertisers when a user "hits" the site while their advertisement is displayed; it charges a higher fee if the user follows a link to an advertiser's website.

The problem with this model is that Search.com needs profiles on its website to encourage people to visit the site, so it has offered some special deals to encourage people to post their profiles. These offers include substantial discounts, even waiving the fee entirely for people who meet certain criteria (for example, an attractive male under the age of 35).

Holly, the engagement partner on the audit of Search.com, has some doubts about the revenue numbers claimed by Search.com in its trial balance. She suspects that some of the profiles are fictitious and the advertising revenue is overstated.

Required

What could Holly do to audit the revenue claimed by Search.com?

11.3 Substantive testing of sales ★ ★

André is seeking your advice on the selection of substantive procedures for the audit of his client, Rock Ltd. (Rock). Rock is a specialist outdoor clothing and equipment retailer and has experienced reasonable growth over the past three years, although this growth has come substantially from the clothing section. Sales of camping and climbing equipment are down significantly so far this year in all stores except the one in Montreal. Early results from audit testing show that controls over the sales process are reasonably effective, resulting in a low to moderate control risk. André believes he will need to do some substantive testing of sales but is unsure about which procedures would be most useful. He has access to Rock's monthly sales budgets for the period, as well as actual sales figures for the eight months of the year to date.

Required

Write a memo to André explaining the substantive procedures for sales that he could choose from and that would be most useful in these circumstances.

11.4 Auditing research and development expenditure ★ ★

Chemo Ltd. (Chemo) is developing a new drug for arthritis. The expenditure does not meet the requirements for deferral as an asset and must be expensed in the current period. The amounts involved are material: the trial balance shows salaries for chemists of $5 million; depreciation of laboratory equipment, $5.5 million; supplies consumed in the laboratory, $4.5 million; and amortization of related patents, $9.0 million. Chemo expects that further development of the drug will allow commercial production and product sales to commence in another three years.

The main difficulty faced by the auditor is deciding whether the expenditure should be classified as research and development expenses or as general administrative expenses. In addition, the auditor is concerned about the accuracy of the amounts claimed by the client.

Required

(a) Explain why the classification of the expenditure is important and needs to be tested.

(b) Suggest to the auditor some techniques for substantiating the expenditure amounts.

11.5 Purchases testing ★ ★ ★

Chris Cho is a veterinary surgeon, specializing in pigs. His customers are pig farmers, large and small, throughout the province. To support his practice, he also operates All Creatures Veterinary Supplies Ltd (ACVS), which supplies drugs and other supplies to pig farmers. Most of the drugs can only be sold on a vet's prescription. The sale of other supplies is unrestricted, although there are safety issues surrounding the storage of some items.

ACVS orders drugs and other supplies in bulk from local and overseas suppliers. Most sales are made to farmers on the receipt of a telephoned purchase order. The sales order is taken by a clerk in the office and entered into the computer system. This generates a packing slip for the storeman, who then takes the supplies from the shelves and packages them for delivery. Often there are not sufficient supplies in stock to complete an order, so that part of the order is held over until more supplies are obtained.

Purchase orders are initiated by the storeman when inventory is running low. The storeman has to be careful not to hold too much inventory, because there are strict regulations regarding "use by" dates for drugs. Sometimes an order of drugs and supplies is not received in full from the suppliers because they are waiting for delivery from the manufacturer. In this case, the storeman makes a note in his diary to follow up and obtain the missing items at a later date.

Clients are often in a hurry to receive their drugs, and Chris often takes drugs with him when he visits a farm. When he remembers, Chris leaves a note for the storeman explaining which drugs he has taken. ACVS maintains a perpetual inventory system, and the storeman is responsible for periodic inventory counts to confirm the accuracy of the inventory records.

Required

(a) What strengths and weaknesses can you identify in the inventory control system at ACVS?

(b) What substantive procedures would you recommend for purchases, given your assessment of the control system?

11.6 Assessing the results of payroll substantive testing ★ ★

The human resources department at Harold Logistics is responsible for selecting and appointing employees, approving pay rates and promotions, and processing employee terminations. The payroll department is responsible for preparing the weekly wages based on the information from the human resources department and according to hours worked by each employee. Harold Logistics has a number of long-term contracts to deliver goods along the eastern seaboard. The company operates a fleet of large trucks and has a number of permanent drivers, who are assisted by other drivers on short-term contracts during busy times of the year (such as the three months prior to Christmas). Drivers work long shifts, and most of the driving is done at night.

During busy times, the human resources department falls behind with its processing of paperwork related to the short-term contract drivers. In particular, there are constant complaints from the drivers that they have to wait several weeks after they start work for their first pay.

William is testing the payroll process. He discovers that the complaints from the drivers are justified; it takes, on average, three weeks from the date the driver starts work for the payroll department to receive the relevant authorization for the driver's pay. However, he also finds that, on average, drivers are paid for one additional week after they actually leave the company because the human resources department does not record the termination date accurately. The payroll department tells William that, because of the confusion, no provision is made for accrued wages at year end.

Required

(a) Based on William's findings, which accounts are likely to be misstated, and which assertions are violated?

(b) What tests would you recommend that William perform to substantiate weekly wages expense?

Questions 11.7 and 11.8 are based on the following case.

Securimax Ltd. (Securimax) has been an audit client of KFP Partners (KFP) for the past 15 years. Securimax is based in Waterloo, Ontario, where it manufactures high-tech armour-plated personnel carriers. Securimax often has to go through a competitive market tender process to win large government contracts. Its main product, the small but powerful Terrain Master, is highly specialized, and Securimax does business only with nations that have a recognized, democratically elected government. Securimax maintains a highly secure environment, given the sensitive and confidential nature of its vehicle designs and its clients.

In September 2011, Securimax installed an off-the-shelf costing system to support the highly sophisticated and cost-sensitive nature of its product designs. The new system replaced a system that had been developed in-house, as the old system could no longer keep up with the complex and detailed manufacturing costing process that provides tender costings. The old system also had difficulty with the company's broader reporting requirements.

The manufacturing costing system uses all of the manufacturing unit inputs to calculate and produce a database of all product costs and recommended sales prices. It also integrates with the general ledger each time there are product inventory movements such as purchases, sales, wastage, and damaged inventory.

Securimax's fiscal year end is December 31.

Source: Adapted from the Institute of Chartered Accountants Australia's CA Program's *Audit and Assurance Exam,* December 2008 and March 2009.

11.7 Substantive procedures for cost of sales ★ ★

Required

(a) What are the principal audit objectives and assertions for Securimax's cost of sales? Explain.

(b) Identify the relevant substantive tests of details that would be appropriate to gather evidence about the assertions in (a) above.

11.8 Substantive testing of income statement and balance sheet accounts ★ ★

Required

Discuss how substantive testing of Securimax's cost of sales expense would relate to substantive testing of the inventory account on its balance sheet.

Questions 11.9 and 11.10 are based on the following case.

Fellowes and Associates Chartered Accountants is a successful mid-tier accounting firm with a large range of clients across Canada. During 2011, Fellowes and Associates gained a new client, Health Care Holdings Group (HCHG), which owns 100 percent of the following entities:

· Shady Oaks Centre, a private treatment centre

· Gardens Nursing Home Ltd., a private nursing home

· Total Laser Care Limited (TLCL), a private clinic that specializes in the laser treatment of skin defects.

Year end for all HCHG entities is June 30.

Shady Oaks Centre is a private treatment centre generating revenue from clients for stays in the facility and provision of nurses, psychologists, social workers, physiotherapists, and occupational therapists.

You are working on the 2011 engagement for Shady Oaks, and your audit manager has requested you use substantive analytical procedures to calculate Shady Oaks' estimated revenue for patients staying in the centre.

You are also completing the planning of the accounts payable and cash disbursement cycle. Accounting staff perform the following procedures:

- A pre-numbered cheque requisition is prepared for all payments.
- The details on the supplier's invoice are matched to the appropriate receiving report.
- The details on the supplier's invoice and receiving report are matched to an authorized purchase order.
- The cheque requisition is stapled to the authorized purchase order, receiving report, and supplier's invoice and forwarded to the appropriate senior staff member for review and authorization.
- The authorized cheque requisition, together with the supporting documents, is passed to accounts payable for payment.

Your controls testing confirms that the above activities are performed effectively.

Source: Adapted from the Institute of Chartered Accountants Australia's CA Program's *Audit and Assurance Exam,* December 2008 and March 2009.

11.9 Tests of details for purchases ★ ★

Required

Design the tests of details for purchases that you would use to supplement the analytical procedures. Relate each test to the relevant assertion for purchases.

11.10 Analytical substantive procedures for revenue ★ ★ ★

Required

Describe all the key information required to estimate Shady Oaks' revenue for patients staying in the centre.

CASES

11.11 Integrative Case Study—Bazaar Company Audit ★ ★ ★

Bazaar Company buys computers, parts, and related equipment and resells them at a markup to a loyal base of corporate customers. Competition is growing, but the market is favourable, and Bazaar offers excellent customer service, giving it a competitive advantage. The owner is very involved in most of the important operating decisions. His capable assistant steps in when necessary. The owner plans to implement a code of ethics at some point and also wishes to improve certain controls.

Bazaar is a medium-sized private company that operates multiple warehouses, each carrying a mix of inventory items. The first type of inventory, which can be costly, consists of specialized computer hardware, desktop computers, and laptop computers. The turnover rate for this inventory is high, since new technology is always emerging. Because the company orders months in advance, Bazaar occasionally overestimates demand. After three or four months, products are difficult to sell, but they are kept because most cannot be returned to the supplier, and Bazaar is reluctant to hold liquidation sales for fear they would negatively affect the sales at regular prices.

This year, Bazaar implemented an integrated computer system to manage the general ledger as well as inventory, purchases, and sales. The system was developed by external consultants and is maintained by Bazaar's IT department.

The sales mix has not changed significantly from previous years. Ten new accounts were opened during the year, with average monthly sales of $5,000 each. Sales also increased because a new representative was hired at the beginning of the fiscal year. Average monthly sales for the 10 experienced representatives are $500,000 each. Rookie representatives normally perform at 50 percent of an experienced representative's level in their first year. Bazaar also lost a customer, who had averaged $90,000 a year in sales, to the competition. Purchases increased and were distributed across the inventory types in amounts similar to the overall sales mix.

The following was documented in the Bazaar Company audit file. You are the manager on the file and you are reviewing the work performed.

SECTIONS FROM THE RECRUIT'S AUDIT FILE

Engagement Risk Assessment

Overall, audit risk is low.

Audit Strategy

A mixed audit strategy would be appropriate because some controls seem to be in place and could be relied on. The controls need to be tested before confirming the strategy.

Audit Sections

Materiality

The partner established a materiality of $250,000 for the engagement, based on 5 percent of net income after tax.

Sales

Sales procedures performed
1. Matched totals on sales listing to sub-ledger and general ledger.
2. Sales variance analysis:

	2010	2011	$Variance	% Variance
Computers	20,000,000	22,000,000	2,000,000	10%
Parts and peripherals	35,000,000	37,500,000	2,500,000	7%
Software	5,000,000	5,500,000	500,000	10%
Total	60,000,000	65,000,000	5,000,000	8%

Credit Notes

Sampled credit notes. A credit was issued for a price adjustment made by a sales representative. The supporting paperwork stated that the credit had been issued in error (which seems to happen often), and the refund cheque was cancelled. However, the details of the refund cheque could not be located. The clerk says he left the cheque copies on his desk and the next morning they were gone. He gave up looking for them.

Expense Analysis

Randomly sampled 10 general ledger expense accounts. Three of the expense account items sampled were traced to invoices and issued cheques. The remaining items were reviewed for reasonableness.

Expense Description	Supplier (purchase details)	Amount
Small tools	Tools & Tools (hammers, screwdrivers, etc.)	$ 1,159.98
Repairs and maintenance	Colder & Sons (air conditioner unit replacement)	106,545.87
Miscellaneous expenses	Design Lavoie (office redecoration and design)	156,985.52

Required

As the manager of the audit file, comment on the following:
(a) Was the risk assessment adequate? If not, what was missing?
(b) Was the documentation of the determination of materiality adequate? If not, what was missing?
(c) Was the work performed over the sales, credit notes, and expense accounts adequate? If not, what else would you expect to be done?

Source: Uniform Final Exam, The Institutes of Chartered Accountants in Canada and Bermuda, Paper 3, Question 2, 2009.

CASE STUDY—CLOUD 9

Answer the following questions based on the information presented for Cloud 9 in Appendix B of this book and in the current and earlier chapters. You should also consider your answers to the case study questions in earlier chapters.

The worksheet you completed for the case study question in chapter 9 includes your estimates of the overall risk assessment (ORA) and the acceptable detection risk (DR) in the sales to cash receipts process. In the case study question in chapter 10, you designed substantive audit procedures to address the DR for the accounts receivables and cash accounts.

Required

Based on your ORA and DR estimates, design substantive audit procedures for Cloud 9 that would address the DR for the sales account.

RESEARCH QUESTION 11.1

The International Accounting Standards Board (IASB) and the U.S. Financial Accounting Standards Board (FASB) were working jointly on a revenue-recognition project with the expectation that the revised standard would be released in 2012. The aim of the project is to develop an accounting standard to govern when revenue from contracts with customers is recognized. The responses from interested parties to the discussion paper *Preliminary Views on Revenue Recognition in Contracts with Customers* revealed several concerns. For example, some respondents felt there would be problems applying one revenue-recognition rule across all industries. In particular, they felt that there would be issues with construction and telecommunication companies.

Required

(a) Choose one of the industries mentioned by the respondents to the IASB/FASB discussion paper as requiring special rules for revenue recognition. Summarize the respondents' concerns and explain how revenue is currently recognized and measured in that industry.
(b) For the industry you have chosen, explain the auditing implications of the (1) current and (2) proposed revenue-recognition rules. Would the auditor's job be easier or harder under the proposed new rules?

Sources: Copies of relevant papers and information on recent developments are available at www.ifrs.org.

SOLUTIONS TO MULTIPLE-CHOICE QUESTIONS

1. c, 2. d, 3. a, 4. d, 5. b, 6. c, 7. c, 8. b, 9. a, 10. d.

CHAPTER 12

Completing and reporting on the audit

LEARNING OBJECTIVES

After studying this chapter, you should be able to:

1. explain the procedures performed as part of the engagement wrap-up, including gathering and evaluating audit evidence

2. understand the considerations when assessing the going concern assumption used in the preparation of the financial statements

3. understand the purpose of and the procedures performed in the review for contingent liabilities and commitments

4. compare the two types of (material) subsequent events to determine what effect they have on the financial statements (if any)

5. analyze misstatements and explain the difference between quantitative and qualitative considerations when evaluating misstatements

6. evaluate conclusions obtained during the performance of the audit and explain how these conclusions link to the overall opinion formed on the financial statements

7. describe the components of an audit report

8. identify the types of modifications to an audit report

9. explain what reporting is required to management and those charged with governance.

AUDITING AND ASSURANCE STANDARDS

CANADIAN	INTERNATIONAL
CAS 230 *Audit Documentation*	ISA 230 *Audit Documentation*
CAS 240 *The Auditor's Responsibilities Relating to Fraud in an Audit of Financial Statements*	ISA 240 *The Auditor's Responsibilities Relating to Fraud in an Audit of Financial Statements*
CAS 250 *Consideration of Laws and Regulations in an Audit of Financial Statements*	ISA 250 *Consideration of Laws and Regulations in an Audit of Financial Statements*
CAS 260 *Communication with Those Charged with Governance*	ISA 260 *Communication with Those Charged with Governance*
CAS 265 *Communicating Deficiencies in Internal Control to Those Charged with Governance and Management*	ISA 265 *Communicating Deficiencies in Internal Control to Those Charged with Governance and Management*
CAS 320 *Materiality in Planning and Performing an Audit*	ISA 320 *Materiality in Planning and Performing an Audit*
CAS 450 *Evaluation of Misstatements Identified During the Audit*	ISA 450 *Evaluation of Misstatements Identified During the Audit*
CAS 500 *Audit Evidence*	ISA 500 *Audit Evidence*
CAS 501 *Audit Evidence—Specific Considerations for Selected Items*	ISA 501 *Audit Evidence—Specific Considerations for Selected Items*
CAS 520 *Analytical Procedures*	ISA 520 *Analytical Procedures*
CAS 560 *Subsequent Events*	ISA 560 *Subsequent Events*
CAS 570 *Going Concern*	ISA 570 *Going Concern*
CAS 580 *Written Representations*	ISA 580 *Written Representations*
CAS 700 *Forming an Opinion and Reporting on Financial Statements*	ISA 700 *Forming an Opinion and Reporting on Financial Statements*
CAS 705 *Modifications to the Opinion in the Independent Auditor's Report*	ISA 705 *Modifications to the Opinion in the Independent Auditor's Report*
CAS 706 *Emphasis of Matter Paragraphs and Other Matter Paragraphs in the Independent Auditor's Report*	ISA 706 *Emphasis of Matter Paragraphs and Other Matter Paragraphs in the Independent Auditor's Report*
CAS 720 *The Auditor's Responsibilities Relating to Other Information in Documents Containing Audited Financial Statements*	ISA 720 *The Auditor's Responsibilities Relating to Other Information in Documents Containing Audited Financial Statements*
CAS 800 *Special Considerations—Audits of Financial Statements Prepared in Accordance with Special Purpose Frameworks*	ISA 800 *Special Considerations—Audits of Financial Statements Prepared in Accordance with Special Purpose Frameworks*
CAS 805 *Special Considerations—Audits of Single Financial Statements and Specific Elements, Accounts or Items of a Financial Statement*	ISA 805 *Special Considerations—Audits of Single Financial Statements and Specific Elements, Accounts or Items of a Financial Statement*
CAS 810 *Engagements to Report on Summary Financial Statements*	ISA 810 *Engagements to Report on Summary Financial Statements*
Rules of professional conduct of each provincial institute/order	*Code of Ethics for Professional Accountants*
IAS 1 *Presentation of Financial Statements*	IAS 1 *Presentation of Financial Statements*
IAS 10 *Events After the Reporting Period*	IAS 10 *Events After the Reporting Period*
ASPE Section 3820 *Subsequent Events*	

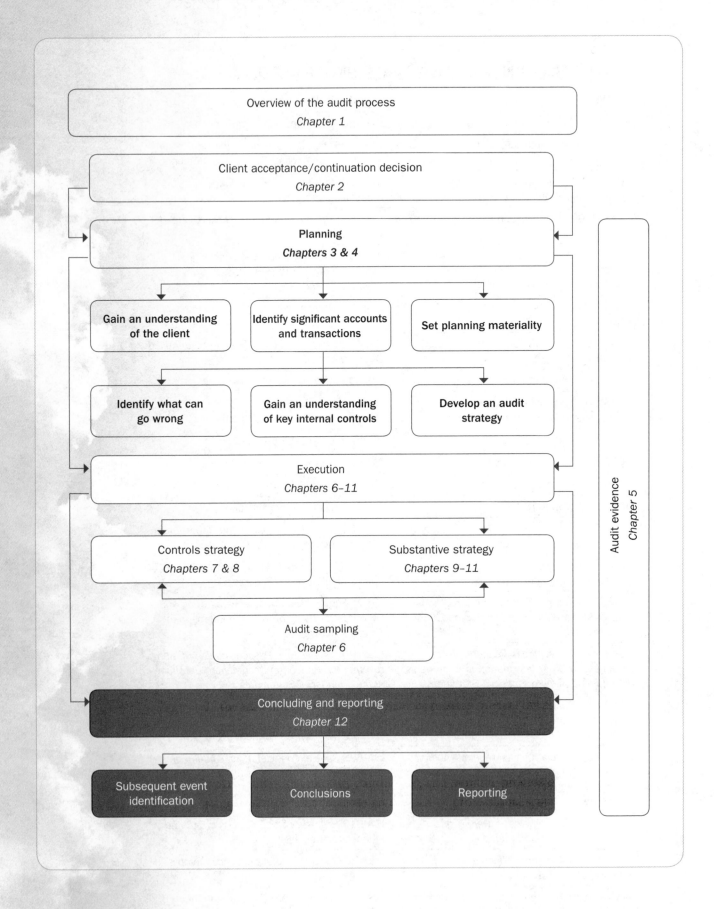

Cloud 9

The partner on the Cloud 9 Ltd. (Cloud 9) audit, Jo Wadley, has called a meeting with the senior staff (Sharon Gallagher, Josh Thomas, Suzie Pickering, and Mark Batten) to discuss the completion of the audit. The partner wants to be sure that all issues are "in hand" and that she is briefed on all contentious matters so that she can resolve them at the scheduled meetings with Cloud 9's board and management. Meetings with clients at the end of the audit can be quite difficult. Sometimes the audit partner considers qualifying the audit report if the client's management will not adjust the financial statements to reflect errors found during the audit.

Sharon, Josh, Suzie, and Mark decide to hold a preliminary meeting to prepare for the meeting with the partner. On the agenda are:
- final evidence and misstatements evaluation
- going concern procedures and assessment
- subsequent events procedures and evidence
- overall conclusion and audit opinion
- legal issues
- communication with Cloud 9's board.

What issues have arisen with Cloud 9's audit? How can they make sure that the partner is fully prepared for the meeting with the client's management?

AUDIT PROCESS IN FOCUS

During the completion phase of the audit a number of procedures are performed. First, the auditor evaluates the audit evidence obtained and reviews the documentation to ensure that it is of a sufficient quality and quantity. Before drawing an overall conclusion on the audit, the auditor also reassesses the going concern assumption, considers the existence of contingent liabilities and subsequent events, performs any additional wrap-up procedures, and assesses any misstatements (sometimes referred to as audit differences) identified throughout the audit and the effect they may have on the overall conclusion (and opinion). The auditor also performs analytical procedures on the adjusted financial statements as a means of assessing their fair presentation.

The final step in the audit process is to evaluate the conclusions drawn from the audit evidence obtained (which will form the basis for the auditor's opinion on the financial statements) and to prepare an appropriately worded audit report. At the same time, a management representation letter is obtained from the client and appropriate communication with those charged with governance is prepared. Consideration is given to compliance with laws and regulations throughout the audit and again as part of the wrap-up and conclusion procedures.

12.1 ENGAGEMENT WRAP-UP

During the wrap-up of an engagement, the auditor finalizes any open items before issuing the audit report, including determining if any remaining procedures are to be completed for the audit. Any remaining audit procedures are assigned to team members, with due dates for completion of the open items. This includes determining that the audit team has properly completed and executed the audit procedures that were planned (as described in chapters 3 and 4) and that all relevant matters have been appropriately considered.

1 Explain the procedures performed as part of the engagement wrap-up, including gathering and evaluating audit evidence.

The following areas are ordinarily covered during the wrap-up of an engagement:

1. Review the audit file to ensure that the planned audit procedures were executed properly and completely. The file is typically reviewed in detail by the manager or above and high-risk areas are typically reviewed by the partner. During the review process, the reviewer makes a list of "review comments" identifying issues not yet resolved, issues requiring futher clarification, and any audit procedures not yet completed. As each working paper is reviewed, it is initialled and dated as evidence that the review was performed.

2. Determine that all necessary matters have been appropriately considered. All significant issues should be documented and conclusions reached. For open items that are no longer relevant to the audit (or necessary to complete), the auditor documents in the audit working papers this fact and the reason(s) why they are no longer relevant.

3. Clear all outstanding review notes and "to-do" items and perform any audit procedures not yet completed. At this stage, if additional audit attention is needed, the auditor performs the necessary audit procedures to resolve open items and issues until they are cleared to the reviewer's satisfaction.

4. Remove all unnecessary documentation, drafts, and cleared review notes from the engagement files. The auditor retains records relevant to the audit, such as audit working papers and other documents that form the basis of the audit opinion, including memoranda, correspondence, communications, and other documents and records (including electronic records) that (1) are created, sent, or received in connection with the audit and (2) contain conclusions, opinions, analyses, or financial data related to the audit. Superseded working papers and financial statements, notes that reflect incomplete or preliminary thinking, and duplicates of documents should be removed.

5. For multi-location engagements, check to ensure that all documents requested from other audit teams have been obtained and reviewed.

6. Consider the amount used for materiality. The auditor considers whether the amount that was used for **materiality** (as discussed in chapter 4 and addressed in CAS 320 *Materiality in Planning and Performing an Audit*) when planning the audit and detecting misstatements (rather than evaluating them) is still appropriate as the basis for their conclusion on the fair presentation of the financial statements taken as a whole. They consider whether, during the course of the audit, they have identified any factors or conditions about the client or its environment (for example, a significant change in anticipated operating results) that would cause them to determine that a different (lower) amount would have been appropriate in establishing their planning materiality. It is important to revisit the amount used for materiality when evaluating misstatements, taking into consideration qualitative as well as quantitative factors.

   When the amount considered material at the end of the audit is significantly lower than at the beginning of the audit (for example, because the basis used for calculating materiality at the planning stage was substantially higher), the auditor considers whether the procedures used throughout the audit were sufficient and whether additional audit procedures need to be performed. To avoid possible surprises at the end of an audit, the auditor should reassess the appropriateness

materiality information that has an impact on the decision-making of users of the financial statements of the materiality set throughout the audit to make sure that sufficient audit procedures are being performed.

7. Reconsider the assessments of internal control at the entity level and the risk of fraud. When planning an audit, the auditor identifies the presence or absence of factors related to the five components of internal control (as discussed in chapter 7) and the risk of fraud and makes an initial assessment of control and fraud risk. They then consider throughout the audit whether additional factors or risks are present and whether they need to revise their conclusion of control risk at the entity level and whether the controls are supportive of the prevention and correction of material misstatements whether due to fraud or error (as discussed in chapters 3 and 8). The auditor specifically reconsiders the assessment of internal control at the entity level when they become aware of significant changes in the client's system of internal controls and after they perform tests of controls. Their conclusions about the effectiveness of internal control at the entity level may be affected by control exceptions that they identify when executing their tests of controls.

When the results of their audit tests identify misstatements in the financial statements, the auditor considers whether such misstatements may be indicative of fraud. The auditor's consideration of fraud risk, and the results of their audit procedures, may indicate that they need to consider withdrawing from the engagement. For example, the auditor may determine that the fraud is so pervasive in the business that they will be unable to complete their audit procedures, or that the fraud will have such an impact on the client's reputation that they no longer wish to have them as a client. In these rare cases, any decision to withdraw from the engagement is not taken lightly and extensive consultation both internally within the audit firm as well as externally with legal counsel will occur before any action is taken. Whether or not the decision is taken to withdraw from the audit engagement depends on (1) whether the evidence suggests that management has been involved in perpetrating the fraud (or there are concerns regarding management's integrity, based on how it dealt with the fraud once it was identified) and (2) the diligence and co-operation of management in investigating the circumstances of the fraud and taking appropriate action.

At the conclusion of the audit, the auditor formally reconsiders their assessment of internal control and fraud risk by considering whether the accumulated results of their audit procedures and other observations affect the assessments they made when planning the audit. This evaluation also considers qualitative matters based on the engagement team and audit team executives' **professional judgement**. (Quantitative and qualitative considerations for materiality are discussed in chapter 4.)

professional judgement the auditor's professional characteristics, such as expertise, experience, knowledge, and training

8. Revisit the planning documentation to ensure that all significant issues identified during the planning phase have been addressed.

9. Perform analytical procedures on the adjusted financial statements. Analytical procedures are used at the end of the audit to evaluate whether the final financial statements are consistent with the knowledge of the business obtained during the audit. Analytics are employed to corroborate the conclusions formed on the individual financial statement elements and the financial statements overall.

10. Perform a review for contingent liabilities and commitments to ensure that they are properly accounted for or disclosed. Specific audit procedures are performed in this area, usually toward the end of the audit. This is discussed further in section 12.3.

11. Perform subsequent events procedures. During the wrap-up of the engagement the auditor performs what is referred to as subsequent events procedures. The objective of subsequent events procedures is to identify those events occurring between year end (that is, the reporting date) and the date of the audit report that may require adjustment to or disclosure in the financial statements. Subsequent events procedures are normally performed through to and including the date of the audit report. Subsequent events are discussed in more detail in section 12.4.

12.1.1 Sufficient appropriate audit evidence

As discussed in chapter 1, the objective of an audit is to obtain sufficient appropriate evidence to reduce the risk of material misstatement in the financial statements to an acceptably low level.

What constitutes **sufficient appropriate evidence** is ultimately a matter of professional judgement. It will be based on the satisfactory performance of audit procedures designed to address the assessed risk of material misstatement (as discussed in chapters 1, 3, and 4 and addressed in CAS 500 *Audit Evidence*). This includes any additional or modified procedures performed to address changes identified in the original assessment of risk. Factors to consider in evaluating the sufficiency and appropriateness of audit evidence (assuming the tests were appropriate to the type of account and assertions most at risk) include:

- materiality of misstatements
- management responses
- previous experience
- results of audit procedures performed
- quality of information obtained
- persuasiveness of the audit evidence
- whether the evidence obtained supports or contradicts the results of the risk assessment procedures.

If it is not possible to obtain sufficient appropriate audit evidence, the auditor should express a qualified, adverse, or disclaimer of opinion, as described in CAS 705 *Modifications to the Opinion in the Independent Auditor's Report*.

12.1.2 Evaluating audit evidence

The goal in evaluating audit evidence is to decide, after considering all the relevant data obtained, whether:

1. the assessments of the risk of material misstatement at the assertion level are appropriate, and
2. sufficient evidence has been obtained to reduce the risk of material misstatement in the financial statements to an acceptably low level.

An audit is an ongoing, cumulative, and iterative process of gathering and evaluating evidence. This requires an attitude of professional scepticism to be applied by each member of the audit team, ongoing discussions among the audit team members

sufficient appropriate evidence quantity (sufficiency) and quality (appropriateness) of audit evidence gathered throughout the engagement, and timely modifications being made to planned procedures to reflect any changes to the original risk assessments.

When misstatements or deviations from controls are found in planned procedures, consideration should always be given to:

- the reason for the misstatement or deviation
- the impact on risk assessments and other planned procedures
- the need to modify or perform further audit procedures.

Before evaluating the results of procedures and any misstatements identified, as discussed previously, consideration should be given to whether the materiality levels established during the planning phase need to be revised. A change in materiality could be a result of:

- new information—for example, the bank supplying the company with funding may have decided to refinance the debt during the year and put in place very restrictive covenants relating to certain balances
- a change in the auditor's understanding of the entity and its operations
- new circumstances—for example, actual profit may be significantly lower than expected profit at the planning stage of the audit.

Cloud 9

Sharon suggests that the members of the team ask themselves whether they believe that sufficient appropriate evidence on which to base an audit opinion has been gathered. Which issues are not satisfactorily resolved? Where do they need to gather additional evidence? Which notes can be cleared and removed from the files? Are assessments of risk and materiality still valid given evidence obtained from substantive procedures?

The team members have performed a final review of the evidence and have identified the major audit differences that the partner will need to resolve with Cloud 9's management. It appears that the only other major outstanding items are the going concern assessment, the search for contingent liabilities, and the subsequent events procedures. None of these can be finalized prior to year end, and certain procedures need to be performed up until the audit report date.

BEFORE YOU GO ON

1.1 Explain why it is important to reassess materiality at the end of the audit.

1.2 What is the goal in evaluating audit evidence?

1.3 Provide three considerations when evaluating the sufficiency and appropriateness of audit evidence.

12.2 GOING CONCERN

As discussed in chapter 3 and CAS 570 *Going Concern*, the going concern assumption is a fundamental principle in the preparation of the financial statements. Under the **going concern** assumption, an entity is viewed as continuing in business for the foreseeable future with neither the intention nor the need for liquidation, ceasing trading, or seeking protection from creditors pursuant to laws or regulations. As a result, assets and liabilities are recorded on the basis that the entity will be able to realize its assets and discharge its liabilities in the normal course of business.

Some financial reporting frameworks contain an explicit requirement for management to make an assessment of the entity's ability to continue as a going concern. For

2 Understand the considerations when assessing the going concern assumption used in the preparation of the financial statements.

going concern the viability of a company to remain in business for the foreseeable future

example, IAS 1 *Presentation of Financial Statements* requires management to make an assessment of an entity's ability to continue as a going concern, and when management is aware of material uncertainties related to events or conditions that may cast significant doubt upon the entity's ability to continue as a going concern, to disclose those uncertainties.

Under other financial reporting frameworks (for example, preparing information in accordance with a joint venture or sale agreement), there may be no explicit requirement for management to make a specific assessment of the entity's ability to continue as a going concern. Nevertheless, since the going concern assumption is a fundamental principle in the preparation of the financial statements, management has a responsibility to assess the entity's ability to continue as a going concern even if the financial reporting framework does not include an explicit requirement to do so.

The following factors are relevant when management is assessing the going concern assumption:

- Generally, the further into the future an event is likely to take place, the greater the uncertainty surrounding that event. For that reason, most financial reporting frameworks specify the period for which management is required to assess all available information when making its going concern assessment. In Canada, this is typically 12 months from the date of the financial statements.
- Any judgement about the future is based on information available at the time at which the judgement is made. Subsequent events can contradict a judgement that was reasonable at the time it was made. Management of clients in industries subject to frequent change face more difficulty when assessing the going concern assumption.
- The size and complexity of the entity, the nature and condition of its business, and the degree to which it is affected by external factors all affect judgement regarding the outcome of events or conditions.

CAS 570 *Going Concern* requires that the auditor consider the appropriateness of management's use of the going concern assumption in the preparation of the financial statements. Consideration of management's use of the going concern assumption is based on knowledge of conditions or events obtained through planning and performing the audit. The auditor considers whether their procedures identify conditions and events that, when considered in the aggregate, indicate that there could be substantial doubt about the entity's ability to continue as a going concern.

The auditor also considers whether there are material uncertainties about the entity's ability to continue as a going concern that need to be disclosed in the financial statements. Usually, material uncertainties relate to an entity's inability to meet obligations as they become due without substantial disposals of assets outside the ordinary course of business, restructuring of debt or equity, or major operational improvements.

The going concern assumption does not apply to the financial statements prepared on a liquidation basis. For example, when owners decide to dissolve the business or bankruptcy proceedings reach a point at which liquidation is probable, they prepare the financial statements on a liquidation basis. When the financial statements are not prepared on a going concern basis, that fact needs to be disclosed, together with the basis on which the financial statements have been prepared and the reason why the entity is not considered to be a going concern.

Cloud 9

Sharon and the team discuss whether there are any issues causing doubt on the appropriateness of the going concern assumption at Cloud 9. The financial ratios indicate no problems with solvency, and the major borrowings are not due to be repaid or refinanced for another four years. However, a loss is expected for this financial year. Cloud 9's management is anticipating a loss because of the costs associated with the new store opening and the sponsorship deal. The team makes a note that these issues have been formally reviewed and they conclude that there are no significant issues casting doubt on the going concern assumption.

BEFORE YOU GO ON

2.1 Provide one consideration management should take into account when assessing the going concern assumption.

2.2 Provide one consideration the auditor should take into account when assessing the going concern assumption.

2.3 Does the going concern assumption always apply to all audits?

12.3 CONTINGENT LIABILITIES

Contingent liabilities are existing or possible obligations on the balance sheet date when the final outcome is uncertain and contingent upon a future event. Most financial reporting frameworks require an entity to record or disclose such contingent liabilities, depending on whether they are "likely" or "probable" and "measureable." While it is management's responsibility to determine the appropriate accounting treatment, given the financial reporting framework under which the financial statements will be prepared, CAS 501 *Audit Evidence—Specific Considerations for Selected Items* requires the auditor to "search" for any litigation and claims involving the entity that the auditor may not be aware of but which may give rise to a material misstatement. The auditor is required to perform the following procedures:

- Inquire of management and others within the entity, including in-house legal counsel, if there are any unreported contingent liabilities.
- Review minutes of meetings of **those charged with governance** and correspondence between the entity and its external legal counsel.
- Review correspondence with taxation authorities.
- Review legal expense accounts for unexpected fluctuations.
- Include in the managment representation letter the fact that all contingent liabilities have been disclosed to the auditor.

If the auditor has assessed a risk of material misstatement regarding litigation and claims, they are required by CAS 501.10 to request permission from the client to contact the entity's external counsel. This is usually done via the legal letter, as discussed in chapter 5. If the client does not grant permission for this communication, then the auditor will look to gather evidence by performing alternative procedures. If the alternative procedures do not provide sufficient and appropriate evidence, then the auditor will need to modify the opinion in the auditor's report.

The procedures for contingent liabilities are usually performed at the end of the audit to ensure that there is sufficient and appropriate evidence in the audit file to support

3 Understand the purpose of and the procedures performed in the review for contingent liabilities and commitments.

those charged with governance generally the board of directors, and may include management of an entity

not only contingent liabilities but also the work performed for subsequent events, as described in the next section. While performing the procedures for contingent liabilities, the auditor will also look for evidence that the entity has entered into long-term commitments that have not been appropriately disclosed.

BEFORE YOU GO ON

3.1 What is a contingent liability?

3.2 What are management's responsibilities with respect to contingent liabilities? What are the auditor's responsibilities?

3.3 List three procedures the auditor is required to perform with respect to contingent liabilities.

12.4 SUBSEQUENT EVENTS

④ Compare the two types of (material) subsequent events to determine what effect they have on the financial statements (if any).

The financial statements are prepared on the basis of conditions existing at year end (that is, the reporting date). However, significant events, both favourable and unfavourable, can occur after year end but before the issuance of the audit report that, unless reflected in the financial statements or suitably disclosed therein, could make the financial statements misleading. Therefore, the auditor is responsible for gathering evidence for subsequent events up to the date of the audit report. Once the audit report has been signed, the auditor is no longer responsible for detecting subsequent events.

There are three key dates that are important when considering subsequent events:

1. The date on which the financial statements are approved. This is the date on which those with the recognized authority assert that they have prepared the entity's complete financial statements, including the related notes, and that they have taken responsibility for the financial statements.

2. The date of the audit report. This is the date on which the auditor signs the audit report on the financial statements. The audit report is not dated earlier than the date on which the auditor has obtained sufficient appropriate audit evidence on which to base their opinion on the financial statements. Sufficient appropriate audit evidence includes evidence that the entity's complete financial statements have been prepared and that those with the recognized authority have asserted that they have taken responsibility for the statements.

3. The date on which the financial statements are issued. This is the date on which the audit report and audited financial statements are made available to third parties, which may be, in many circumstances, the date on which they are filed with a regulatory authority.

Each of these terms become important when considering the date when field work is completed and are further explained below.

CAS 560 *Subsequent Events* establishes standards and provides guidance on the auditor's responsibility regarding subsequent events. This standard describes the two types of **subsequent events** that require consideration and evaluation:

1. events that provide additional evidence with respect to conditions that existed at the date of the financial statements (type 1 subsequent events)

2. events that provide evidence with respect to conditions that arose subsequent to the date of the financial statements (type 2 subsequent events).

subsequent events both events occurring between year end and the date of the audit report, and facts discovered after the date of the audit report

The two types of subsequent events are also defined in IAS 10 *Events After the Reporting Period* and ASPE Section 3820 *Subsequent Events*. Each of these is now discussed in more detail.

12.4.1 Type 1 subsequent events

Type 1 subsequent events provide additional evidence with respect to conditions that existed at year end. Such events may affect the estimates inherent in the financial statements or indicate that the going concern assumption in relation to the whole or a part of the entity is not appropriate. Therefore, the financial statements should be adjusted to reflect any material type 1 subsequent event up to the date of the audit report. This may include revisions to estimates where new information is now available. Examples of type 1 subsequent events (requiring changes of amounts in the financial statements) are:

- the bankruptcy of a customer subsequent to year end, which would be considered when evaluating the adequacy of the allowance for doubtful accounts
- an amount received with respect to an insurance claim that was being negotiated at year end
- deterioration in operating results and financial position after year end that is so significant that it may indicate that the going concern assumption is not appropriate to use in the preparation of the financial statements
- the settlement of a lawsuit after the reporting period for an amount different from what was originally estimated.

12.4.2 Type 2 subsequent events

Type 2 subsequent events are those events that do not result in changes to amounts in the financial statements. However, these events may be of such significance as to require disclosure in the financial statements. Examples of type 2 subsequent events (not requiring adjustment but possibly requiring disclosure in the financial statements) are:

- the uninsured (or underinsured) loss of plant or inventory as a result of a fire or flood subsequent to year end
- the purchase of a business
- the issuance of shares or debt securities.

12.4.3 Procedures used when conducting a subsequent events review

The subsequent events review performed for identifying type 1 or type 2 events requires the auditor to perform specific audit procedures different from the usual examination of transactions after year end (for example, the verification of the cut-off of sales or the collection of trade receivables). However, when the usual examination of transactions after year end is performed as part of the substantive tests of certain account balances, primarily to ensure that routine transactions are recorded in the proper period, or to review the appropriateness at year end of the carrying amounts of assets and the adequacy of provisions for losses or expenses, the auditor will be alert for items that may indicate significant subsequent events. When performing these procedures, the auditor may become aware of significant events occurring subsequent to the balance sheet date that may require adjustment to or disclosure in the financial statements.

The procedures performed to identify events that may require adjustment of or disclosure in the financial statements are performed as near as practicable to the date of the audit report and include some or all of the following:

- gaining an understanding of and evaluating processes that management has established to determine that subsequent events are identified and dealt with
- reading minutes of meetings of the board of directors and executive committees held after year end and inquiring about matters discussed at meetings for which minutes are not available
- reading and analyzing the latest available interim financial statements and, as considered necessary and appropriate, budgets, cash flow forecasts, and other related management reports for events such as changes in accounting principles, significant changes in results or working capital, and noncompliance with loan terms, and reviewing sales, receipts, journals, and other accounting records relating to transactions that have occurred subsequent to the date of the financial statements
- inquiring, or extending previous oral or written inquiries, of the entity's legal counsel concerning litigation and claims
- assessing continued compliance with borrowing limits and loan covenants
- inquiring of those charged with governance as to whether any subsequent events have occurred that might affect the financial statements
- inquiring of management as to whether any subsequent events have occurred that might affect the financial statements. Examples of inquiries of management on specific matters are:
  - whether new commitments, borrowings, or guarantees have been entered into or any other factors have changed the classification of any liabilities
  - whether sales of assets have occurred or are planned, or any other plans have been made that may affect the carrying value or classification of assets
  - whether new shares have been issued, long-term debt financing instruments have been put in place, or an agreement to merge or liquidate has been made, or any of these events are planned
  - whether any change of ownership has occurred or is contemplated
  - whether any assets have been seized (or appropriated) by the government or destroyed—for example, by flood or fire
  - whether there have been any developments regarding risk areas and contingencies
  - whether any unusual adjustments have been made since the date of the financial statements or are contemplated
  - whether any significant changes in foreign exchange rates have occurred that could affect the entity
  - whether there has been any change in the status of related party transactions, including those entered into subsequent to the date of the financial statements
  - whether any significant assessments have been made by tax authorities with respect to tax assessments, fines, and penalties
  - the current status of items involving subjective judgement or that were accounted for on the basis of preliminary information, such as provisions for litigation in progress
  - whether any events have occurred or are likely to occur that will bring into question the appropriateness of accounting policies used in the preparation of the financial statements; for example, if such events call into question the validity of the going concern assumption

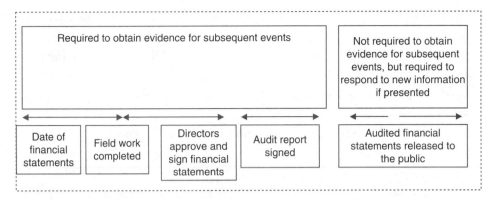

FIGURE 12.1 **Subsequent event timeline**

- sales and profit trends, industry and general economic climate, exceptional bad debt losses, decreases in raw material prices or possible inventory losses, renegotiation of prices under contract, or sales of inventory at a loss.

The auditor obtains written representations (as covered in CAS 580 *Written Representations*) from management as part of the management representation letter (as illustrated in chapter 5) confirming oral representations made with respect to subsequent events and that it is not aware of other relevant subsequent events.

The extent to which the results of these procedures will need reviewing and updating immediately prior to issuing the audit report depends on the length of time that has elapsed since the procedures were carried out and the susceptibility of the matters under consideration to change over time.

Figure 12.1 shows the subsequent event timeline and the responsibility of the auditor to gather evidence up to the release of the audited financial statements.

12.4.4 Auditor responsibility for subsequent events

Subsequent events may require adjustments to the financial statements. For subsequent events occurring *up to the date of the auditor's report*, if the client indicates that it will not change the financial statements in a situation where the auditor believes they should be changed, a qualified or adverse opinion is issued. When the audit report has been released to the entity (but not released to the public), the auditor would notify those charged with governance (generally the board of directors and management) not to issue the financial statements and audit report to any third parties. If the financial statements have been released or are subsequently released anyway (without being changed), the auditor must take action to prevent reliance on the audit report. This is usually done by withdrawing the audit report and the company issuing a communication to those third parties that have received the report.

After the audit report is signed, the auditor is not required to perform any further procedures relating to subsequent events. But if *after the financial statements have been issued* the auditor becomes aware of a fact that existed at the date of the audit report and that, if the auditor had known at that date, could have caused them to modify the audit report, the auditor should:

1. consider whether the financial statements need revision
2. discuss the matter with management and those charged with governance

3. consider whether the actions taken are appropriate in the circumstances. This would include performing any additional audit procedures necessary, and reviewing and approving any revisions to the financial statements. In addition, anyone in receipt of the previously issued financial statements and audit report should be informed of the situation and advised that a new audit report has been issued on the revised financial statements.

The revised audit report may be dated no earlier than the date on which the new financial statements are approved and should include an emphasis of matter paragraph referring to the note in the financial statements that more extensively outlines the reason(s) for the revision to the previously released financial statements. If the impact of the item requiring adjustment is not pervasive to the financial statements overall, the auditor may alternatively choose to double-date the audit report. In this case, the audit report date would be the original date and a new date would be added for the change to the financial statements. For example, if the original audit report was signed and issued on March 15, 20X1, and subsequently the auditor became aware of a lawsuit that should have been disclosed but was not, the financial statements should be amended to include the note disclosure of the contingent liability. As the impact of the subsequent event in this example can be isolated, the auditor can still date the financial statements March 15, 20X1, adding "except for note X dated April 15, 20X1."

When management does not take the necessary steps, the auditor should notify those charged with governance (such as the audit committee or board of directors) of the entity that action will be taken by the auditor to prevent future reliance on the auditor's report. As discussed above, this is usually done through communication with regulatory filers and through the entity's company website.

Cloud 9

Procedures to search for subsequent events at Cloud 9 are documented in the audit program. These include a review of minutes of board meetings in December, January, and February, and analysis of the interim results for these months (including analytical procedures). The partner on the audit will also formally ask management about any subsequent events that have come to its attention in the meetings to be held between year end and the audit report date. The team will also search for additional borrowings or other matters involving significant contracts.

BEFORE YOU GO ON

4.1 Describe the two types of subsequent events that are required to be considered as part of the audit of the financial statements.

4.2 Provide two types of procedures an auditor may perform to identify a subsequent event.

4.3 What should an auditor do when, after the discovery of a subsequent event, the client does not take appropriate action?

⑤ Analyze misstatements and explain the difference between quantitative and qualitative considerations when evaluating misstatements.

12.5 MISSTATEMENTS

As noted in chapters 10 and 11, when performing substantive testing the key objective is to determine whether there are material errors within each account balance and to quantify any identified errors. A **misstatement** is a difference between the amount, classification, presentation, or disclosure of a reported financial statement item and the amount, classification, presentation, or disclosure that is required for the item to be in accordance with the applicable financial reporting framework. An **error** is an unintentional misstatement in the financial statements, including the omission of an amount or a disclosure. When an error or exception is identified during substantive testing, the first response is to find out why the error or exception has arisen. It may require an increase to the sample size to ensure that there are no other errors in the balance (unless the total error in the account balance is able to be quantified without performing additional testing). It is important when errors are identified to continue testing until the error can either be accurately quantified or the balance has been fully tested to an extent that proves that a material error can no longer exist within the balance.

In reaching a conclusion as to whether the misstatements need to be corrected, the auditor evaluates whether the misstatement either causes the financial statements to be materially misstated or requires additional disclosure. This evaluation involves considerable professional judgement. Both quantitative and qualitative considerations are taken into account, including:

- the risk of additional misstatements remaining undetected
- the effects of identified misstatements on the client's compliance with covenants under debt or similar agreements
- whether the proposed corrections result from an error or are the result of a **judgemental misstatement** between the client's and the auditor's application of accounting policies
- the reversing effect of uncorrected misstatements identified in the prior year on the current year's financial statements (see section 12.5.2)
- the likelihood that recurring differences, which currently are immaterial, will have a material effect in the future
- the sensitivity of the circumstances surrounding the misstatements—for example, the implications of differences involving fraud and possible illegal acts, or violations of contractual provisions
- the significance of the financial statement elements affected by the misstatements
- the significance of the misstatements relative to known user needs—for example, the magnifying effects of the misstatements on the calculation of a purchase price in a transfer of interests (buy/sell agreement)
- the effect of the misstatements on segment information or on another portion of the client's business that has been identified as playing a significant role in the client's operations or profitability
- the effects of offsetting misstatements in different financial statement captions (or balance names within the financial statements—for example, cash at bank, prepayments, or payables).

12.5.1 Current-year misstatements

When misstatements identified during the audit are not corrected by the client, the auditor prepares a working paper (sometimes referred to as a schedule or summary of audit differences) that accumulates all identified misstatements in order to be able to consider their aggregate effect on the financial statements as a whole. The auditor also considers these misstatements against individual items or balances, such as profit before tax or net income, trend of earnings, working capital, shareholders' funds, and loan covenants.

misstatement a difference between the amount, classification, presentation, or disclosure of a reported financial statement item and the amount, classification, presentation, or disclosure that is required for the item to be in accordance with the applicable financial reporting framework. Misstatements can arise from error or fraud.

error an unintentional misstatement in the financial statements, including the omission of an amount or a disclosure

judgemental misstatement a misstatement that arises as a result of a difference in the application of judgement by the client and the auditor, such as the use of an estimate the auditor considers unreasonable or the inappropriate application of an inappropriate accounting policy. A judgemental misstatement is not the same as an error

Manitoba Metal Fabricators

Year End: December-31-10

Adjusting Journal Entries

Date: 01/01/2010 To 31/12/2010

						Assets		Liabilities		Net Income	
								Prepared by JT		**Reviewed by** SG	
Number	Date	Name	Account No	Reference		Debit	Credit	Debit	Credit	Debit	Credit
1	31/12/2010	Professional Fees	9800	C5						15,000	
1	31/12/2010	Accounts Payable	4500	C5					15,000		
		To record the audit fee for the year									
2	31/12/2010	Repairs and Maintenance	9500	C10						20,000	
2	31/12/2010	Accounts Payable	4500	C10					20,000		
		To record unrecorded liability at year end									
3	31/12/2010	Accounts Receivable	1200	B5		25,000					
3	31/12/2010	Sales	7100	B5							25,000
		To record cut off error									
4	31/12/2010	Payroll Expense	9900	300						50,000	
4	31/12/2010	Payroll Liabilities	5400	300					50,000		
		To accrue estimate of management bonus									
5	31/12/2010	Amortization Expense	9600	PY						15,000	
5	31/12/2010	Accumulated Amortization	2300	PY			15,000				
		Carryforward from PY due to amortization calculation error									
6	31/12/2010	Utilities	9200	PY						5,000	
6	31/12/2010	Accrued Liabilities	4600	PY					5,000		
		Carryforward from PY due to cut off error									
						25,000	15,000		90,000	105,000	25,000
		Net Income (loss)	80,000.00								

FIGURE 12.2 **Summary of audit differences**

When evaluating the materiality of misstatements, the auditor considers the cumulative effect of the misstatements at the end of the current year on pre-tax income and/or net income, working capital, and shareholders' equity. The auditor also considers whether the matters underlying the misstatements could cause a material misstatement in future years' financial statements if the client should decide to correct all the misstatements in one year, even though the misstatements are not material to the current year's financial statements. This is particularly relevant when the misstatements represent recurring, and generally increasing, differences in particular areas or accounts, such as certain expense accruals. See figure 12.2 for an example of a summary of audit differences.

12.5.2 Prior-year misstatements

Misstatements may not have been corrected by the client in the prior period because they did not cause the financial statements for that period to be materially misstated. As described in CAS 450 *Evaluation of Misstatements Identified During the Audit*, the cumulative impact of immaterial uncorrected misstatements related to prior periods may have a material effect on the current period's financial statements.

When these misstatements in the prior year have been identified, they are considered by the auditor to "reverse" in the following reporting period. For example, if payables are understated due to a cut-off error in the prior period, the misstatement is considered to "reverse" in the following period and therefore overstates payables in that period. Misstatements that are due to errors (or fraud) are always considered to reverse in the following period, whereas misstatements that arise due to judgemental misstatements between the client and the auditor may not necessarily reverse. Assessing prior-period judgemental misstatements is a complex area that requires a high level of professional judgement and experience, and is considered an advanced auditing concept.

The identification and resolution of misstatements is one of the most important responsibilities in an audit and is a critical step in the formulation of the opinion on the fairness of the client's financial statements. Considerable judgement is required when reaching a conclusion on the materiality of unrecorded misstatements, and is influenced by the evaluation of the needs of a reasonable person who will rely on the financial statements. This requires the evaluation of the total mix of information available, both quantitative (the dollar amounts of the misstatements relative to the position and results of the entity) and qualitative (other considerations that are not influenced by the dollar amount of the misstatements). This is why the final evaluations and conclusions formed regarding misstatements are always performed by the partner responsible for the audit engagement. Figure 12.2 shows a summary of audit differences.

PROFESSIONAL ENVIRONMENT

Forensic accounting

One of the more popular television genres in recent years has been crime with a heavy reliance on forensic science to solve cases (for example, the *CSI* franchise). The programs are so popular there are claims that they have led to a jump in enrolments in forensic science courses. According to Long, demand for forensic accounting has also never been higher, although this is more likely due to the fallout from Enron and WorldCom than from any television program. These cases have made boards of directors more aware of their liability for fraud. If a problem is brought to their attention, they appear to be more willing to order an investigation, and forensic accountants are called in to do the work.

Another potential cause of the increased interest in forensic accounting is terrorism. Since the tragedy of 9/11, tracing the money trail behind terrorism has been a high priority for security agencies. Forensic accounting expertise is similar to auditing in the sense that both rely on a deep understanding of double-entry accounting plus a large dose of other skills and attributes; in the case of forensic accounting, these include expert knowledge of legal systems and interview techniques. However, at its heart, forensic accounting relies on accounting knowledge because some fraudsters go to great lengths to hide their trail and a knowledge of double-entry bookkeeping is necessary to keep up.

Forensic accountants need to have an eye on how their findings will be used in court. In fact, "forensic" means something that will be used in, or is suitable to be used in, courts of law. In the past, most forensic accounting work related to accountants appearing in court as expert witnesses for personal injury or divorce cases. Now, forensic accounting practices are focusing more on investigation, fraud risk management, anti-money laundering, and computer forensics.

The world's largest anti-fraud organization and premier provider of anti-fraud training and education, the Association of Certified Fraud Examiners (ACFE), has experienced a sharp rise in membership over the last few years. The fraud investigators say they have been trying for years to get regulators interested in investigating potential fraud cases, such as the Bernard Madoff Ponzi scheme. Now they say they have noticed a recent increase in community appreciation of their work.

Sources: C·PEM, "Amending Audit Reports" (Chapter 13), 2010; C. Long, "Forensic Frenzy," Charter, June 2007

12.5.3 Qualitative considerations

Qualitative considerations may cause misstatements of quantitatively immaterial amounts to be considered material to the financial statements. Examples of this are when correcting the misstatement would affect:

- the client's compliance with regulatory requirements or covenants under debt or similar agreements
- the client's compliance with contractual requirements of operating and other agreements
- management's satisfaction of requirements for the awarding of bonuses or other forms of incentive compensation
- the reported profit, by changing it to a loss or vice versa
- individual line items, subtotals, or totals, by a material amount
- key ratios monitored by analysts or other key users of the financial statements.

Cloud 9

Numerous misstatements have been found during the Cloud 9 audit. Sharon and the team review these items individually as they arise and collectively at the completion of the audit field work.

For any matters they believe are material, either quantitatively or qualitatively, they will prepare a summary for the partner. The partner needs to understand the nature of the item, including the probable cause of the error and whether it is an indicator of more serious issues in the client's systems. The summary will outline the nature of the evidence gathered and the additional work completed to verify the size and nature of the misstatement, including whether there was an expansion of the sample size and the results of any alternative procedures performed. The summary will make a recommendation and outline why the audit team believes that an adjustment should or should not be made to the client's financial statements.

BEFORE YOU GO ON

5.1 What does an auditor do when misstatements identified during the audit are not corrected by the client?

5.2 Why is it important to consider the prior-year unadjusted misstatements?

5.3 Name two qualitative considerations that may be taken into account when assessing misstatements.

12.6 EVALUATING THE CONCLUSIONS AND FORMING AN OPINION

The final phase of the audit is to assess all of the audit evidence obtained and determine whether it is sufficient and appropriate to reduce the risk of material misstatement in the financial statements to an acceptably low level. Forming an opinion on the financial statements involves the following four steps:

1. evaluating the audit evidence obtained
2. evaluating the effects of unrecorded misstatements identified and the qualitative aspects of the entity's accounting practices
3. evaluating whether the financial statements have been properly prepared and presented in accordance with the applicable reporting framework
4. evaluating the fair presentation of the financial statements.

6 Evaluate conclusions obtained during the performance of the audit and explain how these conclusions link to the overall opinion formed on the financial statements.

12.7 COMPONENTS OF THE AUDIT REPORT

The format of an audit report for general purpose financial statements is governed by CAS 700 *Forming an Opinion and Reporting on Financial Statements*. For audit reports that are not prepared for general purpose financial statements but are instead provided on other historical financial information or special purpose financial statements, CAS 800 *Special Considerations—Audits of Financial Statements Prepared in Accordance with Special Purpose Frameworks*, CAS 805 *Special Considerations— Audits of Single Financial Statements and Specific Elements, Accounts or Items of a Financial Statement*, and CAS 810 *Engagements to Report on Summary Financial Statements* detail the required components of the audit report, which are the same as those required by CAS 700.

7 Describe the components of an audit report.

The main components of the auditor's report, which is required by CAS 700 to be in writing, include:

1. Title
2. Addressee
3. Introductory paragraph:
   - identifies the entity whose financial statements have been audited
   - states that the financial statements have been audited
   - identifies the title of each of the statements that comprise the complete financial statements
   - refers to the summary of significant accounting policies and other explanatory notes
   - specifies the date and period covered by the financial statements.
4. Management's responsibility for the financial statements. Management's responsibility includes establishing and maintaining internal controls relevant to the preparation and fair presentation of the financial statements that are free from material misstatements, whether due to fraud or error; selecting and applying appropriate accounting policies; and making accounting estimates that are reasonable in the circumstances.
5. Auditor's responsibility for the financial statements. The auditor must state that the responsibility of the auditor is to express an opinion on the financial statements based on the audit, state that the audit was conducted in accordance with auditing standards (including compliance with relevant ethical requirements),

describe the audit, and state that the auditor believes that the audit evidence obtained is sufficient and appropriate to provide a basis for the auditor's opinion.

6. Auditor's opinion on whether the financial statements give a true and fair view or is presented fairly, in all material respects, in accordance with the applicable financial reporting framework.

7. Other reporting responsibilities; for example, in some cases auditors may be required to report on other matters

8. Auditor's signature either in the firm's name, the personal name of the auditor, or both (depending on the legislative requirements)

9. Date of the report

10. Auditor's address.

The standard wording used when providing an opinion on the financial statements in accordance with an applicable accounting framework and expressing an unqualified opinion is provided in CAS 700. A sample audit report is provided in chapter 1.

BEFORE YOU GO ON

7.1 Name two factors included in the description of management's responsibility for the financial statements, as included in the audit report.

7.2 Name five components of the audit report.

7.3 What is the auditor's responsibility for the financial statements, as included in the audit report?

12.8 IDENTIFY THE TYPES OF MODIFICATIONS TO AN AUDIT REPORT

8 Identify the types of modifications to an audit report.

In some situations, the auditor's report will require modified wording to emphasize a certain matter or to express a qualified, adverse, or disclaimer of opinion (as outlined in CAS 705 *Modifications to the Opinion in the Independent Auditor's Report* and CAS 706 *Emphasis of Matter Paragraphs and Other Matter Paragraphs in the Independent Auditor's Report*). This usually happens when:

1. a significant uncertainty exists that should be brought to the reader's attention,
2. there is an inability to obtain appropriate audit evidence, or
3. the financial statements are materially misstated.

12.8.1 Emphasis of matter

An emphasis of matter does not affect the auditor's opinion and applies where the resolution of a matter is dependent on future actions or events not under the direct control of the entity, but that may affect the financial statements, and the matter is disclosed in the financial statements. The most common emphasis of matter is one relating to an entity's ability to continue as a going concern, which may depend on finance arrangements still in negotiation or the financial support of the parent entity.

See figure 12.3 for an unqualified audit report with an emphasis of matter.

Ernst & Young LLP
Chartered Accountants
Ernst & Young Tower
222 Bay Street, P.O. Box 251
Toronto, Ontario M5K 1J7

Tel: 416 864 1234
Fax: 416 864 1174
ey.com/ca

FIGURE 12.3 **Unqualified audit report with an emphasis of matter**

Source: Ernst & Young LLP, 2011

INDEPENDENT AUDITORS' REPORT

To the Board of Directors of Skyward Ltd.

We have audited the accompanying consolidated financial statements of Skyward Ltd., which comprise the consolidated statements of financial position as at December 31, 2012 and 2011, and the consolidated statements of comprehensive income, changes in equity and cash flows for the years then ended, and a summary of significant accounting policies and other explanatory information.

Management's responsibility for the consolidated financial statements

Management is responsible for the preparation and fair presentation of these consolidated financial statements in accordance with International Financial Reporting Standards, and for such internal control as management determines is necessary to enable the preparation of consolidated financial statements that are free from material misstatement, whether due to fraud or error.

Auditors' responsibility

Our responsibility is to express an opinion on these consolidated financial statements based on our audits. We conducted our audits in accordance with Canadian generally accepted auditing standards. Those standards require that we comply with ethical requirements and plan and perform the audit to obtain reasonable assurance about whether the consolidated financial statements are free from material misstatement.

An audit involves performing procedures to obtain audit evidence about the amounts and disclosures in the consolidated financial statements. The procedures selected depend on the auditors' judgment, including the assessment of the risks of material misstatement of the consolidated financial statements, whether due to fraud or error. In making those risk assessments, the auditors consider internal control relevant to the entity's preparation and fair presentation of the consolidated financial statements in order to design audit procedures that are appropriate in the circumstances, but not for the purpose of expressing an opinion on the effectiveness of the entity's internal control. An audit also includes evaluating the appropriateness of accounting policies used and the reasonableness of accounting estimates made by management, as well as evaluating the overall presentation of the consolidated financial statements.

We believe that the audit evidence we have obtained in our audits is sufficient and appropriate to provide a basis for our audit opinion.

Opinion

In our opinion, the consolidated financial statements present fairly, in all material respects, the financial position of Skyward Ltd. as at December 31, 2012 and 2011, and its financial performance and its cash flows for the years then ended in accordance with International Financial Reporting Standards.

Emphasis of Matter

Without qualifying our opinion, we draw attention to Note 4 in the financial statements which indicates that Skyward Ltd. incurred a net loss of $600,000 during the year ended December 31, 2012 and, as of that date, Skyward Ltd.'s current liabilities exceeded its total assets by $1,220,000. These conditions, along with other matters as set forth in Note 4, indicate the existence of a material uncertainty that may cast significant doubt on Skyward Ltd.'s ability to continue as a going concern.

Toronto, Canada

February X, 2013.

"Ernst & Young LLP"

Chartered Accountants
Licensed Public Accountants

A member firm of Ernst & Young Global Limited

12.8.2 Inability to obtain appropriate audit evidence

A limitation on the scope of the auditor's work could result from an inability to perform procedures (the most common form of scope limitation) or an imposition by the entity (rare). The auditor may not be able to perform procedures believed necessary due to factors such as timing, damage to accounting records, and lack of or restricted access to key personnel, accounting records, or operating locations; or the absence of adequate accounting records to provide sufficient and appropriate audit evidence upon which to rely. For example, it may not be possible for the auditor to verify the existence of inventory if the client has not held an inventory count, or does not have particularly reliable perpetual inventory records. This would then form the basis for a limitation of scope qualification in the audit report. Where a scope limitation is material to the financial statements, a qualified opinion or disclaimer of opinion is expressed. Figure 12.4 shows a sample audit report with a qualification due to a scope limitation.

12.8.3 Material misstatement of financial statements

The auditor may disagree with those charged with governance about matters such as the acceptability of accounting policies selected, the method of their application, or the adequacy of disclosures in the financial statements. Where these disagreements are material to the financial statements, a qualified or adverse opinion is expressed. Examples of such reports are included in CAS 705 and CAS 706. Table 12.1 outlines the circumstances in which a modification would be issued and the type of modification appropriate in the circumstances.

TABLE 12.1 **Types of qualified and unmodified audit reports**

NATURE OF MATTER THAT DOES NOT GIVE RISE TO A QUALIFICATION	UNMODIFIED REPORT
Significant uncertainty—going concern	Emphasis of matter
Significant uncertainty—litigation	Emphasis of matter
Additional disclosures with which the auditor concurs	Emphasis of matter
Early adoption of a new accounting standard with a significant impact on the financial statements	Emphasis of matter
A major catastrophe that has had or continues to have an impact on the entity	Emphasis of matter
Subsequent event resulting in a new auditor's report on revised financial statements	Emphasis of matter

(continued)

NATURE OF MATTER GIVING RISE TO THE QUALIFICATION	AUDITOR'S JUDGEMENT ABOUT THE PERVASIVENESS OF THE EFFECTS OR POSSIBLE EFFECTS ON THE FINANCIAL REPORT	
	MATERIAL BUT NOT PERVASIVE	MATERIAL AND PERVASIVE[a]
Financial statements are materially misstated	Qualified opinion	Adverse opinion
Inability to obtain sufficient appropriate audit evidence	Qualified opinion	Disclaimer of opinion

TABLE 12.1 **Types of qualified and unmodified audit reports** (continued)

[a]Where the circumstances are so material and pervasive that the auditor has been unable to obtain sufficient appropriate audit evidence, or where a qualified opinion is inadequate to disclose the misleading or incomplete nature of the financial statements.

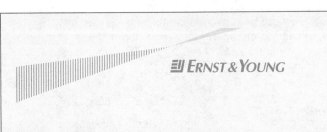

FIGURE 12.4 **Sample audit report with a qualification due to a scope limitation**
Source: Ernst & Young LLP, 2011

Ernst & Young LLP
Chartered Accountants
Ernst & Young Tower
222 Bay Street, P.O. Box 251
Toronto, Ontario M5K 1J7

Tel: 416 864 1234
Fax: 416 864 1174
ey.com/ca

INDEPENDENT AUDITORS' REPORT

To the Board of Directors of Skyward Ltd.

We have audited the accompanying consolidated financial statements of Skyward Ltd., which comprise the consolidated statements of financial position as at December 31, 2012 and 2011, and the consolidated statements of comprehensive income, changes in equity and cash flows for the years then ended, and a summary of significant accounting policies and other explanatory information.

Management's responsibility for the consolidated financial statements

Management is responsible for the preparation and fair presentation of these consolidated financial statements in accordance with International Financial Reporting Standards, and for such internal control as management determines is necessary to enable the preparation of consolidated financial statements that are free from material misstatement, whether due to fraud or error.

Auditors' responsibility

Our responsibility is to express an opinion on these consolidated financial statements based on our audits. We conducted our audits in accordance with Canadian generally accepted auditing standards. Those standards require that we comply with ethical requirements and plan and perform the audit to obtain reasonable assurance about whether the consolidated financial statements are free from material misstatement.

An audit involves performing procedures to obtain audit evidence about the amounts and disclosures in the consolidated financial statements. The procedures selected depend on the auditors' judgment, including the assessment of the risks of material misstatement of the consolidated financial statements, whether due to fraud or error. In making those risk assessments, the auditors consider internal control relevant to the entity's preparation and fair presentation of the consolidated financial statements in order to design audit procedures that are appropriate in the circumstances, but not for the purpose of expressing an opinion on the effectiveness of the entity's internal control. An audit also includes evaluating the appropriateness of accounting policies used and the reasonableness of accounting estimates made by management, as well as evaluating the overall presentation of the consolidated financial statements.

(continued)

FIGURE 12.4 **Sample audit report with a qualification due to a scope limitation** (continued)

We believe that the audit evidence we have obtained in our audits is sufficient and appropriate to provide a basis for our qualified audit opinion.

Basis for qualified opinion

Skyward Ltd's investment in Cumulus Inc., a foreign associate acquired during the year and accounted for by the equity method, is carried at $450,000 on the consolidated balance sheet as at December 31, 2012, and Skyward Ltd.'s share of Cumulus Inc.'s net income of $90,000 is included in Skyward Ltd.'s income for the year then ended. We were unable to obtain sufficient appropriate audit evidence about the carrying amount of Skyward Ltd.'s investment in Cumulus Inc. as at December 31, 2012 and Skyward Ltd.'s share of Cumulus Inc.'s net income for the year because we were denied access to the financial information, management, and the auditor of Cumulus Inc. Consequently, we were unable to determine whether any adjustments to these amounts were necessary.

Opinion

In our opinion, except for the possible effects of the matter described in the basis for qualified opinion paragraph, the consolidated financial statements present fairly, in all material respects, the financial position of Skyward Ltd. as at December 31, 2012 and 2011, and its financial performance and its cash flows for the years then ended in accordance with International Financial Reporting Standards.

Toronto, Canada

February X, 2013.

"Ernst & Young LLP"

Chartered Accountants
Licensed Public Accountants

A member firm of Ernst & Young Global Limited

Cloud 9

Sharon prepares several versions of a draft audit report for the partner. The partner will discuss the audit report possibilities with Cloud 9's management at their meetings. The draft audit reports vary because the appropriate report depends on the outcome of the discussions between the partner and Cloud 9's management. If management refuses to amend the financial statements for the material misstatements found during the audit, the audit report could be qualified. It is possible that a subsequent event could still occur that would require an emphasis of matter. However, there have been no scope limitations.

BEFORE YOU GO ON

8.1 Provide an example of a common emphasis of matter included in audit reports.

8.2 Does the inclusion of an emphasis of matter in the audit report result in the report being qualified?

8.3 Describe one situation in which scope limitation may be appropriate in the audit report.

12.9 COMMUNICATION WITH THOSE CHARGED WITH GOVERNANCE

⑨ Explain what reporting is required to management and those charged with governance.

Communication with those charged with governance is covered in CAS 260 *Communication with Those Charged with Governance*, which requires that the auditor communicate audit matters of governance interest arising from the audit of the financial statements with those charged with governance. Communication with those charged with governance, with management, and with third parties, when applicable, is also covered in several other auditing standards. For example, if the auditor has identified a fraud, or has information that indicates the existence of a fraud, they are required to communicate these matters to an appropriate level of management by CAS 240 *The Auditor's Responsibilities Relating to Fraud in an Audit of Financial Statements*. Similarly, when the auditor has identified material noncompliance with laws and regulations, they are required to communicate their findings to those charged with governance in accordance with CAS 250 *Consideration of Laws and Regulations in an Audit of Financial Statements*.

"Governance" is the term used to describe the role of people entrusted with the supervision, control, and direction of an entity. Those charged with governance are accountable for ensuring that the entity achieves its objectives, with regard to reliability of financial reporting, effectiveness and efficiency of operations, compliance with applicable laws, and reporting to interested parties. Those charged with governance includes management only when it performs such functions.

"Audit matters of governance interest" are those that arise from the audit of the financial statements and, in the auditor's opinion, are both important and relevant to those charged with governance in overseeing the financial reporting and disclosure process. Audit matters of governance interest include only those matters that have come to the auditor's attention as a result of the performance of the audit. The auditor is not required to design audit procedures for the specific purpose of identifying matters of governance interest.

Figure 12.5 shows a sample letter to the board of directors where no significant issues were noted.

FIGURE 12.5 **Sample letter where no significant issues are noted**

Source: PEM Audit Engagements Phase III-Reporting. *C · PEM*, Electronic Templates, Form 515, 2010–2011

To the Members of the Board of Directors,

The matters raised in this report arise from our financial statement audit and relate to matters that we believe need to be brought to your attention.

We have substantially completed our audit of Cloud 9 Inc. financial statements in accordance with Canadian generally accepted auditing standards.

Our audit is performed to obtain reasonable assurance as to whether the financial statements are free of material misstatements. Absolute assurance is not possible due to the inherent limitations of an audit and of internal control, resulting in the unavoidable risk that some material misstatements may not be detected.

In planning our audit, we consider internal control over financial reporting to determine the nature, extent, and timing of audit procedures. However, a financial statement audit does not provide assurance on the effective operation of internal control at Cloud 9 Inc. However, if in the course of our audit, certain deficiencies in internal control come to our attention, these will be reported to you. Please refer to Appendix A1 to this letter.

Because fraud is deliberate, there are always risks that material misstatements, fraud, and other illegal acts may exist and not be detected by our audit of the financial statements.

The following is a summary of findings resulting from the performance of the audit:

1. We did not identify any material matters (other than the identified misstatements already discussed with you that have now been corrected) that need to be brought to your attention.

(continued)

FIGURE 12.5 **Sample letter where no significant issues are noted** (continued)

2. We received good co-operation from management and employees during our audit. To the best of our knowledge, we also had complete access to the accounting records and other documents that we needed to carry out our audit. We did not have any disagreements with management and we have resolved all auditing, accounting, and disclosure issues to our satisfaction.

Please note that Canadian auditing standards do not require us to design procedures for the purpose of identifying supplementary matters to communicate with those charged with governance. Accordingly, an audit would not usually identify all such matters.

This communication is prepared solely for the information of management and those charged with governance and is not intended for any other purpose. We accept no responsibility to a third party who uses this communication.

Yours truly,

W & S Partners

March 15, 20X2

12.9.1 Audit matters of governance interest to be communicated

The auditor meets with management and those charged with governance to discuss the results of the audit. The matters that they discuss are those that arise from the audit and that, in the auditor's opinion, are both important and relevant to those charged with governance. As previously stated, the auditor is not required to design audit procedures for the specific purpose of identifying matters of governance interest.

Matters of governance interest that the auditor may wish to discuss with those charged with governance include:

- the general approach and overall scope of the audit, including any expected limitations thereon, or any additional requirements
- the selection of, or changes in, significant accounting policies and practices that have, or could have, a material effect on the entity's financial statements. (The auditor considers the appropriateness of the accounting policies to the particular circumstances of the entity. They judge these against the objectives of relevance, reliability, comparability, and understandability, but having regard for the need to balance the different objectives and the cost of providing information with the likely benefit to users of the entity's financial statements. They also discuss the appropriateness of accounting estimates and judgements—for example, in relation to provisions, including the consistency of assumptions and degree of prudence reflected in the recorded amounts.)
- the potential effect on the financial statements of any material risks and exposures, such as pending litigation, that are required to be disclosed in the financial statements

- misstatements, whether or not recorded by the entity, that have or could have a material effect on the entity's financial statements
- material uncertainties related to events and conditions that may cast significant doubt on the entity's ability to continue as a going concern
- disagreements with management about matters that, individually or in aggregate, could be significant to the entity's financial statements or the audit report (These communications include consideration of whether the matter has or has not been resolved and the significance of the matter.)
- expected modifications to the audit report. The auditor discusses any expected modifications to the audit report on the financial statements with those charged with governance to confirm that:
  - those charged with governance are aware of the proposed modification and the reasons for it before the report is finalized
  - there are no disputed facts with respect to the matter(s) giving rise to the proposed modification (or that matters of disagreement are confirmed as such)
  - those charged with governance have an opportunity, where appropriate, to provide further information and explanations with respect to the matter(s) giving rise to the proposed modification
- any practical difficulties encountered in performing the audit
- any irregularities or suspected noncompliance with laws and regulations that came to the auditor's attention during the audit
- comments on the design and operation of the internal controls and suggestions for their improvement, particularly if the auditor has identified material weaknesses in internal control during the audit (This is sometimes separately communicated in a management letter, as discussed in chapter 7.)
- any other matters agreed upon in the terms of the audit engagement.

The auditor also informs those charged with governance of those uncorrected misstatements aggregated by the auditor during the audit that were determined by management to be immaterial, both individually and in the aggregate, to the financial report taken as a whole.

12.9.2 Documentation considerations

The auditor retains a copy of the communication with those charged with governance in their working papers, together with details of any responses from management and/or those charged with governance and their intended action(s). If the communication takes the form of a presentation at a meeting or meetings, the auditor files a copy of the presentation material and also gives a copy of the material to management to prevent disputes at a later date. Depending on the nature, sensitivity, and significance of the matters communicated, the auditor may decide to confirm oral communications in writing.

As soon as practicable, the auditor should communicate deficiencies in internal controls to management or those charged with governance. The reporting of internal control deficiencies should always be documented; the most common form is a letter (as discussed in chapter 7). However, depending on the circumstances, documentation in the form of a file note (minutes of meetings) may be appropriate as evidence of the discussion held on internal control deficiencies.

Cloud 9

Sharon also prepares a draft letter to be used for communication with those charged with governance at Cloud 9. The letter is incomplete but will be finalized after the completion of subsequent events procedures and the final meetings between the partner and Cloud 9's management.

BEFORE YOU GO ON

9.1 Name five items of governance interest that would be communicated to those charged with governance.

9.2 Is communication with those charged with governance always in the form of a letter?

9.3 If communication is not always in the form of a letter, what other forms of communication could the auditor use?

SUMMARY

1 **Explain the procedures performed as part of the engagement wrap-up, including gathering and evaluating audit evidence.**

During the engagement wrap-up, the auditor reviews planned audit procedures to ensure they are completed, finalizes any open items (including review notes and to-do items), ensures that all necessary documentation is in the working paper files and removes any unnecessary documentation, reconsiders their risk assessment and fraud risk, reconsiders materiality, performs analytical procedures, assesses misstatements, and performs subsequent events procedures.

2 **Understand the considerations when assessing the going concern assumption used in the preparation of the financial statements.**

The auditor is required to consider whether the going concern assumption is the correct basis upon which the financial statements have been prepared. That is, is the entity viewed by the auditor, management, and those charged with governance as continuing into the foreseeable future with neither the intention nor the need to liquidate, to cease trading, or to seek protection from creditors?

3 **Understand the purpose of and the procedures performed in the review for contingent liabilities and commitments.**

It is the auditor's responsibility to perform procedures to verify that there are no unrecorded or undisclosed lawsuits or claims that could result in the financial statements being materially mistated.

4 **Compare the two types of (material) subsequent events to determine what effect they have on the financial statements (if any).**

There are two types of subsequent events. Type 1 subsequent events are those that provide additional evidence with respect to conditions that existed at year end. These are required to be adjusted for in the financial statements. Type 2 subsequent events are those that provide evidence with respect to conditions that developed subsequent to year end; these are not required to be recorded in the financial statements, but are considered for inclusion as a disclosure note.

5 **Analyze misstatements and explain the difference between quantitative and qualitative considerations when evaluating misstatements.**

Quantitative and qualitative considerations of misstatements include the risk of undetected errors remaining, the effect of the misstatements on compliance with covenants or agreements, whether the misstatements are errors or judgemental misstatements, whether any prior-period unadjusted misstatements exist and could affect the current period's results, the likelihood that these differences will become material in the future, the sensitivity of the misstatements, the significance of the misstatements for the known users of the financial statements, the effect of offsetting differences in financial statement captions, and the dollar amount (quantity) of the misstatements.

6 **Evaluate conclusions obtained during the performance of the audit and explain how these conclusions link to the overall opinion formed on the financial statements.**

The final phase of the audit is to assess all of the audit evidence obtained and determine whether it is sufficient and appropriate to reduce the risk of material misstatement in the financial statements to an acceptably low level. Based on the evidence gathered, the audit opinion on the financial statements will be determined.

7 Describe the components of an audit report.

The audit report includes a title, addressee, introductory paragraph, management's and the auditor's responsibility for the financial statements, audit opinion, other matters including other reporting responsibilities, auditor's signature, date of the report, and auditor's address.

8 Identify the types of modifications to an audit report.

The overall conclusion reached at the end of the audit can be unmodified, unmodified with an emphasis of matter, modified with a qualification, modified with an adverse opinion, or modified with a disclaimer of opinion.

9 Explain what reporting is required to management and those charged with governance.

All audit matters of governance interest, that is items that are important and relevant to those charged with governance in overseeing the financial reporting and disclosure process, should be reported to management and those charged with governance by the auditor. This is a required communication that can be provided verbally or in writing, with written communications (or evidence of such communications) preferred.

KEY TERMS

Error, 475

Going concern, 467

Judgemental misstatement, 475

Materiality, 464

Misstatement, 475

Professional judgement, 465

Subsequent events, 470

Sufficient appropriate evidence, 466

Those charged with
    governance, 469

MULTIPLE-CHOICE QUESTIONS

12.1 At the conclusion of the audit, the wrap-up process involves:

(a) review of proper and complete execution of planned audit procedures.

(b) determination that all necessary matters have been appropriately considered.

(c) revisiting open review notes, to-do items, and open audit procedures.

(d) all of the above.

12.2 If an auditor finds any misstatements or deviations in planned procedures:

(a) the auditor should consider the reason for the misstatement or deviation.

(b) the auditor should not revise the risk assessment.

(c) the auditor should not alter any planned procedures.

(d) the auditor does not have to consider the need to perform further audit procedures.

12.3 The going concern assumption means:

(a) the entity is facing difficulties continuing as a going concern.

(b) the entity is viewed as continuing in business for the foreseeable future with no need for liquidation.

(c) assets and liabilities are stated at liquidation values.

(d) the auditor is concerned about whether the entity is going to change locations.

12.4 Subsequent events are:

(a) events subsequent to the start of the financial year.

(b) events subsequent to the appointment of the auditor.

(c) events subsequent to the end of the financial year.

(d) events subsequent to the going concern assumption.

12.5 The following is a valid type of subsequent event:

(a) an event that provides additional evidence with respect to conditions that existed at year end.

(b) an event that occurred after the start of the year but before the end of the year.

(c) legal action that was settled in the last month of the financial year.

(d) all of the above.

12.6 If an auditor becomes aware after the date of the auditor's report but before the financial statements are issued of a fact that may materially affect the financial statements, the auditor should:

(a) consider whether the financial statements need changing.

(b) discuss the matter with management.

(c) take the action appropriate in the circumstances.

(d) all of the above.

12.7 The following is an example of an event that provides evidence with respect to conditions that developed subsequent to year end:

(a) bankruptcy of a customer subsequent to year end, which would be considered when evaluating the adequacy of the allowance for uncollectable accounts.

(b) loss of plant as a result of fire or flood after year end.

(c) deterioration in financial results after year end, which may indicate doubt about the going concern assumption in the preparation of the financial statements.

(d) an amount received with respect to an insurance claim that was in the course of negotiation at year end.

12.8 Management's responsibility for the financial statements includes:

(a) selecting internal controls tests.

(b) selecting samples for audit testing.

(c) selecting and applying appropriate accounting policies.

(d) selecting experts to assist with testing asset valuations.

12.9 Emphasis of matter is used without an accompanying qualification of the audit report when:

(a) a significant uncertainty exists that should be brought to the reader's attention.

(b) an extreme limitation of the scope of the engagement exists.

(c) there is a disagreement with those charged with governance regarding the selection of accounting policies.

(d) all of the above.

12.10 Communication with those charged with governance:

(a) means that the auditor should write to the board of directors about any matters of governance interest arising from the audit of the financial statements.

(b) is done at the start of the audit.

(c) is done through the audit report.

(d) requires the auditor to write to the CEO at the conclusion of the audit.

REVIEW QUESTIONS

12.1 What is the process of "engagement wrap-up"? Why is it important?

12.2 What is the accounting assumption of "going concern"? Why is it of interest to auditors?

12.3 What procedures must the auditor perform to search for contingent liabilities?

12.4 Explain the difference between the two types of subsequent events. Discuss the auditor's responsibility for detecting subsequent events (a) prior to the completion of field work, (b) prior to signing the audit report, and (c) between the date of the audit report and the issuance of the financial statements.

12.5 What options does an auditor have when material errors are found? Do these options vary for current-year misstatements and prior-year misstatements?

12.6 Why do audit reports contain paragraphs outlining (1) management's responsibility for the financial statements and (2) the auditor's responsibility for the financial statements? What is contained in these paragraphs?

12.7 What is "modified wording" in an audit report? What are the different types of modified wording and when are they used?

12.8 Explain the difference between limitation of scope and disagreement with those charged with governance.

12.9 CAS 260 stresses the importance of communication with "those charged with governance." Who are these people and why is it important that the auditor communicate with them (and not others)?

12.10 What matters does an auditor communicate at the end of an audit to those charged with governance? Why are these matters important?

PROFESSIONAL APPLICATION QUESTIONS

Basic ★   Moderate ★★   Challenging ★★★

12.1 Audit wrap-up ★

Lucy Huang has just finished her first audit assignment. She is now assisting her audit manager, Tom Lucas, in wrapping up the engagement. He has asked Lucy to make a list of all uncleared review notes, to-do items, and audit procedures, and to note for each whether the matter requires more attention, has been resolved (but is not yet noted on file), or is no longer relevant because of other events.

Tom has also asked Lucy to go through the files and remove all unnecessary documentation, drafts, and review notes. Lucy is very nervous about this task because she believes her inexperience will mean that she will not be able to distinguish "unnecessary" from "necessary." She has heard that in a famous case in the United States an audit firm was prosecuted because it shredded files that should have been kept.

Required

(a) What additional attention would open matters require?

(b) Explain why documents in a client's audit files would be "unnecessary." Give examples.

12.2 Assessing going concern ★★

Manitoba Metal Fabricators (MMF) is a company that makes steel components for the construction industry. It specializes in extreme precision manufacturing where tolerances are measured in distances of less than one millimetre. Its products are used in revolving restaurants, automatic doors, and similar construction components. In the past, the majority of its sales have been to international construction companies, particularly in the Middle East. Construction has slowed down in the Middle East, and the extremely expensive buildings requiring high-precision steel components are becoming less popular. In addition, some of the technology used by MMF has been copied by companies in southeast Asia, resulting in extreme price competition in this sector of the construction industry for the first time.

MMF is highly leveraged. Two years ago the company borrowed a large sum of money to fund the purchase of new premises and the latest laser cutting equipment. The loan is due for renewal three months after year end. One week before the audit report is to be signed, the bank has still not agreed to renew the loan and MMF's management has begun negotiations with another bank.

Required

(a) Identify the factors that would raise questions about the going concern assumption for MMF. Are there any mitigating factors?

(b) What reporting options are available to the auditor of MMF? Discuss. Refer to CAS 570 in your answer.

12.3 Subsequent events procedures ★ ★

Mitch Ziegel and Rosie Punter are discussing the audit plan for a large manufacturing company. The company has two main manufacturing plants plus several warehouse and distribution centres (one in each province). The company has a large investment in trade receivables and there are additional concerns this year about whether the tough economic conditions have affected the collectability of the trade receivables. The agenda for the board of directors' monthly meeting includes an item to discuss the effect of the economic crisis on customers. The board is also negotiating a take-over with a competing company. The discussions have been ongoing for some time and one month before year end the board of the other company indicated it would like more progress to be made on this deal. Another matter concerning senior management at the manufacturing company is a threatened labour dispute by the largest union representing workers at the distribution centres. A number of safety issues have been identified for the company, explaining the union's demands for better working conditions and a pay increase. The company management is disputing most of the safety concerns.

Mitch and Rosie are reviewing the draft plan to ensure that adequate procedures are included to meet their obligations for detecting subsequent events during the period from year end to the date of signing the audit report. Mitch is the engagement partner on the audit and Rosie is an audit manager. Rosie admits to Mitch that she has always had trouble distinguishing the two types of subsequent events in IAS 10 and therefore has some trouble applying CAS 560. She also admits to Mitch that she has never been involved in an audit where there was a subsequent event arising after the date of the audit report, so she doesn't know what the auditor is supposed to do in these circumstances.

Required

(a) Explain the difference between the two types of subsequent events. Give an example of each and explain the type of adjustment (if any) to the financial statements that would be required.

(b) List some audit procedures that should be in the audit plan for this company for the detection of subsequent events occurring prior to the date of the audit report.

(c) Explain the auditor's responsibilities for subsequent events that arise after the date of the audit report (after the date the financial statements are issued). What is the difference in the auditor's responsibilities between these events and those arising before the date of the audit report?

12.4 Reporting subsequent events ★ ★

Brad Gokool is reviewing the results of the subsequent events audit procedures. Brad is writing a report for his audit partner based on these results and will be attending a meeting tomorrow with the partner and representatives of the company to discuss them. The issue will be whether the financial statements should be amended or additional notes should be included for these subsequent events.

Many of the items are not material and Brad will recommend that no action be taken with respect to these. However, there are several items that Brad believes are material and should be discussed at the meeting. These are:

· The board is planning to issue shares in a private placement on August 15.
· The share issue is to fund the purchase of a 60 percent stake in another company. The negotiations are in the final stages and although the contract is not yet signed, it will be signed by August 15.
· A statement of claim was lodged in the Supreme Court in the week after year end claiming damages for illness allegedly caused by chemicals used at a subsidiary company's manufacturing plant in the 1990s. This is the tenth such claim lodged and the client has denied responsibility in all cases because it was unreasonable to believe at that time that these chemicals had adverse health effects. The claimant has new scientific evidence that counters this defence.
· The review of subsequent cash receipts has revealed that several of the accounts receivables that were considered doubtful have now been paid. However, the audit procedures have shown that a large customer with a significant receivable balance considered safe on June 30 unexpectedly declared bankruptcy on July 20.

The year end for the company is June 30 and the audit report is due to be signed on August 20.

Required

For each item above:
(a) What type of subsequent event is it?
(b) What is the appropriate treatment in the financial statements ?

12.5 Misstatements and the audit report ★ ★ ★　④ ⑤ ⑦

Katrina Lukacs is the engagement partner of the audit of Champion Securities, an investment company. Most of Champion's assets and liabilities are financial and their valuation is critical to the assessment of the company's solvency and profitability. Katrina has employed two outside experts to value the financial assets and liabilities because they are extremely complex to value, particularly the energy market derivatives and the instruments traded in foreign markets. In addition, the valuations are highly dependent on market conditions and the specific and detailed requirements of the recently revised accounting standards.

Throughout this year's audit, Katrina has had difficulties with the CEO of Champion Securities. He is vehemently opposed to any asset writedowns she has suggested. The CEO has the backing of the chairman of the board and Katrina has been unable to get the CEO to listen to her concerns about the valuations of the financial assets and liabilities the company has made. In past years, Katrina has had an amicable relationship with both the CEO and the chairman and the audits have run very smoothly. Katrina has now realized that this harmonious relationship was mainly due to the boom in the market. It was unlikely that there would be arguments about writing up the value of the company's assets during these good times.

Katrina, with the help of the experts, has prepared a summary of the relevant items, detailing the revised values for the assets and liabilities and the associated effects on income and retained earnings. The CEO has dismissed this summary and the audit recommendations with the comment, "The market has hit the bottom and is recovering. There is no need to show these writedowns because by the time the financial statements are published the values will be back to where they were before the market fell. It is all a waste of time. In fact, I think you are just being difficult to deal with. I think we need an auditor who is a bit more realistic."

Required

(a) Discuss the ethical issues Katrina faces and explain what she needs to do to comply with the code of professional conduct independence requirements.
(b) Explain Katrina's audit report options.
(c) Recommend a course of action for Katrina.

12.6 Misstatements and the audit report ★ ★ ★

The staff at Nguyen and Partners have completed the necessary audit work for Manitoba Metal Fabricators. The partner responsible for the audit is now reviewing the audit file. She has come across the Schedule of Unadjusted Differences and is considering the type of audit report to issue. Referring to figure 12.2, answer the following:

Required

(a) If overall materiality for the engagment were set at $50,000, what type of audit report would be issued? Why?

(b) If overall materiality for the engagment were set at $100,000, what type of audit report would be issued? Why?

(c) Why does the current year Schedule of Unadjusted Differences include entries from the prior year? Explain the impact these entries have on the current year financial statement balances.

12.7 Audit reports and other communication at the end of an audit ★ ★

Steven Erasmus has had difficulties throughout the audit of Kingston Catering. The company is a long-standing client of the audit firm and there have been no problems in the past. However, four months into the start of the financial year the company's computer systems failed. Subsequent diagnostic tests revealed that a particularly nasty virus had infected the computer system and corrupted all the processed data. The IT manager called in an IT specialist for advice as soon as the problem was discovered. The specialist installed a new computer system and additional security programs and the IT manager is confident that the problem will not recur.

The processed data had been backed up and stored in a secure location, but when a restoration was attempted it was discovered that the virus had also corrupted the backups. The Kingston Catering staff tried to reconstruct the computer files based on paper records, but the reconstruction was incomplete because some paper documents had been inadvertently destroyed.

Steven is particularly concerned about sales and trade receivables. Kingston Catering has many "one-time" customers as well as several large accounts. The first four months of the year corresponded with the busiest time of the year for the company. Staff attended many corporate and private functions during this time and made numerous sales of catering equipment to wholesale and retail customers. Or at least they think they did, and they believe that they collected all the accounts. Steven is not so sure. He thinks the chaos caused by the computer virus meant that deliveries were being made in a rush without the completion of the appropriate paperwork and the attempts to collect accounts were ineffectual as customers took advantage of the situation to claim that they had either already paid or had returned goods for credit. Other customers simply "fell off" the system and were never billed.

Required

(a) Discuss Steven's audit report options and recommend the appropriate wording for the audit report.

(b) What matters would Steven include in the letter to those charged with governance at Kingston Catering?

Questions 12.8 and 12.9 are based on the following case.

Fabrication Holdings Ltd. (FH) has been a client of KFP Partners for many years. You are an audit senior and have been assigned to the FH audit for the first time for the financial year end, December 31, 2012.

FH's financial statements for the year ended December 31, 2012, show land and buildings at fair value of $20.8 million. As part of your subsequent events procedures, you become aware that FH sold the property in January 2013 when an independent third party made an unexpected offer of $24.5 million. The difference between the sale price and the amount stated in the financial statements (which has not been adjusted) is material. You have not yet signed the audit report.

Source: Adapted from the Institute of Chartered Accountants Australia's CA Program's Audit and Assurance exam, May 2008.

12.8 Subsequent events ★ ★

Required

Analyze the events surrounding the sale of land and buildings. Is it a subsequent event? If so, which type?

12.9 Audit reports and subsequent events ★ ★

Required

Based on your answer to question 12.8, explain what type of audit opinion you would issue. Why?

Questions 12.10 and 12.11 are based on the following case.

Fellowes and Associates Chartered Accountants is a successful mid-tier accounting firm with a large range of clients across Canada. In 2011, Fellowes and Associates gained a new client, Health Care Holdings Group (HCHG), which owns 100 percent of the following entities:

- Shady Oaks Centre, a private treatment centre
- Gardens Nursing Home Ltd., a private nursing home
- Total Laser Care Limited (TLCL), a private clinic that specializes in the laser treatment of skin defects.

Year end for all HCHG entities is June 30.

You are the audit partner reviewing the audit work papers for HCHG for the year ended June 30, 2011. Today is July 13, 2011, and the audit report is due to be signed in three weeks' time.

During your review you note that the fixed-term borrowings of HCHG totalling $75 million are approaching maturity and HCHG does not seem to have renegotiated any terms of refinancing. You are aware, from your experience with other clients, that banks are reluctant to extend financing on the same terms in the current market. The financing of HCHG was historically managed by the group's treasurer, who left the group six months ago and has not been replaced.

HCHG's financial controller, who has been with the group for nine months, has advised you that he has been busy renegotiating with some of HCHG's key suppliers who recently requested cash on delivery for all orders, rather than extending the normal credit terms.

You are also aware that a fire that occurred in the Shady Oaks cafeteria last week was not adequately covered by insurance. Fortunately, no one was seriously injured in the fire, but the cafeteria was so badly damaged that it had to be closed. When you are discussing this matter with HCHG's law firm, they reveal that the centre is unlikely to have adequate professional indemnity insurance to meet the current demands of several malpractice cases that have been brought against it in the last 12 months.

Source: Adapted from the Institute of Chartered Accountants Australia's CA Program's *Audit & assurance exam*, December 2008 and March 2009.

12.10 Final review issues—subsequent events ★ ★

Required

(a) Explain your responsibilities with respect to the cafeteria fire.
(b) How will this event be handled in the financial statements and the audit report?

12.11 Final review issues—going concern and reporting ★ ★ ★

Required

(a) Are there any going concern issues for HCHG? Explain. If so, what are the mitigating circumstances?

(b) How will you recommend that the issues be handled in the financial statements and the audit report?

12.12 Types of audit reports and modifications ★

Required

For each of the following situations, indicate what type of modification/audit report is most appropriate.

(a) There is a scope limitation and it is material. However, the overall financial statements are still presented fairly.

(b) There is a departure from GAAP and it is pervasively material.

(c) The auditor lacks independence in fact, but not necessarily in appearance.

(d) The uncorrected misstatements are immaterial.

12.13 Disclosure of subsequent events ★ ★ ★

In connection with your examination of the financial statements of Martinson Inc. for the year ended December 31, your post-balance sheet date audit procedures disclosed the following items:

1. January 5: The funds for a $50,000 loan to the corporation made by Mr. Martinson on May 18 were obtained by him with a loan on his personal life insurance policy. The loan was recorded in the account Loan Payable to Officers. The source of the funds obtained by Mr. Martinson was not disclosed in the company records.

2. January 9: The mineral content of a shipment of ore en route on December 31 was determined to be 80 percent. The shipment was recorded at year end at an estimated content of 50 percent by a debit to Raw Material Inventory and a credit to Accounts Payable in the amount of $41,200. The final liability to the vendor is based on the actual mineral content of the shipment.

3. January 31: As a result of reduced sales, production was curtailed in mid-January and some workers were laid off. On February 5, all the remaining workers went on strike. To date, the strike is unsettled.

4. February 20: A contract was signed whereby Whitworth Enterprises purchased from Martinson Inc. all of its capital assets, inventories, and the right to conduct business under the name "Martinson Inc. Division." The transfer's effective date will be March 1. The sale price was $800,000.

Required

Assume that the above items came to your attention prior to completion of your audit work on February 28. For each of the above items, discuss the disclosure that you would recommend for the item.

12.14 Approaches to reporting contingent liabilities ★ ★

Hatami and Partners completed the field work for the December 31, 2011, audit of Harbinger Corporation on March 1, 2012. The financial statements and auditor's report were issued and mailed to shareholders on March 15, 2011.

Required

In each of the two situations below, select from the list possible actions below from the point of view of the auditor. Assume both situations are material.

Situations

1. On January 5, 2011, a lawsuit was filed against Harbinger for a copyright infringement action that allegedly took place in early 2000. In the opinion of Harbinger's lawyers, there is a reasonable (but not probable) danger of a significant loss to Harbinger.

2. On February 15, 2011, Harbinger settled a lawsuit out of court that had originated in 2005 and is currently listed as a contingent liability.

Possible Actions

(a) Adjust the December 31, 2011, financial statements.

(b) Disclose the information in a footnote in the December 31, 2011, financial statements.

(c) Request that the client revise and reissue the December 31, 2011, financial statements. The revision should involve an adjustment to the December 31, 2011, financial statements.

(d) Request that the client revise and reissue the December 31, 2011, financial statements. The revision should involve the addition of a footnote, but no adjustment, to the December 31, 2011, financial statements.

(e) No action is required.

Cases

12.15 Integrative Case Study—Ball Construction Corporation ★ ★ ★

You are the audit senior of Ball Construction Corporation (BC), a small public company that enters into construction contracts with individuals and developers and builds to their specifications. BC is a Canadian company, but recently opened a branch in the south-western United States.

It is September and the audit fieldwork for this year's audit engagement has just been completed. You are in the process of finalizing the audit file. The following is documented in the audit file:

Risk Assessment

Although BC's audit is recurring and we are familiar with its operations and systems, we determined that the audit risk for this year has increased from medium to high. There are three main reasons for the change:

- Recent declines and instability in the U.S. housing market have created a high credit-risk situation.
- BC's controller left in March 2012, and the position had not been filled by year end.
- The bank increased the interest rate on the company's operating line during the year, suggesting that it views BC as a higher risk than before.

Audit Approach

No information systems issues were noted in prior years. While we identified isolated control weaknesses in this year's review of the systems, overall the controls appear reliable. We will use a combined approach, and, because of the increased risk, we will increase the amount of substantive work.

Materiality

Planning materiality was set at $242,000.

1. Internal control

   (a) When the controller left, the finance department staff took on additional duties. We noted that during the latter part of the year, the same individual was creating purchase orders, entering invoices into the system, and preparing the cheque runs. The CFO said the situation was unavoidable, and noted that the accounting manager reviewed the cheque runs and prepared the bank reconciliations.

   (b) We noted that many journal entries had not been approved. The CFO said that he trained most of the employees responsible for the entries, so he knows what the entries are for. He also said, "Our management review of reports and financial statements would uncover any incorrect entries."

   (c) The CFO relies on senior management to review, approve, and sign reports generated by the finance department, such as the "Costing Report by Project." Testing of a sample of reports indicated that most reports had been appropriately approved. However, some reports were found on a construction manager's desk. When asked about them, she explained, "I'm so busy managing the jobs that

I have that I haven't had time yet to look them over." The signed reports were given to the audit team the next day and the audit testing was completed.

2. Accounts receivable and allowance for doubtful accounts

We sent confirmations to a sample of accounts receivable and noted the following issues based on the responses received:

- One confirmation was returned stating that a receivable balance, related to a $1,542,000 contract, was overstated based on the progress report. Upon examination of the relevant report, we noted that a transposition error had occurred (86% completion was used when it should have been 68%). This represents a known error of $277,560. The CFO agreed that it was an error, but was satisfied that this was an isolated issue and would normally have been caught by the supervisor's review. The CFO does not want to adjust for this error.

- The CFO was quite adamant that no adjustments be made to the financial statements, declaring that "the statements fairly and accurately represent the financial situation of BC."

Required

(a) What type of audit report should be prepared, assuming the CFO does not change his position? Discuss.

(b) Prepare the draft managment letter.

Source: Uniform Final Exam (UFE), The Institutes of Chartered Accountants in Canada and Bermuda, Paper 2, 2008

CASE STUDY—CLOUD 9

Answer the following questions based on the information presented for Cloud 9 in Appendix B of this book and the current and earlier chapters. You should also consider your answers to the case study questions in earlier chapters.

Required

Based on everything you know about the audit of Cloud 9, finalize the audit by preparing the audit report and the letter to those charged with governance of the company.

RESEARCH QUESTION 12.1

The global financial crisis led to increasing legal action against auditors as company managers searched for scapegoats and potential places to recover their losses. The tough economic times also likely caused companies that would otherwise have survived to fail, exposing bad management and poor-quality auditing.

Required

Conduct a literature search for reports of threatened and actual legal action against auditors as a result of the global financial crisis. Include in your search articles raising questions about auditors and the quality of their work even though legal action may not have commenced.

Write a summary of your findings and comment on the merits of the cases against auditors. Is there any evidence of poor-quality auditing?

SOLUTIONS TO MULTIPLE-CHOICE QUESTIONS

1. d, 2. a, 3. b, 4. c, 5. a, 6. d, 7. b, 8. c, 9. a, 10. a.

APPENDIX A: SAMPLE DOCUMENTS

BANK CONFIRMATION

(Areas to be completed by client are marked §, while those to be completed by the financial institutions are marked †)

FINANCIAL INSTITUTION (Name, branch and full mailing address) §	**CLIENT** (Legal name) §
Regional Bank of Canada 1234 West Street Toronto, Ontario M5J 2X8	ABC Company Ltd. 987 South Road Toronto, Ontario M8G 3R1 The financial institution is authorized to provide the details requested herein to the below-noted firm of accountants § _John Smith_ _____ Client's authorized signature
CONFIRMATION DATE § December 31, 2012 **(All information to be provided as of this date)** (See Bank Confirmation Completion Instructions)	Please supply copy of the most recent credit facility agreement (initial if required) § _____

1. LOANS AND OTHER DIRECT AND CONTINGENT LIABILITIES (If balances are nil, please state)

NATURE OF LIABILITY/ CONTINGENT LIABILITY †	INTEREST (Note rate per contract) RATE † DATE PAID TO †	DUE DATE †	DATE OF CREDIT FACILITY AGREEMENT †	AMOUNT AND CURRENCY OUTSTANDING †

ADDITIONAL CREDIT FACILITY AGREEMENT(S)

Note the date(s) of any credit facility agreement(s) not drawn upon and not referenced above †

2. DEPOSITS/OVERDRAFTS

TYPE OF ACCOUNT §	ACCOUNT NUMBER §	INTEREST RATE §	ISSUE DATE (If applicable)§	MATURITY DATE (If applicable)§	AMOUNT AND CURRENCY (Brackets if Overdraft) †

EXCEPTIONS AND COMMENTS
(See Bank Confirmation Completion Instructions) †

STATEMENT OF PROCEDURES PERFORMED BY FINANCIAL INSTITUTION †
The above information was completed in accordance with the Bank Confirmation Completion Instructions.

_____   _____
Authorized signature of financial institution   BRANCH CONTACT - Name and telephone number

Please mail this form directly to our chartered accountant in the enclosed addressed envelope.

Name:	Jason Power, Staff Accountant Ernst & Young LLP
Address:	222 Bay Street Toronto, Ontario M5K 1J7
Telephone:	(416) 864-1234
Fax:	(416) 864-1174

Developed by the Canadian Bankers Association and The Canadian Institute of Chartered Accountants

FIGURE 1A **Bank confirmation**

Source: The Bank Confirmation form is copyrighted to CaseWare International Inc., all rights reserved.

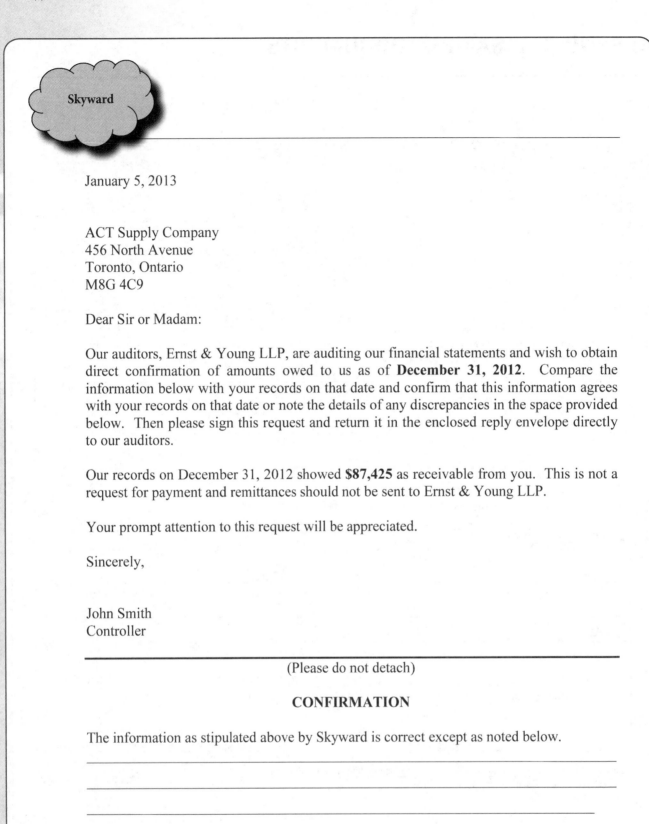

Skyward

January 5, 2013

ACT Supply Company
456 North Avenue
Toronto, Ontario
M8G 4C9

Dear Sir or Madam:

Our auditors, Ernst & Young LLP, are auditing our financial statements and wish to obtain direct confirmation of amounts owed to us as of **December 31, 2012**. If the information is incorrect, please report the details of any discrepancies directly to our auditors in the space provided below. Then please sign this request and return it in the enclosed reply envelope directly to our auditors. If no differences are reported to the auditors, this statement will be considered correct.

Our records on December 31, 2012 showed **$87,425** as receivable from you. This is not a request for payment and remittances should not be sent to Ernst & Young LLP.

Your prompt attention to this request will be appreciated.

Sincerely,

John Smith
Controller

_____

(Please do not detach)

CONFIRMATION

The information as stipulated above by Skyward is correct except as noted below.

_____

_____

_____

Signed: _____   Date: _____

Title: _____   Customer #: ACT-1
Company: _____

FIGURE 3A **Accounts receivable confirmation—negative balance**

Skyward

January 5, 2013

ACT Supply Company
456 North Avenue
Toronto, Ontario
M8G 4C9

Dear Sir or Madam:

Our auditors, Ernst & Young LLP, are auditing our financial statements and wish to obtain direct confirmation of amounts owed to us as of **December 31, 2012**. Compare the information attached with your records on that date and confirm that this information agrees with your records or note the details of any discrepancies in the space provided below. Then please sign this request and return it in the enclosed reply envelope directly to our auditors.

Our records on December 31, 2012 showed the attached list of invoices totaling $4,790 as receivable from you. Please note that these invoices may not represent the entire balance owed to us as of that date. This is not a request for payment and remittances should not be sent to Ernst & Young LLP.

Your prompt attention to this request will be appreciated.

Sincerely,

John Smith
Controller

(Please do not detach)

CONFIRMATION

The information as stipulated above by Skyward is correct except as noted below.

_____

_____

_____

Signed: _____		Date: _____
Title: _____		Customer #: ACT-1
Company: _____		

FIGURE 4A **Accounts receivable confirmation—positive invoice**

Skyward

January 5, 2013

ACT Supply Company
456 North Avenue
Toronto, Ontario
M8G 4C9

Dear Sir or Madam:

Our auditors, Ernst & Young LLP, are auditing our financial statements and wish to obtain direct confirmation of amounts owed to us as of **December 31, 2012**. If the information is incorrect, please report the details of any discrepancies directly to our auditors in the space provided below. Then sign this request and return it in the enclosed reply envelope directly to our auditors. If no differences are reported to the auditors, this statement will be considered correct.

Our records on December 31, 2012 showed the attached list of invoices totaling $4,790 as receivable from you. Please note that these invoices may not represent the entire balance owed to us as of that date. This is not a request for payment and remittances should not be sent to Ernst & Young LLP.

Your prompt attention to this request will be appreciated.

Sincerely,

John Smith
Controller

_____

(Please do not detach)

CONFIRMATION

The information as stipulated above by Skyward is correct except as noted below.

_____

_____

_____

Signed: _____   Date: _____

Title: _____   Customer #: ACT-1

Company: _____

FIGURE 5A **Accounts receivable confirmation—negative invoice**

Soft Soles Inc.
Trial Balance

Account Number	Account Description	Debits	Credits	Account Number	Account Description	Debits	Credits
1020	Cash Operating Account	84,679.00	0.00	2375	HST Paid on Purchases	123,450.00	0.00
1030	Cash Saving Account	2,400.00	0.00	2620	Bank Loans	0.00	787,500.00
1050	Petty Cash	786.00	0.00	3350	Common Shares	0.00	100.00
1055	Store Locations	500.00	0.00	3560	Retained Earnings - Previous Year	0.00	599,622.45
1200	Accounts Receivable	145,180.50	0.00	4200	Sales	0.00	2,057,500.00
1205	Allowance for Doubtful Accounts	0.00	14,518.05	4440	Interest Revenue	0.00	4,543.00
1320	Prepaid Expenses	3,004.00	0.00	5020	COS Stores	1,028,750.00	0.00
1520	Inventory	60,389.00	0.00	5300	Freight Expense	11,511.00	0.00
1530	Goods in Transit	4,530.00	0.00	5410	Wages & Salaries	653,345.00	0.00
1540	Allowance for Obsolescence	0.00	417.00	5610	Accounting & Legal	16,536.00	0.00
1820	Office Furniture & Equipment	17,689.00	0.00	5615	Advertising & Promotions	15,643.00	0.00
1825	Accum. Amort. -Furn. & Equip.	0.00	12,838.00	5620	Bad Debts	5,423.00	0.00
1860	Building	13,248.00	0.00	5625	Business Fees & Licenses	1,357.00	0.00
1865	Accum. Amort. -Building	0.00	3,606.00	5660	Amortization Expense	2,580.00	0.00
1880	Land	1,704,933.00	0.00	5680	Income Taxes	27,807.00	0.00
2100	Accounts Payable	0.00	56,984.00	5685	Insurance	2,065.00	0.00
2120	Other Accrued Expenses	0.00	49,875.00	5690	Interest & Bank Charges	563.00	0.00
2130	Warranty Provision	0.00	9,145.00	5700	Office Supplies	2,450.00	0.00
2160	Corporate Taxes payable	0.00	35,854.00	5760	Rent	23,187.00	0.00
2170	Vacation payable	0.00	15,654.00	5765	Repair & Maintenance	2,643.00	0.00
2180	EI Payable	0.00	14,935.00	5780	Telephone	1,458.00	0.00
2185	CPP Payable	0.00	20,909.00	5784	Travel & Entertainment	1,654.00	0.00
2190	Federal Income Tax Payable	0.00	35,833.00	5790	Utilities	8,973.00	0.00
2370	HST Charged on Sales	0.00	246,900.00				
						3,966,733.50	3,966,733.50

FIGURE 6A Trial balance

Skyward Ltd.
Excerpt from General Ledger
Sorted by: Transaction Number

	Date	Comment	Source #	Trans. No.	Debits	Credits	Balance	
1020 Cash Operating Account							80,000.00	Dr
	1/13/2012	Bank deposit	1	J25	40,254.00	0.00	120,254.00	Dr
	1/13/2012	Soft Soles Inc.	1	J28	0.00	35,575.00	84,679.00	Dr
					40,254.00	35,575.00		
1200 Accounts Receivable							0.00	Dr
	1/1/2012	Sports Galore	1	J1	565.00	0.00	565.00	Dr
	1/1/2012	Cross Country Sports	200	J5	13,750.00	0.00	14,315.00	Dr
	1/4/2012	Grandview Sportswear	201	J6	39,000.00	0.00	53,315.00	Dr
	1/5/2012	Meyer Sports	202	J7	4,950.00	0.00	58,265.00	Dr
	1/5/2012	Meyer Sports	203	J8	15,500.00	0.00	73,765.00	Dr
	1/5/2012	Rebel Sports	204	J9	31,000.00	0.00	104,765.00	Dr
	1/5/2012	Sports Galore	205	J10	19,097.00	0.00	123,862.00	Dr
	1/5/2012	Sports Galore	206	J11	1,864.50	0.00	125,726.50	Dr
	1/9/2012	Rebel Sports	207	J12	13,250.00	0.00	138,976.50	Dr
	1/9/2012	Meyer Sports	208	J13	19,500.00	0.00	158,476.50	Dr
	1/9/2012	Rebel Sports	209	J14	7,125.00	0.00	165,601.50	Dr
	1/9/2012	The Soccer Store	210	J15	19,500.00	0.00	185,101.50	Dr
	1/11/2012	Cross Country Sports	211	J16	20,580.00	0.00	205,681.50	Dr
	1/11/2012	Meyer Sports	212	J17	8,000.00	0.00	213,681.50	Dr
	1/13/2012	Rebel Sports	213	J18	13,850.00	0.00	227,531.50	Dr
	1/13/2012	Grandview Sportswear	1	J20	0.00	4,000.00	223,531.50	Dr
	1/13/2012	Rebel Sports	2	J21	0.00	679.00	222,852.50	Dr
	1/13/2012	Rebel Sports	3	J22	0.00	7,125.00	215,727.50	Dr
	1/13/2012	Meyer Sports	4	J24	0.00	28,450.00	187,277.50	Dr
	1/13/2012	Meyer Sports	5	J29	0.00	19,500.00	167,777.50	Dr
	1/13/2012	Sports Galore	6	J30	0.00	21,526.50	146,251.00	Dr
	1/13/2012	Grandview Sportswear	7	J31	0.00	1,070.50	145,180.50	Dr
					227,531.50	82,351.00		

FIGURE 7A **General ledger**

Soft Soles Inc.
Aged Overdue Sales Invoices Summary
As at 1/13/2012

Name	Total Due	Total Current	Total Overdue	1 to 30 Overdue	31 to 60 Overdue
Cross Country Sports	26,979.00	26,979.00	0.00	0.00	0.00
Grandview Sportswear	31,000.00	30,000.00	1,000.00	1,000.00	0.00
Meyer Sports	17,950.00		17,950.00	0.00	0.00
Rebel Sports	35,225.00	13,850.00	21,375.00	11,375.00	10,000.00
Sports Galore	21,526.50	11,526.50	10,000.00	10,000.00	0.00
The Soccer Store	12,500.00	12,000.00	500.00	500.00	0.00
Total outstanding:	145,180.50	94,355.50	50,825.00	22,875.00	10,000.00

FIGURE 8A **Subsidiary ledger**

Soft Soles Inc.
Customer Master File

Customer Number	Name	Contact	Street	City	Province	Postal Code	Balance Approved Credit Limit
12001	Cross Country Sports	Jack Williams	106 Ave	Vancouver	British Columbia	V2S 9G2	25,000.00
12002	Grandview Sportswear	Frank Johnstone	2315 Erie Road	Toronto	Ontario	L4S 9G3	15,000.00
12003	Meyer Sports	Franklin White	100 Brand Road	Winnipeg	Manitoba	W3R 1Q6	50,000.00
12004	Rebel Sports	Elizabeth Franklin	PO Box 22, Station A	Toronto	Ontario	L4D 9G3	25,000.00
12005	Sports Galore	John Johnson	65 How Street	Guelph	Ontario	Y3E 9H2	10,000.00
12006	The Soccer Store	Cindy Black	66 Charlottetown Place	St. John's	NL	A1A 9N0	15,000.00

FIGURE 9A **Master file**

Soft Soles Inc.

PURCHASE REQUISITION

	Req. No.	322
	Date:	02-Jan-12

SUPPLIER NAME	ADDRESS - CITY, STATE, ZIP:
Skyward Ltd.	Toronto, Ontario

Department	Purchasing
Method of Shipment	
Ship to Attention of:	Merchandising Division
Required Delivery Date:	16-Jan-12
Authorization Number	TBD

Item	Quantity	Part No.	Description	UM	Price	Total
238902	100		Cloud Comfort Walking Shoe	ea		

REQUESTED BY: _____ John King, Merchandising Manager

APPROVED BY: _____

FIGURE 10A Purchase requisition

PURCHASE ORDER

Soft Soles Inc.

100 Anywhere Street	P.O. NO. 322
Vancouver, BC	DATE January 6, 2012
	CUSTOMER ID CLO9

VENDOR		SHIP TO	
	Skyward Ltd.		Soft Soles Inc.
	Toronto, Ontario		100 Anywhere Street
	(416) 999-9999		Vancouver, BC
			604-555-5566

SHIPPING METHOD	SHIPPING TERMS	DELIVERY DATE
Courier		1/16/12

QTY	ITEM #	DESCRIPTION	JOB	UNIT PRICE	LINE TOTAL
100 each	238902	Cloud Comfort Walking Shoe		$ 50.00	$ 5,000.00
				SUBTOTAL	$ 5,000.00
				SALES TAX	600.00
				TOTAL	$ 5,600.00

1. Please send two copies of your invoice.
2. Enter this order in accordance with the prices, terms, delivery method, and specifications listed above.
3. Please notifiy us immediately if you are unable to ship as specified.
4. Send all correspondence to:

   Soft Soles

   100 Anywhere Street

   Vancouver, BC

Authorized by   Date

FIGURE 11A **Purchase order**

Packaging Slip/ Shipping Document

Skyward Ltd.
Toronto, Ontario
Phone 416-999-9999
Fax 416-999-9991

Date: January 12, 2012
Customer ID: SoftSo

Ship to: Soft Soles Inc.   Bill to: Same as Ship To
               100 Anywhere Street
               Vancouver, BC
               604-555-5566

Order Date	Order Number	
1/6/12	322	

Item #	Description	Quantity
238902	Cloud Comfort Walking Shoe	100 ea

Please contact Customer Service at (416) 999-9999 with any questions or concerns.
Thank you for your business!

FIGURE 12A Packaging slip/Shipping document

Skyward Ltd.

Toronto, Ontario
Phone 416-999-9999   Fax 416-999-9991

INVOICE

DATE: 01/16/2012
INVOICE # 214

Bill To:
Soft Soles Inc.
100 Anywhere Street
Vancouver, BC

604-555-5566

Ship To:
Same as Bill to

Comments or Special Instructions: None

SALESPERSON	P.O. NUMBER	SHIP DATE	SHIP VIA	F.O.B. POINT	TERMS
	322	16-Jan-12	Courier		2/10, net 30

QUANTITY	DESCRIPTION	UNIT PRICE	AMOUNT
100	238902 Cloud Comfort Walking Shoe	$ 50.00	$ 5,000.00

SUBTOTAL	$ 5,000.00
TAX RATE	12.00%
SALES TAX	600.00
SHIPPING & HANDLING	-
TOTAL	$ 5,600.00

Make all cheques payable to Skyward
If you have any questions concerning this invoice, call Barbara, Skyward, 604-999-9998

THANK YOU FOR YOUR BUSINESS!

FIGURE 13A **Sales invoice**

Date: 1/5/2012
Statement # 101

Skyward Ltd.
Toronto, Ontario
Phone 416-999-9999
Fax 416-999-9991

To:

Soft Soles Inc.

100 Anywhere Street

Vancouver, BC

604-555-5566

Please Attach with Payment					

Remittance:

Statement #	101
Date	
Amount Enclosed	

Make all cheques payable to Skyward Ltd.

Thank you for your business!

FIGURE 14A **Remittance advice**

C3
Skyward
9/30/2012

BANK RECONCILIATION   DATE 7 October 2012

Prepared by Client   LEDGER ACCOUNT   1006-0-00
                                DESCRIPTION   CHEQUING ACCOUNT
                                BANK NAME   LOCAL BANK
                                RECONCILIATION DATE   30-Sep-12
                                PERFORMED BY   Bill Reds, 2 Oct 2012
                                REVIEWED BY   Noel Smith, 3 Oct 2012

RECONCILIATION

BALANCE PER BANK 30 Sep 2012	200,448.90	B
DEDUCT		
Wire transfer to Supplier XX - recorded by us in Sept 2012	41,909.00	A
Wire transfer to Supplier XX - recorded by us in Sept 2012	63,621.20	A
Wire transfer to Supplier XX - recorded by us in Sept 2012	6,575.00	A
ADD Service charge - recorded by us in Oct 2012	55.80	C
Net interest expense for September 2012 - recorded by us in Oct 2012	752.40	C
BALANCE PER BOOKS 30 Sep 2012 C1 lead	89,151.90	

A   Traced to bank cutoff statements. Processed by bank in Oct 2012. Noted agreement to description and amounts.

B   Traced to bank's statement of accounts at 30-9-2012. Traced to bank response summary in C5

C   Not recorded by client. Amount is however immaterial. Pass further review.

✓   checked totals

FIGURE 15A **Sample bank reconciliation**

Sample Client Ltd.
31-Dec-12
PPE Continuity Schedule

ASSETS

A/C NO	DESCRIPTION	BALANCE 31 Dec 2011	ADDITIONS	CIP reclass	RETIREMENTS	BALANCE 31 Dec 2012
1400	LAND	45,000.00	264,000.00 K2			309,000.00
1410	LAND IMPROVEMENTS	86,096.73	6,292.50			92,389.23
1420	BUILDING	3,170,144.64	1,545,451.90			4,715,596.54
1430	PRODUCTION EQUIPMENT	6,204,856.31	777,197.95 K2	225,152.13 K2	156,142.37 K3	7,051,064.03
1440	DIES & MOLDS	8,420,714.52	440,422.57	254,489.66 K2	117,585.00 K3	8,998,041.75
1450	TOOL ROOM EQUIPMENT	147,767.42				147,767.42
1460	OFFICE EQUIPMENT	28,673.10				28,673.10
1470	FURNITURE & FIXTURE	134,348.55	102,264.95			236,613.50
1475	VEHICLES	81,554.93				81,554.93
1480	ENGINEERING EQUIPMENT	54,171.15	29,927.42			84,098.57
1485	QC EQUIPMENT	14,691.29	3,987.00		3,906.00	14,772.29
1490	COMPUTER EQUIPMENT	283,657.56	53,591.42		13,546.59	323,702.39
1540	CONSTRUCTION IN PROGR	479,641.79	133,489.35	-479,641.79 K2		133,489.35
		19,151,317.99	3,356,625.06	0.00	291,179.96	22,216,763.10

ACCUMULATED DEPRECIATION

A/C NO	BALANCE 31 Dec 2011	PROVISION	RETIREMENTS	BALANCE 31 Dec 2012	FY 12 DEPREC	DIFF	%	NBV 31 Dec 2012	NBV 31 Dec 2011
1610								309,000.00	45,000.00
1620	84,229.19	1,177.32		85,406.51	2,974.65	(1,797.33)	-60.4%	6,982.72	1,867.54
1630	1,296,544.40	133,014.21		1,429,558.61	126,655.17	6,359.04	5.0%	3,286,037.93	1,873,600.24
1634	3,877,675.68	522,430.78 K4	138,939.71 K3	4,261,166.75	420,787.95	101,642.83	24.2%	2,789,897.28	2,327,180.63
1650	5,762,463.15	1,200,780.56 K4	117,585.00 K3	6,845,658.71	1,123,205.04	77,575.52	6.9%	2,152,383.04	2,658,251.37
1660	140,273.72	4,995.30		145,269.02	7,311.33	(2,316.03)	-31.7%	2,498.40	7,493.70
1670	22,786.89	2,351.67		25,138.56	1,291.38	1,060.29	82.1%	3,534.54	5,886.21
1675	97,107.81	20,102.28		117,210.09	14,797.82	5,304.46	35.8%	119,403.41	37,240.74
1680	5,831.18	11,662.35		17,493.53	5,831.18	5,831.17	100.0%	64,061.40	75,723.75
1685	19,549.79	18,814.88		38,364.67	6,916.01	11,898.87	172.0%	45,733.90	34,621.36
1690	13,715.55	1,633.74 K4	3,906.00	11,443.29	1,943.70	(309.96)	-15.9%	3,329.00	975.74
1635	84,196.73	58,826.31 K4	13,546.59 K3	129,476.45	46,833.23	11,993.08	25.6%	194,225.94	199,460.83
								133,489.35	479,641.79
	11,404,374.09	1,975,789.40	273,977.30	13,106,186.19	1,758,547.46	217,241.94	12.4%	9,110,576.91	7,746,943.90

EXPENSE BREAKDOWN

A/C NO		
5370	PROD EQ	1,740,402.80
5371	PROD EQ-NEW	117,000.00
5375	LEASED EQ	0.00
5570	TOOL ROOM	4,995.30
5990	SHIPPING	11,662.35
6170	R&D	18,814.88
6170	QC	1,633.80
7170	SALES	11,414.39
8170	OFFICE EQ	69,865.88
		1,975,789.40

Notes

A   All amounts traced to the Fixed Asset Depreciation-Book Purposes Report (PP&E detail register) for the applicable asset classification.

Tickmarks

√   Clerical accuracy checked. Re-calculated formulas.
PY   Agreed to prior year
TB   Agreed to trial balance

FIGURE 16A **Example working paper (PPE continuity schedule)**

CLIENT: Sample Client Ltd
Period-end: 31/12/2012
Currency/unit: $ 000's

Reference: N04

N04 - SEARCH FOR UNRECORDED LIABILITIES

Section 1: review of subsequent disbursements

| Disbursement type (Disbursements after Year End) | Disbursement reference | Disbursement | | | TM/Ref | Invoice details | | | Delivery Date / Date of service provided | TM/Ref | Accrued at year end? | TM/Ref | Comments |
		Date	Amount	Recipient		Date	Amount	Description					
Wire transfer	123 456	31/Jan/2013	(700)	ABC	⬛	12/Jan/2013	(500)	Electricity bill 12/12	2012	✓	Yes	✗	
Wire transfer	654 293	31/Jan/2013	(1,500)	DEF	⬛	13/Jan/2013	(1,000)	Lawyer's invoices 12/12	2012	✓	Yes	✗	
Cheques	754 633	31/Jan/2013	(2,001)	GHI	⬛	13/Jan/2013	(2,001)	Flight to Las Vegas in FY13	2013		N/A	N/A	
etc...													

Section 2: Review of invoices received after year end

| | Invoice details | | | TM/Ref | Delivery Date / Date of service provided | TM/Ref | Accrued at year end? | TM/Ref | Comments |
	Date	Amount	Description						
	05/Jan/2013	(900)	raw material	⬛	200N+1	✓	N/A	N/A	
	03/Jan/2013	(1,000)	Lawyer's invoices 12/10	⬛	200N	✓	Yes	✗	
	04/Jan/2013	(1,500)	temporary workers Dec 2010		200N		Yes	✗	-
	04/Jan/2013	etc...							

Key to audit tickmarks :
⬛ Agrees to Invoice details
✓ Agrees to delivery note / details of service provided
✗ Agrees to details of accrued liabilities

Comments: No error detected (in addition to the one detected during our cut-off procedures)

FIGURE 17A Completed working paper (search for unrecorded liabilities)

CLIENT:	Sample Client
Period-end:	31/12/2012
Currency/unit:	$ 000's

F01.2 - OBSERVATION OF PHYSICAL INVENTORIES _ COUNTS

Reference	
	F01.2

EY Attendee:	Max Power
Location of Count:	Location C
Date:	30/Nov/2012
Account balance at the date of physical inventory:	50,000 F04

Section 1: Procedures to complete before and during the physical counts

Comments: Please refer to F01.3 for the documentation of our work relating to review of the client's procedures and details of observation during the physical counts. No issue noted

Section 2: Review of entity's counts and test of compilation

Test #	Selection number / tag reference	Item #	Description	Measurement in units	[A] Quantity per EY	[B] Quantity per count teams	TM/ Ref	[B] - [A] Variance	[C] Final quantity verified with the client	[D] Quantity per inventory compilation	TM/ Ref	[D] - [C] Variance	Comments
Count Sheets to Floor													
1	123,453	ABC		Unit	10	10	☑	-	-	10	✓	-	
2	124,556	DEF		Unit	10	15	☑	5	15	15	✓	-	
3	244,537	GHI		Unit	10	10	☑	-	-	9	✓	(1)	A
4	982 345	F450D		Unit	45	45	☑	-	-	45	✓	-	
5	123 444	234F5G		Unit	32	32	☑	-	-	32	✓	-	
6	124 567	WOE902		Unit	78	78	☑	-	-	78	✓	-	
7	128 919	XE9901		Unit	12	12	☑	-	-	12	✓	-	
8	234 001	V34ER		Unit	42	42	☑	-	-	42	✓	-	
9	236 013	B7829D		Unit	111	111	☑	-	-	111	✓	-	
10	878 130	W2340KD		Unit	54	54	☑	-	-	54	✓	-	
11	124 904	1209KKI8		Unit	45	45	☑	-	-	45	✓	-	
12	765 432	72DIKMD		Unit	67	67	☑	-	-	67	✓	-	
13	232 224	O987234		Unit	89	89	☑	-	-	89	✓	-	
Floor to Count Sheets													
1	245,367	JKL		Unit	10	10	☑	-	-	10	✓	-	
2	653.452	MNO		Unit	10	15	☑	5	15	15	✓	-	
3	765.342	PQR		Unit	10	10	☑	-	-	10	✓	-	
4	546 737	12OPEP		Unit	19	19	☑	-	-	19	✓	-	
5	345 792	RED56W2		Unit	102	102	☑	-	-	102	✓	-	
6	932 842	F4020XC		Unit	10	10	☑	-	-	10	✓	-	
7	123 591	FS234VTE		Unit	92	92	☑	-	-	92	✓	-	
8	876 761	AS3290F		Unit	43	43	☑	-	-	43	✓	-	
9	988 238	NN00S		Unit	56	56	☑	-	-	56	✓	-	
10	234 912	MPOO2D		Unit	43	43	☑	-	-	43	✓	-	
11	123 479	AD129MK		Unit	56	56	☑	-	-	56	✓	-	
12	567 230	120LLK		Unit	2	2	☑	-	-	2	✓	-	

FIGURE 18A **Example of an inventory working paper**

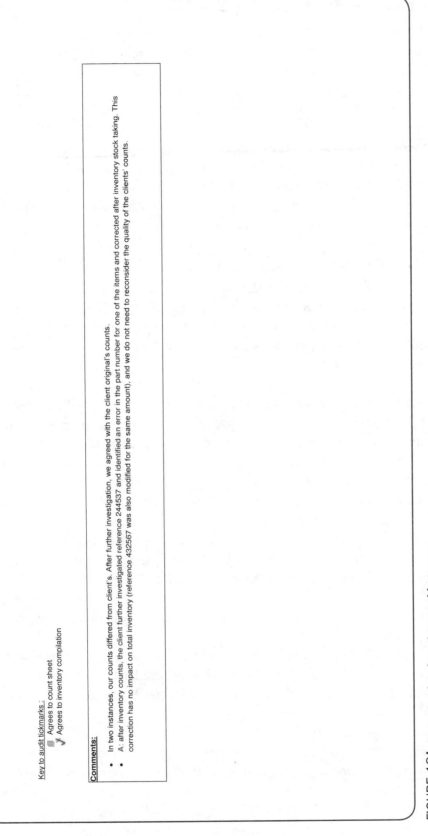

Key to audit tickmarks :
🔲 Agrees to count sheet
✗ Agrees to inventory compilation

Comments:

- In two instances, our counts differed from client's. After further investigation, we agreed with the client original's counts.
- A: after inventory counts, the client further investigated reference 244537 and identified an error in the part number for one of the items and corrected after inventory stock taking. This correction has no impact on total inventory (reference 432567 was also modified for the same amount), and we do not need to reconsider the quality of the clients' counts.

FIGURE 18A **Example of an inventory working paper**

APPENDIX B: CLOUD 9 LTD.

W&S Partners is a Canadian accounting firm with offices located in each of the major cities. W&S Partners has just won the December 31, 2012, statutory audit work for Cloud 9 Ltd. The audit team assigned to the client is Partner, Jo Wadley; Audit Manager, Sharon Gallagher; Audit Seniors, Josh Thomas and Suzie Pickering; IT Audit Manager, Mark Batten; and Audit Juniors, including Ian Harper, Weijing Fei, and you.

Prior-year audits were conducted by Ellis & Associates. As part of the change of auditors process, Jo Wadley met with R.J. Ellis (Managing Partner, Ellis & Associates) to discuss acceptance of Cloud 9 Ltd. as a client and to inquire about access to Ellis & Associates' workpapers. In the discussion, R.J. Ellis stated that there were no issues that W&S Partners should be aware of before accepting the client or commencing the work.

CLOUD 9 LTD. COMPANY BACKGROUND

Originally founded in 1980 by Ron McLellan, the Toronto-based company was a manufacturer and retailer of customized basketball shoes. In 1993, Cloud 9 Inc. (a publicly listed Canadian company) purchased the original company from Ron McLellan and renamed it Cloud 9 Ltd. As part of the sale agreement, Ron McLellan was appointed to the Cloud 9 Ltd. board of directors.

The parent company, Cloud 9 Inc., has wholly owned subsidiaries in the United Kingdom, Germany, United States, China, and Brazil, and has built a reputation around the fact that its shoes have comfort and durability. The company promotes itself using its now well-known tagline, "Our shoes are so comfortable, it's like walking on Cloud 9." Currently, Cloud 9 Ltd. is primarily a wholesaler of athletic shoes to its main customers: David Jones, Myer, Foot Locker, and Rebel Sports.

Cloud 9 Ltd. receives the majority of its inventory from the China production plant, with the remainder coming from the United States. All inventory is purchased on free on board (FOB) shipping terms, which means Cloud 9 Ltd. takes ownership of the products once the international courier accepts the goods for delivery. The inventory is sent to the main warehouse in Richmond, B.C., which is linked to retailers through an electronic inventory system. When retail inventory levels get low, the company ensures that deliveries are made using their own transport trucks, thus ensuring control throughout the entire process.

In February 2010, Cloud 9 Ltd. launched its new product line, which included the "Heavenly 456" walking shoe. Advertising campaigns and media coverage have been very successful and sales for this style of shoe have steadily increased. For Cloud 9 Ltd., the "Heavenly 456" now makes up 20 percent of total sales.

A specific marketing campaign was initiated in 2012 to promote and build the "Cloud 9" brand in Canada. The Canadian company was granted permission from its parent entity to sponsor a new soccer team, the Thompson Thunders, for the 2012 season. Under this sponsorship agreement, Cloud 9 Ltd. is to provide all the athletic footwear for the team, as well as having sole merchandising rights. The agreement also includes general advertising rights at the stadium.

In a separate contractual arrangement, Cloud 9 Ltd. has signed Kevin McDonald, the captain of the Thompson Thunders, as spokesperson for the brand. This arrangement allows Cloud 9 Ltd. to use Kevin's image to promote and build the brand in Canada.

To further establish the brand, the first "Cloud 9" retail store was opened in Toronto, Ontario, on June 1, 2012. The store operates on a just-in-time inventory system linked with the main warehouse in Richmond, B.C. However, the management team reports that there have been a few hiccups in determining ideal inventory quantities for the store to allow optimum availability of merchandise to the customers. There have also been some thefts of merchandise from the store and in order to reduce inventory loss by theft, the company has installed closed-circuit television cameras.

Personnel

Cloud 9 Ltd. has 52 full-time employees. In the retail store, the company employs part-time staff, with casual employees enhancing staff levels in the busier retail period.

To administer the company's finances, Cloud 9 Ltd. employs Finance Director David Collier, Financial Controller Carla Johnson, and Business Systems Manager Justin Reeves. These three employees are entitled to participate in the employee stock-purchase plan and receive stock options in Cloud 9 Inc. if revenue targets are met.

Financial information

Responding to pressure from its parent company, Cloud 9 Ltd. set a goal of increasing its revenue by 3 percent for the 2012 fiscal year. One of the critical success factors for the company achieving this 3 percent increase is to grow its share of the North American footwear market. However, with the new store opening and the subsequent increase in costs, as well as the costs related to the sponsorship deals, the management team is projecting a loss for the year.

In addition, to build customer loyalty and promote sales in the retail store, Cloud 9 Ltd. introduced a loyalty program whereby customers earn one point for every $10 that they spend. Customers can then redeem points by going online to receive coupons that can be exchanged for merchandise in the store.

On October 1, 2011, the company took out an additional loan of $2 million with Ontario Bank to help fund the store costs and to purchase additional delivery trucks and vans. This loan is repayable over five years. The company's other debt relates to loans issued five years ago from a company that is majority-owned by one of the directors.

All inventory is purchased in U.S. dollars, which the company acquires under forward exchange contracts. The company provides a 12-month warranty on all footwear. Historical claims have been 2 percent of total sales.

The prior-year income statement and balance sheet are included below.

CLOUD 9 LTD.
Income Statement
December 31, 2011

	Notes	December 31 2011 $	December 31 2010 $
Revenue	2	34 300 042	32 114 278
Borrowing costs	3	748 106	672 373
Other expenses	3	32 122 122	29 976 827
Proft before income tax		1 429 814	1 465 078
Income tax expense	4	378 074	452 064
Profit		1 051 740	1 013 014

CLOUD 9 LTD. **Balance Sheet** December 31, 2011			

	Notes	December 31 2011 $	December 31 2010 $
Current Assets			
Cash		1 753 765	534 938
Trade receivables		10 701 064	10 091 048
Inventory		6 263 242	6 796 990
Financial assets		4 075 205	8 488 110
Prepayments and other assets		666 054	1 135 416
Total Current Assets		23 459 329	27 046 502
Non-Current Assets			
Property, plant and equipment		852 965	301 667
Deferred tax assets		277 559	326 218
Total Non-Current Assets		1 130 524	627 885
Total Assets		24 589 853	27 674 387
Current Liabilities			
Payables		8 413 818	11 354 152
Bank loan		8 240 091	10 860 940
Current tax liabilities		207 893	12 391
Provisions		189 015	200 188
Total Current Liabilities		17 050 817	22 427 671
Non-Current Liabilities			
Deferred tax liabilities		170 284	136 794
Long-term debt		1 500 000	—
Provisions		79 566	46 890
Total Non-Current Liabilities		1 749 850	183 684
Total Liabilities		18 800 667	22 611 355
Net Assets		5 789 186	5 063 032
EQUITY			
Share capital		5 448 026	5 448 026
Reserves		(259 498)	66 088
Accumulated losses		600 658	(451 082)
TOTAL EQUITY		5 789 186	5 063 032

Following are the September 2012 trial balance for Cloud 9 Ltd., a transcript of a meeting with Carla Johnson, Cloud 9 Ltd. financial controller, and sales and cash control testing support.

CLOUD 9 LTD. Trial Balance				
	Sept 30, 2012		**Sept 30, 2011**	
Cash — Operating Account	184 679		551 583	
Cash — Savings Account	60 000		1 200 000	
Petty Cash	786		2 182	
Cash — Store Locations	500			
Trade Receivables — Stores	217 649			
Trade Receivables — Wholesales	10 704 933		11 218 837	
Allowance for Doubtful Accounts		468 197		637 167
Miscellaneous Receivables	44 789		49 372	
HST Receivable	31 457		23 895	
Employee Receivables	21 478		46 127	
Inventory	5 888 922		6 157 752	
Goods in Transit	453 002		629 235	
Allowance for Obsolescence		417 788		523 745
Derivative Financial Assets	3 987 453		3 592 899	
Amounts Receivable from Parent	482 306		482 306	
Prepaid Rent	300 450		211 699	
Prepaid Insurance	765 702		417 603	
Other Prepaid Expense	45 876		36 752	
Deferred Tax Asset	346 949		277 559	
Furniture and Equipment	1 768 954		1 098 290	
Accum Depr — Furniture and Equipment		1 283 848		757 958
Leasehold Improvements	1 324 875		722 302	
Accum Depr — Leasehold Improvements		360 651		209 669
Trade Payables		1 857 543		1 215 219
Accrued Bonuses		300 000		250 000
Sales Commissions Payable		423 786		398 074
Other Accrued Expenses		1 949 875		1 203 470
I/C Payables		593 457		494 361
Hedge Payable		5 198 524		4 852 694
Accrued Vacation Payable		156 548		111 937
Post-Retirement Benefits		91 198		71 047
Loyalty Program Provision		62 456		
Warranty Provision		91 456		85 597

(continued)

	CLOUD 9 LTD. Trial Balance			
	Sept 30, 2012		Sept 30, 2011	
Payable to Bank		8 872 482		9 560 224
Payable to Directors		149 354		179 867
Provision for Current Tax Liabilities		159 866		207 893
Provision for Deferred Tax Liabilities		198 647		170 284
Share Capital		5 448 026		5 448 026
Reserves	247 638		259 498	
Retained Earnings		600 658	451 082	
Revenue — Stores		640 782		
Revenue — Wholesales		27 255 417		33 987 595
Interest from Bank		45 432		28 642
FX Gain/Loss		35 467		29 568
Proceeds on Disposals				7 714
Other Revenue		188 590		246 523
COS — Stores	480 586			
COS — Wholesales	12 340 046		16 393 394	
Salaries and Employee Benefits	3 813 345		4 842 343	
Storage — Rent Expense Store	125 000			
Storage — Rent Expense Warehouse	2 219 443		2 959 257	
Distribution Expenses	1 551 191		2 008 015	
Telephone	74 654			
Computer and IT Costs	189 352		298 583	
Advertising & Promotion — Print	1 564 359		1 046 668	
Trade Shows	245 765		384 934	
Advertising & Promotion — TV	1 306 426		496 996	
Advertising & Promotion — Sponsorships	1 284 756			
Rent Expense — Office	231 877		309 170	
Bad Debt Expense	56 784		120 000	
Depreciation — Furniture and Equipment	525 890		339 852	
Depreciation — Leasehold Improvements	150 982		96 326	
Entertainment	165 432		320 703	
Professional Fees	238 654		458 903	
Insurance Expense	2 065 096		1 597 463	
Recruitment	264 327		297 190	
Interest Expense — Loan From Bank	763 187		701 576	
Interest Expense — Directors	35 424		46 530	
Tax Expense	278 074		378 074	
	56 850 048	56 850 048	60 677 274	60 677 274

TRANSCRIPT OF MEETING WITH CARLA JOHNSON
Present: Carla Johnson, Financial Controller, Cloud 9 Ltd.,
Josh Thomas, Audit Senior, W&S Partners

JT: **Thanks for seeing me, Carla.**

CJ: You're welcome, Josh. What can I do for you?

JT: **I need to ask you some questions around Cloud 9's process for recording wholesale revenue transactions, including the trade receivables and cash receipts aspects. After I understand the process, I'll need to select a sample transaction to confirm my understanding of the process as you have explained.**

CJ: Well, I can tell you what should be happening, but you may want to go and speak to the sales manager or warehouse managers to confirm that they do what the company policy and procedures say.

JT: **Good point, I'll make appointments to see them. Thanks. So let's start at the beginning—how does a sales transaction get initiated?**

CJ: We've got a pretty complex inventory management software system called Swift. It was designed by some of our tech guys in the United States. It tracks and does everything!

JT: **Sounds impressive!**

CJ: Anyway, the customers—let's say the Sport Mart store in Toronto—complete a purchase order online through a site that is linked to Swift.

JT: **How do the customers decide the quantity and know the price?**

CJ: Swift is linked (don't ask me how) and sends an alert when their inventory balance of our products gets below the predetermined limit they set with us. They can select the quantity based on their needs, but the prices are set in the system. They get sent price lists from the sales manager so they know the current prices.

JT: **How often are prices changed?**

CJ: Depends on the market, really. I don't think they change too frequently.

JT: **What if you don't have the products?**

CJ: The system doesn't allow them to place an order greater than our current inventory levels. If they need more, they need to fill out a separate request form that gets emailed to our warehouse manager so he can place the order with China.

JT: **OK, so they complete a purchase order. Then what?**

CJ: The submitted purchase order goes through a credit check and then becomes a sales order. That's all done behind the scenes in the system. We really don't see anything on our side until the sales order stage.

JT: **Guess that saves a lot of time and trees!**

CJ: Yeah, there's so much that we rely on the system to do for us, it's scary. If we were hit by an electrical storm, we'd be in trouble.

JT: **What happens to the sales orders—how do they get filled?**

CJ: Every day, the warehouse manager downloads the outstanding sales orders to these little handheld computer/scanner thingies. It's very Star Trek. Warehouse personnel use these to select the items off the shelves onto pallets. The pallets are taken to a staging area where each product is then scanned. This establishes the shipping document in Swift, which then gets printed for the delivery.

JT: **Are the shipping documents approved before the goods go out the door? How do you know that what got sent is what was ordered?**

CJ: Swift matches the quantities and products on the shipping document to the sales order. Once they match, the approval box is activated and the shipping supervisor can enter his pass code. This officially approves the shipping document and it gets printed.

JT: **How many orders do you fill in a day? It sounds like a lot for one person to do.**

CJ: We probably complete about 50 orders a day. Shoes aren't perishable items, you know, so it's not like we are sending products to every store, every day. We're trying out the "pit crew" concept, where there's two shipping supervisors with about four to five warehouse employees in their crew team. So they are in the staging area with them and do it right there with the handheld devices. They like to have little contests to see who can do it the fastest. You should go down there; it's quite a lively group. David encourages it and it's been great for productivity and morale.

JT: **Sounds like a great working environment. Better than being stuck in a broom closet sifting through invoices!**

CJ: Ah, the life of an auditor. I remember the good old days . . .

JT: **And the goods are sent out on your own trucks?**

CJ: That's right. We've bought our own trucks and vans rather than relying on couriers. The drivers pick up their loads in the morning and bring back anything undelivered. Because shoes are an easy product to off-load, we have to be careful about theft. So nothing can be left in the back of a truck at the end of the day. It comes back here and gets locked up in the shipping cage until it can be delivered again.

JT: **Why would goods be undelivered?**

CJ: Sometimes the drivers get behind or the store is closed unexpectedly. So there are occasions when all the goods won't get delivered in the day.

JT: **OK, so once the goods are delivered to the customer, how do you bill them?**

CJ: The drivers have the customers sign for the goods and then give us the signed copy. We go into the billing system and pull up the draft invoice that was generated when the shipping document was approved. We match the quantities in the invoice against the shipping document and confirm customer sign-off. This way, we only bill for those goods that were actually received by the customer. At 4 p.m., we do a batch run for the day. The copy is stapled to the signed shipping document and put on file. The running of the batch run posts the invoices to the sales journal and accounts receivable subledger.

JT: **Does finance ever go back to the sales order?**

CJ: No. Since a shipping document can't get generated unless it agrees to the sales order, we don't go back that far into the process. Why, do you think we have to?

JT: **I wouldn't say so at this stage. But you'd have to be sure to have some tight controls around Swift, given that it seems to do everything.**

CJ: Like I said, it does everything.

JT: **What is the cash receipts process?**

CJ: We get most payments via EFT, so my AR clerk downloads the previous day's receipts from online banking. She then goes into the subledger to post the receipts against the customer accounts. When she's finished posting each entry, she runs a batch report of all postings and reconciles it back to the bank statement. I review that reconciliation and sign off.

JT: **Are bank reconciliations done in a timely manner?**

CJ: I do bank recs each month for the operating and savings accounts. David reviews and approves them. Keep in mind what I just explained is for the wholesale transactions. We have separate procedures for the store regarding daily cash balance reconciliations to the deposits in the operating bank account.

JT: **Yes, our graduate will be handling the store side of the sales to cash receipts process. They will probably come and talk to you in a day or two. Well, I think that should do it for now. I may have some follow-up questions for you as I start getting my head around all of this.**

CJ: Door's always open.

JT: **Thanks for your time.**

SALES CONTROL TESTING SUPPORT

CLOUD 9 LTD.
SALES INVOICE

TO: David Jones
23 Main St, Shop 43
Toronto, Ontario

October 13, 2012

132811
Swift Purchase order reference: P00132811
Shipping reference: D00132811

Code	Description	Qty	Price per unit	Total price
786541	Heavenly 456 — Women 9	5	$114.74	$573.70
786540	Heavenly 456 — Women 8	3	$114.74	$344.22
	Total			$917.92
	HST			$119.33
	TOTAL			**$1,037.25**

Payment due on November 27, 2012

CLOUD 9 LTD.
SHIPPING DOCUMENT

TO: David Jones
123 Main St, Shop 43
Toronto, Ontario

October 12, 2012

D00132811
Swift Purchase order reference:
P00132811
Authorized: YES

Code	Description	Qty
786541	Heavenly 456 — Women 9	5
786540	Heavenly 456 — Women 8	3

Driver: R. Williams

I declare that all goods were received and no damage noted.

Customer Signature: _Sally Rose_ 12/10/12

CLOUD 9 LTD.
SALES INVOICE

TO: Rebel Sports — World Square
     680 George Street, Shop 12
     Barrie, ON

October 27, 2012

133410
Swift Purchase order reference: P00133410
Shipping reference: D00133410

Code	Description	Qty	Price per unit	Total price
587241	Maximum Speed — Men 12	4	$123.56	$494.24
786540	Heavenly 456 — Women 8	2	$114.74	$229.48
	Total			$723.72
	HST			$94.08
	TOTAL			**$817.80**

Payment due on December 13, 2012

CLOUD 9 LTD.
Shipping Document

TO: Rebel Sports — World Square
     680 George Street, Shop 12
     Barrie, ON

October 25, 2012

D00133410
Swift Purchase order reference:
P00133410
Authorized: YES

Code	Description	Qty
587241	Maximum Speed — Men 12	4
786540	Heavenly 456 — Women 8	2

Driver: R. Williams

I declare that all goods were received and no damage noted.

Customer Signature: _Jenna Hennesey_ · 26/10/12

SALES CONTROL TESTING SUPPORT

CLOUD 9 LTD.
SALES INVOICE

TO: Myer — Burnaby
     328 Elizabeth Ave
     Burnaby, BC

134063
Swift Purchase order reference: P00134063
Shipping reference: D00134063

November 4, 2012

Code	Description	Qty	Price per unit	Total price
649852	Olympic — Women 6	4	$109.21	$436.84
475125	Thunder 75 — Men 14	2	$157.68	$315.36
	Total			$752.20
	HST			$90.26
	TOTAL			**$842.46**

Payment due on December 19, 2012

CLOUD 9 LTD.
SHIPPING DOCUMENT

TO: Myer — Burnaby
     328 Elizabeth Ave
     Burnaby, BC

D00134063
Swift Purchase order reference:
P00134063
Authorized: YES

November 3, 2012

Code	Description	Qty
649852	Olympic — Women 6	4
475125	Thunder 75 — Men 14	2

Driver: Ted McGinty

I declare that all goods were received and no damage noted.

Customer Signature: _Julie Brown_ .... 4/11/12 ....

CLOUD 9 LTD.
SALES INVOICE

TO: Cross Country Sports
       769 First Avenue
       St. John's, NL

November 6, 2012

134104
Swift Purchase order reference: P00134104
Shipping reference: D00134104

Code	Description	Qty	Price per unit	Total price
786541	Heavenly 456 — Women 9	2	$114.74	$229.48
	Total			$229.48
	HST			$29.83
	TOTAL			**$259.31**

Payment due on December 21, 2012

CLOUD 9 LTD.
SHIPPING INVOICE

TO: Cross Country Sports
       769 First Avenue
       St. John's, NL

November 5, 2012

D00134104
Swift Purchase order reference:
P00134104
Authorized: YES

Code	Description	Qty
786541	Heavenly 456 — Women 9	2

Driver: D. Bredbenner

I declare that all goods were received and no damage noted.

Customer Signature: _Olivia Villagran_   5/11/12

CLOUD 9 LTD.
SALES INVOICE

TO: Wide Road Specialty Retailer
     74 Shore Highway
     Fredricton, New Brunswick

December 12, 2012

135215
Swift Purchase order reference: P00135215
Shipping reference: D00135215

Code	Description	Qty	Price per unit	Total price
587240	Maximum Speed — Men 10	3	$123.56	$370.68
475123	Thunder 75 — Men 12	3	$157.68	$473.04
347586	Heat Seeker — Men 15	2	$174.21	$348.42
	Total			$1192.14
	HST			$154.98
	TOTAL			**$1347.12**

Payment due on January 15, 2013

CLOUD 9 LTD.
SHIPPING DOCUMENT

TO: Wide Road Specialty Retailer
     74 Shore Highway
     Fredericton, New Brunswick

December 11, 2012

D00135215
Swift Purchase order reference:
P00135215
Authorized: YES

Code	Description	Qty
587240	Maximum Speed — Men 10	3
475123	Thunder 75 – Men 12	3
347586	Heat Seeker – Men 15	2

Driver: R. Williams

I declare that all goods were received and no damage noted.

Customer Signature: _Sharon J. Jones_ 11/12/12

CLOUD 9 LTD.
SALES INVOICE

TO: Foot Locker — Pitt St Mall
      435 Pitt St, Shop 4
      London, Ontario

December 20, 2012

135947
Swift Purchase order reference: P00135947
Shipping reference: D00135947

Code	Description	Qty	Price per unit	Total price
649852	Olympic — Women 6	2	$109.21	$218.42
786540	Heavenly 456 — Women 8	5	$114.74	$573.70
786539	Heavenly 456 — Women 7.5	2	$114.74	$229.48
	Total			$1 021.60
	HST			$132.81
	TOTAL			**$1 154.41**

Payment due on January 31, 2013

CLOUD 9 LTD.
SHIPPING DOCUMENT

TO: Foot Locker — Pitt St Mall
      435 Pitt St, Shop 4
      London, Ontario

December 18, 2012

D00135947
Swift Purchase order reference:
P00135947
Authorized: YES

Code	Description	Qty
649852	Olympic — Women 6	2
786540	Heavenly 456 — Women 8	5
786539	Heavenly 456 — Women 7.5	2

Driver: R. Williams

I declare that all goods were received and no damage noted.

Customer Signature: .... 18/12/12 ......

SALES CONTROL TESTING SUPPORT

CLOUD 9 LTD.
System 01 version 1.9
Daily Reconciliation of AR Posting to Bank
as of September 19, 2012

Description	Source	Amount
Cash receipts posted to accounts receivable	Subledger	10 577.23
Total bank deposits	Bank statement	10 577.23
Difference		0.00
		OKAY

Prepared: ...... *Jessica Williams* 19/9/12

Approved: ...... *Carla Johnson* 19/9/12

CLOUD 9 LTD.
Online Banking
EFT payments for September 19, 2012
Passcode accepted:
Carla Johnson

EFT 427	David Jones	$7 856.46
EFT 428	Cross Country	$2 720.77
Total		$10 577.23

CLOUD 9 LTD.
System 01 version 1.9
Daily Reconciliation of AR Posting to Bank Report
as of October 8, 2012

Description	Source	Amount
Cash receipts posted to accounts receivable	Subledger	8 765.49
Total bank deposits	Bank statement	8 765.49
Difference		0.00
		OKAY

Prepared: _Jessica Williams_   8/10/12

Approved: _Carla Johnson_   8/10/12

CLOUD 9 LTD.
Online Banking
EFT payments for October 8, 2012
Passcode accepted:
Carla Johnson

EFT 445	Rebel Sport	$2 963.54
EFT 446	Foot Locker	$1 964.71
EFT 447	Myer	$3 837.24
Total		$8 765.49

CLOUD 9 LTD.
System 01 version 1.9
Daily Reconciliation of AR Posting to Bank Report
as of October 23, 2012

Description	Source	Amount
Cash receipts posted to accounts receivable	Subledger	5 490.61
Total bank deposits	Bank statement	5 490.61
Difference		0.00
		OKAY

Prepared: *Jessica Williams*   23/10/12

Approved: *Carla Johnson*   23/10/12

OZBank

CLOUD 9 LTD.
Online Banking
EFT payments for October 23, 2012
Passcode accepted:
Carla Johnson

EFT 501	David Jones	$1 237.89
EFT 502	Cross Country	$4 252.72
Total		$5 490.61

CLOUD 9 LTD.
System 01 version 1.9
Daily Reconciliation of AR Posting to Bank Report
as of November 12, 2012

Description	Source	Amount
Cash receipts posted to accounts receivable	Subledger	9 302.20
Total bank deposits	Bank statement	9 302.20
Difference		0.00
		OKAY

Prepared: _Jessica Williams_   12/11/12

Approved: _Carla Johnson_   12/11/12

OZ_Bank_

CLOUD 9 LTD.
Online Banking
EFT payments for November 12, 2012
Passcode accepted:
Carla Johnson

EFT 534	David Jones	$2 179.52
EFT 535	Dick's Sports	$1 095.48
EFT 536	Running Shop — Calgary	$2 304.00
EFT 537	Myer	$2 612.72
EFT 538	Foot Locker	$1 110.48
Total		$9 302.20

CLOUD 9 LTD.
System 01 version 1.9
Daily Reconciliation of AR Posting to Bank Report
as of December 3, 2012

Description	Source	Amount
Cash receipts posted to accounts receivable	Subledger	12 567.33
Total bank deposits	Bank statement	12 567.33
Difference		0.00
		okay

Prepared: _Jessica Williams_   3/12/12

Approved: _Carla Johnson_   3/12/12

OZBank

CLOUD 9 LTD.
Online Banking
EFT payments for December 3, 2012
Passcode accepted:
Carla Johnson

EFT 576	Myer	$3 684.53
EFT 577	Foot Locker	$2 087.45
EFT 578	Rebel Sport	$1 832.12
EFT 579	Rebel Sport	$1 971.03
EFT 580	David Jones	$2 992.20
Total		$12 567.33

CLOUD 9 LTD.
System 01 version 1.9
Daily Reconciliation of AR Posting to Bank Report
as of December 19, 2012

Description	Source	Amount
Cash receipts posted to accounts receivable	Subledger	13 874.85
Total bank deposits	Bank statement	13 874.85
Difference		0.00
		OKAY

Prepared: _Jessica Williams_   19/12/12

Approved: _Carla Johnson_   19/12/12

OZBank

CLOUD 9 LTD.
Online Banking
EFT payments for December 19, 2012
Passcode accepted:
Carla Johnson

EFT 635	Wide Road Specialty Retailer	$6130.61
EFT 636	Cross Country	$1456.18
EFT 637	Foot Locker	$6288.06
Total		$13874.85

GLOSSARY

accountability relationship situation in which one party is answerable to another for the subject matter, p. 6

accuracy assertion that amounts and other data relating to recorded transactions and events have been recorded appropriately, pp. 173, 221

advocacy the threat that can occur when a firm or its staff acts on behalf of its assurance client, p. 55

analytical procedures an evaluation of financial information made by studying plausible relationships among both financial and non-financial data, pp. 146, 194, 360, 384, 434

applicable financial reporting framework the financial framework chosen by management to prepare a company's financial statements. For example, an applicable framework for a reporting issuer would be International Financial Reporting Standards (IFRS). An applicable framework for a private enterprise could be Accounting Standards for Private Enterprises (ASPE), or it could be IFRS, p. 7

application controls manual or automated controls that operate at a business process level and apply to the processing of transactions by individual applications, p. 108

assertion statement made by management regarding the recognition, measurement, presentation, and disclosure of items included in the financial statements, pp. 7, 130, 172

asset-test (quick) ratio liquid assets to current liabilities, p. 150

association what occurs when a public accountant is involved with financial information, p. 53

assurance engagement an engagement performed by an auditor or consultant to enhance the reliability of the subject matter, p. 6

attribute sampling a sampling technique used to reach a conclusion about a population in terms of a rate (frequency) of occurrence, p. 319

audit committee a sub-committee of the board of directors. The audit committee enhances auditor independence and ensures that the financial statements are fairly presented and that the external auditor has access to all records and other evidence required to form their opinion, p. 62

audit evidence information used by the auditor to support the audit opinion, p. 7

audit file the file where the evidence and documentation of the work performed is kept as a permanent record to support the opinion issued, p. 7

audit plan a plan that details the audit procedures to be used when testing controls and when conducting detailed substantive audit procedures, pp. 7, 218

audit program a detailed listing of the audit procedures to be performed, with enough detail to enable the auditor to understand the nature, timing, and extent of testing required, p. 351

audit risk the risk that an auditor expresses an inappropriate audit opinion when the financial statements are materially misstated, pp. 7, 130, 218, 254, 348, 384, 434

audit sampling the application of audit procedures to less than 100 percent of items within a population, pp. 225, 357

audit strategy a strategy that sets the scope, timing, and direction of the audit and provides the basis for developing a detailed audit plan, pp. 90, 139, 218

bank confirmation a letter sent directly by an auditor to their client's bank requesting information such as the amount of cash held in the bank (or overdraft), details of any loans with the bank, and interest rates charged, p. 178

block selection the selection of items that are grouped together within the population of items available, p. 231

board of directors the group that represents the shareholders and oversees the activities of a company and its management, p. 53

cash equivalents highly liquid investments that may be quickly converted to cash, p. 388

classification assertion that transactions and events have been recorded in the proper accounts, pp. 173, 221

closing procedures processes used by a client when finalizing the books for an accounting period, p. 91

combined audit strategy a strategy used when the auditor obtains a detailed understanding of their client's system of internal controls and plans to rely on that system to identify, prevent, and detect material misstatements, p. 140

common-size analysis a comparison of account balances to a single line item, p. 148

compilation engagement an engagement in which an auditor compiles a set of financial statements based on the information provided by the client, ensuring mathematical accuracy, p. 16

completeness assertion that all transactions, events, assets, liabilities, and equity items that should have been recorded have been recorded, pp. 172, 221

compliance audit an audit to determine whether the entity has conformed with regulations, rules, or processes, p. 10

component auditor an auditor who, at the request of the group engagement team, performs work on financial information related to a component for the group audit, p. 192

comprehensive audit an audit that encompasses a range of audit and audit-related activities, such as a financial statement audit, operational audit, and compliance audit, p. 11

computational evidence evidence gathered by an auditor checking the mathematical accuracy of the numbers that appear in the financial report, p. 183

confidentiality the obligation that all members of the professional bodies refrain from disclosing information that is learned as a result of their employment to people outside of their workplace, p. 51

consulting firms non-audit firms that provide assurance services on non-financial information, such as corporate social responsibility and environmental disclosures, p. 11

control activities policies and procedures that help ensure that management directives are carried out. Control activities are a component of internal control, pp. 263, 304

control environment the attitudes, awareness, and actions of management and those charged with governance concerning the entity's internal control and its importance in the entity, p. 256

control exception an observed condition that provides evidence that the control being tested did not operate as intended, p. 319

control risk the risk that a client's system of internal controls will not prevent or detect a material misstatement, pp. 130, 218, 260, 348, 384, 434

controls (referring to control activities) the terms "internal control," "control(s)," "system of internal controls," and "components of internal control" may be used to refer to the same process, p. 304

corporate governance the rules, systems, and processes within companies used to guide and control, pp. 58, 91

corporate social responsibility (CSR) a range of activities undertaken voluntarily by a corporation. CSR disclosures include environmental, employee, and social reporting, p. 11

current file a file that contains client information that is relevant for the duration of one audit, p. 198

current ratio current assets to current liabilities, p. 150

cut-off assertion that transactions and events have been recorded in the correct accounting period, pp. 173, 221

debt to equity ratio liabilities to equity, p. 151

detection risk the risk that the auditor's testing procedures will not be effective in detecting a material misstatement, pp. 132, 260, 348, 384, 435

documentary evidence information that provides evidence about details recorded in a client's list of transactions (for example, invoices and bank statements), p. 180

dual purpose tests procedures that provide evidence for both tests of controls and substantive procedures, p. 356

due care the obligation to complete each task thoroughly, document all work, and finish on a timely basis, p. 50

earnings per share (EPS) profit to weighted average ordinary shares issued, p. 144

electronic evidence data held on a client's computer, files sent by email to the auditor, items scanned and faxed, p. 186

emphasis of matter what results when an auditor will issue an unmodified audit opinion when there is a significant issue that is adequately disclosed and there is a need to draw the attention of the user to it, p. 18

engagement letter a letter that sets out the terms of the audit engagement, to avoid any misunderstandings between the auditor and their client, p. 71

enquiry an evidence-gathering procedure that involves asking questions verbally or in written form to gain an understanding of various matters throughout the audit, p. 194

entity-level controls the collective assessment of the client's control environment, risk assessment process, information system, control activities, and monitoring of controls, pp. 256, 304

error an unintentional misstatement in the financial statements, including the omission of an amount or a disclosure, p. 475

evidence information gathered by the auditor that is used when forming an opinion on the fair presentation of a client's financial statements and to confirm amounts recorded in client records, pp. 176, 187

execution stage detailed testing of controls and substantive testing of transactions and accounts, pp. 90, 146

executive directors employees of the company who also hold a position on the board of directors, p. 62

existence assertion that recorded assets, liabilities, and equity interests exist, pp. 173, 221

expert someone with the skills, knowledge, and experience required to aid the auditor when gathering sufficient appropriate evidence, p. 189

extent of audit testing the amount of audit evidence gathered when testing controls and conducting detailed substantive procedures, p. 224

external confirmation evidence obtained as a direct written response to the auditor from a third party, in paper form, or by electronic or other medium, p. 178

externally generated evidence information created by a third party (for example, supplier statements, bank statements), p. 188

fair presentation the consistent and faithful application of accounting standards when preparing the financial statements, p. 8

familiarity threat the threat that can occur when a close relationship exists or develops between the assurance firm (staff) and the client (staff), p. 56

financial statements a structured representation of historical financial information, including the related notes, p. 7

financial statement audit an audit that provides reasonable assurance about whether the financial report is prepared in all material respects in accordance with the financial reporting framework, p. 8

fraud an intentional act through the use of deception to obtain an unjust or illegal advantage, p. 91

general controls controls that apply to a company's IT system as a whole. They include policies and procedures for the purchase, maintenance, and daily operations of an IT system, security, and the staff training, p. 108

going concern the viability of a company to remain in business for the foreseeable future, pp. 91, 467

gross profit margin gross profit to net sales, p. 149

group engagement partner the auditor responsible for signing the audit report, p. 192

haphazard selection the selection of a sample without use of a methodical technique, p. 231

imprest payroll account account established for processing payroll disbursements only, p. 388

independence the ability to act with integrity, objectivity, and professional scepticism maintaining an attitude that includes a questioning mind, being alert to conditions that may indicate possible misstatement due to error or fraud, and a critical assessment of audit evidence, p. 53

independent auditor's report the auditor's formal expression of opinion on whether the financial statements are in accordance with the applicable financial reporting framework, p. 7

independent directors non-executive directors without any business or other ties to the company, p. 58

information risk the risk that users will rely on incorrect information to make a decision, p. 26

information technology the use of computers to store and process data and other information, p. 107

inherent risk the susceptibility of the financial statements to a material misstatement without considering the internal controls, pp. 130, 218, 260, 348, 384, 434

inspection an evidence-gathering procedure that involves checking documents and physical assets, pp. 185, 194

integrity the obligation that all members of the accounting professional bodies be straightforward and honest, p. 50

internal audit an independent service within an entity that generally evaluates and improves risk management, internal control procedures, and elements of the governance process, p. 11

internal auditors employees of the company who evaluate and make recommendations to improve risk management, internal control procedures, and elements of the governance process, p. 63

internal control the process designed, implemented, and maintained by those charged with governance, management, and other personnel to provide reasonable assurance about the achievement of the entity's objectives with regard to reliability of financial reporting, effectiveness and efficiency of operations, and compliance with applicable laws and regulations, pp. 7, 253, 304

internal control exception an observed condition that provides evidence that the control being tested did not operate as intended, p. 279

internally generated evidence information created by the client (for example, customer invoices, purchase orders), p. 187

intimidation threat the threat that can occur when a member of the assurance teams feels threatened by client staff or directors, p. 56

inventory turnover cost of sales to average inventory, p. 150

judgemental misstatement a misstatement that arises as a result of a difference in the application of judgement by the client and the auditor, such as the use of an estimate the auditor considers unreasonable or the inappropriate application of an inappropriate accounting policy. A judgemental misstatement is not the same as an error, p. 475

judgemental selection the selection of items that an auditor believes should be included in their sample for testing, p. 232

key performance indicators (KPIs) measurements, agreed to beforehand, that can be quantified and reflect the success factors of an organization, p. 143

legal letter a letter sent to a client's lawyer asking them to confirm the details of legal matters outstanding identified by management, p. 181

liens legal claims of one person on the property of another person to secure the payment of a debt or the satisfaction of an obligation, p. 389

liquidity the ability of a company to pay its debts when they fall due, p. 144

listed entity an entity whose shares, stock, or debt are listed on a stock exchange, p. 8

management letter a document prepared by the audit team and provided to the client that discusses internal control weaknesses and other matters discovered during the course of the audit, p. 280

management representation letter a letter from the client's management to the auditor acknowledging management's responsibility for the preparation of the financial statements and details of any verbal representations made by management during the course of the audit, p. 183

material an amount or disclosure that is significant enough to make a difference to a user. For example, if a company reports a profit of $100,000 and the auditor finds an error resulting in an overstatement of net income by $10, this probably wouldn't affect an investor's decision. However, if the auditor finds an error overstating revenue by $50,000 or 50 percent of the profit, this likely would affect the user's decision and would therefore be considered material. The concept of materiality is one of the reasons why an audit never provides 100 percent assurance, p. 7

materiality information that has an impact on the decision-making of users of the financial statements, pp. 8, 90, 135, 464

misstatement a difference between the amount, classification, presentation, or disclosure of a reported financial report item and the amount, classification, presentation, or disclosure that is required for the item to be in accordance with the applicable financial reporting framework. Misstatements can arise from error or fraud, pp. 369, 475

moderate assurance assurance that provides negative assurance on the reliability of the subject matter, p. 14

nature of audit testing the purpose of the test and the procedure used, p. 223

negative confirmation a letter sent directly by an auditor to a third party, who is asked to respond to the auditor on the matter(s) included in the letter only if they disagree with the information provided, p. 179

negligence failure to exercise due care, p. 64

no assurance what results when an auditor completes a set of tasks requested by their client and they report factually on the results of that work to their client, p. 15

non-executive directors board members who are not employees of the company. Their involvement on the board is limited to preparing for and attending board meetings and relevant board committee meetings, p. 62

non-sampling risk the risk that the auditor reaches an inappropriate conclusion for any reason not related to sampling risk, p. 228

non-statistical sampling any sample selection method that does not have the characteristics of statistical sampling, p. 229

Notice to Reader the communication issued when the auditor performs a compilation engagement, p. 16

objectivity the obligation that all members of the professional bodies not allow their personal feelings or prejudices to influence their professional judgement, p. 50

observation an evidence-gathering procedure that involves watching a procedure being carried out by another party, p. 194

occurrence assertion that transactions and events that have been recorded have occurred and pertain to the entity, pp.172, 220

operational audit an assessment of the economy, efficiency, and effectiveness of an organization's operations, p. 10

payable confirmation a letter sent directly by an auditor to their client's lender or supplier requesting information about amounts owed by the client to the lender or supplier, p. 178

performance materiality an amount less than materiality that is set to reduce the likelihood that a misstatement in a particular class of transactions, account balances, or disclosures, in aggregate, do not exceed materiality for the financial statements as a whole , p. 137

permanent file a file that contains client information that is relevant for more than one audit, p. 197

physical evidence inspection of a client's tangible assets, such as its inventory and fixed assets, p. 185

planning stage gaining an understanding of the client, identifying risk factors, developing an audit strategy, and assessing materiality, p. 90

pledge something delivered as security for the payment of a debt or the fulfillment of a promise, which is forfeited if there is failure to pay or to fulfill the promise, p. 388

positive confirmation a letter sent directly by an auditor to a third party, who is asked to respond to the auditor on the matter(s) included in the letter in all circumstances (that is, whether they agree or disagree with the information included in the auditor's letter), p. 179

price–earnings (PE) ratio market price per share to earnings per share, p. 144

professional behaviour the obligation that all members of the professional bodies comply with rules and regulations and ensure that they do not harm the reputation of the profession, p. 51

professional competence the obligation that all members of the accounting professional bodies maintain their knowledge and skill at a required level, p. 50

professional judgement the auditor's professional characteristics such as their expertise, experience, knowledge, and training, pp. 282, 348, 384, 450, 465

professional scepticism maintaining an independent questioning mind, p. 99

profit margin profit to net sales, p. 149

profitability the ability of a company to earn a profit, p. 143

projected error extrapolation of the errors detected when testing a sample to the population from which the sample was drawn, p. 238

qualified opinion provided when the auditor concludes that the financial report contains a material (significant) misstatement, p. 18

quantitative materiality information that exceeds an auditor's preliminary materiality assessment, p. 136

random selection process whereby a sample is selected free from bias and each item in a population has an equal chance of selection, p. 230

rate of deviation when testing controls, the proportion of items tested that did not conform to the client's prescribed control procedure, p. 235

reasonable assurance high but not absolute assurance on the reliability of the subject matter, p. 13

recalculation an evidence-gathering procedure that involves checking the mathematical accuracy of client records, p. 194

receivable confirmation a letter sent directly by an auditor to their client's credit customers requesting information about amounts owed to the client by the debtor, p. 178

receivables turnover net credit sales to average net receivables, p. 151

relevance extent to which information is logically connected to an assertion, p. 177

reliability extent to which information reflects the true state of the information, p. 177

re-performance an evidence-gathering procedure that involves redoing processes conducted by the client, p. 194

reporting issuer a public company with a market capitalization and a book value of total assets greater than $10 million, p. 57

reporting stage evaluating the results of the detailed testing in light of the auditor's understanding of their client and forming an opinion on the fair presentation of the client's financial statements, p. 90

return on assets (ROA) profit to average assets, p. 149

return on equity (ROE) profit to average equity, p. 149

review engagement an engagement in which the auditor does adequate work to report whether or not anything came to their attention that would lead them to believe that the information being assured is not fairly presented, p. 14

rights and obligations rights to assets held or controlled by the entity, and liabilities (obligations) of the entity, pp. 173, 221

risk assessment process the entity's process for identifying and responding to business risks, p. 260

roll-forward procedures procedures performed during the period between an interim date and year end (the roll-forward period) to provide sufficient and appropriate audit evidence to base conclusions on as at year end when substantive procedures are performed at an interim date, p. 355

sampling risk the risk that the sample chosen by the auditor is not representative of the population available for testing and, as a consequence, the auditor arrives at an inappropriate conclusion, p. 226

self-interest threat the threat that can occur when an accounting firm or its staff has a financial interest in an assurance client, p. 54

self-review threat the threat that can occur when the assurance team needs to form an opinion on their own work or work performed by others in their firm, p. 55

shareholders owners of the company, p. 61

significant account an account or group of accounts that could contain material misstatements based on their materiality and/or relationship to identified inherent and financial statement risks, pp. 347, 385, 434

significant risk an identified and assessed risk of material misstatement that, in the auditor's judgement, requires special audit consideration, p. 130

specific materiality information that is relevant when some areas of the financial statements are expected to influence the economic decisions made by users of the financial statements, p. 137

statistical sampling an approach to sampling where random selection is used to select a sample and probability theory is used to evaluate the sample results, p. 229

stratification the process of dividing a population into groups of sampling units with similar characteristics, p. 230

subsequent events both events occurring between year end and the date of the audit report, and facts discovered after the date of the audit report, p. 470

substantive audit procedures procedures used when the auditor plans to get a minimum knowledge of the client's controls and conducts extensive substantive procedures that involve intensive testing of year-end account balances and transactions from throughout the year, p. 218

substantive audit strategy a strategy used when the auditor does not plan to rely on the client's controls and increases the reliance on detailed substantive procedures that involve intensive testing of year-end account balances and transactions from throughout the year, p. 140

substantive procedures (substantive testing or tests of details) audit procedures designed to detect material misstatements at the assertion level, pp. 220, 323, 351, 383, 433

sufficient appropriate evidence quantity (sufficiency) and quality (appropriateness) of audit evidence gathered, pp. 8, 91, 176, 466

systematic selection the selection of a sample for testing by dividing the number of items in a population by the sample size, giving sampling interval (*n*) and then selecting every *n*th item in the population, p. 230

technical competence the skills, training, and ability of the internal audit team, p. 63

tests of controls (controls testing) the audit procedures designed to evaluate the operating effectiveness of controls in preventing, or detecting and correcting, material misstatements at the assertion level, pp. 218, 305, 384, 435

tests of details of balances tests that support the correctness of an account ending balance, p. 356

tests of details of transactions tests predominantly designed to verify a balance or a transaction back to supporting documentation; therefore, they usually include vouching and tracing, p. 356

third parties anyone other than the client and its shareholders who uses the financial statements to make a decision, p. 66

those charged with governance generally the board of directors, and may include management of an entity, pp. 11, 469

times interest earned profit before income taxes and interest expense, p. 151

timing of audit testing the stage of the audit when procedures are performed and the date, such as within or outside the accounting period, that audit evidence relates to, p. 224

tolerable misstatement the maximum error an auditor is willing to accept within the population tested, p. 234

tracing tracking a source document back to the underlying accounting records, p. 356

transaction-level controls controls that affect a particular transaction or group of transactions, pp. 267, 304

trend analysis a comparison of account balances over time, p. 147

unmodified opinion a clean audit opinion; the auditor concludes that the financial statements are fairly presented, pp. 8, 18

valuation and allocation assertion that assets, liabilities, and equity interests are included in the financial statements at appropriate amounts and any resulting valuation or allocation adjustments are appropriately recorded, pp. 174, 221

verbal evidence responses of key client personnel to auditor enquiries throughout the course of the audit, p. 184

vouching taking a balance or transaction from the underlying accounting records and verifying it by agreeing the details to supporting evidence outside the accounting records of the company, p. 356

walkthrough tracing a transaction through a client's accounting system, p. 141

WCGWs areas where material misstatements due to error or fraud could occur in a flow of transactions or in the sourcing and preparation of information that affects a relevant financial report assertion, p. 305

working papers paper or electronic documentation of the audit created by the audit team as evidence of the work completed, pp. 8, 196

INDEX